Walking in
FRANCE

Sandra Bardwell
Miles Roddis
Gareth McCormack
Jean-Bernard Carillet
Laurence Billiet
Tony Wheeler

D1056070

LONELY PLANET PUBLICATIONS
Melbourne • Oakland • London • Paris

X56
$3.00

FRANCE

ALSACE & MASSIF DES VOSGES
Magnificent views from the long crest of the Massif des Vosges, with vineyards and fairytale villages below

PARIS REGION
Stately forests, rivers, quiet villages and historic towns far from the hustle and bustle of the city

BRITTANY
Coast-walking par excellence: colourful rock architecture, good paths, rugged cliffs and unspoiled beaches

LOIRE VALLEY
Easy walking in a land of chateaux, wide river valleys and fine wines

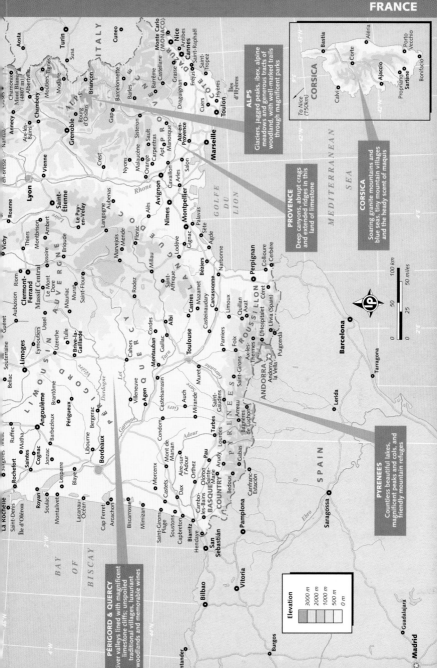

FRANCE

CORSICA
Soaring granite mountains and blue seas, tiny mountain villages and the heady scent of maquis

ALPS
Glaciers, jagged peaks, ibex, alpine meadows and generous tracts of woodland, with well-marked trails through magnificent parks

PROVENCE
Deep canyons, abrupt crags and extended ridges in this land of limestone

PYRENEES
Countless beautiful lakes, magnificent peaks and cols, and friendly mountain refuges

PÉRIGORD & QUERCY
River valleys lined with magnificent limestone cliffs, unspoiled traditional villages, luxuriant woodlands and memorable wines

Elevation
3000 m
2000 m
1000 m
500 m
0 m

100 km
50 miles
0   25   50

MEDITERRANEAN SEA

GOLFE DU LION

BAY OF BISCAY

To Nice (150km)

ITALY

SPAIN

Walking in France
1st edition – July 2000

Published by
Lonely Planet Publications Pty Ltd A.C.N. 005 607 983
192 Burwood Rd, Hawthorn, Victoria 3122, Australia

Lonely Planet Offices
Australia PO Box 617, Hawthorn, Victoria 3122
USA 150 Linden St, Oakland, CA 94607
UK 10a Spring Place, London NW5 3BH
France 1 rue du Dahomey, 75011 Paris

Photographs
All of the images in this guide are available for licensing from
Lonely Planet Images.
email: lpi@lonelyplanet.com.au

Main front cover photograph
Dawn over Lac Rond, Parc National de la Vanoise
(Gareth McCormack)

Small front cover photograph
Looking over the Chamonix Valley from the Grand Balcon Nord,
Northern Alps (Gareth McCormack)

ISBN 0 86442 601 1

text & maps © Lonely Planet 2000
photos © photographers as indicated 2000
GR and PR are trademarks of the FFRP (Fédération Française de la
Randonnée Pédestre)

Printed by Craft Print Pte Ltd, Singapore

Contents – Text

2 Contents – Text

The Walks	Duration	Standard	Transport
Paris Region			
Across Paris	4 hours	easy	yes
Vallée de la Marne	7 hours	medium	yes
Provins	3 hours	easy	yes
Giverny	3 hours	easy	yes
Forêt de Rambouillet	3 hours	easy	yes
Dampierre-en-Yvelines & the Vaux de Cernay	4 hours	easy-medium	yes
Forêt d'Ermenonville	4 hours	easy	yes
Forêt de Fontainebleau	5 hours	easy-medium	no
Brittany			
Côte de Granit Rose	3 days	medium	yes
Presqu'île de Crozon	2 days	medium	yes
Loire Valley			
The Loire from Fontevraud to Gennes	2 days	easy-medium	yes
Around Amboise	4½–5 hours	easy	yes
Cher River to Château de Chenonceau	3¾–4½ hours	easy	yes
Burgundy			
Avallon & Vezelay	2 days	easy-medium	yes
Around Anost	4¾–5¼ hours	medium	yes
Skirting the Côte d'Or	4½–5 hours	easy–medium	yes
Auvergne & Massif Central			
Puy de Dôme	2 days	medium	yes
Puy de Sancy	5¾–6½ hours	medium-hard	yes
Col de Guéry	5–5½ hours	easy-medium	yes
Puy Mary & Jordanne Valley	2 days	medium	yes
Plomb du Cantal	4¼–5 hours	medium	yes
Périgord & Quercy			
Les Eyzies to Sarlat-la-Canéda	2 days	medium	yes
Vers to Cajarc	3 days	medium-hard	yes
Pyrenees			
Lac de Lhurs	5½ hours	medium	no
Around Ansabère	7½ hours	hard	no
Les Orgues de Camplong	7 hours	medium-hard	no
Chemin de la Mâture	5 hours	medium	yes
Pic de Labigouer	8½ hours	hard	yes
In Vignemale's Shadow	3 days	medium-hard	yes
Lacs de Cambalés	5½ hours	medium	no
Circuits des Lacs	5½ hours	medium	no

The Walks *continued*	Duration	Standard	Transport
Pic du Cabaliros	6½ hours	hard	yes
Vallée de Lutour	6 hours	medium	yes
Corsica			
GR20	15 days	hard	yes
Provence			
Les Baux & Chaîne des Alpilles	5¼–6 hours	medium	yes
Les Calanques	5½–6½ hours	hard	no
Gorges du Verdon	2 days	medium-hard	yes
Grand Luberon & Mourre-Nègre	4¾–5½ hours	medium	no
Provence's Colorado	5¾–6¼ hours	medium	no
Southern Alps			
Platary	4 hours	medium	yes
Rochers du Parquet	8½ hours	hard	yes
Plateau d'Emparis	6½ hours	medium-hard	yes
Romanche Valley	5½ hours	medium	yes
Lac du Goléon	6 hours	medium	yes
Col de Saint-Véran	5½ hours	medium	seasonal
Three Cols	8 hours	hard	seasonal
Pic de Château Renard	6½ hours	medium-hard	seasonal
Col de Cerise	5½ hours	medium	seasonal
Lac de Trécolpas	6 hours	medium	seasonal
Mercantour Lakes	6 hours	medium	no
Northern Alps			
Grand Balcon Sud	2 days	easy-medium	yes
Lac Blanc	6 hours	medium	yes
Chamonix Aiguilles	6–7 hours	medium-hard	yes
Montagne de la Côte	6 hours	medium-hard	yes
Vallorcine & Alpages de Loriaz	5 hours	medium	yes
Desert de Platé	6 hours	medium	yes
Tour of the Vanoise Glaciers	5 days	medium-hard	yes
Jura			
Grand Crêt d'Eau	5–5½ hours	easy	no
Above the Valserine Valley	2 days	medium	yes
Around Lac des Rousses	6½–7½ hours	medium-hard	no
Le Mont d'Or	4½–5 hours	easy-medium	yes
Alsace & Massif des Vosges			
Crête des Vosges	4 days	medium	yes
Around the Vineyards	3½–4 hours	easy	yes

Map Index

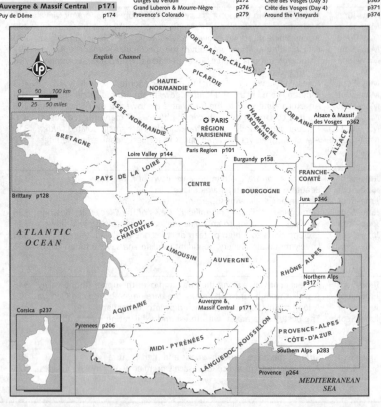

The Authors

Sandra Bardwell

After graduating with a thesis on the history of national parks in Victoria (Australia), Sandra worked as an archivist and then as historian for the National Parks Service and its successors. She has been a dedicated walker since joining a bushwalking club in the early 1960s and became well known through her column in the Melbourne *Age* and as the author of several guidebooks on the subject. In 1989 Sandra and her husband Hal retired to the Highlands of Scotland where they live in a village near Loch Ness. For several years she worked as a monument warden for Historic Scotland until Lonely Planet took over her life. She has walked extensively in Australia and Britain, for Lonely Planet in Italy and Ireland – and now also in France.

Miles Roddis

Always an avid devourer and user of guidebooks, Miles came late to contributing to them. For more than 25 years he lived, worked, walked and ran in eight countries, including Laos, Iran, Spain, Sudan, Jordan and Egypt. He celebrated a new life by cycling nearly 20,000km round the rim of the USA, basing his less-than-best-selling *Riding the Wind* upon his experiences. Convinced that the bike is humankind's greatest invention but for velcro, he enjoys agitating for cyclists' rights and annoying motorists. Happiest when up high, he's trekked, among other trails, the Zagros mountains in Iran, Britain's Pennine Way and the Pyrenees from Atlantic to Mediterranean. Now settled, paradoxically, at sea level beside the Mediterranean in Spain, he has contributed to *Africa on a shoestring*, *West Africa*, *Read This First: Africa*, *Lonely Planet Unpacked* and *Walking in Britain*, and was coordinating author of *Walking in Spain*.

Gareth McCormack

After finishing a degree in law in 1995, Gareth travelled, walked and climbed his way across Asia, Australia and New Zealand for 18 months. This trip inspired a radical career turnaround and he is now a writer and photographer based in Ireland. He is a regular contributor to the magazine *Walking World Ireland* and co-authored Lonely Planet's *Walking in Ireland*. Every year he tries to spend several months of the year photographing wild and beautiful parts of the world.

Jean-Bernard Carillet

After a degree in translation and in international relations, Jean-Bernard joined Lonely Planet's French office in 1995 and is now a full-time author. Diving instructor and incorrigible traveller, he will decamp at the slightest opportunity to travel round the world, but always returns to his native Lorraine in the east of France. As well as coauthoring the last edition of *Tahiti & French Polynesia*, Jean-Bernard has contributed to Lonely Planet's *South Pacific*, *Corsica*, and the French-language guides to *Martinique*, *Dominique et Sainte Lucie* and *Guadaloupe et Dominique*.

9

Laurence Billiet

After five years at Lonely Planet's French office trying to convince the people of France of the many beauties of Lonely Planet guides, Laurence emigrated to Melbourne's head office to take over the very mysterious position of International Marketing Coordinator. Driven by a constant desire to travel, she has trekked over difficult terrain in Iceland, Réunion, Hawaii, Australia and now Corsica. She is fascinated by volcanoes, addicted to vanilla Danette and crazy about football (and greatly missing it).

Tony Wheeler

Tony was born in England but spent most of his youth overseas. He returned to England to do a university degree in engineering, worked as an automotive engineer, returned to university to complete an MBA then dropped out on the Asian overland trail with his wife, Maureen. They've been travelling, writing and publishing guidebooks ever since, having set up Lonely Planet Publications in the mid-70s.

Caroline Guilleminot

Born in Paris, but raised with the memory of her Russian and Columbian ancestors, Caroline discovered the joy of walking on the rocky paths of the Annapurnas in Nepal. Trained as a translator, this real fauna addict worked for several years as a corporate journalist before joining Lonely Planet's French office.

Sophie Haudrechy

Born in 1968, Sophie studied French literature and Hungarian. After living in Hungary and travelling in Central Europe, she settled in Paris where she works as a freelance editor. She has coordinated Lonely Planet's French-language guides to India and New York.

Bénédicte Houdré

Brought up on the edge of the Seine River, Bénédicte never forgot her love for weeping willows. Her passion for walking, open spaces and the 'family spirit' led her towards the French office of Lonely Planet where she works as an editor.

FROM THE AUTHORS

Sandra Bardwell Numerous tourist information organisations provided information: the CDTs for Ariége-Pyrénées, Dordogne, Haute-Garonne, Pyrénées-Roussillon, and similar bodies for Alpes-Provence, Béarn, Briançon, Hautes-Alpes and Queyras. Staff at local tourist offices readily provided information and advice: Bedous, Cauterets, Chichilianne, Clelles, Crozon, Domme, Huelgoat, Lannion, Les Eyzies, Périgueux, Quimper, Saint-Cirq Lapopie, Saint-Cyprien and Saint-Martin Vésubie. Among many friendly hosts, Jean-Pierre Florence (Cauterets), M and Mme Tardegl (Le Boréon) and Mme Turina (Saint-Véran) were particularly helpful. At home, Anne Coombs' language tapes were a great help and Keith helped overcome initial palmtop anxiety. Fritz and Bev's advice, help and

Parisian hospitality have been greatly appreciated. At Lonely Planet in Melbourne, the patient and professional guidance by Lindsay, Teresa, Glenn and Emily, and early encouragement from Nick, Chris and Sally, have been greatly appreciated.

Jean-Bernard's advice has been much appreciated, and it's been good to work with Gareth again. Sharing this project with Miles has always been stimulating, often entertaining, and most rewarding.

During an experience of the walking guide writer's worst nightmare, the hospitality of M and Mme Barthelmy at La Sarette, Besse, the professional attention of Dr François Roques and Les Deux Alpes taxi and ambulance drivers, the insurance company staff in Sydney and Paris, and the professional guidance by Mr D Rutherford and Sara Ralph at Raigmore Hospital minimised the difficulties. Last and very far from least, Hal's company and patient help in a myriad of ways made all the difference.

Miles Roddis Very special thanks to Ingrid, my best mate and companion on the trails. Also to Damon for cheerfully following up loose ends and Tristan for calmly talking me down when the computer plays up.

Thanks too to the invariably efficient, usually goodhumoured staff of so many tourist offices whom I cajoled and pestered. Especially to Magali Masson, Nolay, fellow walker Delphine Zambon in Les Rousses, Claudine Ganter, Riquewihr, and Sandrine Miroir at Espace Massif Central in Clermont Ferrand.

Didier Cornaille, prolific walker and writer, in Burgundy; Andre Salvi, trail blazer in Métabief; and Claude Herrgott, President of the Club Vosgien, Vallée de Saint-Amarin, all communicated useful lore and lowdown.

The walking over, Frogaroos Jacqueline and Robert Pastor plus Kate and Mike Nichols patiently answered an unstaunchable flow of email questions and, throughout the book's own *grande randonnée*, Sandra was a wise, shrewd and particularly congenial writing companion.

Gareth McCormack Much of the preliminary research for the Northern Alps was made very easy by the excellent assistance provided by the Parc National de la Vanoise and the tourist offices of the Savoie and Haute-Savoie departments. In France, Niall Gault provided company and transport on the Desert de Platé walk, and Helen Fairbairn provided company and chocolate on all of the other walks. Thanks especially to Helen, for being good at French, and to all of the little green beers that eased aching muscles in the evening. During the writing up Lindsay Brown and Teresa Donnellan at LP Melbourne gave prompt and tireless replies to my many queries.

Jean-Bernard Carillet Jean-Bernard wishes to thanks his colleagues Caroline, Bénédicte and Sophie for their motivation and involvement in this project. Heartfelt thanks also go to Lindsay Brown for his confidence and Emily Coles for her patience.

This Book

Sandra Bardwell coordinated this 1st edition of *Walking in France* and wrote all but one of the introductory chapters, Brittany, Périgord & Quercy, the Pyrenees and Southern Alps. Miles Roddis contributed Facts for the Walker as well as the Loire Valley, Burgundy, Auvergne & Massif Central, Provence, Jura and Alsace & Massif des Vosges. The Northern Alps was written by Gareth McCormack. Jean-Bernard Carillet coordinated and wrote part of the Paris Region, with coauthors Caroline Guillemot, Sophie Haudrechy and Bénédicte Houdré. He also coordinated the Corsica chapter, a third of which he walked and wrote; Laurence Billiet and Tony Wheeler between them covered the other two-thirds.

Material from the 3rd edition of *France*, updated by Steve Fallon, Daniel Fobinson, Teresa Fisher and Nicola Williams, was used in *Walking in France*, along with material from the 1st English edition of *Corsica* by Olivier Cirendini, Jean-Bernard Carillet, Christophe Corbel, Laurence Billiet and Tony Wheeler, and the 1st edition of *Cycling France* by Katherine Widing, Sally Dillon, Neil Irvine and Catherine Palmer.

From the Publisher

Walking in France was brought to life under the coordination of Emily Coles (editing) and Simon Tillema (design and mapping). Members of the editorial team included Anne Mulvaney and David Burnett, with proofing assistance from Sally Dillon and Lindsay Brown. Chris Andrews translated the Paris Region chapter from French to English, while Jean-Bernard Carillet traced down French translations for the Flora & Fauna section. Arnaud Lebonnois put in a lot of work updating prices for the Corsica chapter. Chris Klep, Helen Rowley, Andrew Smith and Jim Miller all contributed to mapping and Vicki Beale lent a hand with layout.

Thanks to Quentin Frayne for the language section, Leonie Mugavin for checking the Getting There & Away chapter, Sean Pywell for his wildlife expertise, Csanad Csutoros for the climate charts, Kate Nolan, Ann Jeffree, Jane Smith, Reita Wilson-Wright and Lisa Borg for illustrations, Tim Uden for invaluable layout assistance, Fiona Croyden and Matt King from Lonely Planet Images for their help in sourcing images and Jamieson Gross for the cover design.

Foreword

ABOUT LONELY PLANET GUIDEBOOKS

The story begins with a classic travel adventure: Tony and Maureen Wheeler's 1972 journey across Europe and Asia to Australia. Useful information about the overland trail did not exist at that time, so Tony and Maureen published the first Lonely Planet guidebook to meet a growing need.

From a kitchen table, then from a tiny office in Melbourne (Australia), Lonely Planet has become the largest independent travel publisher in the world, an international company with offices in Melbourne, Oakland (USA), London (UK) and Paris (France).

Today Lonely Planet guidebooks cover the globe. There is an ever-growing list of books and there's information in a variety of forms and media. Some things haven't changed. The main aim is still to help make it possible for adventurous travellers to get out there – to explore and better understand the world.

At Lonely Planet we believe travellers can make a positive contribution to the countries they visit – if they respect their host communities and spend their money wisely. Since 1986 a percentage of the income from each book has been donated to aid projects and human rights campaigns.

Updates Lonely Planet thoroughly updates each guidebook as often as possible. This usually means there are around two years between editions, although for more unusual or more stable destinations the gap can be longer. Check the imprint page (following the colour map at the beginning of the book) for publication dates.

Between editions up-to-date information is available in two free newsletters – the paper *Planet Talk* and email *Comet* (to subscribe, contact any Lonely Planet office) – and on our Web site at www.lonelyplanet.com. The *Upgrades* section of the Web site covers a number of important and volatile destinations and is regularly updated by Lonely Planet authors. *Scoop* covers news and current affairs relevant to travellers. And, lastly, the *Thorn Tree* bulletin board and *Postcards* section of the site carry unverified, but fascinating, reports from travellers.

Correspondence The process of creating new editions begins with the letters, postcards and emails received from travellers. This correspondence often includes suggestions, criticisms and comments about the current editions. Interesting excerpts are immediately passed on via newsletters and the Web site, and everything goes to our authors to be verified when they're researching on the road. We're keen to get more feedback from organisations or individuals who represent communities visited by travellers.

Lonely Planet gathers information for everyone who's curious about the planet – and especially for those who explore it first-hand. Through guidebooks, phrasebooks, activity guides, maps, literature, newsletters, image library, TV series and Web site we act as an information exchange for a worldwide community of travellers.

Research Authors aim to gather sufficient practical information to enable travellers to make informed choices and to make the mechanics of a journey run smoothly. They also research historical and cultural background to help enrich the travel experience and allow travellers to understand and respond appropriately to cultural and environmental issues.

Authors don't stay in every hotel because that would mean spending a couple of months in each medium-sized city and, no, they don't eat at every restaurant because that would mean stretching belts beyond capacity. They do visit hotels and restaurants to check standards and prices, but feedback based on readers' direct experiences can be very helpful.

Many of our authors work undercover, others aren't so secretive. None of them accept freebies in exchange for positive write-ups. And none of our guidebooks contain any advertising.

Production Authors submit their raw manuscripts and maps to offices in Australia, USA, UK or France. Editors and cartographers – all experienced travellers themselves – then begin the process of assembling the pieces. When the book finally hits the shops, some things are already out of date, we start getting feedback from readers and the process begins again …

WARNING & REQUEST

Things change – prices go up, schedules change, good places go bad and bad places go bankrupt – nothing stays the same. So, if you find things better or worse, recently opened or long since closed, please tell us and help make the next edition even more accurate and useful. We genuinely value all the feedback we receive. Julie Young coordinates a well travelled team that reads and acknowledges every letter, postcard and email and ensures that every morsel of information finds its way to the appropriate authors, editors and cartographers for verification.

Everyone who writes to us will find their name in the next edition of the appropriate guidebook. They will also receive the latest issue of *Planet Talk*, our quarterly printed newsletter, or *Comet*, our monthly email newsletter. Subscriptions to both newsletters are free. The very best contributions will be rewarded with a free guidebook.

Excerpts from your correspondence may appear in new editions of Lonely Planet guidebooks, the Lonely Planet Web site, *Planet Talk* or *Comet*, so please let us know if you *don't* want your letter published or your name acknowledged.

Send all correspondence to the Lonely Planet office closest to you:

Australia: PO Box 617, Hawthorn, Victoria 3122
USA: 150 Linden St, Oakland, CA 94607
UK: 10A Spring Place, London NW5 3BH
France: 1 rue du Dahomey, 75011 Paris

Or email us at: talk2us@lonelyplanet.com.au

For news, views and updates see our Web site: www.lonelyplanet.com

Introduction

From the Atlantic to the Mediterranean, from Paris to the Pyrenees, walking in France is more an experience of walking in several different countries than just one.

Through the chateau country of the Loire, the massed ranks of vineyards in Burgundy and Alsace, the unspoiled beaches of western Brittany and along the wooded, cliff-lined rivers of Périgord and Quercy, the walking is easy. Farther south, the deep Gorges du Ver-

don, the extraordinary volcanic formations of the Massif Central and the colourful Mediterranean coast of Les Calanques offer adventurous walks in widely contrasting settings. And there's much more to France's mountainous areas than the famous names of the Alps – you can also explore the narrow spines of the Massif des Vosges, the meadows of the rolling Jura, the glaciers of the Northern Alps, the high plateaus, deep valleys and lakes of

France

NORWAY

SWEDEN

North Sea

DENMARK

IRELAND

UNITED KINGDOM

ATLANTIC OCEAN

English Channel

Channel Is

NETHERLANDS

BELGIUM

LUXEMBOURG

GERMANY

POLAND

CZECH REPUBLIC

SLOVAKIA

AUSTRIA

★ PARIS

FRANCE

SWITZER-LAND

HUNGARY

SLOVENIA

CROATIA

Bay of Biscay

BOSNIA HERCE-GOVINA

YUGO-SLAVIA

ANDORRA

MONACO

ITALY

PORTUGAL

Golfe du Lion

CORSICA

SPAIN

Balearic Islands

SARDINIA

ALBANIA

Mediterranean Sea

SICILY

GREECE

MOROCCO

ALGERIA

TUNISIA

Baltic Sea

the Southern Alps, the vast chain of the Pyrenees, and the narrow paths through the wild Corsican mountains.

France is blessed with an incomparable system of walking routes. The famous *grandes randonnées* (long-distance walking routes) and countless other waymarked paths present a tantalising array of choices, from short strolls to odysseys of several months. Many follow age-old paths that open up settled countryside to exploration on foot, yet don't take all the fun out of walking; there's greater freedom to be savoured in sparsely populated mountainous areas.

National parks may be few in number, but in a country with a widely dispersed population, they are invaluable islands of relative wildness and superlative beauty. The many regional nature parks are quite different, with living, working communities and a blend of natural and cultural heritages in scenic landscapes. Walking is the best way to discover these parks, with established paths, camping grounds and *refuges* (refuges or mountain huts).

Providing information about the heritage of these areas is taken very seriously in France. You could spend weeks visiting national park information centres and high-class museums devoted to wildlife and cultural themes. Superb walking guides, along with guides for flora and fauna, geology and history, fill dozens of metres of book shelves; all important maps for walkers are extremely accurate.

Wildlife protection may not be one of France's strong points. Walkers, however, can witness the results of positive achievements: the reintroduction of ibex, bearded vultures and other species once persecuted to near-extinction. Indeed, the wildlife can be a highlight of a walk almost anywhere in France: golden eagles, vultures, chamois (izards) and marmots in the Alps and Pyrenees; sea birds in Brittany; wildflowers in the Alps, Pyrenees and Massif Central; heavily scented maquis in Corsica and Provence; the oak forests of Périgord; and the larch, beech and pine woodlands of the high country.

French walkers may take to their pastime with serious enthusiasm, but out on the grandes randonnées there's always a cheery 'Bonjour' to passing walkers. Meeting French walkers often means meeting families, and staying in walkers' accommodation is a memorable experience, especially for the camaraderie among walkers that makes language differences irrelevant.

Gastronomic delights can enhance a walking holiday in France, as the Burgundy, Loire and Alsace and Vosges regions illustrate. Great pride is taken in the preparation and presentation of good food; sampling regional specialities at small village restaurants, or preparing al fresco feasts from the huge variety of fresh produce, are fitting conclusions to a day on the trail.

You can leave the car behind and use the generally excellent public transport in most areas covered in this book. Fast, reliable train services link the cities and many towns; bus services bring quite remote small towns and villages within reach.

Walking is the unrivalled means of bringing together the best of France's richly diverse natural and cultural heritages, in an absorbing, rewarding experience that can clearly reveal the wisdom of the famous statement that every person belongs to two countries: their own and France.

Facts about France

HISTORY

25,000 BC – Cave-dwelling Cro-Magnon people in Périgord

15,000 – Hunting communities established

5500 – Farming and pastoral communities began to develop in the south

3600 – Peasant farmers settled in the Paris basin

1800 – Trade with southern England, Central Europe and Spain established

1200 – Celtic tribes moved into Alsace, Lorraine and Burgundy

600 – Massalia (Marseille) established as a Greek colony; grapevine introduced

125 – Southern part of 'France' became Roman protectorate

52 – Roman legions took control of the entire territory known today as France; population between five and 10 million

AD 43 – Lugdunum (Lyon) became capital of Roman Gaul

313 – Christianity officially recognised

476 – End of western Roman Empire

486 – Franks became strongest among invading Germanic groups

507 – Paris made capital of Frankish territory under Merovingians

590 – Irish monasticism introduced by Saint Columbanus (Columba)

732 – Charles Martel defeated Moors at Poitiers, saving France from Muslim rule

800 – Charlemagne crowned Holy Roman Emperor

843 – Treaty of Verdun defined boundaries of the Carolingian Empire, covering much the same territory as modern France and Germany

911 – Duchy of Normandy in lower Seine Valley founded

987 – Hugh Capet elected king of areas around Paris and Orléans

1066 – William (the Conqueror), duke of Normandy, invaded England

1096 – First French participation in crusade to the Holy Land

1100 – Population of France about 6.2 million

1120 – University of Paris founded

1152 – Eleanor of Aquitaine married Henry of Anjou (later Henry II of England); one-third of France under English control

1180 – Start of Philip Augustus' reign during which the south was integrated into the French kingdom

1259 – Normandy, Maine, Anjou and Poitou won back from England

1300 – Population of Paris 200,000

1328 – Population of France about 20 million

1337 – Beginning of Hundred Years' War between England and France

1348 – Great Plague reached south of France, eventually killing about one-third of France's population

1415 – French forces defeated at Battle of Agincourt; Henry V of England took control of most of France north of the Loire River

1416 – Henry V became King of France

1429 – French forces led by Jeanne d'Arc (Joan of Arc) defeated the English at Battle of Orléans

1430 – Jeanne d'Arc burnt at stake for heresy

1453 – English ousted from French territory but retained toehold at Calais

1491 – Charles VIII married Anne of Brittany, enabling annexation of Brittany to France

1530s – European Protestant Reformation, strengthened by ideas of exiled Frenchman John Calvin

1534 – Beginning of French imperialism with Jacques Cartier's expedition to Canada

1539 – French made the official language of the state; first canal built along Vilaine River (Brittany)

1562 – Wars of Religion broke out between French Protestants (Huguenots) and Catholics

1563 – St Bartholomew's Day Massacre in Paris, in which 3000 Huguenots were slaughtered

1564 – Edict of Nantes by Henri IV created civil rights for Huguenots; canals and bridges built, renewed economic growth

1599 – 90% of population classed as peasants

1610 – Louis XIII ascended throne; frontiers on Rhine and in Pyrenees consolidated

1631 – *La Gazette*, France's first newspaper, published

1643 – Louis XIV (Sun King) became king at age of five; much later, created first centralised French state

1678 – Treaty of Nijemegen with the Dutch gave France Franche-Comté

1681 – Edict of Nantes revoked and Protestantism banned; about 300,000 Huguenots fled

1700 – Population of France 21 million

1709 – Last major famine in the country; devastatingly cold winter

1720 – Marseille decimated by plague

1720s – Trade with Caribbean and American colonies enabled Atlantic coast towns to prosper, but rural areas remained poor

1760s – Radical ideas of American Revolution spread to France

1768 – Corsica bought from Genoa by Louis XV for 40 million francs

1774 – Louis XVI became king; economic woes worsened

1783 – Montgolfier brothers made first balloon flight

1789 – Storming of Bastille in Paris launched French Revolution; population of France 28 million

1790 – Constitution adopted, providing for parliamentary government with hereditary monarch

1791 – Moderate leaders replaced by radical Jacobins; First Republic established

1793 – Louis XVI guillotined

1799 – Corsican general Napoleon Bonaparte assumed power as First Consul; created Bank of France, reformed education system, introduced new legal system and the franc; population 27 million, making France most populous country in Europe

1806 – 5.4 million people lived in urban areas, 23.7 million in the countryside

1812 – Napoleon abdicated and fled to Elba

1815 – Louis XVIII installed on French throne after Congress of Vienna; Napoleon escaped Elba but was defeated at Battle of Waterloo and exiled to Saint Helena

1821 – Population of France 30.5 million

1824 – Reactionary Charles X followed Louis

1830 – July Revolution, in which Charles was overthrown and replaced by Louis-Philippe, chosen by parliament

1848 – Riots precipitated February Revolution; Louis-Philippe replaced by Second Republic; adult male suffrage introduced; Louis Napoleon Bonaparte elected as president

1850 – 19% of people lived in urban areas

1851 – Population of France 35.8 million

1852 – Birth of Second Empire after coup d'etat by Louis, who became Emperor III

1853 – Baron Haussmann launched modernisation of Paris

1870 – France declared war on Prussia but soon defeated

1871 – Treaty of Frankfurt ratified by elected Assemblée Nationale (National Assembly), but rejected by ordinary Parisians who revolted against the government and were slaughtered; France lost Alsace and Lorraine

1875 – Republican constitution approved by National Assembly

1880 – Free public education across France granted

1889 – 3.2 million visitors to World Exhibition in Paris; Eiffel Tower opened

1895 – Confédération Générale du Travail created, unifying trade union movement; first Peugeot car took to the road; first public cinema showing by Lumière brothers

1904 – Entente Cordiale signed by France and Britain for peace and cooperation

1905 – Church and state legally separated; Parti Socialiste established

1909 – Louis Bleriot made first flight across English Channel

1914 – Germany declared war on France and Russia; start of WWI during which 2.3 million French killed or crippled, large areas of northeastern France devastated and industry almost ruined

1919 – Treaty of Versailles, strongly influenced by France, imposed enormous reparations bill on Germany

1920 – French Communist Party formed, splitting from Socialists, but both refused to participate in government; population of France 39.2 million

1927 – World's first airmail service from France

1931 – Population equally divided between urban and rural areas

1936 – Front Populaire (a coalition of left-wing parties) won national elections but held power for only a few months; introduced holiday pay and 40-hour week. Population of France 41.9 million

1937 – Railways partly nationalised

1939 – Britain and France declared war on Germany

1940 – France occupied by German forces; puppet state set up in Vichy; General Charles de Gaulle installed a French government-in-exile in London, but later moved to Algeria

1944 – Paris liberated in August

1945 – End of WWII; one person in three worked in farming

1946 – Population of France 40 million; new constitution approved by the people after elections in which women voted for first time; Fourth Republic established after brief rule by de Gaulle; comprehensive social security system established; Bank of France nationalised, trade unions strengthened

1949 – Council of Europe set up; precursor of European Economic Community (EEC)

1950s – French industry rapidly modernised and expanded

1954 – Government decided to develop nuclear weapons; outbreak of war in Algeria, nominally a *département* (department) of France; French Indochina lost at Battle of Dien Bien Phu

1957 – French initiative led to setting up of EEC with five other countries

1958 – Fifth Republic founded with de Gaulle as president; industrial production had doubled since 1948

1962 – De Gaulle negotiated end to war in Algeria; refused to sign nuclear test ban treaty

1963 – First nuclear power station built

It All Started in the Vézère Valley

It would be easy to sum up French history in terms of wars and revolutions, with some chateau-building on the side. Yet such events span a mere 2000 years, whereas human beings have lived in France for more than 200 millennia.

The most plentiful evidence of this imagination-challenging presence is in the 50km-long Vézère Valley, in Périgord. Here, the small town of Les Eyzies hosted the first serious excavation of ancient settlement sites in 1863. Since then, archaeologists and their colleagues from a wide range of scientific disciplines have delved back 200,000 years and worked out the broad sequence of civilisations in European prehistory. They have revealed how Neanderthal people discovered the use of fire; the earliest skeleton identifiable as homo sapiens was found in the valley. Cro-Magnon people, from around 35,000 BC and especially during the Magdalenian era (from 25,000 BC), became consummate artists, painting and carving seemingly ceremonial images on the walls of deep caves. The most famous cave paintings in France are at Lascaux in the upper Vézère, dating from about 15,000 BC. This era takes its name froms La Madeleine in the Vézère, where the earliest manufactured small tools and weapons were found.

These people lived in spacious rock shelters, plentifully available in the limestone cliffs lining the valley. Several abris (shelters) at Les Eyzies have been turned into tourist attractions and the village promotes itself as the World Capital of Prehistory; it is also the site of France's National Prehistory Museum (see the Les Eyzies to Sarlat-la-Caneda walk in the Périgord & Quercy chapter). The area's international significance has been recognised in the designation of the Vézère Valley by Unesco as a World Heritage List area.

1966 – Population 49 million; France withdrew from North Atlantic Treaty Organisation (NATO)

1968 – Civil unrest culminated in student uprising in Paris, national strike in May; introduction of reforms by de Gaulle divided the rebels and restored peace; this period saw the rise of women's liberation and environment movements, and relaxation of authoritarianism

1969 – Georges Pompidou succeeded de Gaulle

1972 – Ministry of the Environment established

1973 – International oil embargo impelled development of nuclear power

1974 – Rightist Valéry Giscard d'Estaing elected; new divorce laws, lower voting age

1981 – Election of Socialist François Mitterand as president; socialists won power in National Assembly; first TGV (train à grande vitesse) put into operation

1982 – Growth of rural townships outpaced that of urban areas

1983 – Population of France 54.6 million

1984 – 48% of country's power needs supplied by nuclear power stations (about 73% by mid 1990s); Les Verts (Greens) political party formed

1986 – Right-wing parties under Jacques Chirac took over National Assembly

1988 – Mitterand re-elected; introduced unpopular austerity measures

1989 – Ecologists won 5 to 21% of votes in municipal elections

1990 – New political party, Génération Écologie, formed

1991 – Edith Cresson appointed France's first woman prime minister; lasted a year

1992 – Narrow majority voted in favour of European integration (Maastricht Treaty); law passed requiring setting aside of nonsmoking areas in public places; ecology parties won 17% of votes in regional elections

1993 – Right-wing parties victorious in National Assembly elections; 8% of votes to ecology parties

1994 – Channel tunnel opened for rail freight traffic and passengers

1995 – Chirac elected president; decision to resume testing of nuclear weapons in Pacific caused outrage; public sector strikes against welfare cuts and proposals to trim national railways paralysed the country; extreme right-wing Front National gained control of three towns in local government elections; France rejoined NATO

1997 – Socialist-Communist-Green coalition victorious at parliamentary elections but soon confronted with difficult economic problems (notably social security deficit) and negotiations about European Monetary Union (EMU)

1998 – Premier Lionel Jospin took France into EMU; national celebrations when France won football's World Cup

1999 – A 35-hour working week introduced; disastrous fire in the Mont Blanc tunnel; talks are arranged between the French Government and Corsican nationalists

History of Walking

The origins of France's extraordinary network of paths go back to Gallic and Roman times, when defined routes were developed for communication between settlements. Other paths grew up, all with a strictly utilitarian purpose: paths for shepherds taking stock to summer pastures; ways followed by itinerant tradespeople, worshippers and pilgrims; tracks used by foresters and farmers to their more remote holdings; routes used by customs officers on the lookout for smugglers along the coast. Their legal status was not clear-cut; some were state-owned, some were owned by the local *commune* (the basic unit of local government), others were private, while some merely had a long-established, uncontested tradition of use. It is estimated that in 1945 there were one million kilometres of sentiers and chemins throughout France.

By the mid-20th century, many of these old routes had fallen into disuse or disappeared as the population of rural areas declined, as small farms were amalgamated and as highways and major roads proliferated. Declining use of local tracks removed the incentive to maintain them; many were grafted onto adjacent private properties.

Prior to this in the 18th and 19th centuries, travel for pleasure and for discovery had become popular among the wealthy and leisured. The more hardy eschewed coaches and horses and went on foot. From the late 18th century, climbing Alpine peaks became an increasingly popular activity. Tourist guides began to appear from the mid-19th century, and the Club Alpin Français (CAF; French Alpine Club) was founded in 1874, two years after the Club Vosgien set about methodically marking routes through the Massif des Vosges.

Cyclists set up Le Touring-Club de France (TCF) in 1890, and in 1904 it acquired a specialised section for walkers. The growth of scouting, with its emphasis on camping, and later the youth hostelling movement, helped to stimulate popular interest in the outdoors. The revolutionary granting of paid holidays to French workers in 1936 was a catalyst for the strong growth in walking for pleasure after WWII.

In 1947 the TCF, the CAF, the Camping Club of France and the Club Vosgien, inspired by the visionary Jean Loiseau, established the Comité National des Sentiers de Grande Randonnée (CNSGR) to promote recreational walking. Large numbers of affiliated clubs were formed throughout France and members set about surveying, clearing and waymarking 20,000km of walking routes following recognised chemins and sentiers. With the emphasis on longer-distance routes rather than short local paths, these routes introduced a new term to the French language – *grande randonnée*, or GR, by which the routes are now known. The first GRs developed were GR1 around Paris, GR2 along the Seine and GR3 beside the Loire River, with a 30km section between Orléans and Tavers.

In the late 1950s the CNSGR decided to promote the GRs through guidebooks. The first was published in 1957 for the Mont Blanc area, a simple document lacking maps. Later, the Institut Géographique National (IGN) allowed the use of extracts from its 1:50,000 topographical maps in the guides, thus adding immeasurably to their usefulness. There are now more than 180 titles of these superb guides in print.

In the 1970s the CNSGR recognised that it wasn't enough to simply identify and waymark routes and to publish guidebooks. It had won government financial support to extend the network of routes, but paths and tracks were still disappearing as urbanisation flourished and new roads were built. During the decade, public meetings drew attention to the lack of permanent protection for these paths. A 1977 decree gave legal right of passage exclusively to walkers along the coast; since then more than 1300km of paths have

Pilgrimage Paths

The chemins des Saint-Jacques (Ways of Saint James) were a collection of four pilgrimage routes across France to Santiago de Compostela in Scpain, starting in Le Puy-en-Velay, Arles (south of Avignon), Paris and Vézelay.

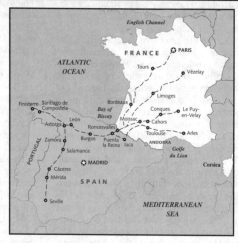

The most famous of these, from Le Puy, is 1500km long. The French section of 735km passes through Cahors, Moissac and Aire to Saint-Jean Pied de Port in the Basque country, at the foot of the pass through the Pyrenees into Spain. This ancient pilgrim's route to the burial place of the disciple Saint James, Spain's patron saint, was pioneered in AD 951. Pilgrims have followed the route ever since, most numerously between 1000 and 1500 when Santiago rivalled Rome and Jerusalem as a Christian site of pilgrimage.

Most pilgrims made the arduous, often hazardous journey on foot, fuelled by the desire to express their faith, seek penance for sins and ensure salvation in the afterlife. *Refuges* (refuges or mountain huts) along the way provided simple comforts for pilgrims and the route became an important channel for spreading political and cultural ideas across Europe. The many churches and shrines built to cater for the pilgrims' spiritual needs established an enduring architectural tradition.

During the 1990s the popularity of the pilgrimage routes enjoyed a renaissance and thousands now make the journey. In 1998 the chemins des Saint-Jacques were designated by UNESCO as a World Heritage List site, thanks to the efforts of the FFRP and several kindred groups. The FFRP revived the route from Le Puy as the GR65 and plans to open the other routes – notably that from Vézelay in Burgundy. A guide to the 1400km GR654 is planned for publication in spring 2001. Vézelay features on a walk described in the Burgundy chapter of this book.

The first guidebook to the chemins des Saint-Jacques was published between 1140 and 1150, to promote Santiago as a pilgrimage centre. For practical purposes walkers now have a choice of modern guides. *The Way of St James: Le Puy to Santiago* by Alison Raju is an exhaustive Cicerone guide; *Paris to the Pyrenees* by Marigold & Maurice Fox is published by the Confraternity of Saint James in its series of Pilgrim Guides; it also produces an annual accommodation list and can be contacted at 1 Talbot Yard, Borough High St, London SE1 1YP. There are three Topo-Guides published by the FFRP: *Le Puy-Figeac* (No 651), *Figeac-Moissac* (No 652) and *Moissac-Roncevaux* (No 653); Rando Éditions (see the Pyrenees chapter) publishes *Le Chemin de Saint-Jacques en Espagne*.

been cleared and opened, thanks to substantial government funding. However, paths elsewhere remain at risk.

The invaluable contribution that walking has made to tourism impelled the creation of *gîtes d'étape*, relatively simple accommodation designed specifically for walkers along the GRs. They were pioneered in 1971 along an alpine section of the GR5 and others soon followed in the Pyrenees. Nowadays, relatively few routes lack a chain of gîtes to welcome walkers at the end of the day.

In 1978 the CNSGR renamed itself Fédération Française de la Randonnée Pédestre (FFRP), to better reflect the involvement of its many local groups.

During the next two decades the FFRP became the recognised protector of France's paths and tracks. However, its tireless efforts to secure their permanent legal protection have met with only limited success, despite numerous high-profile public meetings and a petition with 1.5 million signatures calling for the safeguarding of France's heritage of 800,000km of *chemins* and *sentiers* (both terms for paths). The FFRP gained a generous and influential benefactor in the Gaz de France charitable foundation, especially for a program to provide notice boards with maps and brief descriptions of local walks throughout France. In 1996 a survey revealed that 31 million French people regularly enjoyed walking for pleasure. Another of the FFRP's goals, the designation of the chemins des Saint-Jacques pilgrimage routes as a World Heritage List site, was achieved in 1998 (see the boxed text 'Pilgrimage Paths').

Towards the close of the 20th century, the FFRP had waymarked 180,000km of paths and tracks, either as GRs (60,000km) or as shorter routes (120,000km). For contact details of the FFRP, see Useful Organisations in the Facts for the Walker chapter.

GEOGRAPHY

With an area of nearly 551,000 sq km, and measuring around 1000km from north to south and from east to west, France is the third-largest European country, after Russia and Ukraine. Known to the French as the 'divinely moulded hexagon', it borders Belgium, Luxembourg, Germany, Switzerland, Italy and Spain. The borders generally correspond with distinctive natural features. The Atlantic Ocean and English Channel lie to the west and north-west, and the Mediterranean to the south. In the east, the Rhine River marks the border with Germany. On the Swiss frontier, Lake Geneva (Lac Léman) lies between the long ridges and valleys of the Jura Mountains (rising to 1700m) and the rugged French Alps, which

extend south to the edge of the Côte d'Azur. The Alps are crowned by Mont Blanc (4807m), the highest mountain in Europe. The Pyrenees stretch along the greater part of the 450km border with Spain, Vignemale (3298m) being the highest summit.

France has three other upland areas. The Massif Central, west of the Alps and across the Rhône River valley, is dominated by extinct volcanoes (up to 1465m high), while deep gorges slice through its limestone plateau. The wooded Massif des Vosges in the north-east is cut by steep ice-carved U-shaped valleys in the north; to the south, wide glacial valleys sweep through higher, rockier ground (up to 1424m). The more subdued Massif Armoricain forms the aging spine of Normandy and Brittany, the highest point of which is in the Monts d'Arrée (384m).

Most of the Ardennes plateau is in Germany and Belgium; a small corner lies in France, north of Champagne. Corsica, the third-largest island in the Mediterranean, is largely mountainous, the highest peak touching 2719m; it also has deep gorges, spectacular sea cliffs and sandy beaches.

The greater part of France is, in fact, low and gently undulating, scarcely exceeding 200m in height. This most fertile part of the country is dominated by the valleys of the Seine (forming the Paris basin which comprises about 20% of the country), Loire and Garonne Rivers.

France has five major river systems (extensive sections of which are still navigable); the Atlantic is the main destination, receiving the outflow from three of them. The longest, the Loire (1020km), rises in the Massif Central and flows out at Nantes near the southern edge of Brittany; the Garonne (combining the Dordogne, Lot and Tarn) exits near Bordeaux; and the Seine (775km) flows north-east from Burgundy, through Paris, to the English Channel at Le Havre. Draining the southern end of the Vosges, the Jura Mountains and the Alps, the Rhône system (including the Durance, Isère and Saône rivers) has the greatest outflow. The Rhine gathers in the rivers north and east of Paris and flows into the North Sea.

Signs of a Glacial Past

Many of the world's finest walks are through landscapes which have been substantially shaped by glaciers. As a glacier flows downhill under its weight of ice and snow it creates a distinctive collection of landforms, many of which are preserved once the ice has retreated or vanished.

The most obvious is the *U-shaped valley* (1), gouged out by the glacier as it moves downhill, often with one or more bowl-shaped *cirques* or *corries* (2) at its head. Cirques are found along high mountain ridges or at mountain passes or *cols* (3). Where an alpine glacier – which flows off the upper slopes and ridges of a mountain range – has joined a deeper, more substantial valley glacier, a dramatic *hanging valley* (4) is often the result. In a post-glacial landscape, hanging valleys and cirques commonly shelter hidden alpine lakes or *tarns* (5). The thin ridge which separates adjacent glacial valleys is known as an *arête* (6).

As a glacier grinds its way forward it usually leaves long, *lateral moraine* (7) ridges along its course – mounds of debris either deposited along the flanks of the glacier or left by sub-ice streams within its heart. At the end – or snout – of a glacier is the *terminal moraine* (8), the point where the giant conveyor belt of ice drops its load of rocks and grit. Both high up in the hanging valleys and in the surrounding valleys and plains, *moraine lakes* (9) may form behind a dam of glacial rubble.

The plains which surround a once-glaciated range may feature a confusing variety of moraine ridges, mounds and outwash fans – material left by rivers flowing from the glaciers. Perched here and there may be an *erratic* (10), a rock carried far from its origin by the moving ice and left stranded in a geologically alien environment; for example, a granite boulder sitting in a limestone landscape.

View of area before glacier's retreat

The country's 3200km-long coastline is very diverse. The English Channel is fringed by high chalk cliffs separating bays and estuaries. The north-west peninsula reaching out into the Atlantic, with France's most westerly point at Pointe du Raz, south-west of Brest, has many deep inlets and low granite cliffs. The unwavering Atlantic seaboard of the Bay of Biscay has most of France's sandy beaches, including Europe's longest (228km), and its highest sand dunes (at Pyla, south of the Garonne estuary). In the extreme south of the Atlantic coast, the Côte d'Argent (Silver Coast) is named for the pure white sands of its beaches. The western half of the Mediterranean coast is mainly sandy, but beyond the Rhône delta and the Camargue wetlands, the sand is replaced by pebbles and rocks.

GEOLOGY

About 600 million years ago, the land mass of France was submerged. Then tectonic activity throughout north-western Europe about 300 million years ago created three major mountainous areas: the Massif Central, the Massif des Vosges and the Massif Armoricain (in Brittany), comprising granites, gneiss, mica-schist, sandstones and some volcanic rock. These ancient mountains were subsequently worn down over vast periods of time to much lower levels. The uplands of Corsica were also formed during this era, but were subjected to more violent tectonic movements, thus producing a very rugged, dissected mountainscape.

The Alps, the Pyrenees and the Jura have emerged from several phases of mountain building. They were originally formed about 100 million years ago, but were later subjected to intensive folding, more upthrusting and erosion. It is in these mountainous areas, and in the Vosges, that the impact of the advance and retreat of vast ice sheets during the succession of ice ages of the past two million years is most striking: deep valleys (boldly U-shaped in the Vosges); narrow ridges; cirques (basins sculpted at the heads of glaciers); and low ridges of moraine (debris left behind by retreating glaciers). Glaciers are still active in landscape formation in the Northern Alps (see the boxed text 'Living Glaciers' in the Northern Alps chapter), and to a lesser extent in parts of the Southern Alps and the central Pyrenees.

When the last ice age ended, sea levels rose dramatically and flooded coastal river valleys, notably in Brittany, producing the deeply indented coastline; former hills became the offshore islands.

The large sedimentary basins of the major river systems, the Alsace plain and the Rhône delta began to take shape about 250 million years ago when sediments were laid down in shallow seas; these sediments became the sandstones and limestones now forming the Paris, Aquitaine and Saône-Rhône basins. The youngest of these rocks, the limestones, are only 65 million years old.

The rift valley of the Rhine was formed by movements of massive blocks along fault lines during an Alpine mountain-forming phase. Subsequent disturbances changed the course of the river, diverting it from its westwards and southerly course so that it now flows into the North Sea.

The Massif Central has a complex geological history, distinguished by the presence of relict volcanoes. These originated during a phase of Alpine mountain-building and were active between 20 and three million years ago; the most recent lava flow has been dated between 8000 and 10,000 years ago. The volcanoes have been drastically reduced by erosion to their conical basalt cores *(puys)* and the attendant lava flows; some craters now contain lakes. The Massif Central is also unusual in that it has a considerable area of limestone – not in a basin, but on a plateau, raised as much as 1000m by tectonic upheavals during the last 10 million years.

CLIMATE

Three major influences, modified somewhat by topography, define France's climate.

The Atlantic Ocean is responsible for the maritime climate of the north-west and adjacent inland areas. A procession of low pressure systems and associated fronts brings sharply fluctuating conditions, with mild, cloudy, wet weather. Rain is likely on 200 days per year, the heaviest falls being from

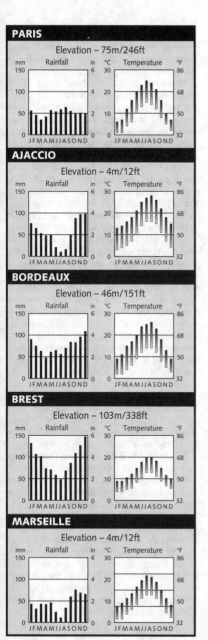

November to January. Hours of summer sunshine are the lowest in the country – seven to eight a day on average – and summer maximum temperatures don't often exceed 30°C.

This maritime pattern extends as far south as the Loire estuary and inland to the western fringes of the Vosges, the Massif Central and the Pyrenees, but these areas also experience a continental climate. Rainfall is more concentrated in summer storms, so spring and autumn are drier. The far south-west is warmer and sunnier than the north-west; winter is mild but summer rather wet, especially in the far south where there are plenty of short, sharp showers.

The continental climate of the inland areas, influenced by the movement of large masses of air (mainly high pressure systems from the north and east), is typified by snowy winters and hot, thundery summers. In areas sheltered from the maritime cloud masses, rainfall can be as low as 600mm per year (compared with mountainous areas where 2000mm per year isn't unusual). Winters are colder than in the north-west; frost and snow are common, especially to the east. Summer is warmest in the south of the region and sunshine can average around nine hours per day. Lyon, for example, has a longer, warmer summer than Paris (four months when the maximum can exceed 36°C) and minimum winter temperatures are lower in Lyon than in the capital (down to -21°C compared with -15°C).

The timing of the wettest season in mountainous areas varies. In the Pyrenees, it's during autumn and winter, while in the Vosges, Jura and the Northern Alps, summer and autumn are the wettest times. Summer in the Southern Alps, the Pyrenees and parts of the Massif Central is relatively fine and fairly warm, although cloud, heavy showers and afternoon thunderstorms are quite common.

The Languedoc and Provence coast, Corsica, the Alpes Maritime, the Rhône Valley and the southern Massif Central all enjoy a Mediterranean climate. Winters are mild and not too damp (although heavy snow on the Corsican mountains can often last well into spring) and summers are hot and dry with up to 12 hours of sunshine daily; any rain is heavy and often thundery. The lower Rhône Valley also endures the sometimes destructive mistral, a cold, dry wind from the north or north-west. Most prevalent in winter and spring and likely on 100 days per year, the mistral is caused by colder, drier air pouring over the Alps and being funnelled at speed (up to 100km/h) down the Rhône Valley towards warmer, less dense air over the Mediterranean.

ECOLOGY & ENVIRONMENT
Conservation
The Ministry of the Environment is the main government agency involved with conservation. It has several directorates concerned with flora, fauna and parks (see the list of contacts later in this section). There are also four regional Conservatoires Botaniques Nationaux (National Botanical Conservatories) – in Brest, Nancy, Porquerolles and Bailleul. They carry out research into rare and threatened species of plants, conserve them (mostly by local cultivation) and educate the public about France's botanical heritage.

While there are nationwide issues which engage environmental groups (see the boxed text 'A Motorway in the Vallée d'Aspe' in the Pyrenees chapter), local issues such as drainage of wetlands and the disappearance of rural tracks are more likely to have an impact on the countryside through which you'll walk. Two issues which cause considerable concern beyond France are the continuing development of skiing facilities in fragile alpine environments and the impact of mountain bikes. If you are simply passing through an area, it's difficult to detect such concerns, although regional newspapers (such as Sud-Oeust in Périgord and Quercy) are an easily accessible and enlightening resource.

From the walkers' point of view, the most striking facet of environmental conservation in France is the creation of legally protected reserves – national parks, regional nature parks and a host of smaller, specialised sites.

The way in which regional nature parks are organised, directly involving local people and giving them a stake in their protection

and funding, goes a long way towards ensuring their wellbeing. The parks have an umbrella organisation, the Fédération des Parcs Naturels Régionaux de France.

However, it is undoubtedly the FFRP which figures most prominently in protecting and promoting walkers' interests and in attempting to safeguard the areas through which its vast network of waymarked routes pass. It sets particular store by the creation of new regional nature parks as an effective means of stemming the decline of rural communities and traditional land uses, plus ensuring the protection of paths and promoting the development of facilities for walkers.

The FFRP strives for the permanent legal protection of paths and tracks and for a dedicated official scheme to fund their protection and maintenance. It rightly sees France's footpath heritage as indispensable to protecting the natural heritage, promoting green tourism and creating jobs. Its campaign is aimed at government agencies responsible for natural and cultural heritage, at the Council of Europe and Unesco. Its 15-point charter, published in 1997, crystallises its aims, namely to seek greater government commitment at all levels to path protection, to open more paths in urban areas, to involve young people in its work and to have a Unesco study done on the best way of saving the entire international heritage of footpaths. This charter was published under the title Le Livre Blanc (15FF) and may be available from the FFRP in Paris.

While the FFRP works for these overarching goals, its local groups maintain existing paths, watch for any threats to access and continue to develop new routes, especially those of special cultural significance.

In 1999 the FFRP launched its Sentier Propre (Clean Paths) campaign to rid the countryside of rubbish and eyesores such as abandoned vehicles and household appliances. It aims also to set up 'alert networks' to get rid of rubbish dumps in the countryside. The idea was pioneered in the Mayenne département (Loire) and in the first year, 12 others joined in.

continued on page 44

FLORA & FAUNA
OF FRANCE

RICHARD MILLS

France has a remarkably rich and diverse natural heritage, despite land clearing and drainage, road building, urbanisation and hunting: nearly 5000 species of flowering plants and ferns, 131 species of mammal, 266 species of nesting birds (and many more which migrate to French territory), 32 amphibian species, 33 reptile species, 73 freshwater fish species, 50,000 species of insects and 1400 of molluscs. A mid-1990s study showed that 140 of the 205 different types of wildlife habitats recognised in Europe were to be found within its boundaries.

National parks, regional nature parks and the many smaller nature reserves are the best places to observe and learn more about the natural world.

The following guide is a select survey of species that walkers are likely to see. Although many species of flora and fauna are confined to one of the five areas or broad habitat types defined here, others range widely and may be seen at sea level and in the mountains, at any time of the year or seasonally.

Field guides are of course indispensable for detailed identification; a selection is given in the Books section of the Facts for the Walker chapter.

Female Ibex (Capra ibex)

Mountains & Uplands

Three broad zones can be identified here: forested uplands between about 1000 and 1600m; subalpine meadows and woods from 1600 to 2500m, and alpine grasslands, heaths and rocky ground above 2500m. The boundaries between these zones aren't clearly defined and can vary according to local soil and climatic conditions. All three feature prominently in several chapters of this book.

Beech forests characterise the uplands. The **common beech** (*Fagus sylvatica*, le hêtre), with its smooth, silvery grey bark, is particularly beautiful during October as the foliage turns from pale yellow to rich orange-brown to reddish brown.

In the lower reaches of the subalpine zone, spruce and pine are the main trees of the forests. **Norway spruce** (*Picea abies*, l'épicéa), widely grown commercially for Christmas trees, is recognisable by its typical triangular shape, long slender cone and branchlets of small leaves (or spines).

The hardy **European larch** (*Larix decidua*, le mélèze) grows right up to the usual limit of tree growth at 2500m, although specimens have been found up to 2800m. Readily distinguished as the only deciduous (true) conifer (turning a beautiful gold in late autumn), it is conical in shape, with the lowest branches often turning abruptly upwards about 2m out from the trunk, and can assume massive proportions. Larches can live up to 500 years; their timber is valued for carpentry, joinery and for roof slates. They may be found in association with the **arolla pine** (*Pinus cembra*, le pin cembro). A slow-growing but long-living pine, its shiny dark green needles uniquely occur in bundles of five; the large seeds in the deep blue cones (only found on old trees) are a favourite food of the **nutcracker** (*Nucifraga caryocatactes*, le casse-noix moucheté), a small bird confined to the central Alps.

Although strictly a forest denizen, the **black grouse** (*Tetrao tetrix*, le tétras-lyre) is found only in the alpine regions. The male is glossy black with a white wing band and lyre-shaped tail; the hen is smaller and has reddish brown plumage. During the spectacular courtship parades, the male raises his red comb.

Above the tree line, in the alpine zone and up to about 3200m, dense thickets of **alpenrose** (*Rhododendron ferrigineum*, le rhododendron sauvage) up to 1m high are interspersed among the grasses and rocky outcrops; the small clusters of bell-shaped, deep pinkish red flowers last through summer.

Very few species of birds can survive long at these

KATE NOLAN

Branch section of the European larch
(*Larix decidua*)

KATE NOLAN

Alpenrose (*Rhododendron ferrigineum*)

elevations. The **ptarmigan** (*Lagopus mutus*, le lago-pède) is happy on rocky ground up to 3500m and blends into its habitat by changing colours at least three times during the year, from spotted grey in summer to pure white in winter. Its legs are protect-ed by a special layer of insulating feathers.

The small **snow finch** (*Montifringilla nivalis*, la niverolle d'Europe) also adapts to its changing sur-roundings, as its brown back and black throat become paler during colder months. It lives in large flocks on stony ground, and in summer may be seen around the highest summits. The **alpine accentor** (*Prunella col-laris*, l'accenteur alpin) frequents mountain slopes and alpine meadows during summer, descending to less harsh environments for the winter. Its plumage remains unchanged – grey head, black-and-brown-barred wings and distinctive speckled throat.

Brown hare (*Lepus europaeus*)

Mammals are more numerous and generally more approachable. The **brown hare** (*Lepus europaeus*, le lièvre commun), its name accurately describing its ap-pearance, is also marked out by its long, black-tipped ears. Although it prefers farmland and nearby grass-land during summer, it is also seen in open woodland and on mountain slopes. The **mountain hare** (*Lepus timidus*, le lièvre variable) is just as adaptable, chang-ing from pale grey-brown in summer to pure white in winter. Although mainly nocturnal, large groups may be seen during the day on scree slopes up to 3000m and in open birch or pine woodland. One of the most endearing alpine dwellers, the **chamois** (*Rupicapra rupicapra*, le chamois) stands about 80cm tall at the shoulder and has a white head with broad black strips across the eyes and shortish, slightly hooked horns. Reversing the habit of the ptarmigan and mountain hare, it exchanges its yellow-brown summer coat for thick dark brown or black winter fur. It is incredibly agile on the steepest cliffs, expertly balancing on its flexible hooves, and if disturbed can climb 1000m in barely 15 minutes. Although it can range up to 4000m in summer, usually in large groups of females and young (born in May-June), it is most likely to be seen up to 2500m; it seeks cover at much lower levels during winter. Its close relation, the **izard** (l'isard), is at home in the Pyrenees; similar in appearance and equally agile, it is slightly smaller than the chamois.

REITA WILSON-WRIGHT
Chamois (*Rupicapra rupicapra*)

Above the tree line don't expect to hear many wildlife sounds, except the shrill, echoing whistle of the **marmot** (*Marmota marmota*, la marmotte). Not unlike a large, dark, chunky squirrel, it has a big rounded head with miniature ears and a short bushy

KATE NOLAN
Marmot (*Marmota marmota*)

Male ibex *(Capra ibex)*

tail. It spends most of the day scampering about on scree slopes and hibernates during winter in deep family-sized burrows. Belying its somewhat lugubrious appearance, the **alpine ibex** *(Capra ibex*, le bouquetin) can perform even more acrobatic feats on cliff faces than the chamois. Unmistakable, with large tapering, ridged horns (shorter in the female), they are usually seen in small groups on sunny slopes between 800 and 3500m. The ibex is very tame, a propensity which puts it at risk from illegal hunting.

The **mouflon** *(Ovis musimon*, le mouflon) has lived in Corsica since prehistoric times, but its numbers are now much reduced from the plentiful population of a century ago. It was introduced to mainland alpine France at various times during the later 20th century. About the size of a small sheep, it is mainly reddish brown. The males have a white saddle patch and sport a fine pair of backward-curving, nearly circular horns. The Corsican female's short pointed horns are generally absent in her mainland counterpart.

France's mountainous areas are the home of a remarkable number of raptors. The biggest and most powerful of all eagles, the **golden eagle** *(Aquila chrysaetos*, l'aigle royale) has a wingspan exceeding 2m, held in a V-shape during its awesome gliding and soaring displays. It dives with wings folded to catch small rodents or carrion and is generally dark brown if seen from below, with white wing patches.

Two of the three species of vulture, most common in the Pyrenees, are equally as impressive. The **griffon vulture** *(Gyps fulvus*, la vauture fauve) spreads its dark broad wings to at least 2.5m, with the wingtip feathers splayed finger-like; the stubby tail is distinctive. Flocks gather around carrion and are often seen gliding high above mountain ridges. Hunting and poisoning caused the extinction of the species in the Cévennes during the 1930s, but during the 1970s local activists and national park staff bred some birds obtained from zoos and wildlife care centres. After their release into the wild during the early 1980s, a self-sustaining population became established. Present also in the Mercantour, the lighter-coloured **lammergeier**, or **bearded vulture** *(Gypaetus barbatus*, le gypaète barbu), has an equally massive wingspan. An important part of its diet is bone marrow which it obtains by dropping bones onto rocks from a great height. The smaller **Egyptian vulture** *(Neophron percnopterus*, le percnoptère d'Egypte) is quite different, with a white body and shorter wings.

Of the smaller raptors, the **buzzard** *(Buteo buteo,*

Griffon vulture *(Gyps fulvus)*

la buse variable) is widespread. Mainly dark brown, it habitually glides and soars, but is also often seen perched on fence posts; it can be identified by its high-pitched whistle. The smaller **sparrowhawk** (*Accipiter nisus*, l'épervier) is another common sighting in most areas, with its grey-blue back and rusty chest. The **peregrine falcon** (*Falco peregrinus*, le faucon péflerin) has pointed wings and dark grey back and wings and is a rather speckled dark blue grey and white beneath. Its presence usually causes great alarm among other birds, which it catches on the wing.

The **adder** (*Vipera berus*, la vipère) ranges very widely; it prefers undisturbed ground and can be found as high as 2750m. Colouring varies between the sexes; the males can be yellowish, pale grey or silvery with black markings and a characteristic inverted V at the back of the head. Up to 65cm in length, they are usually active during the cool of the day, spending the rest of the time basking in the sun. They rarely bite and fatalities are extremely unusual. It's a slightly different story with the **asp viper** (*Vipera aspis*, le vipère aspic), the venom of which is more potent, although it will only strike if taunted. Its colouring varies from light grey to reddish brown with a row of dark crossbars along the length of its body. They may be found up to 3000m and are most active on cooler dry days.

Among the huge array of wild flowers, a few stand out. In the lower woodlands, **yellow anemone** (*Anemone ranunculoides*, l'anemone fausse renoncule) has buttercup-like flowers and notched leaves. The large yellow heads of the **globeflower** (*Trollius europaeus*, la boule d'or) are unmistakable. Strikingly colourful gentians are generally found at higher levels and some species prefer open, stony ground, while others like to keep their roots damp. One of the largest is the **trumpet gentian** (*Gentiana acaulis*, le gentiane printaniefre), its deep blue flowers up to 70cm long. **Spring gentian** (*Gentiana verna*, la grande gentiane) is very much smaller, with conventional flat, five-petalled, pale to deep blue flowers. Not all gentians are blue – the **great yellow gentian** (*Gentiana lutea*, la gentiane-grande) has clusters of star-shaped yellow flowers. The **mountain pansy** (*Viola lutea*, pensée jaune) is fairly common, growing in clusters in both grassy and rocky sites; it has typical yellow, violet or bicoloured blooms. The **alpine snowbell** (*Soldanella alpina*, la soldanelle des alpes) and its relative, the **Pyrenean snowbell** (*Soldanella villosa*, la soldanelle des Pyrénées), grow into low mats with deep green roundish leaves and violet bell-shaped and fringed flowers; the Pyrenean species has very hairy stems.

Peregrine falcon (*Falco peregrinus*)

KATE NOLAN

Alpine snowbell (*Soldanella alpina*)

Woodlands

Woodlands of deciduous trees will probably feature in nearly all lowland walks. There are, of course, conifer plantations, but these are less likely to host popular walks. The main species in any woodland vary widely, depending on soil, climate and elevation.

Oaks are widespread, notably **English oak** (*Quercus robur*, la chêne pédoncule), which can grow to massive proportions with a trunk several metres across, and to a great age. The largish dark green leaves are lobed and slightly tapered. The **common beech** (*Fagus sylvatica*, le hêtre) can grow (on limestone soils) to 25m, with a huge crown; the bright green foliage becomes orange brown by late autumn. During May the ground around the trees is carpeted with the cast-off pale yellow male flowers.

Maples (*Acer* spp, l'érable) are also common, although it may be difficult to pinpoint the particular species; the leaves are typically lobed, each lobe tapering to a point. **Sycamore** (*Acer pseudoplatanus*, le sycomore) is particularly plentiful; it has leathery, dark green leaves. **Elms** (*Ulmus* spp, l'orme) are similarly numerous and potentially baffling; their overall graceful shape and foliage (leaves are often glossy with notched edges) can, with the help of a field guide, provide useful clues. **Common hazel** (*Corylus avellana*, le noisetier) is more of a tall bush, with rather hairy leaves which are deep green on top and whitish beneath. The leaves of the tall **common ash** (*Fraxinus excelsior*, le frêne) are quite different – slender and arranged in pairs along the stem.

A host of wild flowers bring colour and variety to the woodlands from early spring. One of the earliest to appear is the **bluebell** (*Endymion hyacinthoides non-scriptus*, la jacinthe des bois), with sky blue, slender, bell-shaped flowers on fine stems forming beautiful carpets on the forest floor. **Lily of the valley** (*Convallaris majalis*, le muguet) has delicate, white, globular, fragrant flowers; it favours dry ground on lime-rich soil. **Traveller's-joy** (*Clematis vitalba*, la clématite), usually known by its first botanical name, climbs all over the place; its narrow oval leaves tend to conceal the small green-white flowers. **Wood anemone** (*Anemone nemorosa*, l'anémone) has a single white flower on each stem, set off by the slender dark green lobed leaflets.

Elder (*Sambucus nigra*, le sureau) is a small shrub or tree up to 10m high, covered in massed dense clusters of tiny white flowers in spring; the black fruit (which are edible) can be used to make a powerful

KATE NOLAN

Bluebell
(*Endymion hyacinthoides non-scriptus*)

wine. Summer flowering **orange balsam** (*Impatiens capensis*, la balsamine) and **small balsam** (*Impatiens parvilora*) have characteristic five-petalled leaves with a wide lower lip and smaller hood; the flowers of the small balsam are yellow, while the other has orange blossoms with red spots.

Two members of the deer family are among the mammals you're most likely to find literally crossing your path in the woodlands. The **red deer** (*Cervus elaphus*, le cerf élaphe) is the largest wild animal in France. It stands up to 150cm at the shoulder and weighs up to 220kg, and in summer has a generally reddish brown to beige appearance. The winter coat has more grey in it. The male's antlers can grow as many as 16 points from the central spine; they are usually shed in March or April. Red deer generally congregate in large herds, stags and hinds keeping separate except during the autumn-winter breeding season. While naturally preferring woodland, red deer may also be seen in Mediterranean lowlands and in the mountains up to 2500m. At the other end of the scale, **roe deer** (*Capreolus capreolus*, le chevreuil) is Europe's smallest indigenous deer, rarely weighing more than 30kg and reaching just 80cm at the shoulder. Its summer dress is reddish brown with a distinctive white patch on the rump. The stag's mini, three-spined antlers are no more than 30cm long. Less gregarious than red deer, they are usually seen singly in woodland or around cultivated land.

Red deer (*Cervus elaphus*)

The **red squirrel** (*Scioris vulgaris*, l'écureuil roux) divides its time between foraging on the ground for seeds, especially from conifer cones, berries and fruits, and scampering through the branches. With a dark bushy tail as long as its dark chestnut furred body (24cm), it is unmistakable. Its nest of twigs and forest litter is firmly wedged into a tree fork.

The solidly built **wild boar** (*Sus scrofa*, le sanglier) has a grey-brown coat; the male possesses short powerful tusks, crucial weapons deployed during the rut from November to January. Although it forages harmlessly enough for its staple diet of nuts, fruits and roots, it can cause extensive damage rooting for worms and insects with its flexible snout. Fleet-footed despite their weight (up to 150kg), males lead mostly solitary lives, while sows and the lighter-coloured piglets live in groups. A description of the **brown bear** appears in the Pyrenees chapter of this book.

You'll need luck or a moonlit night to spot the **pine marten** (*Martes martes*, le martre des pins), found in both conifer and deciduous forests. Mainly

Red squirrel (*Scioris vulgaris*)

Lynx (Felix lynx)

KATE NOLAN

Red fox (Vulpes vulpes)

KATE NOLAN

Green woodpecker (Picus viridis)

a nocturnal species, it's most likely to be seen during the day in undisturbed areas. About the size of a domestic cat, it is generally dark brown with a yellowish throat and chest patch and pale brown ears.

Other woodland mammals to be on the lookout for include: the **lynx** (*Felix lynx*, le lynx), mainly in the Jura Mountains, larger than a wild cat with brownish spotted fur; the rather rare **genet** (*Genetta genetta*; la genette), long-tailed and catlike, with a foxy head; and the **red fox** (*Vulpes vulpes*, le renard), which may be seen almost anywhere and is instantly recognisable by its red brown coat, long bushy tail and canine profile.

Among the reptiles, the **green lizard** (*Lacerta verdis*, le lézard vert) is a common sight. Growing to 40cm in length, the male is bright green or yellow-green with an attractive black stipple pattern and an obvious blue patch on the throat. It is most in evidence in sunny spots in the mornings and evenings.

Some of the woodland birds are usually heard before they're seen. The monotonously unforgettable call of the **cuckoo** (*Cuculus canorus*, le coucou) is a sure sign that spring has arrived; the bird is much more difficult to spot, with a dark brown, lightly patterned back and a white, brown-striped chest. The **woodpigeon** (*Columba palumbus*, la palombe) takes off and lands with a loud clatter of its wings; it is distinguished by the white wing markings and collar, and has a grey-brown back and pink-and-grey chest. The **jay** (*Garrulus glandrius*, le geai des chênes) is both noisy and colourful, with reddish grey back and black, blue and white wing markings and a head crest which it can raise and lower. The jay's French name points to its role in maintaining a healthy population of oaks by carrying acorns over relatively long distances. The **green woodpecker** (*Picus viridis*, le pic-vert) is probably the most likely sighting among the woodpeckers. Easily identified by its red crown, olive green back and yellow rump, it has a loud ringing call, and rarely makes the woodpecker's trademark drumming sound. The **golden oriole** (*Oriolus oriolus*, le loriot), true to its name, has a brilliant yellow head, back and chest and prefers tall deciduous woodlands. In conifer forests, look out for the **coal tit** (*Parus ater*, la mésange charbonnière), with a black head and buff chest. The **woodcock** (*Scolopax rusticola*, la labécasse), with its red-brown colouring, is superbly camouflaged on the forest floor; it has a long straight beak and a characteristic fast, weaving flight.

Wetlands & Waterways

Although fish are an obvious component of these ecosystems, no mention is made of them here, on the assumption that walkers spend more time pursuing them in restaurants than trying to catch them in the wild.

Weeping willows (*Salix alba*, 'Tristis'; le saule) are plentiful along river banks, trailing their long sinuous branches, laden with slender leaves, in the water. **Lombardy poplars** (*Populus nigra*, 'Italica'; le peuplier) are often seen beside rivers (and roads), with their familiar tall, slender tapering profile and bright dark green leaves. Other common waterside trees are **white poplar** (*Populus alba*, peuplier blanc), also easily recognisable by their lobed dark grey-green leaves with white hairy underside; and the **common alder** (*Alnus glutinosa*, l'aulne), with readily identifiable obovate (spoon-shaped) very dark green leaves.

One of the rarer animal sightings, and most likely along river banks where there is little human disturbance, is the **otter** (*Lutra lutra*, la loutre). Measuring as much as 120cm (half of which is its tail), its sinuous body has mid-brown fur; its head is rather flat with long whiskers. Otters are most active soon after dawn or at dusk and their presence is betrayed by a worn path over the edge of the bank; their tracks show five clawed digits on each webbed foot. The **beaver** (*Castor fiber*, le castor) has been successfully reintroduced to France; it inhabits water bodies surrounded by deciduous woodland, essential to supply material for its massive dams. Easily identified, it has a rounded body, glossy brown on top and tawny beneath, and a flat, scaly black tail. Its dams can consist of a few hundred saplings, each more than 4cm across – a definite hazard to the wellbeing of the woodland. The diminutive **dipper** (*Cinclus cinclus*, le cincle plongeur) is inseparable from fast-flowing streams and pools. Its dark brown-and-black body sets off a white bib, colouring which blends with the rocks and turbulent water where it's usually seen, before or after diving to the bottom in search of larvae and snails.

Despite its name, the **grass snake** (*Natrix natrix*, couleuvre à collier) is commonly found in wet areas (and over a wide range of dry ground up to 2300m). It is generally olive or blueish grey in colour, with a yellow or orange collar and a pair of black crescents behind the head. Up to 150cm in length, the grass snake spends much of the day coiled up in the sun; it also enjoys basking afloat, but retreats to the

European otter (*Lutra lutra*)

Dipper (*Cinclus cinclus*)

Grey heron (Ardea cinerea)

Ringed plover (Charadrius hiaticula)

water mainly when it is threatened. Its bite isn't harmful.

The deep inlets along the Brittany coast are rich in birdlife. Among those you're most likely to see are **grey herons** (Ardea cinerea, le héron cendré), standing quietly in the shallows. They're generally mid-grey with a black V pattern down the white chest, and long orange bill. They look ungainly in flight, with the head tucked right in and legs trailing in the breeze. On a much smaller scale, the **reed bunting** (Emberiza schoeniclus, le bruant des roseaux) spends its time in the rushes and reeds. The male is readily identifiable: a sparrow-like bird with black head and white collar and black-and-rust wings. The **ringed plover** (Charadrius hiaticula, le grand gravelotte), with black, white and brown patterned head and brown back, runs along the shore, pausing often to gather food. There should also be the **little egret** (Egretta garzetta, l'aigrette garzette), all-white with black legs, and overhead the **marsh harrier** (Circus aeruginosis, le busard des roseaux), the adult male of which has narrow pale grey wings and tail and brown back; they habitually glide with wings held in a shallow V.

The vast estuary of the Rhône River on the Mediterranean coast embraces a mosaic of freshwater marshes and drainage channels, étangs (shallow lakes) and a narrow shingle shore. Generally in the triangle between the two branches of the river lies one of the premier wetland areas of Europe, the Parc Naturel Régional de Camargue, 85,000 hectares in area. Despite extensive reclamation for agriculture in

Greater flamingoes (Phoenicopterus ruber)

the north, about 340 species of birds nest or spend the winter in the area. In the saline marshes, **greater flamingoes** (*Phoenicopterus ruber*, le flamant) congregate in their thousands. Their beautiful pinkish plumage and legs are acquired gradually – juveniles have dark brown backs and become white before turning pink at three or four years. They feed in large flocks, steadily advancing in search of food. Other species in the marshes include elegant **avocets** (*Ricurvirostra avosetta*, l'avocette élégante), dressed in white with tasteful black trimmings and a gracefully up-curved bill, and **black-winged stilts** (*Himantopus himantopus*, l'échasse blanche), with spear-like bill, black back, white head and chest and, of course, very long legs. Numerous waders live on the tidal mudflats; **redshanks** (*Tringa totanus*, le chevalier gambette), with their bright reddish legs and grey-brown, dark spotted plumage are among the most plentiful, together with all manner of ducks, terns, the eight species of heron found in Europe, and several raptors, including black kites. The flora of the Camargue is no less important, from the salt-tolerant **glassworts** (*Salicornea* spp, la salicorne) around the étangs to the tall **yellow iris** (*Iris pseudacorus*, l'iris faux-acore) of the freshwater areas.

Black-winged stilt
(*Himantopus himantopus*)

RAY TIPPER

Puffins (*Fratercula arctica*)

GRAHAM BELL

The Coast

Corsica and the rocky shores and nearby islands of the Brittany coast are the best places for coastal bird-watching, while the characteristic flora is best seen in the small reserves and less developed areas.

Among the sea birds, the **fulmar** (*Fulmaris glacialis*, le pétrel fulmar) is easy to spot by its stiff-winged flight as it glides close to the cliffs. The **guille-mot** (*Uria aalge*, le guillemot de Troïl), black of back and head, spends most of its time at sea, nesting on the cliffs during late winter and spring. There's no mistaking the **puffin** (*Fratercula arctica*, le macareux moine), with the bright multicoloured bill of the breeding season, squat black-and-white body and large grey-white face patch. From a distance it's difficult to distinguish cormorants from shags as they both characteristically stand on rocks to dry their wings, although the smaller **shag** (*Plalacrocorax aristotelis*, le cormoran huppé) extends its wings fully and appears to be all-black. The **cormorant** (*Phalacrocorax carbo*, le grand cormoran) has some white on its face and a bronze back. The **gannet** (*Sula bassana*, le fou de Bassan) is a spectacular diver, plummeting arrow-like into the sea from 30m up; a largish, mainly white bird, it has a distinctive yellow head.

Gulls are common: the **herring gull** (*Larus argentatus*, le goéland argenté) is small, noisy and grey-backed, while the larger **great black-headed gull** (*Larus ichthyaetus*, le goéland à tête noire) and the **great black-backed gull** (*Larus marinus*, le goéland marin) are neatly described by their names. **Andouin's gull** (*Larus audounii*, goéland d'Audouin), similar in appearance to the herring gull although paler in colour and with a red bill, is confined to Corsica.

Along the beaches of shingle and sand, flocks of **oystercatchers** (*Haematopus ostralegus*, le huitrier pie), with their very distinctive straight red bill, black head, back and outer wing and noisy call, and the small, busy **common sandpiper** (*Actitis hypoleucos*, le fauvette pitchou), crouching and running or flying low and fast, are often seen. The **turnstone** (*Arenaris interpres*, le tournepierre) has a variegated brown, reddish, black-and-white back and head, and white underparts; a stocky bird, its name describes its feeding habits – in search of worms.

The **osprey** (*Pandion haliaetus*, le balbusard pêcheur), recognisable by its white body and brown back and wings, is a formidable hunter, with talons capable of grasping the slipperiest of prey. It nests in tall trees or on cliffs and breeds in early summer. The

Shag (*Plalacrocorax aristotelis*)

Gannet (*Sula bassana*)

Oystercatcher (*Haematopus ostralegus*)

population on Corsica has grown from only three pairs in 1973 to around 20 birds in 1998.

There's always a chance of seeing **grey seals** (*Halicheorus grypus*, le phoque gris) off Brittany. Despite the name they can be brown or silver, even black, and varying shades of grey; they spend plenty of time basking on sand banks and smooth rocks.

Thrift, or sea pink (*Armeria maritima*, l'armérie maritime), growing in rock crevices, produces masses of striking deep to pale pink flowers from early spring. **Sea holly** (*Eryngium maritimum*; le panicaut maritime), a protected species, resembles a thistle and has spring leaves and blue flowers. **Sea stock** (*Matthiola sinuata*, la giroflée des dunes) colonises sand dunes in low clumps of plants with slender silvery grey, woolly leaves and mauve or lilac flowers. **Sea rocket** (*Cakile maritima*, le cacilier maritime) sprawls across the sand in tall clumps of thick, shiny succulent-leaved plants, with small clusters of white or lilac pink flowers. Another easily identifiable plant is **sea campion** (*Silene maritime*, le silène maritime), which also grows in large clumps on rocky ground and on sand dunes, the white flowers emerging from enlarged pinkish tubes (of the calyx); it has small fleshy leaves.

Grey seal *(Halicheorus grypus)*

Although not confined to the coast, **gorse** (*Ulex europaeus*, l'ajonc) and **broom** (*Sarothamnus* spp, le genêt), both yellow-flowering, are widespread. The former has a particularly strong almond perfume and abundant spiny leaves, growing in impenetrable thickets. Although broom blossoms are similar to those of the gorse, this taller, more graceful bush has long branchlets with trefoil leaves. **Marram** (*Ammophila arenaria*, l'oyat), a rather abrasive grass, naturally serves, and is widely used, to stabilise sand dunes.

At least three species of heather (*Erica* spp, la bruyère) are common on coastal heaths: purple-flowering **bell heather** (*Erica cinerea*, la bruyère cendrée), **Dorset heath** (*Erica ciliaris*, la bruyère ciliée), with bristle-edged leaves and pink flowers, and **Cornish heath** (*Erica vagrans*, la bruyère vagabonde), which has much paler flowers.

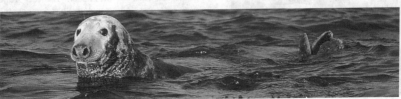

Grey seal *(Halicheorus grypus)*

Corsican pine *(Pinus nigra var. maritima)*

Mediteranean Zone

Taking in the Mediterranean coast, its hinterland and Corsica, this lowland zone hosts distinctive associations of trees, shrubs and wild flowers, home for a great variety of fauna species. Eighty percent of the species of flora in France are in this zone.

Typical woodlands on sandstone, mainly in Provence, comprise evergreen **cork oak** (*Quercus suber*, la chêne liège) reaching 20m in height with characteristic low twisted branches and spongy, fissured bark. This is removed every eight to 10 years and used to make corks. **Tree heather** (*Erica arborea*, la bruyère arborescente) reaches a height of 3m and has white bell-shaped, honey-scented flowers. The **strawberry tree** (*Arbutus unedo*, l'arbousier) is small and bushy and has white flowers; don't be misled by its name – the round dark fruit are edible, but not moreish. On the more widespread limestone, three trees are prominent. **Holm oak** (*Quercus ilex*, la chêne verte) has a dense, grey-black crown, dark bark and dark evergreen, spine-tipped leaves, oval in shape. **Sweet chestnut** (*Castanea sativa*, le châtaignier) is widely cultivated, its timber being used for fencing, although in Corsica production has declined as a result of a fungal disease, inadequate regeneration and damage by domestic pigs. The tree has longish dark green, prominently veined leaves, and the fruit husk, protecting two nuts, is covered with tiny hairs. **White**, or **downy**, **oak** (*Quercus pubescens*, la chêne blanche), a medium-height tree, takes its name from its hairy shoots and leaves. Other trees of the Mediterranean forest include: **Aleppo pine** (*Pinus halepensis*, le pin d'Alep), which has distinctive shiny, bright green leaves and colourful deep purple-brown, orange-streaked bark; **wild olive** (*Olea europaea*, l'olivier), smaller than the commercial variety and with small oval leaves and small black fruit; and **common juniper** (*Juniperus communis*, le genévrier), with needle leaves – the ripe black berries are used to make gin. At higher elevations on Corsica, the tall slender **Corsican pine** (*Pinus nigra var. maritima*, le pin laricio) lives to a considerable age and has grey-green foliage. The tiny **Corsican nuthatch** (*Sitta whiteheadi*, la sitell corse), just 12cm long, is a bird endemic to the island. It lives in conifer forests and is a very agile climber, clinging to slender branchlets in search of seeds and insects. It has a prominent white band above the eye.

Maquis, widespread in the Mediterranean, is a dense association of hardy, generally low-growing

Strawberry tree *(Arbutus unedo)*

aromatic and scrubby plants and small trees, the evolution of which is strongly influenced by fire. Colourful and abundant white and pink **rockroses** (*Cistus spp*, ciste) are prominent in early spring. **White asphodel** (*Asphodelus albus*, l'asphodèle blanche) has small white, narrow-petalled flowers. **Rosemary** (*Rosmarinus officinalis*, le romarin) thrives in the sunny climate and has masses of aromatic lilac flowers. The **mastic tree** (*Pistachia lentiscus*, le pistachier lentisque) produces red fruit with a resinous fragrance. The **kermes oak** (*Quercus coccifera*, la chêne kermes), an evergreen, has spiny leaves and prickly scales on the acorn cup.

Corsican red deer (*Cervus elaphus corsicanus*, le cerf élaphe de Corse) were reintroduced to the island in 1985 from Sardinia, initially into protected enclosures. In 1998 16 adults were released into the wild. Similar to the red deer in mainland forests, they are at home in the maquis, feeding on fruits and nuts. Once very common throughout France, **Hermann's tortoise** (*Testudo hermanni*, la tortue d'Hermann) is now rare, although less so in Corsica. Another maquis denizen, at 19cm long it has a markedly domed and lumpy carapace, and is green yellow or light brown in colour with dark, irregular patches on each plate. It spends most of the day in the sun, except in very hot weather when it retreats to the shade.

Rockrose (*Cistus spp*)

White asphodel (*Asphodelus albus*)

Wild cat

Endangered Species

About 40 species of flora disappeared from France during the 20th century, and hundreds more are rare or threatened with extinction by both natural and human agencies. The latter are far more serious: excessive collection, especially of orchids and medicinal species; destruction of habitat, especially the drainage of wetlands; changing agricultural practices; and road and building construction. Full protection nationwide is now accorded to 400 species of flora, indicating that they are classed as threatened; 36 species are partially protected, and the collection of many more (such as lily of the valley, bilberry and wild daffodil) is controlled at specific sites.

The auroch, bison and wolf have disappeared from France in relatively recent times. The survival of several species into the 21st century is precarious in the face of human intrusion into habitats (in the case of the otter and brown bear); as well, pond drainage threatens waders, and use of insecticides, senseless hunting, trapping and poisoning are universal threats. About 20 species of mammals and birds living in the forests are in danger of extinction or are vulnerable. All bats, the wild cat, hedgehog, beaver, red squirrel, most reptiles and many insects, all raptors, the stork, crossbill, nutcracker, golden oriole and several more birds, have full legal protection. The hunting of game species is regulated season by season, area by area.

Hedgehog

continued from page 26

Here are contact details for some of France's major environmental organisations, including government agencies. For details of the FFRP, see Useful Organisations in the Facts for the Walker chapter.

Fédération des Parcs Naturels Régionaux de France (☎ 01 44 90 86 20, fax 01 45 22 70 78, @ info@parcs-naturels-regionaux.tm.fr, www. parcs-naturels-regionaux.tm.fr) 4 rue de Stockholm, 75008 Paris. The Web site has up-to-date tourist information including details of organised walks and accommodation in parks.

La Ligue pour la Protection des Oiseaux (☎ 05 46 82 12 34, fax 05 46 83 95 86) corderie Royale, BP 263, 17305 Rochefort. Formed in 1912, the league's mission is to protect wild birds in their natural habitats. It acquires land to manage as nature reserves (eg, Les Sept Îles in Brittany), sets up clinics to treat birds injured in oil-spill disasters and establishes special nesting sites. Its quarterly *L'Oiseau* magazine is available by subscription.

Ministère de l'Environnement
  Direction de la Nature et des Paysages (☎ 01 42 19 20 21) 20 ave de Ségur, 75007 Paris. This directorate of the ministry is responsible for national parks, although in practice the best contacts are the *maisons du parc* (park information centres) of the individual parks.

Ministère de l'Environnement
  Direction de la Protection de la Nature (☎ 01 47 58 12 12) 14 blvd du Général Leclerc, 92524 Neuilly-sur-Seine. This directorate is responsible for the protection of flora and fauna.

Office National des Forêts (☎ 01 40 19 58 00) 2 ave de Saint-Mandé, 75570 Paris. The ONF manages state and communally owned forests for timber production and protection of the environment. It has branches in each French region.

NATIONAL PARKS & RESERVES

France was a latecomer to the international community of national parks, even though a reserve had been established at Fontainebleau in 1861. Regretting this dilatoriness, perhaps, a late burst of creative activity began in 1960 when a law was passed enabling the classification of a national park where the natural environment is of special importance and where it is judged necessary to afford it legal protection. Two parks were set aside in 1963:

Parc National de la Vanoise (in the Alps, east of Grenoble) and tiny Parc National de Port Cros, a Mediterranean islet on the Côte d'Azur. The Parc National des Pyrénées followed in 1967, then the Parc National des Cévennes (the largest) in Languedoc three years later, the Parc National des Écrins in 1973 and Parc National du Mercantour in 1979. The total area of national parkland amounts to 1,257,200 hectares, or about 2% of the land area of France.

Each park is surrounded by a much larger *zone périphérique* (periphery zone) where any development must harmonise with the environment. Each is run by a public agency bringing together representatives of local organisations, tourism interests and natural scientists. Funding comes from Parcs Nationals de France. Only the Pyrenees, Port Cros and Cévennes have very small permanent populations in their heartlands.

The national parks are areas of outstanding cultural, ecological and landscape value where biological diversity and landscapes are protected; this may involve supporting traditional activities which have influenced the character of the landscape today. National parks are also regarded as the ideal place for cultivating respect for the natural world.

Development in national parks is not ruled out; activities which promote local development, mainly eco-friendly, or green tourism are possible. Park regulations, however, are pretty strict in prohibiting anything which would change the character of the park (see the boxed text 'National Park Regulations' in the Facts for the Walker chapter).

Programs to reintroduce species of flora and fauna to various parks have been particularly successful; ibex, long absent from the mountains, may now be seen in all the alpine parks. The numerous maisons du parc run education programs and activities to teach people more about the parks.

France takes seriously cross-border cooperation in the management of parks and reserves. It is a major player in the European Natural Sites Twinning Programme, set up in 1987 for cooperation in technical, scientific and cultural research and protection work. At least 14 French reserves are twinned with reserves in other countries, mainly those popular with migratory birds and where habitat management is crucial. Of the national parks, Mercantour and Vanoise cooperate with bordering Italian parks in a wide range of nature conservation and recreation programs.

At the wider European level, France participates in the now-prestigious European Union (EU) Diplôme Européen scheme, set up to encourage the protection and management of areas with exceptional European importance. The granting of a Diplôme is accompanied by recommendations for improvements in various aspects of park management. If these initiatives are successful, the Diplôme is renewed. In the case of Mercantour, granted an award in 1993, greater involvement of foresters and stock farms in the work of the park virtually ensured renewal in 1998. Vanoise and Écrins have also received this award.

Natural Regional Parks

There is much more to France's protection of natural areas than national parks. In 1967 a decree was passed providing for the setting aside of *parcs naturels régionaux*. There are now 36 (covering 10% of the country's land area), whose functions are regulated through the 'Landscapes Law' (enacted in 1993).

Unlike the national parks, which are concentrated in the mountainous periphery, regional nature parks are scattered from one end of France to the other, including Corsica. They protect a very wide range of features, from the gentle mountains of the Queyras and Jura, to the rugged volcanic peaks in the Auvergne, the wetlands of the Camargue, the heathlands of Armorique in Brittany, and many forests. The two largest are in the Auvergne: Volcans d'Auvergne (395,068 hectares), set aside in 1975, and wooded Livradois-Forez in eastern Auvergne (320,000 hectares), created in 1983. The big differences from national parks are that regional nature parks are home to relatively large numbers of people (eg, 105,000 in Livradois-Forez) and that about 90% of their funding comes from the regions.

The main aim of their management is to balance the preservation of natural and cultural heritages with long-term social and economic development based on tourism, environmental education and traditional rural activities. Outdoor recreation is encouraged by the development of low-key facilities such as paths for walkers and trails for horse riders and cyclists. The strict regulations applying in national parks don't cover regional parks, although responsible walking practice is actively promoted.

Other Reserves

There are also numerous *réserves naturelles*, many of which are within national and regional parks (eg, the Écrins and Vercors); most are small areas with special geological or biological features (see the Côtes d'Armor section of the Brittany chapter). Some are privately owned, although many are readily accessible.

The *arrêtés de biotope* are small, distinct reserves which protect habitats critical for the survival of protected flora and fauna species.

Sites of outstanding natural beauty or of artistic, historical, scientific or traditional importance can be protected as *sites naturels classés* (dating from 1930). The many such sites in France range from individual trees to high mountains.

Small, beautiful unspoilt stretches of the coast and inland lakes, notable for their ecological value, may be acquired, protected and managed for people to enjoy by Le Conservatoire de l'Espace du Littoral.

Public Forests

France is one of the most forested countries in Europe – third only to Sweden and Finland – with 14 million hectares of wooded land. However, 70% of this is privately owned and more than likely closed to public access. Of the remainder, forests belonging to the state are known as *forêts domaniales*; numbering about 1500, they comprise 1.7 million hectares. Other public forests are owned by local collectives or public agencies and cover about 4.5 million hectares. Forêts domaniales are managed by the Office National des Forêts, for their ecological, economic, tourism and landscape values.

POPULATION & PEOPLE

France has a population of 61 million people, only 20% of whom live in the greater metropolitan area of Paris. The overall number of people living in mountain areas has been declining since the 1950s, although some rural areas have managed to reverse this trend.

For most of the last 200 years, France's rate of population growth has been considerably lower than that of its neighbours. However, during that time more immigrants have been accepted than into any other European nation. Between 1850 and WWI, France received 4.3 million immigrants. Another three million arrived between the world wars, most coming from other parts of Europe. The economic boom after WWII attracted millions of mainly unskilled workers and their families from French-speaking North and sub-Saharan Africa and Indochina. Millions of non-French-speaking people from the same areas were also welcomed, as a much needed workforce during a prolonged period of rapid economic growth.

Large-scale immigration was stopped by a 1974 law banning all new foreign workers. Immigration laws were again changed in 1993 to make it more difficult for immigrants to become French citizens, while in 1997 legislation legitimised the status of some illegal immigrants but also made it easier to locate and repatriate others. This has been against the background of a backlash against non-white immigrant groups, especially North African Muslims, who have not assimilated into French society as quickly as their European predecessors (Muslims comprise France's second-largest religious group). Particularly in the south, extreme-right political groups have exploited racist sentiment and gained power in local government.

About 80% of French people identify themselves as being Roman Catholics, but although most have been baptised, very few ever attend church.

SOCIETY & CONDUCT

From afar, the French have something of a reputation for brusqueness, arrogance and rudeness. At first hand, you'll find that this is a piece of foreign folklore of little or no substance, especially beyond Paris; a little effort on your part can make all the difference very quickly.

Generally speaking, the French are rather formal and polite in their manners and behaviour, especially when meeting people. Wherever you are – in a shop (especially small ones), the post office, getting onto a bus, arriving at a hostel or camping ground – always say '*Bonjour, monsieur/madame/ mademoiselle*', and '*Merci monsieur/ madame, au revoir*' when you leave. Neglect of this practice will raise barriers and make genuine contact much more difficult. Your attempts at communicating in French, however halting and stilted, will be appreciated. Especially in rural areas, do *not* expect everyone to speak English. Even if they do, it will be a while before they gain the confidence to speak to you. In conversation, the subject of money is just not discussed; not surprisingly, the French do not share the British obsession with the weather. Fruitful topics are food, where you come from (particularly if it is outside Europe) and...food.

LANGUAGE

Around 122 million people worldwide speak French as their first language, and various forms of creole are used in Haiti and French Guiana, and Cajun French is spoken in parts of Louisiana. French is the national language, but pockets of France have their own language: Alsacien (Alsace), Breton (Brittany), Basque (south-west), Catalan (around Perpignan) and Corsican (Corsica).

For an easy-to-use language guide with a list of words and phrases particularly suitable for walkers, see the Language chapter later in this book.

Facts for the Walker

SUGGESTED ITINERARIES

France has a mind-boggling 180,000km of blazed trails. By supplementing the walks described in this book with local way-marked trails, you can easily spend at least a week and often more exploring just one of our regional chapters.

If you're intending to walk in more than one area, bear in mind that while the magnificent high-speed TGV trains can hurtle you from one end of the country to the other, you may spend almost as much time again endeavouring to cover the final 20km to your destination; rural bus services have

Highlights

- Provins and its medieval city above the plains of Brie, like plunging into the 13th century

- The eerie Mediterranean atmosphere of the Gorges de Franchard in Fôret de Fontainebleau

- The wide unspoiled beaches in Finistère, Brittany

- Rounding a towpath bend to see Château de Chenonceau straddling the Cher River

- Munching wild nuts plucked along quiet lanes in the Loire valley

- Setting out, like so many pilgrims across the centuries, from the magnificent facade of Vézelay's basilica in Burgundy

- A juicy Charolais steak, washed down with a glass or two of finest Burgundy wine

- Crunching tiny volcanic cinders underfoot on Puy de la Vache in the Massif Central

- Windy picnics up high in the Massif Central, each day with a different Auvergnat cheese

- Awesome views of Vignemale, the Pyrenees' highest summit; golden eagles; pine woodlands; alpine meadows and beautiful high lakes

- Enjoying the international camaraderie at a Pyrenean mountain refuge with minimal electricity, no showers and cold water only

- Hot sunny days in the wild, wide Quercy Causses, through timeless villages and

- past intricate stone-built walls, dovecotes and farm buildings

- Resisting – well almost – abundant temptations in street markets; discovering the rich, robust red wines of the Cahors

- Crossing the glorious Cirque de la Solitude in the high mountains of Corsica

- Descending through maquis to Conca on the last day of the two-week Corsican traverse

- Every single centimetre of the Gorges du Verdon in Provence

- The scent of wild thyme and rosemary on Provence trails

- Sharing sumptuous meals with lively French walkers at a gîte d'étape in the Parc National du Mercantour

- Reaching the Vercors plateau in the Southern Alps via a secretive pass

- Stepping out onto the ice of the Glacier des Bossons in the Northern Alps

- Getting as close as walkers can get to the world of mountaineers around Chamonix Aiguilles

- Rising above the morning mist in the valley of Valserine, Jura

- Tucking into a steaming plate of *choucroute Alsacienne*, the local sauerkraut

- Looking at the ribbon of path receding along the spine of the Crête des Vosges and feeling really rather small

been cut to the quick and are sometimes nonexistent outside the school year.

If you're planning to explore a couple of regions, check carefully how to get from one to another (Lonely Planet's *France* details the possibilities for trans-France travel in considerable detail). Build a little extra cash into the holiday budget to allow, say, for a 15km taxi ride which will save you a long walk or what might be a wait of several days. And don't discount the idea of hiring a car locally. Although not cheap (see Car & Motorcycle in the Getting Around chapter), it will certainly save you a lot of travelling time.

With a week to 10 days at your disposal, each one of the regions in this book merits a visit. Given the time required to reach the Pyrenees and Alps, however, a more extended visit is recommended. Especially satisfying possibilities include the soul-stirring Crête des Vosges in Alsace and more gentle walking through Burgundy's cereal fields, vineyards and forest trails around Dijon.

If you want to combine culture and walking, consider a week based in Paris, walking a trail or two in the Île de France, the green ring around the capital. Alternatively, enjoy a mix of chateaux and footpaths in the Loire Valley. Gastronomy? Both Alsace and Burgundy with their rich cuisines and fine wines are obvious destinations.

If you can spare two weeks or more, consider combining several days of walking in Provence, primarily in the Luberon area, with a two-day diversion to make an exploration of the Gorges du Verdon canyon.

You can enjoy a satisfying week in the Massif Central, setting out from Clermont Ferrand. But it's even more fulfilling to take a couple of weeks and work your way southwards to enjoy walks in the Monts Dômes, Monts Dore and Monts du Cantal. Alternatively, set out from Aurillac and work your way northwards.

For variety, think of combining a couple of contrasting regions within easy travelling distance of each other, eg, Brittany, with its rugged coastal walks, and the Loire Valley; or either venue in combination with the Paris region. Burgundy is well situated as a prelude or postscript to walking in the Jura to its

east. Similarly, Périgord and Quercy pull west as charming and more gentle counterweights to the imposing Massif Central.

If you have your own transport, Périgord and Quercy can also be combined with walks in Provence and, casting further, the Pyrenees. Similarly, for a high mountain holiday combined with hills or gorges, plan a walk or two from the Provence chapter, then climb into the Parc National du Mercantour in the Southern Alps.

If you're an aficionado of the really high stuff, the Pyrenees probably merit a walking holiday on their own, as do both the Chamonix Valley and Parc National de la Vanoise in the Northern Alps, and their equally impressive and very diverse sisters in the Southern Alps, the Parc National des Écrins, Parc Naturel Régional du Vercors and Parc Naturel Régional du Queyras.

And the island of Corsica? It needn't necessarily be out on its own in the Mediterranean. Although it's satisfying in itself, you can also travel there via Provence, jumping off to do the Calanques walk on the outskirts of Marseille or others further afield.

Wherever you walk, be it a long weekend or a two-month trek, eat, drink and make yourself merry at the end of each day. No country in the world has a greater variety of local cheeses, indigenous wines and regional dishes to restore your energy.

PLANNING
When to Walk

If you're free to determine your dates, avoid the second half of July and August. At this time the pressure upon accommodation can be intense, most of Europe seems to be on the move and prices tend to increase with the volume of visitors. During this period, the need to reserve your next night's bed varies on a scale from highly recommended to downright essential.

In the high mountain areas of the Alps and Pyrenees, the window for walking (unless you're confident on snow and ice) is a fairly small one. Advanced trekkers and mountaineers do attack the high mountain routes in winter, but we assume that most readers aren't so experienced and confine our recommendations to walking at less forbidding times of the year.

Drifts can linger into late June, even mid-July. Until this time, when crossing cols over 2500m you're likely to be tramping on beaten tracks over manageable snow. Summers are brief at this altitude and the earliest snows may fall in the first half of September.

Reducing further the optimum walking season, many *refuges* (refuges or mountain huts), particularly in the Pyrenees, are stretched to the limit and unpleasantly over-crowded in the second half of July and August. (Most *refuges* are open from June until the end of September and some in the Pyrenees and Alps keep a self-contained wing with limited services open all year for passing walkers and skiers). If you're camping you can bypass this problem – away from the *refuges* the slopes are vast enough and trails long enough to accommodate all.

Like the high mountains, parts of the Massif Central and Jura are popular ski areas. They and the Massif des Vosges are also snowbound in winter. But the walking season is longer – generally from early May until mid-October in the Massif Central, and well into November in the Jura and Massif des Vosges. Even at the height of summer, days are rarely too hot to prevent pleasant walking. Corsica is in its prime from May to June and from September to October, away from the summer crowds.

Brittany and the Loire Valley are pleasant between May and September and at their best for walking in late spring and autumn. Always pack a waterproof jacket, however, as rain can be unpredictable and intense. Further south, in Périgord, Quercy and Burgundy, the potential walking season is even longer and rain falls more predictably.

Avoid July and August in Provence. In addition to the pressure on facilities, it's just too darned hot for agreeable walking and many paths are closed because of the risk of forest fire. On the other hand, southern France is ideal walking country for a winter break. Check in advance, however, that your chosen hotel or camping ground is open as many close outside the main tourist season.

What Kind of Walk?

The range of potential walks within France is limitless – from tranquil riverside and coastal strolls to demanding high-mountain treks. Although much of France is now settled with small farms and intensive agriculture, there are still substantial wilderness areas around the Pyrenees and Alps.

France has a huge number of waymarked trails, allowing for easy navigation through a fascinating variety of rural landscapes. And at every turn there is something to delight the senses: small villages, chateaux, historic towns with soaring cathedrals, archaelogical sites and endless gastronomic riches.

The French walk in all sorts of ways: as lone trampers or couples, in small parties or as members of large walking groups, snaking in single file along the trails. It is not unusual to find families walking together, with the small children romping ahead. Weekend walks are very popular, as are week(s)-long walking holidays. Several of the popular long-distance walks in France follow old pilgrimage routes to important Christian shrines.

In France very few people hire a personal guide (except for mountain-climbing) – one certainly isn't required for any of the walks in this book. This said, most professional guides are well informed and congenial company. In popular walking areas, ask at the local tourist office (and check that the guide's English is adequate).

There are quite a few companies which arrange organised walking tours. With some, you walk as a group; with others, you set out with a packed lunch, map and briefing pack, confident that you have accommodation waiting at the end of the day. Others – and it could be worth signing up for this feature alone! – transport all luggage but your day-pack from one overnight stop to the next. You'll find French companies listed in the Guided Walks section later in this chapter.

Camping is very largely confined to French people in their 20s; if you see tents 'in the bush' their occupants are more likely to be British, German, Dutch or American. On the whole, the French enjoy walking hard all day and savouring the comforts of small hotels, *gîtes d'étapes* (walkers' accommodation) or *refuges* at night, especially so they can enjoy a decent meal. Deyhyds cooked over a small stove aren't popular! With sufficient planning, it's possible to undertake extensive walking tours without carrying a tent, given the ready availability of these types of built accommodation.

Maps

Two acronyms worth memorising are IGN, the Institut Géographique National, and FFRP, the Fédération Française de Randonnée Pédestre, a body representing more than 1600 walking clubs and associations. The IGN (ee-zhay-en) covers the nation with several series of maps at differing scales. The FFRP (ef-ef-ayr-pay) produces more than 180 Topo-Guides, guidebooks for walkers illustrated with maps, usually at 1:50,000, which are based upon IGN originals.

The contact details for both are listed under Useful Organisations. For more information on Topo-Guides, refer to Books. You'll find both sections later in this chapter.

Most maps give at least the key in English as well as French. Exceptions are the Rando Éditions maps of the Pyrenees, which are bilingual in French and Spanish, and the otherwise excellent walking maps of Alsace produced by the Club Vosgien in association with the IGN. This is no big deal; most symbols can be interpreted from their form alone.

For information on the custom-drawn walkers' maps in this book, see the Maps in this Book section under Walks in this Book later in this chapter.

Small-Scale Maps The IGN's 1:1,000,000 *France: Routes, Autoroutes* sheet No 901 (22FF) covers the whole country. A much more useful country map for walkers is *France: Grande Randonnée* sheet No 903 (29FF) which carries the same information and has all the country's long-distance trails, known as *sentiers de grande randonnée* (GRs), overprinted. On its rear is a two-tone map of France showing the distribution of every Top 25 and Série Bleue large-scale map (see the Large-Scale maps section).

Among other specialised IGN maps of France at this scale and price are those on mountain biking and cycle tourism (No 906), rock-climbing sites (No 909), inland waterways (No 913), and even golf courses around the nation (No 910). All have basic information in both English and German as well as French. *Vins de France* (No 915) has the principal wine regions highlighted and enough detailed information to keep the most oenophile of walkers delirious for days.

Michelin's Série Rouge (Red Series) *France* sheets, Nos 911 and 989, also cover France with sheets at 1:1,000,000.

If you're simply after a reliable map of the country, most tourist offices can come up with a freebie such as that produced for the French government tourist agency, Maison de la France, or for the Logis de France accommodation chain. Particularly worthwhile if you're driving is the *Bison Fute* (Smart Bison) map, which highlights secondary road alternatives to the busiest national highways and bottlenecks.

The red-covered Top 250 series (29FF) by IGN covers the nation in 16 regional maps at 1:250,000, while Michelin produces 17 maps at 1:200,000.

While ideal for cycling, IGN's Série Verte (Green Series) of 74 maps at 1:100,000 (29FF each) isn't really detailed enough for walking navigation. You might, however, think of picking up the Top 100 map for a region where you're planning to walk – or at least browsing through someone else's. Fairly reasonably priced (29FF), they're rich in tourist information and indicate GR trails. While they currently cover only major tourist areas, they are speedily replacing the Série Verte.

Large-Scale Maps At 1:25,000 and with contours indicated at 10m intervals, two IGN series cover the whole of France. The more recent Top 25 maps (58FF) cover most major tourist areas and will eventually supersede the older Série Bleue (Blue Series) maps (46FF). You don't usually have a choice since Série Bleue prints are almost always withdrawn from the market when an equivalent Top 25 is released.

Maps in each series are impressively detailed in information relevant to walkers; both, however, often fail to indicate isolated buildings – so often a useful navigational clue. Ideal for short walks of up to one day, they have two weaknesses. There's rarely any overlap from one map to another, so you may need to pack several to give full coverage of a day walk. And at 58FF they are expensive.

The numbering system is the same for both IGN series. Each four-digit number has an Est (East) and a Ouest (West) map, indicated by the E and O suffixes on Série Bleue maps and ET and OT on most Top 25s (eg, 3328ET and 3328OT).

The last of the four digits changes in the vertical plane. So you know that map 3327OT covers an area to the north of 3328OT, which in turn has 3329OT to its south. Similarly, the second digit changes in the horizontal plane. Map 3228ET is to the west of 3328OT. East of the latter is 3328ET, then 3428OT.

Clear as mud? Then think of each four-digit number as two sets of two. The first element of each pair represents the east–west axis (32, 33 and 34 in our example); the second half represents north–south (27, 28 and 29 in our example).

Note that a Top 25 map may not cover exactly the same area as its Série Bleue equivalent with the same reference number.

The IGN has all but phased out its Série Orange maps (46FF) which, at 1:50,000, would be ideal for extended walks. They are now only available from six IGN regional centres around the nation (details on its Web site; see Buying Maps at the end of this section). Once stocks are exhausted, they'll become collectors' items.

Private-sector alternatives provide coverage at this scale for several major walking areas. In the south, Rando Éditions (☎ 05 62 90 09 90, fax 05 62 90 67 22) spans the whole of the French side of the Pyrenees and considerable areas of trans-border Spain in 11 maps at 1:50,000. Contours are marked at 20m intervals and areas of steep terrain have elevation shading. Its maps include much other useful information, such

as the position of gîtes and refuges (for an explanation of gîtes, see the Accommodation section later in this chapter), but trails are sometimes more evident on the map than on the ground.

Didier Richard (69FF) gives complete coverage from Lake Geneva to the Mediterranean and from the Rhône River to the Italian border. It also produces a pair of maverick titles in Auvergne, west of the Rhône, and a couple of sheets which cover Corsica. Contour intervals are 20m and both gîtes and GRs are indicated.

Both companies use an IGN base for their maps and superimpose additional features.

There are several maps in two other impressive 1:50,000 IGN series: Plein Air, which is translated as 'Outdoor Activities' (58FF); and Culture et Environnement (48FF). Rich in information, they include both GRs and sentiers de petite randonnée (PRs), together with gîtes, hotels and camping grounds. Unfortunately, they don't cover very many of the most popular walking areas. If one does coincide with the region where you plan to walk, we suggest you make it your first choice at this scale.

Buying Maps In smaller communities, the most likely source for maps, particularly IGN Top 25 and Série Bleue sheets, is Maison de la Presse, a nationwide chain of newsagents and stationers. Often, the local tourist office and librairie (bookshop) will also carry a basic stock. All, with the possible exception of large bookshops, normally only sell maps of the immediate region so you may well need to order other sheets unseen and in advance.

In Paris, Espace IGN (☎ 01 43 98 80 00, fax 01 43 98 85 11, ✆ espace-ign@ign.fr), the massive IGN retail outlet, has more than 10,000 maps and is a mecca for cartophiles. It's at 107 rue de la Boetie, just off the Champs-Élysees (metro George V). You can also order IGN maps directly from its prize-winning, user-friendly Web site at www.ign.fr. Be warned, however, that for smaller orders from outside France heavy postal charges can exceed the cost of the maps themselves.

In the UK, Stanfords (☎ 020-7836 1321, fax 020-7836 0189, @ SALES@Stanfords.co.uk), nearly 150 years in business and a fascinating place to browse around, carries a wide range of IGN and Didier Richard sheets. It also operates an efficient mail-order service and is used to handling requests from far-flung places. Ring, email or write to 12–14 Long Acre, London WC2E 9LP.

What to Bring

When choosing what to bring on your trip, study the Climate section in each walks chapter, then select what's appropriate from the items recommended here. For suggestions about what to include in a basic medical kit, see the boxed text 'Medical Kit Check List' in the Health & Safety chapter.

Clothing If it's hot, wear light, loose clothing such as a T-shirt and shorts or a skirt. A pair of light trousers is preferable if undergrowth is thick and prickly. Stuff another T-shirt into your day-pack for use either as an extra layer or as a change if you become too sweaty. Wear a hat with a brim wide enough to keep the sun off your face. Sunglasses, if there's intense glare, are more than a fashion statement.

The secret of happy walking when it's cold is to wear several layers of light clothing. Although tedious to pull on and off, layers allow you to fine-tune your body temperature; the wind may be knifing into your face, but if you're working hard uphill with a full backpack, the rest of you may feel as though it's in a sauna.

A lightweight, windproof external layer helps to prevent your body from losing too much warmth. A tightly woven cotton or polycotton jacket or a windproof synthetic fleece does the job. Next to the skin, wear a synthetic base layer such as polypropylene, with its ability to wick the moisture away from the body and reduce chilling. Between the two is an ideal space to use those old blouses or shirts that it would pain you to throw out.

Below the waist, many walkers are most comfortable in shorts. Loose-fitting trousers, supplemented if it's really cold by a pair of thermal leggings, will keep you cosy. Leave the Levi's at home; denim is inflexible and, once it's wet, clings around your legs like a cold compress.

Up top (bear in mind that up to 60% of body heat is lost via your head), pull on a cold-weather cap or balaclava and bring along a pair of gloves or mittens.

Against rain, it's well worth investing in a jacket containing Sympatex, Gore-Tex or a similar breathable fabric. It should have a roomy map pocket and a hood which allows some peripheral vision; this can be important in difficult terrain. A good jacket will also have a storm flap over the main zip and drawcords at either waist or hem.

Also to combat rain, a pair of breathable, waterproof overtrousers – with slits for pocket access and ankle zips so that you don't have to pull your boots off when putting them on – are worth the investment. Otherwise, pull on a pair of shorts; legs dry much more easily than soggy trousers.

Footwear You can get by with all sorts of compromises above the ankles, but never sell yourself short on footwear. On easier walks, runners (training shoes), are adequate. For anything more challenging, a pair of good boots will repay the investment time and again.

The heavy, clumping mud-collectors of yesteryear are now extinct, replaced by a wide choice of brands in quality fabric or lightweight leather. In fabric, choose a pair with a waterproof and breathable fabric lining. Firm ankle support is essential, while a sole with widely spaced treads and a stepped heel will help you to negotiate rough terrain. Lastly, make sure you and your boots get to know each other on at least a couple of outings before you head off on a walking holiday; there's nothing worse for morale than throbbing blisters at the end of the first day.

Choose appropriate socks, the vital interface between feet and boots. Synthetic or a wool and synthetic mixture will give the best cushioning and the least friction. Check that there are no seams around the toes; these can cause blisters.

Equipment Check List

This list is a general guide to the things you might take on a walk. Your list will vary depending on the kind of walking you want to do, whether you're roughing it in a tent or planning on staying in a *refuge*, and on the terrain, weather conditions and time of year.

Equipment
- [ ] backpack with waterproof liner
- [ ] camera and spare film
- [ ] emergency, high-energy food
- [ ] gaiters
- [ ] map, compass and guidebook
- [ ] medical kit, toiletries and insect repellant*
- [ ] pocket knife (with corkscrew)
- [ ] sewing kit
- [ ] sleeping sheet
- [ ] small towel
- [ ] sunglasses and sunscreen
- [ ] survival bag or blanket
- [ ] torch (flashlight) with spare batteries and globe
- [ ] water containers
- [ ] water purification tablets, iodine or filter
- [ ] whistle (for emergencies)

Clothes
- [ ] runners (training shoes) or sandals
- [ ] socks and underwear
- [ ] shorts and trousers
- [ ] sunhat
- [ ] sweater, fleece or windproof jacket
- [ ] thermal underwear
- [ ] T-shirt and long-sleeved shirt with collar
- [ ] walking boots and spare laces
- [ ] warm hat, scarf and gloves
- [ ] waterproof jacket or cape
- [ ] waterproof overtrousers

Camping
- [ ] cooking, eating and drinking utensils
- [ ] dishwashing items
- [ ] insulating mat
- [ ] matches or lighter and candle
- [ ] portable stove and fuel
- [ ] sleeping bag
- [ ] spare cord
- [ ] tent (check pegs and poles)
- [ ] toilet paper and toilet trowel

Optional Items
- [ ] altimeter
- [ ] binoculars
- [ ] day-pack
- [ ] emergency distress beacon
- [ ] GPS
- [ ] lightweight groundsheet
- [ ] mobile phone
- [ ] notebook and pencil
- [ ] swimming costume
- [ ] walking poles or stick
- [ ] walkman/radio
- [ ] waterproof, slip-on backpack cover

* see the Medical Kit Check List in Health & Safety

If you're staying out overnight, don't forget to slip some lightweight footwear into your backpack to give both boots and feet a rest at the end of the day.

Equipment If you're limiting yourself to day walks you can happily skip most of what follows, with the exception of our advice on carrying water. Where it's scarce, you'll find springs and sources indicated on individual walk maps in this book, but you should always have a couple of containers in your backpack. They needn't be anything fancy – plastic bottles will do.

For a general discussion of those camping essentials: backpack, tent, sleeping bag and portable stove, refer to the boxed text 'Choosing Gear'.

Other gear requirements include a sleeping sheet if you're hopping from *refuge* to *refuge*, and an insulating mat for the hard, cold ground of the tent floor. This can either be a foam or a self-insulating one, which takes up less space (but costs considerably more).

Choosing Gear

Backpack

Most overnight walks in this book require the use of a dedicated walking backpack. (Travel packs are an efficient way to mix airline-hopping and some trail-walking, but are not really suited to multiday walking in challenging weather.) While styles, constructions and traditions vary from continent to continent, a good backpack should:

- be sturdily constructed from a long-wearing fabric such as canvas or woven synthetic, with high-quality stitching, straps and buckles, a lightweight internal or external frame and resilient and smoothly working zips
- have an adjustable, well-padded harness which distributes weight evenly
- be large enough to comfortably fit all your walking gear, eliminating the need to strap bits and pieces to the outside where they can be lost or damaged
- be water-resistant, with a minimum of external nooks and crannies for water to seep through; stitched seams can be treated with a sealant such as beeswax if the weather is likely to be poor
- be equipped with a small number of internal and external pockets to provide easy access to frequently used items such as snacks, maps etc.

Single-compartment, top-loading packs are generally the most watertight, although some people prefer the convenience of a dual-compartment pack which allows a sleeping bag or tent to be stowed in a compartment separated from the main space. No backpack is utterly waterproof and an internal liner such as a tough garbage bag should be used to ensure at least dry clothes and sleeping bag.

A day-pack or a smaller bum-bag (fanny pack) is perfect for day walks or side trips radiating from a central base camp, when little gear is required. Backpacks with a detachable day-pack can be well suited to this style of travel, although they often suffer the same design compromises as travel packs.

Tent

The choice of a tent largely depends upon the use to which it will be put. An expensive, modern tent may not be appropriate for someone who mostly pitches it in camping grounds or often seeks out hostel or *refuge* accommodation. However, a simple, single-skin canvas tent may be a dangerous choice for bivouacking on a high mountain pass in poor weather. Modern tents are usually dome or tunnel shaped, and have lightweight aluminium poles, a sewn-in waterproof floor and detachable fly, or outer tent. Such tents, while expensive, are roomy, lightweight, stable in windy conditions and pack into a small space.

Sleeping Bag

For serious overnight walking, a good sleeping bag is essential. The two main types differ in the insulating material with which they are filled. Down sleeping bags rely on the extraordinary ability of fine duck or goose feathers to 'loft', or expand, and thus trap a large volume of air within the bag's shell. It is this air, not the fill itself, which is warmed by the body and which insulates you from the cold. Down is extremely light, compresses into a very small volume and has remarkable loft. However, once wet it loses almost all of its insulating ability. A bag with a waterproof, breathable outer shell, while more expensive and a little heavier, can eliminate this drawback.

The alternative is a synthetic-fill bag, in which down is replaced with one of a variety of artificial fibres designed to mimic the lofting ability of the natural product. Early generations of such bags were significantly heavier and bulkier than a down bag of equivalent warmth but this type of bag has the advantage of retaining its loft, and thus warmth, when damp.

Choosing Gear

Sleeping bags are made either in a tapered ('mummy') shape, which minimises surface area and wasted internal space, or are rectangular, which is less constricting but not as warm for the weight. A hood and an internal muff, or heat-seal, around the shoulders and along the zip increases warmth, while a dual-ended, full-length zip allows you to fine-tune the temperature by selectively opening or closing it at the feet and chest.

Stove

Increasingly, with the depletion of wood resources near ever-more-popular camp sites and the growing awareness of the fragility of some wild environments, walkers are abandoning the traditional campfire for one of a range of fuel stoves. These fall into three broad categories.

- Multifuel stoves are small, very efficient and run on a variety of petroleum fuels (including automobile and aircraft fuel), making them ideal for use in places where a reliable supply of one type of fuel is hard to find. They tend, however, to be sootier, more prone to blockages due to contaminated fuel and require some care and experience to use and maintain.
- Methylated spirit (ethyl alcohol) burners are slower and less efficient (requiring more fuel to be carried) but are safe, clean and easy to use. They often come as a complete cooking kit, with integrated compact pots, pans and kettles.
- Butane gas stoves are commonly sold in camping shops around the world and rely on disposable cartridges which must be packed into and out of the wilds. While clean and reliable, they can be slow, awkward to pack and are expensive to run over the long term. Cartridges are widely available, which removes the need to negotiate the often confusing variety of names and unreliable supply of liquid fuels.

Consider also packing a pair of lightweight telescopic poles. Far from being the preserve of the elderly, they're almost a fashion item in the mountains these days. Whatever the terrain, they take most of the weight of your pack away from your back and haunches. The real mountaineer's gear of ice axe and crampons is very much an optional extra, even for some of the highest level walks in this book.

Among smaller but no less vital items is a compass – plus the ability to use it. An altimeter, although by no means essential, can also be a valuable navigational aid. Other useful items include extra plastic bags, a map holder to keep your maps clean and dry, a whistle to call for help in an emergency, a pocket knife and a torch (flashlight). In case of emergency, pack either a polythene 'bivvy bag' or an aluminium 'space' blanket.

With everything assembled, lay it out on the floor, decide what's indispensable and discard the remainder. Once you've tucked the residue back into your pack, reflect upon the advice of Georges Veron, the classic French mountaineer and writer. For comfortable walking, he says, your pack should not exceed 14kg. Like so many before you, spill it all out on the floor again and decide what's *really* essential. Pack everything back in and take off for a strenuous day walk. Back home again, ask yourself how you're feeling. If the answer's less than positive, sling out yet more.

GPS Originally developed by the US Department of Defense for the submarine fleet, the Global Positioning System (GPS) is a network of more than 20 earth-orbiting satellites that beam encoded signals back to earth. Small, computer-driven devices – GPS receivers – can decode these signals to give users an extremely accurate reading of their location – to within 30m. It should be understood that a GPS receiver is of little use to walkers unless used with an accurate topographical map; the GPS receiver simply gives your precise position, which you must then locate on the local map. GPS receivers will only work (properly) in the open. Directly below high cliffs, next to reflective surfaces (such as an expanse of water) or in dense tree-cover, for example, you may get inaccurate readings. GPS receivers are also more vulnerable to breakdowns (including dead batteries) than the humble magnetic compass, so don't rely on one entirely.

Buying Locally The best advice is to bring your gear with you, having tried out everything in advance so that your boots and backpack are comfortable and you can put up that new tent alone in a strong wind with your eyes shut.

In Paris, Au Vieux Campeur (☎ 01 53 10 48 48, www.au-vieux-campeur.fr) is a megacomplex of 18 shops around 48 rue des Écoles, 5e. Just off blvd Saint-Germain, it holds a massive stock. Alternatively, try Passe Montagne (☎ 01 43 29 09 43), 95 ave Denfert-Rochereau.

In Lyon, visit the more modest Au Vieux Campeur (☎ 04 78 60 81 00), at 43 cours de la Liberté, or Ad Hoc Montagne (☎ 04 72 41 75 62), 2 rue Vaubecour.

Popular camping shops in Marseille include Corner Street (☎ 04 91 33 15 83), 30B rue de Rome, and Ilot-Sports (☎ 04 91 33 88 35), 12 rue Euthymènes.

Many quite small towns have a sports gear shop which stocks basic walking and camping equipment. Nationwide chains include Decathlon, Go Sports, Aigle, La Hutte and Intersport.

To buy kerosene *(kerosène)*, methylated spirits *(alcool a brûler* or *alcool dénaturé)* and canisters for Camping Gaz and its analogues, look for the signs *droguerie* or *quincaillerie* (hardware or ironmongers shop), or *bricolage* (do-it-yourself or DIY shop). Make sure, however, that your stove is compatible with the fuel canisters available in Europe. You'll often find gas canisters in the sports and camping sections of large supermarkets. Sniff around their household products shelves for liquid fuels. White gas, or shellite *(essence blanche)*, for MSR-style stoves is difficult to find outside city centres. If you're flying in, don't be tempted to stow away a litre or two since all such fuel products are prohibited items.

Physical Preparation

There's no need to go overboard about preparations for a walking holiday in France. This said, some longish jogs or hikes in the two months before departure to build up stamina and a couple of weeks of preparatory stretching exercises will really pay off. If you plan to take a full backpack on your walking holiday, carry a partially loaded pack on some of your training outings.

WALKS IN THIS BOOK

At the beginning of the book is a table which summarises each walk's duration, standard, accessibility by public transport and the best time to undertake it, while also giving a brief indication of its main features.

Route Descriptions

The duration of each daily stage of a long walk depends upon the location of places to stay overnight on or near the route. Day walks range in duration from 3½ to nine hours of actual walking time. For many walks, there are suggestions for short cuts and easier alternatives.

To get the feel of a walk at a glance, consult the summary information at the head of the description. You'll find the duration, distance and standard indicated, as well as the starting and finishing points, the nearest town and whether or not the walk is accessible by public transport.

We recommend places to stay at the conclusion of each stage of a multi-day walk and at the beginning and/or end of day walks. When dividing up longer walks of several days, we've also taken into account access to public transport and the need to top up your food supplies. Bear in mind that the stages we recommend aren't, of course, immutable. On many of the longer walks several permutations are possible, especially if you're carrying a tent.

Within most walk descriptions, a bold highlight indicates just that: one of the day's highlights. At the end of a number of walk descriptions there are suggestions for side trips, ranging from a 20-minute detour to a full day's outing. Concise descriptions of other recommended walks are listed under the heading Other Walks at the end of each chapter.

Precise compass bearings are only given when there's a possibility of ambiguity. For the most part, we give the general direction you need to take (eg, 'head south', 'at the three-way junction take the path leading north-east' or 'keep heading south-west along the flank of the mountain').

Standards
Each walk is graded into one of five categories: easy, medium and hard plus the intermediate categories of easy-medium and medium-hard. When allotting a grade, we take into account such features as the amount and steepness of uphill walking, the degree of navigational skill required and whether the trail is well formed or rough. These features are more decisive than length: a 10km walk could be graded easy, medium or hard depending upon its other characteristics.

To an extent, the assessment is subjective. A route's difficulty can also vary according to weather conditions and, in the high mountains, the presence or absence of snow. We strongly recommend, therefore, that you read through the whole of a route description before deciding whether to undertake it and how much time to allow.

Easy These walks present no navigational difficulties, don't require the use of all four limbs at any point, last up to five or so hours and can comfortably be undertaken by a family with children over 12 years old.

Medium Medium routes can be walked with a little exertion by someone of average fitness. The relative difficulty may reside in route-finding, the length, changes of elevation, the difficulty of the terrain – or a combination of these factors. It assumes that you're familiar with the use of a compass.

Hard Walks graded hard are just that – tough in terms of navigation, terrain, ascent and length. They're gruelling and you may be finding your way cross-country with no path to guide you.

Times & Distances
On level terrain, moderately fit walkers following a clear path should be able to maintain a steady 4 to 5km/h. By contrast, a steep gradient and roughness underfoot can reduce this rate to as little as 1km/h on a sustained climb over rocky ground.

The times we quote for each walk – this is important – are *actual walking times*. Or, rather, we give a range to allow for the variation in people's walking paces. What we don't do is budget for lunch breaks, pee stops, photo calls, consulting the map, getting temporarily lost, pausing to take in the scenery, brewing a pot of tea and all the other little activities which break up the day and which, cumulatively, can add as much as a third again, or even half, to the net walking time.

Within a walk description we generally give measurements of time rather than distance from the starting point or from the last significant landmark since, on all but the easiest of terrain, the number of kilometres is a fairly meaningless figure.

Maps in This Book
At the beginning of each walks chapter is a regional map which shows main towns and cities, significant natural features and principal transport arteries.

Every walk described has an accompanying map which gives a clear picture of the route and its surroundings. This is best used in conjunction with one of the commercial maps recommended in the Planning section at the head of each walk description (and in the box on individual walk maps).

A continuous brown line indicates the route of a walk, while a broken line indicates either an alternative route or an optional side trip detailed in the text. You'll also find highlighted all significant natural features plus start and finish points, *refuges*, camping grounds, springs and water sources in dry regions and exceptional viewpoints.

Contours also appear in brown and in hilly terrain generally have large intervals (typically 100m). While they provide a broad indication of the topography, we recommend that you don't rely upon them alone for navigation as between each there can be some fairly considerable ups and downs.

Altitude Measurements

Altitude measurements in walk descriptions and on accompanying maps are based upon reference maps which we used while researching the walks. Spot heights sometimes vary from one commercial map to another, but the difference is never more than a few metres – nothing when you've slogged your way up a 500m climb.

Place Names & Terminology

For river banks we either give compass directions such as 'follow the north bank of the stream' or use the terms 'true left' and 'true right'. The 'true left bank' simply means the left bank as you look *down*stream.

You'll find key French words which occur in the names of natural features (such as Lac this or Mont that) in the Glossary at the end of the book.

For a discussion of the French system of walking trails, see the boxed text 'Walking French Trails'.

GUIDED WALKS

In season, most of the national parks including Mercantour, Écrins and the Pyrenees, and regional nature parks such as Armorique, Vercors and Queyras, organise ranger-led half-day and day walks. In each of these areas you should also find several small local companies/individuals who run guided walks. The local tourist office is a useful first point of contact. Among the French companies which run guided walks are:

Chamina (☎ 04 73 92 81 44, ✆ info@chamina.com, www.chamina.com) 5 rue Pierre-le-Vénérable, BP 436, 63012 Clermont Ferrand. Runs walking tours in the Massif Central.
France Randonnée (☎ 02 99 67 42 21, fax 02 99 30 02 96) 9 rue des Portes Mordelaises, 35000 Rennes. Conducts tours all over France.

Terres d'Aventure (☎ 01 53 73 77 77, www.terdav.com) 6 rue Saint-Victor 75005 Paris. Concentrates on mountain areas.
Fédération Unie des Auberges de Jeunesse (FUAJ; ☎ 01 44 89 87 27, fax 01 44 89 87 10, www.fuaj.org) 27 rue Pajol, 75018 Paris. Organises many activities, including guided walks. Chamonix youth hostel, for instance, runs a six-day walking tour of Mont Blanc.
Grand Angle (☎ 04 76 95 23 00, fax 04 76 95 24 78, ✆ GRAND ANGLE@wanadoo.fr) 38112 Méaudre. Runs guided walks and organises independent trips to Provence, the Pyrenees, Auvergne, throughout the Alps and to many other destinations.
La Balaguère (☎ 05 62 97 20 21, fax 05 62 97 43 01, ✆ balaguere@sudfr.com, www.balaguere.com) route d'Argelès Gazost, BP3, 65403 Arrens Marsous. Has an extensive program of guided and independent walks focused on the Pyrenees and surrounding areas.
Club Aventure (☎ 01 46 34 22 60, fax 01 40 46 87 56) 18 rue Séguier, 75006 Paris. Leads treks to, among other destinations, the Pyrenees, Alps, Provence, Périgord and Corsica.

For details of British, US and Australian companies that organise walking tours in France, see Organised Walks at the end of the Getting There & Away chapter.

RESPONSIBLE WALKING

The popularity of walking in rural France, particularly in its wild regions, can place great pressure on the natural environment. Consider the following tips when on the trails and play a small part in helping to preserve the ecology of France's rich countryside. (Take note of the boxed text 'National Park Regulations'.)

Fires

Every summer, hundreds of hectares of Provence and Languedoc-Roussillon in the south of France are ravaged by forest fire. In many areas, campfires are expressly prohibited, both because of the danger of forest fire and because too many campers cooking over wood can rapidly destroy the natural cycle of growth, decay and regeneration.

If you're in an area where wood is plentiful and walkers few, dig a small hole for your fire (to reduce risk of it spreading) and

Walking French Trails

There are four types of French walking trails, lovingly planned, waymarked and maintained by the FFRP; each has its own trail sign and system of classification. It's worth familiarising yourself with the different waymarkers, as on the trail there can be a confusing variety of paint splashes.

GR Trails

An amazing 60,000km of *sentiers de grande randonnée* (GRs) thread their way across the nation. Blazed red and white, these are long-distance routes which tend to be linear rather than circular. The GR4, for example, begins in Royan on the Atlantic coast, works its way down the Massif Central, crosses the Luberon, wriggles its way through the Gorges du Verdon and ends up at the Mediterranean. Others, such as the stunning GR20 (see the Corsica chapter) or the GR54, circling the spectacular Parc National des Écrins in the Alps, are more localised.

Major long-distance trails have a single digit. Offshoots have two or three numbers or a letter prefix. So, for example, the GR1, which circumnavigates the Paris metropolitan area, sprouts the GR11, 11A, 11B and 11C and also the GR111, 111A, 111B and 111C. All GR trails are waymarked with distinctive red and white bars.

International Trails

Some GR trails link in with an extensive system of international walking routes. These are the products of international agreements and run the length and breadth of Europe. The 2600km-long E2, for example, begins on the North Sea coast of the Netherlands, passes through Belgium and Luxembourg and enters France to cross the Massif des Vosges, taking in the spectacular Alpine scenery of eastern France before dipping into the Mediterranean in Nice. While in France, the E2 follows GR5 waymarkers, although occasionally you may see E2 signs.

GRP Trails

At a provincial or regional level are the *sentiers de grande randonnée de pays* (GRPs), sometimes also known as *sentiers de pays*. These are indicated by red and yellow stripes and are often circular. Designed for intense exploration of one particular area, they usually take from a couple of days to a week.

PR Trails

Largely local in nature, *sentiers de petites randonnée* (PRs) – sometimes referred to as *sentiers de pays* – can be anything from an hour to a full day's walking. PR trails are often indicated by a single yellow or green stripe, but you'll also come across blue, yellow-and-purple and other variants, adding local colour. In general, don't assume that because you're walking a designated PR trail it's necessarily well indicated. Most routes are superbly blazed, but a minority are inadequately signed with only the most desultory of markers.

---

use only as many twigs as it takes to cook with; it's amazing how few you'll need to bring water to a brisk boil. Never burn plastics or aluminium foil, and never light a fire in peaty soil, which consists largely of organic matter that can continue to smoulder long after you've moved on. Use only dead, fallen wood and ensure that you *fully* extinguish a fire when dinner's over. Spread the embers and douse them with water. Remember that an extinguished fire is only truly safe to leave when you can comfortably place your hand (or preferably someone else's) in it. In *refuges* in forested areas, it's courtesy to leave wood for those who come after.

In all other areas, use a fuel stove and be sure to pack empty canisters out with you.

Water

Where possible, avoid the use of detergents. That little luxury you allow yourself can play havoc with the fragile ecosystems of high mountain tarns and streams. As a basic rule, never use detergents or toothpaste, even if they claim to be biodegradable, in or near watercourses.

When washing yourself, if you do use soap, be sure that it's biodegradable and take yourself and your water container at least 50m away from the watercourse. Disperse the waste water widely to allow the soil or rock to filter it fully. In the same way, wash cooking utensils a good 50m from watercourses using a scourer, sand, snow or even grit instead of detergent.

Toilets

We all have to go. But contamination of water sources by human urine and faeces can lead to the transmission of all sorts of dire diseases to both humans and wildlife, which often lacks our defence mechanisms. Where you come across a toilet, take advantage of it; the next one could be miles or days away.

Where there's nothing so sophisticated, bury your waste. Dig a small hole 15cm deep and at least 100m from any watercourse. Some people carry a lightweight trowel for this purpose, although a sharp stone serves just as well. Cover the evidence with soil and top it with a rock. In stony, high mountain areas devoid of soil, simply turn over a large stone, perform and replace it. In snow, dig right down to the soil and beneath; otherwise, you risk sullying the pleasure of those who pass by once the snow melts.

Rubbish

Carry out all your rubbish. If you've managed to carry it in, you can pack it out. Don't overlook tiny items such as silver paper, cigarette butts, twist ties and plastic wrappers. Pack a small supermarket plastic bag to hold all such unpleasant bits and pieces. It's also worth making the small if sometimes mildly disagreeable effort to carry out rubbish left by others less responsible than yourself. The aphorism, 'Take only photos, leave only footprints', may be unduly twee, but it's based on sound common sense.

Never bury rubbish, which small animals will snuffle out and scatter almost as soon as you're round the nearest rock. It's also not good for their digestion. If the local fauna spurn it, your trash may take years to decompose, especially at high altitudes. Sanitary towels, tampons and condoms should also be carried out since they burn and decompose poorly.

Erosion

Hillsides and mountain slopes, especially at high altitudes, are prone to erosion. Stick to existing tracks and avoid short cuts that bypass a switchback. If you blaze a new trail straight down a slope, it's certain to become a watercourse with the next heavy rainfall and eventually cause soil loss and deep scarring.

National Park Regulations

Rules and regulations in France's national parks, established in areas of particular natural beauty, are designed to protect their fragile environment. Restrictions include:

- No camping (this said, you're allowed to *faire le bivouac* – put up your tent at dusk, strike camp in the early morning and move on – as long as you're over an hour's walk from a park entrance).
- No motor vehicles.
- No dogs, even on a lead.
- No taking flowers, insects or rock samples.
- No open fires. However, gas stoves are permitted.
- No leaving rubbish. Everything, even the smallest items, should be packed out.
- No mountain bikes.
- No hunting.
- No hang-gliding or parapenting at under 1000m.

Breaches of these restrictions may incur fines.

Where to Camp

The higher you go, the more sensitive the vegetation. Wherever possible, camp lower down in valleys and glens, where the land recovers more easily. Avoid popular places for wild camping. Your abstinence will reduce the pressure upon them – and the alternatives are usually more pleasant anyway.

At the end of the day – or rather, next morning as you prepare to move on – your site should bear no trace of your presence except some flattened grass, which will soon spring back into shape.

Access

If walking through private property, stick to the path and be sure to close all gates behind you, particularly if there is livestock around.

WOMEN WALKERS

You'll be extremely unlucky if you have any problems on the trails related specifically to gender. Like walkers everywhere, French hikers in general tend to be fairly socially enlightened and relaxed.

In *refuges*, toilets and washrooms are unisex and sleeping arrangements are often a single or double-decker bench running from one side of the dormitory to the other where male and female, young and old sleep side by side. If this worries you, pack a tent and retain your independence.

In general, as anywhere, it might be risky for a woman to hitch alone. Take a look also at the brief section on Hitching in the Getting Around chapter. It's advisable, say many sources, not to walk alone – but this applies to men probably as much as women and it's advice that many responsible walkers choose to disregard.

For a general discussion of issues relevant to women travellers, consult the *Handbook for Women Travellers* by M & G Moss.

WALKING WITH CHILDREN

There's no need to hang up your boots until the children are teenagers; walking with them in France is no more or less difficult than elsewhere in Western Europe and you'll see many parents and their children walking *en famille*.

Children are normally well received in French hotels, and camping grounds often have play areas and other facilities for children. Also, an increasing number of *auberges de jeunesse* (youth hostels) now provide family rooms.

Baby food, nappies (diapers), creams, potions and all the other paraphernalia of travelling with the very young are readily available in French towns, although you may not find your favourite brand. If you're planning to walk in less populated areas, stock up in advance.

Children can be slow to adapt to changes of diet, temperature and altitude, so before undertaking a route of several days it might be wise to first establish a base camp and do a number of day or half-day walks to break them – and yourself – in.

Try to choose walks that have plenty of variety, such as spending some time at a *maison du parc* (park information centre), a beach or pool, unusual features such as an archaeological site or a cave, or where there's a good chance of spotting wildlife. Or consider combining a walking holiday with a few days by the sea – plotting so that the more strenuous activity comes first! And if you're camping, check the brochures for a camping ground with a swimming pool.

Think seriously about hiring a car if you haven't brought your own so that you're not reliant upon infrequent or nonexistent rural bus services.

Those a little older can also carry their own pack, which might have a book in it for moments at rest stops when grown-ups get boring. There's a simple rule-of-thumb for calculating what kids can carry on a walk: most can comfortably walk their age and carry half of it. In other words, a 12-year-old should be able to walk about 12km per day in moderate terrain, carrying a pack which weighs 6kg.

Of the regions covered in this book, Brittany and Provence allow you to combine seaside and walking, while both the Jura and Auvergne have enticing lakes. Paris apart, the Loire Valley has perhaps the most interesting cultural distractions, while both the Loire Valley and Burgundy have gentle, undemanding countryside. In Burgundy, there are several gentle walks around Anost, where the municipal camping ground has an open-air swimming pool. Or you could take a family holiday in Paris, sampling its infinite number of distractions for all ages – and fit in a little walking as a secondary activity.

Bear in mind that for many walks we give suggestions for short cuts and easier alternatives which may be better suited to young legs. Many tourist offices can provide brochures and information sheets for short to medium walks within their purview.

Lonely Planet's *Travel with Children* by Maureen Wheeler has lots of practical advice on the subject, along with first-hand stories from a host of Lonely Planet authors and others.

USEFUL ORGANISATIONS
For information about Chamina and the Club Vosgien, both with a regional focus, see the Auvergne & Massif Central and the Alsace & Massif des Vosges chapters, respectively.

Fédération Française de la Randonnée Pédestre
Wherever you walk, you're bound to come across the tracks of the admirable Fédération Française de la Randonnée Pédestre (FFRP; ☎ 01 44 89 93 93, ✉ ffrp.paris@wanadoo.fr), which runs an information centre and bookshop at its headquarters at 14 rue Riquet, 75019 Paris. Its Web site, www.ffrp.asso.fr, in French has some particularly useful links.

The FFRP is a national body representing around 1800 affiliated associations and clubs and their 120,000 members. As well as being an effective national lobby group, it is involved in plenty of grassroots action: some 6000 volunteers maintain the organisation's trails. It also produces Topo-Guides – guidebooks for walkers illustrated with IGN maps – and the walking magazine *Passion Rando*.

Fédération Unie des Auberges de Jeunesse
Fédération Unie des Auberges de Jeunesse (FUAJ; ☎ 01 44 89 87 27, fax 01 44 89 87 10), 27 rue Pajol, 75018 Paris, is the French

youth hostel organisation and a member of Hostelling International. Its Web site, www.fuaj.org, which also has an English version, is well worth stopping by. For more information on hostels, see the Accommodation section later in this chapter.

Club Alpin Français
The national headquarters of the Club Alpin Français (French Alpine Club; ☎ 01 53 72 87 00, fax 42 03 55 60, ✉ club.alpin@wanadoo.fr) is at 24 ave de Laumière, 75019 Paris. It, too, is composed of lots of active regional groups who, among other responsibilities, maintain many of France's high-altitude *refuges*. The CAF also publishes the quarterly subscription magazine, *La Montagne et Alpinisme*.

TOURIST OFFICES
Local Tourist Offices
In towns and large villages, look out for the *office de/du tourisme*. Smaller communities may still use the title *syndicat d'initiative*, while even tinier ones may have a *point d'information*, often co-located with the *poste* (post office) or *mairie* (town hall).

Whatever their size they're usually an excellent resource. Their range of information – about hotels, camping grounds, gîtes, transport etc – is impressive. In particular, they can provide a list of potential accommodation and many will make local reservations for free or for a small fee. Some sell maps and Topo-Guides, while the best also sell nature handbooks. The quality of walking information varies. Some tourist offices have nothing, while others can offer photocopied maps and descriptions (usually only in French) of local trails and PRs.

If you are in a town or village where there is no tourist office and you need information, check with the town hall.

A national park or regional nature park usually has its own visitor centre (the latter often called a maison du parc) which merits a detour if your walk takes you nearby. You can learn a lot about the natural environment in which you're walking. The information, supported by a video or display panels, is usually more useful and relevant to walkers than that held by tourist offices. Here, too, you'll probably find local maps and Topo-Guides on sale.

In walks chapters, regional tourist office details are listed under Information Sources at the beginning of the chapter. Local tourist offices are mentioned under Gateways and Nearest Towns.

Tourist Offices Abroad

French government tourist offices (usually called Maisons de la France) include:

Australia
(☎ 02-9231 5244, fax 9221 8682,
❷ frencht@ozemail.com.au) 25 Bligh St, 22nd floor, Sydney, NSW 2000
Belgium
(☎ 02 513 73 89, fax 02 514 33 75,
❷ maisondelafrance@pophost.eunet.be) 21 ave de la Toison d'Or, 1050 Brussels
Canada
(☎ 514-288 4264, fax 845 4868,
❷ mfrance@mtl.net) 1981 McGill College Ave, Suite 490, Montreal, Que H3A 2W9
Germany
(☎ 069-975 8013 1, fax 745 55 6,
❷ maison_de_la_France@t-online.de) Westendstrasse 47, D-60325 Frankfurt
Ireland
(☎ 01-679 0813, fax 679 0814, ❷ french touristoffice@tinet.ie) 10 Suffolk St, Dublin 2
Italy
(☎ 02-584 8657, fax 584 8622,
❷ entf@enter.it) Via Larga 7, 20122 Milan
Japan
(☎ 03-3582 6965, ❷ oden@mdf.japon.com) 2-10-9 Akasaka, Minato-ku, Tokyo 107
Netherlands
(☎ 0900 112 2332, fax 020-620 3339,
❷ fra_vvv@euronet.nl) Prinsengracht 670, 1017 KX Amsterdam
Spain
(☎ 91-548 9740, fax 541 2412,
❷ maisondelafrance@mad.sericom.es) 8th Floor, Gran Via 59, 28013 Madrid
South Africa
(☎ 011-880 8062, fax 770 1666, ❷ mdfsa@ frenchdoor.co.za) Oxford Manor, 1st floor, 196 Oxford Road, Illovo, Johannesburg, 2196
Switzerland
Zürich: (☎ 01-211 3085, fax 212 1644) Löwenstrasse 59, 8023 Zürich
Geneva: (☎ 022-908 8977, fax 909 8971) 2 rue Thalberg, 1201 Geneva

UK
(☎ 0891-244 123, fax 020-7493 6594,
❷ piccadilly@mdlf.demon.co.uk) 178 Piccadilly, London W1V 0AL
USA
New York: (☎ 212-838 7800, fax 838 7855,
❷ info@francetourism.com) 444 Madison Ave, 16th floor, New York, NY 10022-6903
Los Angeles: (☎ 310-271 6665, fax 276 2835,
❷ fgtola@juno.com) 9454 Wiltshire Blvd, Suite 715, Beverley Hills, CA 90212-2967

VISAS & DOCUMENTS

You're more likely to lose your documents than to have them stolen. In walking country it's extremely unlikely that you'll be robbed. As elsewhere in Europe, however, petty thieves prowl certain parts of large cities, especially around bus and train stations. So before you leave home, it's prudent to photocopy all documents that are important to you (such as your passport, credit cards, travel insurance papers, air ticket, driving licence and even your Hostelling International card). Leave one copy with someone at home and keep another with you, separate from the originals. Also, memorise your passport number; it's surprising how often you need to quote it.

It's also a good idea to store details of your vital travel documents in Lonely Planet's free online Travel Vault in case you lose the photocopies or can't be bothered with them. Your password-protected Travel Vault is accessible online anywhere in the world – create it at the Travel Vault Web site: www.ekno.lonelyplanet.com.

In the Alps and Pyrenees one or two walks run near either the Italian or Spanish border. However, since both countries and France are signatories to the 1997 Schengen agreement, frontier posts are of only historical interest. Additionally, a couple of Jura walks poke a toe into Switzerland. On those days, remember to pack your passport, even though the odds of anyone wanting to see it are minimal.

Citizens of European Union (EU) member states and of Switzerland can travel to and within France on nothing more than their national identity card. Other nationalities must have a passport. This includes Brits, who haven't got around to ID cards. Note too that UK visitors passports are not recognised.

By law, you're meant to have your passport or ID card on you at all times. (If you're reluctant to have your passport on your person for security reasons, carry a photocopy.) In practice, the only occasion when you'll regularly have to flash it is when registering at a hotel or camping ground.

Visas

There are no entry requirements or restrictions on nationals of the EU. Citizens of Australia, the USA, Canada, New Zealand and Israel don't need visas to visit France as tourists for up to three months. Except for people from a handful of other European countries, everyone else needs a visa.

Visas are normally issued on the spot. One valid for a stay of up to 30 days costs around UK£18, and a single/multiple entry visa of up to three months is about UK£21.50/25.50. You will need to produce your passport (valid for a period of three months beyond the date of your departure from France), a return ticket, proof of sufficient funds to support yourself, proof of prearranged accommodation (possibly), two passport-size photos and the visa fee in cash.

If you enter France overland, your visa may not be checked at the border, but major problems can arise if you can't produce one later on (eg, at the airport as you leave the country).

Visa Extensions Tourist visas *cannot* be extended except in emergencies (eg, medical problems). If you're in Paris and have an urgent problem, you should call the Préfecture de Police (☎ 01 53 71 51 68) for guidance.

If you don't need a visa to visit France, you'll almost certainly qualify for another automatic three-month stay if you take the train to Geneva or Brussels, say, and then re-enter France. The fewer recent French entry stamps you have in your passport the easier this is likely to be. If you needed a visa the first time around, one way to extend your stay is to go to a French consulate in a neighbouring country and apply for another one there.

Travel Insurance

A personal travel insurance policy to cover theft, loss and medical problems – particularly if you're walking the high mountains – is important. Look closely at the small print before signing up; some policies specifically exclude 'dangerous activities', which might be construed to include trekking. Ensure that your policy covers the cost of an ambulance and emergency flight home. If you have to stretch out you'll need two, even three, seats and airlines don't give them away!

You may prefer a policy which pays doctors or hospitals directly rather than requiring you to pay up-front and claim later. If you opt for the latter, make sure you keep all documentation. Some policies ask you to call back (reverse charges) to a centre in your home country, where an immediate assessment of your problem is made.

For a discussion of medical cover for citizens of EU countries, see Medical Cover under Predeparture Planning in the Health & Safety chapter.

Other Documents

EU and many non-European driving licences are valid in France. If you're from outside the EU, it's a good idea to also carry an International Driving Permit. Valid for 12 months, they can be picked up from the automobile association in your home country. Note that the permit is not valid unless accompanied by your original licence.

You only need a Hostelling International (HI) card at an official auberge de jeunesse. Just present an HI card from your home country. If you haven't got one, you can enrol at most auberges de jeunesse on arrival (see Hostels under Accommodation later in this chapter for cost details).

EMBASSIES & CONSULATES
French Embassies & Consulates

French diplomatic representations abroad include:

Australia
  Embassy: (☎ 02-6216 0100, fax 6216 0127)
  6 Perth Ave, Yarralumla, ACT 2600
  Consulate: (☎ 03-9820 0944/0921, fax 9820

9363) 492 St Kilda Rd, Level 4, Melbourne, Vic 3004
Consulate: (☎ 02-9261 5779, fax 9283 1210) St Martin's Tower, 20th floor, 31 Market St, Sydney, NSW 2000

Canada
Embassy: (☎ 613-789 1795, fax 562 3735) 42 Sussex Drive, Ottawa, Ont K1M 2C9
Consulate: (☎ 514-878 4385, fax 878 3981) 1 place Ville Marie, 26th floor, Montreal, Que H3B 4S3
Consulate: (☎ 416-925 8041, fax 925 3076) 130 Bloor St West, Suite 400, Toronto, Ont M5S 1N5

Germany
Embassy: (☎ 030-206 3900 0, fax 206 3900 0) Kochstrasse 6–7, D-10969 Berlin
Consulate: (☎ 030-885 9024 3, fax 882 5295) Kurfürstendamm 211, 10719 Berlin
Consulate: (☎ 089-419 4110, fax 419 4114 1) Möhlstrasse 5D, 81675 Munich

Ireland
Embassy: (☎ 01-260 1666, fax 283 0178) 36 Ailesbury Rd, Ballsbridge, Dublin 4

Italy
Embassy: (☎ 06-686 011, fax 860 1360) Piazza Farnese 67, 00186 Rome
Consulate: (☎ 06-6880 6437, fax 6896 490) Via Giulia 251, 00186 Rome

Netherlands
Embassy: (☎ 070-312 5800, fax 312 5854) Smidsplein 1, 2514 BT The Hague
Consulate: (☎ 020-530 6969, fax 530 6988) Vijzelgracht 2, 1000 HA Amsterdam

New Zealand
Embassy: (☎ 04-384 2555, fax 384 3577) 34–42 Manners St, Wellington

Spain
Embassy: (☎ 91-423 8900, fax 423 8901) Calle de Salustiano Olozaga, 928001 Madrid
Consulate: (☎ 91-319 7188, fax 308 6273) Calle Marques de la Enseñada 10, 28004 Madrid
Consulate: (☎ 91-700 7800, fax 700 7801) Ronda Universitat 22, 08007 Barcelona

UK
Embassy: (☎ 020-7201 1000, fax 7201 1004) 58 Knightsbridge, London SW1X 7JT
Consulate: (☎ 020-7838 2000, fax 7838 2001) 21 Cromwell Rd, London SW7 2DQ. The visa section is at 6A Cromwell Place, London SW7 2EW (☎ 020-7838 2051). Dial ☎ 0891-887733 for visa information.

USA
Embassy: (☎ 202-944 6000, fax 944 6166) 4101 Reservoir Rd NW, Washington, DC 20007
Consulate: (☎ 212-606 3600, fax 606 3620) 934 Fifth Ave, New York, NY 10021

Consulate: (☎ 415-397 4330, fax 433 8357) 540 Bush St, San Francisco, CA 94108. Other consulates are located in Atlanta, Boston, Chicago, Houston, Los Angeles, Miami and New Orleans.

Embassies & Consulates in France

All foreign embassies are in Paris. Canada, the UK and the USA also have consulates in other major cities.

Australia
(☎ 01 40 59 33 00; metro Bir Hakeim) 4 rue Jean Rey, 15e

Canada
Embassy: (☎ 01 44 43 29 00; metro Franklin D Roosevelt) 35 ave Montaigne, 8e
Consulate: (☎ 03 88 96 65 02) rue du Ried, La Wantzenau, 12km north-east of Strasbourg
Consulate: (☎ 05 61 99 30 16) 30 blvd de Strasbourg, Toulouse

Germany
Embassy: (☎ 01 53 83 45 00; metro Franklin D Roosevelt) 13 ave Franklin D Roosevelt, 8e
Consulate: (☎ 01 42 99 78 00; metro Iéna) 34 ave d'Iéna, 16e
Consulate: (☎ 03 88 15 03 40) 15 rue des Francs Bourgeois, 15th floor, Strasbourg

Ireland
(☎ 01 44 17 67 00; metro Argentine) 4 rue Rude, 16e, between ave de la Grande Armée and ave Foch

Italy
Embassy: (☎ 01 49 54 03 00; metro Rue du Bac) 51 rue de Varenne, 7e
Consulate: (☎ 01 44 30 47 00; metro La Muette) 5 blvd Émile Augier, 16e
Consulate: (☎ 04 79 33 20 36) 12 blvd Lèmenc, Chambery

Netherlands
(☎ 01 40 62 33 00; metro Duroc) 7–9 rue Eblé, 7e

New Zealand
(☎ 01 45 00 24 11; metro Victor Hugo) 7ter rue Léonard de Vinci, 16e, one block south of Ave Foch

Spain
(☎ 01 44 43 18 00; metro Alma Marceau) 22 ave Marceau, 8e

UK
Consulate: (☎ 01 44 51 31 00; metro Concorde) 16 rue d'Anjou, 8e
Consulate: (☎ 04 72 77 81 70, fax 04 72 77 81 70) 4th floor, 24 rue Childebert, Lyon

USA

Consulate: (for a recorded information service ☎ 01 43 12 23; for 24 hours a day in an emergency ☎ 01 43 12 49 48) 2 rue Saint Florentin, 1er

Consulate: (☎ 04 91 54 92 00, fax 04 91 55 09 97) 12 blvd Paul Peytral, Marseille

CUSTOMS

Duty-free allowances for travel between EU countries were abolished in 1999. Allowances for duty-free goods purchased outside the EU are: tobacco (200 cigarettes, 50 cigars, or 250g of loose tobacco), alcohol (1L of strong liquor or 2L of less than 22% alcohol by volume; 2L of wine), coffee (500g or 200g of extracts) and perfume (50g of perfume and 0.25L of toilet water).

Allowances are generous for duty-paid items (including alcohol and tobacco) bought anywhere in another EU country and brought into France, where certain goods might be more expensive. You can buy up to 800 duty-paid cigarettes, 200 cigars, or 1kg of loose tobacco; 10L of spirits (more than 22% alcohol by volume), 20L of fortified wine or aperitif, 90L of wine or 110L of beer.

MONEY
Currency

France's unit of currency is the franc (abbreviated in this book to FF), which will be superseded by the euro (€) on 1 January 2002. From this date, Euro coins and notes will be used alongside the franc for a few months until 1 July 2002, when the franc will cease to be legal tender. As a rule of thumb, until you get used to it, think of the euro as the equivalent of US$1.

One French franc is divided into 100 centimes. Coins come in denominations of 5, 10, 20 and 50 centimes (0.5FF) and 1, 2, 5, 10 and 20FF; the two highest denominations are easily recognisable by their silvery centres and brass edges. Banknotes are issued in denominations of 20, 50, 100, 200 and 500FF. It's often difficult to get change for a 500FF note.

There are eight kinds of euro coin: 1, 2, 5, 10, 20 and 50 cents (€0.5), plus €1 and €2. Banknotes come in denominations of 5, 10, 20, 50, 100, 200 and €500.

Exchange Rates

The franc's exchange rate was fixed on 1 January 1999 against member states of the EU who signed up for the first round of the euro. While exchange rates against other major world currencies will, of course, fluctuate. Current exchange rates are listed on Lonely Planet's SubWWWay page: www.lonelyplanet.com/weblinks/weblinks.htm.

country	unit		franc
Australia	A$1	=	4.20FF
Canada	C$1	=	4.65FF
euro	€1	=	6.55FF
Germany	DM1	=	3.35FF
Ireland	I£1	=	8.35FF
Italy	L1000	=	3.40FF
Japan	¥100	=	6.35FF
Netherlands	f1	=	3.85FF
New Zealand	NZ$1	=	3.35FF
Spain	100 ptas	=	3.95FF
Switzerland	1SF	=	4.10FF
UK	UK£1	=	10.75FF
USA	US$1	=	6.80FF

Exchanging Money

In large cities, especially Paris, exchange bureaus *(bureaux de change)* are faster, easier, open longer hours and give better rates than banks. However, among the reputable dealers are a number of cowboys. Beware of the small print and if you find, for instance, that the commission is absurdly high or that there are unreasonable hidden extras don't hesitate to ask for your money back

Because of counterfeiting, it may be difficult to change US$100 notes, even in banks

Travellers Cheques Banks and exchange bureaus often give a better rate for travellers cheques than for cash. However banks exact a charge of 20FF to 35FF per transaction or depending, a commission o 1.2 to 2%. Post offices cash travellers cheques and change cash on a commission-free basis.

Lost or Stolen Travellers Cheques If your American Express (www.americanexpress.com) travellers cheques are lost or stolen in France, call ☎ 0800 90 86 00, a 24-hou toll-free number. In Paris, the main American Express office (☎ 01 47 77 70 00; metro Auber or Opéra) is at 11 rue Scribe, 9e; American Express also has offices in 14 other French cities.

If you lose your Thomas Cook cheques, contact any Thomas Cook bureau – in a major train station or one of the Paris offices such as 4 blvd Saint-Michel, 6e (☎ 01 46 34 70 18) – for replacements. The company's customer service bureau can be contacted toll-free by dialling ☎ 0800 90 83 30.

Credit & Debit Cards For withdrawing cash and for general purchases, Visa (Carte Bleue) and MasterCard (Access or Eurocard) are widely accepted. American Express cards are not very useful except at upmarket establishments, but they do allow you to get cash at certain ATMs and more than a dozen American Express offices in France. In general, all three cards can be used to pay for travel by train.

ATMs The most rapid and flexible way to get cash is to use an ATM (automatic teller machine), or cash dispensing machine. Look for the sign Point d'Argent or, less frequently, Distributeur Automatique de Billets (DAB). You'll find them in the wall of most banks and at major train and bus stations. To avoid paying interest, use a card with the international Cirrus or Maestro symbol, where your account is debited instantaneously.

On the Walk
The safest way to travel, in general, is with a modicum of cash and your money accessible via a credit card, supplemented by a reserve of travellers cheques. This said, ensure that you have enough francs or euros to live modestly for four or five days if you're off on a longish linear trek in Corsica, the Pyrenees or Alps.

Costs
Transport costs, which can really skew your budget, needn't be that great if you stick to buses and trains (see the Getting Around chapter). Transport apart, you can live comfortably on 200FF to 300FF a day and on less than 200FF if you're camping wild and free and your only expense is food.

A typical daily budget might include:

Item	cost (FF)
camp site	25 to 50
refuge or gîte	65 to 75
modest hotel	150 to 200
hotel breakfast	20 to 40
dinner in a modest restaurant	55 to 85
loaf of bread and filling	15 to 20
coffee	20
glass of beer, wine or soft drink	7 to 10

Individual travel styles will dictate your budget. Two people travelling together can greatly reduce hotel costs as single room rates are not much lower than doubles. For more information on overnight costs and standards, see the Accommodation section later in this chapter.

Tipping & Bargaining
Cafe and restaurant bills include an element for service. Most people leave a few additional francs in restaurants as a *pourboire* (tip). However, they rarely tip in cafes or bars if they've just had a coffee or drink.

In taxis, the usual tip is 2FF no matter what the fare, with the maximum about 5FF. People in France rarely bargain, except at flea markets.

Taxes & Refunds
France's TVA *(taxe sur la valeur ajoutée)*, known in English as VAT, is 20.6% on most goods except food, medicine and books, for which it's 5.5%. Luxury items such as watches and cameras attract a heavy 33%. Prices that include VAT are often marked TTC *(toutes taxes comprises*; meaning 'all taxes included').

Non-EU residents can get a refund of most of the VAT, provided: they're aged over 15, spend less than six months in France, purchase goods (not more than 10 of the same item) worth at least 1200FF (tax included) at a single shop; and the shop offers duty-free sales. Some shops may refund 14% of the purchase price rather than the full 17.1%

entitlement to cover the expense involved in the refund procedure. They'll explain what you have to do as you leave France.

POST & COMMUNICATIONS

Each of France's 17,000 post offices has a broad yellow sign above it reading 'La Poste'. To mail things in larger branches, go to a window marked *toutes opérations*. In towns, post offices are usually open from 8 am to 7 pm (with a midday break) on weekdays and until midday on Saturday. Those in rural areas often observe much shorter hours, and some may only be open for two or three days each week.

Post

The mail service is fast and efficient. Domestic letters up to 20g cost 3FF. Postcards and letters up to 20g are 3FF within the EU; 3.80/3.90FF to most of the remainder of Europe as well as Africa; 4.40FF to the USA, Canada and the Middle East; and 5.20FF to Australasia. Aerograms cost 5FF to all destinations.

If you're having mail sent to you, ask friends to ensure that the envelope bears the five-digit post code. Addresses should be written as:

John SMITH
8, rue de la Poste
75020 Paris
FRANCE

To have mail sent to you via poste restante (general delivery), available at all French post offices, have it addressed as follows:

SMITH, Jane
Poste Restante
Recette Principale
76000 Rouen
FRANCE

Since poste restante mail is held alphabetically by family name, follow the French practice of having it written first and in capitals. If the long-awaited letter from the folks back home isn't there, ask the clerk to also check under the first letter of your *prénom* (first name). There's a 3FF charge per item up to 20g (4FF up to 100g).

In larger towns and cities, poste restante mail not addressed to a particular branch goes to the *recette principale* (main post office).

A new service appearing in post offices throughout the country is Internet access (for details of the service, see Email & Internet later in this section).

Telephone

The country code for France is 33. France has five telephone dialling areas and all domestic numbers have 10 digits. The first two indicate the region:

01	Paris region
02	north-west
03	north-east
04	south-east (including Corsica)
05	south-west

To call a number in France from abroad, dial your country's international access code, then 33, then omit the 0 at the beginning of the 10-digit local number.

The international access code for dialling overseas from within France is 00. Useful country codes include:

Australia	61
Canada	1
Ireland	353
Italy	39
Germany	49
Japan	81
Netherlands	31
New Zealand	64
Spain	34
South Africa	27
UK	44
USA	1

For directory inquiries ring ☎ 12. Don't be surprised if the operator doesn't speak English. The call is free from public phones but costs 3.71FF from private lines.

Many cafes and restaurants have privately owned, coin-operated Point Phones. To find one, look for a blue and white window sticker bearing the Point Phone emblem.

Phonecards One of your first purchases after arriving in France might well be a phone card since very few public telephones nowadays accept cash. *Télécartes* are sold widely at post offices, *tabacs* (tobacconists), supermarkets, train stations – anywhere you see a blue sticker reading '*télécarte en vente ici*'. Cards worth 50/120 calling units cost 40.60/97.50FF.

Lonely Planet's rechargeable eKno Communication Card (see the insert at the back of this book) is aimed specifically at independent travellers and provides budget international calls, a range of messaging services, free email and travel information – for local calls, you're usually better off with a local card. You can join online at the eKno Web site at www.ekno.lonelyplanet.com, or by phone from within the US (48 states) by dialling ☎ 0800 91 2677.

Check the eKno Web site for customer service and access numbers from other countries and updates on super-budget local access numbers and new features.

Minitel Now being rapidly overtaken by the Web, Minitel – a home-grown, computerised information service accessed via the telephone and a pioneer in its time – remains a way of accessing information. Its addresses (four digits followed by a string of letters) are still frequently quoted in guidebooks and brochures.

Fax
All major post offices can send and receive domestic and international faxes *(télécopies* or *téléfaxes)*. It costs about 15FF to send a one-page fax to anywhere within France, 30FF to within the EU, 45FF to the USA and 50FF to Australia.

Email & Internet
Both La Poste and France Telecom are investing massively in the Internet. La Poste has established around 1000 Cyberposte centres in its branches, where you buy a rechargeable card. Costs are about 50FF for the first hour's connection and 30FF thereafter. France Telecom's Internet stations, although not as widespread, are markedly cheaper. There are Internet cafes in even quite small towns. Ask at the local tourist office. Access rates vary but the norm is 40FF to 50FF per hour. Some cybercafes require a minimum half-hour use.

Free email access while travelling is available through Web-based email accounts such as Lonely Planet's eKno (www.ekno.lonely planet.com), Hotmail (www.hotmail.com), or Yahoo! (www.yahoo.com). This way you can access your mail from cybercafes and other facilities anywhere in the world using any net-connected machine running a standard web browser such as Explorer or Netscape.

Connecting your own modem is more problematical. Phones in France and most of its ex-colonies use a T-shaped jack alien to the rest of the world. You *might* be lucky enough to find the adaptor you need, but even many large hardware shops and supermarkets don't stock them.

INTERNET RESOURCES
Web sites with English versions which are worth a browse include:

Lonely Planet Lonely Planet's site for information about most places on earth, linked to the Thorn Tree bulletin board and Postcards, where you can catch up on postings from fellow travellers. The Web site also has travel news and updates to many of Lonely Planet's most popular guidebooks, and the subWWWay section links you to the most useful travel resources elsewhere on the Web.
www.lonelyplanet.com.au/dest/eur/fra.htm
Maison de la France A wealth of information on and about travel in France.
www.franceguide.com
French Government Tourism Office Also a Maison de la France site, targeted at North American travellers.
www.francetourism.com
Fédération Nationale des Offices de Tourisme et Syndicats d'Initiative Information at a national or village level, on just about any aspect of visiting France.
www.tourisme.fr
Real France Inside information on arts and crafts, nature, leisure, food, restaurants, wine, museums, sights, events, hotels, guesthouses and chateaux.
www.realfrance.com

Fédération des Parcs Naturels Régionaux de France Detailed information on France's 37 regional nature parks.
www.parcs-naturels-regionaux.tm.fr

BOOKS

Books are often published in different editions by different publishers in different countries. As a result, a book might be a hard-cover rarity in one country while it's readily available in paperback in another. Your local bookshop or library is best placed to advise you on the availability of the following recommendations.

For walking guidebooks and natural history titles specific to a region, see Books in the Information section of the individual walks chapters.

Lonely Planet

Lonely Planet's *France*, with more than 1000 fact-packed pages, is an ideal supplement to the general information in this book. If you intend to combine a walking holiday with a visit to the capital, consider picking up the *Paris* guide. *South-West France*, *Provence & the Côte d'Azur*, *Corsica* and *The Loire* guidebooks provide a wealth of additional information that we just don't have room for in this book.

If you're thinking of heading east in the Alps or southwards beyond the frontier in the Pyrenees, think of packing *Walking in Italy* or *Walking in Spain*, both of which have extensive chapters on walks over the border. And if you fancy remaining active yet changing gear, pick up *Cycling France*, with over 35 rides to some of the choicest places in the country.

Lonely Planet's slim-fit but linguistically rich *French Phrasebook* has a range of terms for just about every situation you're likely to meet on the trail and is compact enough to slip into a pocket for instant access.

For foodies, *World Food France* is a full colour pocket-sized encyclopaedia on the culture of eating and drinking in France, boasting mouth-watering photography and authentic recipes. It also features two-way dictionaries, comprehensive menu readers and translations of useful phrases.

Walking Guidebooks

There isn't a great deal available in English with the exception of two British publishers, Cicerone Press and Sunflower Books.

Cicerone specialises in outdoor books, particularly on walking and climbing. Current titles among a dozen or more relating to France include *Walking the French Alps: GR5* by Martin Collins; *Tour of the Vanoise* by Kev Reynolds; and *The Corsican High Level Route*, *Tour of the Queyras* and *Walks in Volcano Country*, all by Alan Castle.

Much slimmer in size and content than Cicerone titles, the Landscapes series from Sunflower Books is also more leisurely in its approach to walks. Typically, these vary from a half-hour stroll to an all-day outing and share space with motoring routes and recommended picnic spots. The quality of the writing varies quite significantly from book to book. Concentrating upon major tourist destinations, titles relating to France include *Landscapes of the South of France*, *Landscapes of Brittany*, *Landscapes of the Pyrenees* and *Landscapes of Corsica*.

Sadly for walkers, the UK publisher Robertson McCarta has gone out of business and its translations of a number of the most popular FFRP Topo-Guides (see later in this section) are rapidly becoming collectors' items. Some bookshops still have residual stocks of these and other titles in the Footpaths of Europe series, but they won't last for long. Regions covered include Normandy and the Seine, Brittany, the Loire Valley, the Auvergne, the Dordogne, the Alps, the Pyrenees, Provence and Corsica.

The FFRP publishes some 180 Topo-Guides in French (75FF to 99FF) describing more than 2000km of waymarked trails. Maps and route descriptions are accurate, although the quality and quantity of background information varies, as you would expect from works compiled in the main by committed volunteers. For a free catalogue write to the FFRP (see Useful Organisations earlier in this chapter for contact details). So far, only one Topo-Guide has been translated into English by the FFRP. May the excellent *Walks in Provence: Luberon Regional Nature Park* (75FF) be the trailblazer for more

In Auvergne, the Massif Central and the Cévennes, Éditions Chamina produces a similar series of equally impressive French-language walking guides.

Guides Franck publishes more than 50 walking guides (98FF each), although they are not always easy to find. Well produced and exceptionally walker-friendly, a guide comes in a ring binder containing descriptions of 45 to 50 half- and one-day walks, each on a separate, removable page.

All three series reproduce IGN 1:25,000 or 1:50,000 maps (although not always the latest edition), upon which route tracings are overprinted. Even if you don't read a word of French, a title may be worth purchasing for the maps alone.

Travel & Exploration

Although it has little specifically about walking, *Travelers' Tales: France* edited by James O'Reilly is a literate, witty collection of writings, ideal for whiling away dead moments.

For an early walking account, read Robert Louis Stevenson's *Travels with a Donkey in the Cévennes*, a wry account of his and his wayward donkey Modestine's 1878 journey in the southern Massif Central.

Natural History

If you like to combine your walking with bird-watching, consider packing either *Birds of Britain and Europe* by Herman Heinzel and others, or *A Field Guide to the Birds of Britain and Europe* by Roger Peterson and others, both published in Europe by Collins. Although the text of *Birds of Europe* by Lars Jonsson is a bit stiff and formal, the illustrations are superb.

Flowers of South-West Europe: A Field Guide by Oleg Polunin & B E Smythies is an excellent guide to France's flowers and shrubs. Compendious and reliable, *Mediterranean Wild Flowers* and *Alpine Flowers of Britain and Europe*, both by Marjorie Blamey and Christopher Grey Wilson, are excellent reference sources, although their weight makes them sluggish companions on the trail.

In French, *Arbres et Fleurs de Nos Montagnes* (Trees and Flowers of Our Mountains;

80FF) is a well-illustrated guide to the trees and plants of Auvergne and central France. *Les Animaux de Nos Forêts* (Animals of Our Forests; 49FF) by the Organisation National des Forêts (ONF) is a good general, if rather didactic, introduction to the fauna of the forest. The ONF produces a number of other illustrated books, including *Les Arbres de Nos Forêts* (Trees of our Forests; 49FF) and *La Vie de la Forêt* (Life in the Forest; 49FF), exploring the forest ecosystem.

Food

Make room for *The Pocket Guide to French Food & Wine* by Tessa Youell and George Kimball, an excellent reference book packed tight with useful information about regional cuisine and wine. You can almost smell the aroma on the pages of *French Cheeses* published by Dorling Kindersley, with more than 350 cheeses photographed in glorious close-up and a detailed description of each to match. Among the indigestion-inducing feast of French recipe books, try the sensible and entertaining *Crafty French Cooking* by Michael Barry – with a chapter devoted to each of the major regional cuisines – and *The Vegetarian Table* by Georgeanne Brennan.

General

Wild France edited by Douglas Botting gives a useful overview of France's wilderness areas and is particularly well informed on flora and fauna. However, with seven contributing authors, the quality of the writing differs markedly from section to section.

Essential Explorer: France published by the British Automobile Association (AA) is far too heavy to pack but it's well worth consulting a library copy.

Michelin *guides verts* (green guides; 69FF each) – which cover all of France in 24 regional volumes, most of which are currently available in English – are full of historical, architectural and touring information. The green guide to all of France (77FF) has brief entries on the most touristed sights.

Many people swear by the red-jacketed Michelin *guide rouge* (red guide) to France (150FF), published each March, which has more than 1200 pages of information on 6400 mid- and upper-range hotels and 3900 restaurants in every corner of the country. It is best known for rating France's greatest restaurants with one, two or three stars. Chefs have been known to commit suicide upon losing a star. The icons used instead of text are explained in English at the front of the book.

Buying Books

In Paris, visit the information centre and bookshop of the FFRP at 14 rue Riquet, 19e. Alternatively, for the most comprehensive range try Au Vieux Campeur at 48 rue des Écoles, 5e, just off blvd Saint-Germain.

In smaller communities, the most likely place to find guidebooks is Maison de la Presse. Often, the local tourist office will also carry a basic stock. FNAC is a nationwide cut-price bookstore chain.

In the UK, you can contentedly spend a day or more of your life browsing around Stanfords in London (see Buying Maps under Planning earlier in this chapter).

Less central, the Travel Bookshop, (☎ 020-7229 5260), 13–15 Blenheim Crescent, W11 2EE, also carries a comprehensive range (check out their Web site at www.the travel bookshop.co.uk).

In the USA, mail orders can be placed with Mountaineers Books (☎ 1800 553 4453, fax 206-223 6306, ✉ mbooks@moun taineers.org), a nonprofit organisation based in Seattle. You can also order books on line through the Adventurous Traveler Bookstore (in the USA and Canada ☎ 1800 282 3963, fax 1800 677 1821, ✉ books@atbook.com; elsewhere ☎ 802-860 6776). Pacific Travelers Supply in Santa Barbara (☎ 888-722 8728, fax 805-564 3138) also provides a mail order service.

NEWSPAPERS & MAGAZINES

France's main daily newspapers are Le Figaro (right wing; aimed at professionals, business people and the bourgeoisie), Le Monde (centre-left; very popular with business people, professionals and intellectuals), Le Parisien (centre; middle-class, easy to read if your French is basic), France Soir (right; working and middle-class), Libération (left; popular with students and intellectuals) and L'Humanité (communist; working-class). L'Équipe is a daily devoted exclusively to sport.

If you read French, the subscription magazine, La Montagne et Alpinisme, published by the CAF, appears four times a year; the FFRP also produces a walking magazine for its members, Passion Rando. (For contact details, see the Useful Organisations section earlier in this chapter.)

RADIO & TV

You can pick up a mixture of the BBC World Service and BBC for Europe on 648 kHz AM. The Voice of America (VOA) is on 1197 kHz AM but reception is often poor. In Paris, you can pick up an hour of Radio France Internationale (RFI) news in English every day at 3 pm on 738 kHz AM. Radio Netherlands often has programming in English on 1512 kHz AM.

France Info broadcasts the news headlines in French every few minutes. It can be picked up on 105.5 MHz FM in Paris.

Upmarket hotels often offer cable and satellite TV access to CNN, BBC Prime, Sky and other networks. Canal+ (ka-**nahl**-ploose), a French subscription TV station available in many mid-range hotels, sometimes shows nondubbed English movies.

WEATHER INFORMATION

If you understand French (or know someone who does), you can find out the météo (weather forecast) by calling the national forecast (☎ 08 36 70 12 34) or regional forecasts (☎ 08 36 68 00 00). For more localised departmental forecasts, dial ☎ 08 36 68 02 plus the two digit departmental number (eg, ☎ 08 36 68 02 75 for Paris). You will need to ask the tourist office or a local for the department number, or Lonely Planet's France guide has a complete list. Each call costs five télécarte units or 2.23FF per minute. In popular walking areas, tourist offices often display the weather forecast for the next 72 hours. Up in the mountains, any refuge warden who merits the title will be au fait with local weather conditions.

You can also go to the nearest post office and dial 3615 Météo on the Minitel. Enter the departmental code when requested, then browse at your leisure the information which appears on the screen.

One of the simplest methods to check the weather, other than look at the sky, is the newspaper. The Météo section is usually on the back page or close to it, and even if you don't speak French, you can look at the universal symbols, and check the predicted high and low temperatures.

VIDEO SYSTEMS

If you're thinking of buying a commercial videotape as a souvenir of your walk, check first that you can play it on your home video player; you won't get a picture if the two image registration systems are different. Nearly all prerecorded videos on sale in France, and also French TV, use the SECAM *(système électronique couleur avec mémoire)* system, which is incompatible with most of the rest of the world. The PAL (phase alternation line) system is common to most of Western Europe and Australia, while North America and Japan use the NTSC (National Television Systems Committee) system. SECAM videos can't be played back on a machine that lacks SECAM capability.

PHOTOGRAPHY
Film & Equipment

Colour-print film produced by Kodak and Fuji is widely available in supermarkets, photo shops and FNAC stores. At FNAC, where prices are at their lowest, a 36 exposure roll of Kodacolor costs 37/46FF for 100/400ASA. One-hour developing is widely available.

For slides *(diapositives)*, count on paying at least 48/60/70FF for a 36 exposure roll of Ektachrome rated at 100/200/400ASA; developing costs 28/32FF for 24/36 exposures.

Kodachrome costs 92FF for a 36 exposure roll of 64ASA, including processing, but it may be a bit difficult to find now that it's no longer developed in France. Processing can take several weeks. Fuji can be turned around in 48 hours.

Restrictions & Photographing People

Photography is rarely forbidden, except in museums and art galleries. Of course, taking snapshots of military installations is not appreciated in any country.

When photographing people or their homes, animals and possessions, it's basic courtesy to ask permission. If you don't know any French, smile while pointing at your camera and raising your eyebrows; they'll get the picture – and you probably will too.

Airport Security

Your camera and film will have to go through the X-ray machine at all airports. The claims that the machines are film safe may no longer be true. Concerns about international terrorism means the United States has led a push to introduce a new type of machine which can fog film. After the first X-ray scan these machines automatically rescan suspicious objects at a higher intensity (to check for explosives). Film manufacturers warn that the silver halide coating on film and its metal casing may trigger this high-intensity scan. These machines can ruin unprocessed film.

These new machines are being used at more than 50 international airports to scan luggage, and in some cases are being used to scan hand luggage. This means you should never pack unprocessed film in checked luggage. Ask for hand inspections where possible.

TIME

France is on GMT/UTC plus one hour during winter and GMT/UTC plus two hours during the daylight-saving period, which runs from the last Sunday in March to the last Sunday in October. Most other Western European countries observe the same time as France year-round. The western fringe countries of Europe – the UK, Ireland and Portugal – are consistently an hour behind France.

French time is normally USA Eastern Time plus six hours, and USA Pacific Time plus nine hours. In the Australian winter (French summer), subtract eight hours from Sydney time to get French time; in the Australian summer subtract 10 hours.

Intercontinental conversions may differ by a further hour for a couple of weeks each year where countries revert to daylight saving on different dates.

Timetables, as in most of Europe, are usually expressed using the 24-hour clock. In France the hours are sometimes separated from the minutes by a lower-case letter 'h' (eg, 15h30).

ELECTRICITY
Voltage & Cycle

France, like the rest of continental Europe, runs on 220V at 50Hz AC.

In the USA and Canada, the 120V electric supply is at 60Hz. Bring a small step-down transformer with you as they aren't readily available locally. While the usual travel transformers allow North American appliances to run in France without blowing out, they cannot change the Hz rate, which determines – among other things – the speed of electric motors. As a result, tape recorders not equipped with built-in adaptors may function poorly and you may notice a certain reduction in the performance of other appliances. While this might be mildly annoying, it won't actually damage your machine.

There are two types of adaptors; mixing them up will destroy either the transformer or your appliance, so be warned.

The 'heavy' kind, usually designed to handle 35 watts or less (see the tag) and often metal-clad, is designed for use with small electric devices such as radios, tape recorders and razors. The other kind, which weighs much less but is rated for up to 1500 watts, is for use only with appliances that contain heating elements, such as hair dryers and irons.

Plugs & Sockets

Old-type wall sockets, often rated at 600 watts, take two round prongs. The new kinds of sockets take fatter prongs and have a protruding earth (ground) prong. Adaptors to make new plugs fit into the old sockets are said to be illegal but are still available at electrical shops. Better, however, to make the small investment in a new plug.

WEIGHTS & MEASURES

France is the originator of the metric system, invented by the French Academy of Sciences after the French Revolution and adopted in 1795. For a conversion chart, see the inside rear cover.

Decimals are indicated by a comma (eg, a marathon is a daunting 42,195km). Conversely, thousands are signalled by a dot (so 2.000 marks the millennium).

LAUNDRY

French *laveries* (laundrettes) are not cheap. They usually charge 18/20FF for a 6/7kg machine and 2/5FF for five/12 minutes of drying. Some laundrettes have self-service *nettoyage à sec* (dry cleaning) for about 60FF per 6kg. Coins are sometimes deposited into a *monnayeur central* (central control box – not a slot in the machine itself). Except with the most modern systems you're likely to need all sorts of peculiar coin combinations – change machines are often out of order, so come prepared. Coins, especially 2FF pieces, are handy for *séchoirs* (dryers) and the *lessive* (laundry powder) dispenser.

Many camping grounds and a few lowland *refuges* have washing machines. They often operate with a *jeton* (token) which you buy at reception.

Outside towns and camping grounds, you'll probably be doing most washing that's needed either at a sink in your accommodation or in the open. If the former, be sure to pack a plug. If the latter, choose a running stream and avoid soap or detergent – and never, ever wash in mountain tarns and pools, where the ecosystem is particularly delicate and easily unbalanced.

BUSINESS HOURS

Don't plan to achieve too much between midday and 2 pm. At lunchtime, just about every French institution, including tourist offices, banks, museums, supermarkets and many tourist offices, closes for between one and two hours as the whole nation stops to feed itself.

Banks are generally open either from Monday to Friday or Tuesday to Saturday.

Hours are variable but core times are usually from 8 or 9 am to sometime between 11.30 and 1 pm and from 1.30 or 2 to 4 or 4.30 pm. Exchange services may end half an hour before closing time.

In towns, post offices are usually open from 8 am to 7 pm on weekdays and until midday on Saturday. Those in rural areas often observe much shorter hours – and indeed may only be open for two or three days each week.

Shops and small businesses are usually open from 9 or 10 am to 6.30 or 7 pm. Food shops, especially bakeries, usually open earlier. Particularly in the provinces, a break between midday and 2 pm is the norm. Smaller food shops are mostly closed on Sunday (although some open in the morning) and all of Monday, so remember to buy provisions by Saturday afternoon at the latest. Large supermarkets usually stay open until 9 or even 10 pm and function from Monday to Saturday.

Although they're becoming more flexible, French restaurants and their clients tend to observe fairly strict hours. Lunch begins promptly at midday and if you arrive later than 12.30 pm you may find the table bare. Dinner may start as early as 7 pm and peak at about 8 pm. In some places, you'll be lucky to get served after 8.30 pm.

In towns, many shops and businesses close down in the latter half of July and August. By contrast, this is the best time for finding shops and restaurants open in popular holiday areas.

PUBLIC HOLIDAYS & SPECIAL EVENTS

The following *jours fériés* (public holidays) are observed in France:

Jour de l'An (New Year's Day) 1 January
Pâques late March/April – Easter Monday
Fête du Travail (May Day) 1 May
Victoire 1945 8 May – celebrates the Allied victory in Europe that ended WWII
L'Ascension (Ascension Thursday) May – celebrated on the 40th day after Easter
Lundi de Pentecôte (Whit Monday) mid-May to mid-June – seventh Sunday after Easter
Fête Nationale (Bastille Day/National Day) 14 July

L'Assomption (Assumption Day) 15 August
La Toussaint (All Saints' Day) 1 November
Le onze novembre (Remembrance Day) 11 November – celebrates the WWII armistice
Noël (Christmas) 25 December

Additionally, Good Friday and Boxing Day (26 December) are holidays in Alsace.

When a public holiday nudges near to a weekend, the French observe the excellent tradition of the *pont* (bridge) which permits them to take the intervening day off, too.

Most French cities have at least one major music, dance, theatre, cinema or art festival each year. Some villages hold *foires* (fairs) and *fêtes* (festivals) to honour anything from a local saint to the year's garlic crop. For precise details about dates, which change from year to year, contact the local tourist office. For a list and information on festivals and events in France, check the Web site (www.viafrance.com).

ACCOMMODATION

France has accommodation of every sort and for every budget. Any tourist office should be able to supply you with a booklet or printed lists of all accommodation and eating places within its ambit. Many will help visitors with reservations, usually in return for a small fee – money well spent.

Whatever the season, it's worth telephoning ahead, even if it's only a call in the morning of the same day, to reserve accommodation – and particularly so if you want dinner. During periods of heavy domestic or foreign tourism (for example around Easter, during the February–March school holiday and, in most walking areas, July and August) it's particularly advisable.

In many parts of France, local authorities impose a *taxe de séjour* (tourist tax) on each visitor in their jurisdiction. The price charged at camping grounds, hotels etc may be from 1FF to 7FF per person higher than the posted rates. Some areas only levy this tax in the summer months, starting around 1 June.

In Cities, Towns & Villages

Camping In this book we call an area with facilities, where a fee is normally demanded, a 'camping ground'. We reserve the term 'camp site' for more informal places where it's possible to pitch your tent.

France has well over 10,000 *campings* (camping grounds). Often the *camping municipal* is your best bet. Prices are very reasonable (rarely more than 50FF for two people and a tent) and their facilities, such as hot water and free showers, can compete with anything in the private sector.

Camping grounds are awarded between one and four stars by the Fédération Française de Camping et de Caravaning (FFCC). These reflect the services and facilities a camping ground offers rather than being an indication of price or the warmth of its welcome. Especially in the high season, some charge by the *emplacement* (pitch or tent site), a fee which includes a car and a tent of whatever size. On top of this, there's a fee per person. Such a system has the virtue of simplicity but it does discriminate against the walker who arrives on foot and with only a lightweight tent.

Nearly all camping grounds close for at least a few months in winter, and some are only open in summer. Hostels sometimes let walkers pitch tents on their premises.

Among several camping guides are Michelin's *Camping-Caravanning: Sélection France* (72FF), which includes 3500 camping grounds; and the FFCC's *Les 11,100 Camping-Caravaning en France* (76FF) – a more comprehensive list. *Camping à la Ferme* (70FF) published by Gîtes de France lists more than 1000 rustic farm camping grounds.

Hostels The great majority of *auberges de jeunesse* (youth hostels) belong to the Fédération Unie des Auberges de Jeunesse (FUAJ) or the smaller Ligue Française pour les Auberges de la Jeunesse (LFAJ). Both are affiliates of Hostelling International (HI). In university towns, you may also find *foyers* (fwa-yei), student dormitories converted for use by travellers during the summer school holidays.

A bunk in a single-sex dormitory generally costs from 50FF to 70FF. Most auberges de jeunesse have self-catering facilities. You'll need sheets or a sheet sleeping bag,

which you can rent at any hostel for about 15FF per stay. If you haven't got an HI membership card or one from the association in your home country, you can join on arrival for about 100FF (70FF if you're under 26). Alternatively, you can pick up a 'guest card' and buy a stamp (19FF) for each night of your stay. Once you've accumulated six stamps, you become a full member.

Chambres d'Hôtes France has about 15,000 *chambres d'hôtes* offering B&B (bed and breakfast), a room in a private house rented by the night plus breakfast. Check the price before you commit yourself – it can vary from little more than that of a hostel to such that you would save money by checking in at the nearest two-star hotel.

Gîtes *Gîte* is a fairly loose term which means little more than 'a place to stay in the country'. You see everywhere the yellow-on-green sign of Gîtes de France, the body which monitors standards and awards a symbol of between one and five *épis* (ears of corn) to affiliated gîtes. A *gîte rural*, rented by the week, is only really of interest if you're thinking of establishing a base and radiating out for day walks. For *gîtes d'étape*, see On the Walk a little later in this section.

Hotels Hotels normally display their prices beside the main entrance. Most have between one and four stars. Ratings are based on strictly objective criteria (eg, the size of the entry hall) so a one-star establishment may prove to be more pleasant than some two- or three-star places.

The majority offer a *petit déjeuner*, a continental breakfast, costing 20FF to 40FF per person – a bit more than you would pay at a cafe. At some hotels, the cost of breakfast is compulsory. Others may insist that you pay for *demi-pension* (half board) in peak season.

Budget hotels are generally a good deal (especially if you're travelling as a couple) and may cost little more than two hostel beds. Most rooms have a washbasin (and usually a bidet) but lack private bath or toilet. Almost all also have more expensive rooms equipped with shower, toilet and other amenities.

Most doubles, which generally cost only marginally more than singles, have only double beds, rather than twin beds *(deux lits separés)*. Taking a shower in the hall bathroom is sometimes free but more frequently costs between 10FF and 25FF. To activate the shower, you may need to ask for a token at reception.

If you're travelling by car, make at least one overnight stop, just for the experience, at a postmodern, pressboard-and-plastic Formule 1 hotel. This chain (central reservations ☎ 08 36 685 685) has ultraclean rooms with TV that will sleep three for between 120FF and 150FF. You'll see its clones strategically positioned near major towns and at motorway exits to catch the itinerant, one-night-stand trade. Only slightly more expensive is the Hôtel Première Classe chain (central reservations ☎ 08 36 688 123, www.premiereclasse.com), with rooms from 160FF.

Double rooms in mid-range hotels invariably come with showers and toilets and typically cost from 170FF to about 350FF. Some 4000 belong to the reliable Logis de France, an organisation whose affiliated establishments meet strict standards of service and amenities.

On the Walk

This book's day walks, and some stages of multiday walks, begin or end at or within a bus/train ride of a population centre, where you'll normally find a range of accommodation and sometimes a camping ground. Other options on many longer walks are camping wild, *refuges* (mountain huts) and gîtes d'étape.

Camping A lightweight tent confers liberty and independence. If it's with you, you can still opt for something more cosy should the mood take you. Camping is generally permitted only at designated camp sites and camping grounds. On longer walks in wild, unpopulated terrain such as the Pyrenees and Alps, camping wild – known as *camping sauvage* – is tolerated if you have a lightweight tent and observe certain sensible rules designed to minimise your impact. As a general rule, don't light a campfire. Erect your tent at dusk at least 1500m from a camping ground (or at least an hour's walk from a road in a national park) and move on next morning. And, of course, if you ever want to pitch your tent on private land, ask permission first.

Refuges & Gîtes d'Étape These are run by organisations such as the CAF and Club Vosgien. Most are staffed and usually open from mid-June until mid-September, although a minority of more accessible ones stay open year-round. In July and August in popular regions such as the Pyrenees and Alps we strongly recommend that you reserve in advance.

Prices are between 50FF and 80FF for a mattress and 160FF to 200FF for half board. Many larger *refuges* set aside an area for cooking, although it may not have equipment. Sleeping is normally on mattresses laid out on long benches running the length of the dormitory. Blankets are provided but not sheets. In many, especially those run by the CAF, lights are out at 10 pm and you'll be lucky to be able to sleep after 7 am.

Refuges are fine for a night or two, but it's worth checking carefully how many sleepers there are to a room. Many are fine – like a high-altitude auberge de jeunesse. Others, where you're squeezed into a dormitory among 35 or more snoring walkers, are less fun.

Gîtes d'étape are usually found in less remote areas, often in villages. Most are privately owned and offer greater comfort and privacy than a *refuge*; some even have showers. Overnight charges average 50FF to 70FF and many serve splendid, filling dinners for about 70FF. *Gîtes d'Étapes et de Séjour*, published annually by Gîtes de France, has an introduction and key in English and is a useful, although far from exhaustive, source of reference.

Two highly recommended smaller chains of gîtes are Rando'Plume with more than 100 gîtes specialising in outdoor and adventure holidays, and the excellent and environmentally aware Gîtes Panda, all of whose accommodation lies within a regional nature park.

FOOD

'Describe French cuisine in not more than 200 words, giving reasons for your answer'. It's like the essays you were set at school – and, when considering the country with the world's richest gastronomic tradition, it's an equally daunting task. Consult one of the culinary titles recommended in the Books section earlier in this chapter, refer to the rich 'Food & Wine' special section in Lonely Planet's *France*, or simply step out of your accommodation, take a sniff and follow your nose. You'll rarely be disappointed.

Local Food

The French have got it right. Eating well is still of prime importance and many spend an immense amount of time thinking about, reflecting upon, consuming and recovering from overindulgence in food.

Just about every region in France has a host of delicious local specialities, including an indigestion-inducing 350 varieties of cheese. French cuisine owes a lot to the variety and freshness of its ingredients. France is blessed with a tremendous diversity of climate and terrain, the result being a range of regional products to satisfy any craving, from olive oil, garlic and tomatoes in the south to the butter, cream and apples of the north. In between you can find anything from *truffes* (truffles) in the Périgord, to *choucroute* (sauerkraut) in Alsace, freshwater fish in lakes and rivers, and abundant seafood and saltwater fish along the coastlines.

For a list of food and menu terms, see the Language chapter at the end of this book. For a more extensive vocabulary to help you navigate a restaurant menu or a trip to the greengrocers, pack Lonely Planet's *French Phrasebook*.

Where to Eat
Restaurants usually open for lunch and for dinner and take a long break in the afternoon. Brasseries stay open all day and, while the choice of food may be more limited, you can grab a meal at any time. Cafes similarly observe long hours and most can rustle up at the very least a sandwich, baguette or *croque monsieur* (toasted sandwich).

Restaurants are obliged by law to display their menus. The service charge is always included but some small change on the saucer will be much appreciated. Most offer a fixed-price set menu, called simply the *menu* or *menu du jour* (menu of the day). Many also have a *plat du jour* (dish of the day).

Restaurant hours are fairly strict, particularly in rural areas. Most people eat lunch on the dot of midday and it's often difficult to get served after 1 pm. Dinner peaks around 8 pm and you may be turned away after 9 pm.

Even the tiniest village usually has a cafe or bar serving sandwiches and snacks. Many will have a restaurant where the quality of the cooking belies its modest appearance. Throughout France you'll find plenty of restaurants serving good, simple food at affordable prices and featuring regional specialities.

On the Walk
Refuges Most staffed *refuges* serve breakfast and dinner, while some of the larger ones which stay open all day offer drinks, snacks and maybe even lunch. It's advisable to reserve dinner at the same time as your sleeping space even though they'll never turn a hungry walker away. You don't have to be staying at a *refuge* to eat there so it's quite possible to enjoy an evening meal then head away to camp somewhere more tranquil.

Buying Food For fresh bread, patronise one of France's more than 36,000 *boulangeries* (bakeries). To top up on supplies, call by an *alimentation* or *épicerie*, general grocery stores which often sell vegetables as well. Go to a *boucherie* (butcher shop) for meat. A *charcuterie*, roughly the equivalent of a delicatessen, sells cold cuts, pâtés and salads.

There's usually at least one shop at the beginning and end of each walk we describe and often a much wider choice. For routes of more than one day's duration we also indicate places to pick up supplies en route.

For wild camping, most of the major equipment shops in Paris, Lyon and Marseille (listed in Buying & Hiring Locally at the end of the Planning section earlier in this chapter) sell special dehydrated foods. However, if you have particular favourites, take the precaution of purchasing them before leaving home. This said, you shouldn't have trouble picking up some form of high-energy food in even the smallest, one-shop village.

Wild Food Don't rely upon it but, in season, munching walnuts, chestnuts and hazelnuts – plucked along quiet lanes in the Loire Valley – or rehydrating on bilberries in the Massif Central and wild raspberries in the Jura, can add immeasurably to the pleasure of walking. Several varieties of wild mushrooms found in woodland areas are used in regional dishes (don't try experimenting without a reliable guide, however, as many mushrooms are toxic).

Cooking Most *refuges* and at least some gîtes d'étape have self-catering facilities. If you're camping wild and eat one meal a day or every other day in a *refuge*, you can dispense with a stove and fuel. On the other hand a stove, like a tent, confers extra flexibility – nothing in the world rivals a post-dawn mug of steaming tea or coffee. There's quite a range of books about camp food and cooking. Outdoor gear shops will usually have a few in stock or will be able to recommend a good title.

DRINKS
The price of a drink in a cafe varies – in ascending order – according to whether you're sitting at the bar, at a table or on an external terrace.

Wines of France

There are dozens of wine-producing regions throughout France, but the eight principal regions are Alsace, the Loire Valley, Bordeaux, Burgundy, Champagne, Beaujolais, Languedoc-Roussillon and the Rhône. Wines in France are named after where they're grown rather than the grape varietal, except in Alsace.

Some viticulturists have honed their skills and techniques to such a degree that their wine is known as a *grand cru* (literally, 'great growth'). If this wine has been produced in a year of optimum climatic conditions it becomes a *millésime* (vintage). Grands crus are aged first in small oak barrels and then in bottles, sometimes for 20 years or more, before they develop their full taste and aroma. These are the memorable (and pricey) bottles that wine experts talk about with such passion.

Under French law, wines are divided into four categories:

Appellation d'origine contrôlée (AOC) These wines have met stringent government regulations governing where, how and under what conditions they are grown, fermented and bottled. They are almost always, at the very least, good and may actually be superb.

Vin délimité de qualité supérieure (VDQS) These are good wines from a specific place or region – the second rank of French quality control.

Vin de pays Wines with this label, whose literal meaning is 'country wine', are of reasonable quality and are generally drinkable.

Vin de table These table wines are also known as *vins ordinaires* (ordinary wines). Spending an extra 5 or 10FF can often make a big difference in quality, drinkability and the severity of your hangover.

LPP

Nonalcoholic Drinks

Tap water everywhere is safe to drink, so you don't have to buy fancy, expensive *eau de source* (spring water) such as Perrier, Vichy or Vittel, which comes either *plate* (plain) or *gazeuse* (fizzy).

Two particularly refreshing drinks on a hot day are a *citron pressé*, a glass of iced water with freshly squeezed lemon juice and sugar; and a *panaché*, a beer and lemonade shandy.

Fizzy soft drinks are widely available. Be warned, however, that a beer on a cafe terrace may work out cheaper – and no bad thing.

Coffee expressed from a machine in cafes is invariably delicious. For a small, strong, hair-curling black coffee, ask for un café noir or simply un café. Un *petit café crème* or *une noisette* is espresso coffee with a dash of steamed milk or cream. Un café au lait is lots of hot milk with a little coffee served in a large cup or bowl and is usually only ordered at breakfast time.

Alcoholic Drinks

Wine remains one of France's great glories and walks in this book take in three of its foremost wine producing regions: Burgundy, Alsace and the Loire Valley, as well as the edge of the Champagne area. You can buy plonk for as little as 12FF or a bottle of something very acceptable for 25FF to 40FF. In restaurants and when shopping, take the opportunity to sample the local vintages.

In bars and cafes, beer is usually served very cold and by the *demi* (about 330mL). It's usually cheaper *à pression* (on draught/tap) than in a *bouteille* (bottle) – the way it will come if you simply request *une bière*. Prices vary quite widely depending upon the establishment. At a decent but modest sort of place, count on paying 12FF to 16FF for a demi on draught.

Pastis, one of a range of *aperitifs*, is refreshing. An anise-flavoured drink which turns cloudy when added to water, it's a particular favourite in southern France. Popular brand names are Pernod and Ricard. *Kir*, chilled white wine with cassis (sweet blackcurrant syrup), is also popular.

On The Walk

All in all, water is by far the best thirst quencher when you're walking. It's also the most readily available way to rehydrate. In some mountain regions, well above the cultivation line and away from areas where livestock graze, it's safe to drink straight from flowing streams. Take advice from locals or gîte and *refuge* staff and always keep purifying tablets (such as iodine) accessible.

Village fountains *(fontaines)* where the water is unsafe to drink usually have a sign reading *eau non potable*. For information on how to treat water that seems suspect, see Water Purification in the Staying Healthy section of the Health & Safety chapter.

Health & Safety

Keeping healthy during your walking holiday depends on your predeparture preparations, your daily health care while travelling and how you handle any medical problems that develop. While the potential problems can seem rather alarming, few travellers experience anything more than an upset stomach. The following sections aren't meant to cause concern and are recommended reading before you go.

Predeparture Planning

MEDICAL COVER
Citizens of European Union (EU) countries are covered for emergency care upon presentation of an E111 form, which you need to obtain before you leave home. In Britain, it's available free at a post office. In other EU countries, check with your doctor or local health service.

Although the form entitles you to free emergency treatment in government clinics and hospitals, you will have to pay for dental treatment, any medicines bought from pharmacies, even if a doctor has prescribed them, and possibly for tests. At home, you may eventually be able to recover some or all of these costs from your national health service.

Anyone at all can receive treatment in the *service des urgences* (casualty ward, or emergency department) of any public hospital in France; any costs are generally less than in many western countries.

HEALTH INSURANCE
Make sure you have adequate health insurance. For more information, see the Travel Insurance section under Visas & Documents in the Facts for the Walker chapter.

IMMUNISATIONS
No immunisations are required for France, but before leaving ensure you're up to date with routine vaccinations. Those for diphtheria, tetanus and polio are usually given in childhood and a booster is required every 10 years.

FIRST AID
It's a good idea at any time to know the appropriate responses to a major accident or illness, and it's particularly important if you'll be walking for some time in a remote area. Consider doing a recognised basic first-aid course or adding a first-aid manual to your first-aid kit. Although detailed first-aid instruction is outside the scope of this guidebook, some basic points are given in Major Accidents later in this chapter. Preventing illness or an accident is the most important thing you can do (see Staying Healthy and the boxed text 'Safety on the Walk – Basic Rules' for more advice). You should also know how to summon help should a major accident or illness befall you or someone with you (see the Rescue & Evacuation section).

Staying Healthy

HYGIENE
Make a point of washing your hands more frequently than you would normally, especially before preparing food and eating.

Take particular care to dispose carefully of all toilet waste when you are on a walk; see Toilets under Responsible Walking in the Facts for the Walker chapter.

NUTRITION
Generally, nutrition shouldn't ever be a problem in France. Nevertheless, once you've been walking for a week or more, you'll find your appetite increases, so it's a good idea to increase your intake of energy-giving carbohydrates (pasta, bread) with the evening meal. The generous range of readily available fruit and vegetables should ensure a balanced diet.

Medical Kit Check List

This is a list of items you should consider including in your medical kit – consult your pharmacist for brands available in your country.

First-Aid Supplies
☐ adhesive tape
☐ butterfly closure strips
☐ bandages and safety pins
☐ elasticised support bandage – for knees and ankles
☐ gauze swabs
☐ nonadhesive dressings
☐ scissors
☐ sterile alcohol wipes
☐ sticking plasters (Band-Aids)
☐ sutures
☐ thermometer
☐ tweezers

Medications
☐ antidiarrhoea and antinausea drugs
☐ antibiotics – consider including these if you're travelling well off the beaten track; see your doctor, as they must be prescribed, and carry the prescription with you.
☐ antifungal cream or powder – for skin infections and thrush
☐ antihistamines – for allergies (eg, hay fever), to ease the itch from insect bites or stings, and to prevent motion sickness
☐ antiseptic (such as povidone-iodine) – for cuts and grazes
☐ calamine lotion, sting relief spray or aloe vera – to ease irritation from sunburn and insect bites or stings
☐ cold and flu tablets, throat lozenges and nasal decongestant
☐ painkillers (eg, aspirin or paracetamol, acetaminophen in the USA) – for pain and fever
☐ rehydration mixture – to prevent dehydration, eg, caused by diarrhoea, important if travelling with children

Miscellaneous
☐ eye drops
☐ insect repellent
☐ sunscreen and lip balm
☐ water purification tablets or iodine

FOOD

The stringent food hygiene regulations imposed by the EU are in force in France, so you should feel confident that the food you eat in restaurants is safe. However, given the popularity of seafood, particularly in Brittany, it's better to be circumspect with such delicacies, especially shellfish.

WATER

Tap water in France is safe to drink. However, the water in most French fountains is not drinkable and may have a sign reading *eau non potable* (undrinkable water), although some may have a welcome notice indicating quite the opposite, especially near cemeteries.

Always beware of natural sources of water. A bubbling Alpine or Pyrenean stream may look crystal clear, but if it's in an area where animals graze it's unwise to drink any, unless you're at the source and can see it coming out of the rocks.

Water Purification

The simplest way of purifying water is to boil it thoroughly. Vigorous boiling should be satisfactory; otherwise use chlorine or iodine, in powder, tablet or liquid form, available from outdoor equipment suppliers and pharmacies. Follow the recommended dosages and allow the water to stand for the correct length of time. Iodine is more effective than chlorine in purifying water, but follow the directions carefully and remember that too much iodine can be harmful. Chemical solutions may not work at all if the water is dirty.

Consider buying a water filter for a long trip. Total filters remove all parasites, bacteria and viruses and make water safe to drink, although they may be expensive. Simple filters, such as a nylon mesh bag, take only dirt and larger foreign bodies out of the water so that chemical solutions work much more effectively. Read the specifications so that you know exactly what the filter removes from the water and what it leaves behind.

TIREDNESS

More injuries happen towards the end of the day when you're tired, than earlier when you're fresh. Although tiredness can simply be a nuisance on an easy walk, it can be life-threatening on narrow, exposed ridges or in bad weather. You should never set out on a walk that is beyond your capabilities on the day. If you feel below par, have a rest day. To reduce the risk, don't push yourself too hard. Take short rests every hour or two, for 15 to 20 minutes, and have a lunch break of about half an hour. Towards the end of the day, moderate your pace and be aware that your concentration is probably wearing out too. Make sure you eat sensibly – several snacks of energy-sustaining food are better than a large, leaden lunch.

BLISTERS

This problem can be avoided. Make sure that your walking boots or shoes are well worn in before your visit. At the very least, wear them on a few short walks before tackling longer outings. Your boots should fit comfortably with enough room to move your toes; boots that are too big or too small will cause blisters. Similarly with socks: be sure they fit properly, and wear socks specifically made for walkers; even then, check that there are no seams across the widest part of your foot. Wet and muddy socks can also cause blisters, so carry at least one spare pair. Stop as soon as you feel the slightest irritation and apply a simple

Everyday Health

Normal body temperature is up to 37°C (98.6°F); more than 2°C (4°F) higher indicates a high fever. The normal adult pulse rate is 60 to 100 per minute (children 80 to 100, babies 100 to 140). As a general rule the pulse increases about 20 beats per minute for each 1°C (2°F) rise in fever.

Respiration (breathing) rate is also an indicator of illness. Count the number of breaths per minute: between 12 and 20 is normal for adults and older children (up to 30 for younger children, 40 for babies). People with a high fever or serious respiratory illness breathe more quickly than normal. More than 40 shallow breaths per minute may indicate pneumonia.

sticking plaster, or preferably one of the special blister plasters which act as a second skin. Don't forget to keep your toenails trimmed; long nails can make descents decidedly uncomfortable.

KNEE PAIN

Most walkers experience strain on long, steep descents. It can be reduced, although never eliminated, by developing a proper descent technique. Take short, controlled steps with your legs slightly bent and make sure your heels come down first. If there is no path, zigzag down, within the safe limits of the terrain, rather than making a beeline for the bottom. Some walkers find that tubular bandages help to reduce strain; others use hi-tech, strap-on supports.

Walking poles are effective in taking some of the weight off the knees, although you may need to adjust the length for maximum effectiveness. Poles also help to maintain balance on potentially knee-jarring scree slopes and rocky ground, and in crossing streams.

Medical Problems & Treatment

ENVIRONMENTAL HAZARDS

There's no doubt that walkers are at risk from some environmental hazards. The risks, however, can be significantly reduced by using common sense and reading the following section.

Altitude

The reduced level of oxygen at altitudes above 2500m affects most people to some extent. The effect may be mild or severe and occurs because less oxygen reaches the muscles and the brain, requiring the heart and lungs to compensate by working harder. Although the likelihood of suffering any significant effects on walks described in this book is very slight, it's still worth taking a couple of days to accustom yourself to altitudes above 2500m if you're planning to cross some higher passes, especially in the Pyrenees.

Warning

Self-diagnosis and treatment can be risky, so you should always seek medical help. The warden or owner of a refuge or gîte d'étape, B&B or hotel, or the local tourist office, can usually recommend a local doctor or clinic.

We have used generic rather than brand names for drugs in this section – check with a pharmacist for locally available brands.

Sun

Protection against the sun should always be taken seriously. Particularly in the slightly rarified air and deceptive coolness of the mountains, sunburn develops rapidly. Apply sunscreen, as well as a barrier cream to your nose and lips, and wear a broad-brimmed hat whenever the sun appears. Protect your eyes with good-quality sunglasses with UV lenses, particularly when walking near water, sand or snow. If you do get burnt, calamine lotion, aloe vera or other commercial sunburn relief preparations will soothe the discomfort.

Heat

Treat heat with respect! Take time to acclimatise to high temperatures, drink plenty of liquids and don't do anything physically demanding until you are acclimatised.

Prickly Heat This is an itchy rash caused by excessive perspiration trapped under the skin. It usually strikes people who have just arrived in a hot climate. Keeping cool, bathing often, drying the skin and using a mild talcum or prickly heat powder, or retreating to an air-conditioned room may help to relieve symptoms.

Dehydration & Heat Exhaustion Dehydration is a potentially dangerous and generally preventable condition caused by excessive fluid loss. Sweating and inadequate fluid intake are the commonest causes among walkers; other causes are diarrhoea, vomiting and high fever – see the entry on Diarrhoea later in this chapter.

The early symptoms of dehydration are weakness, thirst and passing small amounts of very concentrated urine. These may progress to drowsiness, dizziness or fainting on standing up, and finally, coma.

It's easy to forget how much fluid you're losing through perspiration while you're walking, especially if a breeze is drying your skin quickly. Maintain a steady fluid intake – the minimum recommended is 3L per day.

Dehydration and salt deficiency can cause heat exhaustion. Salt deficiency is characterised by fatigue, lethargy, headaches, giddiness and muscle cramps. Salt tablets are unnecessary – just add extra salt to your food.

Heatstroke This is a serious, occasionally fatal condition that occurs if the body's heat-regulating mechanism breaks down and body temperature rises to a dangerous level. Continuous exposure to high temperatures and insufficient fluids can make you vulnerable to heatstroke.

The symptoms are feeling unwell, sweating little or not at all, and a high body temperature (39° to 41°C or 102° to 106°F). When sweating has ceased, the skin becomes flushed and red. Severe, throbbing headaches and lack of coordination also occur and the sufferer may be confused or aggressive. Eventually the victim will become delirious or convulse. Hospitalisation is essential; meantime get the victim out of the sun, remove clothing, cover with a wet sheet or towel and fan continuously. Give fluids if the person is conscious.

Cold

Hypothermia This occurs when the body loses heat faster than it can produce it so that the body's core temperature falls. It is a real threat for walkers – people do die from it. You should always be prepared for the onset of inhospitable conditions in the mountains, no matter how warm and clear the weather when you set out. Always carry spare, high-energy food (see What to Bring under Planning in the Facts for the Walker chapter).

The decline from very cold to dangerously cold can happen with frightening speed if wet clothing, fatigue and hunger are combined with windy conditions. If the weather deteriorates, take precautions immediately: put on extra layers of warm clothing, a wind and/or waterproof jacket, plus wool or fleece hat and gloves. Have something to eat and make sure that everyone in your group is fit, feeling well and alert.

Symptoms of hypothermia are, in approximate order of appearance: lethargy, exhaustion, shivering, cold extremities, stumbling, dizzy spells, slurred speech, irrational or violent behaviour (for example, trying to take off protective clothes), violent bursts of energy, numb fingers and toes.

To treat mild hypothermia, first get the person to the best available shelter, remove their clothing if it is wet, and replace it with dry, warm garments. Wrap the person in a sleeping bag if available, or a space blanket or large bivouac bag; failing those, have other members of your group sit or lie as close to the sufferer as possible. Do not rub victims: instead allow them to slowly warm themselves. Give them warm, sweet fluids (*never* alcohol) and some high-energy, easily digestible food, such as chocolate.

Early recognition and treatment of mild hypothermia is the only way to prevent severe hypothermia, which is a potentially life-threatening condition.

INFECTIOUS DISEASES
Diarrhoea
Simple things like a change of water, food or climate can cause a mild bout of diarrhoea, but a few rushed toilet trips with no other symptoms is not indicative of a major problem. More serious diarrhoea is caused by infectious agents transmitted by faecal contamination of food or water, by using contaminated utensils or by direct contact from one person's hand to another. Paying particular attention to personal hygiene and taking care of what you eat are important in avoiding diarrhoea.

Dehydration is the main danger, particularly in children or the elderly, as it can occur quite quickly. Fluid replacement is the most important response. Weak, black tea with a little sugar, soda water, or soft drinks which have gone flat and been diluted 50% with water are all good. With severe diarrhoea, a rehydrating solution is preferable to replace minerals and salts lost. Commercially available oral rehydration salts (ORS) are very useful; add them to boiled water. In an emergency, you can use a solution of six teaspoons of sugar and a half teaspoon of salt to 1L of boiled water. You need to drink at least the same volume of fluid that you are losing in bowel movements and vomiting. If you pass small amounts of concentrated urine, you need to drink more. Keep drinking small amounts often and stick to a bland diet as you recover.

Gut-paralysing drugs such as diphenoxylate or loperamide can be used to bring relief from symptoms, but they don't cure the problem. Only use these drugs if you don't have access to toilets (eg, if you *must* travel); they are not recommended for children under 12 years, or if you have a high fever or are severely dehydrated.

Seek medical advice if you pass blood or mucus, are feverish, or suffer persistent or severe diarrhoea.

Fungal Infections
Sweating liberally, probably washing less than usual and going longer without a change of clothes all mean that long-distance walkers risk picking up a fungal infection which, although an unpleasant irritant, presents no danger.

Fungal infections are encouraged by moisture, so wear loose, comfortable clothes, wash when you can and dry yourself thoroughly. Try to expose the infected area to air or sunlight as much as possible and apply an antifungal cream or powder, eg, tolnaftate.

Tetanus
This disease is caused by a germ which lives in soil and in the faeces of horses and other animals. It enters the body via breaks in the skin. The first symptom may be discomfort in swallowing, or stiffening of the jaw and neck; this is followed by painful convulsions of the jaw and whole body. The disease can be fatal. It can be prevented by vaccination, so make sure you're up to date with this before you leave.

INSECT-BORNE DISEASES
Lyme Disease
This is a tick-transmitted infection. The illness usually begins with a spreading rash at the site of the tick bite and is accompanied by fever, headache, extreme fatigue, aching joints and muscles and mild neck stiffness. If untreated, these symptoms usually resolve over several weeks, but disorders of the nervous system, heart and joints may subsequently develop. Treatment works best early in the illness. Medical help should be sought.

TRAUMATIC INJURIES
Sprains
Ankle and knee sprains are common injuries among walkers. To help prevent ankle sprains you should wear boots that have adequate ankle support. If you do suffer a sprain, immobilise the joint with a firm bandage, and if feasible, immerse the foot in cold water. Distribute the contents of your pack among your companions. Once you reach shelter, relieve pain and swelling by keeping the ankle elevated for the first 24 hours and, if possible, by putting ice on the swollen joint. Take simple painkillers to ease the discomfort. If the sprain is mild, you may be able to continue your walk after a couple of days, preferably with a lighter pack. Seek medical attention for more severe sprains, as an X-ray may be needed to find out whether a bone has been broken.

Major Accidents
Accidents causing head injuries or fractures, are always possible when walking. Here is some basic advice on what to do if a major accident does happen; detailed first-aid instruction is outside the scope of this guidebook (see the First Aid section earlier). If someone suffers a bad fall:

- Make sure you and your companions are not in danger
- Assess the injured person's condition
- Stabilise any injuries, such as bleeding wounds or broken bones
- Seek medical help (see Rescue & Evacuation later in this chapter)

If the person is unconscious, immediately check whether they are breathing, clear the airway if it is blocked, and check the pulse, by feeling the side of the neck rather than the wrist. If there is a pulse but no breathing, start mouth-to-mouth resuscitation immediately. In such circumstances, the victim should be moved as little as possible in case the neck or back is broken. Keep the person warm by covering them with a space blanket, sleeping bag or dry clothing; insulate them from the ground if possible.

Check for wounds and broken bones; if the victim is conscious ask where pain is felt; otherwise, inspect the body in situ as far as you feel you can with safety. Control any bleeding by applying firm pressure to the wound. Bleeding from the nose or ear may indicate a fractured skull. Do not give the victim anything by mouth, especially if they are unconscious. Most cases of brief unconsciousness are not associated with serious brain damage. Nevertheless, anyone who has been knocked unconscious should be watched closely. Carefully note any signs of deterioration (eg, change in breathing patterns) to report to the rescuers/doctor.

Indications of a broken bone are pain, swelling and discolouration, loss of function or deformity of the limb. You should not try to move a broken bone unless you know exactly what you are doing. To protect from further injury, immobilise a nondisplaced fracture by applying a splint; if the thigh bone is broken, strap it to the good leg to hold it in place. Check the splinted limb frequently to ensure the splint hasn't cut off circulation. Simple fractures take several weeks to heal, so they don't need fixing immediately. Broken ribs are painful but usually heal by themselves and do not need splinting. If breathing becomes difficult, or the victim coughs up blood, a lung may be punctured, so medical attention should be sought urgently.

Fractures associated with open wounds (compound fractures) need more urgent treatment because of the risk of infection.

Dislocations, where the bone has come out of the joint, should be set as soon as possible by a doctor.

Internal injuries are more difficult to detect, and cannot usually be treated in the field. Watch for shock – a specific medical condition associated with failure to maintain the volume of circulating blood. Signs include a rapid pulse and cold, clammy extremities.

CUTS & SCRATCHES

Any cut or graze should be washed thoroughly and treated with an antiseptic, such as povidone-iodine. Dry wounds heal more quickly, so avoid bandages and dressing strips if possible, as they inhibit drying. Infection is present if the skin margins become red, painful and swollen. Serious infection can cause swelling of the whole limb and of the lymph glands and a fever may develop; seek medical attention immediately.

BURNS

Immerse the burnt area in cold water as soon as possible, then cover it with a clean, dry, sterile dressing. Keep this in place by plasters for a day or so in the case of a small, mild burn, but longer for more extensive injuries. Medical help should be sought for severe and extensive burns.

BITES & STINGS
Bees & Wasps

These are usually painful rather than dangerous. However, anyone allergic to these bites can suffer severe breathing difficulties and will need medical care immediately.

Calamine lotion or a commercial sting relief spray will ease discomfort, and ice packs will reduce the pain and swelling.

Snakes

To minimise your chances of being bitten, always wear boots, socks and long trousers when walking through undergrowth where snakes may be present. Don't put your hands into holes or crevices.

A bite by any of the adders or vipers found in France is unlikely to be fatal. Even so, wrap the bitten limb tightly, as you would for a sprained ankle, and immobilise it with a splint. Keep the victim still and seek medical assistance; it will help if you can describe the offending reptile. Tourniquets and sucking out the poison are now totally discredited treatments.

Ticks

Ticks can cause skin infections and more serious diseases (eg, Lyme disease – see earlier), so you should always check all over your body if you have been walking through a potentially tick-infested area. Ticks are most active from spring to autumn, especially where there are plenty of sheep. They usually lurk in overhanging vegetation, so avoid pushing through tall bushes if possible.

If you find a tick, press down around the head with tweezers, grab the head and gently pull upwards. Avoid pulling the rear of the body – this may squeeze the tick's gut contents through the attached mouth parts into your skin, increasing the risk of infection. Smearing chemicals on the tick will not dislodge it and is not recommended.

HAY FEVER

If you suffer from hay fever, bring your usual treatment, as the pollen count in southern France (Périgord, Quercy, Provence and Corsica) is very high in May and June.

WOMEN'S HEALTH
Gynaecological Problems

Antibiotic use, synthetic underwear, sweating and contraceptive pills can lead to fungal vaginal infections, especially when travelling in hot climates. Fungal infections are characterised by a rash, itch and discharge and are usually treated by nystatin, miconazole or clotrimazole pessaries or vaginal cream. If these are unavailable, a vinegar or lemon-juice douche, or yoghurt can help. Maintaining good personal hygiene and wearing loose-fitting clothes and cotton underwear may help prevent these infections.

Urinary Tract Infection

Cystitis, or inflammation of the bladder, is a common condition in women. Symptoms include burning when urinating and having to urinate frequently and urgently; blood can sometimes be passed. Sexual activity with a new partner or with a partner who has been away for a while can trigger an infection.

Drinking plenty of fluids may resolve the problem. Single-dose (nonantibiotic) treatments may be effective in the early stages of mild cystitis. If symptoms persist, seek medical attention because a simple infection can spread to the kidneys, causing a more severe illness.

Safety on the Walk

You can significantly reduce the chance of getting into difficulties by taking a few simple precautions. These are listed in the boxed text 'Safety on the Walk – Basic Rules'; a list of the clothes and equipment you should take on a multiday walk appears in the What to Bring section of the Facts for the Walker chapter.

As emphasised under Equipment in the What to Bring section of the Facts for the Walker chapter, a GPS receiver should not be relied upon in remote areas. It cannot be emphasised enough how important a topographic map and a compass are to any walker.

CROSSING RIVERS
Sudden downpours are common in the mountains and can turn a gentle stream into a raging torrent in minutes. If you're in any doubt about the safety of a crossing, look for a safer passage upstream or wait; if the rain is short-lived, it should subside quickly.

If you decide it's essential to cross (late in the day, for example), try to find a wide, shallow stretch of the stream rather than a bend. Take off your trousers and socks, but keep your boots on – the water will be cold and your feet could easily be injured on the stream bed. Put dry, warm clothes and a towel near the top of your pack. Undo the chest strap and hip belt of your pack and secure them out of the way, in case you have to off-load the pack in deep water. Use a walking pole as a third leg, or go arm in arm with a companion, holding at the wrist, and cross side-on to the flow, taking short steps.

LIGHTNING
If a storm brews, avoid open areas. Lightning seeks out crests, lone trees, small depressions, gullies, caves, doorways and wet ground. If you are caught in the open, curl up as tightly as possible with your feet together, and put a layer of insulation between you and the ground. Keep well clear of metal objects, including framed backpacks and walking poles.

DOGS
During walks in settled areas of France, you're bound to encounter barking dogs – tethered or running loose. Regard any dog as a potential attacker and be prepared to take evasive action; even just crossing the road can take you out of its territory and into safety. A walking pole may be useful, although use it as a last resort, especially if the owner is in sight. Knowing your tetanus immunisation is up to date is reassuring.

Safety on the Walk – Basic Rules

Allow plenty of time to complete a walk before dark, particularly during spring and autumn when daylight hours are shorter.

Don't overestimate your capabilities. Study the route carefully before setting out, noting possible escape routes and the point of no return (where it's quicker to continue than to turn back). Monitor your progress during the day against the time estimated for the walk and keep an eye on the weather.

Unless you're very experienced, it's wise not to walk alone. Always leave details of your intended route, the number of people in your group and expected return time with someone responsible before you leave, and let them know when you return.

Before setting out, make sure you have the relevant map, a compass, medical kit, spare warm clothes, raingear and adequate food and water; obtain the local weather forecast for the next 24 hours. If walking in remote areas, you may like to take along a bivvy bag, torch (flashlight) and spare batteries, whistle, notebook and pencil, an emergency supply of high-energy food and spare gloves and socks.

The Mobile, the Mountain & the Emergency

More and more walkers these days pack a mobile phone *(téléphone portable)* as an additional mountain safety feature rather than a fashion statement (although a reader reports having seen a skier in the Pyrenees hurtling down a red run, ski poles akimbo, one hand clamping a mobile to his ear!).

The Gendarmerie, no doubt weary of being expensively called out for less than life-threatening situations, has issued a guidance leaflet neatly entitled *Appel des Cimes* (Call from the Peaks).

First, it says, pause before you ring and ask yourself if there's anything you can do yourself to improve or solve the problem.

Situations which justify a call include when you or a member of your group:

- are lost and darkness or weather conditions prevent you from continuing
- are stuck because of a landslide or avalanche
- have suffered a serious accident (such as a fracture, broken limb or open wound).

If you're tired, hungry, cold, late and want to get home – well, 'Don't call us, we'll call you' is the message.

RESCUE & EVACUATION

If someone in your group is injured or falls ill and can't move, leave somebody with them while another one or two people go for help. They should take clear written details of the location and condition of the victim, and of helicopter landing conditions. If there are only two of you, leave the injured person

with as much warm clothing, food and water as it's sensible to spare, plus a whistle and torch. Mark the position with something conspicuous, eg, an orange bivouac bag, or a large stone cross on the ground.

If you need to call for help, use the internationally recognised emergency signals. Give six short signals – with a whistle blast, shout or the flash of a light – followed by a minute's rest. Repeat the sequence until you receive a response. If the responder knows the signals, this will be three signals followed by a minute's pause and a repetition of the sequence. Be ready to explain where the accident occurred, how many people are injured and the injuries sustained.

Search & Rescue Organisations

Several organisations are involved in mountain rescue in France. Within an area it can be either the Peloton de Gendarmerie de Haute Montagne (PGHM), the Compagnie Républicaine de la Securité (CRS) or the local *pompiers* (fire brigade; ☎ 18). The Service d'Assistance Médicale Urbain (SAMU; ☎ 15 toll-free anywhere in France) provides an ambulance and emergency medical assistance for which you pay. The national police emergency number is ☎ 17.

Helicopter Rescue & Evacuation

Familiarise yourself with the conventional signals to helicopter crews: Arms up in a V shape means 'I/we need help'; arms in a straight diagonal line (one arm of the letter X) means 'All OK'.

To land, a helicopter needs a cleared space 25 x 25m with a flat landing area of 6 x 6m. It will fly into the wind when landing. In extreme emergencies where there's nowhere to land, a person or harness might be lowered. Take the greatest care to avoid the rotors when approaching a landed helicopter.

Getting There & Away

AIR

Many airlines link Paris with every corner of the globe, and international flights also operate to and from several regional airports.

Airports & Airlines

It's probable that you'll arrive in France at one of Paris' airports. Air France and a few other international carriers use Orly airport, 16km south of central Paris. For flight and other information call ☎ 01 49 75 15 15.

Roissy Charles de Gaulle airport, 27km north of the city, is also used by Air France, and by all other international airlines. For flight and other information call ☎ 01 48 62 22 80.

For information on getting to/from these airports, see Getting There & Away in the introduction to the Paris Region chapter.

Buying Tickets

Return (round-trip) tickets are usually cheaper than two one-way tickets. The cheapest tickets are often burdened with restrictions: minimum and/or maximum stays, advance reservation requirements, nonrefundability etc.

Round-the-world (RTW) tickets enable you to combine a visit to France with trips to other countries; if you live in Australasia, an RTW may be no more expensive than an ordinary return fare, eg, from Australia in the high season it could cost around $A2600, from New Zealand $NZ2799. You usually have to book dates for every sector you want to fly, but these can be changed en route. The departure date from your home country usually determines the fare; RTW tickets are generally valid for one year.

The best way to find cheap tickets is to phone around. Check the total fare, stopovers allowed or required, duration of the journey, period of validity, cancellation penalties and any other restrictions.

You may feel happier paying more than the lowest fare to enjoy the security of dealing with a reputable travel agent. Some of the following firms have offices or agents beyond their base:

Council Travel (USA-based)
www.counciltravel.com
Nouvelles Frontières (France-based)
www.newfrontiers.com
STA Travel
www.sta-travel.com
Travel CUTS (Canada-based)
www.travelcuts.com
usit CAMPUS (Ireland-based)
www.usit.ie
Wasteels (France- and Belgium-based)
www.voyages-wasteels.fr

The UK

Direct flights to Paris operate from most British regional airports. Major carriers are Air France, British Airways (including its budget carrier Go), British Midland, Easy Jet, KLM UK, Ryanair and Buzz. A straightforward and fully flexible London-Paris ticket with Air France will cost UK£163/100

Warning

The information in this chapter is particularly vulnerable to change: prices for international travel are volatile, routes are introduced and cancelled, schedules change, special deals come and go, and rules and visa requirements are amended.

Airlines and governments seem to take a perverse pleasure in making price structures and regulations as complicated as possible. Check directly with the airline or a travel agent to make that you understand how a fare (and ticket you may buy) works. Remember that the travel industry is highly competitive, and lurks and perks abound.

Before you part with your hard-earned cash you should gather opinions, quotes and advice from as many airlines and travel agents as possible. The details given in this chapter should be regarded as pointers and are not a substitute for your own careful, up-to-date research.

one way/return. You should find cheaper fares, however, if you shop around. French provincial airports served include Bordeaux, Lyon, Marseille, Nice and Toulouse.

Ireland
Aer Lingus, Air France, Cityjet and Ryanair operate flights from Dublin to Paris. Discounted return fares from Dublin cost around I£84, or I£134 from Belfast. For people aged 25 and under, usit CAMPUS (☎ 01-602 1600 in Dublin) has one-way/return Dublin-Paris flights for I£55/99. The Belfast-Paris student return fare is I£68. Connections are available to Bordeaux and Toulouse.

Continental Europe
Return fares to Paris include Berlin (266DM), Madrid (38,000 ptas) and Rome (L590,000). The cheapest fares are available in early spring and late autumn. Air France's youth fares often cost only slightly more than charters.

North America
The range of flights across the North Atlantic, the world's busiest long-haul air corridor, is vast. Council Travel and STA Travel in the USA have offices in principal cities nationwide. Major newspapers have weekly travel sections in which you'll find reams of travel agents' ads.

You should be able to fly one way from New York to Paris for US$197 to US$299 in the low season and US$345 to US$510 in the high season. Equivalent fares from the west coast are US$90 to US$200 higher.

In Canada, Travel CUTS (☎ 1-888-838 CUTS) has offices in all major cities. Budget travel agents' ads in the Toronto *Globe & Mail*, the *Toronto Star* and *Vancouver Province* are worth a look.

Australia & New Zealand
STA Travel and Flight Centres International are major dealers in discounted air fares from Australia and New Zealand. The Saturday travel sections of the main newspapers carry many ads offering cheap fares, but these are usually low-season fares on obscure airlines and encumbered with many conditions.

Thai Airways, Malaysia Airlines, Qantas and Singapore Airlines operate flights to Paris from about A$1825 (low season) to A$2449 (high season). Promotional fares are frequently on offer so it pays to scan daily newspapers.

Fares on arilines including Japan Airlines, Emirates, Gulf Air and Korean Air are often cheaper; return fares range from A$1500 in the low season to A$1800 in the high season.

From New Zealand, the cheapest fares are often on routes through Asia; return fares range from NZ$2015 in the low season to NZ$2445 in the high season.

LAND
The UK
Bus Eurolines (☎ 01582-404511, ✉ euro lines@imagenet.fr, www.eurolines.co.uk) runs bus services from London's Victoria coach station via Dover and Calais to numerous French cities including Paris (UK£34/49 one way/return, 7½ hours). Bookings can be made at the Eurolines office (☎ 020-7730 8235), 52 Grosvenor Gardens, London SW1W 0AU; by telephone through the main Eurolines office (☎ 01582-404511) in Luton; or at any office of National Express, whose buses link London and other parts of the UK with the Channel ports.

Eurostar This very civilised passenger train service through the Channel tunnel takes only three hours to travel from London's Waterloo station to Paris' Gare du Nord via Ashford. Passport and customs checks are usually done before you board the train.

There are frequent daily services from London and Ashford to Paris and other stops in France, including Calais Fréthun and Lille. In the UK contact Eurostar on ☎ 0990-186 186, or in France (in English) on ☎ 08 36 35 35 39, or check its Web site at www.eurostar.com.

The excursion 2nd-class return fare on Eurostar's London-Paris service is UK£109. Changes to date and time of travel can be made before each departure and full refunds are available before the outward trip.

Young people aged 25 or under can purchase return tickets for UK£79; dates can be changed but reimbursement is limited to 50%. Children under 12 pay UK£59 return in 2nd class. Special deals may be on offer, so contact Eurostar for current details.

In London, Eurostar tickets are available from some travel agents, at many main-line train stations and from Rail Europe (☎ 0990-300 003), 179 Piccadilly, London W1V 0BA. Owned by the Société National des Chemins de Fer (SNCF), Rail Europe sells other SNCF tickets, but these are refundable only in the UK. In France, ticketing is handled by SNCF (see the Getting Around chapter for contact numbers).

Eurotunnel Eurotunnel's high-speed shuttle trains carry cars, coaches, motorcycles and bicycles from Folkestone through the Channel tunnel to Coquelles, 5km southwest of Calais, in air-conditioned comfort. For information and reservations, try a travel agent or contact Eurotunnel (in the UK ☎ 0990-353 535, in France ☎ 03 21 00 61 00, www.eurotunnel.com).

The regular return fare for a car and all its passengers is around UK£160 from July to late September. Reservations are mandatory. Eurotunnel runs 24 hours per day, every day of the year, with up to four departures hourly during peak periods. Vehicles pass through customs and passport control for both countries before driving onto the train. If you're planning to drive around France, it could be cheaper to take your vehicle through the tunnel (or on a ferry – see the Sea section later in this chapter) than to hire a car there.

Continental Europe
Eurolines Bus Europe's largest international bus network, Eurolines (☎ 01 43 54 11 99, @ euroline@imagenet.fr, www.euro lines.fr), links Paris and other French cities with places throughout Europe, and with Scandinavia. Buses are slower than trains but they are cheaper, especially if you qualify for the discounts available to people who are 25 or under or over 60, or take advantage of discount fares on offer from time to time.

Typical services to Paris and other French cities are: from Amsterdam (340FF, 7½ hours), Berlin (510FF, 14 hours) and Rome (620FF, 23 hours); these are nondiscounted, one-way adult fares. Return tickets are cheaper than two one-way tickets. In summer it's wise to make reservations a few days ahead.

There are Eurolines-affiliated companies in Rome (☎ 06-44 23 39 28), Berlin (☎ 030-86 0960), and Amsterdam (☎ 020-560 87 87).

Busabout With Busabout (☎ 020-7950 1661, fax 7950 1662, @ busabout.info @virgin.net, www.busabout.com) you buy a ticket valid for two weeks, one, two, three or six months, or for unlimited travel, which enables you to leave the bus whenever you choose at numerous destinations in Europe and Scandinavia. The company, based at 258 Vauxhall Bridge Rd, London, operates a system of circuit and point-to-point services. In France, destinations include Paris, Avignon and Nice (all year), and Calais, Reims, Lyon, Tours and Bordeaux (during the warmer months).

Tickets cost about 20% less than comparable Eurail tickets and are available through student travel agencies. As an example, a standard 15-day ticket costs UK£249, or UK£199 for students. You can join the network wherever you choose, but there's an additional fee of at least UK£15 for the trans-Channel bus. Busabout runs year-round, passing through each pick-up point every two days (daily during the warmer months).

Train Rail services link France with every country in Europe; schedules are available from major train stations in France and abroad. SNCF contact numbers are given in the Getting Around chapter.

Thalys (☎ 08 36 35 35 36, www.thalys .com) is a TGV service operated jointly by French, Belgian, Dutch and German railways. It provides services to Paris' Gare du Nord from Amsterdam (4¼ hours, 446FF one way), Cologne (four hours, 428FF one way), Brussels (1½ hours, 355FF) and several intermediate stations. Tickets can be purchased by telephone and at all SNCF stations. Worthwhile discounts are available for children up to 12 years, young people under 26 years and for people over 60.

SNCF and Ferrovie dello Stato (FS; the Italian semigovernment railways) operate the Artesia TGV services from Milan and Turin to Lyon and Paris' Gare de Lyon. The standard one-way Milan-Paris fare (seven hours) is 567FF (a return ticket costs less). The usual range of discounts is available. Contact ☎ 08 36 35 35 35, any FS station, travel agents or www.artesia-geie.com for information and bookings.

Hitching Allostop Provoya (☎ 01 53 20 42 42), 8 rue Rochambeau, 75009 Paris, matches hitchers and drivers going to the same destination. You pay a fixed rate per kilometre (around 25 centimes) to the driver plus a fee to cover administrative expenses. Examples of possible costs are Amsterdam (180FF) and Berlin (330FF).

Hitching is never entirely safe in any country, and we don't recommend it. Travellers who decide to hitch are taking a small but potentially serious risk. For more advice, see Hitching in the Getting Around chapter.

SEA

Reservations and tickets for ferry travel to/from the UK, Ireland and Italy are available from most travel agents in those countries and in France. Return fares generally cost less than two one-ways. Children aged four to 14 or 15 years travel for half to two-thirds of an adult fare. Food is expensive on ferries, so it's worth bringing your own.

The UK & Ireland

Fares vary widely according to seasonal demand; tickets can cost almost three times as much in July and August as in the cooler months. To take advantage of promotional fares, you may have to reserve 24 hours or more in advance. Pricing policies of some companies (eg, Hoverspeed, Brittany Ferries and Condor Ferries) make it more expensive to buy a ticket in pounds than in francs.

Eurailpasses are *not* valid for ferry travel between England and France, but Eurailpass holders pay 50% of the appropriate fare for crossings with Irish Ferries (if you book ahead). Some discounts are available for students (eg, on SeaFrance) and young

people (eg, on Sealink Brittany Ferries), at least for tickets bought in France.

Numerous services operate from ports in England, and from Rosslare and Cork in Ireland, to ports in far northern France, Normandy and Brittany. The shipping lines are:

Brittany Ferries (☎ 0990-360 360, www.brit tany-ferries.com). Services from Plymouth to Roscoff and Saint Malo, Poole to Cherbourg, Portsmouth to Ouistreham and Cork to Roscoff (from April to early October only).
Condor Ferries (☎ 01305-761 551, www.con dorferries.co.uk). Services from Weymouth to Saint Malo (May to mid-October only).
Hoverspeed (☎ 01304-240 241, www.hover speed.co.uk). Services from Dover to Calais and Folkestone to Boulogne.
Irish Ferries (☎ 01-661 0551, www.irish-fer ries.ie). Service from Rosslare to Cherbourg.
P&O European Ferries (☎ 0990-980 555, www.poef.com). Services from Portsmouth to Cherbourg and Le Havre.
P&O Stena Line (☎ 0990-980 980, www .postena.com). Service from Dover to Calais.
SeaFrance Sealink (☎ 0990-711 711, www.sea france.co.uk). Service from Dover to Calais.

Fares range very widely: from UK£24 for a return adult ticket to UK£269 for four adults with a car on peak-season weekends. From Ireland – a journey of at least 14 hours – the range for single fares is from IR£80 (for a single adult without car) to IR£355 (for a car with up to two passengers in high season); many discounts are available. Check with the individual carriers.

Italy

Corsica is linked to Italy by various sea routes (see the Corsica chapter for details of ferries from mainland France). During summer, and especially from mid-July to early September, reservations on all routes must be made well in advance.

On top of the basic fare, each port levies an additional tax on visitors and vehicles, ranging from 24FF to 44FF for a passenger and 35FF to 64FF for a vehicle, depending on the port of departure and arrival. Fares range from 96FF to 190FF for an adult one-way ticket and from 250FF to 420FF for a small car. The companies concerned are:

Corsica Ferries (☎ 04 95 32 95 95 in Bastia, www.corsicaferries.com). Services from Savona and Livorno to Bastia and from Savona to Île Rousse in summer

Corsica Marittima
(☎ 04 95 54 66 66 in Bastia, www.Corsica-Marittima.com). Fast service from Genoa and Livorno to Bastia between April and September.

Moby Lines (☎ 04 95 34 84 94 in Bastia). Services from Genoa and Livorno to Bastia and from Piombino to Bastia from July to September.

ORGANISED WALKS

For a list of French companies running organised walks, see Guided Walks in the Facts for the Walker chapter. Here is a selection of foreign companies providing walking holidays to France.

The UK

Alternative Travel Group (☎ 01865-315 678, fax 315 697, ✉ info@atg-oxford.co.uk) 69–71 Banbury Rd, Oxford OX2 6PE. Walking tours to Provence, the Dordogne Valley and Cévennes.

Exodus Walking Holidays (☎ 020-8673 0859, fax 8673 0779, ✉ sales@exodustravels.co.uk, www .exodustravels.co.uk) 9 Weir Rd, London SW12 0LT. Mountaineering tours in the Northern Alps, walking tours in the Pyrenees, Cévennes and Corsica.

Holiday Fellowship (☎ 020-8905 9388, fax 8295 0506, www.hfholidays.co.uk) Edgeware Rd, London NW9 5AL. Walking tours in the Dordogne Valley, Mont Blanc region, Loire Valley, Hautes Pyrénées and Provence.

Travelbag Adventures (☎ 01420-541 007, fax 541 022, ✉ info@travelbag-adventures.co.uk, www.travelbag-adventures.co.uk) 15 Turk St, Alton, Hampshire GU34 1AG. Walking tours in the Luberon area of Provence, Auvergne volcanoes and the Dordogne.

Waymark Holidays (☎ 01753-516 477, fax 517 016) 44 Windsor Rd, Slough SL1 2EJ. Walking tours on the Alpine High Route, to the Jura, Cévennes, Hautes Pyrénées and Auvergne.

The USA

Backroads (☎ 1-800-462 2848, fax 510-527 1444, ✉ backtalk@backroads.com) 801 Cedar St, Berkeley, CA 94710. Walking tours to Burgundy, Vézère and Dordogne Valleys, and other Provence areas.

Cross Country International Walking Tours (☎ 1-800-828 8768, fax 914-677 6077, ✉ xcintl@ aol.com, www.walkingvacations.com) PO Box 1170, Millbrook, NY 12545. Walking tours in the Lot Valley and Provence.

Walking the World (☎ 1-800-340 9255, fax 970-498 9100, ✉ walktworld@aol.com) PO Box 1186, Fort Collins, CO 80522. Walking tours to Provence.

Wilderness Travel (☎ 1-510-558 2488, fax 558 2489, ✉ info@wilderness travel.com, www .wildernesstravel.com) 1102 9th St, Berkeley, CA 94710. Walking tours in Dordogne Valley, Provence and Burgundy.

Australia

Adventure World (☎ 02-9956 7766, fax 9956 7707, ✉ sydney@adventure.world.com.au) 73 Walker St, North Sydney, NSW 2060. Tours to the Dordogne Valley, Provence and Corsica.

Ecotrek: Bogong Jack Adventure (☎ 08-8383 7198, fax 8383 7377) PO Box 4, Kangarilla SA 5157. Walking tours to the Pyrenees, Loire and Dordogne Valleys, and Chamonix.

Getting Around

Much of France's domestic transport network is state-owned and subsidised: the Société National des Chemins de Fer (SNCF) runs virtually all inter-departmental land transport, and short-haul bus companies are either run by the *département* (department) or grouped so that each local company handles a different set of destinations. Eurolines and other privately owned long-haul bus operators are confined to international routes.

AIR

Any French travel agent can make bookings for domestic flights and supply details of the complicated fare system. Outside France, Air France representatives sell tickets for many domestic flights. The main domestic carriers are:

Air France (☎ 08 02 80 28 02) 40 ave George V, 75008 Paris
Air Inter (☎ 01 45 46 90 00) 119 ave des Champs Élysées, 75008 Paris
Air Liberté (☎ 08 03 80 58 05) 3 rue Pont des Halles, 94656 Rungis
Air Littoral (☎ 08 03 83 48 34) 100 blvd Montparnasse, 75006 Paris
Corsair (☎ 01 49 79 49 79) 24 rue Saarinen, 94150 Rungis

Costs

The cheapest tickets are one-way youth/student air fares, eg, from Paris to Bordeaux is 290FF, to Nice 390FF. Adult tickets cost up to four times as much depending on restrictions and timing of flights. On most flights each passenger is allowed one cabin bag and 23kg of checked luggage. Excess baggage costs 10FF per kilogram.

Discounts

Substantial discounts are available on many flights. As an example, Air France has four regular fare levels (Tempo 1 to Tempo 4) offering discounts to people over 60, married couples and families. Tempo Jeunes fares are available to people aged 24 and under and to students 26 and under.

To/From the Airport

For information on public transport links to Orly and Roissy Charles de Gaulle airports, see the Paris chapter. For information on regional airports, see relevant walks chapters.

BUS

French transport policy is biased towards the state's rail system, so inter-regional bus services are limited. However, there are plenty of short-distance bus services within each département, especially in rural areas with relatively few train lines (eg, Brittany). Bus travel is generally inexpensive and services to even quite remote areas are regular if not frequent. Many services are provided by SNCF where uneconomical train lines have been closed; tickets for these are purchased at the *guichets* (ticket windows) in the train station, and timetables on display include bus services, designated by the word *car*.

TRAIN

France's excellent rail network, operated by SNCF, reaches almost every part of the country. Many towns not on the SNCF train and bus network are linked with nearby stations by intra-departmental bus lines, and timetables generally are organised to provide good connections at peak times. Although the *grandes lignes* (main lines) radiate from Paris like the spokes of a wheel, journeys between provincial towns on different spokes need not involve travelling via Paris. It is possible, for example, to go from Quimper (Brittany) to Périgueux (Dordogne) in one day, via Nantes and Bordeaux.

TGV

The TGV *(train à grande vitesse)*, pronounced 'teh-zheh-veh' and meaning 'high-speed train', is one of the transport wonders of Europe. Its maximum speed is 300km/h and three regional routes provide fast and frequent travel to main junction stations (see also Eurostar and Thalys in the Getting There & Away chapter). Its routes are:

TGV Sud-Est Links Paris' Gare de Lyon with Lyon and the south-east: Dijon, Geneva, the Alps, Avignon, Marseille, Nice and Perpignan.
TGV Atlantique Links Paris' Gare Montparnasse with Brittany, Nantes, the Loire Valley, Bordeaux, the western Pyrenees and Toulouse.
TGV Nord Links Paris' Gare du Nord with Lille and Calais.

Information

Larger train stations have both guichets and information/reservations desks. They can provide details of travel throughout France.

If you'll be moving around within a particular region, ask at a train station for a *Guide Régional des Transports* (Regional Transport Guide), an informative booklet of SNCF bus and intra-regional rail timetables. SNCF's small, free *horaires* (timetables) are available at stations; at first they look complicated, but once you're familiar with the use of the *notes à consulter* (footnotes) to indicate, for example, frequency of service, they're invaluable for efficient travelling. Two sets are issued each year: for summer (end of May to end of October) and winter (November to end of May).

Outside a region, or outside France, information (in English) about schedules and fares is available on ☎ 08 36 35 35 35 (in French) and ☎ 08 36 35 35 39 (in English). The SNCF Web site (voyages.sncf.fr) has timetable and booking information in English.

At the time of writing, most luggage lockers were out of service because of the security threat posed by terrorists.

Classes & Sleepers

Most French trains, including the TGV, have 1st- and 2nd-class sections.

Overnight trains usually have *couchettes* (sleeping berths) for which reservations are necessary, the fee being 90FF. More luxurious *voitures-lits* (sleepers) cost from 259FF to 907FF per person. On some overnight trains a 2nd-class *siège à dossier inclinable* (reclining seat) can be reserved for 20FF.

Check the destination panel beside the door when you board your train – trains are sometimes divided mid-journey, so that some cars head off to a different destination from the rest of the train.

Costs & Reservations

For 2nd-class travel, expect to pay about 60FF per 100km for cross-country trips and up to 100FF per 100km for short journeys. Regular return journeys cost twice as much as one way. Travel in 1st class is 50% more expensive than in 2nd class. Children under four travel free; those aged four to 11 pay 50% of the adult fare.

Reservation Fee This fee (20FF) is obligatory for travel by TGV and for a couchette. To save disappointment, reservation is highly desirable if you're travelling during peak holiday periods and want a seat on a popular train. Reservations can by made by telephone, via the SNCF's Web site, at any SNCF ticket office or from a ticket machine in a train station (see Buying a Ticket). Make sure you specify *non-fumeur* (nonsmoking) or *fumeur* (smoking). For telephone or online purchases you'll receive a reference number which you must quote at any ticket counter to obtain your ticket.

Supplements On certain trains to/from Paris, non-TGV passengers travelling in *heures de pointe* (peak periods) have to pay a supplement of up to 60/120FF for 2nd/1st class. Supplements do not generally apply to travel between provincial stations, but may be levied if you take an international train (eg, one coming from Italy) on a domestic segment. Supplement-liable services are indicated by a hatch symbol (#) below the train number on the small horaires.

Buying a Ticket

At the largest stations there are separate ticket windows for *international*, *grandes lignes* (long-haul) and *banlieue* (suburban) lines. Tickets bought with cash can be reimbursed for cash, so keep them safe.

You can usually use any one of the main credit cards to pay for train tickets, both in person and via the SNCF's Web site. Almost every SNCF station has at least one

Mosquée de Paris, built in an ornate Hispano-Moorish style.

SIMON BRACKEN

The Eiffel Tower, Paris.

JOHN HAY

View of Napoleon's tomb in the Hôtel des Invalides, from the Eiffel Tower.

JOHN HAY

Lamps in the Paris streets.

SIMON BRACKEN

The quiet, green surrounds of the Jardin du Luxembourg.

SIMON BRACKEN

A riot of tulip blooms announce spring at the artistically inspired gardens of Monet's famous pink and green house, Giverny.

easy-to-use ticket machine *(automat pointe de vente* (APV), or *billetterie automatique)* that accepts credit cards.

Rail Passes for Non-Europeans

These can be purchased at a few places in Europe if you're not a resident of any European country. However, prices are very much higher than they would be at home. They do not include reservation fees or couchette charges but do enable discounts on the Eurostar. Most have half-price versions for children aged four to 11.

In France, passes are available from the SNCF offices at Orly and Roissy Charles de Gaulle airports; in Paris at Gare du Nord, Gare de Lyon and Gare Saint Lazare, and at the main train stations in Marseille and Nice. In London rail passes for overseas visitors are sold by Rail Europe (☎ 0990-300 003), 179 Piccadilly, London W1V 0BA, or at Victoria station.

In Australia, contact Thomas Cook (☎ 02-9320 6561); in Canada, Rail Europe (☎ 1-800 361 7245), and in the USA, Rail Europe (☎ 1-800 438 7245). Bookings can be made online at www.raileurope.com.

Eurailpass This offers reasonable value to people who are under 26 on their first day of travel and who aim to travel more than 2400km during the currency of the ticket. Tickets are available for unlimited travel during 15 or 21 days, or one, two or three months. One/two months of unlimited travel with the Eurail Youthpass costs US$605/857.

Europass This provides for travel in France and certain other countries between five and 15 consecutive or nonconsecutive days over two months. The regular adult fare for 1st-class travel ranges from US$326 for five days to US$746 for 15 days. The Europass Youth ticket, available to people aged 25 and under, is cheaper.

Rail Passes for Residents of Europe

The Euro Domino and Inter-Rail passes are available to anyone who can prove residence in Europe for at least six months. They are not valid in your country of residence. In France they are sold at most train stations; elsewhere, contact Rail Europe (see Rail Passes for Non-Europeans). Holders are entitled to discounts on the Eurostar and Thalys but must pay SNCF reservation fees and supplements.

Euro Domino France This gives three, five or 10 days travel over a period of one month plus a 25% discount on travel from the place of purchase to the French border. The youth version (for people 25 and under) offers three/five/10 days of 2nd-class travel for UK£85/115/185; the adult version costs UK£105/145/220. They don't tell you until you're there that a certain number of discount seats are set aside on some TGV services and that once they're full, you'll have to travel at another time; also, some TGV services are not available at all to Euro Domino holders.

Inter-Rail Pass This gives 22 consecutive days of unlimited 2nd-class travel for 1285FF if you're under 26, or 1836FF for adults, and a 50% discount on travel from your home country to France.

SNCF Discount Tickets

SNCF has a range of discount tickets, unencumbered by residency requirements, which give reductions of up to 50%. Full details are available in leaflets at all SNCF stations. Among them are the Découverte series, for people aged 12 to 25, for people over 60 and for couples. Découverte J8 and J30 require reservation of tickets eight or 30 days in advance to attract reductions of up to 60%.

Validating Your Ticket

Before boarding, you must validate your ticket in a *composteur*, an orange post standing between the ticket windows and the platform. Insert the ticket printed side up and the machine will take a nick out of the side and print the time and date on the back.

Reimbursements

Unused tickets bought in France can be reimbursed during their validity (up to two months) at any ticket window. For tickets bought elsewhere, it's back to the office from which they were bought.

CAR & MOTORCYCLE

For a walking holiday, there are advantages in driving your own vehicle – ease of travel, especially when it comes to finding out-of-the-way accommodation, and the savings for a couple or group. However, these have to be balanced against the inconvenience if you want to do through walks, and the fact that the rate of fatalities on French roads is almost double that of the UK or USA.

Riders of any type of two-wheel vehicle with a motor must wear a helmet. Bikes of more than 125cc must have their headlights on during the day. To rent a motorcycle, you usually have to pay a *caution* (deposit) of several thousand francs, which you forfeit, up to the value of the damage, if you're in an accident and it's your fault.

Documents & Equipment

All drivers must carry the following documents with them at all times:

- a national ID card or passport
- a valid driver's permit or licence; many foreign licences can be used in France for up to one year
- original registration document
- proof of insurance

A reflective warning triangle, to be used in the event of breakdown, must be carried in the car. A right-hand drive vehicle must have deflectors fixed to the headlights to avoid dazzling oncoming traffic.

Road Rules

Motoring in Europe (UK£4.99), published in the UK by the Royal Automobile Club (RAC), summarises the road regulations. Motoring organisations in other countries publish similar guides. North American drivers should remember that turning right on a red light is illegal in France.

Fines for serious violations (eg, speeding, driving through a red light) range from 1300FF to 100,000FF. The police can make tourists pay up immediately.

Speed Limits Unless otherwise indicated, a speed limit of 50km/h applies in all designated built-up areas. Outside built-up areas, the limits are:

- 90km/h (80km/h on wet roads) on undivided N and D motorways/highways
- 110km/h (100km/h on wet roads) on dual carriageways (divided highways)
- 130km/h (110km/h on wet roads, 50km/h in foggy conditions) on *autoroutes* (multilane divided highways)

Right of Way Any car entering an intersection, including a T-junction, from a road on your right has *priorité à droite* (right of way), no matter how minor the road it's coming from. If you're turning left you have to wait for cars coming from your right.

Priorité à droite is suspended at *ronds-points* (roundabouts, or traffic circles), where vehicles already in the roundabout have right of way, and on priority roads marked by a yellow diamond with a black diamond in the middle.

Alcohol French police conduct random breathalyser tests to find drivers whose blood-alcohol concentration is over 0.05%. Fines range from 900FF to 30,000FF and licences can be suspended.

Costs

While the cost of any given journey by car (fuel and autoroute tolls) may be more than a single train ticket, it's clearly cheaper with two or more people sharing the cost.

Fuel The fuel price very much depends on where you buy it. Supermarket petrol stations are the cheapest venue, those at rest stops along the autoroutes the most expensive. At the time of writing, *sans plomb* (unleaded) petrol cost from 5.91FF to 6.74FF per litre, and *gazole* (diesel) from 4.18FF to 5.07FF.

Tolls These are charged on almost all autoroutes and many bridges. Some autoroutes have toll plazas every few dozen kilometres, while on others a machine issues a ticket to be handed over at a *péage* (toll booth) when you exit. Expect to pay about 40FF per

100km, by credit card if you prefer. As an example of how they mount up, the total cost of tolls from Paris to Nice is 356.50FF. The Web site of the Association des Sociétés Françaises d'Autoroutes (ASFA) at www .autoroutes.fr has full details.

Parking In most cities and many towns, parking near the centre costs 5FF to 10FF per hour and is commonly limited to two hours.

Rental
Multinational agencies such as Hertz, Avis, Budget and Europcar are very expensive if you hire on the spot, up to 900FF for the smallest model, but prebooked and prepaid rates can be reasonable. Domestic companies such as Rent-a-Car Système and Century, and student travel agencies such as usit CAMPUS offer the best on-the-spot rates.

Most rental companies require the driver to be over 21, or even 23, and to have had a driving licence for at least one year.

Assurance (insurance) for damage or injury you cause to other people is mandatory; other charges, eg, collision damage waiver, vary widely between companies. When comparing rates, the most important thing to check is the *franchise* (excess/deductible) – the amount you're liable to pay if you're at fault in an accident before the insurance takes over.

BICYCLE
If you're combining a cycling holiday with some walking, then you might consider bringing a copy of Lonely Planet's *Cycling France* guide, with all the information you'll need about organising such a visit. For a predominantly walking holiday, a bike could be useful to reach the start of some walks, or could provide the means for a pleasantly different day out in between walks.

There's usually at least one shop in most towns that hires out mountain bikes for up to 100FF per day; a deposit of 1000FF or 2000FF may be required, which you forfeit if the bike is damaged or stolen.

Bicycles must have two functioning brakes, a bell, a red rear reflector and yellow reflectors on the pedals. After sunset and in poor visibility cyclists must turn on a front white light and a rear red one. Cyclists must ride single file when being overtaken.

HITCHING
Hitching is never completely safe anywhere in the world and we don't recommend it. Travellers who hitch should understand that they are taking a small but potentially serious risk. However, it you speak some French (few older people in rural areas know any English), hitching affords opportunities to meet people from all walks of life. Please consider the following advice.

Two women hitching together should be safer than a woman hitching alone – definitely a risk. Two men travelling together may have a harder time than a man travelling solo. The best and safest combination is a man and a woman. Never get into a car with someone you don't instinctively and immediately trust. Keep your pack with you rather than in the boot (trunk).

Allostop Provoya (see the Getting There & Away chapter) may be able to put you in touch with drivers going to provincial cities.

LOCAL TRANSPORT
France's larger cities and towns generally have excellent public transport systems; there are metros in Paris, Lyon, Marseille, Lille and Toulouse, and ultra-modern trams in Paris, Nantes, Strasbourg and Grenoble. Information about routes and fares is usually available at tourist offices and local bus company information counters.

Taxis are generally expensive but in a few areas they're the only means available for reaching the start of a walk if you don't have a car. Most towns have a taxi rank near the train station. Expect to pay between 3.50FF and 10FF per kilometre, depending on the time of day, day of the week and distance you're travelling. An extra charge per piece of baggage may be levied.

Paris Region

Although the Île de France is extensively built up and densely populated, it is a region of great natural beauty and tucked away within it are many wonderful places. Amazing as it may seem, it is still possible to walk in unspoilt surroundings only 50km from the capital.

The nine walks described in this chapter will give you an idea of the amazing variety of cultural, historical and artistic heritage found in the Paris region, as well as the diversity of its flora and landscapes. Rivers, lakes, leafy forests, pine forests, sandstone outcrops, museums, painters, chateaux, writers...these are just a few of the highlights. Paris itself is well worth exploring on foot; it too holds wonderful surprises for the walker.

CLIMATE
The Paris Basin is subjected to both oceanic and continental climatic influences. The Île de France region has the lowest rainfall in France (575 mm per year), spread more or less evenly over the seasons. The yearly average temperature in Paris is 12°C (3°C in January, 19°C in July), with occasionally dramatic variations (the temperature can fall below freezing in winter, and often climbs to more than 30°C in summer). Temperatures are slightly lower outside Paris (by 1°C).

INFORMATION
Maps
The Michelin 1:100,000 *Environs de Paris* sheet No 106 and the IGN *Paris et ses environs* sheet No 90 (at the same scale) cover the Paris region, but not the Provins and Vallée de la Marne walks. For a more complete coverage of the Île de France, you'll need the Michelin 1:200,000 *Île de France* sheet No 237.

If you're planning to spend any time in Paris, you will need a map of the city centre. Lonely Planet's *Paris City Map* is indexed, easy to use and includes a metro guide.

For maps covering individual walks, see Planning in the introduction to each walk.

HIGHLIGHTS

RICHARD l'ANSON

Along the Seine River to the Eiffel Tower

- The medieval town of Provins, for a journey back to the 13th century

- Claude Monet's gardens at Giverny, in full bloom from May to September

- The Vaux de Cernay, near Dampierre, a picturesque valley that inspired the landscape painters of the late 19th century

- The Mediterranean landscape of the Gorges de Franchard, in the Forêt de Fontainebleau

Books
English-language walking guides to Paris include: *Walking Paris* by Gilles Desmons, *Pariswalks* by Alison & Sonia Landes and *Walks in Hemingway's Paris* by Noel Riley Fitch.

To help you identify flora and fauna in the forests of the Île de France, the Office National des Forêts (☎ 01 40 19 58 00, www .onf.fr), 2 ave de Saint Mandé, publishes several books (in French), priced from 29FF.

Au Vieux Campeur (☎ 01 53 10 48 48), a specialist outdoor gear shop on the corner of rue du Sommerard and rue de Beauvais, 5e, keeps a good range of walking books.

Lonely Planet offers two guides to the capital: *Paris*, a complete guide, and the pocket-sized *Paris Condensed*. Both contain detailed information on accommodation and eating options in one of the great gastronomic centres of the world.

Information Sources

The Espace du Tourisme Île de France (☎ 01 44 50 19 98, fax 01 44 50 19 99, www.paris -Île-de-france.com, metro Palais-Royal-Musée du Louvre, 1er) is in the lower level of the Carousel du Louvre shopping mall, next to the inverted glass pyramid. They will supply you with information on the Île de France, but only have basic information on Paris itself. They are open daily except Tuesday.

Tourist offices convenient to walks include:

Provins (☎ 01 64 60 26 26, fax 01 64 60 11 97)
  rue du Vieux Chemin de Paris
Rambouillet (☎ 01 34 83 21 21) place de la
  Libération

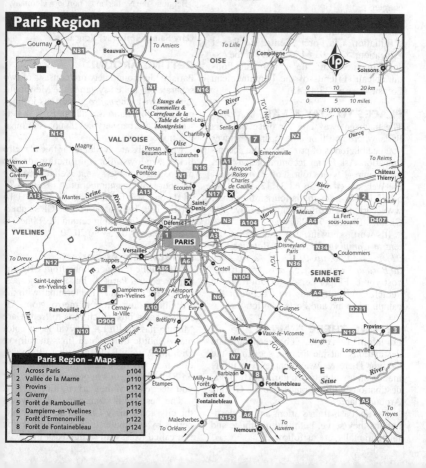

Paris Region

Paris Region – Maps

Dampierre (☎ 01 30 52 57 30, fax 01 30 52 52 43) 9 Grande Rue

Maison du Parc Naturel Régional de la Haute Vallée de Chevreuse (☎ 01 30 52 09 09, fax 01 30 52 12 43) Château de la Madeleine, Chevreuse

Ermenonville (☎ 03 44 54 01 58, fax 03 44 54 04 96) 1 rue René de Girardin

Barbizon (☎ 01 60 66 41 87) 55 Grande Rue

For information on the Fédération Française de la Randonnée Pédestre (FFRP) and the Club Alpin Français, which organises regular walks in the Paris region, see the section Useful Organisations in the Facts for the Walker chapter.

For more detailed information on the Forêt de Fontainebleau, contact the Centre d'Initiation à la Forêt (Centre for Forest Education; ☎/fax 01 64 22 72 59) or the Association des Amis de la Forêt de Fontainebleau (Friends of the Fontainebleau Forest; ☎ 01 64 23 46 45).

PLACES TO STAY & EAT

The main gateway city for these walks is Paris, where you'll be able to find whatever you need in terms of provisions and accommodation. Ask for an accommodation list at the Champs-Élysées tourist office or consult the Web site (☎ 08 36 68 31 12, fax 01 49 52 53 00, ✉ info@paris-touristoffice.com, www.paris-touristoffice.com), 127 ave des Champs-Élysées, 75008 Paris, 8e.

It's worth knowing that you can pitch a tent at *Camping du Bois de Boulogne (☎ 01 45 24 30 00, fax 01 42 24 42 95, Allée du Bord de l'Eau, 75016 Paris, 16e)*. It will cost you 65FF per person (or 96FF with a vehicle). A shuttle bus runs between the camping ground and Porte Maillot.

GETTING THERE & AWAY

For information on travel between Paris and destinations outside France, see Air in the Getting There & Away chapter. For information on travel between Paris and regional destinations within France, see the Getting Around chapter.

The six Paris train stations and the destinations they serve, both within France and internationally, are as follows:

Gare d'Austerlitz (13e) Loire Valley, South-Western France, Languedoc, Roussillon, Pyrenees, Spain, Portugal

Gare de l'Est (10e) Champagne, Alsace, Lorraine, Luxembourg, parts of Switzerland, southern Germany and points farther east

Gare de Lyon (12e) Areas south-east of Paris including Burgundy, Provence, the Côte d'Azur, the Alps, parts of Switzerland, Italy and points beyond

Gare Montparnasse (15e) Parts of southern Normandy, Brittany, places between Paris and Brittany (Chartres, Angers, Nantes, Tours) and TGV to parts of South-Western France

Gare du Nord (10e) Northern France, UK, Belgium, the Netherlands, northern Germany, Scandinavia, Moscow etc and Eurostar to London

Gare Saint Lazare (8e) Normandy

GETTING AROUND

Paris' underground network consists of two separate but linked systems: the Métropolitain, known as the *métro*, which has 13 lines and over 300 stations, and the RER, a network of suburban services that pass through the city centre.

Metro maps are available for free at metro ticket windows. For information on the metro, RER and bus system, call the RATP's 24-hour inquiries number on ☎ 08 36 68 77 14 if you speak French, or ☎ 08 36 68 41 14 for English. Information on SNCF's suburban services (including certain RER lines) is available on ☎ 01 53 90 20 20

To/From the Airports

Of the public transport links from Orly airport to central Paris, Jetbus is the cheapest (about 25FF). It links the terminal with the Villejuif Louis Aragon metro stop. Air France has a bus which runs to/from Gare Montparnasse (40FF). Orlyval is an automated shuttle train which links the airport with the Antony RER (suburban) train station, from where you can travel into the city on RER line B; this approach ensures that you steer clear of the Paris traffic.

The best public transport link between the city and Roissy Charles de Gaulle airport is by commuter train on the RER line B3, called Roissyrail (around 50FF).

ACROSS PARIS

Pigeons and Parisians in the Parc du Champ de Mars with *that* tower in the distance

ACROSS PARIS

The route described here crosses the capital from west to east: from the Bois de Boulogne to the Bois de Vincennes. It's a walk of roughly 19km, mainly on the left bank. You'll see the most famous sights – including the Eiffel Tower – but also some more surprising and lesser-known spots. You'll discover the very different atmospheres of the various *quartiers*, noticing subtle changes as you make your way from the well-heeled 16th *arrondissement* (district) to the more working-class streets of the 12th via the historic centre of Paris (the old Lutetia) and the Latin Quarter, taking in several magnificent parks and gardens. Each section describes a relatively homogeneous part of the city, with convenient points at which to join or leave the walk.

The route is indicated by the red-and-yellow waymarkers, mainly on lampposts or signposts, of the FFRP's Paris Traverse No 1. It's not always easy to follow, so it's best to navigate with the FFRP publication *Topoguide : Paris à pied* or a detailed map of Paris (preferably one at a scale of 1:10,000).

You'll find plenty of snack bars and grocery stores along the way. But remember that many shops are closed on Sunday.

Porte de la Muette to Pont de Bir Hakeim

This section crosses the 16th arrondissement, the poshest part of Paris. The route starts at the Porte de la Muette, on the edge of the Bois de Boulogne, or more specifically on the place de Colombie, just in front of the OECD building (which is hidden by a fence), next to the bus stop, in front of the sign saying 'Porte de la Muette'.

Take the little gravel lane that goes along by the fence of the OECD building and crosses the superb **Jardin du Ranelagh**. You'll come out onto the chaussée de la Muette; turn left and go to an intersection where you'll see La Gare, an old station that has been turned into a fashionable restaurant. Cross the road and follow rue Largilliére, then, after the intersection with ave Mozart, the rue des Vignes; notice the little cinema, Le Ranelagh, at No 5. Fifty metres farther on, turn left into the rue Raynouard; then, after another 50m, go down the little street that heads off to the right, at a lower level (rue Berton). This takes you down a paved lane, with greenery all around, and it's

Paris from the Eiffel Tower with the Parc du Champ de Mars in the foreground

like being in a village. During the 19th century the French writer Honoré de Balzac lived at No 24.

When you get to rue d'Ankara, there's a beautiful view of the Eiffel Tower. Follow ave Marcel-Proust, then rue Charles Dickens, which leads to rue des Eaux. You can visit the **Musée du Vin**, which is on your left, at the foot of a hill. Go under the metro viaduct and cross the Pont de Bir Hakeim across the Seine. Enjoy the view of the Eiffel Tower, just nearby.

Pont de Bir Hakeim to Hôtel des Invalides

Now you're on the left bank, right on the Seine. Go along beside the river to the **Eiffel Tower**. Instead of

Across Paris

looking at it from directly underneath, with hundreds of tourists milling about, it's a good idea to explore the two little parks beside the tower, which are much quieter, with their pretty fountains and trees, and from which the views are superb.

Find your way across the **Parc du Champ de Mars**, which leads away from the Eiffel Tower, preferably down one of the side lanes. This huge park was used as a parade ground in the 18th century. Keep going till you get to the École Militaire building at the end of the park. Facing the École Militaire, go left to the place de l'École Militaire; from there, it's not far along the ave de Tourville to

Across Paris

another military edifice, the magnificent Hôtel des Invalides. This building dates back to the 17th century and was used as a hospital for soldiers wounded in combat. The Église du Dôme has a superb, gilded dome, which looks magnificent lit up at night. The spire is 107m high. Have a look at the Jardins de l'Intendant, in front of the building.

Hôtel des Invalides to Jardins du Luxembourg

This stretch of the walk crosses the 7th arrondissement, where many international institutions and government ministries are concentrated.

From the Hôtel des Invalides, take the **ave de Breteuil**, which is at right angles to ave de Tourville, leading away from the Hôtel. With trees along either side and a grassy strip down the middle, it's one of the most opulent aves in Paris. Turn left into rue d'Estrées. When you get to place André-Tardieu, you'll have a good view of the Tour Montparnasse on one side and the Hôtel des Invalides on the other. Keep going along rue de Babylone, then rue Monsieur (on the right). When you get to the rue Oudinot, turn left, then take the first street on the right (rue Rousselet), which comes out on the rue de Sèvres, a very busy shopping street (the department store Bon Marché is a little bit farther east.

Now you go into the 6th arrondissement, which is also very well-heeled and home to many religious organisations. A hundred metres farther on, turn into rue Saint-Romain, then turn left into **rue Cherche Midi**, a very old Parisian thoroughfare. It has many antique shops, boutiques and mansions dating from the end of the 18th century (notably at Nos 85, 87 and 89). Note also the old street name carved into the stone on the corner of the rue Jean-Ferrandi.

Just before blvd Raspail, leave the rue du Cherche-Midi and turn right into the **rue du Regard**, which is lined with magnificent mansions (at Nos 1, 5, 7 and 13), with carved doors and moulded portals.

Cross rue de Rennes, one of Paris' major shopping streets (with a side view of the Tour Montparnasse on your right) and go down the rue Notre Dame des Champs, which crosses the blvd Raspail 300m farther on. Keep going for another 200m, then turn left into rue Vavin, which will take you to the Jardins du Luxembourg.

Église du Dôme of the Hôtel des Invalides, home of Napoleon's extravagant tomb

The Jardins du Luxembourg, a favourite haunt of Parisians in summer

Jardins du Luxembourg to Jardin des Plantes

This stretch of the walk crosses one of the most famous parks in Paris, the university district and the historic centre of the capital (old Lutetia).

The rue Vavin comes out at the south-west entrance to the **Jardins du Luxembourg**. Take the lane on the left, which goes past the apiary and heads north. You'll pass tennis courts and areas for *pétanque* (a type of bowls), children's games and people playing cards and chess. At the end of the lane, turn right and go along beside the Orangerie (which houses exhibitions) to the **Palais du Luxembourg** which dates from the beginning of the 17th century, and is where the senate sits. Go along in front of this building, and just beyond it, turn right into the lane which goes past the beautiful **Fontaine des Médicis** and takes you out of the park again, onto place Edmond Rostand.

Cross the blvd Saint-Michel and take rue Soufflot, heading towards the **Panthéon**, which houses illustrious tombs. Take the first street on the right (rue Le Goff) then the first on the left (rue Malebranche), which cuts across rue Saint-Jacques, one of the oldest streets in Paris, dating back to Gallo-Roman times. Continue along rue des Fossés Saint-Jacques, and when you get to a littlse square, follow the rue de l'Estrapade, then the rue Blainville, which comes out onto the picturesque **place de la Contrescarpe**. Take rue du Cardinal-Lemoine on the left, then the cobblestone rue Rollin on the right, which leads you via a stairway to the rue Monge. Look for No 49 rue Monge: when you go through the porchway it's like entering another world. Suddenly you're back in Roman times in the **Arènes de Lutéce**, which date from AD 200 and were used for circuses. Make your way through these magnificent remnants, and go out on the right-hand side into the rue de Navarre, which leads to the rue Lacépède. Turn left and walk to the entrance of the Jardin des Plantes (Botanical Gardens), established under Louis XIII in the 17th century.

Jardin des Plantes to Bois de Vincennes

This stretch of the walk crosses part of the 13th arrondissement and continues into the 12th: neither are much frequented by tourists.

Visit the **Jardin des Plantes** and its various amenities as you please (there are hothouses, a minizoo,

The Fontaine des Médicis, an ornate Italianate goldfish pond in the Jardins du Luxembourg

The Panthéon, which houses the remains of Voltaire, Rousseau and Marie Curie, among others

ACROSS PARIS

and the Museum d'Histoire Naturelle). When you've been right round the gardens, go out into rue Geoffroy Saint-Hilaire (via the south-west exit). On the way out, you'll see the **Mosquée de Paris**, just across the way, with its 33m-high minaret.

Go down the rue Geoffroy Saint-Hilaire to the left, then turn into the first street on the left (rue Poliveau), which leads to the blvd de l'Hôpital. Cross it and go into the grounds of the **Hôpital La Pitié-Salpêtriére** (behind the metro viaduct), one of Europe's biggest hospitals, housed in buildings that date back to the 17th century. Originally the complex was an arsenal. Having passed through the entrance hall, head for the large chapel, straight ahead, then turn right and go through the Porche Lassay. Keep going straight ahead for about 400m. You'll come to the hospital's south exit on rue Bruant, which leads to the blvd Vincent Auriol. Turn left and follow the boulevard to the Seine.

As you cross the Pont de Bercy, take a look at the imposing architecture of the gigantic **Ministére de l'Économie et des Finances**. You're entering the 12th arrondissement. On the other side of the bridge, walk to the **Palais Omnisports de Paris-Bercy** (POPB), recognisable by its futuristic architecture and its sloping lawn-covered walls. This venue can hold 17,000 spectators and is used for all sorts of events (concerts, sports etc). The **Parc de Bercy**, which extends beyond the POPB, is pleasant. Walk to the end of it and, when you get to the rue Joseph Kessel, turn left.

Go past place Lachambeaudie, then take the tunnel that goes under the railway lines. At the other end of the tunnel, take rue des Fonds-Verts to the right, then the rue de Wattignies. A hundred metres farther on, turn right into rue de la Bréche aux Loups, then left almost straight away into rue des Meuniers. This brings you to the heart of a working class suburb. Keep following the rue des Meuniers to blvd Poniatowski. Go left along the boulevard until you get to the Porte de Reuilly, beyond which stretches the **Bois de Vincennes**.

Sun and moon on the Mosquée de Paris

Beautiful gardens around the ornate Hispano-Moorish Mosquée de Paris

Lawn roof of the Palais Omnisports de Paris-Bercy, one of Paris' most important new buildings

Vallée de la Marne

Duration	7 hours
Distance	25km
Standard	medium
Start/Finish	Nanteuil-Saâcy
Public Transport	yes

Summary This walk takes you along village streets, with views over the bends of the Marne, before following the river and then climbing up to the vineyards of Champagne.

Fed by a majectic river, the Vallée de la Marne is the nearest wine-growing area to Paris. Less than an hour from the city, this long but relatively gentle circuit allows you ample opportunity to explore the valley – its villages, orchards, woods and vineyards officially within the Champagne region.

HISTORY

Humans have been travelling up and down the Vallée de la Marne for at least 300,000 years. Around AD 1000 the Meaux region belonged to the counts of Vermandois, forbears of two powerful aristocratic families headed by the counts of Brie and Champagne. By the 12th century the county of Brie (from Meaux to Provins) had become so powerful it posed a real threat to the Capetian kings. After concluding an alliance with the Crown, however, Brie was ruined by the Hundred Years' War. Later the county became a principle source of provisions for the capital and the preferred location for the country residences of French kings and princes.

The Marne was hard hit by the wars of the 19th and 20th centuries, blasted in quick succession by Napoleon's 1814 campaign, the war against Prussia in 1870, WWI (with the Battle of the Marne) and WWII.

PLANNING
When to Walk

Summer and autumn are the best seasons, as the fruit ripens and the grapes are harvested.

Maps

The walk is covered by the IGN 1:25,000 *Château-Thierry* sheet No 2613O, *La Ferté-Gaucher* sheet No 2614O and the *Saâcy-sur-Marne* sheet No 2513E.

PLACES TO STAY

If you'd like to spend a couple of days around the Marne, there are hotels at Nanteuil-sur-Marne and at Charly-sur-Marne. There are also various camping grounds open from April to the end of September, including *Les Illettes* (☎ 03 23 82 12 11) at Charly and *Les Monts* (☎ 03 23 70 01 18) at Nogent L'Artaud and another one at Crouttes-sur-Marne. To book one of these gîtes, contact the branch of Gîtes de France at Laon (☎ 03 23 27 76 80, fax 03 23 27 76 88).

GETTING TO/FROM THE WALK

To the start of the walk by train, take the Paris–Château-Thierry line at the Gare de l'Est. Get off at Nanteuil-Saâcy or Nogent-l'Artaud-Charly (Town B). The trip takes about 45 minutes. Trains are not frequent; most run at the beginning and end of the day.

If you're leaving Paris by car, take the A4 autoroute from the Porte de Bercy and follow it to Meaux. After Meaux, head towards Changis-sur-Marne, La Ferté-sous-Jouarre and then Nanteuil-sur-Marne.

THE WALK

From the Nanteuil-Saâcy train station, head for the level crossing and pick up the GR14A on your right. Follow the GR trail to the park surrounding the Château de Citry (which you can't see). Follow the wall of the park (departing from the GR route for a while), then continue along a path between orchards and vegetable gardens. You'll come to a spot overlooking Citry's **Église Saint-Ponce** church.

Once in Citry (which has a *café-épicerie*), take the rue de la Ferme in front of the town hall and schools, and continue along the route de Pavant until you get to a square on your right. Cross this square and go along rue Michaud (joining up with the GR14A again). This street turns into a path which climbs towards orchards and vineyards, from which you have a view over Crouttes and Nanteuil-sur-Marne. This is also where you'll first come across the **Aqueduc de la**

Dhuis which carries water from two rivers to the Réservoir de Ménilmontant in Paris.

When you get to Villaré, take the road that crosses the village (the GR14A goes a round-about way through fields that are not particularly interesting) and follow it till you get to rue Pierreuse on the left, where you'll join up with the GR14A again. You come to a little square; between the houses at Nos 9 and 11 is the beginning of a path lined with fruit trees, which continues into a wood. It follows the Aqueduc de la Dhuis for nearly 4km.

After a good kilometre, you cross the **Vallon de Pisseloup** and several other little gullies. From this path, the views over the Marne below are superb. The GR14A crosses the D82 and follows a path going off to the right into the woods. Turn right onto the third track you cross, climbing up to an abandoned farm, La Baronnerie, then continuing between a wood and pastures to a farm called Marie.

Having skirted round this farm, go along the edge of the Bois de la Folie and then turn right towards another farm, Les Gravelles, which you pass, following a gravel path on the left back down towards the woods. Halfway down, you'll come to the aqueduct again, which you follow for only a short while before deviating from the GR14 to go into Nogent L'Artaud. Here you'll find various food shops, cafes and, near the Marne, a *creperie-grill* (☎ 03 23 70 11 69), which is shut on Sunday evening and Monday.

Go to the place du Marché, which leads to the **Église Saint-Germain**. Following the main street of Nogent L'Artaud, you'll reach a bridge crossing the Marne. Just after the bridge on the left, a track takes you down onto the **towpath**, where horses used to pull heavy barges.

Follow the Marne west until you come to the third path going off to your right: it comes out onto the D969, which you cross before taking the first street on the right.

A little farther on, you get onto the GR11A which passes through **vineyards**.

Follow it to Charly, a small town, which produces champagne and has a good range of shops and restaurants.

Take the time to visit the **Église Saint-Martin**. On the way out of town, take the D114 to the hamlet of Rudenoise. Keep going straight ahead on a path which climbs up through the vineyards. Cross the D842 and remain on the GR11A until you reach the ruined buildings of Champ Ruche; from here, you take a gravel path that goes into the woods and comes out on the D842 above Crouttes-sur-Marne. Woods and vineyards alternate along the GR11A. Quite soon, you come to a road which descends into Nanteuil-sur-Marne (leaving the GR11A).

In Nanteuil, take the rue Alexandre Morlot, then the rue du Bac. Cross the D402 and the Marne to arrive back at the train station.

Vineyards of the Marne

The vineyards along the Marne River, on chalky and clay-rich soil, have the privilege of being included in the region to which the Champagne *appellation d'origine contrôllée* (label of origin) applies. The small land-holders of Charly-sur-Marne, Nanteuil, Saâcy and Citry cultivate Pinot Noir, Pinot Meunier and Chardonnay grapes, the three varieties which are authorised to receive this prestigious label. While you're doing this walk, visit the wine-maker's cellars. For information on vineyards in the area, call in at the tourist office in Charly-sur-Marne (☎ 03 23 82 07 49), 20 place du Général de Gaulle. It's open Monday to Saturday afternoons from 2 to 6.30 pm and, in the summer only, daily except Monday from 9 am to 12.30 pm.

Provins

Duration	3 hours
Distance	12km
Standard	easy
Start	Longueville
Finish	Provins
Public Transport	yes

Summary A short walk through woods and across the plains of the Brie region to the medieval town of Provins.

Eighty kilometres from Paris, Provins and its citadel look over the plains of Brie, the premier wheat-growing area in the Paris Basin. From kilometres away in all directions you can see the Tour César (César Tower) and the rooftops of the Saint-Quiriace church, the most famous historic buildings in a town renowned for its remarkably well-preserved medieval architecture. On this route through the countryside around Provins you'll discover the Brie plains. It's another world, and like the many visitors who come to do the walk, you'll feel you're stepping back in time.

HISTORY

Provins was the old capital of the counts of Champagne. Its influence peaked during the 12th and 13th centuries, when it was famous for the annual fairs which brought within its city walls merchants from as far abroad as Lombardy and Flanders. Its decline began at the beginning of the 14th century as new trade routes opened elsewhere. But this relative oblivion saved its monuments, and today Provins is a remarkably well-preserved medieval town.

PLANNING
When to Walk

Provins is a tourist destination and very busy from April to September. Various interesting activities are organised during this season including jousting, a medieval feast and an August harvest festival.

Maps

The walk is covered by the IGN 1:25,000 *Provins* sheet No 2616O.

PLACES TO STAY

Provins is a town to be savoured at leisure. For walkers wishing to linger overnight there are quite a few accommodation options. For a B&B, contact *Ferme du Châtel* (☎ *01 64 00 10 73, fax 01 64 00 10 99,*

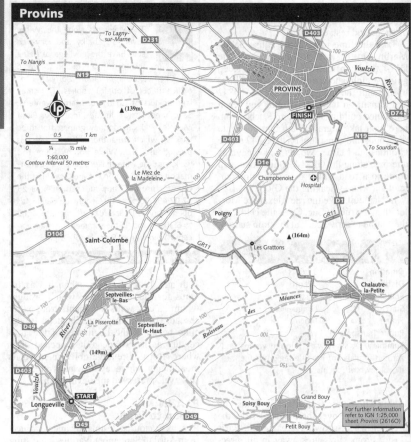

Provins

5 rue de la Chapelle Saint-Jean). This establishment is open year-round and has five rooms from 250FF to 475FF. You need to book a long way ahead.

In the lower part of town, the hotel *Le Clos Saint-Jacques* (☎ 01 64 00 01 10, fax 01 64 60 11 37, 12 ave du Général de Gaulle) charges 239FF for a room (single or double).

GETTING TO/FROM THE WALK

If you're travelling to Longueville, at the start of the walk, by train, take the Paris-Provins suburban line or Paris–Culmont Chalindrey main line *(grande ligne)* from the Gare de l'Est and get off at Longueville train station (one hour). There's a railcar (a single railway carriage) shuttle service between Longueville and Provins. Trains operate frequently right through the day.

If you're leaving Paris by car, take the A4 autoroute from the Porte de Bercy, to the south-east of the centre, and turn off at Serris, then head for Provins along the D231.

THE WALK

Facing away from the Longueville station, go down the street on the right until you get to a bridge, which you go under to get onto the GR11. After a short climb you enter the Longueville wood, before coming out onto a plateau and the village of Septveilles-le-Haut. From here to Chalautre-la-Petite, the GR trail follows a path through croplands, chalk plateaus and undergrowth. **Chalautre-la-Petite** is a quiet village with beautiful Briard-style houses, restored medieval buildings and a charming church.

Leave Chalautre-la-Petite on a winding road, the D1, which takes you through a wood; after 1km turn off on a path to the left, which runs along beside an old quarry. You cross a large expanse of fields before taking a path on the right (east) leading back to the D1, which you follow to Provins (careful, the verge is narrow). Go past the hospital complex on your left and veer right to get to the N19: cross it, then climb up the little bank and follow the path between two fields above the road. You'll have a good **view** of the high part of Provins, the dome of Église de Saint-Quiriace and the Tour César.

To reach the town follow a tree-lined path, the ruelle aux Vignes. Take the route de Chalautre on your right; the Provins train station is to the left. In Provins you'll find plenty of food stores and supermarkets, as well as restaurants. There's a *cafe-restaurant* in front of the Longueville train station.

Side Trip: Tour of Provins
2–3 hours, 2–3km
Don't miss out on visiting medieval Provins. Starting from the train station, follow the 'Centre-Ville' signs, then the rue des Bordes. From the rue des Bordes, take the rue Victor Arnoul, then the rue Edmond Nocard on the right. You'll come to the historic centre of the lower town: the **Place Saint-Ayoul** and its **11th-century church**. Nearby is the **Tour de Notre Dame du Val**, which is a remnant of a 14th-century church. Farther on, following the rue de la Cordonnerie (on the right) you'll see the Église Sainte-Croix.

The rue de la Cordonnerie comes out onto to the place du Général Leclerc, from which a pedestrian street, the rue du Val, leads to the rue Saint-Thibaud at the foot of the upper town. Here you'll find the entry to the **souterrains**, a labyrinth of chambers and

cavities (open daily between April and March, and on weekends between October and March; guided visits can be arranged).

Go up rue Saint-Thibaud till you get to the **Place du Châtel**. Notice the ruins of the 12th-century **Église Saint-Thibaud** on the right: a pillar and part of an arch built against a house. From the square, keep going along rue de Jouy to the **Porte de Jouy**, which is the starting point for a walk around the **ramparts** (11th to 13th centuries), from which there are magnificent views over the old town and surrounding plains.

Don't miss the **Grange aux Dîmes** (literally meaning 'tithe-barn') in the rue Saint-Jean, once used as a covered market for the Provins fairs. Have a wander through the little streets lined with charming houses around the place du Châtel.

To head for the **Tour César**, take the rue Jean Desmarest; you'll come out into **place Saint-Quiriace** with its **collegiate church**. The exhibits in the Provins museum, housed in the **Maison romane**, 7 rue du Palais, illustrate the history of the town from Merovingian times up to the French Revolution. It's open daily between June and October, and on weekends from April to May (22FF). Retrace your steps to the train station.

Giverny

Duration	3 1 hours
Distance	13km
Standard	easy
Start/Finish	Giverny
Public Transport	yes

Summary On this walk, which goes through the Parc Naturel Régional du Vexin, you'll discover the landscapes that inspired the painter Claude Monet.

The small village of Giverny owes its fame to the Impressionist painters. It still has the charm and atmosphere that captivated many artists from the late 19th century to the early years of the 20th. The surrounding countryside is equally attractive and part of it has been declared a *réserve naturelle* (nature

PARIS REGION

reserve). Wooded hills line the valley of the Epte, a little river that inspired Monet, and the more majestic Seine. You'll walk through these hills before descending into the valleys to discover villages that display features typical of the Île de France and Normandy. Unspoilt nature, regional architecture and traces of the past are all highlights of this walk. You can begin or end it with a visit to Claude Monet's marvellous flower and water gardens.

PLANNING
When to Walk
Since Giverny is a major tourist destination, avoid weekends. It's best to go when plants are in bloom (from May to September) so that you can see the gardens in their full splendour.

Maps
The walk is covered by the IGN 1:25,000 *Vernon* sheet No 2113O.

PLACES TO STAY
In the village of Giverny, *La Musardière* (☎ 02 32 21 03 18, fax 02 32 21 60 00) is the only hotel in the village. It has double rooms with showers for 300FF and serves meals.

GETTING TO/FROM THE WALK
By train, take the Paris-Rouen line from Gare Saint-Lazare and get off at Vernon (there are trains every one or two hours). A shuttle bus will take you from Vernon to Giverny, 4km away (the return fare is 20FF), dropping you in front of Monet's house. Bus departures coincide with trains.

If you're leaving Paris by car, take the A13 autoroute at the Porte d'Auteuil and turn off at Bonnières-sur-Seine. Cross the Seine at Bennecourt and head towards Limetz Villez then Giverny on the D201.

THE WALK
Leaving Monet's house behind you, take the path called Blanche Hoschède-Monet

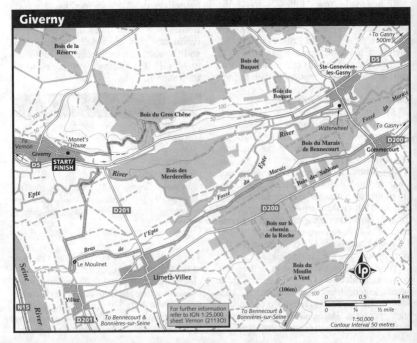

on the right. You pass houses built of *pierres moulières* (stones from a mill), then modern villas and fallow fields. The path overlooks the Seine Valley, but the river remains hidden.

After 400m take a steep dirt track on the left, then, on the right, a path across the hillside into the Bois de Gros Chêne. At the next fork, take the path on the right, which climbs up to a clearing; you are still fairly high up and will be able to admire the views. Follow a loop in the path through an intriguing entanglement of dead trees. At the next fork, take the path on the right which descends to the town of Sainte-Geneviève-les-Gasny. Cross the D5 and follow it to the left for 100m. Turn right down chemin du Moulin Brûlé, then right into the rue des Jacobins and finally right into the rue de l'Eau, which will lead you to a little bridge over the Epte. Look out for the old mill's **waterwheel**.

Two hundred metres down this shady road, you'll come to **Gommecourt**, where you'll see a pretty 1920s house, stone houses and little Norman farmhouses. Take the rue des Sablons, on the right. It turns into a path and goes into the **Bois des Sablons**, a *site naturel classé* (classified natural site). Keep going straight ahead. Turn right, pass the village of Limetz on your left and cross the D201. Fifty metres farther on you'll find a path marked by two white stone posts; follow it.

From here on you follow an arm of the Epte. After going round an imposing building surrounded by trees, you come to the locality of Le Moulinet. Cross the Epte (passing an old washing-place) and follow a path to the right (north), which goes off through fields. This flat expanse of land is surrounded by

Giverny, Monet & Impressionism

In 1874 Claude Monet exhibited *Impression, Soleil Levant* (Impression, Sunrise). This picture was to give its name to a new movement in painting: Impressionism. With the introduction of paint in tubes, painters came out of their studios to work in the open air. They were trying to capture plays of colour, the movement of shades and reflections; they were seeking out the changing aspects of nature, like the light in a field, the flow of a river or the sky at dusk.

In 1883 Monet set up his studio in the Maison du Pressoir at Giverny, near the lake, where he lived up to his death in 1926. At Giverny he undertook an immense artistic and botanical project. He was inspired by the landscapes, waterways and gardens of the area. First he worked on and in the garden adjoining his house, where the banks of flowers (iris, dahlias, clematis, orchids, roses and poppies) make up remarkable chromatic compositions. Then he moved on to the water garden: a little maze of channels and alleys lined with weeping willows and bamboo, leading to the lily pond. Here Monet painted his famous *Nymphéas* (lilies), in which water and plants combine in a marvellous play of colour.

The house and gardens were bequeathed to the state by the painter's descendants, and have become the Fondation Claude Monet. They were restored with financial assistance from America and opened to the public in 1980. They can be visited Monday to Sunday, from 10 am to 6 pm (35FF).

Monet has attracted many American painters to Giverny, fascinated by his approach. Their work is exhibited in the Musée d'Art Americaine (Museum of American Art), at 99 rue Claude-Monet. It's open from the 1 April to 31 October, from 10 am to 6 pm).

Monet's famous water garden features a wisteria-draped Japanese bridge.

JOHN HAY

PARIS REGION

wooded hills. At the first intersection turn right then left after 200m; you'll be within sight of Giverny. Once on the D5, turn left towards Monet's house, which is well worth a visit (see the boxed text 'Giverny, Monet & Impressionism'). There are several restaurants in Giverny, including the *Nymphéas*, in front of the Fondation Claude Monet.

Forêt de Rambouillet

Duration	3½ hours
Distance	14km
Standard	easy
Start/Finish	Saint-Léger-en-Yvelines
Public Transport	yes
Summary A cool haven in the shade of oaks, pines and ferns, at the heart of one of the most famous forests in the Paris region.	

The Forêt de Rambouillet, about 50km to the south-west of Paris, attracts walkers, cyclists and horse-riders. Nearly 2 million people visit it each year, mainly on weekends during spring and autumn. In spite of this, if you get away from the busy areas, it's relatively easy to find quiet paths and unspoilt surroundings. The short walk described below goes through mature forest, over sandy ground, and follows horse-riding tracks for part of the way.

With an area of 13,000 hectares, the Forêt de Rambouillet is the largest remnant of the Grande Forêt de l'Yveline, a wooded expanse that covered the whole south-western part of the Paris region during the Middle Ages. Once a royal hunting ground, Rambouillet was honoured by the visits of François I, Louis XV (at whose behest the largest number of hunts was organised) and finally Louis XVI, who recorded his experiences of the sport of kings in his *Journal du Roi*.

The forest is made up of 75% broad-leaved trees, including oaks, and 25% conifers, notably Scotch firs and laricio pines. Lily of the valley, heather and ferns also grow in the forest. With a bit of luck you'll be able to find edible mushrooms, including *cépes* (cepes) and *girolles* (chanterelles). Deer, foxes and wild boar live in the forest.

PLANNING
When to Walk
This walk can be done year-round, but avoid the hunting days: Tuesday and Saturday in autumn.

Maps
The walk is covered by the IGN 1:25,000 *Forêt de Rambouillet* sheet No 2215OT.

PLACES TO STAY
At Saint-Léger-en-Yvelines, *Le Relais de la Vesgre* (☎ 01 34 86 34 40, 1 rue de la Harpe) has single rooms for 160FF and doubles with shared bathroom and toilets from 200FF. Meals can be arranged.

Three kilometres from the Rambouillet train station, the *Camping Municipal de l'Étang d'Or* (☎ 01 30 41 07 34, fax 01 30 41 00 17), on the route du Château d'Eau, has camp sites for 25FF per night, plus 21FF per day per person. It has a restaurant-bar-grocery store, open during the peak season.

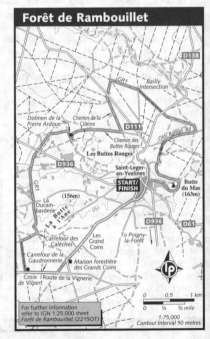

Forêt de Rambouillet

The gîte d'étape at the ***Bergerie Nationale*** (☎ *01 34 83 68 17*), in the Parc du Château, 2km from the centre of Rambouillet, has five rooms at 100FF per person (140FF for two), including breakfast. It's open year-round. Simple meals are served. You have to book.

GETTING TO/FROM THE WALK
A train runs from the Gare Montparnasse in Paris to Rambouillet (41FF). The trip takes 30 minutes on the express train or one hour on the slow train. To get to Saint-Léger-en-Yvelines, you can choose between a bus and paying 100FF for a taxi (available at the station). Buses leave from the Rambouillet bus station on Monday, Tuesday, Thursday and Friday at 7.27 am, but only during the school term. The buses back from Saint-Léger-en-Yvelines leave at 5.59 pm (the trip takes 15 minutes and costs 50.44FF).

If you're going by car from Paris, take the A13 autoroute at the Porte de Saint-Cloud and head for Versailles, Saint-Quentin-en-Yvelines and Rouen. After about 11km, turn off onto the A12, heading for Saint-Quentin, Dreux and Rambouillet, then follow the sign for Trappes and Rambouillet. The autoroute takes you directly to the N10. Turn off at Rambouillet Centre. At the roundabout, take the D937, heading for Saint-Léger-en-Yvelines, then the D936.

THE WALK
The walk begins from the car park at the entrance to the village. On the other side of a small pond next to the car park, you'll find the path which starts at a wash house whose roof is visible from the road.

Follow the path over the little wooden bridge that crosses the stream to the right of the wash house. Turn right, heading east past the picnic tables, and follow the sandy track that leads off to the right. Note that the path isn't marked in any way. Over the next 200m it climbs gently up to the top of a low hill (Butte du Mas). Turn off hard left and go round a hairpin bend. The path gets narrower and overlooks a clearing and a lake.

In the midst of low forest, the path swings to the right. To the west is the park of a small **château**. A sign on a tree on the right points the way to the view from the Butte du Mas. A few hundred metres beyond the chateau, you cross another track at right angles and keep going on a grassy path. A few metres farther on, you'll come out onto another path, which you follow to the right (north-east). Now you're on the route of the old roman road (there's no sign).

Keep going along this path between fences designed to keep game from eating the young seedlings. You'll come to a junction, where you take the path on the left with a white gate across it. This will take you into a low forest planted with pines and ferns. When you get to the fork stay on the left and follow the path till you reach the D138. Cross this road and keep going straight ahead into the forest, heading north-west. Ferns, oaks and Scots pines line the sandy path. When you get to the Bailly intersection, where four paths diverge, keep going straight ahead. You are now on the GR1, indicated by red-and-white waymarkers, which you follow from here on. At the fork ahead, turn left, following the waymarkers, passing a plantation of oaks on your right. Two hundred metres farther on, cross the D111 and keep going straight ahead along the chemin de la Citerne. Go past the old, disused water tank and keep following the horse-riding track.

At the next junction, turn right and follow the chemin des Buttes Rouges, which is sealed for a few metres. At the fork, turn right down a pretty path that has an almost Mediterranean look because of the pines. About 10 minutes later you'll arrive at a three-way junction where you go right and then right again to get to the **Dolmen de la Pierre Ardoue**.

Branch off to the right then to the left. Farther on you'll come to the D936, which you cross, following the GR1 straight ahead. Having passed a splendid carpet of heather, you go into a low forest with a variety of plant species, including oaks, ferns and wild roses. The path widens and comes out at La Ducambarderie. Keep going straight ahead. After about 10 minutes of climbing, you'll come to a fork where you turn to the right. The path takes you through the middle of a vast expanse of ferns to the Carrefour des Calèches. Here you leave the GR1 (which diverges right) and continue briefly to a path on the left which will take you to the route de la Vignerie at the Croix de Vilpert. Turn left on the sealed road. Go through the Carrefour de la Goudronnerie. After 250m turn left and head for Les Grands Coins (300m) and Saint-Léger-en-Yvelines. On the way, pass the Maison Forestiére des Grands Coins on your right and go through a gate to get to an intersection. Here you leave the Forêt de Rambouillet. Follow the path to your left which continues north-east along a sealed road.

The way back to Saint-Léger-en-Yvelines is along a little road lined with houses. If you're feeling hungry after the walk, the restaurant *Le Saint Hubert (☎ 01 34 86 30 40)* has a complete menu for 95FF. As a cheaper option, there's a little *8 á Huit* supermarket on the Grande Rue (it's closed Monday and on Sunday afternoon) and a *bakery* near the post office.

Dampierre-en-Yvelines & the Vaux de Cernay

Duration	4½ hours
Distance	17km
Standard	easy-medium
Start/Finish	Dampierre-en-Yvelines
Public Transport	yes

Summary A walk through woods in the heart of the charming Chevreuse valley and along a rushing stream.

This little walk takes you through one of the most beautiful parts of the Île de France to one of the many sites that have made the Parc Naturel Régional de la Haute Vallée de Chevreuse famous. Set within the park's boundaries, the Vaux de Cernay, near the ruins of the Cistercian Abbaye de Cernay, is a haven of pools, undergrowth and blocks of sandstone over which small waterfalls tumble. The park was created in 1985 to protect the natural environment and the historical heritage of a valley rich in picturesque villages, chateaux and hilly, wooded landscapes. Marked paths crisscross the park, resplendent with oak, chestnut and Scots pine. The walk suggested here will give you an idea of the valley's beauty, remarkably unaffected by nearby suburban developments.

PLANNING
When to Walk
The Vaux de Cernay is best appreciated between spring and autumn. During summer, it's best to go during the week to avoid the weekend crowds. Parts of the walk are very steep and can be slippery when it rains.

Maps
The walk is covered by the IGN 1:25,000 *Forêt de Rambouillet* sheet No 2215OT.

PLACES TO STAY
The *Maison de Fer* (Iron House), rue Pierreuse, is a gîte d'étape with rooms for two, four or six people (60FF per person). Ring the *maison du parc* (park information centre) in Dampierre (☎ 01 30 52 22 29, fax 01 30 52 12 43) between 2 and 6 pm to make a booking. Part of the garden surrounding the lodge is set up as a camping ground.

GETTING TO/FROM THE WALK
To get to Dampierre-en-Yvelines by train, take the RER line B to Saint-Rémy-les-Chevreuse (45 minutes; trains run every 20 minutes), then a bus to Dampierre. Buses are infrequent; check the times with the bus company SAVAC (☎ 01 30 52 45 00).

If you're leaving Paris by car, follow the ring road west and head for Versailles, from where you follow signs to the chateau. Turn left onto the D91 towards Saint-Quentin-en-Yvelines. This road takes you to Dampierre-en-Yvelines.

THE WALK
Facing away from the old chateau at Dampierre-en-Yvelines, take the uphill road in front of you (north) and to the right (rue de Maincourt), then the first little road to the left (rue Pierreuse). This will bring you to the **Maison de Fer**, an iron house built by

the French engineer Duclos, a disciple of Eiffel, for the Universal Exhibition in Paris in 1899. It was subsequently taken apart and reassembled here.

The path comes out onto open ground; take the forest track on the left, which is marked in blue. After about 400m take the GR1C to the left, which is marked with red and white stripes. You are on the Butte Rouge, and the path goes down steeply among oaks and chestnuts.

At the bottom of the hill it joins a sealed path: turn left then right down the rue de Fourcherolles. Then you have to turn right

again onto a rocky path with a barrier across it; follow the marks, one set red-and-white, the other set blue. You go into the woods again. At the end of a long straight stretch, turn left. Soon you cross a sealed road. After the car park, turn left where there's a sign indicating the chemin des Maréchaux, then take the next turn to the right. The GR path is sandy and winds through the forest over uneven ground. At the top of a little hill, tall pines rise over a carpet of ferns and heather; the trail is up and down for a while. At one point you leave the shelter of the tall trees and go along the edge of an old quarry.

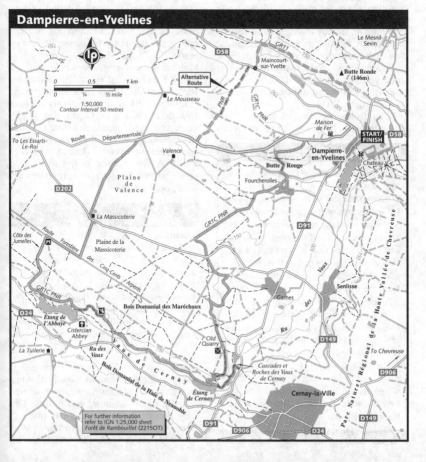

Keep following the path, which leads you back into the trees.

In the end you come to the site known as **Cascades et Roches des Vaux de Cernay**. The path overlooks the valley, then goes down to the Étang de Cernay. To the east of the lake, the route passes a monument to the landscape painter **Léon Germain Pelouse**, who came to live in Cernay in 1872. For a small detour, keep going along the path marked in blue and you'll come to a stream called the Ru des Vaux, which cascades over blocks of sandstone.

Retrace your steps back to the lake and continue along the path round the north shore: the water narrows and the stream continues on its way through dense vegetation. At the information board in the picnic area ahead, turn right. Go up a path of loose earth and stones. From the top of the rubble slope you have a splendid view over the ruins of a **Cistercian abbey** (1138) and a lake (Étang de l'Abbaye).

Keep following the GR waymarkers, which take you back into the valley. When you get to the Côte des Jumelles forest track (there's a sign), turn right, leaving the GR trail. Go to the end of the track, which comes to a picnic area and the Route Forestière Cinq-Cents. Turn right – the track leads off between the edge of the forest and a wide plain. Then you turn left (after roughly 500m) to get to La Massicoterie, a group of farm buildings. Cross the road and go round La Massicoterie, leaving it to your right; you'll come to a dirt path going north across the fields. When you come out onto the *route départementale*, turn right (east) along it to arrive back in Dampierre-en-Yvelines. Alternatively, a more picturesque option is to turn left (north-east) off the road after roughly 800m onto a smaller road, following PNR waymarks. This takes you through orchards to Maincourt-sur-Yvette. From here, you can follow the charming Yvette River along the waymarked GR11 back to the starting point.

Dampierre has several eating options. Near the chateau, in the Grande Rue, is a little crepe and pizza restaurant called *Brocéliande*. Across the road, there's a *boulangerie-pâtisserie* (bakery and cake shop). A few houses past Brocéliande, you'll be able to stock up on provisions at a little *grocery store*.

Château de Dampierre

This chateau, the pride of Dampierre-en-Yvelines, was built for Charles-Honorée de Luynes between 1683 and 1688. Hardouin-Mansart, the architect responsible for the Grand Trianon at Versailles and the place Vendôme in Paris, drew up the plans and designed the facade, while the gardens were planned by Le Nôtre, to whom we owe the park at Versailles.

With its facades of ochre stone and red brick, the chateau is a classic example of the style associated with Louis XIII. It houses a collection of very fine paintings and sculptures, period furniture and rare and precious objects. A 19th-century English garden stretches away on the eastern side.

The chateau is open to the public every day from 2 to 6 pm, and the gardens can be visited from 11 am to 6 pm (entry costs 52FF for the chateau and the gardens, or 34FF for the gardens only).

Forêt d'Ermenonville

Duration	4½ heures
Distance	16km
Standard	easy
Start/Finish	Ermenonville
Public Transport	yes

Summary A pleasant walk that starts off in the shade of broad-leaved trees, continues through pines and finishes with a visit to a magnificent museum, set among lakes and greenery.

In the 9th century Ermenonville was just an anonymous group of houses. Today it's a historic town that charms nature lovers as well as those interested in art and history. This walk outside the town walls has two segments: one takes you through a small part of the 7000-hectare Forêt d'Ermenonville; the other is more cultural, leading through fields to the royal Abbeye de Chaalis. Although the first part of the walk is among broad-leaved trees, the forest is mainly made up of conifers – Scots pines and Maritime pines.

HISTORY

In the 18th century the Marquis René de Girardin, heir to the estate of Ermenonville, came to live on his property and devoted himself to its beautification. Steeped in the theories of the Swiss philosopher Jean-Jacques Rousseau, he wanted to pay homage to nature by creating landscapes that would encourage reverie. The park he designed and its surroundings were one of the most beautiful sites ever produced as a collaboration of humans and nature. He invited Rousseau to come and stay in this Arcadia, and it was here that the writer spent the last six weeks of his life and was buried. This living monument to Rousseau is one of the main reasons why Ermenonville is famous today.

PLANNING

This walk can be done year-round.

Maps

The walk is covered by the IGN 1:25,000 *Forêts de Chantilly, d'Halatte et d'Ermenonville* sheet No 2412OT.

PLACES TO STAY

In Ermenonville, the *Auberge de la Croix d'Or* (☎ 03 44 54 00 04, fax 03 44 45 05 44), 2 rue Radziwill, provides comfortable accomodation and rustic charm. The price for a double room with a shower and toilet is 240FF. The meals are very good too. It's shut Sunday evening and Monday.

GETTING TO/FROM THE WALK

The closest train station (about 4km away) is at Nanteuil-le-Haudoin. You can get there from the Gare du Nord in Paris, but buses from the station to Ermenonville are very infrequent, so it's best to take a taxi (☎ 03 44 88 01 23). To return to Nanteuil-le-Haudoin by taxi, phone Taxi Penel (☎ 03 44 54 01 39).

If you're leaving Paris by car, take the A1 autoroute from the porte de la Chapelle, turn off at the Saint-Witz exit (No 7) and follow the D922 to Ermenonville. To get there from Senlis (10km away), follow the N330.

THE WALK

Leave the Château d'Ermenonville on your right and follow rue René-de-Girardin past the entrance to the **Parc Jean-Jacques Rousseau** and the tourist office (see the end of the walk description for park details). Before the bakery, turn left onto the D84. At the roundabout, take the forest track opposite, which leads off between the D922 and the D84. After walking through low forest for a while, you cross open country on the route de Saint-Sulpice. About 600m farther on, turn left (on the route de l'Éventail); this brings you back to the GR1, which you'll find on your right. Notice the red-and-white waymarkers, which you'll be following from here on in.

After crossing the D922, the path winds under a tangled canopy of branches and creepers. Soon you come onto the chemin des Ermites (Hermits' path). Now you're in the open again. Young birches and ferns line the path to the Petit Carrefour (Little Crossroads). Take the second road on the left (route du Bosquet Rond). Gradually the broad-leaved trees are replaced by pines. After crossing the D126 the forest changes in appearance: tall pines, sand, blocks of sandstone and ferns on hilly terrain.

At the carrefour du Bosquet Rond, take the uphill sandy path opposite and to the right. You'll come to a fork after roughly 250m. The path on the right leads you to a fenced-off plot of land; go along the right-hand edge of this plot to the carrefour de la Cavée. At the next crossroads, a sign on the right points the way to a memorial (a hundred metres away), built in memory of the victims of an air accident during the 1970s. Leave the GR with its waymarkers and take the route du Bosquet opposite and to the left (or straight ahead of you if you're coming back from the Memorial).

Next you turn left down a broad lane which leads to the Baraque Chaalis. Go left along the sealed road for a few dozen metres. Soon you'll come to a path on the right

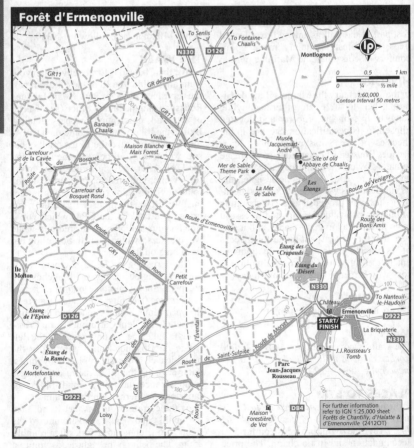

Forêt d'Ermenonville

which takes you back into the forest: it's a pleasant walk through the pines. The path crosses the GR11; for a hundred metres of so you follow the GR de Pays before turning right to get back onto the GR11. The path crosses the D126 and joins up with the Vieille Route.

Before long you'll start hearing noises from the **Mer de Sable** theme park. After crossing the N330 you come to the ruins of the 12th century **Abbaye de Chaalis** and, next to it, a chateau, built during the 18th century. This chateau now houses the **Musée Jacquemart-André**, where, at the beginning of the

20th century, the painter, traveller and collector Nélie Jacquemart-André gathered her various treasures: paintings, furniture and *objets d'art*. It's open on Sunday from mid-November to the beginning of March, and every day for the rest of the year. The museum entry fee is 35/28FF for adults/concessions, or 15/10FF for entry to the park only.

The final section to Ermenonville is along a beautiful path. First, however, you have to go through the car park and turn left onto the N330, walking on the grassy verge for about 700m until you see a path closed off by a wire-mesh gate on the right. Now look to your left (you'll need to look carefully!): there's an overgrown forest track. Follow it into the undergrowth; the path opens out little by little and leads you to a lovely spot where there's an old weir, a little stone bridge, and poplars along the water's edge to the right.

Follow the path to a little stone cross, where you turn right. You'll come back onto the route des Bons Amis, which will bring you to a car park. If you take the sealed road opposite and to the left, you'll end up back at Ermenonville. For those interested in visiting Parc Jean-Jacques Rousseau, it's open every day, except Tuesday, between 2 and 6.15 pm. Stop at the information office (☎ 03 44 54 01 58) near the entrance to the park for more details.

The *Crêperie du Parc*, near the Château d'Ermenonville, does crepes and grills; about 300m past the tourist office you'll find a *bakery*.

Forêt de Fontainebleau

Duration	5 hours
Distance	17km
Standard	easy-medium
Start/Finish	Barbizon
Public Transport	no

Summary This beautiful walk in the eastern part of one of the Paris Basin's most famous forests begins in a well-known town and takes you through a variety of landscapes and terrains.

The Forêt de Fontainebleau, about 50km south of Paris, is the metropolitan region's main air-renewal plant. It's also the region's most popular forest, with about 12 million visitors per year. Even so, and in spite of various development projects and road access from multiple points, there are still some parts of this huge, well-managed and well-loved forest that have an air of mystery and wildness. The landscapes are very diverse, and the large sandstone outcrops attract thousands of amateur climbers each weekend – it's an ideal spot for training.

The region also attracts experienced walkers, who find that some parts of the Massif des Roches de Sablon are a bit like medium-level mountain terrain.

NATURAL HISTORY

The landforms of the region vary markedly, with sandstone rubble slopes, gorges, sandy soil and small plateaus. Forest species include broad-leaved trees (oaks, beeches, sorb apples, birches and chestnuts among others) and conifers (Scots pines, spruces, laricio and Maritime pines). The massif also abounds in game: deer, foxes and wild boars are common.

PLANNING

Avoid this walk on weekends: it's just too busy.

Maps

The entire walk is covered by the IGN 1:25,000 *Forêt de Fontainebleau* sheet No 2417OT.

The Barbizon School

As with Monet and Giverny, painters have made Barbizon famous throughout the world. In 1847 Théodore Rousseau came to live in the town and was followed by Jean-François Millet in 1849. Other painters soon joined them, including Jacque, Corot, Daubigny and Barye. Inspired by the nearby forest and the surrounding countryside, they worked on landscapes and scenes of country life. It was here that Millet painted his famous *The Angelus* (1858) and *The Gleaners* (1857). The movement, often said to be a precursor of Impressionism, has been baptised the 'Barbizon School' by art historians.

The painters used to meet in the Auberge du Pére Ganne, and pay for their food and drink by painting on the walls and the furniture. This inn, which is in the Grande Rue, has now been turned into a museum, where engravings, drawings and photos are exhibited. Don't miss it whatever you do. It's shut on Mondays and entry is 25FF. In the same street, at No 27, you can visit Millet's studio.

PARIS REGION

Forêt de Fontainebleau

PLACES TO STAY

Barbizon, an exclusive holiday town, has 10 or so hotel-restaurants, all rather dear unfortunately. Among the less expensive are *La Clé d'Or* (☎ *01 60 66 40 96, fax 01 60 66 42 71)*, which has rooms from 200FF, and *Les Alouettes* (☎ *01 60 66 41 98, fax 01 60 66 20 69)*, with rooms from 210FF. Book a long way ahead for weekends.

GETTING TO/FROM THE WALK

There is no public transport to Barbizon. You can take a train from the Gare de Lyon in Paris to Fontainebleau, and get a taxi from there to Barbizon (it's a 10km drive and will cost about 150FF).

A better idea is to hire a car in Paris. Take the A6 autoroute at the Porte d'Italie or the Porte de Gentilly, turn off at the Milly-la-Forêt exit (about 50km from Paris), then follow the N37 and the D64, heading for Barbizon.

THE WALK

In Barbizon, follow the Grande Rue to where it ends at the edge of the forest. From there, don't follow the sealed allée des Vaches, take the path called chemin du Bornage that heads off to the right, just after the last house. Soon you'll come to the Maison Forestiére de Barbizon; keep going straight ahead to a fork a bit beyond the Maison Forestiére. Turn right.

After walking for 30 to 40 minutes, you'll come to the Maison Forestiére de Macherin, which is beside the D11. Cross the road and keep going straight ahead. This first part of the walk, along the edge of the forest, is relatively monotonous. You walk on a flat, sandy path through clusters of tall trees, often getting a view out to the west (to the right). Less than an hour after starting, you'll come out onto the D409, which you cross. Two hundred metres farther on, at a fork, take the path to the right called chemin de Milly à Fontainebleau. The landscape changes gradually: clumps of conifers start to appear.

After about an hour and 15 minutes, the path joins up with the GR11, recognisable by its red-and-white waymarkers, which you follow from here onwards. From here, the walk heads into the **Massif des Rochers des Sablons**, among huge blocks of sandstone, broad-leaved trees and more and more conifers, as well as ferns. The path is steeper, with lots of little climbs and descents. For a short stretch the route coincides with that of the Tour du Massif de Fontainebleau (TMF; marked in white and green). At the point where the GR11 and the TMF separate (the TMF heads due north), follow the GR11 towards the Gorges de Franchard and a lookout called **Point de Vue des Hautes Plaines**, from which the view is magnificent. The walk through the **Gorges de Franchard**, which takes you over a high plateau made up of a labyrinth of enormous boulders, is the most difficult and spectacular part of the walk. Some stretches are very steep. The sandstone rubble, the sand and the pine trees give the landscape a Mediterranean air. Be careful not to lose the GR waymarkers.

At the end of this section (which should take between 45 minutes and an hour), the route comes out onto an esplanade, where you turn left to get back on to the GR1. Here you leave the scree and the pines behind and plunge back into a forest of broad-leaved trees. Cross the route de l'Ermitage

and follow the GR1 waymarkers. After 50m the GR1 turns off to the left and follows the route du Monastére, which leads shortly to the D409. Cross it and take the route des Trois-Fréres, which is slightly to the right and signposted (be careful not to take the route des Bois d'Hiver, which is the one directly across from the intersection with the D409).

About 1.5km farther on you'll come to the carrefour des Monts Girard where a number of paths come together. Keep following the waymarkers for the GR1 (which now follows the route du Puits au Géant) to a junction where the route joins up with the TMF again. Here you enter the **Massif des Gorges et Platières d'Apremont**. After a short climb, you come to a lookout, the **Point de Vue des Gorges d'Apremont**, from which the panorama is superb. The path follows a ridge winding through the rocky massif then, after 500m, drops away suddenly to the right and into the valley below. At the junction with route Marie-Thérèse (which is sealed), leave the GR1 and follow the road left to the next intersection, 500m farther on, where there's a sign saying 'l'allée des Vaches, Barbizon 1km'. You're just about back to your starting point.

There are plenty of restaurants along the Grande Rue in Barbizon. Most are gourmet establishments and hence very costly. The **Brasserie Le Royal** at No 50 has sandwiches for 15FF and the *plat du jour* (daily special) for 55FF. In this street you'll also find a **grocery store** (shut on Monday) and a **bakery**.

Other Walks

Across Paris: North to South

This walk is about 20km long. It starts from the Porte de la Villette and ends at the Parc Montsouris, in the south. The route goes through Parc de La Villete and Parc des Buttes-Chaumont, follows the Canal Saint-Martin for a short stretch, then crosses the historic district of the Marais and the Île de la Cité (with the cathedral of Notre Dame), the Latin Quarter, the Butte aux Cailles, and finally the Parc Montsouris.

Tour du Massif de Fontainebleau

The Tour du Massif de Fontainebleau (TMF), created in 1975, is a loop that goes right round the forest of Fontainebleau. It's about 64km long and is indicated by green-and-white trail markers. People generally take three days to complete it. It goes through most of the interesting parts of the forest and shows you how diverse the area is in terms of trees, landforms and atmosphere.

The simplest way to do the tour is to start from the Thomery train station (you can get there from the Gare de Lyon in Paris) on the eastern side of the loop: the route goes past the train station. You can camp for free beside one of the four maisons forestiéres spaced out along the route. Get in touch with the Centre d'Initiation à la Forêt (☎/fax 01 64 22 72 59) for more in-formation. There aren't any shops along the way.

Forêt d'Halatte

The Forêt d'Halatte is part of the wooded massif called 'Les Trois Forêts' (The Three Forests), including Chantilly, Ermenonville et Halatte, about 50km north of Paris. The Mont Pagnotte, which is the highest point on the massif, is 220m above sea level. The area is known for its superb beech trees. There are various possible routes starting from the village of Fleurines.

To get there on public transport take a train from the Gare du Nord in Paris to Chantilly Gouvieux. Then get an SNCF bus to Senlis. From Senlis to Fleurines you'll have to take a taxi.

Use the IGN 1:25,000 *Forêts de Chantilly, d'Halatte et d'Ermenonville* sheet No 2412OT.

Brittany

The farther west you travel in Brittany (Bretagne) the more you realise that its claim to be different from the rest of France is absolutely accurate. The 1300km coastline is crumpled into innumerable bays, beaches and long estuaries separated by rocky headlands; many small islands brave the English Channel and the turbulent western seas. The gently undulating hinterland of Finistère in the west is both quietly rural and wooded, and wild and bare. Breton culture, especially music and language, is practised enthusiastically and the age-old maritime heritage is carefully protected. Most importantly for walkers, there are many accessible, well-organised, and interesting walks along the coast and across the countryside. Two coastal walks are described in this chapter, together with outlines of inland and other coastal walks.

Between 3000 and 1500 BC, Brittany's prehistoric residents left behind an array of stone monuments – tombs, standing stones, forts. Much later the Romans gave the name Armor (or Armorica) to the western reaches of the area and Argoat to the wooded interior, but never established themselves here. Decisive in Brittany's history was the AD 460 invasion of Celts from Britain, who founded Brittany as a nation and developed a distinctive Breton language. The next 1000 years were turbulent and often violent until Brittany was annexed to France in 1532. Gradually Breton language and culture declined as French was entrenched as the official language by centralising national governments. However, in the later 20th century, determination to preserve Brittany's cultural heritage has been renewed, mainly in the west.

Geologically, Brittany began to take shape around 500 million years ago from the Massif Armoricain, a mountain range which was then worn down over eons to form the low-relief interior where the highest point is Roc'h-Trévézel (384m). The deep indent-ations of the coastline were wrought by upheavals of the earth's crust;

HIGHLIGHTS

SANDRA BARDWELL

The wild and rugged Atlantic coastline of Presqu'île de Crozon

- Long, unspoiled sandy beaches, rocky headlands and pine woodlands along the Presqu'île de Crozon coast
- Fantastic red granite boulder formations on the Côte de Granit Rose on a misty morning
- A feast of savoury galettes and sweet crepes, with the Breton cocktail of cider and cassis as a prelude
- Rugged coastal cliffs adorned with mauve thrift, white daisies and orange lichen

when sea levels rose at the end of the last ice age (around 10,000 years ago), the coastal valleys were flooded, forming a series of long, narrow estuaries.

CLIMATE

Atlantic Ocean weather systems and the Gulf Stream are the prevailing influences over coastal Brittany and its hinterland, keeping

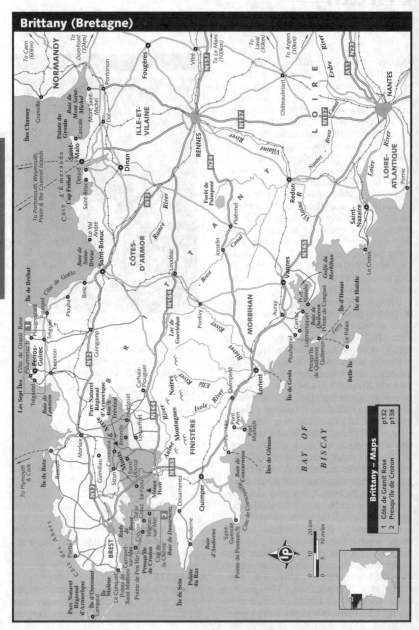

Brittany (Bretagne)

BRITTANY

To Caen (60km)

To Domfront (32km)

NORMANDY

To Laval (30km)

To Le Mans (100km)

To Angers (90km)

Erdre River

Loire River

A11

N23

NANTES

Îles Chausey

Granville

Pointe du Grouin

Baie du Mont Saint-Michel

Mont Saint-Michel

Pontorson

Fougères

Vitré

N157

N137

Châteaubriant

LOIRE

LOIRE-ATLANTIQUE

Pornic

Côte d'Émeraude

Cancale

Dol

ILLE-ET-VILAINE

RENNES

N24

Vilaine River

Nantes

Loire

Saint-Nazaire

To Portsmouth Weymouth, Poole & the Channel Islands

Pointe du Groin

Saint-Malo

Dinard

Cap Fréhel

Saint-Briac

Dinan

N12

Forêt de Paimpont

Ploërmel

Redon

Vilaine R

Le Croisic

Le Val André

Baie de Saint-Brieuc

Côte de Goëlo

Saint-Brieuc

CÔTES-D'ARMOR

Loudéac

Rance River

Canal

Josselin

Vannes

N165

Golfe du Morbihan

Île d'Houat

Île de Hoëdic

Île de Bréhat

Paimpol

Binic

Plouha

Guingamp

Pontivy

Brest

Auray

Port Navalo

Carnac

Belle Île

Le Palais

Ferry

Côte de Granit Rose

Perros-Guirec

Ploumanac'h

Tréguier

Lannion

N12

MORBIHAN

Baie de Quiberon

Presqu'île de Quiberon

Pointe de Conguel

Plouharnel

Locmariaquer

Les Sept Îles

Trégastel

Trébeurden

Baie de Lannion

Parc Naturel Régional d'Armorique

Roc'h Trévézel

Huelgoat

Carhaix-Plouguer

N164

Île de Croix

Lorient

Concarneau

Port Manech

Quimperlé

To Plymouth & Cork

Morlaix

Île de Batz

Roscoff

Commana

Brennilis

Loqueffret

N164

Monts d'Arrée

Monts Noires

Élé River

Isole River

Aulne River

Baie de Concarneau

Îles de Glénan

BAY OF BISCAY

Guimiliau

Sizun

Saint-Rivoal

Ménez Hom

Le Faou

Quimper

Côte de Cornouaille

To Plymouth & Cork

Île Molène

Île d'Ouessant

Lampaul

Parc Naturel Régional d'Armorique

Le Conquet

Pointe de Camaret-sur-Mer

Pointe de Saint-Mathieu-sur-Mer

Pointe de Pen Hir

BREST

Rade de Brest

Presqu'île de Crozon

Cap de la Chèvre

Crozon

Telgruc-sur-Mer

Talar Grarac

N165

Douarnenez

Baie de Douarnenez

Audierne

Saint-Guénolé

Pointe de Penmarc'h

Baie d'Audierne

Pointe du Raz

Île de Sein

Côte des Abers

Portsall

N

FINISTÈRE

Brittany – Maps	
1 Côte de Granit Rose	p132
2 Presqu'île de Crozon	p138

0   10   20 km
0   5   10 miles

HEINRICH WERNER

CHRIS MELLOR

SALLY DILLON

HEINRICH WERNER

HEINRICH WERNER

Orderly rows of lavender and crowded fields of heavy-headed sunflowers – the colours and perfume of Provence in July.

An excellent network of walking paths wind their way around the rugged Breton coastline.

Bay of Cap de la Chèvre.

Colourful facade, Brittany.

Searching for titbits, Brittany.

Interpretive centre in Parc Naturel Régional d'Armorique, Brittany.

temperatures mild in comparison with the rest of the country. Rainfall is fairly evenly distributed throughout the year, although winter is the wettest time. As important as the seasonal pattern is changeability – conditions can alter several times during the day.

Brittany is Different

Plougrescant, Plouguiel, Veryarc'h (typical place names on bilingual road signs), preference for cider over wine at all times, spirited Breton music, the prominence of the black-and-white Breton flag – these are some of the striking features that set Brittany, and especially Finistère in the west, apart from the rest of France.

Immense importance is attached to Brittany's Celtic heritage, shared with Cornwall, Ireland, the Isle of Man, Scotland and Wales. A large flag, comprising those of each of these kindred lands, billowing outside a Celtic shop in Quimper, proudly proclaims this heritage. The nine black and white bands of the Breton flag, designed in 1923, represent former bishoprics, and the rectangle in the upper left corner displays stylised ermines, traditionally associated with Brittany.

The language, now spoken by around 500,000 people, is closely linked to Cornish and Welsh. Although taught in schools, it has been scorned by the central government, which passed a bill in 1992 stipulating that French is the country's only official language. However, the government is now under pressure to sign the European Union Convention on Minority Languages, a commitment which would require a constitutional amendment. The letters BZH displayed on car badges derive from the Breton word for the region, Breizh. Breton music, arts and radio stations are holding their own, if not thriving.

Breton separatism has waxed and waned; fully recovered from the odium of Nazi associations during WWII, it now finds strength in association with other Celtic nations and in the EU, in the hope that a union of regions rather than sovereign states may eventually emerge.

Spring (April and May) is generally mild; May is often settled and, with June, constitutes the driest period of the year. During summer the average daily temperature is around 17°C on the coast, often tempered by a sea breeze. Relatively rare hot weather arrives with easterly winds from the warmer interior; July, August and September are the warmest and sunniest months.

The Atlantic Ocean exerts its influence most forcefully during autumn and winter, in frequent north-westerly and south-westerly gales. Temperatures are relatively mild and snow is uncommon; bitterly cold easterly and north-easterly winds prevail occasionally and sunshine is scarce.

INFORMATION
Maps

IGN 1:100,000 *Brest Quimper* and *Saint-Brieuc Morlaix* sheets, Nos 13 and 14 respectively, cover the areas described in this chapter and are handy for trip planning. The IGN 1:100,000 *Park an Arvorig – Parc Naturel Régional d'Armorique* sheet in the Culture & Environnement series (58FF) shows the routes of the main waymarked walks which pass through the region.

For maps covering individual walks, see Planning in the introduction to each walk.

Books

Although the Michelin *guides verts* (green guides) are aimed at car-borne visitors, they contain a wealth of information about history, topography, architecture and so on; the *Brittany* edition is worth acquiring.

Information Sources

For Brittany generally, contact Comité Régional du Tourisme (☎ 02 99 36 15 15, fax 02 99 28 44 40, www.brittanytourism.com), 1 rue Raoul Ponchon, 35069 Rennes.

Inquiries about Côtes d'Armor can start at Maison du Tourisme (☎ 02 96 62 72 15, fax 02 96 62 72 25, armor@cotesdarmor.com), 29 rue des Promenades, 22046 Saint-Brieuc. For Finistère, contact the Maison du Tourisme in the regional centre of Quimper (☎ 02 98 53 04 05, fax 02 98 53 31 33), place de la Résistance, 29000 Quimper.

BRITTANY

BRITTANY

Côtes d'Armor

Taking its name from the Roman title for the area (Land of the Sea), Côtes d'Armor looks out across a rock-strewn shore to the English Channel. While there is much of interest for walkers away from the coast, along valleys and through woodlands, the focus here is on the beautiful Côte de Granit Rose. Of all the coastal walking in northern Brittany, this section has the lowest density of seaside resorts and the most extensive walking on shore-side paths. Although some towns and villages have sold their souls to tourism and the leisure industry, and are blighted by some truly awful modern buildings, small farms with fields of cereals and vegetables blend easily with the scenic and endlessly fascinating coastline.

Côte de Granit Rose

Duration	3 days
Distance	58km
Standard	medium
Start	Trégastel Plage
Finish	Tréguier
Nearest Town	Lannion
Public Transport	yes

Summary The best of Brittany's north coast: excellent paths, including the famous *sentiers des douaniers* (customs officers' paths), fantastic groupings of pink granite boulders, sandy beaches and rocky headlands. The flexible itinerary gives scope to vary the daily stages.

This three-day walk follows the coast path from the town of Trégastel generally eastwards to Tréguier at the head of the Jaudy River estuary, although you could easily spend five days on the walk, allowing time to visit the *maisons du littoral* (coastal visitor centres) near Ploumanac'h and Pointe du Château. The most prominent features are the broad, shallow reef-filled bay between the town of Perros Guirec and Pointe du Château, and the long, narrow Jaudy estuary. West to east is the preferred direction, so there's a good chance that you'll have the

prevailing winds behind you. Although relatively little ascent is involved, the walk is graded medium, recognising that some sections follow rocky paths or shingle banks – not the easiest of surfaces. It's impossible to avoid some road walking, but overall the distance isn't great and the walk is mainly along paths and tracks. Several of these are sentiers des douaniers; the one near Trestraou is the best known thanks to easy access and fine scenery. These paths are reminders of the days when smuggling was a popular pastime along this coast. The route follows that of the GR34.

The places to stay are mainly camp sites; *gîtes d'étape* (hostel-style walkers' accommodation) are scarce in the area, but there are plenty of hotels, *chambres d'hôtes* (B&B accomodation in a private house) and self-catering places, details of which are available from the tourist offices.

There are no safe, natural sources of water along the way, so make sure you carry drinking water; during summer, bars and cafes are never far away.

NATURAL HISTORY

Four sections of the coast are protected in nature reserves. The pink granite rock formations near Ploumanac'h, with many species of flowering plants and the fringing heathland, are the focus of a small protected natural site. On the shore, yellow-flowering rock samphire and white sea campion are common, while in the shelter of the rocks you'll find wild thyme, orchids, masses of burnet rose and hyacinths. Heather is common in the more open areas.

The nearer tiny islands and the beach between Port Blanc and Plougrescant are within a conservation area; the islets are great mounds of shingle where brackish marshes support unusual associations of flowering plants.

North of Plougrescant, Pointe du Château is another protected natural site, due to the unusual triple shingle bar formation, enclosing two brackish ponds. These harbour some rare vegetation particular to such sites; sea kale, with thick, dark green leaves, and the yellow-horned poppy, with an exceptionally long seed pod, are quite common. The Jaudy estuary is a European conservation area for birds.

PLANNING

During May and June, before the crowds arrive, there's a good chance of settled weather, although some camp sites don't open until June. Good weather is also likely in September.

Maps & Books

You'll need IGN 1:25,000 *Lannion Perros-Guirec* and *Paimpol* sheets, Nos 0714OT and 0814OT respectively. The Fédération Française de la Randonnée Pédestre (FFRP) French-language Topo-Guide *Côte de Granit Rose* (No 346) includes background information, a route description from Saint-Brieuc to Roscoff (in the opposite direction to that of the walk described here) and variants from the main route. The Cicerone guide by Alan Castle, *The Brittany Coastal Path*, is out of date for maps and accommodation, but the excellent description holds good.

NEAREST TOWN
Lannion

Lannion is a sizable town at the head of the estuary of the Léguer River and within easy reach by bus to the start and finish of the walk. The tourist office (☎ 02 96 46 41 00, fax 02 96 37 19 64), 2 Quai d'Aiguillon, 22300 Lannion, is open all year.

There's a Cyberposte Internet service at La Poste, quai de Viarmes (a few hundred metres downstream from the tourist office). It's open from 9 am to noon and 2 to 5 pm

Monday to Friday and 9 am to noon on Saturday. The fee is 50FF for the first hour and 30FF per additional hour.

Places to Stay & Eat Beside the Léguer River, *Camping des Deux Rives* (☎ 02 96 46 31 40), rue du Moulin de Duc, is open from Easter to September. The tariffs are 20FF per pitch and 20FF per person. The site is about 1km upstream from the town centre.

Auberge de Jeunesse Les Korrigans youth hostel (☎ 02 96 37 91 28, 73 rue Territorial) is open all year. The fee is 52FF per person; it's worth ringing ahead as the hostel is popular with large groups.

For self-caterers, there's a *Stoc* supermarket in Rue des Augustines, near Pont Sainte-Anne.

Pizzerias and creperies are plentiful; among the latter is *Crêperie-Grill L'Akene* (☎ 02 96 37 06 59, 8 rue Duguesclin), a short distance north of the supermarket, where there's a good range of generous-sized *galettes* (savoury pancakes) and crepes (the sweet variety; 35FF to 55FF), best washed down with Breton cider.

It's possible to camp close to the start of the walk in Trégastel at *Camping Tourony*

BRITTANY

(☎/fax 02 96 23 86 61, 105 rue de Poul-Palud). The site is open from April to mid-September; a pitch costs 25FF, plus 25FF per person.

There's a *Marché U* supermarket opposite the bus stop at Trégastel and a good *boulangerie* (bakery) nearby, opposite the tourist office.

Getting There & Away By train on the Paris' Gare Montparnasse to Brest service, change at Guingamp for the branch line to Lannion (☎ 08 36 35 35 39 for information). For an extended visit to Brittany, the *Guide Régional des Transports* from any train station is indispensable for planning travel by train.

Brittany Ferries (☎ 09 90 36 03 60) sailings from Portsmouth to Saint-Malo (UK£36 per adult in the high season) and from Plymouth to Roscoff (UK£33) both land you within reasonable distance of Lannion by road. On public transport, go by train from Saint-Malo to Dol (on the Rennes line), then to Saint-Brieuc and to Guingamp for the branch line to Lannion. There's a train from Roscoff to Morlaix for the Compagnie Armoricaine de Transport (CAT) bus service (☎ 02 96 46 76 70) to Lannion.

By road, the N12 dual carriageway from Rennes to Brest passes through Guingamp, from where the D767 leads to Lannion.

GETTING TO/FROM THE WALK
To the Start
Several CAT buses depart from outside Lannion train station from Monday to Saturday; line 15 serves Perros-Guirec, Trestraou and Trégastel (15FF, 17FF and 20FF). *La Route des Cars* timetables are most easily obtained from the tourist office.

From the Finish
CAT bus service line 7 between Lannion and Paimpol (Monday to Saturday) goes

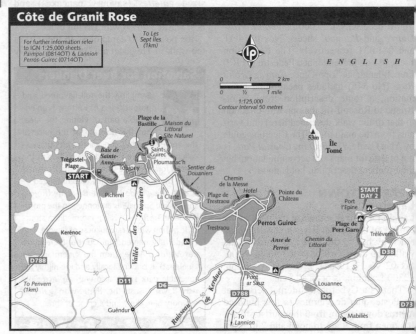

through Tréguier, where the Le Port bus stop is almost opposite Hôtel L'Estuaire 24.50FF). There is also an infrequent but potentially handy service (line D) from Tréguier to Lannion via Port Blanc and Plougrescant, on the route of the walk.

THE WALK
Day 1: Trégastel to Port l'Epine
5½–6 hours, 21km, 200m ascent

It's only a short step from the bus stop in Trégastel to the start of the walk, around the shore of the Baie de Sainte-Anne – along the sand if the tide is out. Follow the waymarkers round the Tourony headland to the main road. Cross the bridge and take to the sand; go on to the villages of Ploumanac'h and Saint-Guirec (where there are creperies and bars).

Continue to Plage de la Bastille to reach the start of the sentier des douaniers (an hour from Trégastel), a broad path winding round the coast past fantastic clusters of rounded, reddish granite boulders. Shortly you come to the maison du littoral for the surrounding Site Naturel de Ploumanac'h (open from 10.30 am to 7 pm mid-June to mid-September and afternoons only during the rest of the year), with a free display and information about the site. After another hour the path ends at a bend in the road above Plage de Trestraou.

As an alternative camp site to either Lannion or Trégastel, *Camping Claire Fontaine* (☎ 02 96 23 03 55) is about 800m south of the beach and is open all year. For a meal there's a choice of creperies or a pizzeria; the nearest supermarket is the *Comod*, in the centre of **Perros Guirec**.

Continue down along the promenade then up and round the outskirts of affluent Perros Guirec. About 15m past the house numbered 44 in chemin de la Messe, turn off on a path down the open slope to the edge of a low cliff (this path is not shown as the way-marked route on the recommended IGN

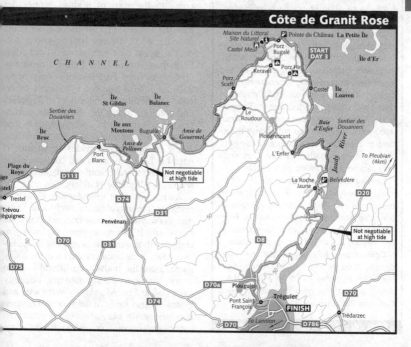

Côte de Granit Rose

1:25,000 map). About 250m farther on, skirt a large hotel, go round **Pointe du Château** and down some steps to the shore. Roadside paths lead round the broad Anse de Perros bay, crowded with moored yachts (1½ hours from Trestraou). From a bend in the road, cross a reclaimed area to a large roundabout. Continue east along the road and after about 1km, and 75m past *Camping Ernest Renan*

Les Sept Îles

On a fine day, looking out to sea from near Ploumanac'h, you can see a cluster of rocky islets sitting just below the horizon. These are Les Sept Îles, one of France's most important bird sanctuaries. It's thought that 'sept' (literally meaning 'seven') could express the sacred significance of the isles, or it may come from the word *saith*, meaning 'saint', of which there were many in Brittany's early history.

It was Brittany's first nature reserve, set aside in 1912 with the aim of putting an end to the decimation of sea birds by hunters. Among the isles, volcanic Rouzic, only five hectares in area, hosts a remarkably wide variety of sea birds (rather elusive on the mainland coast): puffins, cormorants, razorbills, guillemots, kittiwakes, herring gulls, great and lesser black-backed gulls, oyster catchers and fulmars. Puffins were successfully reintroduced with chicks imported from the Faroe Islands. France's only gannet colony, of about 4000 pairs, lives here and petrels visit the island to breed in March before heading for their wintering quarters in July. Grey seals may also be seen basking on the rocks.

Landing is permitted only on the largest island, Île aux Moins (Monks Island), where there are a one-time monastery, the ruins of one of Vauban's forts (see the boxed text 'From Powder Magazines to Nuclear Submarines' in this chapter) and an old gunpowder factory.

Contact the ornithological station on Île-Grande (☎ 02 96 91 91 40) or the tourist office in Perros Guirec (☎ 02 96 23 04 72) for details of boat trips from Trégastel or Perros Guirec to the sanctuary.

(☎ 02 96 23 11 78), open from 1 June, turn off to the *chemin du littoral* (coastal path); this eventually becomes a path along the shingle to the end of the beach (not along the road, as marked on the IGN map), an hour from the roundabout. Then cross a wooded spur to reach **Plage de Porz Garo**.

Less than 500m farther on, *Camping Port L'Épine (☎ 02 96 23 71 94, fax 02 96 23 77 83)* is open from May to mid-September. The tariff is 30FF per tent and 25FF per person. There are a restaurant and bar on site.

Day 2: Port l'Epine to Porz Hir
5–5½ hours, 20km, 210m ascent

Beyond the nearby *Camping Municipal Le Palud (☎ 02 96 91 73 11)*, follow the *sentier littoral* (also coastal path), then roads and paths round Plage de Trestel and on to Plage du Royo – take to the sand if possible. Then, across a low rocky point, follow the shingle bank or better still, the beach. About 200m beyond the end of the sand and shingle, you come to the start of a short sentier des douaniers, which leads to a road to take you past the locality of **Port Blanc** (two hours from the start); diverge 10m beyond a footpath signpost to a path along a field edge. Farther on, beyond the Pellinec causeway (1¾ hours from Port Blanc) – only negotiable at lowish tide but bypassable otherwise – walk through the hamlet of **Buguélès** and continue along the shore, tide permitting. Field-edge paths and quiet roads lead to **Anse de Gouermel** and its vast tidal flats. *Bar Le Gouermel* provides sustenance if need be. Leave the road and continue close to the shore to Porz Scaff – back into a landscape of red granite boulders.

An hour or more from Anse de Gouermel brings you to a road near Castel Meur. From here the waymarked route does not follow the road (as the IGN map suggests) but leads generally north towards the prominent house between two large boulders and on to the rocky shore. Here the **maison du littoral** is open every afternoon during summer, but only from 1.30 to 5 pm Monday to Wednesday and Friday at other times of the year; information about the nearby *site naturel classé* (classified natural site) is available, and guided walks are conducted from the centre on Wednesday morning and Saturday afternoon between mid-June and late August. Make your own way out to the **Pointe du Château** for fine views of the myriad rocky islets just offshore.

Turn inland to follow a narrow road south-east to a wider road. To reach Camping du Gouffre from here, turn right then second left (the camping ground is 500m farther south). Otherwise, leave the road almost immediately to follow a short shoreline path then, back on the road at Porz Bugalé, continue generally south along it for 1.2km to Camping Le Varlen.

Camping Le Varlen (☎ *02 96 92 52 15*), in route de Pors Hir, is open all year; a tent space costs 20FF and it's 18FF per person. *Camping du Gouffre* (☎ *02 96 92 05 95*) has more space for tents, and charges 25FF for a space and 18FF per person; basic supplies are available. The nearest shops are in Plougrescant (2.2km south), with a *boulangerie*, *grocery* and *minimarket* in the main street.

For a meal, it's 10 minutes' walk from Le Varlen to *Crêperie du Castel* by the shore; it's open from noon to 10 pm for oysters (60FF per dozen), galettes (15FF to 42FF) and crepes (15FF to 32FF), accompanied by traditional Breton music.

Day 3: Porz Hir to Tréguier
4½–5 hours, 17km, 180m ascent
Return to the route at Porz Bugalé and continue to Castel, emerging close to the creperie.

The scene is changing now, as you head up the estuary of the **Jaudy River**. From a signposted road junction at L'Enfer, where it's only 30 minutes' walk (uphill) to **Plougrescant**, continue on another sentier des douaniers through woodland and along field edges to a right turn up to the village of La Roche Jaune (1½ hours from Porz Bugalé). Here the well-signposted **Belvédère** looks out over the Jaudy estuary and its low islets to the open sea. In the centre of the village just south of the route, at a sharp bend, there is a bar and *épicerie* (grocery store). Rather than labour around the pointless loop to shore level, fork left, then left again at a T-junction, then right.

Continue along the reasonably well-marked route down to the shore, go upstream for 50m to a minor road, then turn off along a shoreline track. This soon fades and you're left to contend with seaweed and mud for 400m (minor roads can provide a dry inland alternative) to the end of a rough road which climbs to a junction; turn left and continue to **Plouguiel**. Turn left at the D8 main road (not as shown on the IGN 1:25,000 map), then right and on to **Pont Saint-François**, a fine old footbridge. Cross it and follow the riverside path downstream to a busy main road and the anticlimactic approach to **Tréguier** via Le Port, where you will find the bus stop for Lannion.

If you do stay in Tréguier, there are no cheap options, although for couples hotels aren't a bad bet. The first you come to is *Hôtel de l'Estuaire* (☎ *02 96 92 30 25*), with doubles from 150FF. For an end-of-walk treat, a little farther on is *Hôtel Aigue Marine* (☎ *02 96 92 97 00*), where doubles are around 400FF. *Restaurant Grill Le St Bernard*, in rue Marcelin Berthelot, is locally recommended and has set *menus* (fixed-price meals of two or more courses) featuring fish and grills from 52FF to 125FF.

Finistère

At any of the more sharply defined western extremities of the coast, it's easy to understand how Finistère (meaning 'Land's End') acquired its name. The view westwards is filled with the restless grey waters of the Mer d'Iroise and the Atlantic Ocean, breaking ceaselessly against the rocky points – those seemingly inevitable limits of the bare windswept hinterland. The coast is low in profile, indented with long jagged lines of colourful cliffs fringed with heathlands and pine woods, and separated by secluded coves and beaches. Paths closely following much of the coast offer weeks of scenic walking, with the bonus of seeing abundant relics of Finistère's long history, from prehistoric times to the recent past.

In the low rolling hills and valleys of the interior, within Parc Naturel Régional

Parc Naturel Régional d'Armorique

Protection of the natural environment and cultural heritage, alongside development of economic, social and cultural activities linking town and country people, are the aims of this park in Finistère. Created in 1969, its 172,000 hectares extend from the Monts d'Arrée to Pointe de Pen Hir and seaward to France's western extremity, Île d'Oeussant. It is home to more than 56,000 people.

The park comprises four distinct geographical areas: marine, in the International Biosphere Reserve of the Mer d'Iroise, comprising Île d'Oeussant, Île Molène and Île de Sein; Presqu'île de Crozon, especially notable for ancient geology, fossils and many forts; the beautiful estuary of the Aulne River; and the Monts d'Arrée, with small rocky peaks, moorlands, heaths, peatlands, woodlands and hedged fields.

The many ecomuseums and similar places together serve as a multicampus school of environmental discovery. Among them are the Maison des Minereaux at Saint-Hernot (see the Presqu'île de Crozon walk description) and the Musée des Phares et Balises on Île d'Oeussant. The park information centre is at Mènez Hom near Hanvec (☎ 02 98 68 81 71).

Just as important from a walker's point of view is the extensive network of waymarked walks throughout the park, as good a way as any of exploring its features.

d'Armorique (PNRA), there's also scope for many and varied walks of quite a different character from those on the coast.

Brittany's distinctiveness is more clearly delineated in Finistère than elsewhere in the region, particularly in the place names, language and the prominence of the Breton flag (see the boxed text 'Brittany is Different' earlier in this chapter). This is where you're most likely to hear Breton spoken. All in all, Finistère is an area *par excellence* for combining first-class walking with insights into local history and culture.

Presqu'île de Crozon

Duration	2 days
Distance	49km
Standard	medium
Start	Camaret-sur-Mer
Finish	Tal ar Groaz
Nearest Towns	Camaret-sur-Mer and Crozon
Public Transport	yes

Summary An outstandingly scenic cliff-top and beach walk along good paths, through fragrant pine woods, across open heathlands and past many historic defence sites. The daily stages, the start and the finish are all adaptable.

This two-day walk follows the coast of Presqu'île de Crozon, a small peninsula in central western Finistère, from the resort of Camaret-sur-Mer southwards then northeast and eastwards to Plage de l'Aber and the nearby village of Tal ar Groaz. A continuation to Anse du Caon and the small town of Telgruc-sur-Mer is outlined as a possible easy third day, or as a day walk from Plage de l'Aber.

The route is easy to follow along mostly good paths, and many other paths have developed around popular focal points along the way. Waymarking is consistent enough with PNRA 'Sentier Côtier' signposts and large orange dots. You'll also find some of the familiar red-and-white GR *(grande randonnée)* markers – the path is part of the GR34.

Although nowhere on the coast is more than 100m above sea level, the route is punctuated by many relatively short ascents and descents, thus meriting the medium grading. There's scope for varying the pattern of the walk by shortening the daily stages, especially if you are travelling by car, by basing yourself in or near the town of Crozon and doing a number of day walks, using the many quiet roads and tracks for access to the coast. The most suitable of these are highlighted on the IGN 1:25,000 map (see Maps & Books later in this walk). The peninsula is well endowed with camp sites; some of these, as well as a gîte d'étape, are well placed for this walk.

Details of other accommodation are available from the local tourist offices.

NATURAL HISTORY

Depending on your outlook, Presqu'île de Crozon is cruciform- or scarecrow-shaped, the head facing west to the Mer d'Iroise, ending bluntly at Pointe du Toulinguet. The northern arm ends at Pointe des Espagnols on the Rade de Brest (rade in French meaning 'natural harbour'); its southern counterpart, Cap de la Chèvre, is in the Baie de Douarnenez. The dominant rock type is ancient Armorican quartz sandstone, extensively displayed at Pointe du Guern, Pointe de Dinan, Pointe de Pen Hir and at Cap de la Chèvre, while schists are prominent at Anse de Pen Hat and Anse de Porz Naye. These rocks formed from deposits of sand and other material in the sea which once covered Brittany, so fossils are commonly found embedded in them.

The greater part of the peninsula is within the PNRA. Reflecting the diversity of wildlife habitats, six sites are of particular importance for nature conservation. The cluster of islets off Pointe de Pen Hir, Les Tas de Pois, is a bird sanctuary where shags, gulls and kittiwakes nest. The point itself is a protected natural site for its geological features. More than 100 species of birds have been recorded at L'Étang de Kerloc'h, including warblers, reed buntings, owls, buzzards and ducks. This small lake is also home to families of otters and numerous species of dragonfly. At Cap de la Chèvre a rare heathland community comprises bell heather, ling and summer gorse; orchids also are likely to be found on the heathlands. Sea bream and bass breed in the waters of the Aber River, a protected natural site where shelduck, egrets, marsh harriers and some migratory species may be seen. The mixed forest of the Falaises de Guern, between Plage de l'Aber and Anse du Caon, are the habitat of protected plant and animal species.

PLANNING

May and June are the ideal months for Finistère, when there's the best chance of settled weather and the heathland wild flowers are in bloom. Insect repellent is a useful deterrent against flying insects during still evenings; a water bottle is essential as natural sources of water along the walk are almost nonexistent.

Maps & Books

IGN's 1:25,000 Camaret, Presqu'Île de Crozon sheet No 0418ET covers the area. Le Mènez-Hom Atlantique à Pied, Presqu'île de Crozon, Porzay, Châteaulin, Le Faou FFRP Topo-Guide (No P293) describes 35 short walks, including several which cover most of this walk. Individual walks are also available on A4 cards for 5FF each. All three publications are available from the tourist office in Crozon.

NEAREST TOWNS
Camaret-sur-Mer

The tourist office (☎ 02 98 27 93 60, fax 02 98 27 87 22), Quai Kleber, 29570 Camaret, is open all year. For sending and receiving emails, there's a Cyberposte facility at the post office, place Charles de Gaulle; it's open from 9 am to noon and 2 to 5 pm Monday to Friday, and 9 am to noon on Saturday; the fee is 50FF for the first hour and 30FF for each additional hour.

Places to Stay & Eat A good camping option, *Camping Plage de Trez Rouz* (☎ 02 98 27 93 96, Plage de Trez Rouz) overlooks a small beach, 2.5km north of Camaret. The tariffs are 25FF per person and 20FF per tent space; it's open from Easter to the end of September and there's a small restaurant on site. The nearest *gîte d'étape* (☎ 02 98 27 62 30) is at Larrial, about 4km east, on the D55 road to Le Fret.

There are numerous *creperies* and *pizzerias* along the beachfront at Camaret where you can eat inexpensively, and a couple of *bars* where a Guinness deficit can be obliterated.

Getting There & Away Daily CAT bus services (☎ 02 98 90 88 89) run from both the Quimper and Brest bus stations to Camaret-sur-Mer (alight at Le Port bus stop) via Crozon (stops at the tourist office; 65FF).

BRITTANY

BRITTANY

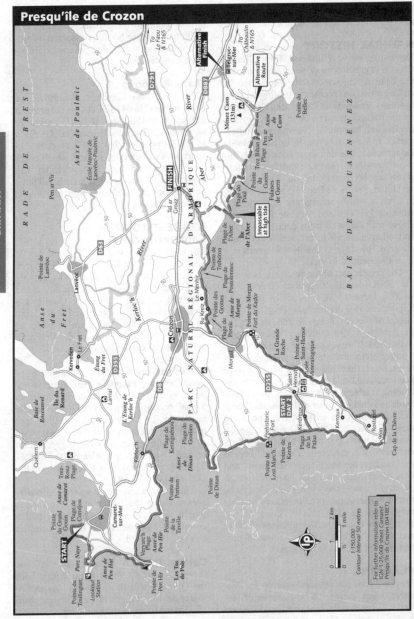

Presqu'île de Crozon

RADE DE BREST

Anse de Poulmic

To Le Faou & N165

D791

River

D887

Alternative Finish

Télgruc-sur-Mer

To Châteaulin & N165

Alternative Route

Ménez Caon (131m)

Pointe du Bellec

Pen ar Vir

Ecole Navale de Lanvéoc-Poulmic

Trez Bihan Plage Pen ar Vir

Anse du Caon

Pointe de Lanvéoc

D63

River

50

Aber

FINISH

Tal ar Grouz

PARC

NATUREL

RÉGIONAL

D'ARMORIQUE

Pointe du Guern Falaises de Guern

Plage du Poul

Île de l'Aber

Plage de l'Aber

Impassable at high tide

BAIE DE DOUARNENEZ

Lanvéoc

Kerloc'h

Pointe de Tréboron

Plage de Postolonnec

Pointe des Grottes

Le Menhir

Ru Kreiz

Pointe du Porzic

Anse de Morgat

Fort du Kador

Pointe de Morgat

Anse du Fret

Le Fret

Kerveden

Crozon

Morgat

La Grande Roche

Pointe de Saint-Hernot

Étang du Fret

L'Étang de Kerloc'h

D8

Larnal

Saint-Hernot

Musée Minéralogique

Baie de Roscanvel

Île du Renard

D355

START DAY 2

Quélern

Kernoch

Plage de Kerzriguénou

Plage de Goulien

Anse de Dinan

Prehistoric Fort

Kerdreux

Plage de la Palue

Kerroux

Rostudel

94m

Cap de la Chèvre

Pointe de Portzen

Pointe de la Tavelle

Pointe de Dinan

Pointe de Lost Marc'h

Pointe de Kerdra

Trez-Rouz Plage

Anse de Camaret

Plage de Corréjou

Camaret-sur-Mer

Pointe du Grand Gouin

START

Vercc'ach Plage

Porz Naye

Anse de Pen Hir

Pointe de Pen Hir

Anse de Pen Hat

Les Tas de Pois

Pointe du Toulinguet

Lookout Station

N

1:150,000
Contour Interval 50 metres

0   1   2 km
0   ½   1 mile

For further information refer to IGN 1:25,000 sheet Camaret Presqu'île de Crozon (0418ET)

Frequent trains from Paris' Gare Montparnasse go to Brest and to Quimper (☎ 02 98 50 50 50; 360FF and 370FF).

By road, turn off the N165 Quimper-Brest route near Châteaulin for the D887, or at Le Faou for the D791; these two roads merge and become the main route to Camaret-sur-Mer via Crozon.

Crozon

Crozon is the closest largish town to the end of the walk and also a potential base for exploring Presqu'île de Crozon in a leisurely fashion. The tourist office (☎ 02 98 27 07 92, fax 98 27 24 89), blvd Pierre Mendes-France, 29160 Crozon, is open year-round.

Places to Stay & Eat The most convenient camping ground if you're on foot is *Pen ar Menez* (☎ 02 98 27 12 36), in blvd de Prologuan, a few hundred metres west of the bus stop and tourist office. The tariffs are 16FF per pitch and 17FF per person and it's open from April to 30 September; the facilities could do with some modernisation. Alternatively, *Les Pins* (☎ 02 98 27 21 95), in route de la Pointe de Dinan, charges 21FF for each person and for each tent space.

L'Oceanic Pizzeria Restaurant (☎ 02 98 27 02 70, 24 rue de Camaret) is just across the road from the entrance to Pen ar Menez camping ground. It's open for lunch and from 7 pm to midnight for pizzas (50FF to 70FF), pasta and grills.

The *Casino* supermarket, on blvd de Prolognan, about 250m east of the camping ground entrance, is open until late, Monday to Saturday.

Getting There & Away For transport information to/from Crozon, see Getting There & Away under Camaret-sur-Mer.

GETTING TO/FROM THE WALK

The walk begins in Camaret-sur-Mer. To return from the end of the walk, there are at least two CAT buses travelling between Quimper and Camaret-sur-Mer via Tal ar Groaz (stopping opposite the boulangerie) and Telgruc-sur-Mer (stopping at the town hall; 52FF).

THE WALK
Day 1: Camaret-sur-Mer to Saint-Hernot

7½–8 hours, 27.5km, 460m ascent

From the north-western end of the Plage de Corréjou, follow the *sentier côtier*, a broad grassed path that soon narrows and meets a minor road. Pass a squat stone building on your right and go round **Pointe du Grand Gouin**. For several kilometres the cliff tops are encrusted with derelict fortifications above and below ground, dating back to the mid-19th century. From the car park near Porz Naye, leave the road (about 150m east of the point shown on the IGN map) to pass the firmly closed entrance to the lookout station on **Pointe du Toulinguet**. Descend to the beach and, diverging from the route mapped on the IGN 1:25,000 sheet, cross the grassed dunes fringing Anse de Pen Hat and climb to the cliff top (1½ hours from Camaret-sur-Mer). The next 2km to **Pointe de Pen Hir** are superb – colourful cliffs riven by deep chasms. The point is dominated by a towering concrete memorial to those Bretons who died defending France in the two world wars. The point itself is inaccessible to all but the rock climbers who flock there.

Leaving the crowds behind, continue to **Veryarc'h Plage** where a welcome *bar* serves crepes, mussels and drinks. Beyond the end of the beach, the better way across the heathland is on the narrow path on the seaward side of the broad, signposted track; en route, Pointe de la Tavelle and Pointe de Portzen are fine vantage points. About 1½ hours from Veryarc'h Plage, cross the bridge at **L'Étang de Kerloc'h**. From the next headland there's an excellent prospect of the natural bridge at Cap de la Chèvre (to be passed later on). Then, if the tide is right, take to the sands of the twin beaches, Plage de Kerziguénou and Plage de Goulien; otherwise, a path crosses the dunes to the road at the southern end of the latter beach (1¼ hours from the Kerloc'h bridge). A clear path leads on to **Pointe de Dinan**; with care you can negotiate rocky ground almost to the actual point.

Southwards now, the route continues in fine style above the rocky shore to **Pointe de Lost Marc'h** and the remains of a prehistoric promontory fort (almost 1½ hours from Plage de Goulien). Having descended from the point, again walk along the sand, easily passing intervening Pointe de Kerdra if the tide is

From Powder Magazines to Nuclear Submarines

Since at least the 14th century, defence against possible maritime invasion has helped to shape the fortunes and landscape of Presqu'île de Crozon. Numerous forts, artillery bases and gunpowder magazines punctuate the coast and hinterland, and are prominent features on walks in the area. Two facts explain this preoccupation: the long, exposed Atlantic coastline and Brest's historic role as a port and arsenal.

Despite devastating raids by the English in the 14th century and by the Spanish two centuries later, it wasn't until the 1680s that engineer Sébastien de Vauban established a system of defence that, with later upgrades, served well until the mid-1940s. The earliest edifices were the Fort de Cornouaille near Trez Rouz (a few kilometres north-east of Camaret-sur-Mer), the battery at Pointe des Espagnols (guarding the Rade de Brest seaway) and the imposing Tour de Camaret which justified its existence by repulsing an attempted landing by Anglo-Dutch forces in 1694. The system was tinkered with during the later alarms of the American War of Independence and Napoleon's adventures, then extensively modernised during the 19th century. Several forts were built, plus the massive Kador battery near Crozon (see the Presqu'île de Crozon walk description).

Between the world wars, an air base was set up at Lanvéoc Poulmic (north of Crozon), and more recently and contentiously, nuclear submarines have been based at Île Longue. Brest is one of France's major naval bases, so naval vessels are a common sight in Anse de Crozon, providing a faintly sinister reminder of modern geopolitics amid the peaceful activities of pleasure cruisers and yachts.

out (otherwise keep to the path above the beach), to **Plage de la Palue**. To reach Saint-Hernot, leave the beach 1.2km south of the latter point along a minor road to a car park, from where a better road goes via Kerdreux to Saint-Hernot (1.7km from the beach).

Gîte d'Étape de Saint-Hernot (☎ 02 98 27 15 00), in the centre of the village, has dorm beds for 55FF or private rooms for around 100FF; meals are available in the attached bar-restaurant where a 70FF *menu* features fresh local seafood. Nearby is the Musée Mineralogique (☎ 02 98 27 19 73) of the PNRA; it's open from 10 am to noon and 2 to 5.30 pm daily except Saturday, and presents displays about the park and its intricate geology. Entry is 25FF for adults and 14FF for children.

Day 2: Saint-Hernot to Tal ar Groaz
6½–7 hours, 21km, 600m ascent
Back at the beach, the sentier côtier leads into more rugged terrain than that already traversed; the wild flowers are more sparse and low stone walls enclose fields where now only gorse and bracken thrive. At the popular **Cap de la Chèvre**, at 96m the highest point on the coast so far (1½ hours from the start), you'll see impressive memorials to members of the air service in western France.

Beyond the cape, the path dips and climbs around small inlets, bypassing the D255 road south-east of Kerroux. About 1½ hours' walking brings you to another worthwhile detour, to **Pointe de Saint-Hernot**. A short distance farther on a signposted path leads to Saint-Hernot. The path continues to wander up and down, usually steeply, and there's another fine vantage point at **La Grande Roche**. Eventually you reach the substantial **Fort du Kador** at Pointe de Morgat, now the peaceful home for a colony of the protected bat species, *chauves-souris grands rhinolophes*. Shortly afterwards you plunge into the incongruous bustle of the port of Morgat (about 1½ hours from the Saint-Hernot turn-off). There's no alternative to the path beside the road (D887) paralleling the shore of Anse de Morgat. At the far end, follow the D887 road north for 300m then turn sharp right to a T-junction; turn left and continue to **Plage de Porzic**. To reach Crozon's centre, head generally north along rue Saint-Pol Roux, rue du Portzic and rue du Menhir to meet the main road near the post office.

Continuing eastwards from Plage du Porzic, the route avoids roads around Pointe des Grottes via a path on the seaward side of the cliff, which rejoins the marked route near Ru Kreiz. After about 30 minutes you come to **Le Menhir**, where a marine version of a topographic map shows all the beacons on the Baie de Douarnenez and the Rade de Brest. The menhir (prehistoric standing stone) disappeared long ago. From here, another new route from the eastern end of Plage de Postolonnec leads south-west round a tennis court and *Bar-Crêperie Le Korrigan* (which boasts an extensive repertoire of crepes). Climb steeply to Pointe de Trébéron, then down to the broad **Plage de l'Aber**. Tidal comings and goings and the depth of the Aber River dictate an inland road walk towards the village of Tal ar Groaz. Rather than end in Tal ar Groaz, the walk can be extended east along the coast to Telgruc-sur-Mer (see the Alternative Route at the end of this walk description).

Camping de l'Aber (☎ 02 98 27 02 96), on the route Plage de l'Aber, is about 450m up the road from the sharp bend where the road turns down to the bridge (1½ hours from Plage du Porzic). With a panoramic view of the coast, it charges 17FF per person and 16FF per pitch and is open all year. Pizzas, hamburgers, quiche and *frites* (chips, or French fries) can be had in the adjacent bar. In the village are a *boulangerie*, small *Spar* supermarket, a *creperie* at Hôtel de l'Aber, and *Le Capri*, a bar-restaurant-pizzeria where grills range from 55FF to 90FF and pizzas from 40FF to 60FF.

Alternative Route
1½ hours, 6km one way
You could continue from Tal ar Groaz to Telgruc-sur-Mer as an alternative finish to the walk (a long day), or do this section as a day's outing from Tal ar Groaz (2½ hours, 10km return). From the sharp bend in the road between Plage de L'Aber and Camping

de l'Aber, descend to cross the bridge over the Aber River; on the left is a lime kiln built in 1839 and abandoned in 1872. About 150m farther along the road, turn off to the signposted shoreline track, which could be submerged at high tide. Just round the first small point, a path leads up to the low cliff top and onto the parking area near **Île de l'Aber**. If the tide is low, it's worth crossing to the isle (a proper island at high tide) to see the massive fort, although only the ground floor survives. Beyond Plage du Poul and the **Falaises du Guern**, about 30 minutes farther on, detour to the crest of Pointe du Guern for a fine view.

The next stretch, down to Trez Bihan Plage, is delightful – heathland with scattered pines and rocky outcrops; continue to Anse du Caon. To reach Telgruc-sur-Mer, walk up the minor road leading north and signposted 'Circuit du Ménez Caon'; turn right up the main road at a crossroads; access to the camping ground is within the next 500m, and the small town another 1.2km farther on.

Of three camp sites, *L'Armorique* (☎ 02 98 27 77 33) charges 44FF for one person and a tent (cheaper than Le Panoramic). In the town, there's a, *8 à Huit* supermarket, a *boulangerie* and a *bar-creperie*, all near the prominent church.

A possible alternative return to Camping de l'Aber is via Ménez Caon (see the IGN 1:25,000 map), from which there are fine coastal views.

Other Walks

Île d'Oeussant
Île d'Oeussant is the most westerly outpost of France (and Europe), a small low island (8 by 4km) bounded by 30km of magnificent coastline protecting a largely unspoiled hinterland. Following paths and quiet roads, you can explore the island (part of the PNRA) in three days of easy walking (around 50km). Oeussant's lighthouses, including the world's most powerful, are the theme of an ecomuseum there, and the island is outstanding for observation of resident and migratory sea birds. You'll need IGN 1:25,000 sheet No 0317OT and the FFRP Topo-Guide *North Finistère: The Path of Lighthouses* (No PR059). Contact the tourist office (☎ 02 98 48 85 83),

BRITTANY

Bourg de Lampaul, 29242 Oeussant, for more information. Compagnie Maritime Penn ar Bed (☎ 02 98 80 24 68), Port de Commerce, 29607 Brest, runs a daily ferry service from Brest and Le Conquet to the isle (April to November).

Coast Path

Brittany's coastal path (GR34) follows the greater part of the English Channel and western ocean shores, from the Normandy border near Mont Saint-Michel to the Morbihan coast in south central Brittany, a distance of around 1000km. Apart from the walks described in detail earlier in this chapter, there's also the chemin des Phares (Path of the Lighthouses), between Portsall and Brest in Finistère. It traverses a very scenic, rocky coast, almost free of unlovely seaside resorts; several lighthouses highlight the area's maritime heritage.

The 86km route (five or six days' walking) has an FFRP Topo-Guide *North Finistère: The Path of Lighthouses* (No PR059); the IGN 1:25,000 sheets are Nos 0416ET and 0417ET. Contact the tourist office (☎ 02 98 44 24 96), 8 ave Georges Clemenceau, 29200 Brest, for accommodation information. Brest enjoys a TGV *(train à grande vitesse)* train service from Paris' Gare Montparnasse (☎ 02 98 80 50 50); buses (☎ 02 98 44 46 73) link Brest to towns along the way.

Other FFRP Topo-Guides for the coast are: *Côte d'Émeraude* (No 345); *Pointe du Raz-Cap Sizun* (No 291) and *Côte de Cornouaille, Pointe du Raz à Lorient* (No 292).

Monts d'Arrée

The rocky hills, woods and heathlands of the PNRA are unlike anywhere else in Brittany. In the area between Brasparts, Commana, Saint-Rivoal and Brennilis, 10 waymarked circuit walks (8 to 18km), based on villages or roadside picnic areas, explore this varied landscape, its traditional villages and farming communities. The relevant IGN 1:25,000 sheets are Nos 0517E and 0617O. Contact the tourist office (☎ 02 98 99 72 32), 29690 Huelgoat, for the *Circuits de Petite Randonnée Autour du Yeun Elez* leaflet and for

accommodation lists. The park office (☎ 02 98 68 81 71) is at Ménez Meur, 29460 Hanvec. Two FFRP Topo-Guides also cover the area: *Pays de Morlaix, Monts d'Arrée et Trégor* (No 056) and *Monts d'Arrée-Cap Sizun* (No 380). Public transport is sparse, so a car is preferable. Major roads cross the area north-south, branching from the N12 Saint-Brieuc to Brest and the N165 Brest to Quimper routes.

Huelgoat & Beyond

Huelgoat, a small town on the eastern edge of the PNRA, can be the starting point for a traverse of the park, and the base for exploring local archaeological and historic sites, forests and the Argent River. Of several waymarked routes for easy to medium day walks, the Circuit du Canal de la Mine takes in the remains of 18th- and 19th-century silver workings. Leaflets about these walks are available from the tourist office (☎ 02 98 99 72 23), 29690 Huelgoat, as is the useful guide *39 Sentiers de Randonnées en Centre Finistère*. You'll need the IGN 1:25,000 sheet No 0617E.

There's a CAT bus service (☎ 02 98 44 46 73) from Carhaix Plouguer to Huelgoat; Carhaix is on a branch train line from Guingamp on the Paris' Gare Montparnasse to Brest line (☎ 02 96 46 76 70 for information). By road from the north (Morlaix), follow the D769 and D14; from the south and west, several roads branching from the N165 (from Brest to Quimper) lead towards Huelgoat.

A two- or three-day traverse of the park, following waymarked routes (GRs 380 and 37) from Huelgoat via Loqueffret and Saint-Rivoal to Le Faou on the Aulne River estuary, provides an interesting and varied walk. Accommodation close to the route is limited (gîtes d'étape in Saint-Rivoal and near Hanvec), and some paths can become very muddy. The IGN 1:25,000 sheets are Nos 0617E, 0617O, 0517E and 0517O. From Le Faou, CAT buses run to Quimper and Brest for train connections. Contact the Huelgoat tourist office or the PNRA (☎ 02 98 68 81 71) for more information.

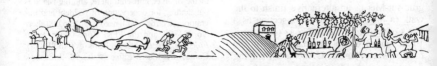

Loire Valley

The Loire Valley is much more than the major chateaux that are mandatory stops on every coach party itinerary. Chateaux there are in plenty, plus abbeys and fine churches. But there's also the more modest charm of slate-roofed villages, their walls built of blocks of mellow tufa, a particularly soft variant of limestone, white and sensuous like clotted cream under the sun.

Grandeur in the valleys of the Loire and its tributaries tends to be artificial rather than a glorious creation of nature. Here, nature is gentle: woods of oak and beech, and flat river valleys sometimes benignly overlooked by low bluffs. Or else it's tamed in the form of lush green vineyards and cereal fields stretching to the broad horizon.

But the Loire, at 1012km France's longest river, can throw a tantrum. Every summer the currents of this deceptively languid watercourse claim an incautious swimmer or two. Engorged in winter and spring, for centuries the river would devastate the low plains, and even today it floods regularly. Notice the *levées* (levies, or dykes), the first of which were built back in the 13th century.

Few people come to the Loire expressly for a walking holiday. But if you're in the area, a day or two on foot can be a pleasant and exhilarating alternative to more conventional and less energetic ways of visiting the sights. A word of warning: if you decide to walk the GR3, which runs through the Loire Valley, we recommend that you do so with caution. The trail's waymarkers are often faded or nonexistent and discrepanies between signing and IGN 1:25,000 maps are frequent.

CLIMATE
Winter days can be dreary and damp but rarely cold, with daily averages no less than 7°C. Spring and autumn offer ideal walking, although there may still be frost on the ground in March and April. Even in the height of summer walking is agreeable, with maximum temperatures around 23°C.

HIGHLIGHTS

SALLY DILLON

The Château de Saumur, reflected in the Loire River

- Marvelling at the mock-ups of Leonardo da Vinci's inventions in the country house of Clos-Lucé

- Rounding a bend to see the Château de Chenonceau straddling the Cher River

- Munching wild walnuts, chestnuts and hazelnuts, plucked along quiet lanes

- Sharing a bottle of cold Saumur wine at the end of the trail

INFORMATION
Maps & Books
IGN's 1:250,000 TOP 250 sheet No 106 and Michelin's 1:200,000 *Angers, Tours et Orléans* sheet No 64 give good coverage of the region. For maps covering individual walks, see Planning in the introduction to each walk.

For a detailed look at the region, see Lonely Planet's *The Loire Valley*.

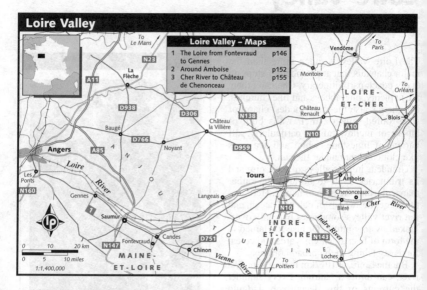

Loire Valley

Loire Valley – Maps

1	The Loire from Fontevraud to Gennes	p146
2	Around Amboise	p152
3	Cher River to Château de Chenonceau	p155

Information Sources

For regional lists of hotels, restaurants, camping grounds and chateau guides, contact one of the two regional tourist offices (Comité Régional du Tourisme) for the Loire Valley:

Pays de la Loire (☎ 02 40 48 24 20, fax 02 40 08 07 10, ✉ crt.promo@wanadoo.fr, www.cr-pays-de-la-loire.fr/FR/tourisme/index.htm) BP 20411, 44204 Nantes Cedex 2

Centre-Val de Loire (☎ 02 38 70 32 74, fax 02 38 70 33 80, ✉ crtl.centre@wanadoo.fr, www.loirevalleytourism.com) 9 rue Saint-Pierre Lentin, 45041 Orléans Cedex 1

GATEWAY
Tours

With wide 18th-century avenues and cafe-lined boulevards, Tours (with a population of 270,000) has the cosmopolitan and bourgeois air of a miniature Paris. The central tourist office (☎ 02 47 70 37 37, fax 02 47 61 14 22), at 76 rue Bernard Palissy, opposite the huge Centre International de Congrès, makes free hotel reservations.

Places to Stay & Eat If you're under canvas, take bus No 5 to Saint Avertin's bus

terminal, 5km south of Tours, and follow signs to *Camping Les Rives du Cher* (☎ 02 47 27 27 60). The cost is 14FF per tent and 14FF per person.

A bed in a room of four or six at the *auberge de jeunesse* (☎ 02 47 25 14 45), in Parc de Grandmont, 5km south of the Tours train station, costs 47FF. Take bus Nos 1 or 6 from place Jean Jaurès, the main square.

Hôtel Le Lys d'Or (☎ 02 47 05 33 45, 21–23 rue de la Vendée), near the station, has rooms from 120FF.

The old city area around place Plumereau, rue du Commerce and rue Colbert is packed with restaurants, bars and cafes.

Getting There & Away There are 10 to 15 TGV trains a day between Gare Montparnasse in Paris and either Tours or Saint-Pierre des Corps (both 201FF), an industrial suburb from where you can take a shuttle to the Tours train station or bus Nos 2 or 3 to the heart of town. Slower and cheaper trains (153FF, five to eight a day) go to/from Paris' Gare d'Austerlitz.

For car hire, call Ada (☎ 02 47 64 94 94), Europcar (☎ 02 47 64 47 76) or Budget (☎ 02 47 46 21 21).

Anjou

The Loire from Fontevraud to Gennes

Duration	2 days
Distance	56km
Standard	easy-medium
Start	Fontevraud
Finish	Gennes
Nearest Town	Saumur
Public Transport	yes

Summary Fontevraud to the confluence of Loire and Vienne Rivers. Along the low escarpment via cereal fields and vineyards to Saumur. A loop through the forest of Amboise and more gentle pastoral walking. Cultural diversions aplenty.

The medium standard of this undemanding walk, which is effectively two one-dayers based upon Saumur, lies only in the length of each stage.

PLANNING
April to June and September to mid-October are ideal, but walking can be agreeable even in the height of summer, when the heat is rarely extreme. Even in August, once you've left Fontevraud and until you reach Saumur, you'll meet few others on the trail.

Maps
Day 1 of the walk is covered by IGN 1:25,000 sheets, Nos 1723OT and 1623ET respectively. Even if you don't read French, consider buying instead the Fédération Française de la Randonnée Pédestre (FFRP) Topo-Guide *L'Anjou à Pied* (No D049) in which the route is indicated accurately at 1:50,000. Costing 75FF, you get an additional 47 walks for good measure.

For Day 2, you need to add the IGN sheet No 1623OT. On both days, the GR3 route differs in several places from the tracing on IGN maps.

In Saumur, these maps are available at Maison de la Presse, 50m from the tourist office, and Librairie du Val de Loire, 48 rue

Orléans. The tourist office sells a loose-leaf guide in English (20FF), describing 22 local walks of between 7 and 15km.

NEAREST TOWN
Saumur
Known as '*la perle d'Anjou*', the bleached, bourgeois Saumur is indeed one of the Loire's jewels. Beneath slate-roofed houses, cobbled pedestrian streets form a lively shopping and social precinct at the base of the fortified chateau. The large Saumur tourist office (☎ 02 41 40 20 60, ✆ infos@ot-saumur.fr) is on place de la Bilange.

Places to Stay & Eat The plus side of the often noisy and overcrowded *Camping de l'Île d'Offard* (☎ 02 41 40 30 00, fax 02 41 67 37 81) is its swimming pool, free to campers. Sprawling at the south-east tip of an island in the Loire, its fees are a hefty 46FF per tent and 28FF per person. The adjacent youth hostel, *Centre International de Sejour*, shares the same reception desk, phone and fax. B&B costs 83FF per person in a dormitory or 106FF for a double.

In town, *Hôtel Bar de Bretagne* (☎ 02 41 51 26 38), on rue St Nicolas, has doubles from 140FF (from 190FF with bathroom) and does sandwiches and pizzas. At the more tranquil *Hôtel Le Volnay* (☎ 02 41 51 25 41, fax 02 41 38 11 04), opposite the main post office, rooms begin at 160FF (220FF with bathroom).

Rivers of Wine

The Loire produces the greatest variety of wines of any region in France: very dry wines to very tart; all manner of colours, from the lightest white to the deepest purple; and all types of sparkling wines. A particular speciality of the region is rosé, the most noted of which is Rosé d'Anjou.

Many of the Loire wines tend to be underrated by the experts, but obvious exceptions to this are the wines of Pouilly-Fumé, Sancerre, Bourgueil, Chinon and, in particular, Saumur.

Le 30 Février, in place de la République, is a great little spot serving organic food and tasty vegetarian dishes.

Getting There & Away There are up to eight trains a day to and from both Angers and Tours (or its satellite TGV station, Saint-Pierre des Corps). All three have regular TGV services to Paris. The Saumur train station is on ave David d'Angers on the right (north) bank of the Loire River.

For car hire, Europcar, Avis and Hertz have offices on ave du Général de Gaulle. For a taxi, call ☎ 06 07 77 07 35.

GETTING TO/FROM THE WALK
To the Start
The morning bus No 16 for Fontevraud leaves the bus stop beside Saumur's San Nicolas church at 8.10 am.

From the Finish
Bus No 5 from Gennes to Saumur via the left bank of the Loire stops on place du 19 Mars beside the camping ground. It leaves Gennes on weekdays at 3.55 pm during the school year and at 5.35 pm in July and August. Alternatively, cross the bridge to Les Rosiers-sur-Loire to pick up the year-round No 11 bus to Saumur (daily except Sunday) which passes at 5.50 pm.

THE WALK
Day 1: Fontevraud Abbey to Saumur Castle
5½–6½ hours, 26km

An abbey, a fine collegiate church, troglodyte dwellings, windmills and a couple of chateaux are the cultural tally for the day as the trail alternates between oak woods, fields of maize, sunflower, wheat and barley, and many a small vineyard.

It's possible to omit the first 7km by starting from Montsoreau. Take the 8.10 am bus from Saumur or the next one at 12.30 pm (weekdays only).

From **Fontevraud Abbey**, head north along ave Rochechouart. Turn right after 200m into rue Saint-Mainboeuf. Go straight ahead where the road bends left to take a dirt lane. At a four-way junction turn left then, around 15 minutes later, right, heading south-east along a track bordered by a ditch. This junction is unsigned but a small strip of vineyard ahead on the left confirms that you're on the right trail.

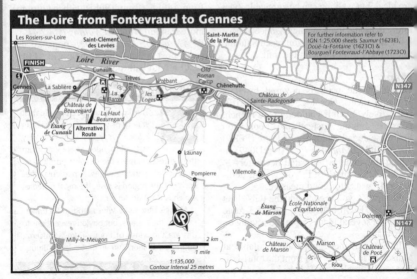

The Loire from Fontevraud to Gennes

Turn left at a T-junction onto a manifest cart track. Some 10 minutes later, turn left onto a sealed lane bordered by walnut trees – which offer fine pickings in season – and cross over the D751.

After passing under the second of two giant electricity pylons, go right, following the sign reading 'Panorama'. From a ruined windmill and orientation table, there's a great vista of the confluence of the Loire and Vienne, and to the north-east, the Centrale Électrique de Chinon nuclear power plant.

An ancient cobbled track winds down from the windmill to Candes Saint-Martin and its fine **collegiate church**. Follow the GR flashes through the hamlet and veer right (north-west) along a walled lane which passes beside the stumps of a couple of ruined windmills before dropping to the village of Montsoreau at river level.

Briefly leave the GR3 to descend rue Françoise de Maridor and wriggle your way through the houses via a series of steps to reach the **15th-century castle**, headquarters of the Parc Naturel Régional Loire-Anjou-Touraine, after about 1½ hours of walking.

Follow the main road downstream and, after perhaps pausing for a drink in one of the several *cafes* in place du Mail, turn left then quickly right to rejoin the GR3 at rue de l'Église. Turn left beside the church then right up the cobbled chemin des Bournais (not rue des Moulins as the recommended IGN 1:25,000 sheet indicates in the first of several discrepancies). At a T-junction, turn right then left just before a squat cone, all that remains of an old windmill. About 100m before the stub of a second windmill, leave the sealed road and fork right along a dusty path between vines. Pass under the legs of a huge pylon and turn right (north) when parallel with a water tower.

After leaving the vineyard, fork left onto a minor path. Take a right as the trail drops down the escarpment passing a series of troglodyte caves cut into the soft tufa. Once at river level, continue along a sealed lane, raised above marshland.

At a left turn before the church of Turquant, you can refill your water containers at a children's playground drinking fountain. (There's also the chance to take a short cut, clipping 2km off the total distance, by continuing straight ahead and rejoining the route at Parnay). Just beyond the church, turn right onto rue de la Mairie to pass more

LOIRE VALLEY

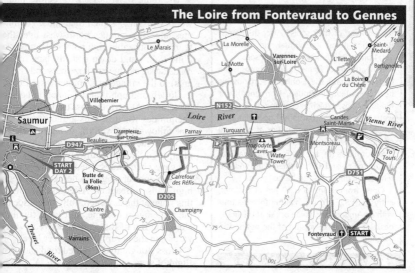

The Loire from Fontevraud to Gennes

Fontevraud Abbey

DIANA MAYFIELD

Fine romanesque detail on the apse of the 12th-century abbey church

Founded in 1099, Fontevraud in its heyday was the largest monastic settlement in Western Europe. One of very few to be 'co-ed', it was headed by an abbess, to whom the monks were subject *pour le salut de leurs âmes* (for the salvation of their souls). After the French Revolution it lost its spiritual role and from 1804 until 1963 functioned as a prison.

Beneath one of four elaborate tombs is the body of Richard the Lionheart – minus his heart (reputedly in Rouen, Normandy) and his intestines, which, according to legend, were buried on the battlefield near Limoges, where he fell. Apply a measure of historical caution, however; within a couple of centuries of his death, the canny French had exported to England at least three skulls and five femurs, all purporting to be his.

Open from 9 am to 6.30 pm in summer, entry costs 32FF. You can either follow a tour with an Anglophone guide or ask at the ticket desk for an English version of the notes, and meander freely.

troglodyte caves. Veer left to follow rue du Val Hulin, then turn right into rue de la Matinière and left onto a dirt track 50m later.

At a T-junction turn right onto an asphalt lane. Where it curves a minute later, continue straight onto dirt track. After 200m, go right to follow a banked sandy track north. At another T-junction, turn left (south-west) onto a sealed road. Be careful not to overshoot a narrow alley rising steeply to the right. Turn into this alley then at its end follow the edge of a field and, where a sign points backwards to Les Hauts de Valbrun, turn right (north-east).

From the tiny church at Parnay, dominated by a magnificent, shady chestnut tree, continue in a generally north-west direction and fork left along rue Antoine Cristal at the next cluster of houses. Just before the top of a small rise, turn sharp right onto a footpath then left (south-west) at a T-junction five minutes later (the GR3 route straight ahead indicated on the IGN 1:25,000 map has clearly been out of commission for years).

Just before reaching a wood the path bends right. At the Carrefour des Réfis crossroads, turn left (south-west) to meet and cross the D205.

The route describes an 'S' before plunging into the welcome shade of an oak wood. Crossing a sealed road about 20 minutes later, it continues north-west over the scarcely noticeable high point of Butte de la Folie (86m) and down a shady lane (more roadside snacks here of hazelnuts and chestnuts) to the village of Dampierre-sur-Loire.

Go left and uphill at a T-junction beside the church. At a white cross turn right along chemin des Ruettes. This attractive walled lane follows the low bluff, giving fine views of the wide Anjou Valley and the first glimpse of Saumur's railway bridge.

Leave chemin des Ruettes at the bottom of a dip and turn right to descend between high walls to Beaulieu. After a steep but, at this stage of the day, mercifully brief ascent, the route again becomes dirt lane, running along the rim of the plateau between vineyards and the abrupt drop to river level.

Cross straight over a sealed road and up a flight of steps onto rue de Bel Air. A couple of minutes later, turn left at a T-junction then right at another crossroads (where the GR3 meets the GR36). After 100m, fork right to follow the quiet rue des Moulins all the way to the **Château de Saumur**, diverging only for the last few hundred metres to enjoy the parallel corniche pathway and its fine views.

Château de Saumur

A fortress in the 13th century, the chateau later became a country residence of the Dukes of Anjou. Open from 9.30 am to 6 pm daily except Tuesday, the admission fee of 38FF allows you to prowl freely around the dungeons and watchtowers. This also includes access to the Collection des Arts Décoratifs, mainly earthenware, porcelain and tapestries, and the Collection Cheval, with examples of just about everything ever used to harness, saddle and bedeck a horse.

Day 2: Saumur to Gennes
6½–7½ hours, 30km

At the time of writing, major roadworks were under way around the Saumur chateau. We describe here what was then the optimum route from the castle to the Thouet River. Order may now have been restored.

From the chateau, take the continuation of rue des Moulins, which becomes rue du Docteur Peton then rue du Petit Mail. Turn left into place Bury and fork immediately right to cross a small public garden and continue straight along rue Fardeau.

At a T-junction, cross the busy road, go briefly left and take a footpath, its entrance marked by two red-and-white bollards, towards the sleepy Thouet River. Turn left to join the GR3 and follow the towpath for about 10 minutes before crossing a couple of bridges to the river's true left bank. Shortly before reaching the busy N347, it's worth visiting **Le Dolmen de Bagneux** (8FF), which at 90 sq m and 500 tonnes is France's biggest dolmen (prehistoric burial tomb).

Once over a bridge spanning the N347, town life is firmly behind you. Go left onto a sealed minor road then straight ahead onto

a wide 4WD track, where the road bends sharply left. Descend rue du Pavé to the picturesque hamlet of Riou, passing caves hewn into the tufa and now used for storing firewood and long-redundant agricultural equipment.

Veer right onto chemin du Moulin. Set back on the right as you enter Marson are some larger caves housing a *champignonnière* (mushroom farm). You can admire the privately owned Château de Marson from the outside. Ascend a flight of wooden steps to follow briefly a *sentier botanique* (botanical path), with labelled trees and bushes.

At a four-way crossroads, go straight, following the sign reading 'Saumur'. Turn left after 25m onto a sandy trail alongside a high wall preventing entrance to the chateau's domains. This is pleasant walking through oak, sweet chestnut, tall Scots pine and, in open glades, ash. At Étang de Marson turn right along an avenue of poplars to follow the lakeside (access is denied by a barbed wire fence). The hoofmarks underfoot and the frequent *propriété privée* (private property) and *défense d'entrer* (no entry) signs indicate that you're passing the grounds of the École Nationale d'Équitation, home to the elite cavalry unit, the Cadre Noir.

Shortly after emerging into open fields, turn left at a T-junction, then make a dogleg right after 250m to pass through Villemolle. Just beyond, bear left at a four-way crossing onto a dirt track to re-enter woodland. About 20 minutes after the village, turn right at a T-junction onto a wider track which heads north-east as far as a bluff above the Loire Valley.

Just before the privately owned Château de Sainte-Radegonde, turn left (north-west) along an overgrown cart track running beside a vineyard.

At a three-way junction take the middle option and stay on a narrow asphalt lane as far as Chênehutte. Turn left to follow the river downstream, then left again up a narrow alley just beyond *Café Restaurant Fontaine d'Enfer*, which does sandwiches (15FF) and a three-course *menu ouvrier* (workers' meal) for 60FF, including drink at weekday lunch times.

Troglodytes

Gleaming white tufa, a particularly soft variant of limestone, is a popular building material in the Loire Valley. Caves and tunnels, gouged into the sheer riverside escarpments to extract the tufa, functioned for centuries as dwellings. Nowadays, a minority are chic bars or restaurants and you can even stay in a *troglogîte*. But most live on as storerooms for some more modern structure erected at their entrance. Still others survive or have been rehabilitated as homes, while in deeper, dark and slightly dank galleries mushrooms are cultivated and wine is aged.

After following the fringe of a wood, make three right turns in quick succession: onto a sealed road, at a sign reading 'La Marquerie' 150m later, then up a steep and indistinct track after a further 75m. This passes the site of an ancient Roman camp. Look out for shards of knapped flint at your feet and, set back from a T-junction where the route turns right (north), the trenches and spoil heaps of a recent archaeological dig. At a crossroads beside a cemetery, turn left along a sealed road and go straight onto a cart track when the road elbows left.

Just before Les Loges, turn right (north) down the track which once served this abandoned farm and follow it as far as the banks of the Loire. Turn left along the D751, perhaps pausing to enjoy the cool of La Cave aux Moines (admission 10FF, including a *dégustation* – tasting), a touristy place where they raise snails, grow mushrooms and sell local wines.

Turn left up a narrow lane 200m later to follow the clearly signed GR3 as it winds through the village of Prébant and its neighbour, Trèves. Just before an imposing tower, all that remains of a once fine castle, turn left up chemin de la Barre.

Once beyond the farm of La Barre, turn right at a T-junction to re-enter woodland shortly after the alternative GR3D takes off south. Follow the main GR3 right along a forest track to pass the ruins of Le Haut Beauregard. (Alternatively, if you want to build in a nifty short cut, continue straight to omit the Cunault rectangle and clip 1.5km off the distance for the day).

The trail drops to the riverside hamlet of Cunault, emerging beside *Camping Municipal de Chênehutte, Trèves et Cunault* (tent 11FF plus 10FF per person) with its fine riverside location. Turn downstream onto the D751 to pass beneath the Château de Beauregard, nowadays a fancy hotel.

Turn left beside the popular *Bar La Cale*. Don't fail to drop into the magnificent 11th-century Romanesque priory church of **Notre Dame**, famous for its murals and exuberant sculpted capitals – all 223 of them.

Follow the GR blazes to leave the village and, once beyond, fork left towards the scattering of houses which constitute La Sablière. Where a cart track intersects with the bitumen lane – the end of the short cut which bypasses Cunault – turn right then, 50m later, left along a broad ride bordered by woodland. (Alternatively, continue along the sealed lane to clip off another kilometre.)

Once past the **Étang de Cunault**, turn right (north-east) along a wide dirt track. Where this intersects with a sealed lane, go left to descend to Gennes, where there's a small tourist office (☎ 02 41 51 84 14), and the Loire River.

Rooms at *Hôtel Le Lion d'Or* (☎ 02 41 38 05 63) begin at 110FF (160FF with bathroom). *Camping Le Bord de l'Eau* (☎ 02 41 38 04 67) charges 11FF for a tent plus 14FF per person.

Touraine

Shaped like a vine leaf, Touraine region spreads out around the town of Tours along the Loire and its major tributaries: the Cher, the Indre and Vienne. Replete with chateaux and outstandingly fine wines, this is one of the culturally richest regions of France. Among the many grand chateaux which crowd Touraine's fertile, picturesque valleys are the Chateau de Chenonceau and Chateau d'Amboise, both highlights of the walks in this section.

Around Amboise

Duration	4½–5 hours
Distance	21.5km
Standard	easy
Start/Finish	Amboise
Public Transport	yes

Summary To the pool at Étang de la Moutonnerie via the Amboise forest. More woodland to Pagode de Chanteloup, then a wriggling course through the fields back to the Loire.

This is an easy, level walk. Once in Forêt d'Amboise, you're mostly on wide rides, struck straight as a ruler through the forest of oak and beech. Thereafter it's minor sealed roads, cart tracks and footpaths amid fields of vines and cereal. With three major monuments and a possible vineyard visit en route, allow plenty of extra time for cultural diversions and distractions.

PLANNING

See Planning in the Fontevraud to Gennes walk earlier in this chapter for information on when to walk. Make sure to bring money – the attractions en route don't come cheap.

Maps & Books

Ask at the Amboise tourist office for the free local 1:40,000 *Val de Cisse, Amboise et ses Environs* map and the free leaflet, *Chemin de la Forêt* (Forest Trail), which are adequate for route following. For greater precision, pick up the IGN 1:25,000 sheet No 1922E (its GR3 tracing, however, mostly obeys some long-abandoned version).

If you plan several walks in the area and read French, consider the FFRP Topo-Guide, *La Touraine à Pied* (No D037). Maison de la Presse, 24 rue Nationale in Amboise, carries this and a reasonable range of IGN maps for the region.

NEAREST TOWN
Amboise

Amboise is 23km east of Tours. The tourist office (☎ 02 47 57 09 28, @ tourisme.amboise@wanadoo.fr) is 200m downstream from the bridge on the Loire's true left bank.

Places to Stay & Eat On an island in the middle of the Loire River facing Amboise, *Camping de l'Île d'Or* (☎ 02 47 57 23 37) costs 29FF for one person and 42FF for two, including tent.

Centre Charles Peguy-Auberge de Jeunesse (☎ 02 47 57 06 36, fax 02 47 23 15 80), at the western tip of the island, costs 50FF. Reserve in advance because it's a popular youth hostel for groups.

Hotels in town are expensive. Just outside town, *Hôtel Les Platanes* (☎ 02 47 57 08 60), 600m from the train station, has doubles for 150FF to 240FF.

Getting There & Away More than 10 trains a day (fewer on Sunday) connect Amboise and Tours (see the Gateway section earlier in this chapter) and five daily trains run to and from Gare d'Austerlitz in Paris. The Amboise train station is on blvd Gambetta, across the river from the centre of town.

The slower bus service (with eight runs a day) to and from Tours stops beside the tourist office.

For a taxi, call AA Taxi Gérome (☎ 02 47 57 01 54), which also rents cars, or Amboise Taxi (☎ 02 47 23 12 51).

THE WALK

From the tourist office, follow the Loire upstream and turn right onto rue François 1 to kick off the day with a touch of culture by visiting the **Château d'Amboise** (see the boxed text).

As you continue along this attractive street (which becomes rue Victor Hugo), spare a thought for King François' more constricted walk. According to legend, François I would slip away from his castle by an underground passage leading to Le Clos-Lucé, the country house where his friend Leonardo da Vinci spent the last three years of his life, and engage in a little intellectual conversation.

Ten minutes' walking brings you to **Le Clos-Lucé** (39FF; open daily in summer from 9 am to 8 pm), which contains around 40 models of da Vinci's inventions, mocked up by IBM.

From here, head south-east along rue de la Malonnière. Around 50m before a crossroads

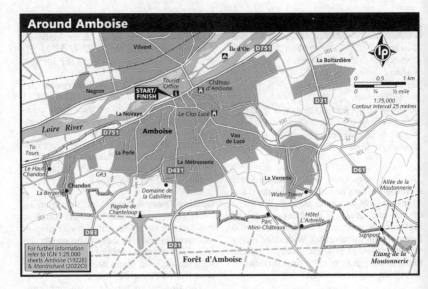

Around Amboise

Vilvent

Île d'Or D751

La Boitardière

Tourist Office

START/FINISH

Château d'Amboise

Negron

La Noiraye

Le Clos Lucé

D31

Loire River D751

Amboise

Vau de Lucé

To Tours

La Perle

La Métrasserie

Le Haut Chandon

GR3

D431

La Verrerie

D61

La Bergerie

Chandon

Domaine de la Gabillère

Water Tower

Allée de la Moutonnerie

Pagode de Chanteloup

Hôtel L'Arbrelle

Parc Mini-Châteaux

D83

D31

Signpost

For further information refer to IGN 1:25,000 sheets Amboise (1922E) & Montrichard (2022O)

Forêt d'Amboise

Étang de la Moutonnerie

0   0.5   1 km
0   ¼   ½ mile
1:75,000
Contour Interval 25 metres

and the last houses of town, turn right onto a dirt track, chemin des Breussollières. Ten minutes later, in quick succession turn right at a stop sign, then left and right again after 175m onto rue des Ormeaux.

At a four-way junction head left up rue des Grands Champs towards a water tower. Beyond the busy D31, continue straight ahead onto a dirt track. At the end of a field, fork to the right, then go straight over allée des Valinières onto a pleasant grassy footpath.

JANE SMITH

Leonardo da Vinci's fabulous 'aerial screw' helicopter on display at Le Clos-Luce

About 10 minutes later and after around 1½ hours of walking, enter a clearing with a wooden post, spiky with signs pointing in every direction. Of the eight possible exits, take the shaded tunnel leading south-east (the second one clockwise after the only sealed road).

Light at the end of this leafy tunnel comes in the form of the glinting waters of **Étang de la Moutonnerie**, a pleasant pond whose banks, even if short on shade, make a great rest stop.

From the pond, turn south-west down allée de la Moutonnerie, then right (west) after 100m to follow the red, blue and sometimes green flashes of a fitness track as it crosses another of the spokes leading away from the signpost and clearing.

At a T-junction, where the fitness track goes right, go briefly left then right (west again) after 50m along a footpath. The path soon joins a wide, straight open ride, allée de Penthièvre. Take the right turn-off where the sandy ride intersects with the gravel allée des Valinières. Next, tack left at a four-way junction to take the least travelled arm, a path heading south-west to run beside a golf course.

At Hôtel L'Arbrelle, go straight across a sealed lane onto another broad ride. This meets a main road at Parc Mini-Châteaux, a bizarre exercise in mini-kitsch where you can visit 43 chateaux of the Loire, none higher than your head. Admission if you're so inclined is an extortionate 45FF, but just think: you could shoot off a reel or two of close-ups and convince the folks back home you've been everywhere in France!

Take a little-walked footpath on the complex's south side as far as the fringe of the forest, where you again pick up a wide trail. Angle sharp right (north) then, three minutes later, turn left beside a lone building onto allée de la Menaudière.

Continue as far as the D31 and car park for the eccentric 18th-century oriental folly, **Pagode de Chanteloup** (30FF; open from 9.30 am to 8 pm in summer). The dead-straight *allées* (lanes) that the route follows were forged through the extensive grounds of the chateau, demolished in 1823, in which the pagoda once sat.

Walk north along the D431, past the *lycée agricole* (agricultural college) where future generations of farmers and wine producers are trained. (A short detour will take you to Domaine de la Gabillère for a little dégustation). Go left along rue du Clos de la Gabillère then, as the sealed road ends, right along a dirt track and left again after 200m onto another sealed road.

At a four-way junction, take the D83, signed 'Saint-Martin-le-Beau'. Just after a bend, turn right along a dirt track signed 'La Talboterie'. Bend left after 75m and follow the wire fence of a large garden to pick up and follow west, then south, the very intermittent red-and-white waymarkers of the GR3. Where the track rejoins the D83, turn right along the broad allée du Châtelier. Ten minutes later leave this broad ride as it curves right, taking instead the minor option heading north-north-west towards the hamlet of La Bergerie, its first red roof already in sight.

Just beyond its neighbour, Chandon village, turn left at a three-way junction signed 'Lussault-sur-Loire' then right towards Le Haut Chandon village, only 500m later. Just

Château d'Amboise

A view of the chateau from the north bank of the Loire

Squatting atop a rocky outcrop dominating the town, this chateau has seen good times. In the late 15th century, Charles VIII, impressed by a visit to Italy where the Renaissance was already in full foment, gave orders for the enlargement of the original modest construction. None too conversant, alas, with the new design, he died aged only 28 when, galloping on horseback to a game of tennis, he struck his head on a low lintel.

A generation later the castle resounded to the noise of masked balls, tournaments and general jollity presided over by the young François I. More sombrely, the chateau was prison in the mid-19th century to Abd el-Qader, an early leader of Algerian resistance to French colonialism.

Admission costs 40FF and the chateau is open from 9 am to 6 pm daily (later in July and August).

behind the village well *(puit)*, descend the Sentier de Guillaume Apollinaire, a narrow alley, and cross straight over the D751 to take a cart track.

Continue east between road and river, past gardens, allotments and summer cabins until you're obliged to turn right and pass through a gravel processing plant. Turn left onto the D751 to return to the tourist office.

LOIRE VALLEY

Cher River to Château de Chenonceau

Duration	3¾–4½ hours
Distance	17km
Standard	easy
Start	Saint-Martin-le-Beau
Finish	Château de Chenonceau
Nearest Towns	Amboise and Tours
Public Transport	yes

Summary From Saint-Martin-le-Beau to the Cher River. A level, towpath walk via Bléré to Château de Chenonceau.

The Cher is perhaps the most attractive of the Loire's little sisters, while Chenonceau is, for many, the region's finest chateau. Rated easy, the only mildly difficult element of the day is negotiating your way down from the bridge west of Bléré to the riverbank.

PLANNING

See Planning in the Fontevraud to Gennes walk earlier in this chapter for information on when to walk.

Maps

The route is so evident that a map is unnecessary. For the record, the walk straddles a fragment of IGN 1:25,000 *Amboise* sheet No 1922E, *Montrichard* sheet No 20220, *Bléré Chenonceaux* sheet No 1923E and the north-west tip of *St-Georges-sur-Cher* sheet No 20230.

NEAREST TOWNS

Both Tours (see the Gateway section earlier in this chapter) and Amboise (see Nearest Town in the Around Amboise walk) are handy bases.

Saint-Martin-le-Beau

There's little to entice you into the small village of Saint-Martin-le-Beau unless you want to visit the tourist office, affiliated to the town hall (☎ 02 47 50 69 65).

Places to Stay & Eat The *Hôtel Restaurant Le Croissant* (☎ 02 47 50 67 01), on rue de Tours, has doubles for between 165FF

Château de Chenonceau

SALLY DILLON

Built in 1513 by Thomas Bohier, financial adviser to François I, the chateau was ceded to the crown upon his death in order to pay off his considerable debts. Henri II, no doubt conscious of the running costs, bequeathed it to his mistress, Diane de Poitiers, who added the first of the magnificent landscaped gardens and built the bridge and ornate rooms spanning the Cher.

Upon Henri's death, his long-suffering widow, Catherine de Médicis, assumed power. Reclaiming Chenonceau, she upstaged her discredited rival by building the impressive 1st-floor gallery and ballroom, where guests danced directly above Diane's bridge.

The gallery, converted into a hospital during WWI, also saw action during WWII. The Cher River marked the boundary between occupied France and the collaborationist Vichy regime and it was frequently used as a clandestine border crossing.

The chateau (admission 45FF) is open from 9 am to 7 pm daily. Allow a minimum of one hour to explore it and the extensive gardens.

and 195FF (210FF and 230FF with bathroom) and *menus* (fixed-price meals of two or more courses) from 85FF. *Camping La Grappe d'Or* (☎ 02 47 50 69 65), 1.25km south of town, is on the banks of the Cher. Open from June to September, it costs 28FF for a tent and up to two people. Its *buvette* (refreshment kiosk) does snacks and has a *menu* costing 55FF.

Getting There & Away It probably means an early start if you're travelling by train from Tours since nothing stops at Saint-Martin-le-Beau between the 7.41 am (weekdays) and 12.25 pm (daily except Sunday). On Sunday only, there's a train at 9.58 am.

Taxi Puce (☎ 02 47 50 26 40) in Saint-Martin-le-Beau charges 80FF to/from Amboise and 140FF to/from Tours. Prices of taxi companies in Amboise and Tours are much the same.

GETTING TO/FROM THE WALK
The walk begins in Saint-Martin-le-Beau. At the end of the walk, trains from Chenonceaux to Tours, from where you can catch a connection to Amboise, leave at 4.44 pm (daily except Saturday) and 6.22 pm (daily).

In July and August, a daily bus for Amboise (line C) leaves Château de Chenonceau at 4.50 pm.

THE WALK
From the train station in Saint-Martin-le-Beau, walk east along the D140. After 200m turn right at a junction to take the considerably quieter D83.

At a bridge over the Cher beside *Camping La Grappe d'Or*, bear left towards the riverbank and follow it eastwards and upstream. The towpath is a tranquil delight compared to the overtrafficked and often inaccessible banks of the Loire. You stand a good chance of spotting heron and other aquatic birds beside the river, and a hawk or falcon hovering expectantly over the cereal fields. And on this stretch of the Cher – again in contrast to

the Loire – you're allowed to take a cooling dip in its waters. Bear in mind, however, the sternly admonitory notices: 'La Baignade est Laissée à Vos Risques et Perils' (Swimming is Entirely at Your Own Risk).

For long periods the only likely intrusions will be the propeller-driven planes or silent, wheeling gliders taking off from Aérodrome d'Amboise-Dierre.

Just under an hour out, the trail passes the first of a succession of identical weirs, locks and locksmiths' cottages. Constructed in the first half of the 19th century at roughly 3km intervals, these locks tamed the river, making it navigable for barge traffic.

About 15 minutes later, the splendid Château de Fontenay rises above the far bank. One kilometre on, mount concrete steps to cross a busy road bridge and scramble down a ramp on the far bank. There's no defined track to the riverside; just forge the way that seems best to you. The footpath, where the route joins the GR41, is firm once you reach it.

Just before the bridge at **Bléré**, *La Belle Époque*, which does a 60FF lunch-time *menu*, is a welcome spot for a drink. Round the corner on rue du Pont, *Pizzeria Trattoria Arlecchino* has pizzas for between 29FF and 48FF.

To bypass the village, walk under the bridge and continue heading upstream beyond another clone weir and lock as the path cuts between a boathouse and a *camping municipal* (municipal camping ground).

Around 45 minutes beyond the camping ground, go straight ahead at Pont de la

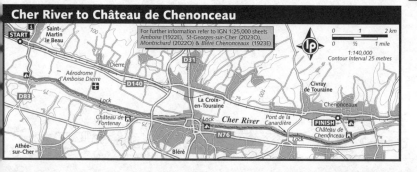

Cher River to Château de Chenonceau

Canardière, where the GR41 leaves the trail, and 250m beyond it, pass another lock.

As you round a bend about 20 minutes beyond the bridge, suddenly there before you and straddling the river is **Château de Chenonceau**, its image reflected in the river. It's a jewel and you've earned that magical view. But don't get too excited too early. Once inside the chateau, you can get a token allowing you out onto the bank where you're standing. But to get *in*, you have to walk another half-hour. (Add your complaints to ours and maybe they'll change the policy.) Continue a farther 900m along the riverbank to the next bridge. Cross to the north bank and continue straight to the railway line, then turn left onto a lane running parallel to the track. This passes the small *camping municipal* (☎ 02 47 23 90 13), which costs 8FF per tent plus 12FF per person, and you reach the main entrance to the chateau and grounds.

Burgundy

Burgundy (Bourgogne) may lack the grandeur and sweeping vistas of the Alps, Pyrenees and Massif Central, but its walking charms are of a less demanding kind. Vineyards and cereal fields sweep broad brushstrokes of colour across a gently undulating landscape. Broadleaf forests of beech and oak are pierced by loggers' tracks and narrow footpaths. And walks often follow ancient, sunken tracks bordered by hedgerows, trimmed tidy or loose and straggling. From one metre to the next, a trail may change from easy, unclogged walking to an overgrown obstacle course – particularly in late spring, when the new grass has grown long and lush.

Once a walk is over, though, there's no better region in all France to replenish energy for the next day's trek. Specialities include *escargots de Bourgogne*, snails plump and sizzling in their sauce of butter and garlic, and *bœuf Bourguignon*, a happy

The Holy Tradition of Wine-Making

This famous wine-growing region is most noted for its great white and red wines. The red are produced with Pinot Noir grapes and white from the Chardonnay. The best reds need 10 to 20 years to age and when mature produce a unique mix of aromas. The four main wine-growing areas of Burgundy are Chablis, Côte d'Or, Chalonnais and Mâconnais.

Burgundy has produced wines since the days of the Celts, but developed its reputation in the reign of Charlemagne, when monks first began to produce wine. With cellars to mature the wine, the inclination to keep records and the organisation to make improvements, the influence of orders such as the Benedictines of Cluny has meant that Burgundy has enjoyed a reputation for great wine ever since.

synthesis of the best local Charolais beef and red Burgundy wine.

Until 1477, when the French king, Louis XI, invaded neighbouring Franche-Comté and annexed Burgundy, the region was a thriving, independent, opulent nation-state. This former wealth is reflected in its indigenous architecture. Just about every village has a fine Romanesque or Gothic church, abbeys and cathedrals abound, and Renaissance manor houses with striking polychrome roofs in geometrical designs pepper the countryside. Nowadays, Burgundy comprises the départements of Côte d'Or, Niévre, Saône-et-Loire and Yonne.

BURGUNDY

CLIMATE

There are no great extremes of climate. Winters, with average temperatures around 6°C, are relatively benign and summers, where temperatures hover around 25°C in August, are not too torrid. Be warned, however, that the Morvan region is known as *le château d'eau* (the water tower) because of its high rainfall, which gives an initial spurt to the Saône, Yonne and Seine.

When the wind blows in from the west, be prepared for rain, sometimes of storm intensity. The prevailing wind from the south blows in warmer Mediterranean air.

INFORMATION
Maps

IGN's 1:250,000 *Bourgogne Franche-Comté* sheet No 109 and Michelin's 1:200,000 sheet No 243 of the same name are both reliable general maps of the region. For maps covering individual walks, see Planning in the introduction to each walk.

Books

Michelin produces a *guide vert* (green guide) in English, *Burgundy Jura*, which, while not pitched at walkers, is impressive for its background information and level of detail.

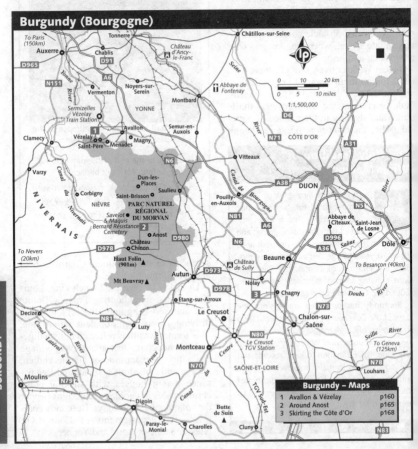

Burgundy (Bourgogne)

Burgundy – Maps	
1 Avallon & Vézelay	p160
2 Around Anost	p165
3 Skirting the Côte d'Or	p168

Avallon & Vézelay

Duration	2 days
Distance	37.5km
Standard	easy-medium
Start/Finish	Avallon
Public Transport	yes

Summary Following the Cousin River. Woods, hamlets and vineyards to Saint-Père and the plateau of Vézelay. Saint-Père again and the Cure River up to Tharoiseau and Le Grand Island. Deep woodland and back to the Cousin Valley.

Tread in the footsteps of tens of thousands of medieval pilgrims who, after attending mass in Vézelay's magnificent basilica (see the boxed text 'The Basilica at Vézelay'), set out on the long journey to Santiago de Compostela on the trail of Les Chemins des Saint-Jacques.

PLANNING

Any season is walking season in Burgundy, although you need to wrap up warmly between November and March. June to October, when the weather's warm but rarely uncomfortable, is the optimum period.

Maps & Books

The route features on IGN 1:25,000 sheets *Vézelay* and *Avallon*, Nos 2722E and 2722O respectively. In Avallon, the best source for maps is Maison de la Presse at the junction of rue de Lyon and rue du Maréchal Foch. In Vézelay, the tourist office and the Librairie L'Or des Étoiles on rue Saint-Étienne each sell a few titles.

Of walking books in French, Chamina's excellent *Le Morvan* is a better investment than the slim Fédération Française de la Randonnée Pédestre (FFRP) Topo-Guide *Traversée du Morvan* (No 111).

NEAREST TOWN
Avallon

From a hilltop site, the walled town of Avallon overlooks the Cousin River, which snakes round its base. The tourist office (☎ 03 86 34 14 19, fax 03 86 34 28 29) is in the old city of Avallon, at 4 rue Bocquillot.

Places to Stay & Eat Beside the Cousin River, *Camping Municipal Sous Roche* (☎/fax 03 86 34 10 39), 1.5km south-east of the old town, charges 13FF for a tent and 18FF per person.

Hôtel du Rocher (☎ 03 86 34 19 03), just off the route at Cousin-le-Pont, has simple doubles/two-bed quads for 100/150FF. *Hôtel du Parc* (☎ 03 86 34 17 00, fax 03 86 34 28 48), opposite the train station, has similarly basic singles/doubles without hall showers for 115/130FF.

Le Gourmillon (8 rue de Lyon) has *menus* (fixed-priced meals of two or more courses) for between 80FF and 172FF, including a particularly lip-smacking *menu gastronomique* for 138FF.

Getting There & Away Four buses daily (two only on Sunday) link Avallon's train station and the TGV *(train à grande vitesse)* hub at Montbard, from where there are frequent trains to/from Paris' Gare de Lyon.

From June to late August, one bus a day from Mombard continues to Vézelay town (not the train station, which is 10km from the town), passing by Avallon train station at 9.45 am. The return bus (useful if you prefer to return to Avallon at the end of Day 1) leaves Vézelay at 5.26 pm.

If you're moving to or from the Around Anost walk later in this chapter, two buses a day, usually requiring a change in Saulieu, link Avallon and Autun.

For taxi hire in Avallon, ring ☎ 03 86 31 60 00. The taxi fare between Vézelay and Avallon is 120FF per vehicle.

THE WALK
Day 1: Avallon to Vézelay

4½–5 hours, 18.5km

From the tourist office, take rue Bocquillot to the town ramparts. Turn left, then left again after the first bend to follow a pedestrian lane downhill. Descend to the bridge over the river at Cousin-le-Pont.

Go under the road bridge and cross a small footbridge to the river's true left bank. Here, you pick up the red-and-white waymarkers cut by an oblique white stripe which indicate the alternative GR13 route.

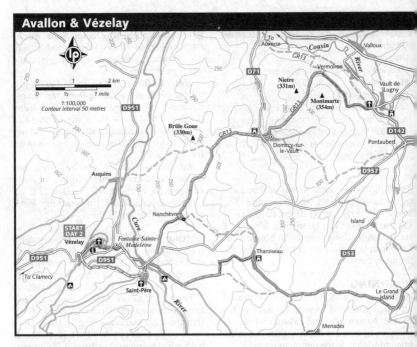

Avallon & Vézelay

There are also less frequent yellow flashes, which continue all the way to Vézelay.

As you follow the trail downstream, notice on the opposite bank the weirs and raceways channelling water to small water-powered flour mills *(minoterie)*, a couple now converted to hotels. It's gentle, shaded woodland walking beside the gurgling river, with the occasional bit of scrabbling over rocks and tree roots.

About an hour from the bridge, walk beside a mossy wall to enter Pontaubert. Go straight across the D957 (perhaps pausing to take water on board at the roadside fountain) and take chemin de Ronde, a narrow lane which curves around the village.

At a T-junction, turn right onto the D142 towards Vault de Lugny. The road runs beside the boundary wall of *Château de Vault de Lugny*, these days housing a four-star hotel. With rooms starting at 850FF, and the grounds and gourmet restaurant the preserve of hotel guests only, it's not every walker's

choice. Phone ☎ 03 86 34 07 86, should you be tempted.

At Vault de Lugny, the route finally leaves the Cousin River, which has been a constant companion since Avallon. However, before turning left along chemin de Borland, make a slight detour to visit the 16th-century **parish church of Saint-Germain**, with its frescoes and finely carved pulpit.

Back on route, go straight ahead and pass the village wash house. After a brief rise, the track levels out to give fine views of the patchwork plain to the east, before curling round the wooded hill of **Montmarte**. Descend to a T-junction with the true GR13, coming in from the north-east. Turn left to follow its stripes, which from here onwards lose their oblique white bar.

Turn right at a T-junction then left a few minutes later, aiming for the red-roofed village of Domecy-sur-le-Vault. Go right down rue de l'Église, beside which are a couple of water troughs and a handsome chateau. Fork

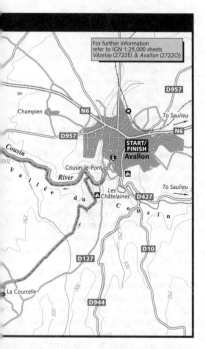

For further information
refer to IGN 1:25,000 sheets
Vézelay (2722E) & Avallon (27220)

D957

Champien   N6   To Saulieu

D957   N6

Cousin   START/
FINISH
Avallon

Cousin-le-Pont

V a l l é e   River

d u   Les
Châtelaines   To Saulieu
D427

C o u s i n

D10

D127

La Courcelle

D944

right beside the church, cross the main village street and head straight up a narrow footpath, which merges with a wide 4WD track just beyond a stone cross.

The track performs a tight 'S' to run beside the first of the Côte de Vézelay vineyards. Roughly three minutes beyond a pair of ailing ash trees, choked with mistletoe and strangled by creeper, go through the hamlet of Nanchèvre. Turn left onto a narrow sealed road and almost immediately right to mount a grassy footpath, with the basilica of Vézelay now prominent on the hilltop to the west.

Where the trail rejoins the road from Nanchèvre, turn left towards Saint-Père and its prominent church spire, perhaps calling by the **caves** (cellars) of Henry de Vézelay (open from 9 am to noon and 2 to 6 pm on weekdays, from 10 am to 12.30 pm and 2.30 to 7 pm on weekends).

Thus fortified, press on to Saint-Père, briefly joining the D957. Cross the bridge

over the Cure River to leave the GR13 as it heads away south-west (absurdly, it bypasses one of France's finest examples of ecclesiastical architecture). The route returns through St-Père on Day 2. If you've time in hand and prefer to visit its magnificent **church** now, go down the main street and turn left.

Otherwise, turn right (north-west) just beyond the bridge to take a quiet road round the rear of the village. Turn right again on rejoining the main road. At a fork very soon after, take the lower option, signed 'Asquins'.

Go left onto a cart track then left again after 50m beside the stagnant Fontaine Sainte-Madeleine (note the traces of a large stone building which would once have enclosed it).

Five minutes beyond, turn briefly left along a sealed road then right after 25m to attack an overgrown footpath which rises towards Vézelay's ramparts. After another five minutes, go right up a flight of stairs penetrating the ramparts (if you come to a small grey metal gate on the right, you've overshot the turning). Wriggle through narrow lanes to emerge into the square in front of the **basilica's** magnificent facade.

On rue Saint-Pierre are Vézelay's tourist office (☎ 03 86 33 23 69, fax 03 86 33 34 00), *Centre Sainte Madeleine (☎ 03 86 33 22 14)*, where a bed in a room or dormitory costs between 55FF and 100FF, and *Restaurant Le Bougainville*, with a range of *menus* starting at 80FF.

Of the cluster of hotels in place du Champ de Foire, just outside the town gates, the most reasonable is *Le Cheval Blanc (☎ 03 86 33 22 12)*, with rooms from 160FF to 250FF and *menus* from 65FF.

Both the municipal *Camping de l'Ermitage* and *auberge de jeunesse*, which share a common telephone *(☎/fax 03 86 33 24 18)*, are 0.5km along the road towards the hamlet of L'Étang.

It's essential to reserve accommodation in July and August and at weekends throughout the year. Alternatively, abridge or extend Day 1 by staying at Saint-Père (see the Day 2 route description for accommodation details).

BURGUNDY

The Basilica at Vézelay

NICKY CAVEN

On the road to salvation

The Basilique Sainte-Madeleine is a Unesco World Heritage List site. Now assailed daily by throngs of tourists, it has known more exciting times and more exotic visitors.

In 1146 Saint Bernard preached the Second Crusade from a nearby hillside. Half a century later, King Philippe-Auguste of France and Richard the Lionheart arranged to meet in its shadow before setting out on the Third Crusade.

More peaceably, as the repository of relics of Sainte Madeleine (Mary Magdalene) and a reputed place of miracles, it drew pilgrims by the thousand and became one of the main French departure points for the Chemins des Saint-Jacques pilgrimage to Santiago de Compostela in north-west Spain (see the boxed text 'Pilgrimage Paths' in Facts about France).

Vézelay and its basilica began to decline in the 13th century when word spread (miraculously, one might say) that other parts of Mary Magdalene had turned up at Saint-Maximin in Provence.

Ransacked by Huguenots during the 16th-century Wars of Religion, desecrated and deconsecrated during the French Revolution, neglected and on the point of collapse, it was restored in the 1840s by Viollet-le-Duc, the famous and, for many, controversial 19th-century restoration architect.

Day 2: Vézelay to Avallon
4½–5 hours, 19km

From Basilique Sainte-Madeleine's western facade, take rue Saint-Pierre, which then becomes rue Saint-Étienne.

Once through the town gates, turn left onto the D957. At the first left-hand bend go straight to take a cart track, then the second turning on the left. This heads south-east towards Saint-Père, giving impressive views north of Vézelay and its basilica.

About 30 minutes out, turn left at the first houses of Saint-Père. At a T-junction with rue de la Mairie, make a 100m diversion to the right to visit the village's superb 12th- to 14th-century Gothic church of **Notre Dame**, the inspiration for Vézelay's basilica.

Hôtel-Bar à la Renommée (☎ 03 86 33 21 34, fax 03 86 33 34 17), on the main street, has a single room for 120FF and doubles for between 190FF and 295FF.

Continuing, turn right to cross the Cure River then immediately right again to follow its lazy course upstream, passing the *camping municipal* (☎ 03 86 33 36 58), where prices are a bargain 8FF for a tent and 10FF per person. A favourite with canoeists, it's a pleasant alternative to Vézelay's camping ground, which can be very crowded.

A little under 10 minutes later, turn left up a narrow sealed lane. Head left up a stony overgrown track then, five minutes later, sharp right along a narrow footpath bordered by unkempt hedges to reach the hamlet of **Tharoiseau** (290m).

Go right, following the high walls and neatly shaped hedges of the privately owned chateau. Beyond the last houses – where you pick up the yellow blazes of the PR2 which links Vézelay and Avallon – take a last glance backwards at the basilica of Vézelay and Saint-Père nestling in its cushion of trees.

Around 15 minutes beyond Tharoiseau, fork left onto a dirt track. Cross straight over the D53 as the trail continues to follow the fringe of a wood. Bear left onto a sealed minor road, then left again a couple of minutes later to pass through Le Grand Island. This is a pretty hamlet, but too many of its houses (used as country retreats by absent

Keeping Paris Warm

From the 16th century until after WWI, the fires and furnaces of Paris were kept alight by wood from the forests of Le Morvan. It's estimated that in the early 19th century, 60% of the capital's firewood was floated down the Seine.

Far upstream, quite small brooks would be dammed. Trimmed logs from nearby woods were tipped into the resulting pond. When the dam was opened and the stream briefly gushed, the logs would be swept down to join a deeper watercourse. With numbers swelling at each major confluence, logs would be sorted by owner and accumulated into convoys at *ports de triage* (sorting stations). The waterborne journey continued to the Yonne River, on to the confluence with the Seine and downstream to Paris.

It took 60 years to dig all 180km of the Canal du Nivernais with its 110 locks (completed in 1843). Connecting the Loire River basin with the waters of the Seine, it extended the long watery supply line to the capital and opened up fresh forests for exploitation.

town dwellers) are boarded up for too much of the year.

Just beyond the last house, turn right (north-east) down a track which crosses a tiny stream then mounts the opposite eastern flank of the shallow valley.

Go left along a minor road to bypass La Courcelle, no more than a cluster of houses. At a junction with another sealed road five minutes later, go straight ahead along a cart track to re-enter a more open, oak forest.

After about 30 minutes of forest walking, there are a couple of tricky navigational moments. Turn right at a grassy track then almost immediately left, bearing due north (not as on the recommended IGN 1:25,000 map). Five minutes later, at a T-junction with a meadow before you and Avallon in sight, turn right, then left a couple of minutes later, ignoring a confusing yellow cross painted on a tree.

Turn left at a bitumen road to reach the friendly **Les Châtelaines** (☎ *03 86 34 16 37, fax 03 86 34 55 95)*, a working farm with a simple camping ground, costing 12FF per person and 5FF for a tent. Arrive between Thursday and Sunday (July and August only) and you can enjoy a meal of fresh farm produce – from its *petit menu* (70FF), ample despite the name, to the gargantuan '*grand où il y a tout*' (the big one with everything) at 100FF.

Continue north-west along the track, which becomes less defined as it heads towards the edge of a wood. Here a signpost and blue dots direct you east along the field boundary then left and down towards the **Cousin River** and the intersection with the alternative GR13. Turn right to retrace the early steps of Day 1 back to the bridge at Cousin-le-Pont and up the hill to Avallon.

Around Anost

Duration	4¾–5¼ hours
Distance	17.5km
Standard	medium
Start/Finish	Anost
Public Transport	yes
Summary	A circular route around the hills, hamlets and farms of Le Morvan in the vicinity of Anost.

'Rien de bon, ne vient du Morvan. Ni bon vent, ni bonnes gens.' (Nothing good comes from Le Morvan. No good wind, no good folk.) Such was the judgement of its neighbours on this once harsh, inhospitable land.

Le Morvan is a giant slab of granite surrounded by the more typical limestone of Burgundy. Its most common sound is the buzz of a chainsaw, its natural vegetation of oak and beech nowadays being supplanted by faster-growing spruce and Scots pine.

The walk takes you through typical Morvan forest. It also crosses plenty of open spaces, offering wide views of the gentler aspects of this once forbidding terrain.

The walk can be divided into two segments – or extended to take in an extra viewpoint. At roughly the halfway point

BURGUNDY

(see the walk description for details), you can turn back to Anost. Not far from the end, at Joux, there's the possibility of a 1.5km, 30-minute round-trip detour for a fine view from Notre Dame de l'Aillant.

PLANNING
See Planning in the Avallon & Vézelay walk earlier in this chapter for information on the best times to walk.

Maps
The route is covered by the IGN 1:25,000 *Arleuf Haut-Folin* sheet No 2824O. The Anost *mairie* (town hall) produces a smudgy pamphlet detailing four fine walks radiating from the village. For a more decipherable version, refer to the map on the wall of the Camping du Pont de Bussy reception area (see Places to Stay & Eat in Anost).

NEAREST TOWN
Anost
Although Anost (pronounced ah-noh) is much more village than town, it has a small tourist information office (☎ 03 85 82 73 26) in the mairie. Its potential for easy, enjoyable walks makes it a good base for a family walking holiday.

You'll be lucky to patronise the bank, which is open only from 9 am to noon on Thursday and has no ATM.

Places to Stay & Eat The municipal *Camping du Pont de Bussy* (☎ 03 85 82 79 07) costs 12FF per tent and 13FF per person.

Anost's one hotel, the sole *gîte d'étape* (hostel-style walkers' accommodation), its only major restaurant and the *Sherlock Holmes* would-be 'pub' belong to the same family. *Hôtel Fortin* has quite reasonable doubles for 200FF to 250FF. *Gîte d'Étape Fortin*, opposite the church, costs 75FF for a bunk and 180FF for half board. If it's closed, inquire at the hotel, pub or restaurant. Contact all on ☎ 03 85 82 71 11, fax 03 85 82 79 62.

Restaurant La Galvache has *menus* at 88FF, 125FF and 175FF. Opposite, *Pizzeria Grill* does pizzas for 40FF to 45FF, pasta for 30FF to 45FF and grills from 55FF to 62FF.

Of the two small supermarkets, *Proximarché* sells a few maps and guidebooks. There's also a *butcher* and a *baker*.

Getting There & Away Outside the school year, bus service No 62 leaves Autun for Anost at 6.10 pm on weekdays. The return service (No 63) departs from Anost at 8.18 am and there's a second run on Wednesday and Friday.

Les Galvachers

Masters of their teams of twin oxen and inured to loneliness, they'd set out on 1 May, heading for what they called '*les pays bas*', the low countries – not the Netherlands, but nearby *départements* (departments) such as Yonne, Allier and Côte d'Or. Some would travel much farther: to Auvergne, Les Vosges, Lorraine and the Ardennes.

They were the *galvachers*, the itinerant carters of Le Morvan, whose rocky infertile soil obliged its best to leave a land which could not sustain them. In some communities, up to 70% of the able-bodied men would take to the trails.

Their animals were Morvandelles, the famous russet oxen of the area. A pair would be yoked together for the whole of their working life. A frisky newcomer would be set in harness with an experienced animal. When the older one became too old for active service, his partner (they were all male) would induct another young ox.

On the road for up to six months, transporting wood and charcoal, maybe topped up with wine, salt, wooden clogs or metal pots, all would aim to be home for Saint Martin's day (11 November) or at the latest by 1 December, the day of Anost's great fair. The last team of oxen were released from their yoke as recently as 1984.

Anost's small excellently documented museum, La Maison des Galvachers (10FF), is well worth a visit. It's open daily except Tuesday in July and August and at weekends in June and September. Hours are from 2 to 5 pm.

From the bus shelter next to the train station in Autun, five buses a day link with TGV trains to/from Paris and Lyon at nearby Le Creusot station. A bus also leaves Autun for Beaune and Dijon at 5.10 pm daily, calling by Nolay (see the Skirting the Côte d'Or walk) at 5.55 pm.

If you're moving to or from the Avallon & Vézelay walk, two buses a day, usually requiring a change in Saulieu, link Autun and Avallon.

In Autun, cars are rented by Europcar (☎ 03 85 52 13 31), at Grande Rue Marchaux (closed Sunday and holidays).

THE WALK

From the mairie in Anost, head south on the D2 and then turn right onto the D88 after 400m. At the municaipal camping ground (see Places to Stay & Eat in Anost), go round the west side of its swimming pool and turn right onto a gravel path. Where it ends, turn left down a lane, then right after 50m onto a grassy footpath. Bear right where this merges with a 4WD track and pass beside the farm of Prébien. The track nowadays seems unexceptional, but you're following a slice of the old route of the *galvachers* (itinerant carters – see the boxed

Around Anost

For further information refer to IGN 1:25,000 sheet *Arleuf Haut-Folin (2824O)*

Les Miens

Rude de l'Enfer

(691m)

Les Ropbe

(668m)

GR13

Notre Dame de l'Aillant (625m)

Side Trip

Joux

Les Bigeards

D88

Montcimet

D88

(587m)

(554m)

Varin

START/ FINISH Anost

Les Places

Le Creux

GR13

Alternative Route

Les Gilets

D88

Prébien

To Arleuf

Bussy

(549m)

Long Bois

Dront

(428m)

D2

Sanceray

Le Mont

La Bussière

Les Gaudry

D88

GR13

La Maison de l'Étang

Corterin

Le Pommoy

River

To Autun

D2

To Autun

0   0.5   1 km
0   ¼   ½ mile
1:45,000
Contour Interval 25 metres

BURGUNDY

text), beaten down over the centuries by thousands of feet and hooves.

Just after crossing the western extremity of a small spruce wood, the path turns sharply west towards the hamlet of Bussy. Go left beside the first house, where you briefly pick up the red and white stripes of the GR13 and head south along a wide, level cart track. When the GR13 peels away south into the deep wood, stay with this track, following it as it curves and descends towards the hamlet of Sanceray.

Just beyond its first houses, turn right beside a white cross and fork left along a level track 100m later. Turn left at a T-junction to cross the tiny Corterin River and go right along the D2, which descends from Anost.

After 600m turn left beside La Maison de l'Étang, a solitary house with a glass veranda, cross a stream and ascend to the small village of Le Mont. Fork right beside a wooden *travail*, a traditional device found only in this part of Le Morvan and used to immobilise a pair of oxen while they were shod.

Just after a sign indicating the hamlet of Dront, turn left up a cart track to join the GRP Tour du Morvan then go left again at a four-way junction 15 minutes later.

At a five-way junction just before a wooden cross overshadowed by a magnificent lime tree, you have a choice. Going straight (west) with the red and yellow blazes of the GRP brings you back to Anost. Otherwise, to continue the route, take the first exit on the right, doubling back on yourself slightly as you head north-east and downhill. Go straight over a sealed road and descend to Le Creux.

Where the road turns sharp right beside another dilapidated travail, go straight to follow a sealed lane as far as **Montcimet**.

At the far (north-west) end of the village, turn left along the D88 at a four-way junction. Around five minutes later, go right, opposite a high yew hedge. Turn left beside the last house of the village to take a wide cart track, and take a footpath to go straight ahead at its first bend after barely 100m.

About 20 minutes later, cross a sealed road to plunge again into forest on a narrow

and none too evident path. (If you miss the turning, it's no great matter; simply turn right along the road, which the path rejoins just before the hamlet of Les Miens.)

Some 250m beyond the village cross, turn sharp left (south) to descend **La Ruée de l'Enfer** (Hell's Headlong Rush), a melo-dramatic name for a pleasant, shaded and not excessively steep descent.

Where the path splits at the end of the steepest stretch of the descent, take the minor branch to the right, signed 'Joux'. The trail bends left 30m later before veering right to cross a small stream and continue to Joux.

In Joux, turn left beside a wooden cross at the first T-junction. (A right turn and a 30-minute, 1.5km round trip detour will take you to the splendid viewpoint at **Notre Dame de l'Aillant**, crowned by a Virgin and child). For Anost, go straight over a wider road to join the GR13 and follow its red and white flashes back to the village.

Skirting the Côte d'Or

Duration	4½–5 hours
Distance	19km
Standard	easy-medium
Start/Finish	Nolay
Public Transport	yes

Summary Up to the plateau of Mont de Rème via Épertully. Down to the Cozanne Valley, gently up to Montagne des Trois Croix and return to Nolay via the GR7.

The walk meanders between the *départements* (departments) of Saône-et-Loire and Côte d'Or. In the former lies the small village of Charolles, which gave its name to the world-famous Charolais cattle, while the latter is fertile soil for Burgundy's greatest wines.

According to the season, green or beige dominates the cereal fields, the streaks and patches of ancient broadleaf woodland and vineyards producing Hautes Côtes de Beaune wine.

Bear in mind that, following negotiations with landlords, small changes may have been made to the trail – notably to the route over the plateau of Mont de Rème, where signing at the time of writing was nonexistent.

As a variation on the walk described here, by making a wide loop between Mont de Rème and Montagne des Trois Croix, you can take in the summit of Mont de Rome-Château (540m), distinguished by its tall telecommunications aerial. This adds an extra 6km to the day.

PLANNING

See Planning in the Avallon & Vézelay walk earlier in this chapter for information on the best times to walk.

Maps & Books

You could buy the IGN's 1:25,000 sheet No 2925ET, but you're better off investing in the *Sentier Jean-Marc Boivin* map. Also at 1:25,000, it highlights walking trails and is available in Nolay from the tourist office or Librairie Papeterie Boulay, 29 rue de la République.

The FFRP Topo-Guide *La Côte d'Or à Pied* (No D021) is rich in suggestions for one- and two-day walks. For more gentle walks, pick up *Circuits Pédestres Autour de Nolay* or *28 Circuits de Randonnée Pédestre dans le Pays Beaunois* from the Nolay tourist office. All are in French but have explicit, easy-to-follow maps.

NEAREST TOWN
Nolay

The friendly tourist office (☎ 03 80 21 80 73, ✉ ot@nolay.com), in place des Halles, is well used to walkers.

Places to Stay & Eat Of easy access for campers, *Camping Les Chaumes du Mont* (☎ 03 80 21 79 61), on the route 750m south-west of town, charges 23FF for a tent and 16FF per person.

On rue du Try, *Le Carnot* (☎ 03 80 21 70 73), which calls itself a motel, is a rather characterless place where rooms with bathroom cost 165FF. *Hôtel de la Halle* (☎/fax 03 80 21 76 37), opposite the tourist office, has much more soul. Doubles with bathroom cost between 220FF and 260FF. If no one's around,

ask at the Auberge du Centre (run by the hotel owners), in the same square.

The cheerful *Hôtel Restaurant du Parc*, opposite the Hôtel de Ville (town hall), has a range of *menus* from 90FF. *Hôtel Restaurant Sainte-Marie* (36 rue de la République) has *menus* for between 75FF and 130FF.

Getting There & Away A morning bus leaves Beaune for Nolay at 7.41 am. In the reverse direction, one leaves Nolay at 8 am. A second service leaves Beaune at 1.10 pm and Nolay at 1.15 pm. All go daily except Sunday. The third and last run departs at 6.05 pm daily from Beaune and 5.55 pm from Nolay.

The 1.10 pm from Beaune continues to Autun (for the Around Anost walk), leaving Nolay at 1.50 pm.

From Beaune there are six trains a day to Lyon and a couple of TGVs to Paris. For Paris, however, it's often quicker to go to Dijon (at least 14 trains a day) and pick up one of the frequent TGV services there.

For a taxi in Nolay, call Taxi Hermary (☎ 03 80 20 20 09).

THE WALK

From Nolay's Hôtel de Ville head south-west along ave de la Liberté. Turn right at the lake beside Camping Les Chaumes du Mont (see Places to Stay & Eat in Nolay) to take route d'Épertully. After 150m, go left at a sign, 'Épertully par la Riotte'. Shaded footpath opens out to give fine views south and west from the **Croix Carnot** cross, erected in 1648.

Go left just after the old village pump of Épertully and a stone cross, then left again at a T-junction. As the road bends beside a former wash house, go right along an overgrown footpath where saplings, brambles and nettles all make a grab for your clothing.

Around the half-hour mark, go through a stile where the now grassy track bends sharply to the right. The path channels you between a hedge and a barbed-wire fence.

Turn left beside the first house of Viécourt to pass under a swag of high-tension electricity cable. Five minutes later, go through a metal gate and head north-east (here the *Sentier Jean-Marc Boivin* map is incorrect) up the grass to meet a rickety wooden stile. On emerging from a copse of trees, cross over the first footpath that intersects the trail at right-angles, then turn right (south) along the second.

Now comes the only challenging navigation of the day – but since views are broad it doesn't matter much if you veer a little off the route. Leave the yellow flashes of the Sentier Jean-Marc Boivin trail as it begins to descend south-westwards. Strike out north-east across the plateau of **Mont de Rème** (514m). On its far side, look for a gap in a crumbling wall and head for a stile bearing

the first of the faded blue and white blazes, symbol of the Circuit des Trois Monts.

Once over the stile, it's an easy descent to the hamlet of Marcheseuil. Turn left beside a *fontaine* (fountain or spring) and cross the D1 onto a grass track. At the first house in Change (286m), it curves round the base of a vineyard then, becoming asphalt, drops to the Cozanne River.

Cross a bridge and ascend to the village church. Go straight ahead (north-west) at a junction then right a minute later to cross an iron bridge over an abandoned railway track. Sealed road becomes fine, cobbled

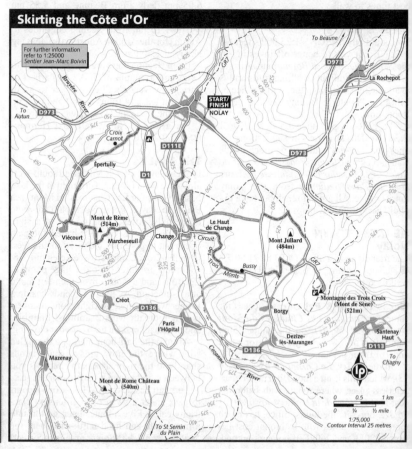

Skirting the Côte d'Or

For further information
refer to 1:25000
Sentier Jean-Marc Boivin

track beyond the scatter of houses of Le Haut de Change. This soon turns sharp right, giving great views westwards of the squares and patches of vineyard and the flat plateau of Mont de Rème above them.

At the imposing farm of Bussy, turn left then immediately right. At a T-junction do another left-right jinx to leave the sealed road and take a track which heads initially south-east. (This section is appallingly signed.) Go left at an intersection and turn right (south-east) five minutes later to double back on yourself. Where the trail meets a pair of bitumen roads, choose the right-hand one, signed 'Montagne des Trois Croix'.

At a bend, the route joins the clearly signed GR7. Turn right to follow it and, after five minutes, head straight uphill along an evident footpath to the summit of **Montagne des Trois Croix**, also called Mont de Sène (521m).

Topped by the three crosses which give it its popular name, the summit of the hill (mountain is far too flattering a term) affords great views: of the Jura Mountains to the south, the Saône Valley to the east and westwards to Le Morvan.

Retrace your steps to the bend where you met the GR7, which you follow all the way back to Nolay. Go straight ahead. Once parallel with Mont Jullard (484m), topped by a couple of spinneys, ignore the flashes of the GR variant which continue straight. Instead, fork left (north-west) onto a grassy track, also blazed with the familiar red and white stripes, which curves round the base of the hill.

Turn left onto a narrow sealed road then right after 125m to take a dusty track between cereal fields. At a junction about 20 minutes later, turn right onto another dirt track, with Nolay's church steeple soon visible straight ahead.

At a T-junction just beyond a lone tree, go left onto a grassy (in places overgrown) footpath and recross the long-abandoned railway a couple of minutes later. Follow this pleasant path as it edges its way round a small vineyard. Take the sealed road on the field's western side and, where it bends left, fork right (north) onto a dirt track.

Where the track joins the D111E, turn right. If your destination is the Camping Les Chaumes du Mont, take rue des Pierres left after 100m, then rue du Meix to rejoin ave de la Liberté. Otherwise, continue straight to return to the heart of Nolay.

Other Walks

Canal du Nivernais

A 107km circuit, from Clamecy to Vézelay, usually divided into five or six walking days. Mostly easy walking, following the canal, passing by its holding ponds and returning via a tranche of the GR13. For an overview, ask for the pamphlet *Sentier du Flottage du Bois* at any Nièvre tourist office. For details contact Randonièvre (☎ 03 86 36 92 98, fax 03 86 36 36 63). More modestly, the 12km canal-side walk from Chevroches to Clamecy will also give you a feel for the life the wood transporters led (see the boxed text 'Les Galvachers' earlier in this chapter).

Sentier Jean-Marc Boivin

This two-day, 45km trail, blazed (not always adequately) by yellow rectangles with a black border, starts and finishes in Nolay. It's highlighted on the map of the same name (see Maps & Books under Planning in the Skirting the Côte d'Or walk) and also features in the FFRP Topo-Guide *La Côte d'Or à Pied* (No D021). Stay overnight at *Camping des Sources (☎ 03 80 20 66 55)* in Santenay.

Auvergne & Massif Central

The Massif Central is the spine of central France, its vertebrae the plugs and cones of extinct volcanoes, known as *puys*. In the relatively rich volcanic soil of its plains and valleys, maize, tobacco and vines thrive. Its rumpled slopes are either clad in dense forest or sweet pasture where cattle and sheep graze, producing some of France's finest and most varied cheeses.

There are two theories for the origin of the massif: that it was created by the clash of European and African tectonic plates at the beginning of the tertiary era, a recoiling of the colossal force which thrust up the Alps; or that it was the consequence of a 'hot spot', a heat surge of indescribable intensity from the earth's mantle which broke through its crust.

The three regions of the massif, in ascending order of age, are the Monts Dômes, Monts Dore and Monts du Cantal. Formed during very different periods of volcanic activity, each has its own character. Much of the area falls within the Parc Naturel Régional des Volcans – at 395,000 hectares sq km, France's largest regional nature park.

You should always set out with plenty of water in the Massif Central. While almost every community at the base of the volcanic massifs boasts a flowing *fontaine* (fountain or spring; often the focal point of the village), rainfall percolates quickly through the thin soil and streams flow only briefly after heavy rainfall.

Also note that in certain fragile moorland areas, it's forbidden to leave the waymarked route. This restriction limits the amount of incidental damage caused by walkers to the vulnerable vegetation.

CLIMATE

Unlike elsewhere in France, the Massif Central receives the major part of its rainfall in summer, frequently in the form of late afternoon storms. While lower-altitude places such as Clermont Ferrand may experience summer temperatures in the high 30s, the mountains normally remain temperate.

INGRID RODDIS

Volcanic Puy de Sancy (1885m), highest mountain in the Monts Dore range

- The sudden vista of Puy de Sancy and its cirque from the Roc de Cuzeau's narrow plateau

- Crunching across volcanic cinders – tiny and light as Rice Krispies – on Puy de la Vache

- Windy picnics up high, sampling each day a different Auvergnat cheese

- The postcard-perfect view of the gentle valley between the pinnacles of Roche Tuilière and Roche Sanadoire

By contrast, the Cévennes and Grands Causses mountains at the southern limit of the Massif Central have a more Mediterranean and more constant climate. Winters are milder and summer – when midday temperatures can make walking uncomfortable – is the extreme season.

In the north of the range, it's wise to check the weather forecast before setting out each day; the mountains can be capricious in their sudden changes of mood.

INFORMATION
Maps

The region is covered at 1:200,000 by Michelin *Auvergne-Limousin* sheet No 239, and by IGN's 1:250,000 *Auvergne* sheet No 111. For maps covering individual walks, see Planning in the introduction to each walk.

Books

Trails in the region are described in detail by both English and French titles. Alan Castle's excellent *Walks in Volcano Country* (Cicerone Press) describes a 15-day traverse of the high crests following, in the main, the GR4 and the GR441, plus an eight-day circuit of the Velay region around Le Puy-en-Velay, based closely upon the GR40. Castle's equally evocative *The Robert Louis Stevenson Trail* in the Cévennes, is discussed in Other Walks at the end of the chapter.

For day walks, Maurice Turner in the Pathmaster Guides series adopts a different, equally thorough (although more stylistically plodding) approach in his *The Auvergne: 30 Circular Walks from Regional Centres*.

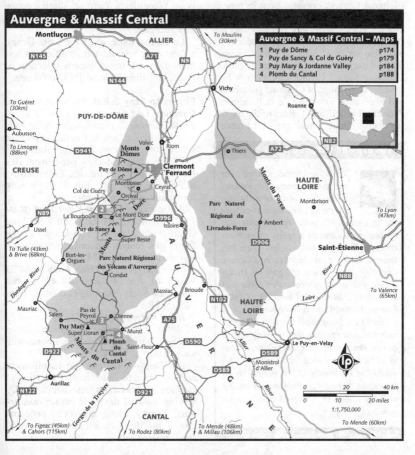

Auvergne & Massif Central

Auvergne & Massif Central – Maps	
1 Puy de Dôme	p174
2 Puy de Sancy & Col de Guéry	p179
3 Puy Mary & Jordanne Valley	p184
4 Plomb du Cantal	p188

If you read French, the best book for gaining an overview of walking possibilities is *Week-ends Massif Central*, one of Chamina's extensive range of great guidebooks to the region.

Lavishly illustrated, *Arbres et Fleurs de Nos Montagnes: Auvergne, Massif Central* by G Joberton & T Dalbavie is a detailed and guide to the region's trees and plants.

Information Sources

The superlative Chamina (☎ 04 73 92 81 44, @ info@chamina.com, www.chamina.com), 5 rue Pierre-le-Venérable, BP 436, 63012 Clermont Ferrand, operates from its base at the heart of the Massif Central. It researches and waymarks trails, vets and approves accommodation for walkers and produces its own fine series of walking guides, mainly (but not exclusively) of the Massif Central.

Espace Massif Central in Clermont Ferrand has a full range of Chamina guidebooks and Fédération Française de la Randonnée Pédestre (FFRP) Topo-Guides of the region. It's open without a break (rare for France!)

Auvergnat Cheeses

The volcanic geology, which gives rise to such spectacular walking, is also the source of a thriving cheese industry. From as early as the 1st century AD, fertile volcanic soils have enabled production of a range of excellent cheeses. Auvergne has no less than five cheeses classified as Appellation d'Origine Contrôlée (the highest category of French cheese, with an officially controlled declaration of origin): Salers, Saint-Nectaire, Cantal, Fourme d'Ambert and Bleu d'Auvergne.

The Bleu d'Auvergne is a rich blue cheese, with a creamier texture than its much-touted cousin, Rocquefort. Given appellation status in 1975, the story goes that it was first developed in the middle of last century by an Auvergnat farmer dubiously experimenting with the effects of rye bread mould on his milk curd. Enjoy!

from 9 am to 6.30 pm Monday to Friday (until 7 pm in summer), plus 9 am to noon and 2 to 6 pm on Saturday.

GATEWAY
Clermont Ferrand

The heart of Clermont Ferrand, largest town in the Massif Central, sits on a long-extinct volcano. With its large student population, it's alive and animated with plenty of interesting places to eat. It makes a good base for exploring the Monts Dômes and the northern part of the massif. The tourist office (☎ 04 73 98 65 00, fax 04 73 90 04 11) is on place de la Victoire, sharing space with Espace Massif Central (see Information Sources).

La Cartographie, at 23 rue Saint-Genès, a short walk from the tourist office in Clermont Ferrand, has a superb selection of maps, including all local 1:25,000 sheets.

Places to Stay & Eat Not far from town, *Camping Le Chanset* (☎/fax 04 73 61 30 73, @ Camping.Lechanset@wanadoo.fr) is on ave Jean Baptiste in Ceyrat, virtually a suburb of Clermont Ferrand. Rates are 20FF for a tent and 15FF per person. Bus No 4C stops right outside (see Getting to/from the Walk in the Puy de Dôme walk for details of the bus route).

At the modern *Corum Saint Jean* (☎ 04 73 31 57 00, fax 04 73 31 59 99, 17 rue Gaultier de Biauzat), also known as the Foyer des Jeunes Travailleurs, B&B accommodation costs 80FF.

The cheery, central *Hôtel Foch* (☎ 04 73 93 48 40, fax 04 73 35 47 41, 22 rue Maréchal Foch) has singles/doubles from 145/155FF.

Hôtel Ravel (☎ 04 73 91 51 33, fax 04 73 92 28 48, 8 rue de Maringues) is a reliable place close to the train station. Rooms with shower start at 150/170FF.

Rue Saint-Dominique and its offshoots north of place de Jaude have a selection of inexpensive *brasseries* (restaurants usually serving food all day) and *ethnic restaurants*. Nearby, along medieval, pedestrianised rue des Chaussetiers are several small *restaurants*.

Getting There & Away Clermont Ferrand's train station, on ave de l'Union Soviétique, is the most important rail junction in the Massif Central. There are more than five long-haul trains a day to Paris' Gare de Lyon and Lyon, plus two or three to Nîmes and a daily service to Toulouse (via Aurillac).

For other walking areas in the Massif Central, four or five trains a day serve La Bourboule (for the Monts Dore) and also Murat (for the Monts du Cantal).

Car rental possibilities include Ada (☎ 04 73 91 66 07), 79 ave de l'Union Soviétique; Europcar (☎ 04 73 92 70 26), rue Émile Loubet; and Budget (☎ 04 73 92 22 66), 106 ave du Brezet.

Monts Dômes

The Monts Dômes are the babies of the Massif Central, thrust up by the range's most recent volcanic activity during the late quaternary period. Their oldest rocks, formed about 100,000 years ago, are youngsters in geological terms, while the most recent eruptions were probably only 7000 years ago, well after the first humans had arrived in Auvergne.

Puy de Dôme

Duration	2 days
Distance	36km
Standard	medium
Start	Ceyrat Robinson car park
Finish	Royat
Nearest Town	Clermont Ferrand
Public Transport	yes

Summary Mainly woodland tracks with a more strenuous diversion over the Puy de la Vache and Puy de Lassolas. Up Puy de Dôme and level striding home above the Tiretaine Valley.

In addition to the Puy de Dôme, Clermont Ferrand's round-shouldered sentinel, the walk takes in a couple of minor and more tranquil puys. Below their bare upper flanks, it passes through typical mixed woodland and a selection of small Auvergnat villages.

You can shorten Day 1 if you bypass the Puy de la Vache and Puy de Lassolas and continue along the GR4, which runs along their base. However, if you do so on a clear day, you'll miss some spectacular scenery.

PLANNING
The walk is normally possible and pleasurable from April to November. However, cloud and rain can obscure the splendid summit views at any time of year.

Maps
The IGN 1:25,000 *Chaîne des Puys* sheet No 2531ET covers the whole walk.

GETTING TO/FROM THE WALK
To the Start
Ceyrat Robinson, at the beginning of the walk, is at the end of the bus No 4C line. Take a bus from the train station in ave de l'Union Soviétique, from place de Jaude or from the bus station on blvd Gergovia. There are at least two buses an hour throughout the day, all of which stop right outside Camping Le Chanset.

From the Finish
Bus No 14 for Clermont Ferrand passes by Royat's post office (at the end of the walk) two or three times an hour on weekdays, the last one leaving at 9.30 pm (9.48 pm on Saturday, 8.36 pm on Sunday).

If you want to leave or join the route in Laschamp, at the end of Day 1, phone Monsieur Montmory (☎ 04 73 62 11 96), who runs a taxi from Villars, about 10 minutes' drive from Laschamp.

THE WALK
Day 1: Ceyrat to Laschamp
4½–5 hours, 18km
From the Ceyrat Robinson car park and bus terminus follow a sign reading 'Gorges de l'Artière' and yellow waymarkers. After five minutes, turn left at a stone bridge to bear away from the stream up a series of zigzags leading to a long, flat stroll through woodland then open pasture.

At about the half-hour mark, go round a metal barrier and pass through the farm of

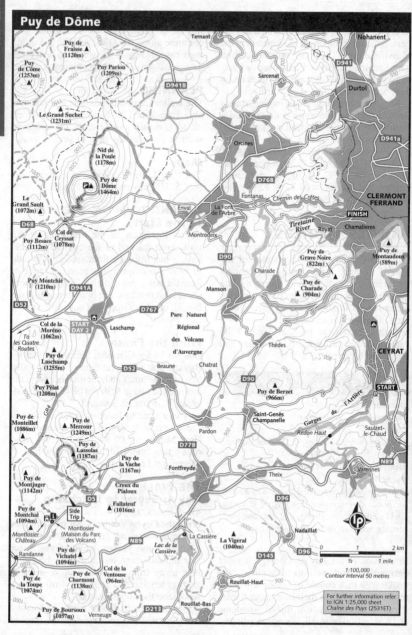

Puy de Dôme

Ternant

Nohanent

Puy de Fraisse (1120m)

Puy de Côme (1253m)

Puy Pariou (1209m)

D941

D941B

Sarcenat

Durtol

Le Grand Suchet (1231m)

Orcines

D941a

Nid de la Poule (1178m)

Le Grand Sault (1072m)

D768

Puy de Dôme (1464m)

Chemin des Crêtes

CLERMONT FERRAND

Fontanas

FINISH

Enval

La Font de l'Arbre

Tiretaine River

Royat

Chamalières

D68

Col de Ceyssat (1078m)

Montrodeix

Puy Besace (1112m)

D90

Puy de Grave Noire (822m)

Puy de Montaudoux (589m)

Charade

Puy Montchié (1210m)

D941A

Manson

Puy de Charade (904m)

D52

Parc Naturel

Col de la Moréno (1062m)

START DAY 2

Laschamp

D767

Régional

des Volcans

CEYRAT

To les Quatre Routes

Puy de Laschamp (1255m)

d'Auvergne

Thèdes

Puy Pélat (1208m)

D52

Beaune

Chatrat

D90

START

Puy de Monteillet (1086m)

Puy de Mercour (1249m)

Puy de Berzet (966m)

Gorges de l'Artière

Puy de Lassolas (1187m)

Pardon

Saint-Genès Champanelle

Redon Haut

Saulzet-le-Chaud

Puy de Montjuger (1142m)

Puy de la Vache (1167m)

D778

N89

Puy de Montchal (1094m)

Creux du Pialoux

Fontfreyde

Theix

D96

Varennes

D5

Side Trip

Fallateuf (1016m)

Nadaillat

Montlosier (Maison du Parc des Volcans)

Montlosier Château

Randanne

Puy de Vichatel (1094m)

N89

Lac de la Cassière

La Cassière

La Vigeral (1040m)

D145

D96

Puy de la Toupe (1074m)

Col de la Ventouse (964m)

Rouillat-Haut

Puy de Charmont (1138m)

Puy de Boursoux (1057m)

Verneuge

D213

Rouillat-Bas

0   1   2 km

0   ½   1 mile

1:100,000
Contour Interval 50 metres

For further information refer to IGN 1:25,000 sheet *Chaîne des Puys* (2531ET)

Redon Haut to join a 4WD track. At a four-way junction, leave the yellow blazes to go straight ahead up a cinder track and bear right after 200m where it joins a narrow road which winds down to the N89. Turn right to skirt the village of Theix. After 500m, go right onto the D52, signed 'Fontfreyde'.

Bear left onto the D778 and cross the D90 10 minutes later to enter the village of Fontfreyde, keeping straight where the main road turns sharp right. At place de la Fontaine (indeed with a flowing fountain), take rue de la Souche, which is the first exit on the right, and leave the village by a muddy cart track. You're now following intermittent green flashes, positioned very much in favour of walkers coming from the opposite direction.

Turn left beside a large barn and sustain a westerly bearing as tracks join from right and left. About 10 minutes beyond the open meadow of Creux du Pialoux, watch out for the sharp left turn onto a footpath which heads south-west to intersect with the GR30.

At a large parking area and a post bristling with signs, take the GR4 in the direction of Laschamp. Less than five minutes later, you have three choices: to continue along the main route, to go straight ahead along the GR4 (saving 2km and about an hour's walking) or to visit the impressive exhibition in the **Maison du Parc des Volcans** at Mont-losier. For Montlosier, continue straight for 400m then turn left (see the side trip at the end of this day's walk description).

To stay with the main route, go right to mount a flight of log steps and walk round the rim of a small side crater (the path differs from the recommended IGN 1:25,000 map). Where a fence bars progress, turn right and north to begin the steep, rugged ascent, assisted by more log steps.

The ancient volcanic vents, chimneys and cones of the range of puys to the south and south-west reveal themselves, plus Puy de Dôme, topped by the giant finger of its radio and TV mast. Once at the highest point of Puy de la Vache (1167m), follow a bare, cinder path round the lip of its crater. Drop north-west to a small pass. Here, where the main path heads away left, go straight

(north) up a much narrower footpath to **Puy de Lassolas** (1187m). The path threads along the rim of this second crater before descending steeply southwards to rejoin the GR trail beside a particularly fine oak, where you turn right.

At a T-junction around 10 minutes later, turn right and north-east, the direction this easy woodland track maintains through pine forest all the way to Laschamp (4km).

At route de la Moreno in **Laschamp**, turn right to reach the *gîte d'étape* (☎ 04 73 62 12 50), just before the church, where a bunk costs 60FF and a copious dinner 70FF.

Go left for *Espace Volcan* (☎ 04 73 62 26 00, fax 04 73 62 16 41, ✉ espace.volcan@wanadoo.fr), which has gîte-type accommodation for 60FF and singles/doubles for 185/240FF. The *menu* (fixed-price meal of two or more courses) at its restaurant costs 80FF. The other eating alternative in the village is *Bar-Restaurant GR*.

Side Trip: Maison du Parc des Volcans
45 minutes, 3.75km return
Turn left (south-west) and follow the marked trail to the Maison du Parc des Volcans information centre, with its visitor-friendly exhibition, 'Des Volcans et Des Hommes' (Of Volcanoes and Men). Open daily from May to October, it closes between 12.30 and 1.30 pm (2.30 pm in July and August). Admission is 18FF and each display has an accompanying English translation on hand-held boards. Retrace your steps to rejoin the main route.

Day 2: Laschamp to Royat
4½–5 hours, 18km
Turn left beyond the church onto Route de Clermont (D767A) to stay with the GR4. Bear left onto a dirt track at the second of two metal crosses to pass beside serried ranks of Scots pine, grown for the wood-cutter's chainsaw. Cross a main road and continue straight (north-west) beyond a metal barrier along a forest track bordered by more phalanxes of pine.

Col de Ceyssat (1078m), around 45 minutes out, is a popular parking spot for walkers attempting the Puy de Dôme. A couple of roadside *auberges* serve drinks, snacks and breakfasts. Cross the car park beside Auberge des Muletiers to join the footpath heading upwards and turn right after 100m onto Sentier des Muletiers (Mule Drivers' Trail).

A series of regular bends and zigzags leads you up the 368m of vertical ascent from the col to the Puy de Dôme summit. As you gain height, the views, particularly of the chain of volcanic summits extending south, become increasingly splendid, the dark stains of implanted spruce and Scots pine contrasting with the lighter green foliage of endemic oak.

At the **summit** (1464m), don't expect quiet contemplation of nature. There's a seething car park, a huge *bar-restaurant*, souvenir shop, picnic room and a small but informative display about volcanoes, captioned in both French and English. Above is a ruined Gallo-Roman Temple of Mercury, and most windy days – which means most days – you'll see hang-gliders and *parapentistes* wheeling overhead, enjoying a bird's-eye view of some 70 extinct volcanoes and the Clermont Ferrand conurbation to the east, the twin black spires of its Gothic cathedral prodding the air like a toasting fork.

Leave by the cinder track which runs beside the vehicle road. Less than 10 minutes from the top, go right beside a rocky spur and drop north-west along a grassy track. Shortly after the small side crater of **Nid de la Poule** (The Chicken's Nest; 1178m), turn right (north-east) beside a battered signpost, where the GR4 heads away westwards. From here on, yellow waymarkers, sparse in places, lead all the way to Royat. The path soon becomes a wide cinder track, descending through forest of beech, which gives way to hazel, ash and hawthorn. Fifteen minutes beyond the junction, keep straight ahead where the dominant path goes east.

Turn right onto chemin des Gouris then almost immediately left along a grassy path bordered by a fence, keeping to the west side of a field with a windsock, a favourite landing area for parapentistes. The path joins a wide, shaded track which heads south-east to the junction of the Puy de Dôme access road and the D68.

Turn left and take a cinder lane to the right after 150m. Go left at a T-junction to follow a sealed road through the hamlet of Enval (passing a pair of fountains) and join rue de l'Étang. Go right up a lane between two huge electricity pylons, then left along a cinder track as far as Montrodeix.

Turn right beside *Bar-Restaurant Le Petit Graillou* and continue south-east along a lane just beyond the village fountain. Cross a wider road and take chemin des Charrioux beside the old village wash house.

About 15 minutes beyond Montrodeix, join a sealed road and go left where it meets the D90. Just before the first houses of La Font de l'Arbre turn right onto the D768. Just before a bend bear right along a track. Where it divides, take the right fork, signed 'Royat par le chemin des Crêtes', to enjoy an easy, agreeable stroll along the western flank of the Tiretaine Valley as far as Royat, the pleasure marred only by the constant growl of traffic from far below.

On the outskirts of Royat, turn right where the track meets ave du Paradis, then left into rue Docteur A Petit, which ends in a cul de sac. Go down a flight of steps, cross the road and, once in the park which runs along the valley bottom, follow it downstream (east). Where it ends at a car park, take a steep path up the south flank to emerge in front of a post office and bus stop for Clermont Ferrand.

Monts Dore

The Monts Dore, wedged in the centre of the Massif Central, are also in the middle of the age band. Formed by successive eruptions between three million and 100,000 years ago, they are considerably older than the Monts Dômes to the north, yet defer to the more ancient Monts du Cantal.

PLANNING

The following planning information is relevant to both walks in this section.

When to Walk

In most years it's possible to walk the heights of the Monts Dore from mid-May,

Le Clos-Luce, Leonardo da Vinci's residence in Amboise, Loire Valley.

Sunflowers in the Loire Valley.

Climbing roses, Loire Valley.

Landscapes of the Loire Valley.

Château de Chenonceau on the Cher River, Loire Valley.

A welcoming restaurant in Vézelay, Burgundy.

Ewes' milk cheeses, Burgundy.

Street light, Burgundy.

Burgundy wines – French oak and solid traditions.

The brightly coloured tiled roofs of Burgundy.

Wine-tasting by candlelight.

The jagged peak of Puy de Sancy, highest of the now-extinct Auvergne volcanoes.

Stock-grazing is still an important way of life in the Massif Central.

Water fountain, Massif Central.

Accommodation comes with breath-taking views at Puy de Sancy, Auvergne.

Medieval Saint-Cirq Lapopie, a picture-postcard village on the Lot River, Périgord.

Château Les Milandes, Périgord.   Traditional house, Vézère Valley.   Saint-Cirq Lapopie.

The fortified village of Domme – one of the highlights of walking in the Dordogne Valley.

once most of the snows have melted, until late November. For the Col du Guéry, the walking season is extended into December.

Maps

The excellent 1998 Chamina/IGN 1:30,000 *Massif du Sancy* sheet (35FF) has clear contour markings. IGN 1:25,000 sheet No 2432ET (1997 edition) covers both walks but fails to represent the most recent diversions made to trails. Maison de la Presse, opposite the Établissement Thermal (Thermal Baths) in Le Mont Dore, sells both.

NEAREST TOWNS

Le Mont Dore and its neighbour, La Bourboule, 7km away, are both spa towns, small winter ski stations and popular summer resorts in the upper Dordogne Valley.

Le Mont Dore

The tourist office (☎ 04 73 65 20 21, fax 04 73 65 05 71) is in a square just off the ave de la Libération.

Places to Stay & Eat Roughly 1.5km north of town and beside the route, *Camping L'Esquiladou* (☎ 04 73 65 23 74) charges 15FF per tent and 18FF per person. At *Les Crouzets* (☎ 04 73 65 21 60), opposite the train station, prices are much the same.

Below Station du Mont Dore at the end of the walk, the *Chalet Grand Balcon* (☎ 04 73 65 03 53, fax 04 73 65 26 39) is an *auberge de jeunesse* charging 51FF for a bunk. At the Club Alpin Français (CAF) *Refuge du Sancy* (☎ 04 73 65 07 05), 300m along the road to Le Mont Dore, a bunk costs 64FF and half board is 164FF. Both are open all year and it's wise to reserve in advance. For details of the bus between Le Mont Dore and Station du Mont Dore, see Getting to/from the Walks later in this section.

In town, *Les Hautes Pierres* (☎ 04 73 65 25 65), on chemin des Vergnes, is a friendly, popular gîte where a bunk costs 65FF. Half board with excellent, copious food is 155FF and full board (including picnic lunch) is a reasonable 190FF.

The *Hôtel Terminus* (☎ 04 73 65 00 23), near the train station, has 26 rooms, with average, rather dowdy doubles from 105FF (170FF with bathroom).

There are over 25 restaurants to choose from. For a snack, try *Au Petit Paris (8 rue Jean Moulin)*.

Getting There & Away There are seven trains a day between Le Mont Dore and La Bourboule, the last leaving Le Mont Dore at 5.30 pm (4.55 pm on Saturday) and La Bourboule at 9.27 pm. Le Mont-Dore's train station is on ave Guyot Dessaigne and La Bourboule's on ave des États Unis. Four trains daily continue beyond La Bourboule to Clermont Ferrand.

For a taxi, call Allo Claude Taxi (☎ 04 73 65 01 05, 06 08 83 34 20).

La Bourboule

The tourist office (☎ 04 73 65 57 71, fax 04 73 65 50 21) is in the *mairie* (town hall), on place de la République.

Places to Stay & Eat La Bourboule has six camping grounds. The municipal *Camping Les Vernières* (☎ 04 73 81 10 20), on ave Maréchal de Lattre de Tassigny, charges 14FF for a tent and 17FF per person. *Camping Les Cascades* (☎ 04 73 81 02 72), smaller and more basic, is even cheaper.

There's an equally wide selection of budget hotels. *Les Princes* (☎ 04 73 81 04 34, fax 04 73 65 58 14) has rooms for between 100FF and 150FF. Those at *Hôtel des Anglais* (☎ 04 73 81 02 39) cost from 100FF to 160FF. Both places, plus a handful of others, are on ave Gueneau de Mussy.

Getting There & Away For trains, see Getting There & Away under Le Mont Dore. To call a taxi, ring Allo Bourboule Taxi (☎ 04 73 65 52 38).

GETTING TO/FROM THE WALKS

Between mid-May and the end of September a shuttle bus runs between Station du Mont Dore, Le Mont Dore and La Bourboule. The shuttle bus leaves Station du Mont Dore at 2.25, 3.30, 4.40 and 5.45 pm. The last return bus leaves La Bourboule at 6.15 pm and terminates in Le Mont Dore.

Puy de Sancy

Duration	5¾–6½ hours
Distance	19.5km
Standard	medium-hard
Start	Le Mont Dore
Finish	Station du Mont Dore
Nearest Towns	Le Mont Dore and La Bourboule
Public Transport	yes

Summary A 600m height gain to Puy de la Tache. A roller-coaster ridge walk via five more puys to Puy de Sancy, the highest in Auvergne. A descent to Station du Mont Dore via Val de Courre.

The difficulty of this walk resides in both its length and overall height gain. However, you'll find several possible cut-out points indicated within both the side-trip entries and the walk description. These enable you to shorten the route or make it a less rigorous two-day walk.

Routes around both Le Mont Dore and La Bourboule are superbly signed. A post at every major junction bristles with arrows indicating distance or time to the next landmark and each has a simplified overview map tacked to it. Occasionally the signed route is diverted in order to limit erosion and encourage new growth. Our walk map reflects such recent changes, but others may have been introduced since we took the trail.

THE WALK

From Le Mont Dore train station, turn left (east) along ave Guyot Dessaigne and left again onto ave de la Bourboule. At the far end of the hamlet of Le Queureuilh, take a right fork, signed 'Camping L'Esquiladou'.

Beyond *Camping L'Esquiladou* (see Places to Stay & Eat in Le Mont Dore), fork right along a narrow sealed road. Where it bends sharply left, go straight then veer left and pass the base of Cascade du Queureuilh waterfall. The route heads north-west then turns sharply north-east to run parallel with a burbling stream.

Go over the D983 and up a narrow sealed road. Where it veers left towards Ferme de

la Tache, keep straight ahead on a grassy track. Just beyond a stile, the route does a brief dogleg.

The path, broad and springy, enters a maturing conifer wood then emerges onto the D996, where it joins the GR4. After 250m of roadwork, curl right to bypass the bleak car park and trashed buildings at Col de la Croix Morand (1401m), reached after 1½ hours of walking. Here, the small *Bar Buron du Col* serves drinks and snacks. (If you have wheels, you might consider omitting these first 6.5km, leaving your vehicle here and enjoying an entire day of vast, open vistas.)

Turn right to follow the well-defined path which zigzags up the steep flank. The vegetation is now strictly moorland: heather, bilberry and, in late spring, a positive brass band of miniature alpine daffodils nodding their trumpets. The trajectory differs from the straight line, tracing a long-abandoned ski lift, marked on the recommended IGN 1:25,000 map. As you ascend, Lac de Guéry comes into view, watched over by Roche Tuilière just beyond it. Also in view is the town of La Bourboule, well to its west, dominated by the escarpment of Puy Gros (see the Col de Guéry walk later in this chapter for details on all these features).

A wooden post marks the summit of **Puy de la Tache** (1629m). Follow a zigzagging course west of the crest (this too differs from the tracing on either of the reference maps) to reach Puy de Monne (1692m). Shortly beyond, the splendid Lac Chambon reveals itself way over to the east.

The roller-coaster route lands you on top of Puy de Barbier (1702m), from where it's an easy ascent to **Puy de l'Angle** (1738m), topped by a wind gauge.

The path angles away along the ridge to a white cross then descends steeply southwest to the small unnamed col at the foot of Puy de Mereilh. It then describes a short dogleg (not marked on either recommended reference map) before meeting the D36 near Col de la Croix Saint-Robert (1451m).

From here, an alternative route along the signed descent to Le Mont Dore via La Grande Cascade falls (see Alternative Route A at the end of this walk description) is both

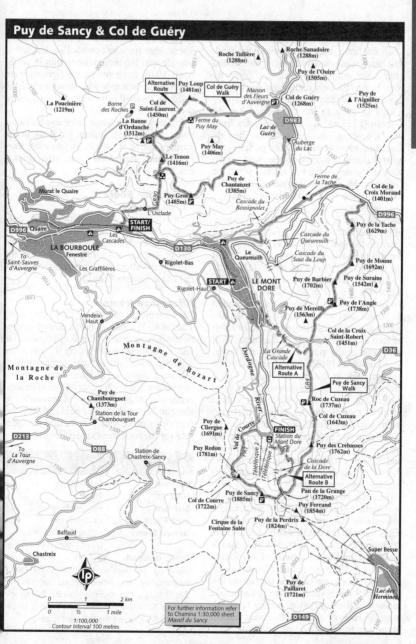

Puy de Sancy & Col de Guéry

Roche Tuilière (1288m)

Roche Sanadoire (1288m)

Puy de l'Ouire (1505m)

Alternative Route

Puy Loup (1481m)

Col de Guéry Walk

Maison des Fleurs d'Auvergne

Col de Guéry (1268m)

Puy de l'Aiguiller (1525m)

La Poucinière (1219m)

Borne des Roches

Col de Saint-Laurent (1450m)

Ferme du Puy May

Lac de Guéry

D983

La Banne d'Ordanche (1512m)

Le Tenon (1416m)

Puy May (1406m)

Auberge du Lac

GR30

Puy de Chantauzet (1385m)

Ferme de la Tache

Col de la Croix Morand (1401m)

Puy Gros (1485m)

Cascade du Rossignolet

D996

Murat le Quaire

L'Usclade

D996

Quaire

START/ FINISH

Les Cascades

Puy de la Tache (1629m)

D130

Le Queureuilh

Cascade du Queureuilh

LA BOURBOULE

Fenestre

Les Graffilières

Rigolet-Bas

Cascade du Saut du Loup

Puy de Monne (1692m)

START

LE MONT DORE

Puy de Barbier (1702m)

Puy de Surains (1542m)

Rigolet-Haut

Puy de l'Angle (1738m)

Vendeix-Haut

Puy de Mereilh (1563m)

Col de la Croix Saint-Robert (1451m)

Montagne de Bozart

Dordogne

D36

Montagne de la Roche

La Grande Cascade

Alternative Route A

Puy de Sancy Walk

Puy de Chambourguet (1373m)

Station de la Tour Chambourguet

CR4

Roc de Cuzeau (1737m)

Col de Cuzeau (1643m)

D213

To La Tour d'Auvergne

D88

Station de Chastreix-Sancy

Puy de Cliergue (1691m)

Val de Courre

FPT

FINISH

Station du Mont Dore

Puy des Crebasses (1762m)

Puy Redon (1781m)

Téléférique 2

Téléférique 1

Cascade de la Dore

Alternative Route B

Col de Courre (1722m)

Puy de Sancy (1885m)

Pan de la Grange (1720m)

Baffaud

Puy Ferrand (1854m)

Cirque de la Fontaine Salée

Puy de la Perdrix (1824m)

Super Besse

Chastreix

N

0   1   2 km

0   ½   1 mile

1:100,000
Contour Interval 100 metres

Puy de Paillaret (1721m)

Lac des Hermines

D149

For further information refer to Chamina 1:30,000 sheet Massif du Sancy

AUVERGNE & MASSIF CENTRAL

pleasant in itself and an opportunity to spread the walk over two days.

To continue, take the short sealed track that heads south-east and bear right at a bend after 300m onto a narrow, grassy footpath. Now begins the only really hard work of the day as the path climbs steeply with scarcely a kink or twist to the flat-topped **Roc de Cuzeau** (1737m). Around 40 minutes from the D36, drag yourself onto the Roc de Cuzeau's narrow plateau for perhaps the most stunning and certainly the most sudden view of the day as the Puy de Sancy and the cirque below, snow still streaking its gullies until well into June, spread before you.

Descend to the Col de Cuzeau. From here, don't take the GR trail which hugs the edge of the precipice. Instead, opt for the safer and more trodden path that follows the contour of the hill to rise to the top of twin ski lifts at the summit of Puy des Crebasses (1762m).

Another half-hour of undemanding walking brings you to Pan de la Grange (1720m). From here a wide track descends to Station du Mont Dore (see Alternative Route B at the end of this walk description). A farther 750m of hard ascent brings you to the magnificent panorama at the summit of **Puy de Sancy**, also known as Pic de Sancy, at 1885m the highest peak in the Massif Central. You'll probably be in the company of crowds of huffing, puffing visitors who have walked 500m up the 850 wooden steps from the top of the *téléférique* (cable car or funicular), by which you can descend, cutting out the last hour of the walk. It operates between 9 am and 5.20 pm (closed, in true French style, from 12.30 to 1.30 pm for lunch) and costs 31/38FF one way/return.

Take the steps, in summer as crowded as any Metro escalator. Where they veer right towards the téléférique, go straight to follow signs for both the GR30 and PR1. Less than 10 minutes later, stay with the GR as the PR makes a detour to the summit of Puy Redon then rejoins the main path at Col de Courre (1722m). Leave the GR30 at the pass to follow the PR down Val de Courre, a former ski run where the vegetation is now being allowed to recover. An initially rocky descent gives way to meadow. Just before the scat-

ter of buildings of Station du Mont Dore, pause at a ruined *buron* . It's far from being just another summer cowherd's cabin, left to subside into the mountain: within it, on 27 April 1944, three resistance fighters were shot by the Gestapo, who then torched the building; its shell is preserved in their memory.

For buses to Le Mont Dore and La Bourboule, see Getting to/from the Walk in the introduction to this walk. As you wait, *Bar-Restaurant Azur Sancy* can offer drinks, snacks or a full meal.

Alternative Route A
45 minutes, 3km
From Col de la Croix Saint-Robert, bear away south-west along the PR12, waymarked with green stripes. With a net height loss of 450m, it's a pleasant descent to the Dordogne Valley via the impressive waterfall of La Grande Cascade.

Alternative Route B
35–45 minutes, 3km
The GR4E leads down past a craggy wilderness where several winter ski lifts meet. Go under a tunnel beneath a drag lift and down a rocky track. Resist the temptation to short-cut down a ski-season red run; the vegetation needs every second of convalescence it can get before next season's onslaught. The track may be bald and ugly, but fine views of the valley more than compensate for the roughness underfoot.

Col de Guéry

Duration	5–5½ hours
Distance	19km
Standard	easy-medium
Start/Finish	La Bourboule
Nearest Towns	La Bourboule and Le Mont Dore
Public Transport	yes

Summary Up through woodland to high pasture and Puy Gros. Around Lac de Guéry to the Col de Guéry. Flat meadow walking and an ascent of La Banne d'Ordanche. Return to La Bourboule retracing the outward route.

It's a day of variety; meadow and woodland, a pair of peaks with fine panoramas, a lake, and the Col de Guéry, from where more film must have been shot than anywhere else in France, apart from the Eiffel Tower.

THE WALK

Set out from the roadside parking area of Les Cascades, on the D130, 1.25km east of *Camping Municipal Les Vernières* and even handier for *Camping Les Cascades* (for details see Nearest Towns in the Puy de Sancy walk). Cross the Dordogne River, here no more than a beck. Don't be misled by the sign 'Lac de Guéry 9km', which points upstream. Instead, follow the GR30 blazes north, over both the D996 and the railway line. After 50m, turn sharp right onto a footpath. Once in open meadow, turn left (north-east) at a T-junction with a broad cart track then right to pass through the sparse houses of the hamlet of L'Usclade, with its pair of flowing water troughs.

Continue due east as the trail, now running between fields bright with wild flowers and a small brook, begins to steepen, elbowing north to enter the welcome shade of a beech wood, springy underfoot from the thick carpet of last year's leaves.

Emerging from the wood, bear right (north-east) onto an ancient track bordered by crumbling walls. Turn right where it joins a wider track beside a flowing trough just west of the remnants of an abandoned buron, on which a couple of tall trees now perch.

Around 250m from the turning, go right onto a grassy footpath which climbs the north-west spur of **Puy Gros** (1485m), from where it's easy, scenic walking along a cliff edge. Below is La Bourboule and the rich valley of the upper Dordogne. To the north-west is the wedge-shaped summit of La Banne d'Ordanche, a goal for later in the day. And then, as you round a bend, Le Mont Dore reveals itself to complete the picture.

After a brief, steep descent to a junction, continue straight ahead to a point where three fences meet. Climb over a stile to follow the path as it winds around the shoulder of Puy de Chantauzet.

Around 30 minutes later, clamber over another stile as the trail, hemmed in between a pair of fences, descends beside a conifer plantation. Turn left at a T-junction along a broad logging track. This leads to shore of Lac de Guéry (1247m), where a right turn soon brings you to the *Auberge du Lac* (*menus* from 95FF).

From here, there's no alternative to a 1.25km slog up the D983 since no footpath runs along the lake's western bank. The traffic's an intrusion but there's more than adequate compensation at **Col de Guéry** (1268m), with its magnificent and much photographed picture-postcard vista northwards of the twin volcanic pinnacles of Roche Tuilière and Roche Sanadoire and the gentle valley between.

At the pass, build in time to visit **Maison des Fleurs d'Auvergne** (18FF), open weekends only from 1 May to mid-June and between 10 am and 7 pm daily from then to mid-September. Although information is only in French, the display is highly visual and in its *jardin écologique* (ecology garden) are many examples of flowers and trees encountered on the walk.

To return to La Bourboule, take the sealed lane heading south-west and, at a three-pronged fork after less than five minutes, choose the left-hand cinder track. This runs through rolling, open pasture, bobbing in season with wild daffodils, to the derelict house and outbuildings of **Ferme du Puy May** (1390m). (See the side trip at the end of this walk description for an alternative route which bypasses the farm and takes in an extra peak.) The track now becomes grassy lane, leading after 20 minutes to Col de Saint-Laurent (1450m), a junction fussy with signs for walkers, cyclists, horse riders, even model aeroplane enthusiasts.

For La Banne d'Ordanche, a worthwhile 20- to 30-minute round trip, turn left. There's an easier option to the tough path which heads straight up the hill's steep eastern slope; follow the narrow trail that curls more gently around to the western flank to meet a footpath coming up from the car park at Borne des Roches. Climb a series of wooden steps to the **summit** (1512m) with its superb views of the Chaîne des Puys, blocking the horizon to the north-east like a rippling sea monster, its central, largest hump topped by the TV mast of Puy de Dôme.

On the way down, turn right to take a footpath 200m before Col de Saint-Laurent. This follows a fence which drops south-east then tacks south-west. Join the broad track near the water trough and ruined buron passed on the outward leg and retrace the

route back to Les Cascades, 40 to 50 minutes' walk away.

Side Trip: Puy Loup
30 to 40 minutes, 2km
A detour from the farm track which passes the ruins of Ferme du Puy May takes in the summit of Puy Loup (1406m), offering great views to the north, then rejoins the main route at Col de Saint-Laurent.

Walking a Little History

In Spain's Pamplona they run before the bulls. But one Sunday in late May, Ingrid, I and around 100 others walked behind the cows.

When the last snows melt on the Monts du Cézallier and the new season's grass starts to shoot, it's traditionally time for L'Estive, the driving of the cattle up to their summer pastures. Until WWII, herds converged upon Allanche from miles around, many having been on the road for days, for the last thrust to the hilltops. Nowadays, they're mainly transported by truck or tractor. But not yet quite all. Every last weekend in May a small herd is driven through the village of Allanche towards the hills, followed by a slipstream of interested walkers.

To a trumpet fanfare and an idiosyncratic rendering of *Roll out the Barrel* from the village band, we set out. The air is filled with the base lowing of the cows, brindle and big horned, the hollow clonk of their bells and the stern call of the cowherds (Oh EH, weh, weh, weh, WEH!) when a beast tries to break loose.

As both cows and people start to pant in the mid-morning heat, the cortege pauses at the hamlet of Pradier to take on water. As is only proper, it being their day, the cattle are the first to sup. The bull, lording it over his harem, pulls rank, drinking deep before his favourite concubines shove their way to the front, while the young heifers on their first Estive hold back in deference to their elders. We humans have the option, denied to bovines, of robust Auvergnat red wine to sluice down the thick, sugary wedges of cake baked by the women of the village on sale for a bargain 5FF.

The band, having lingered too long over morning coffee, fortified with high octane local moonshine, finally catches up. The entertainment resumes as they compensate in volume and enthusiasm for the occasional bum note. The snare drum player thumps his instrument so hard that its strap breaks and his instrument rolls back down the road towards Allanche. The saxophone players, septuagenarians to a man, have trouble sustaining the beat. But what the hell? Everyone's chatting, no one's listening and the cheery rhythms are just what we walkers need to lift ourselves.

A couple of hours later the cows are released beside a ruined *buron* (summer cabin) and fan out over the flanks of the Cézallier. For us too, the feeding begins; shots of Salers, a local liqueur distilled from the roots of the yellow gentian flower, milky pastis and yet more red wine, coarse country sausage, slices of ham thick as a cow's tongue and chunky pâté are passed around to the band's increasingly dissonant rhythms.

Then, as the sound of the band is whipped away by the sharpening breeze, walkers, satiated and with navigating skills none too sharp after such agreeable excess, begin to drift down the hill, heading contentedly back to Allanche.

To join in next year's fun, ring Allanche's tourist office on ☎ 04 71 20 48 43.

Miles Roddis

Monts du Cantal

The 2700 sq km Cantal caldera represents the largest volcanic massif by area in Europe. Peak volcanic activity occurred between nine and seven million years ago, when the whole central area of a giant volcano collapsed in on itself. As its magma chamber emptied, it created the huge caldera. Its rim, still discernible in many places today, includes the Col de Cabre, Puy Mary, Puy Chavaroche and Plomb du Cantal, all of which feature in the walks in this section.

PLANNING
Both walks in this section are possible from the second half of June to early November. Since accommodation is so limited in the Jordanne Valley, it's essential to reserve in July and August.

Maps
The route is covered on the IGN 1:25,000 *Monts du Cantal* sheet No 2435OT, available from Maison de la Presse, on rue Saint-Martin in Murat.

NEAREST TOWN
Murat
The friendly tourist office (☎ 04 71 20 09 47, fax 04 71 20 21 94) is at 2 rue Faubourg Notre Dame, near the mairie.

Places to Stay & Eat Next to Alagnon River, *Camping Municipal Stalapos* (☎ 04 71 20 01 83), on rue du Stade, is only 750m south from the train station. It charges 10FF for a tent and the same per person.

L'Auberge de Maître Paul (☎ 04 71 20 14 66, fax 04 71 20 22 20), in place du Panol, has singles (180FF), doubles (200FF) and triples (250FF). The cheery staff serve *menus* at 85FF and 95FF and pizzas (also available as take aways) for 40FF to 45FF.

Hôtel Les Messageries-Bredons (☎ 04 71 20 04 04, fax 04 71 20 02 81, 18 ave du Dr Mallet) has rooms for 260FF to 280FF.

Getting There & Away There are at least four trains a day between Clermont Ferrand

(see the Gateway section earlier in this chapter) to the north and Aurillac to the south-west.

For a taxi in Murat, call ☎ 04 71 20 04 08 or 04 71 20 03 75.

Puy Mary & Jordanne Valley

Duration	2 days
Distance	31.5km
Standard	medium
Start/Finish	Le Lioran
Nearest Town	Murat
Public Transport	yes

Summary Up to Col de Rombière. Magnificent ridge-walking to Puy Mary, Puy Chavaroche and down to Mandailles. From Col de Pertus into forest, emerging to skirt Puy Griou. Down the northern flank of the upper Alagnon Valley.

The walk takes in two of the massif's finest peaks with the opportunity of side trips to bag another pair. There are also superb extended views, particularly on Day 1, from the intervening ridges. It's possible to leave the walk at Mandailles, at the end of Day 1 (for public transport details, see Getting to/from the Walk).

GETTING TO/FROM THE WALK
The one-way train fare between Murat and Le Lioran is 14FF (15 minutes). A convenient train leaves Murat at 8.33 am daily in July and August, and from Monday to Saturday the rest of the year (the first Sunday train between September and June is at 11.25 am). To return, take the 4.49 pm (daily) or 6.31 pm (not Saturday) train from Le Lioran.

Should you want to leave the route at Mandailles, there's at least one bus a day (two in July and August) to/from Aurillac (25km). For a local taxi, call ☎ 04 71 47 94 51.

THE WALK
Day 1: Le Lioran to Mandailles
4¾–5¼ hours, 17km
From Le Lioran train station, turn left onto the busy N122 then right after 300m onto the

D67, signed 'Super Lioran'. Fork right after 600m beside a large parking area. Go right 75m beyond the Font d'Alagnon car park – with plenty of space for those with their own transport – to take the track signed (perhaps confusingly) 'Font d'Alagnon'. Veer sharp left after 20m to follow a path southwards up a firebreak. A couple of minutes later, turn right onto a broader trail, which crosses a sealed road at a hairpin bend.

Shortly after merging with a wider track coming in from the right, this trail reaches Col de Font de Cère (1289m). Turn right (north-west) beside *Auberge le Buron* to join the GR4 and a wide dirt track. Stay with the track, ignoring a brief and unnecessary GR divergence to the right.

Just before Col de Rombière (1530m), curl round the top of a chair lift to take a more northerly bearing which leads you up to an anonymous pass (wrongly labelled 'Col de Rombière' on the recommended IGN 1:25,000 map). The narrow path, where

patches of snow are possible until early June, gives great views eastwards over the wooded bowl of the Alagnon Valley.

Once over an intervening hillock, the wider, more open basin of the upper Jordanne Valley suddenly reveals itself to the west, with a thin thread of path unravelling itself beneath the rim.

Beyond **Col de Cabre** (1528m), from where there's a fine plunging view northeastwards, the path continues its level course, running beneath the crags of Puy de Peyre Arse. About 25 minutes later, there's a second surprise vista as the valley to the north stretches before you with the village of Le Claux snug at its heart and, on the horizon, Puy de Sancy.

A short, steep descent to the **Brèche de Roland** and a clamber to regain height bring hands and feet into play. Around 10 minutes later, just before the final steep push to the summit of Puy Mary, never dangerous but fairly lung-bursting, there are two alterna-

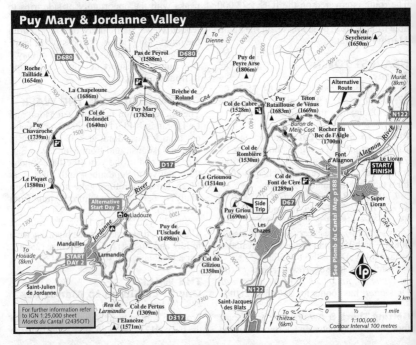

tive route options which bypass the steep climb: a diversion around the puy's eastern flank to the D680, or the less evident but quite manageable westbound path which descends to the D17, thus bypassing Pas de Peyrol and shortening the route by 1.5km.

Once you've heaved your way to the top of **Puy Mary** (1783m), you'll probably be sharing the orientation table with those who have taken the easier way up – a flight of hideous concrete steps from the car park at Pas de Peyrol. Surely there must be some more sensitive way of protecting the thin soil from human traffic.

Pas de Peyrol at 1588m is the highest road pass in the Massif Central. Here, you can rehydrate with a drink on the terrace of **Chalet du Puy Mary**. Turn left (south) to leave the milling crowds and savour the relatively quiet D17 as it snakes round the western flank of Puy Mary. Around 20 minutes from the Pas de Peyrol, turn off the road at a hairpin bend and strike out westwards up a grassy track. After 75m, bear left at a sign reading 'Puy Chavaroche'.

At Col de Redondet (1640m), bear left (south-west), heading for Puy Chavaroche, unmistakable with its pair of tall rounded cones protruding like rabbits' ears from its flat top. To your right is the contrasting craggy, irregular summit of La Chapeloune (1686m). Twenty to 30 minutes of easy ascent brings you to the summit of **Puy Chavaroche** (1739m), with a stone windbreak at the base of twin cairns.

Continue south-west, following the intermittent flashes of the GR400. In season, the moor is a riot of wild flowers breaking free from the clutches of winter snow – alpine daffodil, narcissus, small violet pansies, buttercups and white heather.

After 20 minutes, fork left (south-east) at the pass of Le Piquet, leaving the GR400 to pick up green blazes and descend towards the Jordanne Valley. After dropping steeply the path runs along the western fringe of a beech wood before diving into its shade. On emerging, with Mandailles now clearly in sight, it runs down a spur where patches of eye-high broom alternate with lush grass; at times the trail is scarcely discernible.

Descend a rocky, unkempt path where dog roses tear and nettles lie in wait. Take a sealed lane beside a welcome fountain to drop to the D17 and Mandailles village in the valley bottom. In **Mandailles**, overnighting opportunities are excellent but limited, so it's wise to reserve in advance. The village has a small *grocery*.

Doubles with bathroom at the homely *Auberge du Bout du Monde* (☎ 04 71 47 92 47, fax 04 71 47 95 95) are 200FF. Well used to walkers, it does a great-value half board (215FF) with copious meals. Doubles at *Hôtel aux Genêts d'Or* (☎ 04 71 47 96 45, fax 04 71 47 93 65), which also does meals, are between 180FF and 230FF.

Camping Le Luc (☎ 04 71 47 90 39 in season, 04 71 47 94 71 all year), up the valley (north-east) along the GR400 or D17, is open in July and August. A little farther on is *Gîte d'Étape de Liadouze* (☎/fax 04 71 47 93 81), also highly recommended, where a bunk costs 50FF. It has self-cooking facilities and does a bargain packed lunch for 35FF. (See the walk map for an alternative way of beginning Day 2, avoiding a return down the valley to Mandailles.)

Day 2: Mandailles to Le Lioran
4–4½ hours, 14.5km

Leave Mandailles by crossing the road bridge to the Jordanne River's true left bank. After 50m, turn left (north-east) up a lane then, after a farther 50m, right between two gateposts to take a narrow footpath, signed 'Col de Pertus'.

At the hamlet of Larmandie, tack left onto a cobbled lane. Beside a gushing waterpipe and troughs, turn briefly right then left (initially south) at another sign for Col de Pertus. The path, in its time a finely cobbled track but now much deteriorated, climbs steadily with meadows to the right and mixed wood to the left. After rain or snowmelt, a positive stream dances down towards you, but it's nothing that a stout pair of boots can't repel.

About 15 minutes from Mandailles, the path merges with a wide cart track which turns east to cross the Reu de Larmandie stream and wriggle its way up the valley's eastern flank. Just beyond a buron with a red-tiled roof, bear away northwards, ignoring a wider track on the right. The path expands into a wide track which you soon leave to turn right up a narrow rocky gulley. Pass to the right of a buron with a corrugated iron roof to meet, at a T-junction one minute later, the GR400 alternative route coming up from Liadouze and the Jordanne Valley.

Turn right to follow this broad grassy track as far as the D317 and an information panel proclaiming 'Col de Pertus'. Not so, however, since the pass is still a good 15 minutes' walk away up the road.

The Wolf Trap

Wolves have long ago been hunted and hounded from the Massif Central. But until the end of the 19th century, villagers of the upland villages of Cantal would dig wolf traps, deep pits camouflaged with twigs and leaves and baited with carrion. If a wolf which fell into the trap was not killed, it might be muzzled and paraded through the streets of Aurillac, the nearest town, to show it off and, no doubt, pick up a few centimes.

A 10- to 15-minute round trip from Col de Pertus, following the sign 'Piége au Loup' brings you to one such pit, recently cleaned out and restored.

From **Col de Pertus** (1309m) head north-east along a path signed 'Col du Gliziou' and 'Le Griou'. The route alternates between deep shaded beech wood (look out for violets peeking through the leaf mould) and open meadow, bright with broom and wild flowers.

About 30 minutes from the col, continue straight ahead (north-north-east), passing to the right of a solitary service tree as the GR describes a short and needless loop up into the woods.

Ten minutes later, again keep straight as the main path descends to meet a wider 4WD track coming up from the valley. Col du Gliziou (1350m), without a halfway decent view in any direction, is one of the Massif Central's less dramatic passes. From it, continue north-east along a graded forest

track signed 'Puy du Griou par Rocher Vert' (via Rocher Vert) to remain with the GR400 variant. At a second fork after three minutes, bear left, then immediately right and uphill, again heading north-east onto what becomes narrow footpath.

At a small col (1400m) where the path joins an alternative route coming up from Col du Gliziou, veer slightly right along a forest track, then after 25m, right again and steeply upwards.

The trail meets another (ambiguously signed 'St Jacques' in both directions) at a hairpin bend. Choose the left-hand option. The path now levels out, even dipping a little here and there, before emerging from forest onto open ground at a pass slung between Le Griounou to the north-west and Puy Griou, its much bigger sibling. Turn right to curve round the western slopes of the latter as the trail ascends parallel to a barbed-wire fence.

At a T-junction with a broad, well-trodden dirt path, you can make a short but taxing diversion to bag Puy Griou (see the side trip at the end of this walk description).

To continue, go left, staying with the GR. About 15 minutes from the junction, pass through a spring gate at Col de Rombière and turn left, briefly retreading the Day 1 route. A little over five minutes later, go right (north-east) to leave the main trail where a sign indicates 'Puy Mary par Col de Cabre' for walkers going straight ahead. After 50m, follow a second sign, indicating 'Bec de l'Aigle'. Three minutes later, fork right, following the familiar red-and-white GR waymarkers, plus others in yellow and yet more in a particularly sickly shade of mauve. Here, if you want to stay up high and extend what is a relatively short walking day by an additional hour, take the alternative route to Rocher du Bec de l'Aigle, outlined at the end of this walk description.

The trail drops steeply to the Buron de Meig-Cost (1450m) with its roof of grey slate and a welcome waterpipe and trough. Follow the zigzagging track which leads generally south-eastwards from the cabin into yet more beech wood, interspersed with Scots pine and ash, fighting the conifers for its share of the light.

At a T-junction with a dirt road, turn right. Around 20 minutes later, go left at a sealed road to retrace your first steps of Day 1 and return to Le Lioran. Le Lioran and Super Lioran are bleak places, in or out of season. There's a small *supermarket*, open only in the skiing and summer high seasons. *Bar-Restaurant La Chazotte* does snacks and pizzas. *Hôtel Auberge du Tunnel* (☎ 04 71 49 50 02) has rooms for between 130FF and 220FF, and also serves meals.

Alternative Route
1½–2 hours, 8km
At the junction before Buron de Meig-Cost, continue straight, staying with the GR400 to pass by Puy Bataillouse, Le Téton de Venus (Venus' Breast) and the **Rocher du Bec de l'Aigle** (The Eagle's Beak).

Take a pronounced path to the right at the 1493m spot height. Bend sharply southwest beside a ruined buron onto a track and descend to the N122 and an anticlimactic last kilometre along the busy highway.

Side Trip: Puy Griou
40–50 minutes, 1.25km return
To reach the summit of Puy Griou (1690m), it's a strenuous ascent over basalt, requiring a little clambering here and there, along an unsigned trail. The effort is well worthwhile – both because you've had its rounded peak in your sights for so long and because the views surpass those from either Puy Chavaroche or Puy Mary. Retrace your route back to the main trail.

Plomb du Cantal

Duration	4¼–5 hours
Distance	15km
Standard	medium
Start/Finish	Super Lioran
Nearest Town	Murat
Public Transport	yes

Summary A steep ascent to the ridge just below Plomb du Cantal's summit. A more gentle descent to Col de Prat de Bouc. Back over, varying the route and enjoying the superb views from the peak.

From Plomb du Cantal (1855m), a giant hunk of basalt and the highest peak in the Cantal range, there's a magnificent panorama in every direction. If you want to retain the views longer, stay up high to undertake part or all of the out-and-back Puy Gros side trip outlined at the end of this walk description.

You can bisect this circular route by catching the cable car between Super Lioran and its upper station, 50m below the summit of Plomb du Cantal. Operating from early June to early September, it costs 32FF one way (42FF return).

GETTING TO/FROM THE WALK
See this heading in the Puy Mary and Jordanne Valley walk for information on transport as far as Le Lioran. From Le Lioran train station, turn left onto the busy N122 then right after 300m to take the minor D67 as far as Super Lioran (2km).

THE WALK
From the rear of the lower téléférique station – beside which is a small tourist office (☎ 04 71 49 50 08, fax 04 71 49 51 01) – take the GR4 up a path signed 'Plomb du Cantal'. This runs parallel to the easternmost of the ski lifts which radiate like spokes from the valley. It emerges from wood into open grassland just before the top of the drag lift to follow the poles of a red ski run, signed 'Les Bruyères'.

Fork left (south-east) at a col to join a blue run, signed 'Les Alpins', and a well-defined track. As you ascend, the puys to the north-west and the west reveal themselves: Puy Griou and its smaller neighbour Le Griounou, Chavaroche, Mary, Peyre Arse and Bataillouse. Then, of a sudden as you cross the **ridgeline** after an hour to 1¼ hours of walking, the green bowl of the Prés Marty meadows presents itself, with the cluster of buildings marking Col de Prat de Bouc at its lower, open end.

Postpone for the moment the ascent to the summit of Plomb du Cantal. Instead, descend a path occupied in season by a green ski run, signed 'Prat de Bouc'. At a sign for this, break free from the ski runs to follow intermittent yellow flashes as far as the valley

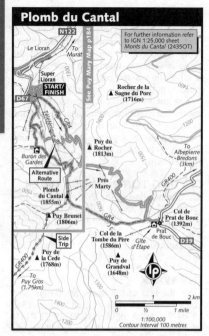

Plomb du Cantal

For further information refer to IGN 1:25,000 sheet *Monts du Cantal* (2435OT)

0   1   2 km
0   ½   1 mile
1:100,000
Contour Interval 100 metres

floor. Go straight ahead beneath a *téléski* (ski lift) to take a much older track, the original route over Plomb du Cantal, predating the advent of leisure skiing by several hundred years. Ignore a more deeply gouged trail which takes off to the right and, two minutes later, pass through a fence and stile.

At valley level, join a cart track and describe a tight loop north-eastwards (deviating from the recommended IGN map's more direct route, which is no longer used). At **Col de Prat de Bouc** (1392m), *Bar-Restaurant Le Buron* does *menus* for 75FF. A bunk at the *gîte d'étape* (☎ *04 71 20 10 05*) costs 55FF, while half board is 140FF.

To regain the ridge, follow the red and white bars of the combined GR4 and GR400, which lead you up the valley's southern flank. Retrace your steps and, just before a cattle pen, strike left through a swing gate to follow the manifest scar of this popular trail. After passing below Col de la Tombe du Père take a north-westerly course beside the

stakes of an old fence to veer almost due north for the last 25m of height gain. Turn left up a flight of wooden steps, laid to protect the summit from erosion caused by the multitude of visitors. Reach the crest of **Plomb du Cantal** 60 to 75 minutes after leaving Col de Prat de Bouc.

Drop down to the téléférique station, with its small *cafe*, open only when the cable car is operating. From here, the route drops by a PR trail to Buron des Gardes. The early part of the descent is rocky and steep in places but quite manageable. (For an easier descent to Super Lioran, see the alternative route at the end of this walk description.)

Just beyond a small weather station a couple of minutes after the cafe, head left towards a post bearing a green footpath marker. Turn left (south-west) to follow an unmaintained track, its rocks daubed here and there with green flashes. Buron des Gardes, distinguishable by the small **reservoir** beside it, is clearly visible.

The trail, now a single-file footpath, follows the boundary fence of the buron to meet a broad track coming from the reservoir. Turn right and pass beneath the base of Téléski du Slalom. Just beyond, turn right (north) to head down a broad break between the trees, following the 'Le Buron' red run to its conclusion before the unharmonious architecture of Super Lioran.

Alternative Route
1 hour, 4.25km
For an easier route back to Super Lioran from the Plomb du Cantal, head north-east from the top of the téléférique. Retrace the morning's GR4 route in reverse until you reach the col, about 30 minutes above Super Lioran. From here, a trail leaves the main route and winds down to Buron de Baguet, at the meeting point of two ski lifts, and continues to Téléski du Slalom, where it rejoins the main route back to Super Lioran.

Side Trip: Puy Gros
2 hours, 8km return
You can follow the GR400 south-west along the ridge for as long as you find comfortable. Puy Gros (1594m) makes a discernible goal.

Other Walks

MONTS DÔMES
Traverse of the High Auvergne

This 15-day, 293km linear route mainly follows the GR4 across the high peaks of the Massif Central from Volvic, just north of Clermont Ferrand, to Langogne, on the main railway line between Paris and Nîmes and accessible by bus from Le Puy-en-Velay. For a shorter walk, which still includes all the major summits of the Parc des Volcans, cut out at Saint-Flour, on the railway line between Paris and Béziers, at the end of Day 10. The route is described in detail in Alan Castle's *Walks in Volcano Country* (see Books under Information at the beginning of this chapter).

MONTS DU CANTAL
Robert Louis Stevenson Trail

This trail, officially recognised and signed as a long-distance route in 1991, follows (but for minor variations to avoid tedious or overtrafficked sections) the itinerary of Robert Louis Stevenson and his wayward donkey, Modestine, in the autumn of 1878.

From Le Monastier-sur-Gazelle south-east of Le Puy-en-Velay, it meanders for 232km as far as Saint-Jean du Gard, west of Alès in the Cévennes Mountains of the southern Massif Central.

Alan Castle, in *The Robert Louis Stevenson Trail*, divides the walk into 13 stages – one more than the pioneering Stevenson, whose wry account of his own journey, *Travels with a Donkey in the Cévennes*, also makes stimulating reading.

Trains link Le Puy-en-Velay with Lyon, Clermont Ferrand and Toulouse. At journey's end, a daily bus operates between Saint-Jean du Gard and Alès, from where there are several trains daily to Nîmes, on the TGV *(train à grande vitesse)* line to Paris.

Gorges du Tarn

A linear 200km route stretches from the source of the Tarn River on the slopes of Mont Lozère to Albi, from where there's a frequent train service to Toulouse. Divided into 12 stages, it's described in Chamina's *Vallée et Gorges du Tarn* in French, together with seven other circular routes in and around the gorges, varying in duration from one to three days.

There's a daily bus between Alès (see the Robert Louis Stevenson Trail) and Florac, home to the Maison du Parc National des Cévennes and a good jumping-off point for the start of the trail.

Périgord & Quercy

PÉRIGORD & QUERCY

Tucked away in south-western France, the adjacent regions of Périgord and Quercy (pre-French Revolution but still commonly used names) cover an extensive area between Bordeaux, Limoges-en-Quercy and Toulouse; each region has a distinctive landscape, ambience and cuisine. Among the cliff-lined valleys and wooded plateaus, with their vineyards, renowned prehistoric sites and historic towns, walkers are presented with an abundance of riches. A wide-ranging network of waymarked routes offers opportunities to visit the famous places and many that are little known in these two areas.

CLIMATE
The dominant influence over Périgord and Quercy are weather systems from the Atlantic Ocean, creating a mild, damp climate. These are modified by drier systems moving across the continent, which bring warm summers and cold winters.

Average annual rainfall over the whole area ranges between 850 and 900mm; in the area around Sarlat-la-Canéda (Périgord), the total edges towards 950mm. Summer is the driest season (160 to 180mm) and winter the wettest (around 275mm).

Prevailing winds are generally from the western quarter; south-westerlies bring thundery weather but little rain, while north-westerlies are the rain-bearers.

From June to early September the average daily maximum temperature ranges between 23°C and 26°C; highs exceeding 30°C are quite common. Light snowfalls are not unknown during winter but average temperatures are relatively mild, from 9°C to 11°C.

INFORMATION
Maps
Two IGN 1:100,000 *Périgueux* and *Cahors Montauban* sheets, Nos 48 and 57 respectively, are useful for planning.

For maps covering individual walks, see Planning in the introduction to each walk.

HIGHLIGHTS

At day's end – medieval Saint-Cirq Lapopie, on the banks of the Lot River

SALLY DILLON

- Sheer limestone cliffs along the Vézère and Dordogne River valleys
- Luxuriant woodlands and farmlands of the Périgord Noir
- Unspoiled traditional villages and hamlets
- Ingeniously intricate stone buildings in the Quercy Causses
- Fortifying Cahors red wines

Books
Many lavish books have been published about Périgord in particular. Perhaps the definitive reference is Freda White's beautiful book, *Three Rivers of France* – the rivers being the Dordogne, Lot and Tarn. Chapters cover history, land and people, weather, buildings, and food and drink. Lonely Planet's *South-West France* covers both regions in detail, while Michelin produces a *guide vert* (green guide) entitled *Dordogne, Berry, Limousin.*

190

Warning

Since the walks described in this chapter pass through many settled areas, dogs are an inevitable hazard. Suggested tactics are outlined in the Health & Safety chapter.

Information Sources

For information about Périgord generally, contact Comité Départemental du Tourisme de la Dordogne (☎ 05 53 35 50 24, fax 05 53 09 51 41, *e* dordogne.perigord.tourisme@ wanadoo.fr), 25 rue du Président Wilson, 24009 Périgueux. The Web site at www .perigord.tm.fr offers a comprehensive introduction to the area and provides numerous contact addresses. For information on camping in the Dordogne area, contact Camping Information Dordogne (☎ 05 53 31 28 01, fax 05 53 28 35 29).

The Comité Départemental du Tourisme du Lot (☎ 05 65 35 07 09, fax 05 65 23 92 76, *e* le-lot@wanadoo.fr), BP7, 46001Cahors, produces useful guides to accommodation and activities in Quercy.

Périgord

The present *département* (department) of Dordogne occupies much the same area as the pre-Revolution region of Périgord. These days it's promoted as the harmonious union of four distinct regions, each identified by the most striking colour of its countryside.

Périgord Vert (Périgord Green) is the northernmost region, all verdant rolling hills and tree-filled valleys (the main river being the Dronne). In the centre, limestone plateaus and cliffs define Périgord Blanc (Périgord White), in which you'll find the old town of Périgueux, the capital of Dordogne. To the south-west Périgord Pourpre (Périgord Purple), bisected by the Dordogne River, takes its identity from the vineyards around

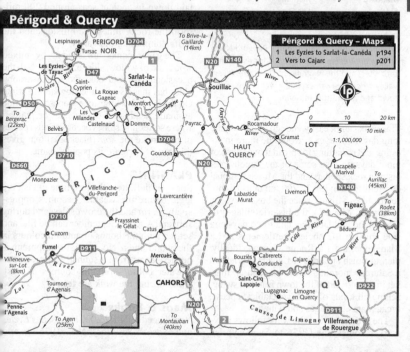

Bergerac. Farther upstream along the Dordogne, and taking in the Vézère Valley, Périgord Noir (Périgord Black), with its dark wooded valleys, is the cradle of prehistoric France (see the boxed text 'It All Started in the Vézère Valley' in the Facts about France chapter) and the venue for the walk described here. It's easy to appreciate why people have been attracted here for countless centuries: it has an equable climate, sheltered valleys now valued for their scenery, and fertile soils producing a wealth of good food and wine. Consequently, it's a prosperous and popular area, where walkers are well catered for and there's ample scope for ranging beyond the often crowded main attractions.

Les Eyzies to Sarlat-la-Canéda

Duration	2 days
Distance	48km
Standard	medium
Start	Les Eyzies
Finish	Sarlat-la-Canéda
Public Transport	yes

Summary A tour through central Périgord Noir, linking the Vézère Valley, famous for its prehistoric sites, and the magnificent Dordogne River valley where you can explore a walled medieval town and an unusual museum.

This walk can fit easily enough into two quite long days; however, it would be more interesting and rewarding to spread it over three or more days, to visit some of the famous prehistoric rock shelters and the Musée National de Préhistoire in Les Eyzies, an unusual museum at Les Milandes (see the boxed text 'Le Village du Monde'), the historic villages of Castelnaud and Domme, and to do day-long side trips to the ancient settlements at La Madeleine and La Roque Gageac. Ideally, plan to finish at Sarlat-la-Canéda (Sarlat) on a Saturday morning, when the open-air market in the old part of the town is in full swing, selling all kinds of fruit, vegetables, cheese, bread, hams, sausages and wines.

The greater part of the walk follows waymarked routes: the GR36 to Saint-Cyprien and sections of the GR64 and GR64A via Domme to Montfort. From there, one possible route among several to Sarlat is described. The waymarked routes make use of paths and quiet roads, providing easy walking, although the amount of ascent merits a medium grading. A bus service along the Dordogne Valley (see Getting There & Away under Nearest Towns) could be used to avoid the road walk into Sarlat or to start from Saint-Cyprien and concentrate on the Dordogne Valley. Camping grounds and gîtes d'étape are the recommended accommodation, but there are plenty of alternatives.

NATURAL HISTORY

The Dordogne, of which the Vézère is a major tributary, rises in the Massif Central and flows generally west for 475km to join the Garonne River near Bordeaux. The valley lies in the extensive Aquitaine basin, between the Pyrenees, the Atlantic and the Massif Central. It is filled with sediments laid down in ancient seas around 200 million years ago, and worn down over time to form the rocky limestone hillsides and the cliffs dominating the valley.

The river banks are shaded by mixed woodland of willow, alder and maple with the occasional ash and oak; the more shrubby elder has masses of white flowers in spring. On the hard, dry limestone slopes you'll find aromatic heathlands of lavender or juniper; where softer limestones occur various species of oak create the *noir* (blackness) that gives this part of Périgord its popular name.

PLANNING

Spring is definitely the best time to visit the area, before the weather becomes oppressively warm and the crowds descend during July and August. September can be fine and settled with the bonus of autumn colours in the woodlands. No special equipment is needed, apart from a sunhat, sunscreen and a water bottle – reliable sources of fresh water during the walk are few.

Maps & Books

You'll need IGN 1:25,000 sheets, *Les Eyzies* and *Sarlat Souillac*, Nos 1936ET and

2036ET respectively. The Fédération Française de la Randonnée Pédestre (FFRP) Topo-Guide *Traversée du Périgord* (No 321) includes a description of the route from Les Eyzies to Saint-Cyprien.

NEAREST TOWNS
Les Eyzies
The tourist office (☎ 05 53 06 97 05, fax 05 53 06 90 79) is open all year. It provides a currency exchange service and a vast array of local information, maps and guides. There is also a small library of serious reference books (in French) about the area's prehistory and history.

An excellent bookshop, opposite the tourist office, stocks maps and all manner of guides (closed Sunday afternoon).

The Musée National de Préhistoire (☎ 05 53 06 45 45), overlooking the town, was being extensively modernised during 1999. It's open daily (except Tuesday) from March to November; entry costs 25FF.

Places to Stay & Eat Open from April to mid-October, *Camping La Riviere (☎ 05 53 06 97 14, fax 05 53 35 20 85)* charges 26FF per person and 38FF per pitch. Alternatively, you can stay in a fine old building on site; B&B is 195FF for a double with private facilities. The spacious restaurant offers *menus* (fixed-price menus of two or more courses) from 68FF.

If you're travelling by car, *Camping La Ferme de Pelou (☎ 05 53 06 98 17)*, about 2km north-east from Les Eyzies on the route of the GR36 (at Le Pelou), would be a quieter alternative.

The nearest *gîte d'étape* (hostel-style walkers' accommodation) is *Les Eymaries (☎ 05 53 06 94 73)*, 3km from town beside the minor road which branches south from the D47 on the western side of the Vézère River bridge. The price per night is 45FF and it's open from April to November.

Les Eyzies is not short of bars and restaurants, many of them expensive. At *La Milanaise (☎ 05 53 35 43 97)*, in the main street opposite Abri Pataud, the range of pizzas includes Périgord-style; Périgordin *menus* are offered for 95FF and 125FF.

In Les Eyzies itself there are *boulangeries* (bakery), *gourmet food shops* and, next to the bookshop, an *épicerie* (grocery store) which can help with Camping Gaz.

Getting There & Away Les Eyzies is on the Paris' Gare d'Austerlitz to Agen railway line via Périgueux (300FF). Connections are possible from Bordeaux, Nantes and Quimper (☎ 08 36 35 35 39).

By car the town is about 40km southeast of Périgueux or about 56km southwest of Brive.

Sarlat-la-Canéda
The tourist office (☎ 05 53 59 27 67, fax 05 53 59 19 44, ✆ ot24.sarlat@perigord.tm.fr), place de la Liberté, is open throughout the year with information about accommodation and local attractions; some local walking guides are available. Maps and guides can also be found in the Maison de la Presse, at 34 rue de la République (next to the Casino supermarket).

Places to Stay & Eat In addition to *Les Acacias* camping ground (see the walk description), there are several *chambres d'hôtes* (B&B accommodation in private houses) and not-too-expensive hotels in Sarlat, including *Hôtel Marcel (☎ 05 53 59 21 98, 50 ave de Selves)*, with doubles from 250FF; full details are available from the tourist office. Try *Napoli Pizza (☎ 05 53 31 26 93, 2 blvd Eugène Le Roy)* for inexpensive pizzas and pasta.

Getting There & Away Sarlat is at the end of a small branch railway line which has a service from Bordeaux (☎ 08 36 35 35 39; 120FF). The Conseil-Général de la Dordogne (☎ 05 56 33 16 73) runs a daily bus service between the train stations at Sarlat, Souillac (on the line from Cahors in Quercy; 28.50FF) and Brive. By car, the N20 is about 20km east via the D703, near Souillac.

Voyages Rey (☎ 05 53 07 27 22), route de Campagne, 24260 Le Bugue, provides a Monday to Saturday bus service between Le Bugue and Sarlat via Saint-Cyprien, Beynac and Vézac.

THE WALK
Day 1: Les Eyzies to Castelnaud
6½–7 hours, 25.5km, 565m ascent

Walk north-eastwards through Les Eyzies; bear right at the junction of the D47 and D706 and 150m farther on turn right (as indicated by waymarkers). Go round a stone house on a narrow path, up to the hamlet of Beune. From there, the route follows quiet roads southwards and across the largely wooded plateau separating the Vézère and Dordogne Rivers. After 1½ hours (from Les Eyzies) you come to the pretty hamlet of **Pechboutier**.

Go to the right of the first building, then along narrow lanes; 200m south of the village the route leads between open fields to a road. Continue southwards, soon starting to descend towards the broad Dordogne Valley. As the gradient sharpens (3.5km from Pechboutier), bear right down a steep track to a narrow road and go right again, into Saint-Cyprien. This alley bends round and down to the left to rue de la Petite Feineire; in quick succession then go right and left along rue des Arcades towards the church in rue Bertrand de Got. Pass the church on your left, then it's right and down

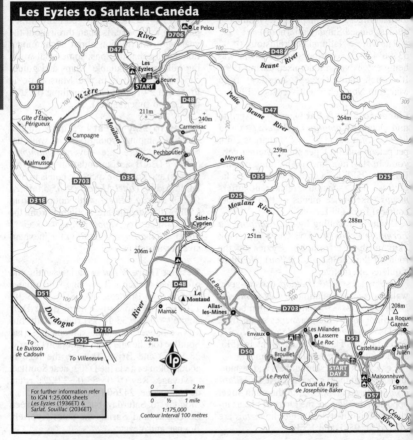

Les Eyzies to Sarlat-la-Canéda

For further information refer to IGN 1:25,000 sheets Les Eyzies (1936ET) & Sarlat. Souillac (2036ET)

0   1   2 km
0   ½   1 mile
1:175,000
Contour Interval 100 metres

ue de la Justice de Paix, and similarly own rue du Terme to place de la Liberté opposite the town hall. From here go left en take the first right down to the main ad (1¼ hours from Pechboutier); *bars* and *staurants* are within easy reach.

To continue, head south via the D48 and en rue du Garrit and, at a major junction ith the D703, cross the road and the rail- ay line and go on to the river near *Camp- g Le Garrit* (☎ *05 53 29 20 56*), where the riff is 22FF per person and 30FF per tent. ollow the willow-lined track upstream and rn away at a junction near Le Bout (rather

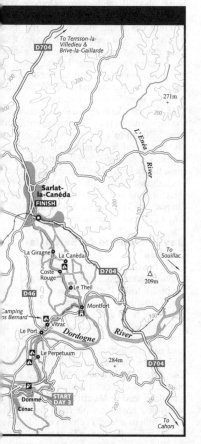

than continuing farther south-east as on the 1:25,000 map). Cross the river to Allas-les- Mines, where there is a rather attractive *restaurant* (1¼ hours from Saint-Cyprien). From the roundabout in the village follow the road signposted to Envaux and Les Mi- landes, temporarily leaving the waymarked route. About 30 minutes' walking brings you to the hamlet of **Envaux**, with some fine old houses and farm buildings.

Leave the river here and continue up the road signposted to Les Milandes. Turn off about 250m south of Le Peytol (not at Le Peytol, as shown on the IGN 1:25,000 map) and rejoin the waymarked route. Cross two streams and climb through forest to a minor road at Le Brouillet. You then join the Cir- cuit du Pays de Josephine Baker (see the boxed text 'Le Village du Monde'), gener- ally east and north-east through fields and on to **Château Les Milandes** (about an hour from Envaux).

From here, take the short cut just round a sharp bend to the D53 and continue briefly towards Castelnaud. Turn right towards Lasserre and Le Roc (as signposted) and follow minor roads across the wooded spur and down towards Castelnaud. From a T- junction at a sharp bend follow a grassy path to another road and turn left towards the prominent church. Pass it on the left, turn right at a T-junction and go steeply down to the riverside part of the village (1½ hours from Les Milandes).

Camping Maisonneuve (☎ *05 53 29 51 29, fax 05 53 30 27 06*) is accessible from the D57 Daglan road about 1km from the riverside centre of the village; the tariff is 25FF per person and 38FF per pitch. It's open from April to October. Attached to the site is a well-equipped gîte d'étape where a dorm bed costs 52FF.

There's also the *gîte d'étape municipal* (☎ *05 53 29 51 21*) in the village, but it's in strong demand by canoeists and often full. In the village are a somewhat expensive gro- cery store, a *boucherie-charcuterie* (butcher shop and delicatessen) and a couple of restaurants, including *Le Jardin Gour- mand*, which serves pizzas (40FF to 58FF, including Périgordin) and *menus* from 76FF.

Le Village du Monde

Any connection between a one-time star of the Paris *Folies-Bergère* and a walking route (Circuit du Pays de Josephine Baker) in the peaceful countryside around Les Milandes seems improbable. Yet it is a very tangible connection indeed.

Josephine Baker, born in an impoverished black ghetto in Missouri (USA), settled in Paris in 1925 and became the sensational, much-feted star of the Folies during the 1930s. In 1946 she bought 15th-century Château Les Milandes, and, to promote her commitment to racial and religious tolerance, set up Le Village du Monde (World Village). Between 1954 and 1963 she adopted 12 children from various countries and of various religions, and brought them to live together at Les Milandes, moving there herself in 1956. However, local disquiet about her community, the disloyalty of some of her followers and financial ruin forced her to sell Les Milandes in 1969. She died in 1975.

The chateau (☎ 05 53 07 16 38) now houses an exhibition about Baker and her colourful life, supported in part by the Association de Josephine Baker. It's open daily from March to October.

Day 2: Castelnaud to Domme
2¾–3 hours, 8.5km, 210m ascent
From Castelnaud walk south along the D57 and turn off after 450m towards Camping Maisonneuve. At a bend in the minor road turn left and follow forest tracks north and east to the cluster of old houses at Saint-Julien. Go on towards Simon but diverge after 1km east down a steep track and soon you're back beside the Dordogne River for a while. Continue to a main road at Cénac, fortuitously reaching it beside a *creperie* which serves draught cider.

To head directly to *Camping Beau Rivage* (☎ 05 53 28 32 05), one of the accommodation choices for the night, turn left and cross the river. The camping ground charges 27FF per person and 40FF for a pitch; it's open from March to October.

Otherwise, head south to the roundabout follow the D43 briefly, then the road sign posted to La Poste, then the first left (passing en route a good *boulangerie* and *supermarket*). The road climbs steeply to L Porte del Bos, a gateway to **Domme**; hea for the 'Centre Ville' and place de la Rod (see the boxed text 'Domme').

Nouvel Hôtel (☎ 05 53 28 38 67, fax 05 5 28 27 13), near the tourist office, has double for 240FF and is open from Easter to Octo ber. *Le Perpetuum* camping ground (☎ 05 5 28 35 18, fax 05 53 29 63 64), on the eas bank of the river, is on the Day 3 route t Sarlat, about 40 minutes from Domme. Wal along rue des Portes from place de la Rod to Porte des Tours, then follow the lowe road to the right, under an overpass. Cor tinue down a succession of paths to a min road and on to the river bank track – th camping ground is 1.3km farther on. You' pay 18FF per person and 20FF for the pitch it's open from Easter to October.

In Domme, *Sodi Épicerie* in Grande Ru (on the corner of rue G Vivans) is open dail from 8.30 am to 1 pm and from 3 to 8 pn Of the several restaurants, one of the leas expensive, *Le Belvédère*, has the best vie (near the lookout). It offers crepes, omelette (including a Périgordin speciality with trut fles) for 95FF and *menus* for 68FF and 98F On place de la Rode, *Le Médiéval* (☎ 05 5 28 24 57) does crepes and salads.

Day 3: Domme to Sarlat-la-Canéda
2–2½ hours, 14km, 205m ascent
Continue north from Le Perpetuum and cros the bridge to Le Port. Turn right then left u the D46 then first right between L Belvédère hotel and some houses. Go up t a minor road which leads to Vitrac; cross th church forecourt and continue left along road past a cemetery, before returning to th D55 for a few hundred metres, passin *Camping Clos Bernard* (☎ 05 53 28 33 44 on the way. Tracks through and fringin woodland lead to **Montfort**, dominated by handsome castle dating from the Middl Ages, with its attendant cluster of old house There's a friendly *bar* and a *creperie* nearby

Here you leave the waymarked route. From the village follow the road signposted to Sarlat-la-Canéda for 400m, turn left up a forest track and go on to a minor road near Le Theil. Continue north for about 800m to a crossroads at Coste Rouge.

To reach *Camping Les Acacias* (☎ 05 53 59 29 30, fax 05 53 31 08 50), turn right here then first left and it's 400m farther on. The camp site is about 300m south of the hamlet of La Canéda, itself 2.5km south of Sarlat. The tariff is 26FF per person plus 23FF for the tent space. During summer there is a bar-restaurant which offers a *menu régional* on site; the nearest alternatives and shops are in Sarlat, 45 minutes' walk away.

For a direct run into **Sarlat** from Coste Rouge, continue generally north-west and north via La Giragne, then left at a Y-junction along a road which meets the D704 below the railway viaduct. To reach the station, go under the viaduct and almost immediately right for 250m. For the town centre, turn right at the roundabout almost below the viaduct and continue on for about 1km.

Domme

Domme, perched on an isolated plateau above the Dordogne River, is regarded as one of the finest *bastide* towns in Périgord. During the Middle Ages these fortified settlements were established to bring scattered communities together for security, taxation or indoctrination. The heart of the walled bastide was the central square, the obligatory place for all trade in the town. Domme was founded in 1281 and began to prosper during the 14th and 15th centuries.

Today, visitors flock to Domme to see the immaculately preserved covered market and other buildings, and inevitably to patronise the souvenir shops. Among the delicacies on offer are (*pâté de fois gras*) goose liver pàté, ducks in many guises and walnuts transformed into liqueur, oil, cakes, biscuits and sweets. These, together with wines, truffles and honey are abundantly available everywhere you turn.

Quercy

The deep sinuous valley of the Lot River is the dominant feature of Quercy, which embraces the départements of Lot and Lot-et-Garonne. To the north and south is the gently undulating Causse de Limogne, a wooded, sparsely populated limestone plateau. It's an area with a distinctly remote feeling, where the villages reveal little change and traditional architectural treasures are seen at every turn. Endearingly perhaps, prosperity is less obvious than in Périgord; rather, you will detect a gritty determination to survive and prosper on a modest rather than a lavish scale.

Dolmens (prehistoric burial tombs), some still well preserved, testify to the antiquity of settlement. The most striking historic features are the numerous derelict stone buildings and stone walls enclosing fields once tilled or grazed (see the boxed text 'Building With Stone'). However, old paths and tracks have survived and provide the main means of exploring the area on foot.

Vers to Cajarc

Duration	3 days
Distance	68.5km
Standard	medium-hard
Start	Vers
Finish	Cajarc
Nearest Town	Cahors
Public Transport	yes

Summary A wonderfully varied walk, from the limestone cliffs of the Lot River valley to the wild and remote plateau of the Causse, a mosaic of woodlands and fields with old tracks linking traditional villages.

The southern reaches of Quercy are the venue for this varied tour between two small towns along the valley of the Lot River via the Causse de Limogne plateau rising from the river to the south. The route passes through several delightful villages, notably Saint-Cirq Lapopie, a superbly preserved medieval village, worth much more than a passing glance.

The distances covered on the first and second days are quite long. If you're travelling by car, it's possible to cover much of the same ground by making a base in the vicinity of Saint-Cirque Lapopie or Limogne-en-

Building With Stone

The distinctive conical architecture of a Quercy borie

Rural buildings in Quercy exhibit a fine understanding of the efficient and aesthetically pleasing use of limestone. Combined home and farm buildings have a slightly sunken ground floor with an arched ceiling; this is where sheep can be housed or crops stored. Above is the family home, reached by an outside staircase leading to a veranda, its roof resting on timber posts or stone pillars. Large slabs set on a strong timber framework form the roof, although tiles are more common nowadays.

A distinctive feature of many houses in Quercy is the dovecote tower. These date back to the 13th century when they were built by the nobility to provide the highly prized fertiliser from pigeon droppings. The towers proliferated during the more egalitarian 19th century and are now retained purely for their architectural value.

Dotted about in fields or in farmyards, small circular or oval buildings with conical roofs of slabs are a common sight in Périgord and Quercy. Known as *bories* (derived from the Occitan word for farm), *gariotes*, *cazelles* or *capitelles*, they were used as shelter for animals or people, or for storage. They are completely cement-free – miracles of construction.

Quercy and doing day walks from there (see Other Walks later).

The walk follows the GR36, GR46 and GR65. Waymarking is generally adequate; the few places where it's vague are clarified in the description. Cyclists and, in places, horse-riders also use these tracks, but it's unlikely that traffic (outside the holiday season) will be congested.

NATURAL HISTORY

The Lot River, like the Dordogne, is within the sedimentary Aquitaine basin. Its narrow valley is adorned with limestone cliffs. The Causse de Limogne, a broad, subtly undulating plateau, is also in limestone territory. Almost all the streams intersecting the plateau are either intermittent or underground. The plateau supports large tracts of oak woodland mixed with birch and juniper. Among the wild flowers lining the old tracks, orchids are unusually common, and bright red common poppies make a colourful springtime display in the deep green fields.

PLANNING

Temperatures can be too high for enjoyable walking during summer, making spring and autumn the ideal seasons to visit the area. A hat and sunscreen should still be carried and don't forget a water bottle of at least 1L capacity, as drinking water is very scarce.

Maps & Books

The IGN's 1:50,000 *Le Lot Randonnée, Les Marches du Sud Quercy* in their Plein Air series is better for planning than following the walk on the ground. The alternative is six 1:25,000 sheets: Nos 2138O, 2138E, 2139O, 2139E, 2238O and 2239O.

Two FFRP Topo-Guides include descriptions and information about parts of the walk: *Traversée du Périgord* (No 321) and *Sentier de Saint-Jacques, Figeac-Moissac* (No 652), at 90FF each.

NEAREST TOWN
Cahors

Transport to the start and from the finish is based in the bustling town of Cahors. The tourist office (☎ 05 65 53 20 65, fax 05 65

53 20 74, @ cahors@wanadoo.fr), place François Mitterand, is open all year and is particularly useful for accommodation and walking guides, and a town map. Maps are available from Halle de Presse, on the corner of blvd Gambetta and rue Victor Hugo, and farther north in the same street and close to the town hall, at the Maison de la Presse.

Places to Stay & Eat With excellent facilities, *Camping Rivière de Cabessut (☎ 05 65 30 06 30, fax 05 65 23 99 46, rue de la Rivière)* charges 40FF for one person and a tent and is open from April to the end of October. There's a bar and small shop on site. It's 1km north of Pont de Cabessut on the east bank of the Lot River.

The *auberge de jeunesse (☎ 05 65 35 64 71, fax 05 65 35 95 92, 20 rue Frédéric Suisse)* has beds for 51FF per person or 68FF for B&B.

Vegetarians can feel at home at *L'Orangerie (☎ 05 65 22 59 06, 41 rue Clément Marot)* with crepes, omelettes and tofu dishes, and *menus* for 68FF and 98FF (closed Sunday and Monday). The popular *Bar-Brasserie La Comédie (☎ 05 65 35 03 04, 40 blvd Gambetta)* is a good place to watch the passing parade and to order from the *menus* which include regional specialities (from 65FF); it's open daily.

There's a *Champion* supermarket, on place Émilien Imbert just south of the tourist office.

Getting There & Away The SNCF service from Paris' Gare d'Austerlitz to Toulouse calls at Cahors (324FF); it passes through Souillac (see the Périgord section earlier) en route. Toulouse is a major junction for services from Bordeaux, Nice and Lyon (☎ 08 36 35 35 39 for information).

By car from Paris or Toulouse, follow the N20 or A20 to Cahors.

GETTING TO/FROM THE WALK
The SNCF daily bus service from Cahors to Capendac goes along the Lot Valley via Vers (18FF), Bouziès, Tour de Faure and Cajarc (43FF). For intermediate points, SARL Cars Delbos (☎ 05 65 34 00 70) runs a daily bus

Heritage Protection in Quercy

Quercy's outstanding cultural and natural heritage was recognised during 1999 by the creation of Parc Naturel Régional des Causses du Quercy. Extending from the southern side of the Dordogne River in the north, southward through the Causse de Gramat, across the valleys of the Célé and Lot Rivers and the Causse de Limogne to the *département* (department) boundary, it takes in 175,000 hectares with a population of only 24,000 (a few thousand more than Cahors).

For an area blighted by population decline and supporting a precarious rural economy, the aim of the park's locally based managers is to ensure that the remarkable cultural and natural heritage of the area is preserved, at the same time as economic, agricultural and social development schemes are promoted. Industrial enterprises will have no place in the park. The emphasis is on bringing pastures back into use, rebuilding stone walls, restoring buildings, opening more paths for walkers, promoting tourism and forestry and discouraging the enclosure of more land for hunting.

A *maison du parc* (park information centre) will be opened in Gramat, between the Dordogne and Célé valleys; meantime contact the tourist office (☎ 05 65 35 09 56) in Cahors for more information.

service between Villefranche de Rouergue and Cahors via Limogne-en-Quercy and Concots, Monday to Friday.

THE WALK
Day 1: Vers to Saint-Cirq Lapopie
5½–6 hours, 22.5km, 410m ascent
Head west through Vers and cross the Lot River bridge. The route round the hamlet of Béars differs from that on the recommended IGN 1:25,000 map, largely avoiding the road, via a series of waymarked left turns. Then climb steeply, bearing left about 600m from Béars, to an open summit past a communications tower.

PÉRIGORD & QUERCY

Continue south-eastwards; about 1.6km from the tower, turn left at a minor road, then first left then right down to another road. Along this road, the route cuts off three sharp bends on the descent to the church in the hamlet of Pasturat (1¼ hours from Vers; no refreshments). Continue to a nearby road junction and turn right to parallel the river. About 1.4km from Pasturat leave the river and walk south-eastwards up an old road; bear left at the second track you meet. After about an hour the direction changes to north-east as the old track generally parallels the D8 for 1km (apart from a short stretch along the road itself) to a small clearing where there is a cross and picnic tables.

The Wines of Cahors

Although the vineyards of the Lot Valley are concentrated downstream from Cahors (and out of the area covered by walks in this chapter), you'll find Cahors reds on the shelves of almost any *épicerie* (grocery store) or supermarket, and in innumerable speciality shops. They're surprisingly inexpensive: around 40FF for a bottle of late 1990s vintage.

Known to aficionados as *liqueur du feu*, which could be translated as firewater, they're the product of the fortuitous combination of good vines, an equable climate, the right type of soil and expert vignerons. Auxerrois grapes yield dark, very robust reds, strong in tannin and with remarkable ageing properties. Those produced on the valley terraces aren't worth drinking under three years old, and wines from the limestone plateau vineyards need at least five years in the bottle; the best vintages can improve for another 10 years. Ideally, any bottle should be opened and allowed to breathe an hour or so before drinking.

The coveted *appellation d'origine contrôlée* (label of origin) was granted in 1971 to around 200 Cahors producers, signifying the meeting of stringent growing, fermenting and bottling standards, and virtually guaranteeing good, if not superb wines.

Continue left from here and descend sharply to the tree-lined river. Shortly, woodland and field-edge paths lead to a junction – keep left to return to the river. An hour's walk brings you to the bridge at Bouziès, which has only two *hotels*, a *wine shop* and a tap (marked *eau potable*) beside the cemetery gate. Continue close to the river to the amazing *chemin de halage* (scanal towpath), literally cut into a cliff which drops straight into the water. The wall is adorned with a striking bas relief sculpture (18m long), inspired by the waters of the river. The path extends upstream for several hundred metres to the Ganil lock (see the boxed text 'Navigation on the Lot River').

About an hour from Bouziès you come to a sign pointing up a steep path to **Saint-Cirq Lapopie** (about 200m west of that shown on the 1:25,000 map). The path emerges in place du Sombral. The helpful tourist office at Saint-Cirq Lapopie (☎/fax 05 65 31 29 06, ℮ saint-cirq-lapopie@wanadoo.fr), place du Sombral, provides local accommodation information, historical references, maps and walking guides.

Maison de la Fourdonne (☎/fax 05 65 31 21 51), rue Droite, is a gîte d'étape in a fine old building. It costs 60FF per night, has a self-catering kitchen and is open from February to December. It shares the building with the Musée de la Mémoire du Village.

To reach *Camping de la Plage* (☎ 05 65 30 29 51, fax 05 65 30 23 33), rather than turning onto the path into Saint-Cirq Lapopie, continue by the river for about 1km; turn right and the entrance is 300m farther on. The camping ground charges 30FF per person and 20FF for a tent space. It has shady pitches close to the river, a bar and, in the high season, a restaurant; it's open all year.

Of the several restaurants in Saint-Cirq Lapopie, *Auberge du Sombral* (☎ 05 61 31 26 08, place du Sombral) has *menus* ranging from 95FF to 145FF featuring regional specialities. Close to the place and more informal is *La Peyrolière* (☎ 05 65 30 23 72), which offers crepes and *menus* from 70FF.

More convenient for campers is *Auberge Roucayral* (☎ 05 65 30 23 02) in Tour de Faure (about 2km east across the Lot River

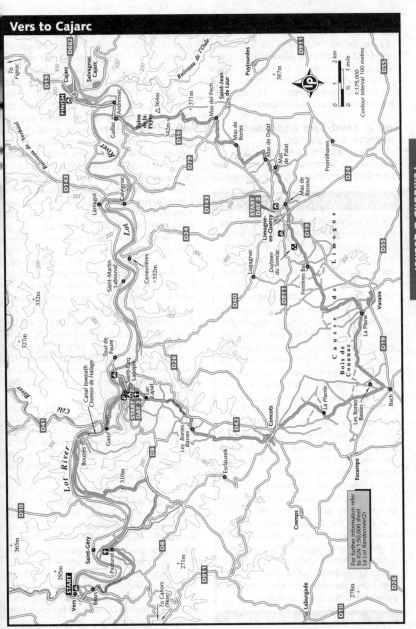

Vers to Cajarc

PÉRIGORD & QUERCY

Ruisseau de l'Oule

To Figeac

D662

Cajarc

Salvagnac Cajarc

D19

FINISH

Gaillac

Andressac

Saint-Jean de Laur

Puyjourdes

+ 387m

△ 364m

+ 371m

Mas del Pech

Talon de la Peyre

342m

D19

Mas de Bories

Mas de Dalat

D79

Mas de Palat

Promilhanes

D24

Ruisseau de Vers

D143

Larnagol

Calvignac

Lot

River

Mas de Bassoul

D55

START DAY 3

D143

300

Limogne-en-Quercy

D19

D24

Saint-Martin Labouval

Cenevières +352m

D40

Lugagnac

Dolmen du Soncar

Ferrières Bas

Causse de Limogne

D55

332m +

327m +

Tour de Faure

Saint-Cirq Lapopie

D26

AC Lapat

Varaire

La Plane

Bois de Couanac

D19

La Plante

Bach

Canal towpath Chemin de Halage

START DAY 2

Ganil

Les Bories Basses

Esclauzels

Concots

D42

Les Bories Basses

Escamps

Bouziès

Cele River

D41

310m

D8

Cremps

D10

365m +

Saint-Géry

Pasturat

295m +

Béars

D911

271m +

To Cahors (9km)

Laburgade

278m +

D26

START DAY 1

Vers

D8

D10

For further information refer to IGN 1:150,000 sheet Le Lot Randonnée(2)

N

0   1   2 km
0   ½   1 mile

1:175,000
Contour Interval 100 metres

from Saint-Cirq Lapopie), which has *menus* from 75FF to 95FF.

There are no food shops in Saint-Cirq Lapopie (apart from a *pâtisserie*, or cake shop, near the church). In Tour de Faure there's an *épicerie* (grocery store), open from 9 am to 8 pm Monday to Saturday and 1 pm on Sunday, and a *boulangerie*.

Day 2: Saint-Cirq Lapopie to Limogne-en-Quercy

7–7½ hours, 28.5km, 440m ascent

From place du Sombral, walk down the road on the right. Turn first right, soon passing the

---

Navigation on the Lot River

The Lot was the first river in France to be used for navigation. The Romans developed an efficient system of barges and ferries with 'ferrymen' who also handled overland transport on treacherous reaches. All this fell into disuse after the Romans departed and it wasn't until the 13th century that river traffic began to revive.

In the early days the river was known as the Olt – its present name being a misspelling of the original. Locks and towpaths were built around rough reaches, providing a passage downstream to the junction with the Garonne River, not far from Bordeaux. Local enterprises flourished: sawmillers (to supply oak for barge building), carpenters, rope-makers, freight carriers, boat crews, innkeepers, and the all-important providers of horses to haul vessels along the canals. All the necessary canals were complete by about 1800. Freight included coal, timber and wines; on the return, manufactured goods and overseas imports were carried. However, the railway line from Cahors to Capendac (near Figeac) opened in 1886 and swiftly extinguished canal traffic.

In 1989 the Conseil-Général du Lot launched an ambitious project to revive use of the river for recreation. Now 64km have been resurrected, between Saint-Cirq Lapopie and Luzech (downstream from Cahors), 13 locks have been restored and one rebuilt, and towpaths have been opened for walkers.

---

gîte d'étape. Shortly, cross a road and climb a steepish path, along which are the 12 Stations of the Cross, to the Calvary and a small chapel. Once on high ground, the route is southwards along minor roads via Lac Lapat, to the locality of La Gravette (1¼ hours from Saint-Cirq). Then follows a stretch of 1.5km on a path, minor roads and an old track to the farming community of Les Bories Basses; turn right on a bend opposite a large building. The way is now southwards for 4km via numerous well-marked track junctions to the village of Concots (about 1½ hours from La Gravette). Here you'll find an *alimentation* (open daily, with a long lunch break), a *boulangerie*, *bar* and *Restaurant Les Voyageurs* (☎ 05 65 31 52 02), open for lunch with 90FF and 150FF *menus*.

Although Limogne-en-Quercy is almost due east from Concots, the route now swings south-eastwards for about 6.5km. Oak woodland and scattered small clearings line the way along very minor roads and old tracks between mossy stone walls. Between La Plante (about 3.5km from Concots) and the crossroads 350m south-west (297 on the map) there's a perfectly preserved **borie** (small stone building) beside the shady track. On through the Bois de Couanac, it's clear that the area was once home to several small communities, judging by the number of ruinous stone buildings.

At Les Bories Basses a cluster of signposts announce the welcome news that Limogne-en-Quercy is only 10.5km farther on. Here the route turns north-eastwards. After about 1km, a forbidding sign dictates a right turn and soon Limogne comes into view on the skyline (2½ hours from Concots). At La Plane there's a minor change from the mapped route to cross the D52. Continue north-eastwards for nearly 2km to a right turn into more open country. Around point 287 on the 1:25,000 map you come to a wire gate *(cledo)* across the track – it must be closed behind you, as must another 250m farther on. Continue past the spacious fields of Ferrières Bas; then 1.1km from the junction 292 (where there's a cross) you reach a signposted path to **Dolmen du Joncas (**about 200m through the trees). It's an impressive arrangement of limestone slabs about 4m long. Back on the track and it's only another 1km to Limogne-en-Quercy. Turn left at a main road (D19) then, at the next junction, either right along the D911 to reach the gîte d'étape, or left along a minor road to the camping ground. *Gîte d'Étape de Limogne-en-Quercy* (☎ 05 65 31 73 25, *route de Lugagnac*) is beside the D911, 200m along from place Yves Ouvrieu. It has beds in small dorms and smaller bedrooms for 40FF per night, a self-catering kitchen, and is open all year.

To the left, *Camping Bel-Air* (☎ 05 65 31 51 27, fax 05 65 24 73 59) charges 17FF each per person and per tent space. In the high season this includes use of the adjacent pool.

The tourist office (☎/fax 05 65 24 34 28), La Maison du Pays de Limogne, provides accommodation contacts and a small selection of maps and local guides. There's a larger collection of maps and guides at Maison de la Presse, on the D40 near the central place Yves Ouvrieu.

For a meal there's *Le Vieux Quercy* (☎ 05 65 31 51 17), on the D41 near place Yves Ouvrieu, which offers *menus* featuring local specialities for 80FF and 125FF. The Sunday market is a memorable event with numerous stalls overflowing with local produce.

For self-caterers, there's a *supermarket*, in place Yves Ouvrieu, a *boulangerie*, and near the church, *Le Trèfle à Quatre Feuilles*, an organic food shop open daily.

Day 3: Limogne-en-Quercy to Cajarc

4–4½ hours, 17.5km, 210m ascent

To rejoin the route, reach the junction of the D911 (to Concots) and D19 (to Varaire) on the south-western edge of Limogne-en-Quercy; follow the D19 south for 300m to a crossroads and turn left. From there the direction is generally eastwards along minor roads through Limogne-en-Quercy's mainly agricultural outskirts. Across the D911, follow old paths and tracks to the community of Mas de Palat (75 minutes from Limogne-en-Quercy). Aim for a prominent cross (not on the map) and continue to the minor road junction. Having

left this road after 300m, the route leads north-east through Mas de Dalat, then northwards for 1km down to a minor road. Turn right and go onto Mas de Bories (40 minutes from Mas de Palat), and a little farther on turn left. Soon you're back on old tracks which lead north and east to a short section of road around the next hamlet, Mas del Pech. Continue northwards; good views north across the Lot Valley open up. The several junctions en route to the highest point of the day (near point 361 on the IGN 1:25,000 map) aren't all mapped, but are waymarked, although the way is more obvious in places where the possible alternatives are distinguished by large crosses.

From a high point (1¼ hours from Mas de Bories) the descent is straightforward, except for a devious way through the knot of tracks just north of Talon de la Pèyre, but keep heading north if in doubt. At the edge of the forest in the valley, turn right to go through Gaillac, then cross the bridge over the Lot River. About 350m farther on, branch right off the main road (D19) and head through Andressac. Continue north to La Capelette, where the road rejoins the D19.

On the other side of the river, continue to a T-junction where you turn right then left for the bus stop in place du Foirail (40 minutes from Gaillac). The Cajarc tourist office (☎ 05 65 40 72 89), place du Foirail, is open from May to the end of August.

Camping Municipal (☎ 05 65 40 65 20, *rue du Couzal*) is open from Easter to November and charges 13FF per person and 18FF per tent. To get there, from the junction at La Capellette follow the D19 for about 300m to a path (right) down to a track beside the railway. This leads to a minor road, along which is the camping ground.

The *Gîte d'Étape Communal* (☎ 05 65 40 71 51, *place du Foirail*) is open from Easter to November.

Around the central place du Foirail are a *Petite Casino* supermarket, a *boulangerie* and *Bar-Café Sympa*, open daily for pizzas, salads and *menus* from 55FF to 135FF. On the main road into town (ave de la Capellette) is *Thomson* hardware shop, which sells Camping Gaz.

Other Walks

PÉRIGORD

Vézère Valley

Upstream from Les Eyzies, the valley is equally renowned for its archaeological sites. La Madeleine, a less visited but no less interesting rock shelter, is the highlight of a 16km, four-hour day walk (which can be extended to 24km, or 5½ hours) from Les Eyzies. The shelter was originally settled 40,000 years ago, and inhabited continuously from about the 2nd century AD to the beginning of the 20th century. La Madeleine Village Troglodytique Médiéval museum (☎ 05 53 06 92 49) is open from 10 am to 6 pm daily; entry is 30FF. Guide sheets in several languages are provided.

From Les Eyzies the route is via Tursac, Lespinasse, La Madeleine, Lespare, La Cour and Laugerie Haute, from where the shorter walk returns directly to Les Eyzies. For the longer journey, continue via Gorge d'Enfer, Le Grel, Les Eymaries and back to Les Eyzies. You will need to carry food and drink for the entire trip.

The walk, part of which follows the GR36, is described in *Sentiers Petites et Moyennes Randonnées*, a booklet available from the tourist office in Les Eyzies (15FF). The relevant IGN 1:25,000 map is No 1936ET.

La Roque Gageac

This is a lovely old village beside the Dordogne River, overlooked by an ancient cave shelter, accessible by a vertiginous flight of steps. The site was settled about 7000 BC and used as a stronghold between the 12th and 15th centuries AD to protect the local base of the Bishops of Sarlat. The shelter is also important for the species of birds, rare in Périgord, which can be seen there. These include the peregrine falcon, a tiny wren and the wallcreeper. The Fort Troglodytique Aerien is open from 10 am to 7 pm daily June to August, and from 10 am to 6 pm at other times (25FF); printed guides in several languages are provided. La Roque Gageac has several bistros and a good boulangerie.

Leaflets Nos 10 and 11 in *Promenades et Randonnées en Périgord Noir* (46FF), available from Les Eyzies tourist office, can be used to devise a walk of 17km (4½ hours) from a base near Domme to La Roque Gageac. The route is via Vitrac Port, Les Veyssieres, La Servantie, Le Cap Long and La Roque Gageac, then back via Gageac, Les Combes and Le Colombier to Vitrac Port. The relevant IGN 1:25,000 map is No 2036ET.

QUERCY

Célé Valley

The Célé River joins the Lot River near the village of Bouziès. The lower reaches are lined with steep limestone cliffs, at the foot of which traditional villages cling to scraps of flattish ground. The GR651 winds round the valley, mainly on the northern side, between Conduché and Béduer, 54km upstream; Béduer is 800m from Mas de la Croiz on the GR65 (the Figeac – Cajarc – Limogne-en-Quercy – Cahors route). The full distance requires four or five days' walking; a side trip from Bouziès (see the Vers to Cajarc walk earlier in this chapter) to Cabrerets and back makes a scenic day's outing of 14km (200m ascent) and a good introduction to the valley. The best return route is simply to retrace your steps; alternatives on the opposite side of the valley are not recommended.

You'll need IGN 1:25,000 sheet Nos 2138E and 2238O. The booklet *Entre Lot et Célé* (37FF) in the excellent Promenades et Randonnées series by the Comité Départemental du Tourisme du Lot, available in Cahors and Saint-Cirq Lapopie, includes several short walks in the valley. Near Cabrerets the Pech Merle Centre du Préhistoire (☎ 05 65 31 23 33) features cave paintings and rock carvings.

There are gîtes d'étape in Cabrerets and Béduer and camp sites along the valley. *O'Louise Bar & Bistro* (☎ 05 65 30 25 56) in Cabrerets is recommended. For more information contact the Cahors tourist office (☎ 05 65 53 20 65).

AROUND LIMOGNE

Of the walks based on Limogne-en-Quercy and described in the booklet *Les Marches du Sud Quercy* in the Promenades et Randonnées series, an easy 12km outing takes in the old village of Lugagnac (with a fine pigeons loft and other old buildings), Dolmen du Lac d'Aurié and Dolmen du Ramel (not mappesd but about 500m west of Mas de Rastouillet), several intact bories, and oak and juniper woodlands.

The route, from the Limogne-en-Quercy swimming pool, is shown on IGN 1:25,000 sheet No 2139E. Clockwise, it's waymarked with yellow waymarkers from Lugagnac almost back to Limogne-en-Quercy, and with occasional red-and-white waymarkers. You'll need to carry food and drink – there are no bars or cafes along the way.

Pyrenees

Many walkers believe the Pyrenees offer the finest walking in France. Surprisingly less well known and much less developed than the higher and world-famous Alps, its towns and villages are also smaller and fewer in number than in the Alps. For walkers, the overwhelming attractions of the Pyrenees are the continuity of its mountainous country – hundreds of virtually uninterrupted kilometres of peaks, ridges, cols and valleys – and the immense variety between and within three broad geographical sections.

The Pyrénées Atlantiques rise steadily through the lush forests of the Pays Basque to France's westernmost summits and valleys. The Hautes Pyrénées are a dense mosaic of steep peaks, rugged ridges and deep valleys, high cols and innumerable lakes, largely within the Parc National des Pyrénées. The Pyrénées Orientales are lower as the ranges taper down towards the Mediterranean, and distinctly warmer and drier than the rest of the ranges.

In the Hautes Pyrénées in particular there are plenty of *refuges* (refuges or mountain huts), and a variety of accommodation is available in valleys within easy reach of the mountains. But it's also possible to disappear into the mountains for several days at a time and have no contact at all with settlements.

This chapter concentrates on two areas: the Vallée d'Aspe on the eastern fringes of the Pyrénées Atlantiques, and the Vallée de Cauterets in the heart of the Hautes Pyrénées, with a variety of day walks and a three-day tour. Suggestions are also provided (see Other Walks at the end of the chapter) for other walks in these areas, and outlines are given of the two end-to-end routes, right through the Pyrenees from the Atlantic Ocean to the Mediterranean.

NATURAL HISTORY

The Pyrenees form an almost unbroken barrier of hills and mountains 400km long, straddling the border between France and Spain, from the Atlantic to the Mediterranean.

The rocky trail through the Vallée du Marcadau, Hautes-Pyrenées

- A path cut into intimidating, vertical rock walls, hundreds of metres high

- The great variety of lakes, large and small, many high in the mountains; beautiful alpine meadows and groves of hardy pines

- Awesome cascades and waterfalls tumbling kilometres down deep valleys

- The international camaraderie among walkers in remote *refuges*

- In the shadow of Vignemale, the Pyrenees' highest peak; the strong feeling of being in the heart of a mountain wilderness

Geologically complex, the range consists essentially of granite and gneiss in the east and limestone capped by granite in the west. A vast ice sheet once covered most of the area, leaving behind a myriad of glacial landscape features, although only very small glaciers (for a description of glacial features, see the boxed text 'Signs of a Glacial Past'). The

205

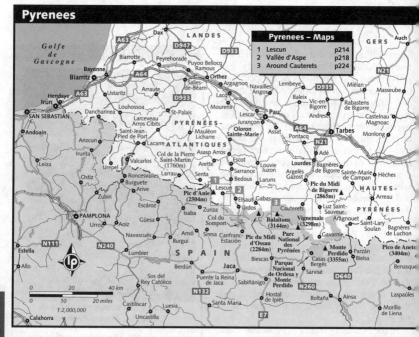

Pyrenees

Pyrenees – Maps

1	Lescun	p214
2	Vallée d'Aspe	p218
3	Around Cauterets	p224

largest of these is the Glacier d'Ossoue on Vignemale in the Hautes Pyrénées; there are also miniature glaciers on Balaïtous (west of Vignemale) and a handful of other peaks. Here too are magnificent cirques, the head-walls of glaciated valleys, of which the Cirque de Gavarnie (its cliffs more than 400m high) and the nearby Cirque de Trou-mouse, around 5km across, are the finest. Lakes, both large and small and always colourful, are numbered in the hundreds. Waterfalls are probably even more numer-ous, from the huge fall on Cirque de Gavarnie to tumbling cascades in mountain streams.

Rolling foothills rise steadily from the At-lantic for 70km to the threshold of the moun-tains, guarded by Pic d'Anie (2504m), a few kilometres west of Vallée d'Aspe. The Hautes Pyrénées are a veritable maze of rugged ridges and long, spiny spurs, many summits rising above 2800m but only a handful topping 3000m. Vignemale (3298m) is the highest, straddling the Franco-Spanish

border. The highest Pyrenean peak wholly within France is Pic Long (3192m), north-east of Gavarnie. The supreme Pyrenean summits are in Spain: Pico d'Aneto (3404m) and Monte Perdido (3355m). To the east, the general elevation begins to decrease; Pic Carlit (2921m) and Pic Canigou (2784m) are the two most substantial peaks in the Pyrénées Orientales.

Several long valleys – the Aspe, Ossau, Azun, Cauterets, Luz-Gavarnie and Aure – reach deep into the mountains. Some lead to high passes, only a handful of which carry roads across the border, notably Col du Som-port. The Garonne River slices through the range from Spain along Val d'Aran.

Above the large oak woodlands of the foothills, forests of beech and European sil-ver fir clothe some of the lower mountain slopes of the Hautes Pyrénées. Above about 1500m and up to 2600m are hardy Scots pine, some birch and Norway spruce, with alpen-rose and juniper scattered about the alpine

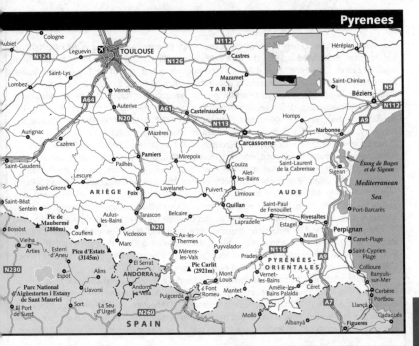

meadows. At the limits of plant growth, dwarf willow creeps among the rocks.

The Parc National des Pyrénées in particular is exceptionally rich in both flora and fauna: about 160 species of flora are endemic, including Pyrenean gentian, the yellow Turk's-cap lily, purple flowering ramonda and Pyrenean pheasant's-eye (of the buttercup family). This is one of the best places in Europe to see large birds of prey such as golden eagles, griffon and bearded vultures (lammergeiers), booted eagles, buzzards and falcons. Plenty of smaller birds are also present: alpine accentors, alpine choughs, ptarmigan, rock buntings and alpine swifts.

The fauna population includes 42 of the 110 species of mammals present in France. Izards (relatives of the chamois) are fairly numerous, marmots are well established, having been introduced from the Alps in the 1950s, and you may see badgers, red squirrels and perhaps pine martens in wooded areas. Brown bears, once numerous in the Pyrenees, are now very scarce indeed and confined to the foothill forests (see the boxed text 'Last Refuge for the Brown Bear'). Reptiles, including grass snakes and vipers, are quite common; their bite can cause an unpleasant reaction but is most unlikely to be life-threatening.

CLIMATE
From the Atlantic coast eastwards at least as far as the wild Ariège region on the edge of the Hautes Pyrénées, the Pyrenees are subject to Atlantic weather patterns. This means that overall the climate is moist and relatively mild (except in the mountains), and that the prevailing winds are south-westerly. East from the Ariège, the range is under the influence of the much drier and warmer Mediterranean climate. However, the dividing line between these two zones isn't clearcut, and conditions in the central Pyrenees are also strongly influenced locally by altitude and aspect. Snowfalls are likely at

Pyrenees National Parks

The most spectacular scenery in the whole of the French Pyrenees is protected in the Parc National des Pyrénées. Established in 1967, the park extends for 100km along the border with Spain, from south of Lescun, above the Vallée d'Aspe, to the Nouvelle massif, east of the Luz-Gavarnie valley. Its entire core zone of 45,700 hectares is above the 1100m level and includes the superb Réserve Naturelle de Néouvielle, a rugged beautiful area of granite peaks (topped by Pic de Néouvielle; 3091m), and many deep, dark lakes; there are no permanent settlements in this large area. The extensive peripheral zone (206,300 hectares) has a population of about 40,000. The park (its core and periphery) is the venue for all the walks described in detail in this chapter.

Next door across the border is Spain's Parque Nacional de Ordesa y Monte Perdido. A small national park was created in the outstandingly spectacular Ordesa canyon area in 1918, and enlarged in 1982 to 15,600 hectares, including Monte Perdido (3355m), the highest peak in the Pyrenees.

Following the example of cooperation between Parc National du Mercantour and Italy's Parco Naturale delle Alpi Marittime (see the Southern Alps chapter), French and Spanish Pyrenean park authorities joined forces in 1988 to create another 'parc sans frontières' embracing one of the finest natural heritage areas in the world. A formal charter commits the parks to working together to solve common problems, and to protect and conserve indigenous wildlife species, especially the ibex and large birds of prey. In 1997 a start was made on studies to reintroduce the Pyrenean ibex – or at least mammals as closely related to the species as possible – which had disappeared from the French side in the 19th century and had dwindled close to extinction in Spain.

Cooperation between the parks was rewarded by the designation of a Unesco World Heritage List site – Pyrénées-Mont-Perdu, cirques et canyons – in 1998. Centred on the massif of the Cirque de Gavarnie and Monte Perdido, the site covers around 30,700 hectares, half of which is in Spain. To achieve this highly prestigious status, it was necessary to demonstrate that the site is of 'exceptional universal value' for its natural features, and that its cultural sites have unique or universal significance.

any time of the year over higher ground and guaranteed from early October until April. Snow may lie in high, north-facing valleys all year and can linger on the highest passes (over 2500m) until early July.

During summer, and especially in August, conditions are bound to be changeable, with regular afternoon thunderstorms and heavy downpours. In the valleys of the central area temperatures reach 25°C or more and can exceed 30°C farther east.

September often brings more settled conditions with excellent visibility. Short-lived storms aren't unknown around the middle of the month, a prelude to the more tempestuous weather of late autumn and winter.

INFORMATION
Maps

For planning purposes, two in the IGN 1:100,000 series are useful: *Pau Bayonne* and *Pay Bagnères de Luchon*, Nos 69 and 70 respectively.

For maps covering individual walks, see Planning in the introduction to each walk.

Books

Of the relatively few English titles devoted to the Pyrenees, Trailblazer's *Trekking in the Pyrenees* by Douglas Streatfield-James covers Spain as well; it describes the GR10 and several shorter walks and is excellent value. The much older Cicerone guide, *The Pyrenean Trail GR10* by Alan Castle, is still useful for a more detailed analysis of the route. *100 Walks in the Pyrenees* by Terry Marsh is also dated, but invaluable if you want to explore the less frequented areas of the Hautes Pyrénées. Useful for the same purpose is Kev Reynolds' *Walks & Climbs in the Pyrenees*. Chris Townsend's *Long Distance Walks in the Pyrenees*, although published in 1991, best conveys the wildness and magnificence of the area through accounts of do-it-yourself extended walks on both sides of the border.

Inevitably, the list of French titles is huge. *Haute Randonnée Pyrénéenne* by Georges Véron (110FF), the originator of the high-level route through the range, provides a most informative and entertaining description of the journey. Four Fédération Française de la Randonnée Pédestre (FFRP) Topo-Guides cover the low-level route (the GR10) and some linked routes.

The national park publishes a series of walks leaflets, *Randonnées dans le Parc National des Pyrénées*, for each of the six valleys within the park. Each set comprises 10 to 12 leaflets, with clear planimetric (contourless) maps, somewhat generalised descriptions of the walks and enlightening background information. Details on leaflets relevant to walks are given in the introduction to regions later in this chapter.

Of the many natural history books (in French) for the Pyrenees, two are recommended. *Fleurs des Pyrénées: Faciles à Reconnaître* by Philippe Mayoux (49FF) is published by Rando Éditions, as is *Rochers et Paysages des Pyrénées: Faciles à Reconnaître*, also by Mayoux (89FF).

Information Sources

For tourist information purposes, the Pyrenees is divided into several regions. Below is a list of the main offices (from west to east) which may be useful starting points for inquiries about accommodation and services. The general Web site for the Pyrenees is www.lespyrenees.com.

Pays Basque
  Agence Touristique du Pays Basque
  (☎ 05 59 46 46 64, fax 05 59 46 46 60)
  BP 811, 64108 Bayonne
Béarn
  Agence Touristique du Béarn (☎ 05 59 30
  01 30, fax 05 59 84 10 13) 22 ter, rue Jean-
  Jacques de Monaix, 64000 Pau
Hautes Pyrénées
  Hautes-Pyrénées Tourisme Environnement
  (☎ 05 62 56 48 00, fax 05 62 93 69 90,
  ✆ tourisme.hautes-pyrenees@cg65.fr) 6 rue
  Eugène-Ténot, 65004 Tarbes

Last Refuge for the Brown Bear

LISA BORG

The brown bear was widespread in Europe 3000 years ago, but merciless hunting, capture for public display and loss of its habitat have severely reduced numbers. In France, it disappeared from the Alps in 1937; there is now only a tiny relict population of a particularly localised subspecies *(Ursus arctos pyrenaicus)* in the Aspe and Ossau valleys of the Pyrenees, where it has been totally protected since 1958. Local reports suggest the chances of the bear's survival are now very slim, with too few females to guarantee successful breeding.

The colour of the brown bear varies widely, from yellow-brown to almost black fur. With a humped back and thick neck, males stand around 2m tall and can weigh up to 240kg, but have a surprising turn of speed over short distances – up to 50km/h. Mainly nocturnal and solitary in habits, they are confined to dense forests, and each individual has an extensive home range or territory, up to 15km in diameter. Although they are naturally shy, they can become aggressive if threatened or injured; acute hearing and a good sense of smell compensate for poor eyesight and enable the bears to steer well clear of inquisitive visitors.

They are omnivorous, although with a strong preference for cereals and berries – another reason for its perilous status. As the area under cereal crops in the upper valleys continues to decline, as fields are turned over to grazing or just left to return to nature, the bear's sources of food continue to dwindle. However, in ideal circumstances, during autumn the bears consume vast quantities of food, storing up for the winter, when they retreat to a natural cave or excavated and lined hollow, and stay in a deep torpor until spring.

PYRENEES

Haute-Garonne
  Comité Départemental du Tourisme (CDT)
  de la Haute-Garonne (☎ 05 61 99 44 00,
  fax 05 61 99 44 19) 14 rue Bayard, 31000
  Toulouse
Ariège
  CDT de l'Ariège (☎ 05 61 03 30 70, fax 05
  61 65 17 34) 31 ave du Général de Gaulle,
  BP 143, 09004 Foix
Pyrénées Orientales
  CDT des Pyrénées Orientales (☎ 05 59 30
  01 30, fax 05 59 84 10 13) 7 quai de Lattre de
  Tassigny, BP 540, 66005 Perpignan

Inquiries about the national park should go
to the Parc National des Pyrénées office
(☎ 05 62 44 36 60, fax 05 62 44 36 70), 59

route de Pau, 65000 Tarbes. Details of the
various local *maisons du parc* (park information centres) are given in the relevant
sections later in this chapter.

Vallée d'Aspe

The Vallée d'Aspe thrusts right into the
heart of the Pyrénées Atlantiques to the
broad Col du Somport on the Spanish border. Southwards to the pass for about 16km,
it's a deep, precipitous valley with forested
slopes, embellished with some spectacular
crags on either side. Villages huddle on

A Motorway in the Vallée d'Aspe

No, this isn't the theme for a horror story, but a real-life threat, until late 1999. To start at the beginning…A railway was built through the Vallée d'Aspe in the 1920s to link the French network at
Oloron Sainte-Marie with the Spanish system via the Col du Somport. It was an engineering marvel
of track laid across precipitous mountainsides, through tunnels cut into cliffs, culminating in the huge
tunnel under Col du Somport. The track between Oloron and the border was damaged – some say
suspiciously – in 1970 and was closed, although the line from Canfranc through Spain remained open.

During the 1980s, as the Spanish (especially Aragonese) economy surged ahead, this trans-Pyrenean
transport route became a public issue. It was claimed that the best way to augment and speed up the
flow of freight traffic into France was to widen the road through Vallée d'Aspe to four or six lanes and
carve a road tunnel under Col du Somport to supplement the road over the 1600m-high pass.

Opponents of this plan pointed to the existence of the abandoned railway and the relative ease
of reopening it. They highlighted the danger posed to wildlife and stock by fast, heavy traffic, the
polluting intrusion of vehicles, the increased consumption of fossil fuel (compared with a railway
which could be powered by locally generated hydroelectricity), and the risk of dreadful accidents
involving hazardous freight. Support for the Aspe autoroute was based on its perceived economic
benefits, especially increased tourism, to the valley.

Some sections of the road were widened, and vast sums of money poured into construction of
the 8km road tunnel. One such widening was at the village of Etsaut; the old narrow road through
its centre – grossly unsuitable for modern heavy goods vehicles – is now bypassed, leaving the village in peace and safety. The tunnel construction site at the Col du Somport was the scene of many
violent protests during the 1990s; a large rally in the valley, and lack of funds, slowed progress. Then,
in March 1999 the disastrous fire in the Mont Blanc tunnel obliterated support for the tunnel and
hugely boosted backing for the railway. A major demonstration was held in the valley in May, and
the French government promptly announced that the road plan would be scrapped (even though
the tunnel was almost complete), that the abandoned railway would be modernised and reopened,
and that the necessary money would be forthcoming.

However, this may not be the end of the saga. Late in September 1999, a noon bus from Etsaut
to Oloron, several trucks and numerous cars were delayed in Bedous by a demonstration on the
road. With police outnumbering protesters by three to one, the road was reopened – just in time to
ensure that the bus passengers made their train connection at Oloron.

small, more or less flat patches. The contentious road and the former railway snake round the mountainsides (see the boxed text 'A Motorway in the Vallée d'Aspe').

To find the best of the first-class walks in the area, you need to go into the smaller although no less dramatic tributary valleys, east and west of the Aspe. Tiny Lescun, surrounded by a dramatic ring of cliffs, the Cirque de Lescun, is the base for three one-day walks described in this section: Lac de Lhurs, Around Ansabère and Les Orgues de Camplong. From the twin villages of Etsaut and Borce in the main valley, it's easy to reach the valleys and peaks to the east and west, as a further two one-day walks, chemin de la Mâture and Pic de Labigouer, illustrate.

GATEWAY
Bedous

Bedous is a small town spread out along the main road (N134) through the Vallée d'Aspe, just within the peripheral area of the Parc National des Pyrénées. Bedous has more variety and choice than the towns closer to the trailheads: Lescun, Etsaut and Borce (see Nearest Towns).

The helpful tourist office (☎ 05 59 34 71 48, fax 05 59 34 52 51), place Sarraillé, is open throughout the year. Here you can obtain comprehensive local information, topographical maps, and the useful folder of 11 walks leaflets *Randonnées dans le Parc National des Pyrénées – Aspe* for 40FF. The weather forecast is on display.

Also in place Sarraillé (signposted from the main road) is VTT Nature (☎ 05 59 34 75 25), open daily during summer; its main interest is cycling but it does stock the IGN 1:25,000 maps for the area.

For *accompagnateurs* (local guides) providing excellent introductions to the natural and cultural history of the area (in French), the most direct contact is Aspe Accompagnateurs en Montagne (☎ 05 59 34 71 48), Office du Tourisme, 64490 Accous (between Bedous and Etsaut).

The local branch of Crédit Agricole has an ATM.

The mountain rescue contact for the area is ☎ 05 59 39 86 22.

Places to Stay & Eat The *Camping Municipal de Carole* (☎ 05 59 34 70 45) is 300m west of the main road (where its location is signposted); it's open from March to November and the tariff for a walker and tent is around 25FF.

Le Choucas Blanc (☎ 05 59 34 53 71), on the main road, charges 48FF for a bed in one of its various-sized rooms; half board is 110FF. *Le Mandragot* (☎ 05 59 34 59 33), on place Sarraillé, charges 50FF per night for a bed in a small room or a dorm, and half board costs 140FF.

Among the few places to eat, *Chez Michel* (☎ 05 59 34 52 47), in the main street, offers *menus* (fixed-price meals of two or more courses) for 45FF to 95FF or, for a taste of Brittany, try *Crêperie du Gabarret* (☎ 05 59 34 76 22), on place Sarraillé, open from noon till late daily in summer, serving crepes, galettes (round, flat cakes made of puff pastry) and salads.

For self-caterers, there's a well stocked *Petit Casino supermarket* in the main street, which carries Camping Gaz, and a *boulangerie* (bakery) and *boucherie* (butcher shop) nearby.

Getting There & Away The TER Aquitaine region of SNCF (☎ 08 36 35 35 35) operates a daily bus service through Vallée d'Aspe from the town of Oloron Sainte-Marie to Canfranc in Spain. The single adult fare from Oloron to Bedous is 26FF. This service connects with regular trains on the branch line linking Oloron with Pau, on the Toulouse-Bayonne railway line.

Pau has a small airport (☎ 05 59 02 45 05) served by flights from Paris and several provincial cities, and nearer European cities including Turin, Amsterdam and Geneva. There's a bus service from the airport to the town centre.

By road, Bedous is 25km south of Oloron Sainte-Marie. The petrol station at Bedous (Garage Lepetre) is the last one before the Spanish border.

PLANNING

The planning information in this section is relevant to all the walks in the Vallée d'Aspe.

PYRENEES

The walking season is from late May to mid-October, except for the highest summits; some snow may linger on the higher passes until well into June. The universal rule (that July and August are busy) applies. From mid-September onwards, bus services may be less frequent and some mountain *refuges* will be closed; this is the time when sheep are brought down from the high pastures into the valleys. Seeing rivers of sheep trotting through the villages, hurried along by barking dogs and whistling shepherds, is an unforgettable spectacle.

Maps & Books

The IGN 1:25,000 *Ossau* sheet No 1547OT covers the valley and is the best map for these walks. Rando Éditions 1:50,000 *Béarn* sheet No 3 is handy for an overview of the area.

The *Randonnées dans le Parc National des Pyrénées* set of 11 leaflets is worth reading (in French) for descriptions of more walks, although they're too vague to be used without the 1:25,000 map.

The general guides listed under Books in the introduction to this chapter could also be useful. In addition, there's a small library of excellent local guides (in French) to walks, climbs, flora, fauna and geology, at least some of which you'll find in newsagents and other outlets in the area. The walking guides include *Randonnées Choisies en Béarn: Ossau-Aspe-Anie* by Georges Véron.

Regulations

National park regulations will apply to some of the areas you'll be walking through; see the boxed text 'National Park Regulations' in the Facts for the Walker chapter for details of regulations.

NEAREST TOWNS
Lescun

The beautiful old village of Lescun, neatly gathered around its large church, huddles below the cliffs of the Cirque de Lescun, to the west of and above Vallée d'Aspe and within the periphery of the national park. This quiet place has a surprising range of services.

The small post office, open Monday to Saturday, will exchange travellers cheques.

Depann' Sports (☎ 05 59 34 52 70) is open from 9 am to 12.30 pm and 4 to 7 pm daily; it sells fruit and vegetables, local products, maps, guides and basic camping gear, including Camping Gaz. To find it, follow the signs from various points around the village.

Places to Stay & Eat The *Gîte & Camping du Lauzart* (☎/fax 05 59 34 51 77) is about 2km south-west of the village. The gîte is open all year (except October) and costs 55FF between May and late September (59FF at other times). The spacious camping area is open from mid-April to late September; the fee for a walker and tent is 37FF. There is a small grocery store on site.

In the centre of the village, *Refuge du Pic d'Anie* (☎ 05 59 34 71 54, fax 05 59 34 53 22) has a twin room and a dormitory. The tariff is 60FF per night, and the kitchen is spacious if sparsely equipped. It's open all year. *Maison de la Montagne* (☎ 05 59 34 79 14), also in the centre of the village, is similarly worth a try.

When the *Hôtel du Pic d'Anie* is open, from mid-April to mid-September, you should be able to have a meal there. The *Bar des Bergers*, in the lower part of the village, serves sandwiches and drinks.

For supplies, in addition to Depann' Sports there's a small *grocery store* open Monday to Saturday that has canned and dry foods, bread, meat and cheese.

Getting There & Away The daily Oloron-Canfranc bus stops on the main road 6km south of Bedous, at the junction of the steep D340 road up to Lescun, a distance of 5km. However, there's no bus service to Lescun itself. A taxi from Garage Lepetre (☎ 05 59 34 70 06) will take you from Bedous to Lescun for 110FF.

Etsaut & Borce

The twin villages of Etsaut and Borce, particularly proud of its medieval heritage, are set back on either side of the main road (N134), 10km south of Bedous. One or the other can serve as the base for the chemin de la Mâture and Pic de Labigouer walks described in this section.

The *maison du parc* (park information centre; ☎ 05 59 34 88 30) in Etsaut, in the old train station, is open from 9.30 am to 12.30 pm and 2 to 6.30 pm most days between May and late September. Local guided walks and climbs (100FF per adult per day) are organised from here during summer and there's a display about the brown bear in the Pyrenees.

Etsaut's small post office, open Monday to Saturday, can exchange travellers cheques. In Borce, the phone next to the Gîte Communal is coin-operated; you'll find card phones over in Etsaut.

Places to Stay & Eat Scenically located 1.5km from the main road, *Camping Aire Naturelle du National Parc* (☎ 05 59 34 87 29) is open from June to mid-September and charges around 20FF per tent and occupant. There's also a *gîte* on site, where a bed in summer costs 48FF; meals are available in the *restaurant* next door.

Gîte Maison de l'Ours (☎ 05 59 34 86 38), in the village square, has family rooms and small dorms at 95FF for B&B or 130FF for half board. The four-course evening meal, with wine, is excellent. Part of the building dates from the 12th century.

Also in Etsaut, the *Vallée d'Aspe Auberge de Jeunesse* (☎ 05 59 34 88 98) has rooms and dorms for 50FF; the kitchen is well equipped and the wardens can offer plenty of advice about local walks and services.

In Borce, there's the modern, well set up *Gîte Communal* (☎ 05 59 34 86 40), beside the prominent church. The tariff is 50FF per night; open all year, it's popular with groups, so it would be wise to ring ahead and reserve a space. When you arrive in Borce, check in at the *bar-tabac* (bar-tobacconist) first.

In Etsaut, the *grocery store* and adjacent *Le Randonneur* bar-tabac are open daily during summer, but closed on Monday at other times. Both have basic supplies, local maps and guides. The *épicerie* (grocery store) in Borce has much more limited opening hours.

Getting There & Away The Oloron–Sainte-Marie–Canfranc bus run by SNCF stops in Etsaut; the one-way adult fare from Oloron is 33FF. To reach Borce you have to walk back to the main road then up the side road to the village (not quite 1km).

Lac de Lhurs

Duration	5½ hours
Distance	10km
Standard	medium
Start/Finish	Lescun
Public Transport	no

Summary An ingenious and, in places, precarious path en route to a small, isolated lake, one of the very few near Lescun, surrounded almost entirely by towering peaks.

This lake is hidden in a high valley between the formidable ranks of cliffs on the western side of the Cirque de Lescun and the equally impressive crags along the Franco-Spanish border. The walk could conceivably be fitted into a half-day, but a full day is recommended as the going, on forest tracks and narrow paths, is quite rough, including a section across a relatively recent landslip.

The route is waymarked with pairs of yellow stripes from the parking area at 'Napia' up through the forest; cairns mark the way higher up. The statistics for the walk assume a start in Lescun; by driving to the parking area, you'd save about 100m of climbing, 5km and 1½ hours. Cattle and sheep graze the area through which you pass, so carry all the drinking water you'll need.

THE WALK
See the Lescun map (p214).

Walk south-west through the village, past the post office on your right, to a crossroads and follow the road signposted 'Lhurs (Lac)'. This leads down and across a small stream (at Pont de Lauga); about 150m farther on bear right towards the parking area at 'Napia' and towards 'Cayolars d'Anaye'. Follow this road south and west and take the third turn right along an earthen track to a Y-junction (at the 'P' shown on the IGN 1:25,000 map). Here there's no doubt – go to the left towards Lac de Lhurs. The track winds round the steep-sided hill, Aloun; just before a stream

PYRENEES

crossing, turn right along a waymarked track. This leads north beside the stream, crosses at a ford and continues upwards beside the stream, soon with a field on the left. Watch for a left bend away from the stream and, now in the forest, go on up the track; bear right at a fork, past a barrier across the track.

Waymarkers show the direction at two more junctions, as the path leads generally south-west up the steep forested slope. Occasional openings in the trees give dramatic views of the cliffs on the peak of Le Dec de Lhurs (2176m) to the south. Bear left at a forest road (not shown on the map); the climb-ing continues a little farther to a rocky path built across a landslip. Then comes an aston-ishing section of path seemingly blasted or cut across the base of a towering, somewhat precarious-looking cliff. The rocky path then goes on up through beech forest and emerges into the open to cross a steep slope. Follow cairns and the occasional waymarker across the stream bed and up a spur covered with low scrubby vegetation. Keep on, through a defile in the cliffs, leading to open rocky ground and, at last, the partly grassed sur-roundings of the lake (2½ to 2¾ hours from Lescun). Return by the same route.

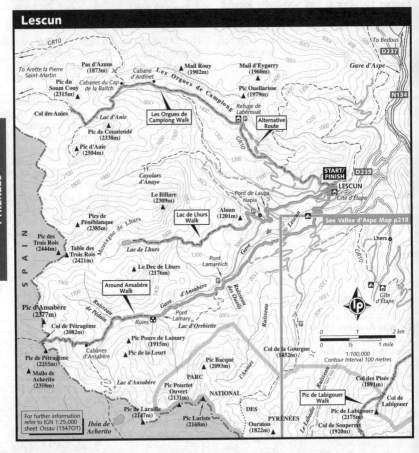

Lescun

Around Ansabère

Duration	7½ hours
Distance	22km
Standard	hard
Start/Finish	Lescun
Public Transport	no

Summary The awe-inspiring trio of Ansabère peaks is the objective of this outstandingly scenic walk – for the views not the ascent. Two shorter but equally scenic alternatives are available.

The Grand and Petite Aiguilles d'Ansabère and the Pic d'Ansabère (2377m) stand on the Spanish border at the head of the Gave d'Ansabère (where 'gave' means mountain stream), south-west of Lescun. The spectacular pinnacles of rock, the long Gave d'Ansabère valley and Col de Pétragème (2082m) are the focus of this fairly demanding walk. It can, however, be shortened (by 8km, 200m ascent and two hours) by driving to Pont Lamareich, at the end of the sealed road. Alternatively, walk only as far as the Cabanes d'Ansabère, at the foot of the Aiguilles, rather than right up to the pass (saving 3km, 400m ascent and 1½ hours). While the entire walk from Lescun definitely earns the hard rating, either of the shorter versions would be easy to medium.

The route of the walk follows quiet country roads, forest and pastoral tracks and finally a steep, well-cairned path up to the pass. When this walk was surveyed, the path wasn't actually followed right to the col. Beyond the scree slope, the path ahead was undeniably hazardous; when we walked to it, driving rain and gusty winds prevented us making the climb to the pass, so this final ascent cannot be accurately described here. However, the walk is the subject of leaflet No 6 in the *Randonnées dans le Parc National des Pyrénées – Vallée d'Aspe* folder; you could perhaps feel reassured by the carefree description of the final climb: 'From the cabines, turn towards the col, left of the Petite Aiguille. Follow the pastoral path which climbs across a stony slope.'

With sheep almost everywhere, you'll need to carry drinking water for this walk.

THE WALK
See the Lescun map.

Follow the route of the GR10 (clearly waymarked) down through Lescun past the Bar des Bergers and across the Gave de Lescun. Continue up past Camping du Lauzart to a crossroads and turn right (leaving the GR10), as directed by a green sign reading 'Masousa-Ansabère'. Follow this quiet road through farmland, south-west and south-south-west to **Pont Lamareich** (1¼ to 1½ hours from Lescun); there's a large informal parking area just to the right. Cross the bridge over Ruisseau des Oueils and walk up the forest track, gaining some height. A little more than 30 minutes through the forest (where forestry activities may be under way) brings you to the edge of open grassland and signs, pointing south to Col de Laraille and south-west to Cabanes d'Ansabère and Col de Pétragème. Soon you cross **Pont Lamary**, with Pic Poure de Lamary (1915m) towering overhead.

The track climbs steeply from here to another spacious, secluded meadow round the junction of two streams and almost enclosed by rugged peaks (about 30 minutes from Pont Lamary). Follow the parallel wheel tracks south-south-west and south across the lesser of the two streams, Ruisseau de Pédain, and up into beech woodland. Less than 30 minutes' steepish climbing brings you to the magnificent valley of grassed hummocky slopes below the Aiguilles d'Ansabère, their neighbours and the two stone-built **Cabanes d'Ansabère**, used by local shepherds during summer. The more easterly one is unlocked and can provide shelter in poor weather.

To head for the pass, work your way up the slope north of the cabins and soon a clear path materialises, rising towards the Petite Aiguille. Leaving the grass and rock behind, follow the cairned route across a scree slope of small black boulders. From here the very narrow path dips somewhat alarmingly across a stony slope then rises to cross the truncated grassy spur ahead. The col is (apparently) not far beyond the spur.

The return to Lescun is simply a matter of retracing your steps.

PYRENEES

Les Orgues de Camplong

Duration	7 hours
Distance	18.5km
Standard	medium-hard
Start/Finish	Lescun
Public Transport	no

Summary The massive cliffs of the Orgues, frequented by golden eagles, form the spectacular backdrop to this walk towards prominent Pic d'Anie. Buy cheese from a traditional *fromagerie* (cheese-maker's) high in the mountains.

The main features of this flexible walk into the upper reaches of the Lauga Valley are the vast cliffs of Les Orgues de Camplong and the birds of prey, the resident fromagerie at Cabanes du Cap de la Baitch, and Col des Anies on the limestone plateau extending north from the massive Pic d'Anie (2504m). It's not difficult to climb to the peak itself,

580m above Col d'Anies (although this is not described here), but you would need to start from the parking area at the end of the road to Refuge de Labérouat (about 4km from Lescun) rather than from Lescun itself. The **refuge** (☎ 05 59 34 50 43), a short distance from the car park, is open from spring to mid-September; the tariff is 60FF per night or 150FF for half board.

An easy day's outing (2½ hours less and only 630m ascent) could involve starting from the *refuge* and walking up to the Cabanes du Cap de la Baitch and back. Allow plenty of time for eagle and vulture-watching near Les Orgues de Camplong, and for lunch with some freshly cut cheese from the fromagerie. You'll need to carry drinking water, and/or wine to accompany the cheese.

From Lescun to the *cabanes* (cabins), the walk follows the route of the GR10 and is thus adequately waymarked. From the *refuge*, the track on up the valley to the cabanes isn't

Cheese-Making in the Mountains

The sturdy, weather-beaten shepherd at Cabanes du Cap de la Baitch is one of a dwindling breed of hardy people carrying on the centuries-old tradition of spending summer in the high mountain pastures with their flocks of sheep. These resilient animals certainly aren't bred for their wool but for the ewe's milk which goes to make distinctive cheeses, right at the source.

Every year in May the sheep are taken from their winter quarters in the valleys to nearby pastures. Then in late June or early July, once the snow has thawed, they are taken on up into the mountains under the watchful eyes of their dogs and shepherds. This is usually a major local event, with special traffic controls set up, and is a magnificent sight as rivers of sheep, most with tinkling bells round their necks, trot through the villages towards the start of the mountain paths. At the end of September or early in October, shepherds, flocks and dogs return to the valleys. Once threatened by the convenience of road transport, *transhumance*, this summer migration on foot, has revived in recent years thanks to greater concern for animal welfare and an increased commitment to keeping traditional cultural practices alive.

The *cabanes* (cabins) dotted about the mountainsides, always in sheltered sites, are simple structures, usually built of stone and these days equipped with a slab of solar panels to provide electricity. This makes the cheese preparation easier: the milk is first heated to 30°C and rennet added to coagulate it. At the right time, it's stirred, then reheated and strained. Next it's put into moulds and drained then salted, ready to go into storage. The cheeses are put in a cool, damp place for two to three months and regularly turned around to settle properly.

Connoisseurs claim they can taste the mountain grasses in these cheeses – of subtle rather than sharp flavour. They're best at room temperature, with a baguette and a bottle of good local red. The shepherd at Cap de la Baitch, like many others, keeps a pair of donkeys who regularly carry cheeses loaded into a pair of wooden panniers 5km down the steep path to the road above Lescun; he keeps some to sell to passing walkers.

waymarked; beyond the cabanes, the route is fairly consistently cairned.

Wild flowers are another feature of this walk, and not only during spring. In early autumn, pink and purple heathers, purple and white crocuses, bright yellow gorse and the distinctive blue-stemmed and blue-flowering queen of the Alps (resembling a thistle) all adorn the rocky ground above and west of the cabanes.

No 9 of the *Randonnées dans le Parc National des Pyrénées* leaflets describes the walk to Pas d'Azuns and Pas de l'Osque, north of the Cabanes du Cap de la Baitch, and thus is handy for the walk covered here.

THE WALK

See the Lescun map (p214).

In Lescun, pick up the GR10 just west of the church and walk up rue Henri Barriot to a T-junction and turn left up a track in the direction of the sign reading 'Refuge de l'Abérouat' (this is an alternative spelling). Next, go right when you come to a road then left again at a fork less than 150m farther on. Leave the road another 200m farther on and follow a path between fields which soon leads to the left and enters some woodland. Climb steeply to a minor road and bear left; continue for about 75m, then turn right along a path which winds quite steeply up a partly wooded hillside. When you meet an old track along a grassed terrace, turn left (50 minutes from Lescun).

Here you can either faithfully follow the GR10 up to Refuge de Labérouat, along a somewhat circuitous route through meadows and woodlands, or head directly for the *refuge* up the track (about 30 minutes' walk), with magnificent views of the Lescun Valley and the distinctive Pic du Midi d'Ossau, with its split peak clearly visible to the east. Here too you'll undoubtedly see vultures and perhaps golden eagles floating effortlessly above the crags.

From Refuge de Labérouat, the track leads into beech woodland; it's rocky in places, so if it has been raining remember that wet limestone is very slippery. Less than an hour's walking takes you up and out of the woodland to the open valley below the

well-concealed Cabane d'Ardinet. The fromagerie is barely 30 minutes farther on.

To continue from the fromagerie towards Col des Anies, cross the bare ground where the sheep are gathered and pick up a clear path which leads generally south-west; after a few hundred metres cross a stream, just above the point where the water spurts out of the rocks. The clear path climbs steadily over mainly rocky ground to the left of a large bluff to a tiny valley, then up on a rocky path to another grassy bowl. Cairns and light blue waymarkers point the way on the south side of the valley; fantastic views of Les Orgues de Camplong and of the plains far below will slow your progress. Cross the limestone pavement, threading through the gaps between the blocks of stone, up towards the col as far as time and inclination permit. Allow about 1¼ hours up to the col from the fromagerie.

The return is simply a matter of retracing your steps. From the col all the way back down to Lescun should take between 2¼ and 2½ hours.

Chemin de la Mâture

Duration	5 hours
Distance	10.5km
Standard	medium
Start/Finish	Etsaut
Public Transport	yes

Summary An exhilarating and outstandingly spectacular walk centred on the historic chemin de la Mâture, a path cut into vertical cliffs; superb views of the Vallée d'Aspe on the return.

This is one of the best-known paths in the Pyrenees, although it's only about 1km long. Cut into a sheer rock face on a fairly steep gradient, it climbs through the deep gorge of Le Sescoué Ruisseau, a tributary of the Gave de l'Aspe. At its narrowest the *chemin* (track) is an unnerving 1.8m wide, but most of it is closer to 3m across and perfectly safe and reassuring. The chemin, on the route of the GR10, is the centrepiece of a fine day walk from Etsaut, which returns from high above the valley via Col d'Arras down to the vil-

PYRENEES

lage. The walk is in the peripheral area of the national park and is part of the longer walk to Pic du Midi d'Ossau (see Other Walks at the end of the chapter).

HISTORY

The chemin de la Mâture was built in 1772 to transport timber from the forests on the southern side of the gorge. Built by convicts using primitive equipment, the path was, for its time, a miracle of surveying, engineering and construction. Timber was in great demand for beams, pulleys and *mâts* (masts) for vessels of the royal navy, hence the name

chemin de la Mâture. Each load of logs was hauled by a team of oxen: two in front and two pairs behind to act as brakes on the descent. The timber was stockpiled near Lees Athas, shipped downriver to Bayonne and on to the royal navy yards.

Of more recent date is the nearby Fort du Portalet, in the main valley, built in the 19th century and used as a prison cduring WWII.

PLANNING
Maps

The route of the GR10 south-eastwards from Etsaut has changed from that shown on the

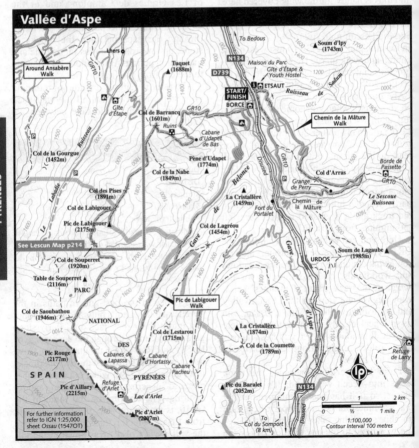

IGN 1:25,000 *Ossau* sheet No 1547OT, and on the Rando Éditions 1:50,000 sheet No 3. It no longer follows the main road (which itself has been widened and realigned here), but goes along paths through the woodland above the road, as described below.

THE WALK
See the Vallée d'Aspe map.

The GR10 leaves Etsaut from the south side of the village square, directly opposite the bridge across the stream. Walk along the lane then go up to the left, and soon right along an old, well-graded path which zigzags up through deciduous woodland. After about 35 minutes you pass a ruinous stone building on the right to arrive at a road beneath a power transmission line. Turn right and continue downhill. This mildly frustrating descent – at least with good views of the valley – persists for about 2km to a small parking area where there are several signs, including one for the chemin de la Mâture. Follow this good path, which leads onwards, overlooking the massive Fort du Portalet and one of the narrowest parts of the Vallée d'Aspe.

The path then abruptly turns into the gorge and the **chemin de la Mâture** stretches improbably ahead under, or rather through, the overhanging cliff. The views all round are spectacular and several vantage points, on wider parts of the chemin, invite photo stops. Eventually the path swings away from the gorge as the valley widens. About 1½ hours after starting on the chemin, you'll come to the stone buildings of **Grange de Perry**, where there's piped fresh water at a trough in the courtyard. From here a mostly excellent path climbs steeply through woodland to a signposted junction (25 minutes from Grange de Perry). Here you leave the GR10 and west to Col d'Arras.

Continue uphill through forest, soon emerging into meadows on the steep hillside, with magnificent views across Vallée d'Aspe. After a few hundred metres the route crosses the inconspicuous **Col d'Arras**, leads into trees and begins to descend. Some care is needed to follow the best route as the path splits, and splits again – red and yellow waymarkers are helpful. At a track junction

(75 minutes from where you left the GR10), bear right following yellow waymarkers. Shortly you come round a corner and Vallée d'Aspe lies ahead with Borce in view far below. The path takes you steeply down to the end of a minor road; follow this across the steep hillside for about 2km to a tight bend. A narrow path takes off from here and descends steadily to reach Etsaut at the information board close to the bridge in the centre of the village (about 1¾ hours from the start of the yellow waymarked route).

Pic de Labigouer

Duration	8½ hours
Distance	21km
Standard	hard
Start/Finish	Etsaut or Borce
Public Transport	yes

Summary A superlatively scenic and challenging walk off the beaten track, across a ridge above Vallée d'Aspe; possible variations can moderate the difficulty without sacrificing any of the rewards.

Pic de Labigouer (2175m) caps a long ridge on the western side of the Vallée de Belonce, which parallels the Vallée d'Aspe above Borce and Etsaut; Pic de Labigouer also overlooks the Cirque de Lescun. Although not a particularly high summit by Pyrenean standards, its comparative isolation from the peaks along the Spanish border and from other nearby high ridges means that the views from the undulating ridge are truly panoramic in scope: from the lowlands to the north, to Pic d'Anie, the Ansabère peaks, Col du Somport, Balaïtous (3144m) to the south-east, Pic du Midi d'Ossau and the deep trench of the Vallée d'Aspe.

Waymarking along the route of the walk is variable – from the familiar GR markers to none at all along the main ridge.

The walk as described is, admittedly, rather long for one day. Alternatively, you could climb Pic de Labigouer and return to Borce by the same route, involving about the same amount of climbing but saving 1½ hours and at least 7km.

PYRENEES

Another possibility would be to stay overnight at **Refuge d'Arlet** (☎ 05 59 34 70 72) beside Lac d'Arlet, above the head of Vallée de Belonce. The *refuge*, run by Parc National des Pyrénées, is open from mid-June to late September. The tariff is 50FF per night or 150FF for half board. In this case, it might be preferable to do the walk in reverse, as the climb up Vallée de Belonce is more gradual than the climb to Col de Barrancq and on to the main ridge. Finding the route should not present any difficulties, and may even be easier than it is coming down the valley.

PLANNING

The route of the GR10 and the network of minor roads immediately west of Borce have changed slightly since the publication of the relevant maps for this walk, ie, IGN 1:25,000 *Ossau* sheet No 1547OT and Rando Éditions 1:50,000 sheet No 3. These alterations are described in the following notes. The route marked on the Rando Éditions 1:50,000 map between the summit of Pic de Labigouer and Col de Souperret is not that described here, and is too steep to be safely recommended. Neither map shows all the tracks and paths in Vallée de Belonce.

THE WALK

See the Vallée d'Aspe map (p218).
Walk northwards out of Etsaut along the road, cross the N134 and go on up to Borce. At the entrance to the village bear left at a fork – this way takes you past the best of the well-preserved old buildings and narrow lanes to a large church. Pass it to your left (along the GR10), cross over the road ahead and climb a track, shortly turning left at a junction. Continue up a winding path to a road and turn right, soon crossing a stream. A little farther on at a crossroads bear left towards 'Maison Sayerse-Nardet GR10', and shortly recross the stream. About 30m farther on, turn right, then right again in the same distance up a path.

There's little respite from climbing now, as the route soon crosses the stream and rises up the open hillside. Then comes a stretch, generally southwards, on waymarked forest roads through mixed woodland, crossing a few streams. This takes you on to expansive meadows with the small **Cabane d'Udapet de Bas**, used by shepherds during summer, on the far side (1½ hours from Borce). Continue up, mainly across open ground, to the ruins of the Haute Udapet cabins. A faint path heads up across the grass and clumps of heather and bilberry towards the lowest point on the skyline. About halfway up this meadow the route veers to the right (north) and enters woodland to soon reach **Col de Barrancq** (1601m), 30 minutes from Udapet de Bas.

Continue southwards through the closely spaced trees and along the narrow ridge – a path soon becomes clear, and in a few minutes you leave the trees on your left behind. It's a steep climb up to the broad and grassy ridge crest (at '1913') – the ideal place for a good break with the mountain panorama now spread out before you.

Follow the ridge down across **Col des Pises** (1891m), then steeply up along the well-cairned path and down a narrow rocky spine to **Col de Labigouer** (2040m); this is on the boundary of the national park's heartland, identified by the national park logo (the red head of an izard on a white background) painted on rocks. From here choose your approach to the top of **Pic de Labigouer**; on a very windy day, the western side was sheltered and not too steep (about 75 minutes from '1913').

Return to Col de Labigouer. To continue south along the ridge, join a narrow path traversing the western flank of the pic; it starts strongly, fades for a few hundred metres on steep ground, then coalesces on the next prominent spur and descends to **Col de Souperret**. A thread-like path picked out with white-and-red waymarkers leads on, now on the eastern flank, maintaining a good height across grassed slopes then along the base of some low cliffs. Two small crags, separated by a short open stretch, are easily passed, then it's down to **Col de Saoubathou** (an hour from Col de Labigouer).

A well-trodden route crosses beneath the colourful **Pic Rouge**, its name coming from the deep-pink rock prevalent around here.

There's also a great deal of very dense conglomerate – multicoloured stones and pebbles embedded in the pink matrix. The path becomes diffuse as it descends towards **Cabanes de Lapassa** (occupied during the summer), but is clear again beyond the cabins. About 500m farther on, you reach the signposted turn-off to Refuge d'Arlet. Continue down to the head of the Belonce Valley and on to **Cabane d'Hortassy**. Here, pass below the buildings and enclosures and follow a narrow path towards then into the trees. The descent continues, back out into the open; keep on the eastern side of the valley, following the route defined by the red-and-white waymarkers.

Continue past the signposted path leading up (right) to Col de Lagréou and go on into the forest. The next turn, onto a path waymarked with the now-familiar white-and-red markers, is easy to miss – it's worth backtracking if you suddenly realise you haven't seen one for a couple of hundred metres. The waymarked path leads down to a bridge over the Gave de Belonce and continues through open country; one or two electric fences across the route may need to be negotiated.

About 30 minutes from the col turn-off you come to the end of the road, where there are signs to various destinations, including Refuge d'Arlet. From here it's just a matter of following the road down through the narrow gorge (where some landslips looked distinctly precarious) and on to the bitumen road, where a large sign designates the road you've been following as route Forestière de Belonce. Turn right and go on down to Borce and Etsaut – about 1½ hours from the end of the road.

Vallée de Cauterets

The Vallée de Cauterets, in the heart of the Haute Pyrénées, isn't a name that appears on local maps. We use it here as a convenient general title for the area around the several streams which flow north through deep valleys from high in the mountains to form the Gave de Cauterets, which tumbles through the town of the same name. Thus the Vallée de Cauterets embraces the valleys of the Gave du Marcadau and the Gave de Gaube which come together in spectacular fashion at Pont d'Espagne at the head of Val de Jéret. This in turn meets the Gave de Lutour at La Raillère (a cluster of bars and restaurants about 2km south of Cauterets), where the cascading rivers unite to become the Gave de Cauterets.

Vignemale (3298m), the French Pyrenees' supreme summit, commands the head of Vallée de Gaube, and is at the crux of a complex pattern of extremely rugged ridges forming the mountainous chain along the Spanish border. The boundary of the Parc National des Pyrénées core area lies just south of Cauterets, so most of your walking will be within the park.

Walks there are in abundance, along wooded valleys, past beautiful lakes, up to high passes on or close to the border, and to some of the summits, although most require scrambling or rock-climbing skills and equipment. The main walk described, In Vignemale's Shadow, starts and finishes in Cauterets. It's a three-day outing, focusing on Vignemale, and is accompanied by two day walks (Lacs de Cambalès and Circuit des Lacs) which can be added to the longer walk or done independently.

With Cauterets as a base, two other day walks are described: Pic du Cabaliros and Vallée de Lutour. The Other Walks section includes suggestions for doing the long walk in easier day walks and outlines the scope for walks in the Gavarnie area to the east.

PLANNING
The planning information in this section is relevant to all the walks in the Vallée de Cauterets.

When to Walk
Overall, the walking season in this area is fairly long; below about 2300m snow should not be an obstacle from late May or early June until about mid-October. Above 2300m, and subject to local advice, you'll probably be glad of an ice axe or walking poles in late spring or late October. July and August are very busy, so you'd definitely

PYRENEES

need to book ahead to ensure a bed in the *refuges* and gîtes d'étape (essential for Refuge Wallon). Late September is particularly beautiful with the deciduous trees starting to change colour. Unfortunately, the useful local bus service has stopped by then (see Getting To/From the Walks below).

What to Bring

If you plan to stay at a *refuge*, you'll need a sleeping bag or sheet, as only blankets are provided. It's wise to take a torch, preferably a head torch, especially at Refuge Wallon where lighting away from the dining room after dark is the minimum needed for safety.

Maps & Books

The best map for all the walks described is IGN 1:25,000 *Vignemale* sheet No 1647OT. Waymarked and publicised walks or walking routes are highlighted in red; the few places where these have changed since the map was published are noted in the walk descriptions. The Rando Éditions 1:50,000 *Bigorre* sheet No 4 also covers the area; it's useful for an overall view, but is less reliable for the waymarked walks and is more difficult to read than the IGN sheet.

The set of 15 leaflets, *Randonnées dans le Parc National des Pyrénées – Vallée de Cauterets*, describes a variety of walks and at 35FF is the best local, French-language guide. Several others are available, published by Rando Éditions and others; the appropriate sections of the GR10 FFRP Topo-Guide, the Trailblazer guide and Georges Véron's book are also useful (see Books under Information at the beginning of this chapter).

NEAREST TOWN
Cauterets

At the foot of the valleys, Cauterets is a fairly large and prosperous town with many fine public and private buildings. It caters generously for walkers (and in winter for skiers) and throughout the year for devotees of the thermal spas.

Information The tourist office (☎ 05 62 92 50 27, fax 05 62 92 59 12, @ espaces .cauterets@cauterets.com), place Foch, is

open daily throughout the year. It produces a detailed accommodation guide and posts the daily weather forecast by the front door.

SOS Touriste (☎ 05 62 42 77 40), operating from 9 am to 7 pm Monday to Saturday and from 10 am to 6 pm on Sunday, is an emergency service provided by the tourist offices of the Haute Pyrénées to assist walkers in difficulty.

The maison du parc for Parc National des Pyrénées (☎ 05 62 92 52 56), route de Pierrefitte (near the bus station), is open from 9.30 am to noon and 3 to 7 pm Monday, Tuesday, Friday and Saturday, and on Thursday afternoon and Sunday morning. This is the best place to go for maps, walking and natural history guides, and general information about the park, including details of the guided walks program during July and August (100FF per adult per day). There's also a comprehensive display on the park's flora and fauna.

Another good source of maps and guides is the Maison de la Presse in place Foch.

For specialised information about the condition of routes over the high passes – particularly valuable in spring and early summer – and about weather in the mountains, contact the Bureau des Guides (☎ 05 62 92 62 02), 8 rue de Verdun. This is also the place to go if you're interested in climbing Vignemale with a guide.

Places to Stay & Eat Of the several camping grounds in the vicinity of Cauterets, *Le Mamelon-Vert* (☎/fax 05 62 92 51 56, ave du Mamelon-Vert) is the most convenient for bus travellers as it overlooks the bus station; it's open from January to late September. The tariff for two people and tent is 68FF (reduced out of season). For car travellers, *Le Cabaliros* (☎/fax 05 62 92 55 36, Pont de Secours), on the north-eastern edge of town beside the main road (N21), is open from June to the end of September and has grassed, shady pitches for around 40FF for a tent and occupant.

The comfortable *Gîte Beau Soleil* (☎ 05 62 92 53 52, 25 Rue Maréchal Joffre) offers two- and four-bed rooms with private facilities for 180FF per night. There's a small kitchen for self-caterers, or you can enjoy the friendly and helpful owner's half board for 185FF per person.

Gîte Le Pas de l'Ours (☎ *05 62 92 58 07, fax 05 62 92 06 49, 21 rue de la Raillère)* has rather cramped dorms and a small kitchen; the overnight fee is 60FF.

For a meal, the many hotel restaurants have *menus* in the 85FF to 150FF range, featuring local specialities. More informally, **Pizzeria Giovanni** (☎ *05 62 92 57 80, 5 rue de la Raillère)* is open daily from 7 pm. The pizzas (45FF to 55FF) are superior, a generous steak costs 65FF and the irresistible home-made desserts 35FF to 45FF. After all this, patrons are welcome to (try to) log onto the Internet to check email and send messages (free).

Another attractive restaurant is **La Bodega** (☎ *05 62 92 60 21)*, in rue de la Raillère, for genuine, tasty Spanish cooking offered in *menus* (65FF to 85FF) or a la carte; it's open from 6 pm.

In ave Maréchal Foch, the main street linking the bus station and the town centre, you'll find a **boulangerie**, a good **boucherie** and two supermarkets, of which **Huit à Huit** (open daily except Thursday) has a larger range than **Petit Casino** (closed Tuesday).

Getting There & Away SNCF runs a daily bus service from Lourdes (outside the train station) to Cauterets (38FF one way). In the handsome bus station there are some fascinating old photos of electric trains on the now-disused line in the early years of the 20th century. Lourdes is on the busy Toulouse-Pau-Bayonne line, with good connections to Paris' Montparnasse train station and Marseille.

GETTING TO/FROM THE WALKS

The great majority of the walks in this section start from Cauterets. Pont d'Espagne, at the end of the D920 road, 8km south of and 600m higher than Cauterets, is an alternative in most cases, with the obvious advantage of saving time and energy. Between June and early September, Excursions Bordenave (☎ 05 62 92 53 68, fax 05 62 92 01 23), place de la Mairie, Cauterets,

operates a useful *navette* (minibus) service from the centre of town to Pont d'Espagne. The return adult fare is 30FF, and there are six departures from each end daily, starting at 8 am from Cauterets and finishing with a 7 pm departure from the large parking area at Pont d'Espagne. There's a national park information centre, telephone and toilets at the parking area. Out of season, Bordenave will take walkers up to Pont d'Espagne for 70FF one way (irrespective of the number of passengers).

In Vignemale's Shadow

Duration	3 days
Distance	30km
Standard	medium-hard
Start & Finish	Cauterets or Pont d'Espagne
Nearest Town	Cauterets
Public Transport	yes

Summary With Vignemale a constant, compelling presence, possibly one of the finest circular walks in the Haute Pyrénées includes stays at two very different *refuges*, and opportunities for day walks from one of them.

This flexible three-day walk from Cauterets takes in a wealth of varied scenery: the cascades of the Gave de Cauterets, the beautiful Vallée du Marcadau, the granite formations and lakes high in the Arratille Valley, two narrow cols on the Spanish border, Vignemale with its glaciers and moraines dominating the head of Vallée de Gaube, and the Gaube's own cascades and tranquil lake.

For overnight accommodation and meals there are two Club Alpin Français (CAF) *refuges* – Refuge Wallon and Refuge des Oulètes de Gaube, quite different in style and setting but both almost guaranteed to foster camaraderie among fellow walkers. Areas are set aside for tents near both and campers are welcome to have meals at the *refuges*.

The paths and tracks followed vary greatly from smooth and level to rough, steep and rocky, but all are clearly defined. Yellow signposts at critical junctions give destinations and estimated times. These times are

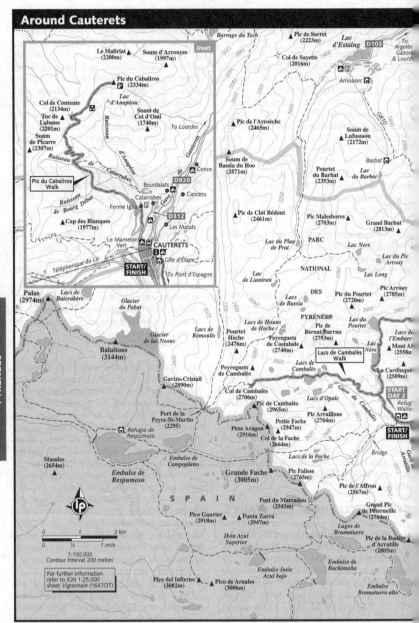

Around Cauterets

Barrage du Tech

Pic de Sarret (2223m)

Lac d'Estaing

D103

To Argelès Gazost & Lourdes

Col de Sayette (2016m)

Arriousec

Inset

Le Maliriat (2200m)

Soum d'Arrouyes (1997m)

Pic du Cabaliros (2334m)

Lac d'Anapéou

Col de Contente (2134m)

Tuc de Labasse (2201m)

Soum de Picarre (2307m)

Soum de Cot d'Omi (1740m)

To Lourdes

Pic de l'Arcoèche (2465m)

Soum de Lufusssou (2172m)

Ruisseau de Catarrabes

Ruisseau d'Anapéou

Gave de Cauterets

Conce

Soum de Bassia du Hoo (2571m)

Pourtet du Barbat (2353m)

Barbat

Lac du Barbat

Pic du Cabaliros Walk

Ruisseau de Bourg Débat

Bourdalats

Catarrabes

Canceru

D920

Pic de Clot Bédout (2461m)

Pic Maleshores (2703m)

Grand Barbat (2813m)

Ferme Igau

D312

Les Matats

Cap des Blanques (1977m)

Le Mamelon Vert

CAUTERETS

Gîte d'Étape

Lac du Plaa de Prat

PARC

Lac Nere

Lac du Pic Arrouy

NATIONAL

Lac de Liantran

Lac de Bassia

Lac Long

Téléphérique du Lis

START/ FINISH

To Pont d'Espagne

DES

Lacs de Bassia

PYRÉNÉES

Pic du Pourtet (2720m)

Pic Arrouy (2785m)

Palas (2974m)

Lacs de Batcrabère

Glacier du Pabat

Glacier de las Neous

Lacs de Rémoulis

Pourtet Hèche (2476m)

Lacs de Hòuns de Hèche

Peyregnets de Costalade (2740m)

Pic de Bernat Barrau (2793m)

Lac du Pourtet

Lac Nère

Lacs de l'Embarr

Mont Ai (2558m)

Lacs de Cambalès Walk

La Cardinquè (2509m)

Balaïtous (3144m)

Gavizo-Cristail (2890m)

Peyregnets de Cambalès

Col de Cambalès (2706m)

Lacs de Cambalès

Gave de Cambalès

START DAY 2

Refug Wallo

Pic de Cambalès (2965m)

Lacs d'Opale

Pic Arraillous (2704m)

START/ FINISH

Port de la Peyre-St-Martin (2295m)

Refugio de Respumoso

Pène Aragon (2916m)

Petite Fache (2947m)

Col de la Fache (2664m)

Lacs de la Fache

Bridge

Gave Arraille

Musales (2654m)

Embalse de Campoplano

Embalse de Respumoso

Grande Fache (3005m)

Pic Falisse (2765m)

Pic de l'Affron (2567m)

S P A I N

Port du Marcadau (2541m)

Grand Pic de Péterneille (2764m)

Pico Gaurier (2918m)

Punta Zarra (2947m)

Lagos de Bramatuero

Pic de la Badète d'Arratille (2805m)

Ibón Azul Superior

Embalse de Bachimaña

0   1   2 km

0   ½   1 mile

1:100,000
Contour Interval 200 metres

For further information
refer to IGN 1:25,000
sheet Vignemale (1647OT)

Pico del Infierno (3082m)

Pico de Arnales (3006m)

Embalse Inón Azul bajo

Embalse Bramatuero alto

PYRENEES

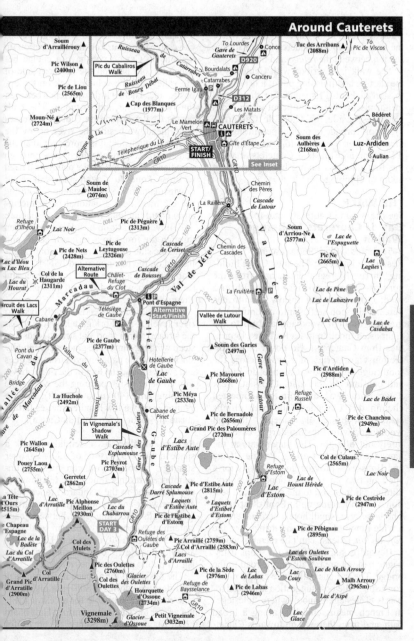

Around Cauterets

Soum d'Arraillérouy ▲

Pic Wilson (2400m) ▲

Pic de Liou (2565m) ▲

Moun-Né (2724m) ▲

Ruisseau de Catarrabes

To Lourdes

Gave de Gauterets

Conce

Tuc des Arribans (2088m) ▲

To Pic de Viscos

D920

Bourdalats

Catarrabes

Ferme Igau

Canceru

D312

Les Matats

Bédéret

Cap des Blanques (1977m) ▲

Ruisseau de Bourg Débat

Pic du Cabaliros Walk

Le Mamelon Vert

Téléphérique du Lis

Cirque du Lis

CAUTERETS

Gîte d'Étape

Soum des Aulhères (2168m) ▲

Luz-Ardiden

Aulian

GR10

START/ FINISH

See Inset

Soum de Mauloc (2074m) ▲

Chemin des Pères

La Raillère

Cascade de Lutour

Refuge d'Ilhéou

Lac Noir

Pic de Péguère (2313m) ▲

Cascade de Ceriset

Soum d'Arriou-Ne (2577m) ▲

Lac de l'Espuguette

Pic de Nets (2428m) ▲

Pic de Leytugouse (2326m) ▲

Chemin des Cascades

Pic Ne (2665m) ▲

Lac Laguès

Lac d'Iléou

Lac Bleu

Col de la Haugarde (2311m) ▲

Alternative Route

Châlet-Refuge du Clot

Cascade de Bousses

La Fruitière

Lac de Pène

Lac de Lahazère

Lac du Hourat

Circuit des Lacs Walk

Cabane

Marcadau

Pont du Cayan

Téléphérique de Gaube

Pont d'Espagne

Alternative Start/Finish

Vallée de Lutour Walk

Lac Grand

Lac de Casdabat

Bridge

Pic de Gaube (2377m) ▲

Hotellerie de Gaube

Soum des Garies (2497m) ▲

Pic d'Ardiden (2988m) ▲

Lac de Badet

La Hucholé (2492m) ▲

Lac de Gaube

Pic Méya (2533m) ▲

Pic Mayouret (2668m) ▲

Cabane de Pinet

Refuge Russell

Pic de Chanchou (2949m) ▲

In Vignemale's Shadow Walk

Pic Wallon (2645m) ▲

Cascade Esplumouse

Pic Peyrot (2703m) ▲

Pic de Bernadole (2656m) ▲

Grand Pic des Paloumères (2720m) ▲

Lacs d'Estibe Aute

Col de Culaus (2565m) ▲

Lac Noir

Pouey Laou (2755m) ▲

Gerretet (2862m) ▲

Cascade Darré Splumouse

Pic d'Estibe Aute (2815m) ▲

Refuge d'Estom

Lac de Hount Hérède

Lac d'Estom

Pic de Cestrède (2947m) ▲

La Tête d'Ours (2515m) ▲

Lac d'Arratille

Pic Alphonse Meillon (2930m) ▲

Lac du Chabarrou

Laquets d'Estibe Aute

Laquets d'Estibet d'Estom

Chapeau l'Espagne

Lac de la Badète

START DAY 3

Refuge des Oulétes de Gaube

Pic Arraillé (2759m) ▲

Col d'Arraillé (2583m)

Lacs d'Arratille

Pic de Pébignau (2895m) ▲

Lac des Oulettes d'Estom Soubiran

Col du Col d'Arratille

Col des Mulets

Pic des Oulettes (2760m) ▲

Glacier des Oulettes

Pic de la Sède (2976m) ▲

Lac de Labas

Lac Couy

Lac de Malh Arrouy

Malh Arrouy (2965m) ▲

Grand Pic d'Arratille (2900m) ▲

Col d'Arratille

Col des Oulettes

Hourquette d'Ossoue (2734m)

Refuge de Baysselance

Pic de Labas (2946m) ▲

Lac d'Aspé

Vignemale (3298m)

Glacier d'Ossoue

Petit Vignemale (3032m)

GR10

Lac Glace

PYRENEES

generally an accurate guide for reasonably fit walkers, except in the Vallée de Gaube where the time is seriously underestimated for the section between the *refuge* and the lake.

The walk is described with Cauterets as the starting and finishing point; it is possible to start at Pont d'Espagne, but this would mean missing the magnificent chemin des Cascades beside the Gave de Cauterets. Transport (private or public) permitting, the ideal solution would be to start from Pont d'Espagne and finish at Cauterets, making the first day less taxing by saving about 600m of climbing.

THE WALK
See the Around Cauterets map (p224–5).
Day 1: Cauterets to Refuge Wallon
5–5½ hours, 10km, 960m ascent
Reach the imposing Thermes César building on rue Maréchal Foch and from the northern entrance go right up a path to a road; cross over and follow chemin des Pères. This soon settles into a comfortable gradient through woodland and up to the signposted junction to La Raillère (45 minutes from Cauterets). Go down in that direction via a series of zigzags, cross the footbridge just below Cascade de Lutour and continue to the road. Cross it, walk down a little way, and join the signposted chemin des Cascades. The path climbs steadily, occasionally steeply, through woodland, with the thundering cascades rarely out of sight. The viewpoints at the named cascades – Ceriset, Pas de l'Ours and Bousses – provide good reasons for a spell or two en route. About 1½ hours' climbing brings you to the short paved section of path leading up to **Pont d'Espagne**. The *hôtellerie* (small hotel) here advertises a wide range of snacks and drinks, but the *café au lait*, at least, can't be recommended.

If you're starting from the Pont d'Espagne parking area, walk up the road to the bridge. The various paths here can be rather confusing – the best suggestion is to head towards 'Télésiège Gaube' (where 'télésiège' in French means chairlift) along a broad path, and from there go on towards Châlet-Refuge du Clot. Nearly 1km from the Pont d'Espagne you come to a bridge across Gave du Marcadau. For the next section up to Pont du Cavan, you have a choice between the old path on the northern side of the valley and the vehicle track on the opposite side. There's little difference between the two in time and distance. The path passes Châlet-Refuge du Clot then crosses wide meadows beside the river below the steep mountainside; it is more open than the vehicle track, part of which goes through woodland. If you follow the path you'll need to cross **Pont du Cavan** and walk back downstream for a short distance to join the vehicle track near a national park information board (an hour from Pont d'Espagne).

Follow the track up beside a stream then through the forest in a series of bends and round the side of a tall crag. The route highlighted on the recommended IGN 1:25,000 map is that of a more direct but steeper and rougher path which leads off just past the stream crossing.

The track then descends slightly, back to river level. A solid bridge takes you across the stream, then a short flat stretch leads to a steep winding climb. The gradient eventually slackens and the path emerges from the trees and swings round the foot of the ridge above. You come to a sign pointing the way to the camping area (400m to the left); **Refuge Wallon** is only a few hundred metres farther ahead (1½ hours from Pont du Cavan).

Refuge Wallon It's essential to book a space in this *refuge* (☎ 05 62 92 64 28) over summer, although you can turn up unannounced at other times. The telephone is not connected to the standard France Telecom network and a conversation is carried on with disconcerting gaps between each statement. Alternatively you can send a fax (fax 05 62 92 06 90) or write to Le Gardien at Boite Postale 25, 65111 Cauterets. There isn't a public phone at the *refuge*.

The basic rate for a space in the modern, well-designed dorms is 80FF per night; private rooms are available for an extra 15FF, but are far too small for comfort. Half board (200FF) guarantees plenty of bread for breakfast and a substantial, three-course, no-frills evening meal. Drinks are extra: 1L of wine (40FF), beer and coffee (both 15FF). Let them know in advance if you're a vegetarian (and be prepared for an omelette). Lunch can be ordered the night before (50FF). These prices may seem high; However, everything must be helicoptered (costing 10,000FF per hour) or backpacked in by staff. In theory, there's a limit of three nights to any one visit, but this may not be enforced out of season. The *refuge* is open from March to early November.

In keeping with the minimal electricity and spartan style of the *refuge*, showers are not provided, so be prepared for just a large basin and cold water. Following the rather old-fashioned CAF rules, everyone is sent off to bed by 10 pm, and the *gardien*'s (caretaker's) assistant stomps around the dormitories at 7 am shouting 'Bonjour' in a very loud voice. You have been warned! Nevertheless, the camaraderie and good humour among walkers is infectious and helps to make a stay at Refuge Wallon a very memorable experience.

The camp site by the stream below the *refuge* is free and campers are welcome to eat inside (and therefore to use the toilets and washing facilities); meals may be prepared there too, with the gardien's permission. National park regulations prescribe that tents may not be left standing during the day – they must be struck by 9 am. Everyone staying in the area is asked to take their rubbish away with them.

Refuge Wallon

Refuge Wallon has several claims to fame among Pyrenean mountain *refuges*: its superb location high in the Vallée du Marcadau, its status as one of the four busiest *refuges* in France, and its age – around 90 years old. Some would add grimly that it is also notorious for its minimal facilities – but that's another story (see the In Vignemale's Shadow walk).

The *refuge* takes its name from a true man of the mountains, Paul Edouard Wallon. Born in 1821 near Montauban (north of Toulouse), he became a lawyer – and then discovered the Pyrenees. During the 1840s and 1850s he spent all his spare time there fishing and studying the how, when and where of local farming.

At the same time, botanists and geologists were discovering, recording and puzzling over the exceptionally rich flora and the extremely complex rocks of the Pyrenees, although they rarely ventured beyond the security of the valleys and into the mountains.

Then, through a chance meeting, Wallon joined a small band of men whose enthusiasm for the mountains led them up to the summits. They dedicated themselves to gaining a complete picture of the very intricate geography of the central Pyrenees – no easy task, as this was long before the days of aerial photography. One fascinating result of this commitment was Wallon's map, *Central Pyrenees, from Navarre to the Vallée d'Aure* published in 1880 at a scale of 1:150,000. A copy of this detailed work of cartographic art is on display in the *refuge*.

Wallon made many pioneering and adventurous ascents of Pyrenean peaks; a formidable summit, Pic Wallon (2645m), nearly east of the *refuge*, is named in his honour. In 1874 he helped to found the Club Alpin Français (CAF) in Paris. Undaunted by age, he climbed and walked in the Pyrenees until at least 1890.

The refuge bearing his name was opened in 1911, built of stone with gravel and sand from the nearby stream. This building still stands, with progressive enlargements extending from its eastern side. The dining room walls are covered with illustrated accounts of Wallon's life and work, and early photos of the refuge. Some show elegant ladies on horseback – perhaps explaining the origin of the well-built track up the Vallée du Marcadau. Quite what they would think of bathing in ice-cold water is interesting to contemplate.

Day 2: Refuge Wallon to Refuge des Oulètes de Gaube

5 hours, 8km, 840m ascent

From the *refuge* walk back down the path towards Pont d'Espagne for 500m to a signposted junction and head towards Lac d'Arratille and Col d'Arratille, across a footbridge. The fairly rocky path pursues a not too steep route up through scattered pines, and after about 30 minutes emerges into a very scenic bowl, where waterfalls tumble between sprawling granite slabs, small patches of grass, juniper and alpenrose.

The path then negotiates a dissected rocky bluff, climbs again to a footbridge across a small chasm and a little farther on you come to the beautiful **Lac d'Arratille** (1½ hours from the *refuge)*. Wander along the western shore then continue generally south, across the outlet from a small pond on the right (a difficult crossing only after heavy rain) and on, across two more normally shallow fords. The climbing then resumes seriously; white-and-red waymarkers mark the way up through a succession of crags, boulders and large scree. Then comes **Lac du Col d'Arratille**, seeming inordinately large just below the **Col d'Arratille**, on the Spanish border (an hour from the lower lake). On a fine day, the spectacle of **Vignemale**, just across the wide valley below, is riveting and awe-inspiring.

To continue, follow the waymarked path into Spain, southwards at first, then contouring the steep scree slope north-eastwards; the path is narrow but well built and sloping into the mountainside, so there's very rarely any feeling of exposure above the sharp drop on the right. Beyond a small stream, the path climbs a rocky spur to the narrow **Col des Mulets** with Pic des Oulettes towering directly overhead (an hour from Col d'Arratille).

The initial drop towards Vallée de Gaube is steep, down scree and rock; after a few hundred metres cross the base of Pic des Oulettes, still on loose rock with bits of grass, and then the streamlet from Col des Oulettes. Zigzag down to the edge of the scree and fallen rock and pick you way down the edge of this unstable footing to the val-

ley floor. The easiest approach to Refuge des Oulètes de Gaube, rather than weaving through the boulders littering the edge of the valley – and the camping area – is directly across the flat area at the foot of Vignemale's skirts of moraine and scree. A set of stepping stones immediately below the *refuge* should enable you to keep your feet dry to the last (an hour from Col des Mulets).

Refuge des Oulètes de Gaube This is another CAF *refuge* (☎ *05 62 92 62 97),* smaller than Wallon and with full electricity. The tariff is 80FF per night in a dorm; half board is 193FF and drinks are extra. Helpfully, the daily forecast is posted on the notice board. There's a thought-provoking display of photos illustrating the dramatic retreat of Vignemale's glaciers since about the 1960s. The same rules apply in the *refuge* and for camping as at Wallon. The *refuge* is open from April to early October.

Day 3: Refuge des Oulètes de Gaube to Cauterets

4½ hours, 12km, 1250m descent

This is a pretty straightforward day, starting with a long, sometimes steep descent from the *refuge*, firstly down through a broad rock barrier to a lovely high meadow. Then it's on down past the impressive **Cascade Esplumouse**, through mixed woodland of pines and rowans. The well-graded path negotiates the steep, rock-encrusted mountainside and goes on to a solid bridge over the tumbling stream, Gave des Oulettes de Gaube. The path loses more height, reaches serene **Lac de Gaube**, then settles down to cross the scree fringing the lake.

At the far end of the lake there's a choice of routes. Leading on more or less straight ahead is the path to the Télésiège de Gaube, which rises gently to the top of the lift; from there a broad track (evidently a piste for skiers in winter) winds down to the base of the télésiège, from where you continue to the right, then left to reach the hôtellerie at **Pont d'Espagne**. Alternatively, from the end of Lac de Gaube, turn right, towards *Hôtellerie de Gaube*. It's open from noon for snacks, drinks and meals, with *menus* from 70FF to

150FF. From the hotel, follow the path for a short distance then bear right to continue down the valley. Soon the path enters pine woodland and makes its way fairly steeply down to the road just below Pont d'Espagne (75 minutes from the lake).

If you're returning to Cauterets on foot, make your way to the start of the **chemin des Cascades** (also the GR10) in front of the hôtellerie, and follow it down to La Raillère. One last choice now presents itself. Rather than retrace the outward route (up to Cascade de Lutour and up to the chemin des Pères), you can avoid all this climbing by firstly walking down the road towards Cauterets, past the souvenir shops (although not immediately past one of the bars). Go round a sharp right bend (with a derelict hotel on the left); a few yards farther on, the traffic road goes to the right. Instead, bear left along a road closed to traffic and follow it down for about 400m, then turn off along a clear path to the right. This leads on to a bridge (where the main road comes in from the right). Cross the bridge and turn left almost immediately along a quiet road (rue Raillère), and continue into Cauterets (about 25 minutes from La Raillère).

Lacs de Cambalès

Duration	5½ hours
Distance	10km
Standard	medium
Start/Finish	Refuge Wallon
Nearest Town	Cauterets
Public Transport	no

Summary A not-too-taxing walk to a diverse collection of colourful lakes ringed by soaring crags, with the possibility of continuing to Col de Cambalès for views to the mighty peak of Balaïtous.

Roughly westwards from Refuge Wallon lies the wild, rock and scree-encrusted valley of the Gave de Cambalès, nearly enclosed by a horseshoe of precipitous crags, crowned by Pic de Cambalès (2965m). Hidden in this somewhat forbidding fastness are more than a dozen lakes of all shapes and sizes, some

little more than puddles, and the three Lacs d'Opale, a brilliant turquoise in colour.

An exploration of these lakes makes a medium day walk from the *refuge*. Col de Cambalès is about 150m vertically and 750m horizontally beyond the highest of the lakes and is worth the climb, on a fine day, for a comprehensive view of the lakes and for the prospect westwards to mighty Balaïtous (3144m).

There are several unbridged stream crossings to negotiate; most have a line of stepping stones, interspersed with what seem to be firmly wedged, flattened old petrol drums. After heavy rain only one is impassable (the unnamed northern tributary of the Gave de Cambalès) – unless you're happy to walk in wet boots and use a safety line.

Sheep and cattle don't venture up the valley, so it should be safe to rely on the streams for drinking water.

There's every chance you'll hear and see marmots and izards along the way; vultures, eagles and smaller raptors are a fairly common sight overhead.

THE WALK
See the Around Cauterets map (p224–5). From the terrace of the *refuge*, follow the path indicated by the yellow signposts to Lacs de Cambalès, up through the pines, keeping to the zigzags as far as possible, to a signed track junction (30 minutes from the *refuge*). Continue across the meadows, over a minor stream and on to the potentially difficult crossing at the foot of a cascade. With this safely behind, there's a steep climb up and over the pronounced southern lip of the valley sheltering the lakes. The first, nearby, is of rather modest dimensions (ie, a large pond); press on for about 20 minutes, across two more fords and then up beside some low cliffs to overlook a cluster of lakes below the path to the north (1½ hours from the *refuge*).

The well-cairned route carries on, generally westwards and down to the north-west shore of the largest of the lakes; another 30 minutes' ascent, past lowish cliffs on your right and over scree, shattered rock and sections of a well-built path, takes you up to a vantage point above a small, anvil-shaped

lake (just west of the point '2582' on the recommended IGN 1:25,000 map).

To reach the Col de Cambalès (2706m)
from here (another 45 minutes), press on
across the sea of shattered rock, then bear
south, to the left, across the scree at the foot
of the cliffs immediately north of the col,
and finally up to the small stony gap in the
otherwise unbroken line of cliffs.

For the return to the *refuge*, allow about
2½ hours from the col or about two hours
from the top lake. This is definitely the more
scenic half of the walk, looking down the
Vallée de Cambalès and across to the beautiful Vallée d'Arratille valley with majestic
Vignemale towering above. On the way, it's
well worth making a shortish detour to have
a look at the Lacs d'Opale (an extra 75 minutes and relatively minimal climbing). There
is a fairly well-cairned route from the eastern
tip of the largest lake (point '2342' on the
IGN map), south-eastwards over rock and
some grass to overlook the smaller lake; the
route leads a little farther west-south-west to
a point above its larger companion.

Circuit des Lacs

Duration	5½ hours
Distance	12km
Standard	medium
Start/Finish	Refuge Wallon
Nearest Town	Cauterets
Public Transport	no

Summary A contrasting quartet of lakes and
many attractive waterfalls among the rugged
crags of the upper Vallée du Marcadau; a fine
circuit with views of Vignemale and other
border peaks.

Each of the tributaries of the Gave de Marcadau tumbles down from a cluster of lakes
and tarns high among the peaks; those to the
north of Refuge Wallon – Lac Nère, Lac du
Pourtet and the twin Lacs de l'Embarrat (on
Ruisseau de Pourtet) – provide the focus of
a fine circuit from the *refuge*. The walk is described in a clockwise direction, but it can
just as well be done the other way, depending on the weather, and whether you prefer

to start by climbing towards the lakes or
going down Gave de Marcadau and beginning the climb from there, at Pont du Cavan.
The walk can also serve as the second day of
a two-day walk up to the *refuge* and back
from Cauterets.

From the *refuge* northwards to Lac du
Pourtet (2420m), the highest point on the
walk, then eastwards down to Pont du
Cavan, the path is well defined although
mostly rocky and slow going; but the spectacular views, especially of Vignemale, are
more than adequate compensation. The
route is cairned throughout and there are
white waymarkers between Lac du Pourtet
and the signposted turn-off to 'Col de la
Haugarde' (about 1km east of the lake).

Several stream crossings are involved between the *refuge* and Lac du Pourtet – those
just south of Lac Nère could be a bit tricky
after some rain, and can be avoided by keeping on the western side of the stream. The
crossings below the Lacs de l'Embarrat
should not present any difficulties.

THE WALK

See the Around Cauterets map (p224–5).
Just to the west of the *refuge*, set out along
the path signposted to several places, including Lac Nère. It winds north-westwards up
the steep, wooded slope and just beyond the
last of the trees, crosses a small stream. A
short distance farther on, in a pleasant flat
meadow, bear right to **Lac Nère** (as signposted; 35 minutes from the *refuge*). The
climb then continues steadily to Lac Nère (an
hour from the track junction), well worth a
decent pause.

To resume, there is more climbing, then
the path makes a safe crossing of a small
cliff face and continues to gain height
steadily to **Lac du Pourtet** (half an hour from
Lac Nère). The path changes direction abruptly here and turns east to start the descent
to Gave du Marcadau. Many zigzags farther
on, having passed the lower of the two **Lacs
de l'Embarrat**, the path swings north and
crosses a spur. Shortly, pass the turn-off to
Col de la Haugarde and follow the path as it
zigzags consistently down into the pine forest and at length reaches Pont du Cavan,

bridging Gave du Marcadau. No more than 1¼ hour's walk from here brings you back up to Refuge Wallon.

Pic du Cabaliros

Duration	6½ hours
Distance	14km
Standard	hard
Start/Finish	Cauterets
Public Transport	yes

Summary A long but rarely steep climb on good paths to a truly exceptional mountain summit from where the panorama embraces nearly all the peaks of the Haute Pyrénées.

Two very substantial peaks overlook Cauterets from the west and north-west: Moun-Né is the larger, more rugged and more southerly of the two and reaches 2724m, a daunting 1800m above Cauterets. Pic du Cabaliros (2334m) is about 3km north-east of Moun-Né, is within reasonable reach on a day's walk from the town. Standing apart from the main mountain massif, it affords an absolutely magnificent view of the Hautes Pyrénées peaks, extending from around Pic du Midi d'Ossau in the west, past Balaïtous with its small glacier and pivotal Vignemale to the south, to the Pic de Troumouse to the east. There's a splendid topograph on the summit, leaving you in no doubt about which peak is which as far as you can see.

Yellow signs show the way in the lower reaches of the route; higher up, there are cairns, but they're superfluous beside a clear path. The pic is within the periphery of the national park. Although the path crosses several streams, you should carry drinking water – the pic is grazing country for sheep and cattle.

A fine clear day is essential for this walk – there's no point in doing it if the visibility is poor. Beware of summer thunderstorms – the summit ridge is very exposed. The map to carry, just in case, is IGN 1:25,000 *Vignemale* sheet No 1647OT.

If you're travelling by car, it's possible to shorten the walk by driving to the car park at the entrance to Ferme Igau (shown on the recommended IGN 1:25,000 map), thus saving about 75 minutes, 200m of climbing and about 2.5km horizontally.

Ferme Igau is a welcome sight on the return; at the small *cafe* you can buy cold drinks (including beer), coffee, ice cream and even crepes.

Above the fine beech woodland on the lower slopes, you'll pass clumps of juniper and alpenrose; pink-flowering heather (or ling) and mauve crocuses are colourful in autumn. In marked contrast to the peaks farther south, Pic du Cabaliros isn't covered with rock and scree – it's grassy almost everywhere above the trees, with only one small rocky outcrop on the summit ridge. Characteristically spiky crags decorate some of the pic's spurs, but they're part of the view rather than obstacles to get around. On the day this walk was surveyed, a pair of golden eagles were obviously enjoying themselves, rising effortlessly on thermals into a brilliant blue sky.

THE WALK
See the Around Cauterets map (p224–5). From the centre of Cauterets, head west to the Pont d'Espagne–Le Mamelon Vert road junction and turn right along the roadside footpath. After 15 minutes, on the edge of town, leave that road and walk up a minor road to the left towards 'La Ferme Igau'. Shortly, turn left again, then on the second sharp bend, turn right along a path signed to Pic de Cabaliros. A steepish climb takes you up to Ferme Igau's entrance, from where you continue south-westwards on a vehicle track, past a tall aerial. This climbs steadily, occasionally steeply, around a few bends and ends near a small stream. A wide path leads on, gaining height quickly in and out of the woodland and past hay meadows. Go through a gate at the entrance to a signed 'Zone Pastorale', reserved for grazing sheep and cattle; the path contours the hillside and dips slightly to cross **Ruisseau de Bourg Débat**. The climbing continues through the last of the woodland, to **Ruisseau de Catarrabes** (1¼ hours from Cauterets).

A steep path goes straight up from here beside the stream, but it's easier (if that's the word) to stick to the older path which copes with the rise in a series of short zigzags. Then, at an acute angled junction, continue up to the right. Many zigzags farther on, you reach a narrow spur (point '1870' on the 1:25,000 map, 75 minutes from Ruisseau de Catarrabes). This is a fine place for a rest, especially as the view to the south now takes in Vignemale. A few hundred metres farther on, the path levels out on a fine traverse, providing a brief rest before the final rise to the broad summit ridge, which you reach a little east of Col de Contente. Continue past the substantial ruins of an elongated stone building to the start of the really final, mainly steep climb to the spacious **summit** (1¼ hours from the narrow spur).

Eventually – it's not easy to leave such a magnificent lookout – return to Cauterets, for which you should allow about 2½ hours.

Vallée de Lutour

Duration	6 hours
Distance	13km
Standard	medium
Start/Finish	Cauterets
Public Transport	yes

Summary By Haute Pyrénées standards, a moderately undemanding walk to a *refuge* beside a beautiful lake; refreshments are available en route at an excellent restaurant and bar.

Looking directly south from Cauterets, your eyes are drawn to the deep valley extending far into the mountains. This is the very scenic Vallée de Lutour, the venue for a fine day walk up to Lac d'Estom, high in the valley. It's a walk that feels much easier than the bare statistics suggest. The climbing – through deciduous forests, Scots pine and spruce woodland, and open valley – comes in stages, rather than one long haul. The route, on clearly defined paths, is not waymarked, but the standard yellow signposts point the way at each junction. For most of the walk, you're right on the edge of the national park heartland; the lake itself is within the park.

The walk can be shortened to an easy half-day, suitable for a family outing, by driving to La Fruitière (20 minutes from Cauterets), saving three hours and 470m ascent.

The IGN 1:25,000 *Vignemale* sheet No 1647OT is the one to take for this walk. There's been one change since it was published: the path to follow south for the first 1.5km from La Fruitière in Vallée de Lutour is now on the eastern side of the stream.

THE WALK
See the Around Cauterets map (p224–5). The walk starts just above the northern entrance to the imposing cream building of the spa **Thermes César** – go to the right, following yellow signs up a path to a road. Cross over and continue along the chemin des Pères. After a few more zigzags this settles into a comfortable gradient up to the signposted junction above La Raillère (45 minutes from Cauterets). The path continues its zigzagging way up through beech woodland to the meadows at Le Pradet (15 minutes farther on), finally reaching *La Fruitière (☎ 05 62 92 52 04)* 1½ hours from Cauterets. It's a small hotel with a restaurant which specialises in local dishes. *Menus* range from 80FF to 150FF and include *garbure* (a thick soup of vegetables, beans and ham); crepes, sandwiches and drinks (including excellent hot chocolate) are also available. The hotel is open from April to mid-November and charges 240FF for half board.

From here, the route on the eastern side of the stream continues very pleasantly for nearly an hour, past the tiny **Cabane de Pouey-Caut** with its domed iron roof and wooden front door, past the turn-off to 'Russell' (which is Refuge Russell) and then across a footbridge to the western side of the stream. The towering **Pic de la Sède** (2976m), at the head of the valley, dominates the view ahead. A spell of fairly steep climbing through pines and beside the cascading stream leads into the open again, and soon you come to the *Refuge d'Estom*, perched most attractively on a grassy apron at the northern end of **Lac d'Estom**. This is one of the most attractive of the many lakes in the area – the steep slopes rising from its eastern and western shores wearing a blend of scree, crags, grass and small clumps of low pines, with soaring crags in between. The refuge is open from June to the end of September and has similar fare to La Fruitière.

Allow about 2½ hours' walking time back to the signposted junction above La Raillère. From here, as a change from returning to Cauterets along the chemin des Pères, you could descend to La Raillère past the impressive cascades of the Gave de Lutour. From La Raillère, walk down the road and follow the route described in the In Vignemale's Shadow walk earlier in this section back to Cauterets (about 40 minutes from the junction).

Other Walks

VALLÉE D'ASPE
Pic du Midi d'Ossau
The distinctive split spire of Pic du Midi d'Ossau (2884m) is prominent in views eastwards from the walks around Lescun and above the Vallée d'Aspe. This spectacular, isolated granite peak within the national park, a few kilometres north of the Spanish border, stands at the head of the Vallée d'Ossau, the next north-south valley eastwards from the Aspe.

The circuit round its base – not necessarily including a climb to the top – is one of the finer walks in the Pyrenees. It commonly provides a day's outing for GR10 walkers based at nearby Lac de Bious-Artigues; alternatively, it can be the highlight of a three- or four-day walk from Etsaut in Vallée d'Aspe.

Of the various possible itineraries, here is one suggestion. A lot of climbing (1600m) on the first day, following the GR10 via the chemin de la Mâture takes you to **Refuge Pyrénéa** (☎ 05 59 05 32 12) beside Lac de Bious-Artigues (meals provided). Alternatively, there's **Camping de Bious-Oumette** (☎ 05 59 05 38 76) nearby. The next day, the circuit of the peak from the lake (1200m ascent) could include Pic Peyreget (2487m), above Col du Peyreget, for spectacular views of Pic du Midi. Pic Peyreget is much more approachable for walkers than Pic du Midi, which is notorious for the looseness of its rocks and for which some climbing skill is highly desirable. The return to Etsaut could be direct, or you could stay at **Refuge d'Ayous** (☎ 05 59 05 37 00), south of the GR10 between Lac de Bious-Artigues and the chemin de la Mâture, and have a good look at the many nearby lakes.

IGN 1:25,000 sheet *Ossau* No 1547OT and/or Rando Éditions 1:50,000 sheet No 3 cover the area of the circuit. The Trailblazer guide (see Books under Information at the beginning of this chapter) is helpful in this area.

VALLÉE DE CAUTERETS
Vallée du Marcadau
The long walk described earlier (In Vignemale's Shadow) is actually made up of four shorter (half-day or day) walks, which you can do from a base in or near Cauterets, starting in the town or at Pont d'Espagne. All are covered by the IGN 1:25,000 *Vignemale* sheet No 1647OT. The *Randonnées dans le Parc National des Pyrénées* leaflets published by the national park (see Books under Information in the introduction to this chapter) is useful. Here is a summary of these possibilities.

Chemin des Cascades This is the well-made path beside the Gave de Cauterets between La Raillère (2km south of Cauterets) and Pont d'Espagne, a distance of about 8km return with 500m ascent. The thundering cascades, several of which are named, are very fine indeed and there are good vantage points from which to contemplate their unbridled power. The permanent veils of fine spray around the cascades have created a seemingly subtropical forest nearby, festooned with mosses and lichens, and crowded with ferns and lush vegetation.

Vallée du Marcadau The topographic map shows the name 'Paradis' at the entrance to the valley (opposite Châlet-Refuge du Clot) for good reason. The valley extends south-westwards for about 5km from Pont d'Espagne to the spacious bowl where the three tributaries of the Gave du Marcadau unite near Refuge Wallon. Pines and some beech in small and large stands, crags, cliffs and verdant meadows, all framed by soaring peaks and rugged ridges, make this one of the most beautiful valleys in the Haute Pyrénées.

An easy day walk from Pont d'Espagne to Refuge Wallon and back occupies four to five hours for a distance of about 12km and only 320m climbing. A longer variation involves the Circuit des Lacs (see the description of that walk earlier in this chapter) either on the way out or on the return; allow at least 5½ hours for this.

Vallée d'Arratille Generally south-east of Refuge Wallon is the superbly wild and beautiful Arratille Valley with cascades, huge granite slabs, copses of pines and two secluded lakes. At the top is Col d'Arratille, where you're on the Spanish border and almost at the foot of mighty Vignemale. A comfortable day walk up to the col and back could start from Pont d'Espagne; allow seven hours for the 18km walk with 1100m ascent.

Vallée de Gaube With Lac de Gaube near its threshold, fine cascades along the Gave des Oulettes de Gaube, and Vignemale presiding over its uppermost reaches, Vallée de Gaube makes the most scenic of venues for a day walk. And there are two bonuses – Refuge des Oulètes de Gaube, at the foot of Vignemale, for lunch perhaps, and Hôtellerie de Gaube, beside the lake, for a drink on the way back. Ideally, start from Pont d'Espagne; the path to Lac de Gaube is signposted below the Pont, beside the road leading up from the car park.

Allow three hours for the walk right up to the *refuge* and about the same for the return; the distance is approximately 14km and the ascent 650m. The times given on the signposts along the well-defined path are very fast indeed, and don't make sufficient allowance for the relatively slow going along rough sections of the path above the lake.

Gavarnie

High in the Luz-Gavarnie Valley, the largish village of Gavarnie is another excellent base or starting point for fine walks in the Hautes Pyrénées.

The magnificent Cirque de Gavarnie, soaring 1500m into the sky about of 6km to the south, on the Spanish border, draws thousands of visitors during the summer who ride donkeys or walk to vantage points nearby. Fortunately it's possible to escape the crowds and to walk up to the foot of the huge waterfall, an easy half-day walk.

However, the best walks take you right away from the village. To set the scene, Pimène (2801m), a peak east of Gavarnie, is a superb vantage point; it's usually reached on a fairly energetic day walk from the village via Plateau de Pailla, Refuge des Espuguettes and the Col de Pimène.

Refuge de la Brèche de Roland (☎ 05 62 93 37 20), also known as Refuge des Sarradets, is spectacularly located close to the western edge of the cirque and is very popular. It's a demanding climb from Gavarnie to the *refuge*, from where some of the 3000m peaks along the rim of the cirque are within reach: Le Taillon (3144m) and Pic du Mabore (3248m).

The Brèche de Roland (2807m) is a deep, geometric cleft in the border ridge, almost directly above the *refuge*. It's the gateway into Spain for a spectacular tour through Ordesa canyon via (or up and over) Mont Perdu (Monte Perdido; 3355m) – the second-highest summit in the entire Pyrenees – within Parque Nacional de

Ordesa y Monte Perdido. Until well into summer an ice axe should be carried for negotiating the small glacier above the *refuge*; walking poles should suffice from then until mid-autumn.

From *Refuge des Oulètes de Gaube* on the three-day In Vignemale's Shadow walk described earlier, it's a day's walk to Gavarnie on the Haute Randonnée Pyrénéenne (HRP; see the High-Level Route later in this chapter). The route crosses the high pass of Hourquette d'Ossoue (2734m), where you can leave your backpack and make the uncomplicated climb to the top of Petit Vignemale (3032m). From the pass it's down to, or past, *Refuge de Bayssellance* (☎ 05 62 92 40 25), open until mid-September, and on to Gavarnie along the southern side of the Gave d'Ossoue valley.

There are gîtes d'étape, a camping area, several hotels and an adequate range of shops in Gavarnie. For more information about accommodation and facilities, contact the tourist office (☎ 05 62 92 49 10); the postcode is 65120.

Two sheets in the IGN 1:25,000 series cover the area – Nos 1748ET and 1748OT; in the 1:50,000 series you'll need Nos 4 and 5. The guides by Streatfield-James and Véron (see Books under Information at the beginning of this chapter) are both useful; the former includes the route through Spain. Parc National des Pyrénées publishes *Un Sentier Pour Deux Parcs – Cirque de Gavarnie, Ordesa, Mont Perdu*, describing a three- to five-day walk (68FF). There's also *Le Guide Rando. Gavarnie-Luz* by M Record.

During summer, access by public transport is good. A regular bus service to Gavarnie connects with the Lourdes-Cauterets service at Pierrefitte Nestalas; the service is much reduced – if it exists at all – during the rest of the year. For more information, ring ☎ 05 62 92 48 60.

THE PYRENEES END TO END

It is entirely possible to walk from the Atlantic Ocean to the Mediterranean through the Pyrenees, following either one of two recognised routes. Alternatively, it wouldn't be difficult to devise the ideal – a third line of traverse making use of both routes, since they intersect or run parallel in several places.

The Low-Level Route

Best known as the GR10, this route devised, waymarked and described by the FFRP, is one of the longest of the really long-distance routes in France. With about 860km between the end points at Hendaye on the Atlantic coast and Banyuls-sur-Mer on the Mediterranean (both close to the Spanish border), it is considerably longer than the Pyrenees themselves. This is because it avoids quite a lot of the highest ground, along or close to the crest of the range, and wanders up and down valleys. Nevertheless, the total ascent *and* descent is a respectable 47,000m.

It seems that walkers' opinions about this meandering route are divided – there are those who enjoy the contrast between the mountains and the valleys, and the experience of visiting the many villages, and those who feel frustrated or short-changed at being wrenched away from the mountains just when they're becoming addicted to the experience.

Many walkers spread their traverse over more than a single visit, since at least six weeks in total is needed, and there are many unmissable side trips – climbing some of the peaks or visiting the Cirque de Gavarnie. Generally the route is well waymarked and well used. It is shown on the IGN 1:25,000 and Rando Éditions 1:50,000 map series. Of the English-language guides, Trailblazer's is more up-to-date. Four FFRP Topo-Guides cover the walk: *Pyrénées Occidentales* (No 1086), *Pyrénées Orientales* (No 1089), *Pyrénées Ariègsoises* (No 1090) and *Pyrénées Centrales* (No 1091).

Gîtes d'étape and *refuges* are generally spaced a day's walk apart along the route, except for a section in the Ariège region (outside the national park) between Goulier (south-east of Aulus-les-Bains) and Refuge de Rulhe (above the Ariège River). Here a tent would be highly desirable and it's essential to carry at least two days' supplies and cooking equipment. There are also camp sites in most of the towns and villages along the way; remember that wild camping is restricted in the national park.

The best times for the whole route are from mid-June to mid-July and during September; snow may lie on higher ground until well into June and from early October. During most of July and August, gîtes and *refuges* become very crowded; some *refuges* close in mid-September. Accommodation lists are available from the tourist offices listed under Information Sources in this chapter.

Both Hendaye and Banyuls-sur-Mer are accessible by train and there are bus services from several large towns in the foothills (such as Pau, Lourdes and Tarbes) to towns and villages in the valleys along the route.

Among the many towns through which the GR10 passes is Saint-Jean Pied de Port, on the chemins des Saint-Jacques (Ways of St James), the famous pilgrimage walking trail between Le Puy-en-Velay on the edge of the Auvergne and Santiago de Compostela in Spain. The French section is designated as the GR65; for more information, see the boxed text 'Pilgrimage Paths' in the Facts about France chapter.

The High-Level Route

The Haute Randonnée Pyrénéenne (HRP) was pioneered by Georges Véron in 1968 and has become one of the classic high-level walks in Europe. Measured in daily stages – a minimum of 43 (average duration around 6½ hours) – rather than horizontal distance (about 800km), it involves 43,400m of climbing, much of it steep and over difficult ground. Sharing its end points with the GR10, the HRP follows the watershed of the Pyrenees, essentially along the divide between rivers flowing north into France and south into Spain. Thus, sections of the route cross the border and go through Spain, so some knowledge of Spanish can be useful.

For the greater part of the distance (at least 34 stages) the HRP stays above the 1000m level and crosses several passes over 2500m. Variants bypass hazardous or potentially snow or ice-covered sections, but the HRP in full remains an undertaking for experienced walkers who are used to crossing rough ground and exposed ridges and are equipped for sudden changes in the weather – from warm and sunny to wet, windy and misty. Although the route is not officially waymarked, it shares a few sections with the GR10, and the Spanish Pyrenean route, the GR11, but a degree of navigational skill is still required to follow it safely.

Gîtes d'étape and especially *refuges* serve many of the stages, but a tent is also virtually essential. You also have to be prepared to carry a few days' supplies at a time – restocking places aren't always plentiful and may not be open when you arrive.

The relevant maps are the same as those for the GR10; Georges Véron's guide, *Haute Randonnée Pyrénéenne*, is indispensable; without the benefit of detailed local knowledge, it may be prudent to allow a little extra time for each of his stages. SNCF trains serve both ends of the route, at Hendaye and Bayuls-sur-Mer, but it is much more remote from intermediate links than is the GR10.

With ice axe and crampons, the route is feasible from mid- to late June to the end of September, or with only an ice axe, from early July to late September. Some *refuges*, especially those serving the GR10 and GR11, could be crowded between mid-July and mid-August.

PYRENEES

Corsica

Corsica (Corse in French) is the most mountainous and geographically diverse of the Mediterranean islands, earning it the perfectly justified title of L'Île de Beauté (The Island of Beauty). Although it covers only 8720 sq km, Corsica in many ways resembles a miniature continent, with 1000km of coastline lapped by azure seas, soaring granite mountains, desert, flatland marshes and a 'continental divide'.

Walking is one of the best ways to explore Corsica. An extensive network of paths crisscrosses the island, ensuring access to remote parts of the interior. Described in detail in this chapter, the GR20 is the most famous of the *grandes randonnées* (long-distance, waymarked walking routes), attracting 10,000 brave souls from all over Europe to take on its heights every year. It was created in 1972, linking Calenzana, in the Balagne, with Conca, north of Porto Vecchio, and has since become something of an institution.

NATURAL HISTORY

Corsica's main attraction is its beautiful and remarkably well-preserved natural environment. Its isolation from the mainland makes it home to many endemic species; of its 2000 plant species, 8% grow nowhere else. In the mountains, nearly half all known species are endemic.

In 1972 350,500 hectares of the mountainous interior were set aside as a nature reserve, the Parc Naturel Régional de Corse (PNRC). With a charter to protect and encourage 'the survival of the natural, cultural and human heritage of the region for the future', the PNRC management has constructed 2000km of signposted footpaths and actively promotes environmental protection on the island.

In addition to the PNRC, there are four nature reserves on Corsica: the Îles Finocchiarola, Îles Lavezzi, Îles Cerbicale and the Réserve Naturelle de Scandola (a Unesco World Heritage listed site).

HIGHLIGHTS

Heading across a shallow valley towards the Bergeries de Ballone on the GR20

- Navigating the treacherous climb out of the glorious Cirque de la Solitude

- Walking along the pozzines around Lac de Ninu, and to the Auberge de la Passerelle, at the foot of Mount Incudine

- Crossing the Aiguilles de Bavella along the alpine route

- Passing through heavily scented maquis on the way to Conca on the last day

Flora

The rich Corsican flora is divided into three zones. The Mediterranean zone (up to about 1000m) is dominated by maquis, holm and cork oaks, olive and chestnut trees. Olives, mass-planted by the Genoese centuries ago, have largely been left to grow wild.

The coastal fringe is covered by the maquis, characterised by low, shrubby, mostly evergreen vegetation. It combines a

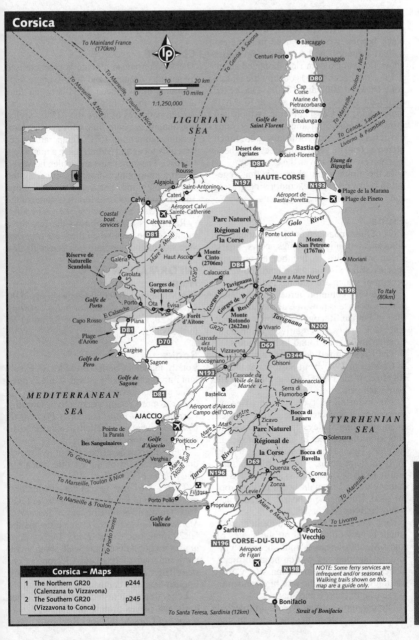

Corsica

LIGURIAN SEA

To Mainland France (170km)

To Genoa & Savona

To Marseille, Toulon & Nice

Barcaggio
Centuri Port
Macinaggio
Cap Corse
Marine de Pietracorbara
Sisco
Erbalunga
Miomo

To Genoa, Savona, Livorno & Piombino

Golfe de Saint Florent

Bastia
Saint-Florent

Désert des Agriates

HAUTE-CORSE

Île Rousse
Algajola
Saint-Antonino
Cateri
Calvi

Étang de Biguglia

Aéroport de Bastia-Poretta
Plage de la Marana
Plage di Pineto

Aéroport Calvi Sainte-Catherine
Calenzana

Parc Naturel Régional de la Corse

Ponte Leccia
Golo River
Monte San Petrone (1767m)
Moriani

Réserve de Naturelle Scandola
Galéria
Girolata

Haut Asco
Monte Cinto (2706m)
Calacuccia

Mare a Mare Nord

Gorges de Spelunca
Ota
Évisa
Gorges du Tavignanu
Gorges de la Restonica
Corte

To Italy (80km)

Golfe de Porto
Porto
Forêt d'Aïtone
Monte Rotondo (2622m)
Vivario
Tavignano River

Piana
Capo Rosso
Cascade des Anglais
Vizzavona
Ghisoni
Aléria

Plage d'Arone
Cargèse
Golfe de Pero
Sagone
Bocognano
Cascade du Voile de la Mariée
Ghisonaccia
Serra di Flumorbo

MEDITERRANEAN SEA

Golfe de Sagone
Bastelica

Aéroport d'Ajaccio Campo dell'Oro

AJACCIO

Pointe de la Parata
Îles Sanguinaires
Golfe d'Ajaccio
Porticcio

Zicavo
Bocca di Laparu

TYRRHENIAN SEA

Parc Naturel Régional de la Corse

Solenzara

To Genoa
Verghia
Taravo River
Bocca di Bavella
Quenza
Conca

To Marseille, Toulon & Nice
Filitosa
Levie
Zonza

To Marseille & Toulon
Porto Pollo
Propriano
Golfe de Valinco

To Marseille

To Porto Torres
To Livorno

Sartène

CORSE-DU-SUD
Aéroport de Figari

Porto Vecchio

NOTE: Some ferry services are infrequent and/or seasonal. Walking trails shown on this map are a guide only.

Bonifacio
Strait of Bonifacio

To Santa Teresa, Sardinia (12km)

Corsica – Maps	
1 The Northern GR20 (Calenzana to Vizzavona)	p244
2 The Southern GR20 (Vizzavona to Conca)	p245

CORSICA

variety of sweet-smelling species, including rock rose, myrtle (treasured for its blue-black berries, which are used in some excellent liqueurs) and tree heather, whose white flowers exude a rich, honeyed scent.

Pine and beech forests occupy the middle zone between 1000 and 1800m. One of the dominant species in these superb forests is the *laricio*, or Corsican pine, which can grow to around 50m and up to 800 years old. Their long, straight trunks were much prized as boat masts and the trees have been extensively logged over the centuries.

In the alpine zone, above 1800m, vegetation is low and sparse, comprising grasses and small ground-hugging plants.

Fauna

Most of the fauna seen on Corsica today are domesticated animals – pigs, cows, goats, sheep and mules. A number of endemic species still exist on the island, however, several of which are endangered.

Once very common across Europe, Hermann's tortoise is now one of the rarest reptiles in France. Recognisable by its orange and black stripes, it is relatively common in Corsica and can be found in the maquis.

The Corsican red deer was reintroduced to Corsica in 1985 from Sardinia at the instigation of the PNRC. Some 20 fawns are born each year.

The mouflon, a type of short-fleeced sheep, now a protected species, can be seen in south-facing valleys from December to February, but retreats to higher altitudes in summer. The males are easily recognisable by their huge horns. Along walking trails you're likely to come across some extensive damage caused by wild boars as they root for food. Hunting wild boar is a traditional winter activity in Corsica.

Bird species include Audouin's gull, which is now only found on the shores of small Mediterranean islands; bearded vulture, or lammergeier, which nests in rocky niches in the mountainous massifs; Corsican nuthatch, one of the rare birds endemic to the island; osprey and shag.

The common rorqual whale, a protected species, can sometimes be seen in the triangle of sea between Nice, the Île de Porquerolles and Corsica.

CLIMATE

The Mediterranean climate is characterised by summer droughts and sun. Average temperatures often exceed 25°C between June and September, while July and August can see temperatures of more than 35°C. Spring and autumn are both fine, with average temperatures of around 15°C. Temperatures between October and March reach a maximum of 20°C. The mountains are cooler, however, and the temperature drops significantly the higher you climb. Snow can be seen above 1600m from October to June and some of the island's peaks are snow-capped year-round.

Rainfall is highest during the last three months of the year, when there are often severe storms and flooding. July is usually dry.

INFORMATION
Maps

The Michelin 1:200,000 *Corse* sheet No 90 covers the entire island. For maps covering the GR20, see Planning in the introduction to the walk.

Books

Lonely Planet's *Corsica* provides an excellent introduction to the island, while *France* has a chapter devoted to Corsica.

For a more recent perspective, Dorothy Carrington's *Granite Island: a Portrait of Corsica* gives an excellent background to Corsica's history and culture.

Paul Theroux describes a visit to Corsica during his circuit of the Mediterranean in *The Pillars of Hercules*.

There are two excellent Fédération Française de la Randonnée Pédestre (FFRP) Topo-Guide titles on Corsica: *A Travers la Montagne Corse* (No 67), which details the GR20 route, and *Corse: Entre Mer et Montagne* (No 065), describing walks both in the north and south of the island. Cicerone's *Corsican High Level Route: GR 20* is a handy English-language companion for the trail.

For walkers interested in exploring other trails and places around the island, *Landscapes of Corsica* by Noel Rochford lists a number of short walking excursions as well as tours suitable for visitors with their own transport.

Information Sources

The Maison d'Information Randonnée du PNRC (PNRC Walking Information Office; ☎ 04 95 51 79 00, fax 04 95 21 88 17, infos@ parc-naturel-corse.com, www.parc-naturel-corse.com), 2 rue Sergent Casalonga, Ajaccio, publishes a wealth of information about the park in French, English and Spanish, along with a number of walking guides (mostly in French). It also provides sensible advice on walking routes. It is open from 8.30 am to noon and 2 to 6 pm (5 pm on Friday), Monday to Friday. Other information centres are listed under Gateways and Nearest Towns.

WARNING

Take note of and observe PNRC rules and regulations; in particular, lighting fires at any point along a route in the park is strictly forbidden, as is camping outside the designated areas near refuges.

As far as water from streams is concerned, safety is not guaranteed: do not use it unless strictly necessary, and then purify it.

PLACE NAMES

Two names exist for most places in Corsica: the original, Genoese-based *corsu* (Corsican) names, which often end in 'u', and the 'Frenchified' names, where the 'u' translates to 'o'. Some signs will carry both names; others just the Corsican.

GATEWAYS

The three towns most convenient to the GR20: Bastia, Ajaccio and Calvi, have both air and sea links with the mainland. For information on travelling between these towns and the mainland, see Getting There & Away later in this chapter.

Bastia

The second largest town on the island, Bastia is Corsica's economic centre and has the fourth most important port in France. Although not a tourist hub, Bastia has a lively and busy town centre, a pretty port, long beaches and a rich cultural life.

Information On the northern side of place Saint Nicolas, the small tourist office (☎ 04 95 55 96 96, fax 04 95 31 81 34) is open to the public from 8 am to 8 pm daily in summer, and from 9 am to noon and 2 to 6 pm in the low season.

Maps and walking books are on sale in the Librairie Jean-Patrice Marzocchi (☎ 04 95 34 02 95), at 2 rue du Conventionnel Saliceti.

Places to Stay Although few tourists stay in Bastia, it can still be difficult to find accommodation, especially in summer.

Camping Casanova (☎ 04 95 33 91 42), in Miomo, is about 5km north of Bastia next to the coastal road. It opens from mid-May to mid-October and charges 12/24FF per tent/person and 20FF per car. To get there, catch a bus for 7.50FF to Erbalunga from the bus stop opposite the tourist office.

Hôtel de l'Univers (☎ 04 95 31 03 38, fax 04 95 31 19 91, 3 ave Maréchal Sébastiani), virtually opposite the post office, has basic, old doubles for 190FF and more comfortable, refurbished rooms with all mod cons for 310FF.

Hôtel Central (☎ 04 95 31 71 12, 3 rue Miot) has some of the town's most comfortable rooms; some have a small balcony. A basic double in low/high season costs 200/260FF.

Places to Eat The *Solo Pizze* (☎ 04 95 31 07 15, 4 place de la Fontaine Neuve) is a great place for inexpensive food in a shady part of the square. Pizza and pasta prices range from 35FF to 50FF (not open on Sunday evening).

It is worth making a detour to *La Voûte* (☎ 04 95 32 27 82, 6 rue Luce de Casabianca) for its rich and varied menu. For a meal that won't cost the earth, choose the excellent pizzas cooked over a wood fire (50FF).

Local traders and producers set up their stalls in the *market place* (place de l'Hôtel de Ville) each morning from around 8.

CORSICA

Ajaccio

The busy port city of Ajaccio, birthplace of Napoleon Bonaparte (1769–1821), is a pleasant enough place, despite having some very busy roads and rather unattractive parts which rub shoulders with the old town.

Information The tourist office (☎ 04 95 51 53 03, fax 04 95 51 53 01), 1 place Foch, is open from 8.30 am to 6 pm (Saturday from 9 am). From July to mid-September it's open from 7 or 8 am to 8 pm. There's also an information counter at the airport.

The large stationery store and bookshop La Maison de la Presse (☎ 04 95 21 81 18), at 2 place Foch, has a wide selection of books, including a small section of English and German publications.

Places to Stay It is difficult to find cheap accommodation in Ajaccio, so you should book ahead during the summer months.

Camping de Barbicaja (☎ 04 95 52 01 17), next to a beach on the Route des Sanguinaires, about 4.5km from the town centre, is open from April to the end of September. Its washroom facilities are adequate. Expect to pay 40/12FF per person/tent and 14FF per vehicle. To get there catch the No 5 bus from blvd Lantivy.

The cheapest place to stay in town is the *Hôtel La Pergola* (☎ 04 95 23 36 44, 25 ave Colonel Colonna d'Ornano). Rooms cost 170FF for a double with hall shower or 200FF for doubles with shower. It's open year-round.

Hôtel Kallisté (☎ 04 95 51 34 45, fax 04 95 21 79 00, 51 cours Napoléon) is a favourite haunt of independent travellers, with a wide range of facilities. A single room costs 200/220FF/300FF, depending on the season. Expect to pay 250/275/340FF for a double room and 325/365/450FF for a triple. The owner speaks English.

Places to Eat With a few eat-in tables, *Fast-Food Asiatique* (☎ 04 95 21 23 31, 1 rue Maréchal Ornano) offers fried noodles for 22FF, chicken curry for 30FF and a daily special at 30FF. It's open daily from 11 am to 3 pm and 5.30 to 11 pm.

Several restaurants and pizzerias along rue des Anciens Fossés, a narrow street in the old town, cater for tourists. The setting is pleasant and the food cheap. *U Borgu* (☎ 04 95 21 17 47), rue des Anciens Fossés, has pasta from 37FF, good pizzas from 44FF, salads for around 40FF and *menus* (fixed-price meals of two or more courses) from 65FF.

There are plenty of supermarkets. The well-stocked *Monoprix* in cours Napoléon is open from 8.30 am to 7.15 pm Monday to Saturday (to 8 pm in summer).

Calvi

Calvi, the capital of the Balagne, is a thriving little town stretched out along a bay under the watchful eye of two giants: the Citadelle and Monte Cinto (2706m).

Information The tourist office (☎ 04 95 65 16 67, fax 04 95 65 14 09) is in the marina, above the harbour master's office *(capitainerie)*. It is open daily between June and October, but is closed Saturday afternoon and Sunday during winter.

There are two bookshops of note: Press'Infos (☎ 04 95 65 17 43), place de la Porteuse d'Eau, and Black 'n' Blue (☎ 04 95 65 25 82), blvd Wilson.

Places to Stay Close to the beach, *Camping La Pinède* (☎ 04 95 65 17 80, fax 04 95 65 19 60), about 2.5km from the town centre, is a quiet, pleasant choice. Sheltered by pine trees, the camping ground has a restaurant, bar, laundrette and supermarket. Prices are 36/14FF per person/tent and 14FF per car. The camping ground is open from 1 April to 15 October.

Auberge de Jeunesse BVJ Corsotel (☎ 04 95 65 14 15, fax 04 95 65 33 72, ave de la République), open from the beginning of March to the end of November, is practically opposite the station. A dormitory bed costs 120FF and includes a generous breakfast. Evening meals cost 60FF.

Hôtel Belvédére (☎ 04 95 65 01 25, fax 04 95 65 33 20, place Christophe Colomb), open year-round, has comfortable doubles with bathroom for 230FF in the low season, 280FF in July and September and 380FF in August.

Places to Eat Away from the restaurants near the harbour is *Le Chalet du Port* (☎ *04 95 65 46 30)*, a pleasant little bar. The food is simple, good and affordable: grilled pizzas (35FF), kebabs (30FF), chips (15FF) or a plate of cold cooked meats (48FF).

A real institution, *Tao* (☎ *04 95 65 00 73)* was set up by Tao Kanbey de Kerekoff, who left his native Caucasus to accompany Prince Lousoupov (who took part in the assassination of Rasputin) into exile. Main courses cost from 95FF to 140FF, with desserts for between 35FF and 45FF. To get there, take the little road off to the right when you get to place d'Armes. Ring ahead for opening times.

The *Super U* supermarket is on ave Christophe Colomb.

GETTING THERE & AWAY

Visitors are charged a 'regional tax' of 30FF upon arrival and departure in Corsica. It is not included in the prices quoted below, but will usually be included in your quoted air or ferry fare. Ferry passengers are also charged a variable port tax.

For information on ferry transport between Corsica and destinations outside France, see the section on Italy under Sea in the Getting There & Away chapter.

Air

The standard fare from Paris to any Corsican city is around 2000FF return, regardless of the season (student fare 1100FF). However, airlines offer various discounts. From April to October, and particularly during summer, charter flights meet the increase in passenger demand.

Air France (☎ 08 02 80 28 02) offers daily direct flights from Paris. Together with regional airlines, it also offers flights from Lyon, Marseille, Nice and Montpellier. Air Littoral (☎ 08 03 83 48 34) flies to Bastia from Paris, Bordeaux and Lyon, and to Ajaccio from Paris.

Charter flights are cheaper (1450FF from Paris), but don't always guarantee confirmed departure times or even days. For high-season charter flights, try Nouvelles Frontières (☎ 08 03 33 33 33).

Bastia-Poretta airport (☎ 04 95 54 54 54) is 24km south of the town. A shuttle bus runs frequently (50FF). The Campo dell'Oro airport is 8km south-east of Ajaccio and is well served by public transport, with an hourly airport bus (20FF). Calvi's airport (☎ 04 95 65 88 88) is 7km south-west of the city centre and is serviced by taxis.

Boat

Details on ferry services are available from many French travel agents. During the summer (late June to September), reservations for vehicles and *couchettes* (sleeping berths) must be made well in advance.

Almost all ferry services between the French mainland (Nice, Marseille and Toulon) and Corsica (Ajaccio, Bastia, Calvi, Île Rousse, Porto Vecchio and Propriano) are handled by the state-owned Société Nationale Maritime Corse-Méditerranée (SNCM; ☎ 08 36 67 95 00 in Marseille, 04 93 13 66 99 in Nice, www.sncm.fr). Schedules and fares are comprehensively listed in the free SNCM pocket timetable, distributed at tourist offices, some hotels and SNCM offices.

In the height of summer there are up to eight ferries a day. *Fauteuil* (literally, 'armchair') seats cost from 240FF and overnight cabins cost an additional 66FF. In winter there are as few as eight services a week and fares are substantially cheaper. Discounts are available for people aged under 25 and seniors. Children under 12 pay 50% less than the adult fare.

Transporting a small car costs between 214FF and 612FF depending on the season. Motorcycles cost from 136FF, and bicycles from 91FF.

Daytime crossings take roughly 6½ hours. Corsica Ferries and SNCM also run a 70km/h express NGV (Navire à Grande Vitesse; ☎ 08 36 64 00 95) service from Nice to Calvi (2¾ hours) and Bastia (3½ hours). Fares on these zippy NGVs are similar to those charged for passage on regular ferries.

GETTING AROUND
Bus

Numerous bus companies offer services all over Corsica, but this does not mean it's

CORSICA

easy to get around by bus. Working out which buses stop at any given place can be quite a challenge because many companies offer only a single service, and many services are infrequent (once or twice a day, often early in the morning) or seasonal.

Although distances are short, fares are relatively high because the demand is so seasonal. You can buy your ticket from the bus driver.

Train
The Corsican rail network (Chemins de Fer de la Corse; CFC; ☎ 04 95 32 80 57, 04 95 32 80 61) has four year-round services: Bastia-Ajaccio, Bastia-Corte, Ajaccio-Calvi and Calvi-Bastia. Prices are very reasonable. Services are slightly reduced in winter.

The CFC produces its own rail pass – La Carte Zoom – which is well worth buying if you intend making more than a couple of train journeys within Corsica (290FF for seven days).

Car Rental
Without a doubt, the best way to get around the island is by car or motorcycle. Some people bring their own cars to Corsica, but it is very easy to hire one on arrival. There are fewer motorcycle hire companies, but you can hire a motorcycle in most of the big towns.

As well as the car rental companies found in towns, all the international car rental companies (Avis, Budget, Europcar and Hertz included) are represented at the airports and this is where you will get the widest choice. You need to have a credit card to hire a vehicle. Expect to pay between 1600FF and 1800FF for a Category A vehicle (three doors, four seats) for a week. The daily rate is about 500FF, while the monthly rate is 4500FF to 5000FF. It pays to shop around.

Bicycle
Cycling around Corsica can add an extra dimension to your holiday, and get you to many of the more remote trail heads without having to rely on infrequent public transport. However, Corsica is hilly on all

but the east coast, so you need to be reasonably fit. Some ferry companies transport bikes for free; others charge around 91FF; it costs 74FF to take your bike on the train. Lonely Planet's *Cycling France* details two tours on the island, which pass several access points for the GR20 and the Mare e Monti routes.

The GR20

Duration	15 days
Distance	168km
Standard	hard
Start	Calenzana
Finish	Conca
Nearest Towns	Calenzana and Porto Vecchio
Public Transport	start only

Summary A legendary, if demanding, walk through the granite ranges of inland Corsica. Experience the isolation and grandeur of the mountains well away from the coastal crowds.

The GR20 stretches diagonally from northwest to south-east, following the island's continental divide (hence its Corsican name, Fra Li Monti, which means 'Between the Mountains'). The diversity of landscapes makes this an exceptional walk, with forests, granite moonscapes, windswept craters, glacial lakes, torrents, peat bogs, maquis, snow-capped peaks, plains and névés (stretches of ice formed from snow).

Consider using the resources available close to the route. Villages linked to the GR20, where you can stop off and stock up, are detailed in the text. The paths linking the GR20 to the villages below are marked with yellow painted lines (these can sometimes be confusing or inadequate on some of the less frequently used paths). For a discussion of villages where you can join or leave the GR20, see the boxed text 'Alternative Access Points'.

PLANNING
When to Walk
The GR20 can be comfortably walked any time between May and October, although

some parts of the route remain snow-covered until June. The peak-season months of July and August are best avoided if you have an aversion to crowds.

What to Bring

The GR20 is a long and challenging walk, and requires some preparation. You will need to carry food with you for at least part of the trail as some of the *refuges* (refuges or mountain huts) only provide light snacks. Depending on the amount of time at your disposal, plan on making detours to local villages for further supplies. Don't forget to carry a good supply of cash.

Water and thirst can also be real problems on the GR20. You will be able to find water at every *refuge*, but between stops there are very few sources of drinking water. These have been detailed in the text.

Camping gear is also essential, as there are only a limited number of places available in *refuges* along the way. When camping you do not have access to equipment inside the huts and fires are prohibited, so bring your own stove and fuel.

Weather in the mountains can fluctuate quickly between extremes, so come prepared for all conditions. A length of rope is a handy addition, as it will allow you to lower your backpack down particularly steep sections of the trail, leaving you free to descend without extra bulk.

Maps

Choose IGN 1:25,000 maps or, at 1:50,000, Didier Richard's *Corse du Nord* and *Corse du Sud*.

NEAREST TOWNS
Calenzana

Thirteen kilometres from Calvi, Calenzana is the northern starting point for the GR20 and is also on the route of the Mare e Monti Nord (Sea to Northern Mountains) walk, making it very popular with walkers.

Places to Stay & Eat The *gîte d'étape municipal* (☎ 04 95 62 77 13) is a few hundred metres along the road to Calvi, on the right-hand side, with hostel-style walkers' accommodation. It has clean, comfortable dormitories for eight people and costs 50FF a night per person. You can also pitch a tent (15FF, plus 25FF per person). There's a *cafe* which serves simple meals, including breakfast for 30FF. The gîte is open year-round and the showers are hot.

Hôtel Bel Horizon (☎ 04 95 62 71 72, 04 95 62 70 08), opposite the church, offers clean rooms with en suite shower and shared toilet. It's open from April to September. Single/double/triple rooms cost 180/200/300FF

WARNING

The GR20 is a genuine mountain route that requires physical commitment and should not be taken lightly. The changes in altitude are unrelenting, the path is rocky and sometimes steep, the weather conditions can be difficult and you have to carry enough equipment to be self-sufficient for several days. Good physical condition and advance training are essential.

Some stretches of the traverse, in particular navigating rickety bridges, snow-covered ground, granite slabs and slippery rock faces, require sure-footedness and a reasonable head for heights.

A walker uses a chain to help cross a granite slab on the GR20

The Northern GR20 (Calenzana to Vizzavona)

Golfe
de Calvi

Calvi

N197

To
Île Rousse
(19km)

D151

START
Calenzana (275m)

GR20

Refuge d'Ortu
di u Piobbu
(1570m)

START
DAY 2

Parc Naturel
Régional de
la Corse

To
Île Rousse
(42km)

N197

To
Bastia
(46km)

Bergerie de
Mandriaccia

Side Trip

Auberge
de la Forêt

Monte Corona
(2144m)

Gorges de l'Asco

Ponte Leccia

Cirque de
Bonifatu

Bocca d'Avartoli
(1898m)

Asco

D147

N193

Alternative
Route

START
DAY 3

Refuge de
Carrozzu
(1270m)

Mare e Mori Nord

Lac de la
Muvrella
(1860m)

Refuge
d'Asco Stagnu
(1422m)

Castirla

A'Muvrella
(2148m)

GR20

Haut Asco

START
DAY 4

Monte Cinto
(2706m)

Cirque de
la Solitude

Bocca Minuta

START
DAY 5

Refuge de Tighjettu
(1640m)

Golo River

Paglia Orba
(2525m)

Bergeries de Ballone
(1440m)

Side
Trip

Corte

Refuge de
Ciottulu di i Mori
(1991m)

Calasima

Albertacce

Calacuccia

Bergeries de Tula
(1700m)

Vallée du Golo

Cascade et Bergerie
de Radule (1370m)

D84

Mare a Mare Nord

To
Aleria
(37km)

Hôtel Castel
di Verghio

Tavignano River

Col de Verghio
(1404m)

Castel di Verghio

Mare a Mare Nord

START
DAY 6

Evisa

D84

Col de
Saint-Pierre
(1452m)

GR20

Lac de Ninu
(1760m)

Bocca a Reta
(1883m)

To
Porto
(21km)

D70

Bergeries
de Vaccaghja
(1621m)

Lac de Melu
(1711m)

Monte Ritondu
(2622m)

Refuge
de Manganu
(1601m)

Lac de
Capitellu
(1930m)

Side
Trip

Refuge de
Pietra Piana
(1842m)

N193

START
DAY 7

Brèche de
Capitellu
(2225m)

START
DAY 8

Bergeries de Gialgu
(1609m)

Soccia

Lac
de Creno
(1310m)

Orto

Bergerie de Tolla
(1011m)

Side
Trip

Vallée du
Manganellu

GR20

Guagno-les-Bains

D23

Guagno

Canaglia

Vico

To
Ajaccio
(51km)

Parc Naturel
Régional de
la Corse

See Southern GR20
Map p245

Refuge
de l'Onda
(1430m)

START
DAY 9

Tattone

Alternative
Route

Monte
d'Oro
(2389m)

Vizzavona (910m)

Vallée de l'Agnone

START
DAY 10

To
Ajaccio
(46km)

For further information refer
to Didier Richard 1:50,000
sheets Corse du Nord (20) &
Corse du Sud (23)

CORSICA

0   5   10 km
0   3   6 miles
1:335,000

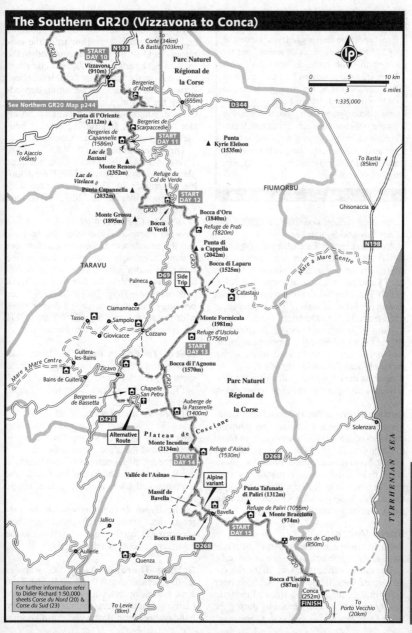

The Southern GR20 (Vizzavona to Conca)

GR20

START DAY 10
Vizzavona (910m)

To Corte (34km) & Bastia (103km)
N193

Bergeries d'Alzeta

See Northern GR20 Map p244

Ghisoni (655m)

D344

Parc Naturel Régional de la Corse

Punta di l'Oriente (2112m)

Bergeries de Scarpaccedie

START DAY 11
Bergeries de Capannelle (1586m)

Punta Kyrie Eleison (1535m)

To Ajaccio (46km)

Lac de Bastani

Monte Renoso (2352m)

Refuge du Col de Verde

FIUMORBU

To Bastia (85km)

Lac de Vitelaca

Punta Capannella (2032m)

Monte Grossu (1895m)

GR20

Bocca di Verdi

START DAY 12

Bocca d'Oru (1840m)

Refuge de Prati (1820m)

Ghisonaccia

Punta di a Cappella (2042m)

TARAVU

D69

Side Trip

Bocca di Laparu (1525m)

N198

Mare a Mare Centre

Palneca

Ciamannacce

Catastaju

Tasso

Sampolo

Giovicacce

Cozzano

Monte Formicula (1981m)

Refuge d'Usciolu (1750m)

START DAY 13

Guitera-les-Bains

Mare a Mare Centre

Zicavo

GR20

Bocca di l'Agnonu (1570m)

Bains de Guitera

Chapelle San Petru

Parc Naturel Régional de la Corse

Bergeries de Bassetta

D428

Auberge de la Passerelle (1400m)

Alternative Route

Plateau de Coscione

Monte Incudine (2134m)

Refuge d'Asinao (1530m)

Solenzara

D268

START DAY 14

Vallée de l'Asinao

Alpine variant

Punta Tafunata di Paliri (1312m)

Jallicu

Massif de Bavella

Bavella

Refuge de Paliri (1055m)

Monte Bracciutu (974m)

Bergeries de Capellu (850m)

Aullerie

Bocca di Bavella

START DAY 15

GR20

D268

Quenza

Zonza

To Levie (8km)

For further information refer to Didier Richard 1:50,000 sheets Corse du Nord (20) & Corse du Sud (23)

Bocca d'Usciolu (587m)

Conca (252m)
FINISH

To Porto Vecchio (20km)

0   5   10 km
0   3   6 miles
1:335,000

TYRRHENIAN SEA

CORSICA

North-South or South-North?

From what direction should you tackle the GR20? Nearly two-thirds of walkers opt for the north-south route, as does this guide. There are various reasons for this – access to Calenzana is easier, the main guide to the route is in this direction, habit – but logic would dictate going from south to north. The southern section between Conca and Vizzavona is easier, giving your body a chance to get used to the effort. Going in this direction also means that you don't have to walk with the sun in your eyes.

in the low season and 200/240/350FF between July and September.

A popular spot is *La Calenzana* (☎ *04 95 62 70 25*), on the main road behind the church. It serves grilled pizzas (36FF to 45FF) and has a Corsican *menu* for 90FF, which includes wild boar with spaghetti during the hunting season. The restaurant is open from April to October.

Housed in an old forge, *U Stazzone* (☎/*fax 04 95 62 80 44*) is open year-round and serves more sophisticated meals, with a *menu* of local delicacies for 90FF.

Spar, at the edge of the village on the road towards Calvi, is a well-stocked supermarket.

Getting There & Away From July to mid-September Les Beaux Voyages bus company (☎ 04 95 65 15 02) has a service from Calvi to Calenzana (25FF, 30 minutes) twice daily except Sunday and public holidays. Buses leave from Calvi opposite the agency's offices in place de la Porteuse d'Eau. In winter the school bus will take you to Calenzana every weekday except Wednesday.

Porto Vecchio

Porto Vecchio is the nearest town of a reasonable size to Conca, at the end of the walk.

The tourist office (☎ 04 95 70 09 58), rue du Deputé Camille de Rocca Serra, is open daily in the summer, and from Monday to Friday and on Saturday morning during the rest of the year.

Places to Stay The quiet *Camping Arutoli* (☎ *04 95 70 12 73*), with all facilities and shaded pitches, is 1km from the carrefour des Quatre Chemins crossroad on the road to L'Ospedale and Zonza. There are signposts to the site from the D368. Allow between 29FF and 35FF per adult, depending on the season, and 15FF per tent or car. On-site bungalows cost between 1500FF (for four people) and 2000FF (for six people) per week, depending on the season.

The *Hôtel Panorama* (☎ *04 95 70 07 96, 12 rue Jean Nicoli*) is one of the cheapest places in the town, costing 240FF for a double in summer, or 330FF for a room with bathroom. Prices fall to 220/310FF in June and September.

Hôtel Le Goéland (☎ *04 95 70 14 15, ave Georges-Pompidou*), between the harbour and the roundabout before the carefour des Quatre Chemins, is a family-run hotel on the waterside and a good choice: it's quiet and has a lovely garden. Double rooms without bathroom cost from 280FF to 330FF, depending on the season, while a double room with bathroom costs from 330FF to 440FF. It's open between Easter and November.

Places to Eat In the Ville Haute, *Les 40èmes* is a creperie on rue Borgo. It serves savoury crepes costing between 20FF and 54FF and is open from 3 pm to midnight, June to September.

Le Bistro du Port (☎ *04 95 70 22 96, route de la Marine*) has a good reputation for fish and its 85FF *menu*. The setting is pleasant and the atmosphere nautical.

There are also a number of restaurants in rue Borgo (Ville Haute) that back on to the ramparts and have lovely terraces facing over the sea.

The *Hyper U* supermarket, on the carrefour des Quatre Chemins, and the *Géant* supermarket, on the next roundabout to the north, are a boon to self-caterers.

Getting There & Away Les Rapides Bleus-Corsicatours (☎ 04 95 70 10 36), 7 rue Jean Jaurès, operates a twice-daily service (daily in winter except Sunday and public holidays) between Bastia and Porto Vecchio via Sainte Lucie de Porto Vecchio (115FF; leaving Bastia at 8.30 am and 4 pm, and Porto Vecchio at 8 am and 1.30 pm).

Île de Beauté Voyages (☎ 04 95 70 12 31), 13 rue du Général de Gaulle, has a service to Ajaccio (110FF) via the mountains (daily except Sunday and public holidays in July and August, and Monday and Friday only in winter). The bus leaves Porto Vecchio at 7 am from outside the bus company's office.

Alternative Access Points

Completing the GR20 will give you a sense of pride and achievement, and rightly so. It is a demanding course which requires commitment. But while the goal of many is to walk it end to end, there is no shame in biting off just a small section. Even a couple of days on the traverse will allow you to experience the beauty of Corsica's mountain wilderness and sample the physical challenges of the trail.

The obvious way to divide the GR20 is into two sections: from Calenzana to Vizzavona (over nine days), and south from Vizzavona to Conca (in six days). Vizzavona is the most convenient midway point, with train and road links to Ajaccio and Bastia.

Between Calenzana and Vizzavona, it's possible to join the trail at several villages along the way: Haut Asco (at the end of Day 3), Castel di Verghio (at the end of Day 5) and Tattone, a short side trip from the main trail (on Day 8). For just a small taste of the GR20, Days 4 and 5 take in some of the most spectacular scenery of the whole walk, across the Cirque de la Solitude.

In the southern section of the GR20, Cozzano (Day 12), Zicavo (Day 13), and Quenza and Bavella (Day 14) are all popular access points for walkers. Reaching Cozzano, Zicavo and Quenza inolves a detour from the GR20, but these traditional villages, tucked away in remote valleys, are the very soul of Corsica and well worth exploring in their own right.

For details of transport links to places along the GR20, see Getting To/From the Walk.

GETTING TO/FROM THE WALK
From the Finish

There is no public transport from Conca, at the end of the walk, to Porto Vecchio. However, staff at La Tonnelle in Conca (see the walk description for contact details) can arrange a shuttle service on request to Sainte Lucie de Porto Vecchio (15FF) to connect with the bus operated by Les Rapides Bleus-Corsicatours (☎ 04 95 70 10 36) between Bastia and Porto Vecchio.

There are also a number of alternative access points to the GR20, some of which are served by public transport.

Haut Asco Haut Asco, at the end of Day 3, is accessible on the D147, which meets the N197 2km north of Ponte Leccia.

Castel de Verghio A bus service runs once daily in each direction between Corte and Porto via Castel de Verghio, on Day 5.

Tattone Tattone (Day 8) is on the Bastia-Vizzavona-Ajaccio railway line. It takes just seven minutes and 8FF to get from Tattone to Vizzavona by train.

Vizzavona Vizzavona (Day 9) is on the railway line between Ajaccio and Bastia. Trains stop four times a day in each direction. Two of the services continue beyond Bastia to Île Rousse and Calvi.

Cozzano Autocars Santini (☎ 04 95 37 04 01) buses run between Cozzano (Day 12) and Ajaccio daily except Sunday.

Zicavo Autocars Santini (☎ 04 95 37 04 01) provides a service between Ajaccio and Zicavo daily except Sunday (70FF).

Bavella In the peak season, Bavella (Day 14) is served by an Autocars Balesi (☎ 04 95 70 15 55) bus daily except Sunday on the Ajaccio–Porto Vecchio line.

Quenza If leaving the GR20 in Quenza, on Day 14, Autocars Balesi (☎ 04 95 70 15 55) buses stop twice daily on the Ajaccio–Porto Vecchio service.

CORSICA

Day 1: Calenzana to Refuge d'Ortu di u Piobbu

7 hours, 10km

You are confronted with the tough conditions of the GR20 from the very outset. This stage is one long ascent, crossing a series of ridges, with hardly a downhill break and long stretches without shade. There's no guaranteed source of water, so bring at least the recommended 2L per person.

The walk starts in Calenzana by winding up to the top of the village, then the path starts to climb steadily through ferns, with good views back to Calenzana and Moncale, another hillside village. At the well-signposted 'Carrefour de Sentiers' (550m), less than an hour from Calenzana, the Mare e Monti Nord route (see Other Walks at the end of this chapter) splits from the GR20. Soon after, the trail reaches the rocky Bocca di Ravalente at 616m.

From the pass, the trail skirts a wide terraced valley, staying fairly level and passing a few small streams that usually dry up later in the season, before climbing relatively gently to 820m. After this easy stretch the trail becomes steeper, zigzagging uphill to another pass, the **Bocca a u Saltu** (1250m). About 3½ hours from the start, this is a perfect spot for lunch. Over the other side of the ridge, on the north-eastern face of Capu Ghiovu, the trail starts to climb even more steeply. About halfway up this stretch is a stream that may be a good source of drinking water.

The wide grassy col at the **Bocca a u Bassiguellu** (1486m), 5½ hours into the walk, is dotted with shady pine trees and makes another good place for a rest stop. From here the trail crosses a rather rocky and unsheltered stretch but stays fairly level. The *refuge* comes into view across a valley, into which you descend before a final short climb brings the day to an end.

The *Refuge d'Ortu di u Piobbu* (1570m) has 30 beds and plenty of camping space. However, it has just one rather primitive toilet and shower; there is a water source about 200m beyond the *refuge* along the GR20. Beds in the *refuge* cost 50FF, and camping or bivouacking costs 20FF per person.

Side Trip: Monte Corona
2½-3 hours

Walkers who still feel strong may want to climb nearby **Monte Corona** (2144m). A trail, marked by cairns and flashes of paint, goes up the slope directly behind the **Bocca di Tartagine** (1852m) *refuge*. From there head south and climb the rocky ridge until the rounded summit, which is covered in loose stones and marked by a cairn, comes into view. The spectacular view stretches from the *refuge* below to the north coast. Allow 2½ to three hours to get to the summit and back.

Day 2a: Refuge d'Ortu di u Piobbu to Refuge de Carrozzu

6½ hours, 8km

Two routes exist for this day. The one fully described in this section is graded difficult. It cuts across a range of mountains, with rocky and often spectacular scenery. The alternative low-level route skirts the mountain range crossed by the main route. It leads off to the west from the Refuge d'Ortu di u Piobbu, meeting a road after a couple of kilometres, which it follows for about 5km down the valley to **Bonifatu** (540m). From Bonifatu retrace your steps up the road for 1.5km before climbing to rejoin the GR20, just beyond the Refuge de Carrozzu.

The day's walk starts with a gentle ascent through pine forest to a ridge (1630m). In front of you is a sharp drop to the valley bottom and then a long, steep ascent (500m) to a much higher ridge on the other side.

The trail descends quickly to the valley floor, passing the ruined **Bergerie de Mandriaccia** (1500m) shepherd's hut and the Mandriaccia stream, then starts the long climb up the other side. About halfway up the unrelenting ascent there's a good source of drinking water, probably the only one you'll come across all day.

Eventually, about three hours from the start, you'll come to the **Bocca Piccaia** (1950m). There's very little shade.

The trail does not actually cross the ridge immediately but stays on the northern side, remaining fairly level until it crosses to the other side and gently descends to the **Bocca** d'Avartoli (1898m). Traversing the southern and western faces of the next ridge, the trail drops steeply before climbing sharply to cross the next pass to the eastern side of the ridge and then crosses back again to the western side at the **Bocca Carrozzu** (1865m), five hours into the walk.

From here the route begins the long and somewhat tedious descent to the *refuge*. At the start of the descent it's worth looking back at the wonderful views enjoyed in the last couple of hours of the walk. A short distance before the *refuge* the trail crosses a stream.

Refuge de Carrozzu (1270m) is in a magnificent setting, hedged in by sheer rock faces on three sides, but with an open terrace looking down the valley. It sleeps 26 and there are plenty of camp sites in the surrounding woods. The standard 50/20FF charges for dormitory/camping apply. In 1998 the young couple who ran the *refuge* prepared soup, cake and other food. They also sold beer, wine, soft drinks, sausage, cheese and other supplies.

A steep path down from the *refuge* brings you to a stream with a series of delightful swimming pools.

Day 3: Refuge de Carrozzu to Haut Asco
6 hours, 6km
This stage is graded medium. Note that there is little water once you've left the Spasimata River behind.

The day starts with a short, rocky zigzag up through the forest to a ridge, then a slightly longer drop to the Spasimata River at 1220m. This is crossed on a rickety suspension bridge that is not for the faint-hearted. At first the trail edges along above the river, crossing long sloping slabs of rock. At some points plastic-coated cables offer handholds – particularly reassuring when it rains.

Leaving the river with its tempting rock pools, the trail then starts a long, rocky ascent to **Lac de la Muvrella** (1860m), which is reached after three to 3½ hours. The lake water is not safe to drink. If you look back during the final stages of the ascent, you'll see Calvi on the north coast. From the lake

it's only a short scramble to the knife-edged ridge. After a short drop on the other side, the trail soon starts to climb again, skirting around the side of A'Muvrella to the Bocca a i Stagni (2010m). The total time of ascent from the river is roughly four hours.

The day is less taxing than the previous two, ending with a 600m descent to Haut Asco, visible far below. Haut Asco looks like any ski resort in the off season – bare, dusty and forlorn – but it's a haven for walkers after the spartan conditions of the last couple of days.

Refuge d'Asco Stagnu (1422m) has 30 beds in rooms for two, four or six people (50FF). It also has hot showers, a kitchen and dining area. There's plenty of camping space on the grassy ski slopes (20FF per person).

There's also a *gîte d'étape* with beds for 40FF (160FF half board). Showers in the gîte cost an extra 10FF.

Two small *shops*, open from 11 am to 8 pm, sell trekking essentials, including freeze-dried food, sausage, cheese, bread, energy bars, chocolate, cereals and fresh fruit.

Side Trip: A'Muvrella
1 hour
This detour from the Bocca a i Stagni takes you to the summit of **A'Muvrella** (2148m) and back. You can also get there from Lac de la Muvrella, rejoining the GR20 at the Bocca a i Stagni, but it's probably easier to leave your backpack at the ridge and make the ascent from there.

Day 4: Refuge d'Asco Stagnu to Bergeries de Ballone
7 hours, 8km
This is generally held to be the most spectacular day on the GR20, crossing the Cirque de la Solitude, which requires some technical climbing. There is water at the Refuge d'Altore, and from there to the bergerie the trail follows a mountain stream.

From Haut Asco the trail starts on the left (south) side of the ski run. It's easy to lose the trail when it runs off the ski slope into the trees. If you do wander off the trail, it's not a problem: you can rejoin the route when it climbs above the valley and the ski slopes

A Taste of Corsica

Corsican food is essentially Mediterranean food embellished with local produce. Some of its more characteristic dishes are best eaten in the winter: game, stews, soup with green beans, potatoes and ham bones, and sumptuous casseroles (*stufati*). Pigs are allowed to range freely through the inland forests, feeding on acorns and chestnuts, and their meat is turned into excellent *lonzu* (preserved pork fillet), *prisuttu* (cured ham) and sausages. Local preserved meats (*charcuterie*) are rarely supplied commercially, but can be sampled in the B&B farmhouses around the island.

Brocciu, a Corsican version of fromage frais, is an indispensable ingredient in many Corsican dishes. Best tasted very fresh (within three days of making), it features in omelettes, lasagnes, sweet and savoury fritters, or is served simply with a sprinkling of maquis herbs.

No discussion of Corsican gastronomy is complete without mention of its superb seafood. Sea urchins, grilled moray eels, sardines stuffed with brocciu and bouillabaisse are some of the fresh local delicacies available.

to cross the glacial moraines. The views over the valley and Haut Asco are stunning.

Allow about two hours to reach the site of the old **Refuge d'Altore** at 2000m. From the small lake at the site, a steep 45-minute climb takes you to the **Bocca Tumasginesca**, or Col Perdu (Lost Pass), at 2183m. From the pass the Cirque de la Solitude falls dramatically away beneath your feet. For most walkers this is the highlight of the entire GR20, and one's first reaction is probably sheer amazement that its navigation is possible.

The descent and ascent of the **Cirque de la Solitude** is more of a rock climb than a walk. However, there are chains bolted into the rock face to make the climb easier. Since other walkers are often almost vertically below you, it's important to take great care not to dislodge rocks or stones as you climb. Typically it takes about 2½ hours to

cross the cirque (a steep-sided basin formed by the erosive action of ice).

From the Bocca Tumasginesca it's 200m down to the scree-covered valley floor, where many walkers pause for lunch. On the other side the route crosses rock slabs, often guided by fixed cables, and makes a series of steep, rocky, chain-assisted ascents before emerging into an equally steep gully (or couloir) filled with loose rocks and stones. Towards the top the climb becomes a little gentler, before emerging 240m above the valley floor at the **Bocca Minuta** (2218m), the second-highest point on the GR20.

Past the ridge the scenery is dramatically different: much wider and more open. The trail makes a long and at times steep descent down the **Ravin de Stranciacone** before reaching the Refuge de Tighjettu about 1¼ hours after leaving the Bocca Minuta.

Refuge de Tighjettu (1640m) charges the standard 50FF for a bed and 20FF for camping or bivouacking. As there is limited camping space around the *refuge*, many campers prefer to pitch their tents lower down, by the river.

It's only another 30 minutes' walk down the valley to the *Bergeries de Ballone* (1440m), open from June to October. There are lots of good spots at which to pitch your tent around the bergerie and camping or bivouacking is free. Beds are also available in a large tent for 10FF.

The bergerie has a popular restaurant and bar, with beer from 12FF, wine for 7FF a glass or 60FF a bottle, and three-course Corsican meals for 80FF. You can also get breakfast the next morning for 30FF and there is a useful range of food and supplies for sale.

The only drawback to this pleasant spot is that there are no toilet or washing facilities. A short walk from the camp site are unpleasant reminders that the lack of toilets could easily be a serious health risk.

Day 5: Bergeries de Ballone to Castel di Verghio
7 hours, 13km
Day 5 contains a half-day option, with the possibility of breaking the journey at the Refuge de Ciottulu di i Mori, with access to

the villages of Calasima and Albertacce. It has been graded medium.

The day begins with a gently undulating ascent through pine forests where streams tumble down from the hills to the west to join the Viru River at the valley floor. Across the valley to the east you can see the road up from **Albertacce** through **Calasima**, at 1100m the highest village in Corsica. The trail turns west round the eastern slope of Paglia Orba and then emerges from the forest for the steep and rocky slog up to the **Bocca di Foghieghiallu** (Col de Fogghiale; 1962m) after about three hours.

On the other side of the pass a wide valley opens out to the south, but the route continues west, crossing the slopes of Paglia Orba and climbing slightly to reach the *refuge*.

Refuge de Ciottulu di i Mori (1991m) charges standard rates: 50FF for one of 28 beds or 20FF to camp or bivouac. Along one side of the building there's a terrace looking out over the valley below. Directly behind the *refuge* is **Paglia Orba** (2525m), the third-highest peak in Corsica. Climbers may want to make the three-hour round trip to the summit of the mountain via the Col des Maures, but the final stretch includes some reasonably challenging rock climbing. This is not an ascent for beginners.

The route continues round to the western side of the Vallée du Golo, descending slightly to 1907m before dropping steeply down to the river at 1700m, just below the ruins of the **Bergeries de Tula**. For the next couple of hours the walk follows the impressively rocky ravine of the **Golo** River, passing a series of appealing rock pools. The path tracing the lower part of the valley was, for many centuries, a traditional route along which farmers took their livestock when migrating to summer pastures.

The valley narrows before the trail reaches the **Cascade de Radule** (1370m) and the **Bergeries de Radule**, after five to six hours. For the final hour you walk through the beech forests of the Valdu Niellu, passing the signposted turn-off to the Fer à Cheval bend (many walkers choose to join the GR20 at this point) and crossing the Mare a Mare Nord trail (see

Other Walks) before finally emerging on the D84 just 100m west of Castel di Verghio (1404m). The ski slopes are on the other side of the road. Older maps show the GR20 crossing the D84 at the Fer à Cheval bend but the trail has been realigned.

Hôtel Castel di Verghio (☎ 04 95 48 00 01) has 29 rooms, each with a shower and sink, that cost 330FF per person for a single room at half board, 250FF per person for a double room and 170FF per person in the gîte d'étape. Bed-only accommodation costs 60FF per person and there's camping for 25FF per person (with a free hot shower).

The hotel's *restaurant* offers a 90FF *menu* that attracts hordes of hungry walkers every evening. The hotel bar sells a good range of basic foodstuffs. Credit cards are not accepted and there is only one (unreliable) phone line to the hotel.

For information on transport from Castel de Verghio, see Getting To/From the Walk earlier in this chapter.

Side Trip: Calasima & Albertacce
1½ or 2½ hours
You can get to Calasima (1100m) in 1½ hours from the Bergeries de Ballone. About 2km before the village you pass a **memorial** to three firefighters killed in an aircraft crash during a forest fire in 1979. The only facility in Calasima is the *Bar du Centre*, but it's only another 5km downhill to Albertacce, which is on the D84. Albertacce has shops, cafes, bars and several places in which to eat, including the *Restaurant Paglia Orba*, the *Auberge U Cintro* and the popular little *Chez François*, all on the main road through town.

Day 6: Castel di Verghio to Refuge de Manganu
5½ hours, 14km
This stage of the GR20 follows a particularly shady route and is of medium difficulty. Water is available at a spring in a shrine just above Lac de Ninu and from a stream from the lake close to the night's stop.

The GR20 runs gently through pine and beech forests, dropping very slightly to 1330m before making a sharp turn to the right (west) and climbing to the small shrine at the **Bocca San Pedru** (Col de Saint Pierre; 1452m), reached after about 1½ hours.

From the pass the route continues to climb, following the carefully laid stones of an ancient mule path. The trail climbs to a ridge, drops off it, climbs back on to it and eventually reaches the **Bocca a Reta** (1883m). It then descends to **Lac de Ninu** (1760m), about 3½ hours from the start. Surrounded by grassy meadows and *pozzines* (interlinked waterholes – see the boxed text), the lake makes a wonderfully tranquil stop for lunch.

The trail continues east, following the course of the Tavignano stream draining the lake, across meadows and then through patches of beech forest past the remains of an abandoned *refuge* to the **Bergeries de Vaccaghja** (1621m), one to 1½ hours from the lake. The bergerie sells wine, cheese and bread. From here you can see the Refuge de Manganu, less than an hour's walk across the valley. The trail drops gently from the bergerie to the **Bocca d'Acqua Ciarnente** (1568m) and finally makes a short, sharp ascent, crossing a bridge over the Manganu stream to the *refuge*.

The pleasant *Refuge de Manganu* (1601m) has 25 beds and plenty of grassy camping space around the building, good showers and toilets and a selection of tempting swimming spots in the Manganu stream. The prices are no surprise: 50FF for a bed and 20FF to camp or bivouac.

Day 7: Refuge de Manganu to Refuge de Pietra Piana
6 hours, 10km

This is a hard day, as the route climbs to the highest point on the GR20 before teetering round a spectacular mountain face. Water is available from streams during the first ascent and from another stream on the final descent to the Refuge de Pietra Piana.

After crossing the bridge from the *refuge*, the GR20 immediately begins to climb, emerging onto a small meadow after 30 minutes, climbing again to another brief, horizontal break at around 1970m and then ascending even more steeply up a rocky gully. This finally becomes a scramble to the

Brèche de Capitellu (2225m), a spectacular small slot through the spiky ridge line of peaks. Around 2½ hours from the *refuge*, this crossing is the highest point on the GR20 and the view to the east is breathtaking.

The trail bends to the south-east and edges round the eastern face of the ridge, high above the lake. There's often snow on the path well into the walking season, so take great care; it's a long way down. Just before another small pass at 2000m, where the trail crosses to the southern side of the ridge, another trail diverges off to the east and drops down to Lac de Capitellu. It's possible to continue down from there to Lac de Melu and then climb back up to the GR20 at the Bocca a Soglia.

The main route climbs slightly to reach the **Bocca a Soglia** (2052m), about an hour's walk from the Brèche de Capitellu. Lots of day-trippers drive into the valley from Corte to walk up to the lakes.

The trail then bends to the north-east, high above Lac de Melu, climbing to the soft-edged little Bocca Rinosa (2150m) and passing Lac de Rinosa before reaching the Bocca Muzzella, or Col de la Haute Route (2206m), about five hours from the start of this stage. From here it's less than an hour, downhill all the way, to the Refuge de Pietra Piana.

The small, 24-bed *Refuge de Pietra Piana* (1842m) is nicely situated right on the edge of the ridge, looking south down the Vallée du Manganellu. There's plenty of grassy camping space and good facilities. As usual, the beds cost 50FF, with camping and bivouacs for 20FF per person.

The *refuge* is used as a helicopter rescue base and there's a landing pad nearby.

Side Trip: Monte Ritondu
3 hours

Walkers may consider climbing Monte Ritondu (2622m), the second-highest mountain in Corsica. This is not a technically difficult climb, although the 800m ascent may be a little tiring at the end of the day.

Cairns mark the route to a meadow and dried-up lake just above the *refuge*. The trail then zigzags uphill before crossing the ridge at 2260m, south of the peak. Don't descend from the ridge towards the small lakes below – continue north along the eastern side of the ridge, crossing patches of snow until the large Lavu Bellebone lake comes into view. The trail drops down to the lake's southern end and edges round the south-eastern side before starting the steep climb up the loose scree slope of the rocky gully that leads to the spiky rock marking the Col du Fer de Lance. From here the trail turns west and climbs to a small metal-roofed shelter, huddled just below the summit. There are superb views in all directions from the summit.

Day 8: Refuge de Pietra Piana to Refuge de l'Onda
5 hours, 10km
An easy, mostly shady day's walk, the trail follows streams almost all day so water is no problem.

After the dramatic ascents and descents of the previous day, this stage of the walk is gentle and predominantly downhill. As soon as the trail leaves the *refuge* there's a choice between following the main GR20 through the Vallée du Manganellu or taking an alternative high-altitude route, marked in yellow, which follows ridges to the Refuge de l'Onda. The high-altitude route is quicker but less interesting and is not covered in any detail here.

The main GR20 starts to drop almost immediately and soon reaches the ***Bergeries de Gialgu*** (1609m), where bread, cheese and wine can be purchased. The trail continues to drop, following an ancient mule track of neatly laid stones that winds down the hill to the Manganellu stream at 1440m. It then continues through often dense forest to the ***Bergerie de Tolla*** (1011m), about three hours from the start. This pleasant little haven sells the usual supplies, and also serves snacks and meals.

Just below the bergerie a bridge crosses the Manganellu stream (940m). From here you can detour off the GR20 to the villages of Canaglia and Tattone (see the side trip).

The GR20 turns upstream from the bridge and almost immediately passes over the Goltaccia, which flows into the Manganellu. Do not cross over this bridge but continue

High-Altitude Lakes & Pozzines

Corsica's 40-odd high-altitude lakes, formed from the glaciers that used to cover the mountains, were unknown to scientists until the 1980s but are now actively monitored by PNRC agents. A number of different analyses have shown that some are endangered by the digging of pigs and the pollution caused by tourist overpopulation in the summer. The PNRC has implemented a protection program for the most popular lakes – Melu, Ninu and Creno – in the summer. Seasonal workers collect the rubbish left by walkers and ensure that the camping bans are upheld. The GR20 has even been diverted so that it does not contribute to the destruction of the grassy areas around Lac de Ninu. Respect the rules: no fires, no rubbish and no walking at inappropriate times.

The pozzines (from the Corsican *pozzi*, meaning pits) are also a fragile environment, threatened by intensive farming. Pozzines are little water holes that are linked together by small streams and are on an impermeable substratum – they're like peat bogs. They feel like a carpet of cool moss to walkers. They are found near Lac de Ninu and on the Plateau de Coscione, between the GR20 and the Refuge de la Bergeries de Bassetta.

upstream and uphill beside the Goltaccia. Eventually the trail crosses the river and climbs away to the north side, soon reaching the busy ***Bergeries de l'Onda***, a hive of activity next to the Refuge de l'Onda's grassy camping site. The bergerie sells wine, bread, cheese and sausages. It is surrounded by fences to keep out the many pigs poking around the site.

The ***Refuge de l'Onda*** itself is higher up the hill, overlooking the bergerie and camp site from 1430m. It charges 50FF for a bed or 20FF to camp or bivouac.

Side Trip: Canaglia & Tattone
2 hours
It's about an hour's easy walk from the Manganellu bridge on the GR20 to the pretty village of Canaglia. The wide track running

CORSICA

alongside the river and the string of little pools make this a popular route with walkers. At Canaglia's small restaurant, the *Osteria u Capitan Moru*, trout is a speciality. There's a phone in the restaurant.

From Canaglia it's 4km by road to Tattone. For a taxi call Alain (☎ 04 95 47 20 06, 04 95 47 23 17) in Vivario.

The *Bar du Soleil Camping* (☎ 04 95 47 21 16), near the Tattone train station, charges 24FF per adult plus 10FF for a tent, 10FF for a car and 5FF for a motorcycle. The camping ground has a snack bar and supplies and also operates a *navette* (shuttle bus). There's another camping ground, *Camping Savaggio*, 2km beyond Tattone.

Day 9: Refuge de l'Onda to Vizzavona
5½ hours, 10km

This is traditionally the mid-stage of the GR20, and ends in Vizzavona, the best-equipped stop along the GR20. Water is plentiful along the trail.

The route sets off northwards, following the high-level alternative route to the Refuge de Pietra Piana, but soon doubles back to head south up the long climb to the **Crête de Muratellu** (2020m), reached after two to 2½ hours. From this bleak height the rest of the day's walk is a long downhill descent.

An alternative route, marked only by stone cairns, continues up the Crête de Muratellu and turns slightly north-east to the Bocca di u Porcu (2159m), from where it turns south-east to climb to the summit of Monte d'Oro (2389m), the fifth-highest mountain in Corsica. There are stretches of difficult rock climbing on this route, which should not be attempted by inexperienced climbers. It finally rejoins the main GR20 route just before Vizzavona and adds about three hours to the day's walk.

The main GR20 makes a steep and rocky descent from the Muratellu ridge into the upper heights of the Vallée de l'Agnone. The descent becomes less steep and the surroundings greener as the route drops below 1600m and passes the remains of an abandoned *refuge* at 1500m. The trail passes a high waterfall, the **Cascades des Anglais**

(1150m), roughly four hours from the start. The trail continues through pine forests, sometimes high above the tumbling stream. Monte d'Oro broods over this scene from the north-east.

A *snack bar* and a bridge over the Agnone hint at the proximity of civilisation, and from here into Vizzavona the route makes the transition from walking path to a track quite suitable for cars. There are several turns, several bridges and what seems like an interminable trudge before the trail finally emerges on to the road right in the middle of the village of Vizzavona, only a short distance from the train station.

Vizzavona (910m) is a tiny health spa at the foot of the massive Monte d'Oro. Those who tackle the whole of the GR20 consider it a welcome return to civilisation and generally make the most of the opportunity to restock with provisions and have a decent meal and a good night's sleep in a hotel.

Vizzavona is situated at the heart of one of the prettiest forests in Corsica, an excellent setting for a number of well-marked shady walks.

Hôtel I Laricci (☎/fax 04 95 47 21 12), looking like a big Swiss chalet, has 12 spacious double rooms that cost 465FF for half board with bathroom (425FF without bathroom), as well as dormitories costing 145FF per person, including an evening meal. The simple yet generous *menu* costs 85FF (wine included). You can do your washing for 50FF. It is open from April to October and you'll need to reserve ahead.

Just opposite the station is the friendly, family-run *Resto Refuge de la Gare* (☎/fax 04 95 47 22 20), home to a restaurant and two clean and simple dormitories that accommodate six people each (60FF per person). Meals are optional (there's a *menu* for about 70FF), but there are no self-catering facilities. It is open from the beginning of June to September.

Campers tend to pitch their tents on a flat piece of land behind the station, which is often full to bursting in summer. Camping is free here but there are no toilets or washing facilities. An official camping ground is being considered.

You can do some serious stocking up at the grocery store, *Épicerie Rosy*, which is in the station and run by Madame Zagnoli. It's open from 7.30 am daily, including Sunday and public holidays, and sells just about everything walkers could want at quite reasonable prices.

Just opposite is the *Restaurant-Bar l'Altagna*, which has *menus* for 65FF and 85FF. Local specialities and tasty snacks are also served all day.

For information on public transport services between Vizzavona and the coastal towns of Ajaccio and Bastia, see Getting To/From the Walk earlier in this chapter.

Day 10: Vizzavona to Bergeries de Capannelle
5½ hours, 13.5km
This section of the walk is punctuated by magnificent views as you approach Monte Renosu against a background of laricio pine and beech trees.

From the station in Vizzavona, follow the marked route for the GR20 Sud, which passes in front of Hôtel I Laricci. It crosses the access path to the GR20 Nord on the right and then crosses a little bridge before climbing to rejoin the N193 and the ONF (Office National des Forêts; National Office for Forests) house. A sign tells you that Bergeries de Capannelle is 4½ hours away, but this is somewhat optimistic. This sign marks the beginning of the dirt track that climbs gently through the woods. The trail goes left at a fork (the right fork leads to a spring, 450m away).

The route quickly leaves the dirt track behind and makes a twisting ascent to a high-voltage power cable that marks the start of a long, flat trek through the undergrowth. The steep little path leads straight ahead until it reaches a junction: here the GR20 goes off to your left, but make a detour 100m down the right fork for a wonderful view of Monte d'Oro and Vizzavona below.

Back on the GR20, the path emerges from the undergrowth into a bare, almost lunar landscape from where you can see **Bocca Palmente** (1647m) ahead. Pay attention to the markings and the junction where the

GR20 turns right to the pass, just over 15 minutes' climb away.

The path goes back down towards the **Bergeries d'Alzeta** before continuing level. After about 30 minutes a hairpin bend marks the left turn-off that leads to **Ghisoni**, where you can stop. This turn-off is an ideal spot for a picnic, with a stunning view over the Monte Renosu massif.

The GR20 continues along the hillside and goes through a forest of laricio pines, some of which are an impressive size. About 1¼ hours later it reaches the three charming **Bergeries de Scarpaccedie**.

A short distance on, the route bears to the right before a steep uphill stretch (a good 20 minutes of solid effort) to a wonderful view of Monte Renosu (2352m). The route then follows a sealed road uphill for about 100m before coming to a sign detailing the services available at the Bergeries de Capannelle (1586m).

Straight ahead, the *Gîte U Fugone* (☎ 04 95 57 01 81), run by Paul Maurizi and his wife and open from mid-May to the end of September, offers the better value of the two, with dormitories for 55FF per person (half board 158FF only). The rooms have recently been renovated and have toilets and hot showers. Those staying at the PNRC *refuge* can come here for a shower (20FF). There is a little grocery selling basic foodstuffs and a restaurant with *menus* based on Corsican specialities for 65FF and 110FF.

The *Gîte U Renosu*, 300m away, is generally only open in winter.

Just before the Gîte U Fugone is the *PNRC refuge*. It is made entirely of stone and is somewhat dubious in terms of comfort. One night costs 35FF per person, collected by the warden of the Gîte U Fugone. Whether you stay here or not, it is worth having a look at the PNRC information here about the rest of the GR20.

It's a 20-minute walk from the sign to the bergeries, which are at the foot of the ski lifts in the resort of Ghisoni. Although there is only one remaining shepherd, all the bergeries kept by local families now serve as cottages for holidaymakers and hunters.

CORSICA

DAY 11:
Bergeries de Capannelle to Bocca di Verdi
5 hours, 11.5km

This stage is relatively short and easy, keeping largely to a plain at around 1500m. If you wish to extend the day, a two-hour detour to the Pozzi plain is an attractive option. The route begins at the foot of the ski lift and rapidly retreats into a forest of beech trees that suggest the Bergeries de Capannelle must have been in an idyllic setting before the construction of the ski resort.

It will take less than 30 minutes to reach the **Bergeries de Traggette** (1520m) and the D169. Fifty metres farther on there is a sign to the Bocca di Verdi and the route heads uphill again. There are views over the Fiumorbu region and the Kyrie Eleïson range before the path enters a thick forest of pine and beech.

After 45 minutes, the GR20 rounds a hairpin bend to the right. When the snow is melting you will have to cross a string of streams here, some of which require some acrobatic skills. Another 45 minutes later there's a second hairpin bend, this time in the open.

You are now halfway through the day's walk and right next to **Punta Capannella** (2032m); above you, the Lischetto stream, which flows from the little Lacs de Rina (1882m), cascades down in a profusion of small waterfalls.

Once you have crossed the **Lischettu**, it will not take more than 30 minutes to get to the **Plateau de Gialgone** (1591m), where the view over the Bocca di Verdi is invigorating. In front of you is **Monte Grossu** (1895m) and, at the edge of the plain, a wooden sign directs you to the Pozzi, a magnificent grassy plain that may be worth the detour (allow two hours to get there and back).

The GR20 itself carries straight on towards Bocca di Verdi and begins an impressive descent that culminates some 30 minutes later in a little wooden bridge straddling the Marmanu stream, which flows from the Fiumorbu.

A few metres on, a simple wooden sign on the ground indicates a giant fir tree that rises to the amazing height of 53.2m. The path soon bends to the right and widens out in the middle of a forest of fir trees. After about 20 minutes the trail reaches a large picnic area.

To the right is a path through the forest which goes to the village of Palneca, while a path to the left leads to the Bocca di Verdi (Col de Verde) after about 300m.

Relais San Pedru di Verde (☎ *04 95 24 46 82, 04 95 24 50 32*), better known as the Refuge du Col de Verde, is in a lush green setting on the edge of the D69. It's open from 1 May to the end of September and has capacity for 18 people. It's fairly basic: a wooden cottage equipped with a stove, a table and three wooden planks topped by mattresses. However, there is absolutely nothing wrong with the sanitation facilities and the shower is hot. A night is only 20FF with hot shower, but *camping* is free.

One of the best things about this *refuge* is its lovely terrace, where you can treat yourself to generous salads for about 25FF, sandwiches (25FF) and drinks (13FF). In the evening grilled meats (40FF) and pizzas are on offer.

Day 12: Bocca di Verdi to Refuge d'Usciolu
7–7½ hours, 14km

This is one of the longer and more difficult days of the GR20, including some very steep sections and sometimes high winds on the exposed ridge sections.

After crossing a minor road, the trail ascends gently through a pine forest to a turnoff (10 minutes). Once it turns left, the real climbing begins. It takes 20 minutes of sustained effort to reach an intermediate plateau – the end of the first section.

A stream marks the start of the second steep section (which is at least shaded by beech trees). After another hour of tough climbing, the trail reaches the **Bocca d'Oru** (1840m), with its excellent views over the eastern plain.

A very pleasant walk then leads, after about 15 minutes, to the **Refuge de Prati** (1820m), or at least what is left of it: the *refuge* was destroyed by lightning in 1997, but there were plans at the time of research to start rebuilding it. It is well worth filling your flask at the *refuge's* water fountain, as

Cauterets and the Vallée de Lutour from Pic du Cabaliros, Pyrenees.

Cows on the verge, Pyrenees.

The long climb up the Vallée de Marcadau.

The clear mountain waters of the Lac de Gaube, Hautes Pyrénées.

View from Monte Ritondu (2622m), Corsica.

The steep and rocky GR20.

Following the trail signs.

Col de Foggiale, Corsica.

Lac de Ninu, one of a string of high-altitude, glacial lakes along the GR20.

there are no other water sources for the rest of the stage. The GR20 follows the path to the right (a path to the left marked in yellow goes down to the village of Isolacciu di Fiumorbu, 1km below to the east) and leads straight on to the ridge.

This very steep stretch only lasts about 20 minutes, but the path remains steep and rocky. Make the most of the view because you will need all your strength to negotiate the next 30-minute section up through large rocks (this could be dangerous in bad weather conditions – so take great care). For the next 1¼ hours the path along the ridge is rock and difficult, coming very close to some frightening precipices at times.

Once past **Punta di a Cappella** (2042m), the trail skirts round the Rocher de la Penta before moving off the ridge and into a little forest that is an ideal spot for a picnic. From here it's less than 30 minutes to the **Bocca di Laparu** (1525m), where the route crosses the Mare a Mare Centre walk (see Other Walks at the end of the chapter). There's a sign to a spring and nearby is a very basic *refuge* (no warden; closed at time of research). The trail to Cozzano leaves the GR20 from here (see the side trip).

After the pass, the trail continues along the ridge, this time climbing steadily up to **Monte Formicula** (1981m), the highest point of the day and a little less than 500m above Laparu. Allow between 1¾ and two hours for the climb.

Once past Monte Formicula, it is not much farther to the Refuge d'Usciolu (roughly 30 to 45 minutes) and, rather like a Sunday afternoon walk, it's downhill all the way.

Leaning against the mountain, the *Refuge d'Usciolu* has a bird's-eye view over the whole valley. The *refuge* has 32 beds (50FF) and is clean and well kept. The *camp site* is just below the *refuge* (20FF per person). The warden offers light refreshments – sheep's milk cheese (40FF), drinks (13FF), sausage, chocolate and hard-boiled eggs.

Side Trip: Cozzano
5 hours
The route to Cozzano forms part of the Mare a Mare Centre walk. It descends from the

Bocca de Laparu for about 20 minutes before entering a splendid forest of laricio pine and leading to a forest track. Turn left and before long you'll pass a fast-flowing stream. There's a natural spring next to the path 200m farther on. Follow the path, which becomes much wider, until you see a sign for Cozzano pointing towards a little path heading down into the forest.

Half an hour later the trail joins a forest road, which it follows for a short time before turning off to the left on a bend to follow the course of a dry river bed. You now see the first chestnut trees *(châtaignier)*. The path keeps crossing the forest road, so look carefully for the orange markings.

After about 30 minutes of this crisscrossing, you come first to a wooden gate across the path, then, a few metres on, to a large stream, and finally to a tarmac road. Turn left and the road will take you into the centre of Cozzano. The gîte is on the right-hand side.

On the other side of the village, towards Palneca (to the north), a large building houses the *Gîte Rural Bella Vista (☎ 04 95 24 41 59)*, which has six dormitories for six people each (60FF per person) and three doubles at 150FF. You can also camp in the garden for 33FF and there is a self-catering kitchen. An evening meal costs 70FF (breakfast 30FF).

There are two bars in Cozzano, the *Central Bar* and the *Snack Bar Terminus*.

Cozzano is the only village in the area with a pharmacy (☎ 04 95 24 40 40), in the main square, open from 9.15 am to 7.30 pm daily except Sunday. The main square also contains a petrol station and a well-stocked *grocery*, both open from 9 am to 7 pm, Monday to Saturday, and on Sunday morning.

For information on public transport links to Cozzano, see Getting To/From the Walk earlier in this chapter.

Day 13: Refuge d'Usciolu to Refuge d'Asinao
7½ hours, 14.5km
It's possible to do this stage over two days, with a detour to the village of Zicavo (not described here) or a stop-off at the Bergeries de Bassetta or the Auberge de la Passerelle, climbing Monte Incudine on the second day.

From the Refuge d'Usciolu, a short, steep path leads back up to the ridge. There's a sign to Cozzano, where it is possible, but not very practical, to stop off. From here it's a tightrope walk along the **ridge**, which is particularly steep at this stage, for a good two hours.

The altitude is an almost constant 1800m, but the trail goes up and down in a continual series of tiny ascents and descents, making the going very hard, particularly across large slabs of rock. The signs are not always easy to find, but the views are sublime.

The trail passes a distinctive U-shaped gap, then drops down towards a grove of beeches on the western side of the ridge.

After about three hours you'll reach a wonderful, huge clearing – an ideal place for lunch. The pastoral setting, with streams and majestic beech trees, is in stark contrast to the barren austerity of the route along the top of the ridge. There's also a spring, which is signposted. About 10 minutes from here the trail reaches the crossroads at the **Bocca di l'Agnonu**, about 3¼ hours from the start of this stage.

At the crossroads there's a sign for Asinao with the words '*Ravitaillement, gîte, camping à 1 heure*' (Refreshments, accommodation, camping – 1 hour). This refers to the Auberge de la Passerelle, but the time is an underestimation.

The route continues among the beeches for about 20 minutes, leading to an overhang with wonderful views. The trail then moves out of the hedges and onto the hilly plain. The route is easy until it reaches the foot of Monte Incudine, which you summit later in the day. After about an hour the trail reaches the junction with the alternative route via Zicavo and the **Refuge de la Bergeries de Bassetta**, 1½ hours' walk to the west. There is a sign indicating that the Auberge de la Passerelle is 200m away. Follow the GR20 towards Asinao (signposted); it will take less than 15 minutes to get to the Casamintellu stream and the *Auberge de la Passerelle*, just next to it.

Essentially a group of wooden shacks on the edge of the Casamintellu stream, the *refuge* stands out in comparison with the PNRC *refuges* as a veritable Ali Baba's cave: biscuits, chocolate, soup sachets, cheese, sausage, bread, pâté, hard-boiled eggs, apples and hot and cold drinks are all available, along with a generous meal of salad, wild boar casserole and pasta (60FF). There's also a water point. However, the 10-bed dormitory (30FF a night) is basic, showers are cold and the sanitation facilities are sadly lacking.

Another option, if you would rather complete this stage over two days, is the impeccably run *Refuge de la Bergeries de Bassetta* (☎ 04 95 25 74 20, 04 95 24 44 50), roughly 1½ hours' walk off the GR20 (with only a slight change in altitude). This private *refuge* is a converted old bergerie and is well worth the detour. It is 1.5km from the Chapelle San Petru and is also accessible by road from Zicavo, which is about 14km away along the D428 and D69. It costs 60FF (or 170FF for half board and 220FF full board). Excellent meals, served in a big communal room with a fireplace, cost 110FF.

After the Auberge de la Passerelle, the trail crosses a rickety wooden footbridge over the Casamintellu and the ascent of Monte Incudine begins. After about 30 minutes, you reach the **Aire de Bivouac i Pedinieddi**. This little plateau used to be home to the Refuge de Pedinieddi, until it was destroyed by lightning. It's possible to *bivouac* here and there is a water supply.

About one hour's walk from the footbridge, you reach the **Bocca di Luana** (1800m), which is on a ridge. The route turns to the right and begins the difficult climb to the ridge leading to the summit. After just over two hours of climbing, the cross on the summit of **Monte Incudine**, at 2134m, comes into view. It is not uncommon for there to be snow here until June.

All that's left now is the descent to the *refuge*. The first 15 minutes is an easy walk along the ridge. The trail reaches a junction and you can see what lies ahead: the path plummets down to the *refuge* 500m below. The slope really is impressive, and your joints will certainly feel it.

Allow 1¼ to 1½ hours to descend from the summit to the Refuge d'Asinao.

Refuge d'Asinao (1530m) only has room for 20 people. It costs 50FF (camping 20FF) and sells basic refreshments (cooked meats, honey, cheese, beer and wine). From the *refuge* you can see the Bergeries d'Asinao below; they are still used and bivouacking is not allowed here.

Day 14: Refuge d'Asinao to Refuge de Paliri via the Alpine Route

6¼ hours, 13km

Deviating from the official trail to follow the Alpine Route, this stage of the GR20 is one of the most beautiful. However, it is also difficult technically, passing through fallen rocks and stones and requiring you to use your hands across a chained slab of rock in one section. If you get vertigo or you are not happy with this, it is advisable to take the main route. It is also worth avoiding this option in the wet, as there is a risk of slipping.

From the Refuge d'Asinao, the GR20 path heads west before gradually turning south to reach the valley, where you ford the Asinao after about 30 minutes' walk. On the way you will pass a sign indicating a turn-off to Quenza, three hours away.

Quenza is a jewel among villages on the Mare a Mare Sud trail (see Other Walks at the end of the chapter), and is three to four hours from the GR20. It boasts a *refuge* and several *hotels*, as well as two *grocery stores*, a post office and telephone boxes.

On the other side of the Asinao River the path climbs gently and then evens out along the side of the mountain at an average altitude of 1300m. The route is easy and pleasant, following a ledge above the Asinao for about one hour. In places you can just about see through the foliage to the towering foothills of the Bavella massif.

After about 1½ hours of walking you reach a crossroads. Straight ahead is the main GR20 route, which skirts the mountainside to the south-west of the massif. Taking off at 90° to the normal path, the **alpine route** (described here) takes you to the heart of the massif and is marked out in yellow – it is, without doubt, one of the highlights of the GR20.

The climb up the mountainside is very steep. There is a short respite for about 10 minutes, then the path leaves the wooded section and continues to climb towards the **Bocca di u Pargulu** (1662m), reaching it after an hour. Towards the end, the knife-edge points of the rock faces can feel overwhelming. When you get to the top and see the panoramic views, however, it will all seem unimportant. In the jagged landscape surrounding you you can make out peaks that look like huge sharp teeth – these are the Aiguilles de Bavella (Bavella Needles).

From here the path descends steeply through a stony gully for about 30 minutes until reaching the famous chain across a smooth, steep slab, about 10m in width. After another 30 minutes of tricky progress along rocky slopes you reach a pass, where you have a wonderful view of the peaks and the village of Bavella, close by to the east. The path to Bavella plunges through a deep gully of pink granite. The markings are sometimes less than adequate during this difficult descent.

Roughly four hours after you set out, the path rejoins the normal route of the GR20. It is then only a short stroll through a pine forest to the Bocca di Bavella car park.

Go past the Madone des Neiges (a statue of the Virgin Mary) and take the tarmac road (one of the few concessions to civilisation on the GR20) to the left for about 300m. This leads into the village of **Bavella**.

It may be worth stopping off in Bavella, as the Refuge de Paliri, at the end of the day, does not provide refreshments. Some walkers choose to leave the GR20 here, although this is a shame as the last stage of the traverse is particularly picturesque.

Les Aiguilles de Bavella (☎ 04 95 57 46 06), near the Madone des Neiges, is open from 1 April to 15 October and provides food and shelter. It costs 70FF in a room shared between four (half board 180FF) and 190FF for a double room. There is also a kitchenette. The restaurant provides Corsican meals for 65FF.

About 300m farther towards the village, on a hairpin bend, is the *Auberge du Col de Bavella* (☎ 04 95 57 43 87), which has an excellent reputation, especially for its food. It costs 80FF in a room for six people (180FF half board). The auberge is open from April to October and accepts credit cards.

Next door is *Le Refuge*, another *refuge*-restaurant-bar, open from May to September. A room for up to four people will set you back 150FF. The restaurant serves pizza, sandwiches and omelettes; there are also *menus* for 65FF or 120FF.

There's a *grocery* opposite the Auberge du Col de Bavella, but it's not particularly well stocked.

For information on public transport services to Bavella, see Getting To/From the Walk earlier in this chapter.

If you wish to continue to the Refuge de Paliri, allow another 2¼ hours. The only difficult section is around the Bocca di Foce Finosa.

When you reach the Auberge du Col de Bavella on the road into Bavella, take the turn-off to the right, which changes into a forest track 50m farther on.

The walk is pleasant and easy, and follows a level route through a forest of pine trees and silver birch for 15 minutes. The path then narrows before forking to the left and descending to a small stream. About 10 minutes later you come to a forest track – follow it to the right for 50m. Turn left at the fork and cross the **Volpajola** stream on the small concrete bridge.

Opposite, to the east, is a long range of mountains, which you will cross via the Bocca di Foce Finosa. Five minutes from the stream, the path forks to the right to begin the ascent. It takes 45 minutes to climb 200m in altitude to the **Bocca di Foce Finosa** (1214m).

The last section of the route is the hour's walk to the Refuge de Paliri, down the east face of the range. The descent starts sharply, then turns north-east and levels out. A small peak just before you reach the Refuge de Paliri (1055m) marks the end of this long stage.

Built on the site of, and with the stones of, a former bergerie, the little *Refuge de Paliri* (20 beds) is not lacking in style. It is also in a magnificent setting. On a clear day you can see as far as Sardinia to the south. The warden has looked after the *refuge* since 1981. It costs 50FF (20FF for camping, with toilets and use of a kitchenette area with equipment). This *refuge* does not sell any food, however, and the showers are cold.

Day 15: Refuge de Paliri to Conca
5 hours, 12km

From the *refuge* the path descends briefly before coming to the heart of a superb forest of maritime pines and silver birch. On the left is the imposing spectre of the **Anima Damnata** (Damned Soul) at 1091m, with its distinctive sugar-loaf shape. After a short walk along a ledge, you can easily make out the Monte Bracciutu massif to the east and Monte Sordu to the south-east (25 minutes away). The path then follows a ridge that curves north-east round a cirque, in the middle of which are the peaks of the **Massif du Bracciutu**.

To the north-east you can see the hole in the Punta Tafunata di Paliri, which almost looks like a bull's-eye in the line of mountains extending from north-east to south-west. Follow this ledge for about 30 minutes (there's no shade), until you reach the **Foce di u Bracciu** (917m). At this point the trail turns to head due south.

The trail follows the contour line for about 10 minutes before tackling the ascent of the **Bocca di Sordu** (1065m). It takes 30 minutes of difficult climbing to reach the pass, with its distinctive masses of fallen rock. The view from here stretches as far as the sea.

Just after the pass you climb 50m down across a relatively steep granite slab (it could easily become a natural slide in the wet). This leads to a sandy path that slices through a pine forest. Five to 10 minutes later the trail emerges at a little plateau dotted with granite domes and strangely shapted piles of rocks. In the background is maquis, a few maritime pines and the trunks of trees destroyed by forest fires. After about 15 minutes in this setting the path starts to descend. About 2½ hours after setting out you will reach the (ruined) **Bergeries de Capellu** (850m). A signpost leads to a spring about

300m to the left of the main path, a good spot for a picnic.

The path climbs steadily down to the **Punta Pinzuta** stream, which you can hear running through the valley. The scorched trunks bear witness to the violent forest fires and create a ghostly atmosphere.

The trail fords the stream, then follows its course for a while before crossing back at a large bend. A good 20-minute climb takes you out of this steep-sided valley and up to a pass. The path continues along the mountainside, almost level, until it reaches the **Bocca d'Usciolu** (587m), a narrow U-shaped passage through a wall of granite.

The descent into Conca in the valley below (20 to 30 minutes) passes through thick undergrowth, emerging at a tarmac road. Turn left, follow the road to a cross-roads and then take the road leading down. You will soon be able to see the main road.

On the way into Conca, just opposite the cemetery, is the gîte d'étape, *La Tonnelle* (☎ *04 95 71 46 55*), which is clean, functional and open year-round. A night in a room, with en suite, sleeping two/three people costs 100/80FF and 70FF for four. It's also possible to camp for about 30FF per person. Breakfast costs 30FF, lunch or dinner 70FF, and there is a kitchenette. Foreign currency can be changed here.

There's a choice of *snack bars* and *restaurants* in the centre of the village. Conca also has a post office and a well-stocked *grocery*, open daily in summer.

Other Walks

Walking in Corsica is by no means limited to the GR20. Other well-known and much enjoyed walks across the island include the Mare e Monti and Mare a Mare trails, outlined briefly here. Although less publicised than the GR20, these routes take in some spectacular mountain and coastal scenery, with the added bonus of ending each day comfortably in a village. For those who doubt their ability to cope with the GR20, they also offer a shorter and less daunting physical challenge.

THE MARE E MONTI ROUTES

As the name suggests, these are paths between the sea *(mare)* and the mountains *(monti)*.

Mare e Monti Nord

This is a superb (and not very difficult) walk which links Calenzana in the Haute-Balagne region to Cargèse, south of the Golfe de Porto. It is divided into 10 stages of four to seven hours each, and its highest point is 1153m. It passes through several exceptional natural sites, such as the Forêt de Bonifatu, the Réserve Naturelle de Scandola and the Gorges de Spelunca, and stops in some charming villages.

The Mare e Monti Nord is passable year-round, but the periods before and after the main season (May to June and September to October) are preferable to avoid the worst of the heat. The path crosses the Mare a Mare Nord in two places: Evisa and Marignana.

Mare e Monti Sud

This path runs between the bays of two well-known seaside resorts in the south-west of Corsica – Porticcio and Propriano. It's divided into five stages of five to six hours and ascends to a maximum height of 870m. There are stops in Bisinao, Coti-Chiavari (which towers above the two bays), Porto Pollo and Olmeto. The walk ends in Burgo (7km north of Propriano).

There are only two *gîtes* on the route: in Bisinao (☎ *04 95 24 21 66*) and Burgo (☎ *04 95 76 15 05*). In the other villages you can either stay in a *hotel* or at a *camping ground*.

The highlights are the views over the bays, the historic Genoese towers and the beaches (the Baie de Cupabia and Porto Pollo). Like its northern counterpart, this path is passable year-round and is not very difficult. Spring and autumn are the best times. The path meets the Mare a Mare Sud in Burgo.

THE MARE A MARE ROUTES

Three Mare a Mare (Sea to Sea) paths link the west and east coasts via the mountains in the centre of the island.

Mare a Mare Centre

The Mare a Mare Centre provides an excellent opportunity to explore the more traditional, inland areas of Corsica. The walk can be completed in seven days of three to seven hours each. Starting in Ghisonaccia, on the east coast, and finishing in Porticcio, on the west coast, it passes through the little-known districts of Fiumorbu and Taravu before crossing the hinterland of Ajaccio.

CORSICA

Unlike the GR20, which stays high in the mountains away from settlements, the Mare a Mare Centre passes through some of the prettiest villages on the island. The route is generally less taxing than the GR20, as well as less crowded. It offers considerable comfort with *gîtes* (with restaurants) and **hotels** every night.

Mare a Mare Nord

From Moriani on the east coast to Cargèse in the west, this path passes through vastly contrasting areas and is split into 10 days, each lasting from four to six hours and reaching altitudes of up to 1600m. For the final section of the walk, between Evisa and Cargèse, the route merges with that of the Mare e Monti Nord.

It is better to avoid the period between November and April, when parts of the route may still be under snow.

Mare a Mare Sud

This route is passable year-round. It is a famous, easy walk that links Porto Vecchio in the south-east to Propriano in the south-west. The walk is divided into five days, each of which lasts an average of five hours, and reaches a maximum altitude of 1171m. A stone's throw from the Aiguilles de Bavella and Monte Incudine, it crosses through the magnificent region of Alta Rocca and many of the most beautiful villages on the island. An alternative route goes via Zonza (allow one extra day).

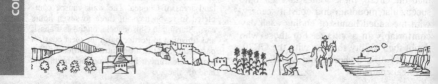

Provence

Provence occupies the south-eastern corner of mainland France. It is the country's most varied area. Cosmopolitan coastal centres like Marseille contrast with inland areas where tiny villages are linked by deserted mountain roads. Many of the region's towns date from at least Roman times and offer a wonderful array of cultural treasures, from Roman theatres and medieval fortifications to outstanding art museums.

For walkers, rural Provence is a delight of colour, light and scent. The same light which fired the palette of the Impressionists enhances the greenness of the Luberon's gentle hills, the turquoise and cobalt blue of the Mediterranean and the dusty beige of the dry, sun-drenched plains and plateaus.

The typical vegetation is *garrigue*, a pot-pourri of kermes oak and holm oak, gorse, thistle, cistus, broom – and headily scented rosemary, lavender and thyme.

Once the walking's over, consider lingering for a few more days to explore Provence's rich Roman legacy; the watery Camargue, one of Europe's most fruitful areas for bird watching; or the brassy Côte d'Azur, its bloom nowadays a little faded.

For other walks in the Alpine regions of Provence, see the Southern Alps chapter.

CLIMATE

Over 2500 hours of sunshine, an average of some seven hours a day, bathe Provence each year. Most of the region enjoys hot, dry summers, with midday maximums up in the high 30s, compensated for by mild winters. Rainfall is low and, while intense showers in spring and autumn can drench, they're usually brief. It's three-season walking, avoiding the torrid months of July and August, when many trails are closed by law because of the risk of fire. If you are walking at the height of summer, watch out for late afternoon thunderstorms which, although usually brief, can be violent.

The infamous mistral is a biting north-westerly wind that howls southwards down

HIGHLIGHTS

NEIL IRVINE

Looking over the Gorges du Verdon from the Balcons de la Mescla

- Unwinding over a seafood dinner in a Cassis quayside restaurant after walking Les Calanques
- Every single centimetre of the Gorges du Verdon
- Savouring the Alps-to-Auvergne panorama from the summit of Mourre-Nègre
- The scent of wild thyme and rosemary

the Rhône Valley and can reach over 100km/h – 'A wind strong enough to pull the tail off a donkey' is the way Provençals describe it. A dry wind which chills and chaps the skin, it blows in spring and winter, although summer gusts are not unknown. Notice how many of the older houses and windbreak trees in the Rhône Valley are positioned to counter its effect. But let's think positive: when the mistral rampages, skies are cloudless and blue.

Provence

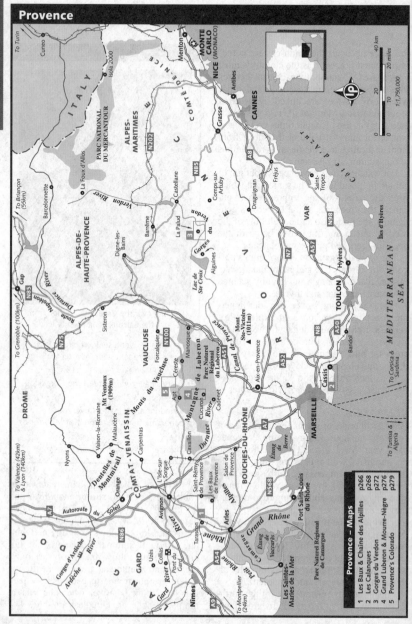

Provence – Maps

WARNING

Many walking trails in the dry south are closed between 1 July and 15 September because of fire risk. These dates may be extended if the danger is deemed to be high. Inquire at the nearest tourist office, and remember the fines for transgressors can be savage.

INFORMATION
Maps
The IGN 1:250,000 *Provence et Côte d'Azur* sheet No 115 and Michelin's 1:200,000 sheet No 245 of the same title are both good overview maps. For maps covering individual walks, see Planning in the introduction to each walk.

Books
Lonely Planet's *Provence & the Côte d'Azur* is rich in detailed, practical information and local background; it's compact enough to slip into a pocket and includes a guide to Provençal wine. The enormously successful *A Year in Provence* and its sequels, written by Peter Mayle, local resident and very Brit, offer a fairly arch vision of the Luberon area.

Les Baux & Chaîne des Alpilles

Duration	5¼ to 6 hours
Distance	27.25km
Standard	medium
Start	Saint-Gabriel
Finish	Saint-Rémy de Provence
Nearest Town	Tarascon
Public Transport	yes

Summary Along the GR6 to the spine of Chaîne des Alpilles. Level walking to the limestone jumble of Les Baux. Down the Gaudre du Rougadou valley and past the remains of Roman Glanum to Saint-Rémy.

Les Baux de Provence (usually called simply Les Baux) swarms with day visitors. But on the route, you'll be almost alone to savour the splendid ridge-top views.

PLANNING
The route is closed between 1 July and 15 September, when it's disagreeably hot and fire danger is high (see the warning).

Maps
Pick up IGN 1:25,000 *Châteaurenard, Saint-Rémy de Provence* sheet No 3042OT at Librairie Mireille, on rue des Halles in Tarascon. Note, however, that the current GR6 route diverges significantly from the map's tracing as it leaves Les Baux.

NEAREST TOWN
Tarascon
Tarascon, built along the murky grey waters of the Rhône river on the border with Languedoc, is dominated by the gaunt mass of the Château du Roi René, built during the 15th century to defend Provence's political frontier. Across the river is Beaucaire, with its own mighty chateau. The tourist office (☎ 04 90 91 03 52, ✉ tourisme@tarascon.org) is at 59 rue des Halles.

Places to Stay & Eat The rather scruffy *Camping Tarascon* (☎ 04 90 91 01 46), just north of the castle, is open from April to October and charges 20/18FF per person/tent. *Camping Saint-Gabriel* (☎ 04 90 91 19 83), at the start of the walk and in the village of Saint-Gabriel, is a more pleasant option. Open May to September, it charges 20/19FF per person/tent and has a swimming pool.

B&B at the *auberge de jeunesse* (☎ 04 90 91 04 08, fax 04 90 91 54 17, 31 blvd Gambetta) costs 67FF.

Rooms at *Hôtel Le Provençal* (☎ 04 90 91 11 41, fax 04 90 91 19 29, 12 cours Aristide Briand) are between 140FF and 220FF.

If you draw a blank in Tarascon, walk over the bridge to Beaucaire on the Rhône's west bank. Its tourist office (☎ 04 66 59 26 57), at 24 cours Gambetta, can provide accommodation information.

Getting There & Away Around 10 trains daily link Tarascon and both Avignon and Marseille (☎ 04 90 91 59 06). From Avignon, there are good rail connections northwards to Lyon and Paris (358FF to 418FF).

PROVENCE

France's Garden

Provence is sometimes called 'the garden of France' because of its superb spices, fruits and vegetables. Regional dishes are prepared with *huile d'olive* (olive oil) and *ail* (garlic), and you can safely assume that any culinary delight *à la provençale* will be prepared with generous quantities of herbs and garlic-seasoned tomatoes.

Provence's most famous soup, *bouillabaisse*, is made with at least three kinds of fresh fish or seafood cooked in broth with onions, tomatoes and saffron, and seasoned with the heady flavours of laurel (bay leaves), sage and thyme.

The region is also famous for its *truffes* (truffles). Known as 'black diamonds', these delectable fungi are so sought after that their trade is controlled by brokers, an exceptional truffle fetching up to 3000FF.

GETTING TO/FROM THE WALK
To the Start
During the school year only, buses (not Sunday) run from Tarascon to Saint-Gabriel at 7.10 and 8.20 am and 1.20 pm. You need to buy a ticket in advance at Librairie Mireille, on rue des Halles. A taxi between Tarascon and Saint-Gabriel costs about 30FF. Ring Taxi Tarasconnais (☎ 06 11 55 90 00, ☎ 04 90 91 15 93).

From the Finish
From Saint-Rémy de Provence, a bus departs for Tarascon from Bar du Marché at 5.45 pm on weekdays (plus Saturday during the school year). Buses (not Sunday) leave for Avignon at 4.25 pm (plus 6 pm during July and August). For confirmation of timetables, ring Rapides du Sud-Est (☎ 04 90 14 59 00).

THE WALK
From the Camping Saint-Gabriel entrance, turn right along the D32 then left along a

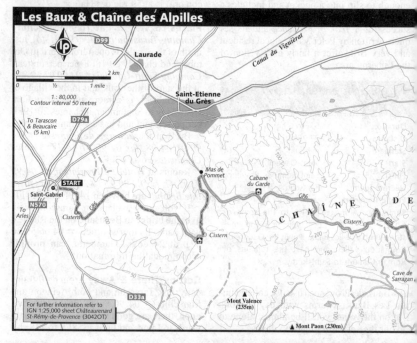

Les Baux & Chaîne des Alpilles

1 : 80,000
Contour interval 50 metres

For further information refer to IGN 1:25,000 sheet *Châteaurenard St-Rémy-de-Provence* (3042OT)

footpath to pass beside a chapel. Turn left at a GR6 sign for Les Baux. After about 30 minutes, a brief detour to the left brings you to a flat rock and sweeping views northwards.

About 40 minutes later, fork north-east at a cabin with a red tiled roof. Soon after, turn left (north) beside a cistern. Around the 90-minute mark, turn right along a lane serving Mas de Pommet. Follow the valley bottom beside rich pasture where bulls graze, noting a lamentably small sign reading 'Danger: Taureaux Sauvages' (Danger: Bulls at Large).

The track passes above Cabane du Garde. Once beyond a five-way junction where the route turns sharply southwards, the scarcely arduous uphill work of the day is all but over as you stride the spine of the Chaîne des Alpilles. As you emerge from a thicket of pines, before you on the south-eastern horizon are the jagged peaks of Les Baux.

After curling round a small hillock, turn briefly north. At a junction 300m later, the path veers abruptly south-east – the dominant

Bauxite

Les Baux has given its name to bauxite, the clay-like white, brown – even red – ore from which aluminium is extracted.

It was first identified in 1821 at a site about 1.5km from what was then a sleepy pastoral village, but it was decades before its commercial potential was realised. Mining, ripping away swathes of the hillside, began at the end of the 19th century and the last digger fell silent as recently as 1990.

direction to Les Baux. Very soon (roughly 50m) after meeting a sealed road, leave the GR6 as it swings east. Continue instead along the road as far as Les Baux, passing a series of caves cut deep into the rock. Just off the route is the Cave de Sarragan cellar with, implausibly, a wine-tasting booth at its deepest limit, where a glass of chilled white wine works wonders.

Les Baux, reached after about 3½ hours' walking, is pandemonium. Visitors, disgorged from coaches and cars, throng its narrow streets. But the detour (for which both time and distance have been factored into the walk statistics) is still worthwhile for the plunging views of the limestone anarchy of Val d'Enfer (Hell's Valley) and perhaps lunch or a drink, albeit at premium tourist prices, in one of its several *restaurants* and *cafes*.

Retrace your steps to rejoin the GR6 and ascend to an orientation table with a magnificent panorama. Navigation is easy beyond a chain barrier as the trail heads towards and skirts beneath a fire watchtower.

An hour beyond the orientation table, look out for a secondary track on the left which descends to join the Gaudre du Rougadou valley. Barely 150m beyond the forbidding walls of Mas de Gros, turn right down a footpath which drops to Barrage des Peiroou. Follow the path hugging the lake's eastern shore then turn right to climb – really climb, using all four limbs in places – up the limestone crags. At the steepest point, steps have been hacked into the rock, plus metal rungs and a cable handhold. It isn't nearly as daunt-

ing as it sounds and the final brief clamber through a natural tunnel in the rock makes a dramatic conclusion to the last of the day's off-road walking.

Soon after turning left along the D5, the extensive remains of the Roman settlement of **Glanum** merit a short detour.

Continue along the D5 for a farther 1.75km to Saint-Rémy de Provence. If you plan to stay overnight here, the tourist office (☎ 04 90 92 05 22), on the way into town on place Jean Jaurès, can supply details of accommodation, including camping grounds.

Les Calanques

Duration	5½–6½ hours
Distance	15.25km
Standard	hard
Start	Cassis
Finish	Morgiou
Public Transport	start only

Summary A classic walk, challenging and unrivalled for its seascapes, with a measure of scrambling from Cassis to the tiny harbour of Morgiou, ascending and descending the intervening *calanques*.

In Provençal, a calanque is a steep-sided rocky inlet. This coastal walk is in three tones – green pine, bright white limestone and, beneath all, the cobalt-blue, sometimes turquoise Mediterranean. We grade the walk as hard because of the very steep descent to Calanque d'En Vau and one or two other briefer but equally demanding stretches.

PLANNING

Unlike most wooded areas of southern Provence, the calanques trail remains open during the summer months of maximum fire risk. A year-round walk, it's at its best during spring and autumn. Pack plenty of water since there's none en route.

Maps

The route is well blazed and, once beyond the first bay, the only way is forward or back so a map is far from essential. The IGN 1:15,000 *Les Calanques* sheet (a hefty 62FF) shows every coastal dimple. The route falls within Didier Richard's 1:50,000 *Collines Provençales* map.

You can pick up both at Astrée, on ave Victor Hugo, or Librairie Preambule, 8 rue Pierre Eydin, in Cassis.

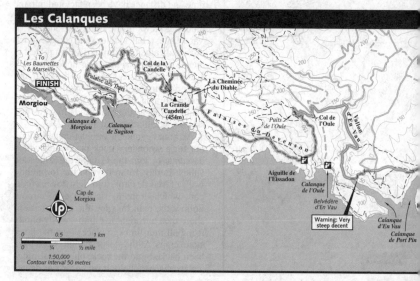

Les Calanques

NEAREST TOWN
Cassis

Cassis, a picturesque fishing port, complete with a 14th-century chateau and France's highest cliff, is noted for its white wine – and as the starting point for boat trips to view the calanques. Unfortunately, it tends to get overrun by tourists in summer. The tourist office (☎ 04 42 01 71 17, @ omt-cassis@en-provence.com) is on place Baragnon.

Places to Stay & Eat The *Camping Cigales* (☎ 04 42 01 07 34), 1km from the port and just off route de Marseille, charges 30FF for a tent and the same per person. The *auberge de jeunesse* (☎ 04 42 01 02 72) is 3.5km west of town, within easy reach of the walk. One-star hotel options include *Hôtel du Commerce* (☎ 04 42 01 09 10, fax 04 42 01 14 17), just north of the port at 1 rue Saint Clair, with doubles between 180FF and 320FF, and *Hôtel de France Maguy* (☎ 04 42 01 72 21), ave du Révestel, where doubles start at 230FF.

Cassis' quayside restaurants serve fine fish and seafood. *Midday Express*, on rue Alexandre Gervais, does reasonable snacks and take-aways.

For further information refer to IGN 1:15,000 sheet *Les Calanques*

Getting There & Away Regular trains link Marseille's Saint-Claude train station and Cassis, whose train station is 3km east of town on the D1.

Buses (to confirm schedules, ring ☎ 04 42 08 41 05) leave for Cassis from Marseille's Gare du Prado bus station. Weekend services depart from Marseille at 9.15 and 11 am plus 4.30 pm. On weekdays, they run at 12.20, 5.20 and 6.45 pm. Convenient return buses leave Cassis at 8.50 am and 2.15 pm (weekdays) and 10 am (weekends).

GETTING TO/FROM THE WALK

The walk begins in Cassis. At the end of the walk, between 15 June and late August, when cars cannot descend beyond the small parking area 2.5km above Morgiou, it's a 3km walk from Morgiou to Les Baumettes. From there buses leave every 25 minutes for Marseille's Gare du Prado bus station, where you can pick up the 6.45 pm run to Cassis.

Another option is to take the 10 am boat (90FF) from Cassis to Morgiou and do the walk in reverse. Tell the crew in advance that you want to land at Morgiou.

THE WALK

In Cassis, at the port's northern limit, turn right up ave de l'Amiral Ganteaume, which swings left, signed 'Les Calanques'. After Plage du Bestouan, turn right up the steep traverse du Soleil, which joins ave du Père Jayne. You soon pick up the GR98 waymarkers, which accompany you all the way to Morgiou.

PROVENCE

The sealed road ends at **Calanque de Port-Miou**. Deepest of the inlets, its quarries were exploited until 1981 and prized Cassis limestone was used on projects as distant as the Suez Canal.

Turn left at a sign, 'Port de Morgiou', and hug the path nearest to the cliff edge to cross the neck of land separating Calanque de Port-Miou from Calanque de Port-Pin.

A steep climb is followed by a dizzying, four-limbed descent to **Calanque d'En Vau**, reached after about 1½ hours of walking. With its jagged limestone pinnacles and near-vertical cliffs, it's a mecca for climbers. Its sandy beach and emerald water are an equally strong pull for day visitors who disembark in droves from pleasure boats.

Head north up Vallon d'En Vau along perhaps the only flat track of the day. About 30 minutes from the bay, turn west towards Col de l'Oule, distinguished by a cistern and battered Club Alpin Français (CAF) sign. Here, ignore the seductive path leading straight ahead to the Belvédère d'En Vau viewpoint. Instead, turn back on yourself to descend to the dried-out well at Puits de l'Oule, where the route runs southwards down a tight, winding valley.

Before reaching the calanque, veer right to climb the valley's steep western flank. The reward for some 10 minutes of lung-searing ascent is the first of many plunging views of the Mediterranean and the Aiguille de l'Eissadon, through whose twin holes the sky winks. Shortly after, the boot-shaped Cap de Morgiou and the offshore islands – Île de Riou with its smaller sisters, Plane and Jarre – reveal themselves in the distance.

After 15 tough minutes of half-walking, half-scrambling beyond the first viewpoint, the payoff begins as you stride the flat cliff top of **Falaises du Devenson**, with magnificent seascapes and views backwards to the Baie de Cassis and the pinkish sandstone Cap Canaille.

Descend northwards to curl round the great bowl of La Cheminée du Diable (the Devil's Chimney). Tack briefly north-west at a rusting pole marking Col de la Candelle. Around 20 minutes later, painted arrows on a rock indicate *éboulis* (scree) to the right

and *rocher* (rock) to the left. Provided that your boots have a sound tread, the scree alternative is easier.

A four-limbed clamber down a steep chimney is followed by easy walking at the base of Falaise des Toits, where the only potential danger is from an unhitched climber falling on your head.

At the west side of Calanque de Sugiton, climb an iron ladder set into the steepest part of the very last of the day's promontories to enjoy a final, gentle descent to the tiny port of Morgiou. Here you can enjoy a well-deserved drink or snack at **Restaurant Le Nautic**.

Gorges du Verdon

Duration	2 days
Distance	26.75km
Standard	medium-hard
Start	La Palud-sur-Verdon
Finish	Point Sublime
Nearest Towns	Castellane and La Palud-sur-Verdon
Public Transport	yes (very limited)

Summary A steep ascent over open hillside. A wooded descent to Belvédère de Maireste viewpoint. The vertiginous sentier du Bastidon. The classic sentier Martel ravine walk/scramble, off road all day, to Point Sublime.

Many walkers only undertake the classic sentier Martel (see Day 2) following the bed of Europe's largest canyon, the Gorges du Verdon, first explored as recently as 1905. At the height of summer, walkers are almost as dense as ants on the march. Day 1, by contrast, affords some fine plunging views, and the sentier du Bastidon, much less trodden, is in places just as breathtaking.

Strangely for such a wonder, the Gorges du Verdon were only given statutory protection as recently as 1997 when the Parc Naturel Régional du Verdon was inaugurated.

PLANNING
When to Walk

Any time is possible. The canyon's steep walls and its cladding of woolly oak, maple, boxwood and ash give shade in summer, although the early part of Day 1 can make the sweat trickle. Many camping grounds and hotels are open only between April/May and September/October.

What to Bring

Take enough water for each day. Unless you drop purifying tablets into Verdon River water, there's no natural supply. Pack a torch (flashlight) to negotiate the two dark, damp tunnels on Day 2.

Maps

The trail is so well blazed that a map is far from essential. Indeed, once down in the canyon, there's only one way out apart from retracing your steps. The route is covered by IGN 1:25,000 sheet No 3442OT and Didier Richard 1:50,000 *Haute Provence, Verdon* sheet No 19. Produced locally in several different languages, including English, *Canyon du Verdon – The Most Beautiful Hikes* (35FF) describes 28 walks in the region.

NEAREST TOWNS
Castellane

Castellane is an unmomentous place, which owes its limited fame to its position as a gateway to the gorges. The tourist office (☎ 04 92 83 61 14) is on rue Nationale.

Places to Stay & Eat Take your pick from the *camping grounds* – around 15 of them – which line the nearby river. A bunk at *L'Oustaou* (☎ 04 92 83 77 27), chemin des Listes, costs 60FF. *Grand Hôtel du Levant* (☎ 04 92 83 60 05, fax 04 92 83 72 14), on place Marcel Sauvaire, has singles/doubles with bathroom for 150/180FF. *La Main à la Pâte* does pizzas and other Italian dishes

Getting There & Away From 1 July to mid-September, Autocars Sumian (☎ 04 42 54 72 82) runs between Castellane and Marseille on Monday, Wednesday and Saturday, leaving Bar L'Étape in Castellane at 12.15 pm, calling by Point Sublime and La Palud-sur-Verdon and continuing to Marseille via Aix-en-Provence. Return departure times are Marseille (8.30 am),

Aix-en-Provence (9 am), La Palud-sur-Verdon (11.20 am), Point Sublime (11.30 am) and Castellane (noon). Outside this period, there's only a Saturday service.

From Switzerland, a daily bus leaves Geneva's train station (7 am), calling by Grenoble (9.45 am) and Castellane (2.40 pm), then continuing to Nice. The return service leaves Nice's train station at 7.30 am, passing by Castellane at 9.35 am.

La Palud-sur-Verdon

Tiny La Palud-sur-Verdon (La Palud), dead as a doornail out of season, is a popular centre for walkers from late spring to autumn. The tourist office (☎/fax 04 92 77 32 02), open from April to September, is in Château de Demandocx.

Places to Stay & Eat Campers have two options: the *camping municipal* and *Camping Bourbon*; both are on the D952, just east and west of town, respectively. The *auberge de jeunesse* (☎/fax 04 92 77 38 72), 500m south-west on the La Maline road, has B&B for 66FF; it's also possible to camp.

The *Hôtel Restaurant Auberge des Crêtes* (☎ 04 92 77 38 47, fax 04 92 77 30 40), 1km from the village, has doubles for 275FF (half board also 275FF).

For a filling snack, *Lou Cafetie* does sandwiches (20FF to 30FF), pizzas (25FF to 38FF) and other dishes, to eat in or take away.

Getting There & Away For the very limited public transport options, see Castellane under Nearest Towns earlier.

Additionally, in July and August Girieud Voyages (☎ 04 92 83 40 27) runs two convenient buses (daily except Sunday) between Castellane (departures at 7.45 am and 4 pm) and La Maline, calling by both Point Sublime (8.15 am and 4.30 pm) and La Palud (15 minutes later). Return buses for Castellane leave La Maline at 9.30 am and 5.15 pm.

GETTING TO/FROM THE WALK

The walk starts in La Palud-sur-Verdon. For information on the bus from Point Sublime at the end of the walk, see Getting There & Away for La Palud-sur-Verdon.

Gorges du Verdon

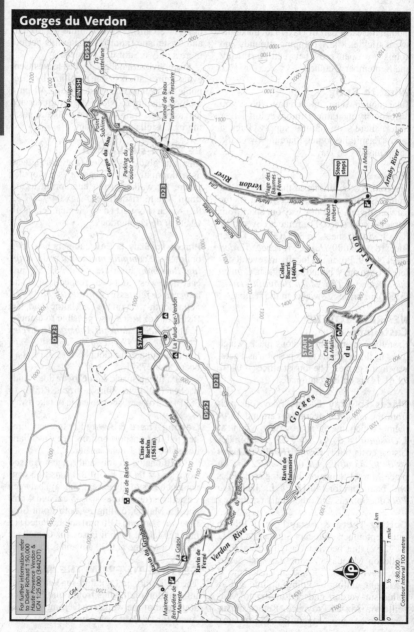

For further information refer
to Didier Richard 1:50,000
Haute Provence Verdon &
IGN 1:25,000 (3442OT)

1:80,000
Contour Interval 100 metres

0   2 km
0   ½   1 mile

FINISH
Rougon
To Castellane
D952
Point Sublime
Gorges du Bau
Parking du Couloir Samson
Tunnel de Baou
Tunnel de Trescaïre
D23
Verdon River
Martel
Sentier
Plage des Baumes Féres
Brèche Imbert
Steep steps
La Mescla
Arrubly River
Route de Crêtes
Collet Barris (1460m)
START
La Palud-sur-Verdon
D23
D952
START DAY 2
Chalet La Maline
Gorges
du
Verdon
Cime de Barbin (1561m)
Jas de Barbin
Sentier du Bastidon
Ravin de Mainmorte
La Graou
Ravin du Grabau
Ravin de Ferpé
Verdon River
Maireste
Belvédère de Maireste
GR4

You can also call Taxi Adrien (☎ 04 92 77 38 20) from the public phone (phonecards only) at Point Sublime. Day/night prices between La Palud-sur-Verdon and Point Sublime are 79/113FF, La Maline 72/100FF and Castellane 200/295FF.

THE WALK
Day 1: La Palud-sur-Verdon to Chalet La Maline
5–5½ hours, 16.25km

Head north-west from La Palud up the D123. At the first bend, turn left onto a side road. A couple of bends later, take a footpath leading straight up the hillside to pick up the GR4. Cross a gravel track and go up a steep, wooded valley before rejoining open terrain. As you ascend, views of La Palud at the heart of its fertile plain become increasingly impressive, while the thin line of the D952 with its toy vehicles snakes to the south.

At something over the hour mark, the path curls around a large bare limestone bluff to reach its highest point. Shortly after the gradual descent begins, fork left (west) along a grassy trail, which soon joins a logging track. Fork left then left again at a sign reading 'Moustiers-Sainte-Marie', as the ruins of Jas de Barbin peek through the trees ahead.

A couple of minutes after crossing a gravel logging trail, turn right and almost immediately left onto a footpath, signed 'Maireste', to leave the GR4. This pleasant, grassy path lined with boxwood soon drops vertiginously south-west down the Ravin du Grinhan.

At a hairpin bend of the D952, take the right-hand prong to reach the seething car park for the Belvédère de Maireste viewpoint, a worthwhile 15-minute detour via spiky karst for a fine first view of the Gorges du Verdon. Just east of the car park is the farm of La Graou with a simple *camping ground*.

The sentier du Bastidon leads away initially south-east. Starting as an easy, fairly level cliff-top path, it gives magnificent views of the canyon below. After about 15 minutes, it begins a steep, zigzagging descent to avin de Ferné, the first of several steep valleys cutting in from the north.

Between 1¼ and 1½ hours after leaving the car park at Maireste, the scooped bowl of

Ravin de Mainmorte comes into view with, high on its eastern flank, the winding D23 corniche road. The path switchbacks steeply up to meet the road – where it's possible to cut out, turn left and return to La Palud (2.5km). To continue, go right to reach **La Maline** after about an hour of roadwork.

The friendly CAF *Chalet La Maline* (☎/fax 04 92 77 38 05), also known as Refuge des Malines, is open from Easter to early November. A bunk costs 74FF and half board is 170FF. There's also limited provision for camping (125FF including dinner and breakfast). There's a public telephone and phonecards are sold – useful if you want to call a taxi from Point Sublime. Advance reservation is advisable at any time and essential for campers.

Day 2: La Maline to Point Sublime
4½–5½ hours, 10.5km

Leave by the path which heads initially north-east from the flowing fountain at the *refuge*. Curl around the coomb (deep hollow), dropping gently towards the canyon floor down a banked, well-maintained path. About 15 minutes out, take the first of the day's metal ladders, positioned along the route, together with hawsers and rope, to help you over the most difficult stretches.

The latter stages of the descent are inadequately signed. Pick the best option from the tangle of descending paths, avoiding wherever possible the vertical short cuts which contribute so much to erosion.

Around 45 minutes' walking brings you to river level and Pré d'Issane, a small pebble beach where the milky emerald waters of the Verdon River race by. Take a last glance back at the *refuge*, perched at the top of the crag.

A little over 30 minutes later just about every device possible (a metal stairway, iron railings, cable and rope) help the brief downwards passage over a steep scree field. After about 15 minutes a signed path to the right leads to La Mescla (see the side trip at the end of this walk description).

A brief, steep ascent leads to the narrow defile of **Brèche Imbert**, approximately halfway from the point of view of distance, but considerably more in terms of energy spent. From here, steep flights of steps lead down a tight chimney. If you find the drop unnerving, simply turn around and take them backwards, facing into the rungs.

About 30 minutes beyond the Brèche Imbert the path begin a series of bends, even doubling back briefly southwards to run back up the gorge. Ten minutes later, the briefest of detours leads to **Plage des Baumes Fères**, a minuscule pebble beach which makes an agreeable lunch stop.

Once beyond a small promontory with plunging views both north and south – another potential lunch spot – it's almost level walking through sun-dappled woodland for the next 45 minutes all the way to the first of two tunnels. (Don't be tempted into the gloom of the first tunnel the route passes. With a pair of narrow-gauge tracks leading in, it's blocked after some distance.)

Enter Tunnel de Trescaire (110m) and, after the briefest interlude of sunlight (pause to look at the whirling waters beneath), plunge into Tunnel de Baou, considerably longer (670m) and often flooded in places.

As you emerge, steps lead down to river level. Cross a footbridge over the minor Gorges du Bau and ascend to Parking du Couloir Samson. Turn left and leave at its north-west corner, still following the GR4 flashes. Less than a minute later, turn right beneath an overhang (where a sign indicates footpath No 16) to reach **Point Sublime** about 45 minutes later.

A roadside *buvette* (refreshment kiosk) serves drinks at a price (10FF for a small water, 15FF for something sweet and fizzy). A fountain just beside the hotel entrance gushes cool water for free.

Auberge du Point Sublime (☎ *04 92 83 60 35, fax 04 92 83 74 31)*, open from Easter to early November, has half board with shower for 260FF and full board for 280FF.

Side Trip: La Mescla
45 minutes, 1.5 km return
For a great view of the confluence of the Verdon and Artuby Rivers, take an easy diversion to the lone rock at La Mescla then retrace your steps to the main trail.

The Luberon

The Luberon range is split by the deep bowl of Combe de Lourmarin into the Petit Luberon to the west and Grand Luberon to the east. The Grand Luberon, of softer limestone and culminating in the peak, Mourre-Nègre (1125m), has been eroded into gentle, rounded contours. The Petit Luberon, lower and more brittle, has weathered into crags, ravines and sharp, spiky angles. There's a similar contrast between north- and south-facing slopes. Woolly oak, needing a cooler, more humid climate, clads the former. Holm oak and garrigue populate the more sparsely vegetated south-facing slopes.

Parc Naturel Régional du Luberon, established in 1977, includes 67 towns and villages within its 165,000 hectares – plus one or two villages.

PLANNING
Unlike the more desiccated areas of southern Provence, the Luberon's more temperate climate makes it suitable for walking year-round. Trails remain open even during periods of maximum fire risk.

Maps & Books
The Grand Luberon & Mourre Nègre walk is covered by IGN 1:25,000 *Pertuis, Loumarin* sheet No 3243OT, while IGN's 1:25,000 *Apt* sheet No 3242OT covers Provence's Colorado. Didier Richard's at 1:50,000 covers all the Parc Naturel Régional du Luberon and much more beyond.

A rare and welcome Fédération Française de la Randonnée Pédestre (FFRP) Topo-Guide in English, the excellent *Walks in Provence: Luberon Regional Nature Park* (No PN07), describes 24 walks in and around the Luberon. Its French Topo-Guide, *Tour du Luberon et du Ventoux* (No 905), describes the GR trails which crisscross the two massifs – the main GR9 and its offshoots.

In Apt, Librairie Dumas, opposite the *mairie* (town hall), plus the tourist office and the *maison du parc* (park information office) carry maps and guidebooks (see Apt under Nearest Town for details).

A Small Yet Acute Problem

Seldom can a tiny speck on the page have aroused such – albeit mild – controversy. In defiance of local custom and preference, this part of Provence was usually spelt *Lubéron* (note that acute accent) in maps and texts, more often than not emanating from distant Paris.

As always, we run with the locals – and also in the good company of the IGN, FFRP and Parc Naturel Régional. Welcome to free, unaccented Luberon!

NEAREST TOWN
Apt

The town's tourist office (☎ 04 90 74 03 18, @ tourisme.apt@avignon.pacwan.fr) is at 20 ave Philippe de Girard. The small Parc Naturel Régional exhibition (entrance 10FF) at the maison du parc (☎ 04 90 04 42 00), in place Jean Jaurès, is very visual in its approach and houses a stunning selection of fossils downstairs. The maison closes on Sunday and, between October and March, also on Saturday afternoon.

Places to Stay & Eat Conveniently central, *Camping Municipal Les Cèdres* (☎ 04 90 74 14 61), on ave de Viton, is open from mid-February to mid-October and charges 8/11FF per tent/person.

The nearest *gîte d'étape* (☎ 04 90 04 88 88, fax 04 90 74 14 86), offering hostel-style walkers' accommodation, is M Rousset's at Le Chêne, 4km west on the Avignon road. The *auberge de jeunesse* (☎ 04 90 74 39 34) is in the village of Saignon, 5km south-east of town.

Hôtel Restaurant Pizzeria Le Palais (☎/fax 04 90 04 89 32), on place Gabriel Péri, is open from April to September. A friendly, family place, it has doubles from 180FF to 220FF and triples at 230FF and 260FF. *Menus* (fixed-price meals of two or more courses) in the restaurant below begin at 90FF. Nearby in place de la Bouquerie, the *plat du jour* (daily special) at *Brasserie Le Gregoire* is 45FF and the two-course *menu* 60FF.

Getting There & Away There are five daily buses between Avignon and Apt, plus an additional weekday service during the school year. For information ring Autocars Barlatier (☎ 04 90 74 20 21), Autocars Villardo-Bernard (☎ 04 90 74 36 10) or the bus station in Avignon (☎ 04 90 82 07 35). From Avignon, there are good road and rail connections both northwards to Lyon and Paris and south to Marseille.

For a taxi ring Apt-Taxi (☎ 04 90 74 34 00) or call by the rank in place de la Bouquerie, near the tourist office. Car rental agencies Apta Location (☎ 04 90 74 10 17) and Ada (☎ 04 90 04 67 90) are both on ave Victor Hugo.

Grand Luberon & Mourre-Nègre

Duration	4¾–5½ hours
Distance	21.5km
Standard	medium
Start/Finish	Cucuron
Nearest Town	Apt
Public Transport	no

Summary A steady haul up Vallon de la Fayette to the Grand Luberon ridge and Mourre-Nègre. More open ridge-walking before descending Vallon de Vaunière to Vaugines and continuing to Cucuron.

The walk's only potential difficulty is the long, constantly uphill walk for over two hours to the summit of Mourre-Nègre, the day's highest point. This accomplished, the rest of the day is all flat or downhill.

GETTING TO/FROM THE WALK

If you're prepared to rise early, it's possible to get to Cucuron and back without your own wheels. The morning bus for Marseille leaves Apt at 6.45 am daily, calling by Cadenet at 7.35 am. From there, you can take a taxi to Cucuron for 70FF. Ring Taxi Arcole (☎ 04 90 08 58 58) in Cadenet or Mme Morra (☎ 04 90 77 20 69) in Cucuron and ask them to meet you at the bus stop. When you're dropped off, agree upon a time to be collected for the return journey to Cadenet,

PROVENCE

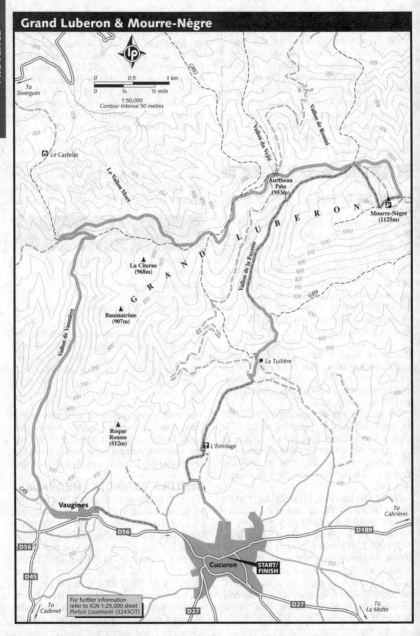

Grand Luberon & Mourre-Nègre

0   0.5   1 km
0   ¼   ½ mile
1:50,000
Contour Interval 50 metres

To Sivergues

Le Castelas

Le Vallon Mort

Vallon de Vaumière

GR282

Vallon du Velié

Vallon de Roumi

Auribeau Pass (953m)

GR9

Mourre-Nègre (1125m)

G R A N D   L U B E R O N

La Citerne (968m)

Baumatrône (907m)

Vallon de la Fayette

La Tuillière

Roque Rousse (512m)

L'Ermitage

GR9

Vaugines

D56

To Cabrières

D56

D45

Cucuron

START/ FINISH

To Cadenet

D27

D27

To La Motte

D189

For further information refer to IGN 1:25,000 sheet Pertuis Lourmarin (3243OT)

from where the evening bus for Apt departs at 6.55 pm. A taxi all the way to or from Apt will set you back a hefty 250FF or more.

THE WALK

From the pool in place de l'Étang in Cucuron, head north up rue de Berard du Roure. After about five minutes, at a point where the road ahead is signed as a cul de sac, fork left onto a gravel track. A few minutes later, the route, blazed in yellow plus red-and-white GR waymarkers, goes briefly left (west), then right to bypass the farm of a famously cantankerous landowner (this waymarked side step doesn't feature on either the recommended IGN map or FFRP Topo-Guide).

The trail then hairpins up to the **chapel of Notre Dame de Beauvoir**, reached after about 30 minutes of walking. From here, a wide, stony track heads northwards up a spur then descends and contours round a fruit orchard.

Where it meets another track, kink left and almost immediately right onto a narrow

linking footpath. This soon merges into a wide, sunken 4WD track which ascends northwards, bypassing the farm of La Tuilière. Continue up the Vallon de la Fayette when the GR9 heads away north-east. As the track climbs, woolly oak gives way to holm oak, fighting its corner with the more temperamental beech above 800m, where the first pines put in an appearance.

About two hours from Cucuron, the path emerges onto the high ridge beside a sign warning of the perils of the *chenille processionaire* (pine processionary caterpillar) – see the boxed text. Turn right onto the unpaved service road for the TV relay station at the summit of **Mourre-Nègre** (1125m). The looming structure, looking like a giant space station, leaves you feeling dwarfed. But if the air's clear, nothing can diminish the panorama as far as the Alps on the eastern horizon and the Massif Central to the west.

Follow a path which drops south-west from the summit. Turn north after 200m onto a track which takes you back to the caterpillar warning board. (Don't be tempted by the broad, seductive track which heads west, following the crest; it soon peters out). Continue westwards along the service road which gives fine vistas of the Vallon de la Fayette, up which you earlier toiled.

At the Auribeau Pass and cistern No 28, a large circular underground water reservoir, there's scope for confusion at a seven-way junction. Go straight ahead (west) on a gently rising track between the GR92, to your right, and the service road which contours along the western flank of Vallon de la Fayette. Follow this track for around 45 minutes as far as cistern No 30. Here the route turns sharply east then south to descend Vallon de Vaunière as far as the hamlet of **Vaugines**, a blessed spot with a *cafe* and several fountains.

Just before Vaugines, you pick up the blazes of the GR9 again. Follow them through the village and eastwards onto a farm track which runs parallel to the D56 as far as the outskirts of Cucuron. Leave the GR9 as it heads northwards, take a side road to the left and follow a spattering of orange blobs back to place de l'Étang.

The Pine Processionary Caterpillar

Between October and March you can see their nests hanging like filigree nets from branches on the sunnier side of pine trees. Inside each, seethe over 200 caterpillars of the *Thaumetopoea pityocampa*, an innocuous-looking greyish yellow butterfly. Huddled together for winter warmth, the caterpillars can survive temperatures down to -15°C as they suck and sap the energy of their host tree.

Come spring, they're on the march. Now as fat as your little finger and 5cm long, they set out in single file: along the branch, down the trunk and into the roots, burying themselves in the ground and entering their chrysalis stage.

The cycle recommences in July when female butterflies fight their way loose to lay their eggs in another tree victim.

Devastating for trees and bristling with highly irritating, mildly poisonous hairs, pine processionary caterpillars can be unpleasant for humans and are best left to march alone.

Provence's Colorado

Duration	5¾–6¼ hours
Distance	20.5km
Standard	medium
Start/Finish	Rustrel
Nearest Town	Apt
Public Transport	no

Summary Through Le Colorado's one-time ochre quarries, round the rim of Les Gourgues and back to Rustrel. Up an ancient packhorse track to Marinier. A steep, zigzagging descent to a broad trail which drops to Rustrel.

The walk is essentially two circles which intersect in the village of Rustrel. The southern one takes you through and around the now-abandoned ochre quarries of Le Colorado. The northern loop, where the vegetation gradually changes from Mediterranean to mountain as you ascend, is mainly through forest. The walk is easily divided into two halves and can be spread over a couple of days.

At the time of writing, negotiations over access to an alternative route to Marinier along an ancient track round the southern side of La Grande Montagne were in progress. This potential alternative is indicated with a broken line on the walk map and may have now opened (inquire at the tourist office in Apt).

GETTING TO/FROM THE WALK

A taxi between Apt and Rustrel costs 90FF (see Getting There & Away under Apt for details). If you're game for some supplementary exercise, you could hire a bicycle for the easy 13km round trip. Cycles Agnel (☎ 04 90 74 17 16), 86 quai Général Leclerc, and Cycles Ricaud (☎ 04 90 74 16 43), 44 quai de la Liberté, rent bikes for 80FF per day.

THE WALK

Head eastwards from a notice board, just opposite the village war memorial, illustrating walking routes around Rustrel. Where the red-and-white flashes of the GR6 lead right down blvd de Colorado, continue straight along the D30A to pass over a crossroads and through an extensive car park. Resist the blandishments of its insistent owner, who will attempt to sell you a map of the ochre extraction area that you don't need at a price you'd never dream of paying. At its extremity, turn south-east to descend towards an easily forded stream, the Doa. After passing through lavender fields the route curls around a bowl of contorted yellow whorls and pinnacles, the first ochre outcrop of the day.

Stay on this compacted 4WD track, following yellow flashes once the GR6 bears away to the left. As you ascend, there are increasingly fine views of Rustrel and the yellow gash of the ochre combe now far below.

Turn left at a junction with a sealed road then right at the next intersection, following a sign reading 'Viens' and 'Caseneuve'. At a left-hand bend, take a cart track to the right and follow the edge of the plateau with more great vistas both to the north and to Grand Luberon topped by its TV relay station in the south-west.

After a brief descent, turn right at a T-junction along a sandy path which runs beside a long, narrow cultivated field and curls round the rim of the ravine of Les Gourgues.

Ochre

Ochre, essentially a blend of sand and clay modified by iron oxides, was mined until quite recently in the low hills to the north of the Luberon.

About 100 million years ago, not far from today's village of Rustrel, a thick layer of green sand was deposited, grain by grain, upon a bed of grey marl. The harsh atmosphere and raging rainstorms high in acid content turned the sands white, yellow and red, metamorphosing the mixture into ochre. Millennia later, these primal colours inspired the name 'Provence's Colorado'.

On the first part of the walk, look out for the former sediment settling beds just before recrossing the Doa. Shortly after, between Istrane and Bouvène, you can see an old ochre processing plant.

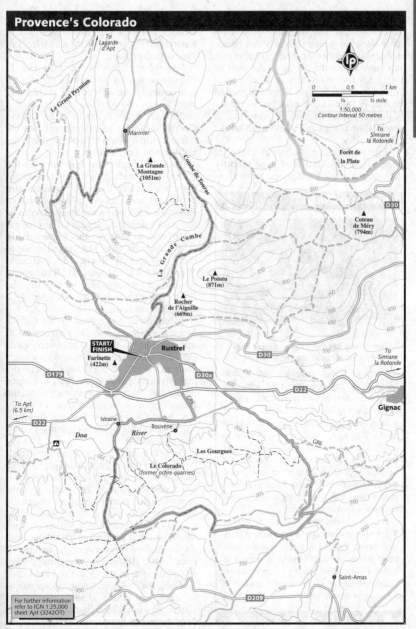

Provence's Colorado

To
Lagarde
d'Apt

Le Grand Peymian

1050

Marinier

To
Simiane
la Rotonde

Forêt de
la Plate

1000

La Grande
Montagne
(1051m)

Combe de Touras

1050

900

800

D30

1000

Coteau
de Méry
(794m)

La Grande Combe

900

850

Le Pointu
(871m)

800

Rocher
de l'Aiguille
(669m)

750

700

650

600

START/
FINISH

Rustrel

D30

To
Simiane
la Rotonde

Farinette
(422m)

D30a

550

500

D179

400

D22

450

GR6

D22

To Apt
(6.5 km)

Istrane

Doa   River   Bouvène

Gignac

Les Gourgues

Le Colorado
(former ochre quarries)

GR6

350

400

500

450

550

500

550

Saint-Amas

D209

0   0.5   1 km
0   ¾   ½ mile
1:50,000
Contour Interval 50 metres

For further information
refer to IGN 1:25,000
sheet Apt (3242OT)

Turn right at a sign for Istrane to descend through juniper and maritime pine, both hardy varieties which thrive in this inhospitable soil. Another sheer ochre cliff comes into view across the cirque to the west as pine gradually gives way to woolly oak. Cross a bed of rich burnt ochre and recross the muddy Doa. Take the sealed road as far as the hamlet of Istrane, no more than a couple of dwellings and an old wash house, long since dry.

At the sign reading 'Bouvène', turn right along a sparsely trafficked road. Shortly after the side track for Bouvène leads away

Provençal Bories

Two-storey beehive shaped bories constructed without mortar, near Apt

It's estimated that there are about 3000 *bories* in the Luberon. Dry stone huts, they come in a variety of sizes and shapes – round, square, rectangular, even ovoid.

Evidence suggests they may go back as far as the Iron Age, when they were used as dwellings. Permanent? Refuge in times of strife? Seasonal? Historians still quibble over their function. Many are of much more recent provenance and even today function as temporary sheepfolds, tool sheds or repositories for general junk.

In their construction, natural or shaped flakes of limestone called *lauzes* were skilfully interleaved without a single wooden roof beam and not a trace of mortar or cement to create a natural, roofed, dry stone structure.

Great shelter if you're caught unawares in a Provençal downpour.

south beside a pipe gushing fresh water, turn left to follow the GR6 blazes back to **Rustrel** and the notice board which marked your departure point.

Just west of this board, take rue de l'Église northwards to pass the tiny church and cemetery. Scramble up a short bank, cross a road and continue straight along a sealed lane into the mouth of **La Grande Combe**. Behind a forbidding fence on the left is a military bunker, sunk deep into the hillside, and a helipad.

At a fork, take the left-hand option which soon leads into an ancient packhorse track which linked the communities of Rustrel and Lagarde d'Apt. Note the fine stone banking on the steeper bends as the track climbs the western flank of the steep valley, densely and impenetrably clad with holm oak. The jagged spike to the north-east is Rocher de l'Aiguille (Needle Rock). The rounded hilltop above it – called paradoxically Le Pointu (The Pointed One) – was once occupied by a Gallo-Roman fort.

Turn right at a sign reading 'La Grande Montagne'. Beside a similar sign around 30 minutes later, the potential alternative route (see the introduction to this walk) bears away to the left. To continue, stay with the main track as it ascends the flank of Combe de Touras, levelling out as the woodland becomes sparser. Beyond a copse of woolly oak, head for a power line and follow it south-westwards to reach the ruined buildings of **Marinier**.

Go left (south) along a bitumen road. After 300m turn right at a couple of plain metal posts onto an indistinct track and follow it westwards across flat, relatively open ground. Soon after passing an enigmatic hump across the path, the trail widens into a well-defined cart track which plunges south-west and once more into woodland. At the first of several zigzags, an area of open forest, cleared for parapenting, gives splendid views of the Grand and Petit s.

Where the trail joins a wider, perpendicular track, just beside a large underground cistern, turn left for the final uncomplicated 2km descent to Rustrel.

Other Walks

Cap Canaille

This 21km, four- to five-hour circular walk circumnavigates the spectacular pink sandstone promontory of Cap Canaille. A coloured pamphlet *Balade au Cap Canaille*, available from Cassis' tourist office, has a good map of the cliff walk from Cassis to La Ciotat. The route is highlighted in full on Didier Richard's 1:50,000 *Collines Provençales* sheet.

Leave Cassis following signs for Route des Crêtes and take a footpath, waymarked in yellow, at Pas de la Colle. If you only want to do the more spectacular outward cliff-top leg, a daily bus leaves La Ciotat for Cassis at 4.35 pm in summer (at weekends year-round). During the school year, there's also a weekday service at 6.15 pm.

The Carmargue

A 22km out-and-back walk, including a 7.5km walkway along the *digue de la mer* (sea dyke), takes you from Les Saintes-Maries de la Mer to the Gacholles lighthouse. En route there are magnificent views of the Réserve Naturelle de l'Étang de l'Impérial and its rich birdlife.

For details, consult the small tourist office in Saintes-Maries (☎ 04 90 97 82 55), 5 ave Van Gogh. For information about other walking trails in the Camargue, visit the larger of the two tourist offices in Arles (☎ 04 90 18 41 20), just off blvd des Lices.

Mont Ventoux

You probably won't be alone on top of Mont Ventoux (1909m), accessible by car and a popular destination for the tougher kind of cyclist. Satisfaction comes as much from the quieter contemplation of equally splendid views from its 25km ridge as from reaching the peak, which remains snowcapped from December to April. Possible routes feature on Didier Richard's 1:50,000 *Massif du Ventoux* and the IGN 1:25,000 sheet No 3140ET. For further information, contact the tourist office at Malaucène (☎ 04 90 65 22 59), 10km south of Vaison-la-Romaine.

Southern Alps

Extending from the city of Grenoble southwards to within sight of the Mediterranean coast, the Southern Alps essentially comprise two major mountain groups: the Alpes Dauphiné and Alpes Maritime. Within their compass are four key conservation reserves: Parc National des Écrins, Parc National du Mercantour, Parc Naturel Régional du Vercors and Parc Naturel Régional du Queyras. Perhaps less well known – and less frequented – than the Mont Blanc range in the Northern Alps, these parks nevertheless offer just as much variety: alpine meadows and plateaus, high passes, lakes, valleys both broad and narrow, and some summits that don't demand mountaineering skills and equipment. There are also many unspoiled, traditional villages, and some of the wildest country in France in the remote reaches of the Parc National du Mercantour. The network of waymarked routes, including traditional paths and byways, provides an almost inexhaustible array of walks, from day-long outings to extended journeys of several weeks.

The great chain of the Alps was pushed up during very prolonged phases of mountain-building, extending back 100 million years. The present landforms owe much to the erosive impact of ice sheets and glaciers during successive ice ages, the last of which ended around 10,000 years ago. The surviving glaciers and snowfields are still active forces of change in the mountain landscape.

CLIMATE

The climate of the Southern Alps is conditioned by both Atlantic and Continental (or eastern European) weather systems, and in the far south by the Mediterranean. These bring dry, warm summers and wet, mild winters with a wide seasonal range of temperatures. The weather is essentially changeable, although the occasional anticyclone (high pressure systems) ensures extended settled periods.

During summer, interruptions by cloud, rain and thunder are unlikely to be prolonged.

HIGHLIGHTS

The high country of the Parc National des Écrins

- The striking rock massif of Mont Aiguille beside the awe-inspiring limestone walls of the Vercors plateau

- The alpine meadows and lakes of the Écrins; deep, steep-sided valleys, with La Meije and its glaciers high above

- A walk fom Europe's highest commune in the Queyras to a 3000m peak on the Italian border

- Surprisingly easy walks in Mercantour through woodlands to a high pass and secluded lakes

- Wild flowers from spring to autumn, the bird-like whistles of marmots, and chamois grazing peacefully

Even after a fine morning it is common for cloud to descend over high ground around noon, while the valleys remain sunny and very warm. It is virtually guaranteed that a spell of fine weather will bring an afternoon or evening thunderstorm, preceded by a build-up of cumulus (billowing) cloud and rising humidity. However, the spectacular lightning, heavy rain and even hail usually clear to another fine day.

At any time of the year, there are marked differences between temperatures in the valleys and on high ground – with every 100m rise in altitude the temperature drops by about 1°C. During summer, the average daily maximum temperature at 850m is around 24°C, while at 2500m it's 7°C. The wettest months in the valleys are from September to November, whereas June to August is the period of highest rainfall in the mountains (except in the far south).

Local winds can be as influential as winds derived from major pressure systems. In fine, settled weather, winds tend to blow up the valleys during the day and down the valley at night, while winds may come from quite different directions higher up. Overall, colder more settled weather is accompanied by winds from the north and east, and wetter, less settled conditions arrive with westerlies.

Snowfalls can be expected above 1200m from October until May; snow may lie in the higher passes, above 2500m, until late July.

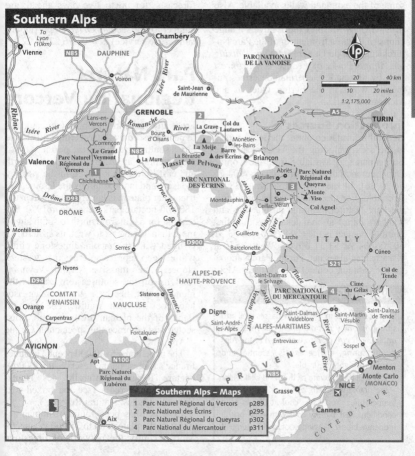

Southern Alps – Maps

1	Parc Naturel Régional du Vercors	p289
2	Parc National des Écrins	p295
3	Parc Naturel Régional du Queyras	p302
4	Parc National du Mercantour	p311

INFORMATION
Maps
IGN 1:100,000 *Valence, Grenoble* and *Nice, Barcelonnette* sheets, Nos 52, 54 and 61 respectively, cover the area and are useful for planning. For maps covering individual walks, see Planning in the introduction to each walk.

Books
Cicerone's *Walking in the Alps* by Kev Reynolds has four chapters wholly or partly devoted to France. Descriptions are brief but serve to give a feel for each area and some of the extended walks available. Also published by Cicerone, *Walking the French Alps: GR5* by Martin Collins covers a large chunk of the area from north of the Parc Naturel Régional du Queyras to Nice. *Walking the Alpine Parks of France & Northwest Italy* by Marcia R Lieberman describes numerous walks in the Écrins, Queyras and Mercantour parks.

Information Sources
General information about the Isère, which is the area including the Vercors and the Écrins parks, is available from the Comité Départemental du Tourisme (CDT; ☎ 04 76 54 34 36), 14 rue de la République, 38019 Grenoble. For the Hautes-Alpes (including the Parc Naturel Régional du Queyras and southern Parc National des Écrins), the first point of contact is the CDT (☎ 04 92 53 31 60, fax 04 92 53 31 60). Its Web site is at www.hautes-alpes.net. For the Parc National du Mercantour, contact the CDT des Alpes

WARNING

Snow can linger in the higher passes well into spring and may not disappear above 2500m until July. If you plan to walk high in the Alps during spring, an ice axe is essential and crampons highly desirable.

It is well to be aware of the wind chill factor – the dramatic cooling effect of wind at low temperatures. You'll feel cool at 0°C in calm conditions, but bitterly cold with even only a moderate breeze. A windproof jacket is a must!

de Haute-Provence (☎ 04 92 31 57 29), 19 rue du Docteur Honnorat, BP 170, 04005 Digne-les-Bains.

Bureau Information Montagne (☎ 04 76 42 45 90) is a specialised mountain advice service on the 1st floor of the tourist office, 14 rue de la République, 38019 Grenoble. It's open from 9 am to noon and 2 to 6 pm Monday to Friday, and 10 am to noon and 2 to 6 pm on Saturday. Here you can obtain advice about the condition of high passes, buy maps and guidebooks and consult a comprehensive library.

France Météo's special mountain weather forecasts, for up to five days ahead, are available by phoning ☎ 08 36 68 04 04. The number for the *secours en montagne* (mountain rescue service) is ☎ 04 76 22 22 22.

Parc Naturel Régional du Vercors

From anywhere in Grenoble you can't fail to be impressed by the towering cliffs to the city's south-west; this is the northern tip of the Vercors plateau. Bounded in the north and east by the Drac River, in the west by the Isère and in the south by the Drôme, this triangular plateau is largely contained in the 180,000-hectare park, set aside in 1970. Extending for 63km from north to south but no more than 40km east to west, its eastern rim is lined with spectacular limestone cliffs, while deep gorges pierce the western slopes. The massive Grand Veymont (2341m) on the south-eastern edge is the highest point; nearby is the amazing, isolated rock of Mont Aiguille. The southern flanks of the plateau are much more dissected and embrace the spectacular Cirque d'Archaine.

The park, home to 30,000 people, includes France's largest nature reserve, the 17,000-hectare Réserve Naturelle des Hauts-Plateaux du Vercors (see the boxed text 'France's Largest Natural Reserve').

Evidence has been found of human activity on the plateau up to 35,000 years ago. More recently the network of limestone caves provided shelter for resistance fighters during WWII, memorials to whom are dotted around the plateau. The traditional practice of taking sheep up to the plateau during summer continues strongly.

The park has an extensive network of waymarked paths (2850km) affording a wide variety of walks, from a full-length plateau traverse to numerous day outings from the several villages and small towns on the plateau and scattered round the foot of its walls.

NATURAL HISTORY

The flora and fauna of the Vercors are best described in three zones, based on elevation, aspect, rainfall and the plateau's location on the dividing line between the Northern and Southern Alps.

In the foothills up to around 900m, the wetter areas have woodlands of downy and sessile oak, Scots pine and ash, sheltering an understorey of box and laburnum. Poplars, willows and alders grow along the streams, and honeysuckle creepers, laurels, knapweeds and helleborines (of the orchid family) bring colour to the woodland floor. The drier south-eastern slopes support oak, beech, fir and Scots pine, with lavender and wild thyme emphasising the Mediterranean character of the area. Throughout the foothills, hedgehogs, moles, shrews, wild rabbits, hares, badgers and wild boars make their homes.

Forests dominate the gently undulating plateau between 900 and 1500m; beech, fir and spruce are the main species, in varying combinations depending on exposure, rainfall and past forestry activities. These woodlands provide shelter for some of the several species of mammals introduced to the Vercors: red deer, roe deer and *mouflons* (wild sheep), together with squirrels and mice. The park's emblem bird, the black capercaillie, is also at home in the forests.

The subalpine areas, above 1700m, merge with the very small extent of alpine habitat above 2200m. Spruce and silver fir survive, although not on the highest ground. Wild flowers are very numerous and colourful in the spacious meadows: yellow wild

Mont Aiguille

This extraordinary, massive block of rock, its walls rising sheer from the surrounding forest for many hundreds of metres, dominates the landscape around Chichilianne. It exercises a magnetic fascination, constantly drawing your gaze as the lighting on the cliffs changes or as the clouds shift to reveal the face, then close in again.

Long ago part of the main Vercors massif, this limestone block was gradually detached by the forces of erosion. The extensively eroded base of the mountain, about 300m east-west and 500m north-south, is built of layers of limestone, on top of which stands the main block of hard, dense rock. Its height is now 2086m, 11m lower than it was about 60 years ago, as the result of periodic rock falls from the sloping summit plateau.

The mountain is closely linked to the origins of rock climbing. In 1492 Charles VIII of France, entranced by what was then known as *Mont inascensibilis* (unclimbable mountain), ordered Antoine de Ville, an army captain, to reach the summit. With eight companions, he obeyed, using ladders and ropes, although it was never revealed where he placed the ladders. More than three centuries passed before a local shepherd made the next ascent, and in 1877 a tourist route was opened. There are now more than 30 climbing routes with fixed aids on the north face, and guided climbs are organised every week from the *maison du parc* (park information centre) in Chichilianne.

tulips, buttercups, narcissus (daffodils), mauve alpine snowbells, white edelweiss (a protected species), orchids (including the *sabot de Venus*, or lady's slipper orchid, France's largest), brilliant deep blue gentians, alpine speedwells, white Saint Bruno's lilies and purple alpine asters. The range of mammals in these areas is relatively small: hares, weasels, foxes and ermines. The chamois has survived, thanks to stringent controls on hunting, while the marmot and ibex have been reintroduced.

SOUTHERN ALPS

The golden eagle (a protected species) is very much at home on the steep cliffs; other denizens of the higher ground include grouse, quails, swifts and peregrine falcons.

GATEWAY
Grenoble

Grenoble, spectacularly overlooked by the northern cliffs of the Vercors, is the natural gateway to the area. It provides services

France's Largest Natural Reserve

Within the regional park is the Réserve Naturelle des Hauts-Plateaux du Vercors, France's largest such reserve, protecting 17,000 hectares of the plateau. It extends southwards from a point a few kilometres from the village of Corrençon to the plateau rim overlooking Châtillon-en-Diois; the rim also forms the eastern and southern boundaries, and includes Mont Aiguille. Altitudes range from 1200m to the Vercors' highest peak, Le Grand Veymont (2356m).

The reserve, set aside in 1985, is of outstanding importance for its ecological diversity, at the crossroads of Mediterranean, Continental and Atlantic climatic influences, and for the ways in which its landscape has evolved as a result of forestry and summer grazing (up to 20,000 sheep each year). No less important are the karstic limestone features – the intricate mosaic of channels in the flat rock beds – and the absence of surface water.

Walkers are more than welcome in the reserve, though several regulations, much the same as those for national parks, must be heeded. Camping is allowed only close to designated waymarked routes: the GR91, the GR93, the sentier Central and the Tour du Mont Aiguille; tents mustn't be pitched until the evening and must be taken down early the next day. Portable radios are not allowed, nor are dogs, even on a lead. Fires are forbidden, as is the collection of minerals, fossils and flowers. A hefty fine can be imposed for breaking any of these regulations.

otherwise lacking in Clelles and Chichilianne, the towns nearest to the walks described in this section (see Nearest Towns).

Information The tourist office (☎ 04 76 42 41 41), 14 rue de la République, is open daily all year. Apart from accommodation information, it sells the particularly useful *Guide Practique de la Montagne* (Practical Mountain Guide), with contact details of just about everyone involved with the mountains in and around Grenoble.

The Bureau des Guides de Grenoble (☎/fax 04 76 03 28 63) is on the 2nd floor of the tourist office and is open from 2 to 6 pm on Thursday. It can offer guide services for walking and mountaineering.

For maps and guides, the best place to go is Glénat Librairie (☎ 04 76 46 34 60), in 19 ave Alsace Lorraine (open from 10 am to 7 pm Monday to Saturday). Of the numerous outdoor equipment shops in Grenoble, the most useful is Clavel Sports (☎ 04 76 87 19 11), 54 cours Jean-Jaurès, open from 9.30 am to noon and 2 to 7 pm Monday to Saturday; on Friday it doesn't close for lunch.

Cybernet Café (☎ 04 76 51 73 18, fax 04 76 03 20 33, ✉ services@neptune.fr), 3 rue Bayard, is open from noon to 1 am Monday to Saturday; the charge is 30/47FF for a 30-minute/one-hour connection. Le New Age Cybercafé (☎ 04 76 51 94 43), 1 rue Frédéric Taulier, is open from 9.30 am to 9 pm and charges the same rates.

Places to Stay & Eat Open all year, *Camping Les Trois Pucelles* (☎ 04 76 96 45 73, 58 rue des Allobroges), in the suburb of Seyssins, charges 30FF for one person and a tent. From the train station, take the tram towards Fontaine and alight at the Maisonnat tram stop, then take bus No 51 to Mas des Îles and walk east along rue du Dauphiné.

The *auberge de jeunesse* (☎ 04 76 09 33 52, fax 04 76 09 38 99, ✉ grenoble-echirolles@fuaj.org, 10 ave du Grésivaudan, Echirolles) is 5km south of the town centre. The tariff is 68FF for B&B and it's open all year. To get there catch bus No 8 from cours Jean-Jaurès (about 200m east of the train station) to the Quinzaine bus stop.

Care in the Vercors

Play safe and carry all the water you'll need for the day right from the start. Being limestone country, there are only a very few possible sources of fresh water on the plateau and they aren't completely reliable.

Watch out for sinkholes and fissures on the plateau – some are deep and narrow and it would be very difficult to extricate someone who has fallen in. It is foolish to attempt any walk on the Vercors plateau in mist or poor weather; check the forecast beforehand if in doubt.

It is essential to carry a compass and the topographical maps for the Rochers du Parquet walk. The landscape is very intricate and distances are deceptive.

For more comfort, **Hôtel Alizé** (☎ 04 76 43 12 91, fax 04 76 47 62 79, 1 rue Amiral Courbet), near the train station, has clean modern doubles with shower and toilet for 202FF, plus 25FF for breakfast.

Close to the hotel is **Chez Pierre** (☎ 04 76 43 47 88, 4 place de la Gare), open daily for reasonably priced pizzas (average 45FF), pasta dishes and grills (75FF to 105FF). For a more pleasant outlook, wander across to Quai Pierre beside the river, where you'll find shoulder-to-shoulder competitively priced *pizzerias*.

For self-caterers, there is a **Petit Casino** (38 cours Jean-Jaurès), between ave Alsace Lorraine and cours Berriat on the western side of the road.

Getting There & Away Lyon-Satolas airport (☎ 04 72 22 72 21, fax 04 72 22 74 71), 45km north of Grenoble, is a destination for flights from London Heathrow, Amsterdam, several cities in Germany, plus Canada, Spain and Italy. From the airport it's just over an hour by train (TGV) or by bus (Satobus; ☎ 04 72 68 72 17) to Grenoble.

There is a TGV service from Paris' Gare de Lyon direct to Grenoble train station, in rue Émile Gueymard. Other SNCF trains connect Grenoble via Lyon with destinations in the north and south of France. The *Guide Régional des Transports* for Rhône-Alpes is a useful guide to services between Grenoble and Gap, along the eastern edge of the Vercors plateau.

Intercars (☎ 04 76 46 19 77, fax 04 76 47 96 34) has an office in the bus station (next to the train station) and handles Eurolines international bus services from such places as Amsterdam, Geneva, London, Milan, Munich, Rome, Turin and Zurich.

PLANNING

The following information is relevant to both the walks in this section.

Snow may still lie above 1400m during May but should not present any difficulties; June is probably the best month for the Vercors, when the wild flowers are most abundant and before the high summer crowds. Prolonged sunny weather is most likely from October to mid-November.

Maps & Books

The IGN's 1:25,000 *Villard-de-Lans* and *Glandasse* sheets, Nos 3236OT and 3237OT, and Didier Richard's 1:50,000 *Vercors* sheet No 12 cover these two walks, the former giving more local detail, the latter identifying more of the surrounding features. The park publishes a 1:40,000 map *Sentiers du Vercors, Vercors Sud* which describes 78 walks in the southern part of the Vercors.

The Fédération Française de la Randonnée Pédestre (FFRP) Topo-Guide *Tour et Traversée en Vercors* (No 903) is invaluable for walks in the area. The IGN's guidebook *Vercors, Diois, Buëch*, although covering a wider area, has more background information. *Le Guide du Vercors* by Maguy Dupont is strong on the cultural and natural history of the area. Didier Richard's *Randonnées en Vercors Nord* and *Randonnées en Vercors Sud* have planimetric maps.

Information

For information about the park, contact the Lans-en-Vercors *maison du parc* (park information centre; ☎ 04 76 95 40 33), chemin des Fusillés, BP14, 38250. Ask for the timetable of summer guided walks.

Regulations

Strict regulations apply in the nature reserve (see the boxed text 'France's Largest Natural Reserve').

NEAREST TOWNS
Clelles & Chichilianne

The nearest town to the village of Chichilianne, the starting point for the walks described in this section, is Clelles on the Grenoble-Gap railway line. The helpful Clelles tourist office (☎ 04 76 34 43 09), place de la Mairie, provides local maps, guides and accommodation information, and posts the current local weather forecast in the front window; otherwise, phone ☎ 08 36 68 02 38 for weather information.

The Maison du Parc et du Mont Aiguille in Chichilianne (☎ 04 76 34 44 95) is open from 10 am to noon Monday to Saturday year-round. It's on the 2nd floor of the *mairie* (town hall), the most prominent building in the village. Here you can pick up books, maps and guides for the park. At the time of research, the only public telephone in Chichilianne was coin-operated.

Places to Stay & Eat The nearest camping grounds are several kilometres from Chichilianne near Saint-Martin de Clelles; try *Camping Municipal la Chabannerie* (☎ 04 76 34 00 38), which is open from May to the end of September.

The *gîte d'étape* (hostel-style walkers' accommodation) in Chichilianne is run by the park and occupies part of the town hall. It's open all year and has modern large and small dorms for 74FF per night; the large and very well-equipped kitchen is in a separate building across the road. They like you to be there before 5 pm, or at other times by prior arrangement.

There is a good hotel in Chichilianne, *Château de Passière* (☎ 04 76 34 45 48), which has doubles in a fine old building from 280FF, and offers an excellent evening meal with *menus* (fixed-price meals of one or more courses) at 120FF and 160FF.

Bar Jere Nico in Chichilianne keeps unpredictable hours, but when it is open you can have pizzas (38FF to 45FF), salads, omelettes or the 70FF *menu*. The same unpredictability governs Chichilianne's one and only *alimentation* (grocery store). Fortunately, there are reliable alternatives in Clelles: a *boulangerie* (bakery) and two *alimentations*, one in place de la Mairie and the other opposite Hôtel Bourgeat.

Getting There & Away Clelles-Mens, on the highly scenic Grenoble-Gap railway line, has a daily service (50FF/87FF one way/return from Grenoble). For more information, phone ☎ 08 36 35 35 39.

A subsidised taxi service operates from Clelles to Chichilianne by arrangement; phone ☎ 04 76 34 42 42 no later than the night before your journey to make arrangements. The tariff is 15FF (normally 81.50FF); the same applies for the return journey.

By road, Clelles is close to the N75, 48km south of Grenoble. Chichilianne is 8km west of the town, via the well-signposted D8 and then minor roads.

GETTING TO/FROM THE WALKS

Both walks described in this section start and finish in Chichilianne; the hamlet of Richardière, about 4km north-west of the village, is an alternative base for the first walk. To reach Richardière follow the signposted minor roads from the centre of Chichilianne.

Platary

Duration	4 hours
Distance	10.5km
Standard	medium
Start/Finish	Chichilianne
Nearest Town	Clelles
Public Transport	yes

Summary An excellent introduction to the Vercors area on a steepish climb to a long grassy ridge with superb panoramic views of the plateau's cliffs and adjacent lowlands.

Platary mountain is within the Parc Naturel Régional du Vercors and is a miniature sample of the topography of the main Vercors plateau. Its long western slope sweeps up to an abrupt eastern escarpment, and the

Provençal poppies in springtime.

Europe's largest canyon, the Gorges du Verdon.

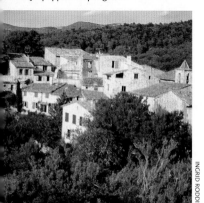

A typical Provençal village.

The Roman settlement of Glanum, Provence.

The high country of Parc National des Écrins, Southern Alps.

The pitted limestone plateau of Vercors is France's largest nature reserve.

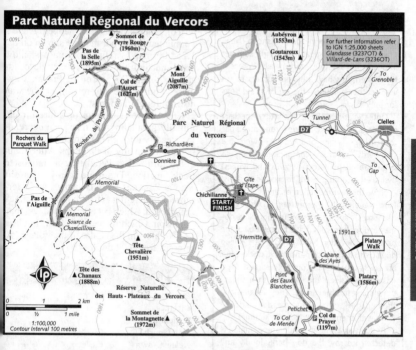

Parc Naturel Régional du Vercors

elongated, narrow crest is pitted with the fissures, ravines and sinkholes characteristic of limestone country.

This walk provides a comparatively easy (by local standards) introduction to the area; the grading reflects the steepness and duration of the ascent (590m vertical). It can be done in half a day but the open grassy summit ridge invites exploration, which can comfortably fill an extra hour or two.

Although the route is described as a circuit from Chichilianne, with a car you could start from Col du Prayer on the D7. From there, blue waymarkers indicate the route up through the forest, more or less clearly enough, past several forestry track junctions.

Maintaining a long tradition, sheep graze the meadows during summer and are protected by specially trained guard dogs. As prominent signs on the approach tracks explain, these large woolly chaperones normally pose no threat to walkers (see the boxed text 'Sheep May Safely Graze').

THE WALK

See the Parc Naturel Régional de Vercors map.

From Chichilianne walk down the road towards Clelles, to the T-junction with the D7, and turn right towards Col de Menée. A few metres along this road turn off to the right, as signposted, towards Le Platary; a little farther on, fork left to cross a stony river bed. Walk up to the road, cross over and start climbing towards Le Platary on a broad, well-graded path, through the beech forest. After about 1¼ hours from Chichilianne, you come to **La Chanas** (Cabane des Ayes on the map) – a couple of buildings used by the local shepherds and collectively known as a *bergerie*. It's a fairly steep climb from here on a stony path to the end of the trees, then up to the open ridge crest (an hour from the bergerie). The views westwards to the cliffs of the Vercors plateau, and of Mont Aiguille, repay the effort generously.

SOUTHERN ALPS

Sheep May Safely Graze

Traditionally, large herds of sheep have grazed high alpine meadows during summer in peace and safety. Unfortunately, in recent times predators have obliged farmers to revive another tradition – the use of guard dogs for their flocks.

Until the end of the 19th century, specially bred dogs knows as *pastous* (pronounced pa-**too**) – large, white and woolly – were the shepherds' invariable companions. Then, as large natural predators (wolves and lynxes) dwindled or disappeared, so did the pastous.

Now, the reintroduction of the wolf to the Parc National du Mercantour (in the Alpes Maritimes), and attacks by uncontrolled domestic dogs generally, have brought back the pastous. They don't replace ordinary sheep dogs (who help muster and move flocks), but are solely protectors. From their earliest days, pastous eat, sleep and live with their sheep, developing mutual trust. They accompany their charges to the alpine meadows and remain with them throughout the summer.

As soon as a stranger (human or animal) is detected nearby, the dog barks loudly and moves between the flock and the intruder. If the intruder persists, the dogs will launch an attack. Should you find yourself in sight of a barking pastou, it is best to stay calm and quiet, and not to brandish your walking pole – you'll probably come off second best. Just steer a wide berth around the flock and continue on your way.

From about point 1573 (as marked on the recommended IGN 1:25,000 map), blue waymarkers identify the best route around clusters of small crags to the airy highest point (1591m) on the ridge. It's worth spending some time wandering along the ridge for different aspects of the views, and perhaps to watch the hang-gliders for which Platary is a popular launching place.

Make your way to the summit (1586m), towards the southern edge of the ridge, and head down over the trackless grassed slope,

south-westwards to the forest edge, the pattern of which is accurately mapped. There's no marked route, but the line shown on the 1:25,000 map is reliable. From a shallow bowl touching the forest, a track descends steeply to the D7 at **Col du Prayer**, waymarked only once you're well on the way down through the forest.

Cross the road and pick up a forest track, initially paralleling the road then descending steadily through the forest. This route is not shown on any of the maps. After about 500m turn left at Petichet at a signposted track junction. The route then joins a dirt road at Pont des Eaux Blanches. At L'Hermitte turn right at a T-junction along a gravel road, which becomes sealed less than 1km from Chichilianne. This leads to place Louis Thiers in the centre of the village (50 minutes from Col du Prayer).

Rochers du Parquet

Duration	8½ hours
Distance	23km
Standard	hard
Start/Finish	Chichilianne
Nearest Town	Clelles
Public Transport	yes

Summary A truly magnificent but challenging walk, with Mont Aiguille ever-present, up to a pass leading to the beautiful meadows, pine groves and limestone crags of the Vercors plateau.

This route is only one of several ways of exploring the Vercors plateau, making use of miraculous passes through the seemingly impenetrable cliffs of the eastern side of the plateau. This is a strenuous (1000m vertical) but immensely rewarding walk, which can be modified to suit different levels of fitness. Richardière is an alternative starting point (not serviced by public transport), reducing the distance by 9km. Col de l'Aupet is a worthy objective in itself, especially if the plateau is mist-bound.

On the plateau the route along Rochers du Parquet (the cliffs of the plateau rim) is virtually trackless, apart from the myriad paths made by wandering sheep. There is a cairned route from a point about 500m north of Pas de l'Aiguille, down into the broad valley at the top of the pass. Alternatively, from Pas de la Selle a less scenic route continues generally eastwards to the Carrière Romaine (Old Roman Rd). Follow that road south to the route of the GR91 and GR93, and on to 'Les Quatre Chemins de Jasneut', from where a somewhat indistinct track leads north-east to Pas de l'Aiguille.

Beech forest covers large parts of the slopes below Pas de la Selle, and pines, mainly Scots pines, are the most prominent trees on the plateau. Wild flowers are quite plentiful, including the relatively rare edelweiss and the distinctive stemless carline thistle, with deeply serrated leaves and a flat white flower with a dark centre. Listen for the shrill whistles of the marmots – they're easy to spot as they scamper about the rocky ground.

THE WALK
See the Parc Naturel Régional du Vercors map (p289).

In Chichilianne, start at place Louis Thiers by following the signs to Richardière; bear left at Bar Jere Nico and, after 300m, right at a fork. Then, it's left at a T-junction and right after a few metres. With broad fields on your left, turn left at a fork along a grassy track (which also serves as a challenging fitness trail). This leads through forest to a stony river bed (usually dry in summer); bear right on its far side to a road. The quickest way to Richardière from here is down this quiet road (the way-marked route was unclear at the time of survey). You'll soon pass through the hamlet of Donnière and reach a T-junction; turn right, then left at the next junction across a bridge. Walk up past the hotel – the main building in **Richardière**; beyond the end of the sealed road, bear right at a fork near an informal car park (1¼ hours from Chichilianne).

Beyond the signposted boundary of the nature reserve and then a clearing further on, there's a not very obvious signposted path on the right (at the locality of Les Serres on the recommended IGN map). This climbs steadily on a superb grade through the forest

on the steep wooded slope falling away from the southern ramparts of **Mont Aiguille**. After about 1½ hours, you'll emerge into the open at a broad rocky gully, where water may be flowing. The path on the right is slightly hazardous – the alternative on the left rejoins it farther up for a zigzag climb up the steep slope, with Mont Aiguille towering above. Continue towards **Col de l'Aupet**, at a junction, and up to the col itself (1627m; another 20 minutes). Follow the sign to Pas de la Selle along the ridge; the narrow path, muddy in places, soon swings to the right across to a wooded spur. Beyond this, the route negotiates a scree slope, then a steep rocky hillside, and at last you reach grassy **Pas de la Selle** (1895m), an hour from the col.

It's impossible to precisely describe the way from here, generally southwards from Pas de la Selle along or close to the plateau rim, to Pas de l'Aiguille (2½ hours). It's best to keep fairly close to the rim, across the grandly undulating meadows, through scattered clumps of pines and across small patches of scree or rock. The views along the way are fantastic, especially north to the overhanging cliffs of Le Grand Veymont. With luck, about 500m before **Pas de l'Aiguille** you'll meet the cairned route described in the introduction to this walk which leads to the rim of the wide valley above the pass. Here the **Source des Chaumailloux** a small natural spring, fills a built-up pond, a rare source of water on the plateau. Nearby are two small huts and an impressive **memorial** to eight local members of the resistance (Maquisards) who died in a battle at the pass in July 1944. There should be water in the nearby stream.

The track starts just below the memorial; at the foot of the towering cliffs, it's quite rough and stony and rather hard on the legs late in the day. Once you reach the forest, take a narrow path through the trees, avoiding what is nothing more than a rocky chute seemingly devastated by the passage of vehicles. Nearly an hour from the pass, you reach the end of a road in a large clearing, where there's another **Maquisard memorial**. Follow the road down to Richardière and retrace your steps back to Chichilianne (1¼ hours from the clearing).

Parc National des Écrins

The Écrins is a rugged collection of peaks containing the most southerly glaciers in the whole of the Alps. A small national park, set aside in 1913 in the Vénéon Valley, was extended eastwards and southwards between 1914 and 1924 and named Parc National du Pelvoux. Renamed in 1973, the park consists of a central, fully protected zone of 91,000 hectares and a peripheral zone around twice that area, home to about 27,000 people. The Parc National des Écrins contains the three highest peaks in France outside the Mont Blanc massif, all in the northern Massif de Pelvoux (these are Barre des Écrins, 4102m; La Meije, 3983m; and Mont Pelvoux, 3932m). Altogether in the Parc National des Écrins more than 100 summits top 3000m. These peaks cluster at the heads of a complex array of ridges separating several deep valleys penetrating the icy heartland from all directions: the Romanche in the north, Guisane in the northeast, Durance in the east, then Vallouise (most developed), followed by Drac in the south, Valjouffrey and Valgaudemar in the west, and the Vénéon in the north-west.

Les Écrins

The original, or earliest, name on record for this rugged mountainous area appears to be Massif de Pelvoux; Mont Pelvoux, in the north, was long believed to be the highest peak. It's thought that the name now used, which literally means 'casket' in French, derives from early mapping surveyors' understanding of the local dialect, and in particular the name for the highest point, now known as La Barre des Écrins. In conversations with prospectors in the hills north-east of Mont Pelvoux (parts of the area are quite rich in minerals), mention was made of écrins, the wooden casks placed in streams below a small cascade, to catch the fine mineral deposits carried in the water.

Full-length traverses of the range demand mountaineering skills and equipment. However, the valleys shelter several villages which serve as bases for day walks or as staging points on longer expeditions. There are 1000km of paths, including the GR54 Tour de l'Oisans, a middle-level circuit of the park, and the outlying GR50. Here you'll find some of the most remote walking areas in the Alps in glorious alpine meadows surrounded by soaring peaks and their attendant glaciers.

NATURAL HISTORY
The park is of outstanding importance for nature conservation; six nature reserves within its boundaries protect special habitats or landforms. The ibex, almost hunted to extinction in the past, was successfully reintroduced to the Valbonnais area in 1989. Among the other mammals, chamois, marmots and mountain hares are the most common. Of the 110 species of birds in the park, you might be lucky enough to spot a golden eagle above the cliffs or to come upon a capercaillie in the forests; jackdaws are more common, and you'll probably hear a black woodpecker before you see one.

Of the 2000 species of flowering plants, the most striking include orange lily, purplish martagon lily, and white and purple crocuses. Among the more prominent spring flowers are the brilliant blue spring and southern gentians; glacier crowfoot (one of the buttercups) appears miraculously in the rocky debris near glaciers and snowdrifts.

Reflecting the very different climatic influences impinging on the park, the wetter western side has forests of copper beech and fir, spruce woodland in the colder north, and larch on the drier eastern slopes where Mediterranean conditions prevail.

PLANNING
The following information is relevant to all three walks in this section.

When to Walk
By late June the passes should be free of snow and should stay that way until early October. Early July is a good time to visit,

when the flowers are at their best and just before the crowds arrive. September is also recommended, although bear in mind that most *refuges* (refuges or mountain huts) close around the middle of the month.

What to Bring

You may want to take an ice axe (or at least good walking poles) in early summer, and a water bottle. With large numbers of sheep and cattle grazing the meadows during summer, it's unsafe to drink water from streams.

Maps & Books

All the walks in this section are covered by Didier Richard's 1:50,000 *Écrins* sheet No 6. Alternatively, in the IGN 1:25,000 series, maps relevant to the Plateau d'Emparis walk are Nos 3435ET and 3335ET. For the Romanche Valley, you'll need No 3436ET, and for Lac du Goléon, No 3435ET is required.

Cicerone's *Tour of the Oisans, GR54* by Andrew Harper is out of date (1993), but nevertheless useful for giving an overall feel for the area and background information. The FFRP Topo-Guide *Tour de l'Oisans* (No 508) includes helpful details of variants of the GR54. Didier Richard's guide *Écrins, Oisans, Briançonnais* describes numerous walks but lacks maps. The IGN guide *Écrins, Queyras* is more of a guide to the national park than to particular walks.

Regulations

Please make sure you're aware of the strict national park regulations which apply to most of the areas covered by the walks here. They're set out in the boxed text 'National Park Regulations' in the Facts for the Walker chapter.

NEAREST TOWN
La Grave

Clinging to the steep southern side of the Romanche River, the small town of La Grave is the base for the walks described in detail in this section. It is a comfortable combination of the traditional and not too modern, and has all the facilities walkers will need.

The tourist office (☎ 04 76 79 90 05, fax 04 76 79 91 65), on the main road beside the bus stop, is open daily all year. It provides local information about accommodation facilities and has a *bureau de change* (exchange bureau). The daily France Météo forecasts are displayed beside the door.

Bureau des Guides de la Grave (☎ 04 76 79 90 21, fax 04 76 79 96 90), place Victor Chaud (at the eastern end of town), offers a range of short instruction courses on rock, snow and ice climbing during the summer. Two outdoor equipment shops, both in the main street, sell a wide range of clothing, equipment and maps: Technicien de Sport (☎ 04 76 79 92 21) and Matériel de Montagne. Easily the best place for maps and all kinds of guidebooks is the Tabac-Presse (a combination of tobacconist and newsagency), in place Victor Chaud.

The head office of Parc National des Écrins (☎ 04 92 40 20 10, fax 04 92 52 38 34) is at Domaine de Charance, in Gap, a town at the southern end of the Écrins park. The nearest maison du parc is open year-round in Briançon (☎ 04 92 21 42 15), at place Médecin-Général Blanchard; there's a collection of excellent displays, and information about the park, including maps and guides, is readily provided.

Places to Stay & Eat The riverside *Camping de la Meije* (☎ 04 76 79 93 34) is open from early May to the end of September; the tariff for two people and a small tent is around 40FF per night. Access is clearly signposted from the eastern end of town.

Le Refuge (☎ 04 76 79 91 00, place de l'Église) is up in the old part of town, on the GR54. It's open all year and has 12 beds (or rather mattresses) and a small kitchen in a single large room – traditional alpine *refuge* style; the fee is 60FF per night. To reach Le Refuge on foot from the main road, the least steep way is via the narrow road branching from the main road almost opposite the Sherpa alimentation.

Of the many restaurants in La Grave, *Au Vieux Guide* (☎ 04 76 79 90 75), just below the main road, offers *menus* for 98FF to 130FF, including local specialities.

Of the two grocery stores, *Alp'Serv'It*, by the main road in the centre of town, has a greater range than the *Sherpa*. It also has its own *boucherie* (butcher shop) and *fromagerie* (cheese-maker's), and stocks Camping Gaz; it's open daily from 8.30 am to 12.15 pm and 3.30 to 7.30 pm. There's also a good boulangerie on the main road.

Getting There & Away VFD bus service No 306 (☎ 04 76 47 77 77) linking Grenoble and Briançon passes through La Grave twice-daily throughout the year (50FF one way). In La Grave the bus stop is outside the tourist office. For the Romanche Valley walk you'll need to catch the morning bus on the same service to Col du Lautaret (14FF one way). See Getting There & Away under Grenoble earlier in this chapter for details of transport links between Grenoble and other parts of France.

In the other direction, from Briançon, the trip to La Grave costs 43FF one way. The bus station in Briançon is next to the train station, at the southern end of ave du Général de Gaulle. Briançon has fairly good train links with Paris, Grenoble and Marseille. There is also a useful twice-daily bus service run by Société des Cars Alpes Littoral (SCAL; ☎ 04 92 51 06 05) between Briançon and Marseille.

Glaciers of the Écrins

Although about 10% of the area of the national park is covered by ice, conditions are less than ideal for the formation and survival of glaciers and large snowfields – the Parc National des Écrins is just too far south, and rainfall is too high.

Nevertheless, glaciers are very numerous and widespread, if individually small, and certainly spectacular. The comparatively small size is a sign that they may well be in retreat – a condition which may be tested if global warming or climate change exert a strong influence here. The most common type of glacier is that lying in a cirque at the glacier's original headwall. Many of these, above 3000m and in sheltered sites, are not visible from down in the valleys.

Plateau d'Emparis

Duration	6½ hours
Distance	18km
Standard	medium-hard
Start/Finish	La Grave
Public Transport	yes

Summary An extremely scenic walk across alpine meadows to two tiny lakes hidden among clusters of crags, with uninterrupted views of the peak La Meije and its attendant cliffs and glaciers.

Belying its name, the Plateau d'Emparis is an area of rolling alpine meadows and clusters of crags and rocky hillocks, high above the steep-sided Romanche Valley. Hidden away among the crags are tiny Lac Noir and Lac Lérié, perched on the precipitous edge of the plateau. These, and perhaps the Col du Souchet, are the objectives for this walk. Towering La Meije and its flanking glaciers and cliffs are the ever-present, fascinating backdrop.

The route is described from La Grave; alternatively, if you have a car, you can start from the village of Le Chazelet, saving about 5km and 350m of climbing, but bypassing the old almost unspoiled village of Les Terrasses (between La Grave and Le Chazelet). From the lakes, you can return to the main path across the plateau either by the same route or by a less well-used path which leads to Col du Souchet, about 500m north-west on the plateau path.

The amount of ascent involved is considerable (1140m) but it's accumulated in distinct stages: to Les Terrasses, from Le Chazelet to the plateau, and from a stream crossing on the plateau to the lakes. Although the route largely follows the GR54 and GR50 (which are waymarked, sparsely, with the standard red and white stripes), it is also defined by yellow signs and waymarkers. The route to the lakes has the yellow markers only.

The plateau is named Plateau de Paris on the topographical maps, but local signposts and literature refer to the same place as Plateau d'Emparis.

Parc National des Écrins

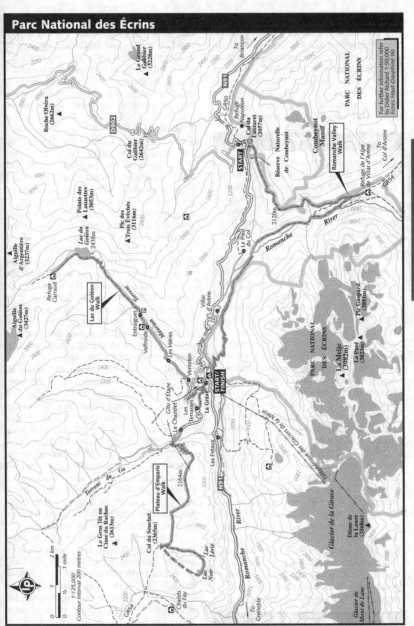

SOUTHERN ALPS

For further information refer
to Didier Richard 1:50,000
Écrins Haut-Dauphiné (6)

PARC NATIONAL
DES ÉCRINS

To Briançon

Le Grand
Galibier
(3228m)

Roche Olvéra
(2662m)

Col du
Galibier
(2642m)

D902

Refuge
Napoléon

Col du
Lautaret
(2057m)

Combeynot
Massif

Romanche Valley
Walk

To
Col d'Arsine

Refuge de l'Alpe
de Villar d'Arène

GR54

N91

GR50

START

Réserve Naturelle
de Combeynot

Le Pied
du Col

2120m

Romanche   River

Pointe des
Lauzettes
(3053m)

Pic des
Trois Évêchés
(3116m)

Aiguille
d'Argentière
(3237m)

Lac du
Goléon
2438m

Refuge
Carrand

Lac du Goléon
Walk

Aiguille
du Goléon
(3427m)

Entraigues

Torrent du Ga

Maurian

Valfroide

Les Hières

Ventelon

Villar
d'Arène

PARC NATIONAL
DES ÉCRINS

Pic Gaspard
(3881m)

La Meije
(3982m)

Le Pavé
(3823m)

Gîte d'étape

Les
Terrasses

Le Chazelet

START
FINISH

La Grave

Téléphérique des Glaciers de la Meije

Les Fréaux

N91

Plateau d'Emparis
Walk

2164m

Le Gros Têt ou
Cime du Ruchas
(2613m)

Col du
Souchet
(2365m)

Lac
Lérié

Lac
Noir

Chalets
du Fay

GR54

Torrent du Ga

Dôme de
la Lauze
(3568m)

Glacier de la Girose

Romanche   River

To
Grenoble

Glacier de
Mont de Lans

0   2 km
0   1   1 mile
1:125,000
Contour Interval 200 metres

NATURAL HISTORY

The plateau was declared a *site naturel classé* (classified natural site) in 1992, in recognition of its outstandingly important landscape. Within an area of 2900 hectares (between Serre Bernard in the east, Le Gros Tet in the north, Les Clots in the south-west and the Romanche Valley), any development must have ministerial approval.

The geology and landforms of the area are very diverse: sedimentary and crystalline rocks, synclines and faults, features carved out by glacial and water erosion, peatlands and scree slopes. In meadows, the continued grazing by thousands of sheep and hundreds of cattle and goats maintains a very rich variety of alpine, wetland and steppe species.

La Meije

Although not the highest peak in the Parc National des Écrins, La Meije (3982m) reigns supreme: for its spectacular beauty, as a respected challenge for climbers and for the saga of early attempts to conquer its summit (such was the 19th-century philosophy, that mountains had to be subdued). It consists of three summits: the Grand Pic de la Meije in the west (the highest), the central Doigt de Dieu and the eastern Meije Orientale. The name 'La Meije' derives from a word in the local dialect meaning 'midday'.

By 1870 most of the major summits in the Alps had been climbed, including Mont Pelvoux (3943m) as early as 1848, and La Barre des Écrins (4102m) in 1864 by a party including Edward Whymper (of Matterhorn fame). However, La Meije remained inviolate, despite attempts by various notable mountaineers. In 1877 the young Baron Emmanuel Boileau de Castelneau rose to the challenge and hired locals Pierre Gaspard and his 20-year-old son to accompany him; they set out from La Bérarde near the head of the Vénéon Valley. The Gaspards were determined to win the summit for local guides rather than surrender it to their Chamonix rivals. The glacier guarding the southern face was easily surmounted, but the party hesitated just below the summit. Boileau retreated but the Gaspards, not to be beaten only a few metres from victory, found a route round the northern face and up to the top. Other ascents soon followed and the first all-woman party to climb La Meije was led by the British mountaineer Nea Morin in 1933. Nowadays, ascents are almost daily events, weather permitting.

THE WALK

See the Parc National des Écrins map (p295). From the northern corner of place de l'Église in La Grave, follow the GR58 uphill; turn left at a signposted junction and climb to a broad track. After a few bends, continue on a well-used, narrow, slightly sunken path. It rises steeply at first then eases to cross the slope and reach the edge of the village of **Les Terrasses**. Follow a stony path in the direction of Le Chazelet, then a steep concreted road past the church, across the road and up a lane. Bear left and go on up to a road and follow it to **Le Chazelet** (1¼ hours from La Grave). At the entrance to the village is an *épicerie* (grocery store) which sells local produce; farther on take note of the location of *Relais d'Emparis*, a bar-restaurant just below the main road and a good place to stop for a beer on the way back.

Walk through the village and down towards the valley immediately to the west; fork left at a junction and continue to a bridge. Cross it and climb the path winding up the steep, grassed slope. It takes a good hour to reach the top of this climb (at 2164m) where signposts point to 'Les Lacs', among other places. The path continues westwards, then north across the meadows which slope steeply to the cliffs above the Romanche Valley, and down into a broad valley. A steady climb leads to a signposted junction; turn south here for the lakes (about 40 minutes from the top of the climb).

The path is clear as it rises gradually through rocky knolls and meadows, past another junction (for Col du Souchet) and on to **Lac Lérié** (20 minutes), well hidden beneath low bluffs. One last quite steep climb, partly close to the precipitous cliff edge, takes you to a fine vantage point above **Lac Noir**.

The direct return is simply a matter of re-tracing your steps; allow about 1¼ hours to Le Chazelet (and the bar) and about 75 minutes down to La Grave.

Romanche Valley

Duration	5½ hours
Distance	15km
Standard	medium
Start	Col du Lautaret
Finish	La Grave
Public Transport	yes

Summary Follow the Sentier des Crevasses, a scenic heritage path in Parc National des Écrins, to a *refuge* for lunch, then descend the spectacular valley of the Romanche River through larch woodlands.

For a change, this walk starts at a point (Col du Lautaret; 2057m) which is higher than the finish (La Grave; 1430m). In Col du Lautaret you'll find a couple of **snack bars**, a *fromagerie* and maison du parc, in the historic *Refuge Napoléon* (open summer only).

The first part of the walk is along the well-defined sentier des Crevasses, across the north-western flank of the Combeynot massif. Beside the first part of this path, several detailed interpretive signs (in French) describe the salient features of the local geology, topography, flora, fauna and history (the area has been inhabited since Roman times). Farther on, a fixed cable provides a measure of security along one narrow section. From the *refuge*, it's downhill virtually all the way, following the Romanche River.

Waymarking along the walk is variable. The medium grading reflects the total distance and the steepness of part of the descent beside the Romanche. When the walk was surveyed, a family with two children aged under seven made good time from Col du Lautaret to the Refuge de l'Alpe de Villar d'Arène. The walk could be shortened by finishing at the village of Villar d'Arène, returning to La Grave by the evening Briançon-Grenoble bus, thus saving about 4km and 100m ascent.

NATURAL HISTORY

Col du Lautaret and the surrounding area lie at the junction of Mediterranean and Continental climatic influences, and at the convergence of distinct geological zones (crystalline and sedimentary rocks). As a result, an unusually large number of species of flora – up to 1500 – are found here. This richness is one of the main reasons for the creation of the Réserve Naturelle de Combeynot, through which the first section of the walk passes.

THE WALK

See the Parc National des Écrins map (p295). From Col du Lautaret, walk back down the road towards La Grave for about 400m to a car park on the left, where there is a national park information board. Follow the broad path, along which interpretive signs describe a wide variety of local features. After about 400m signposts point the way to 'L'Alpe de Villar d'Arène'. The path climbs almost imperceptibly along the boundary of the **Réserve Naturelle de Combeynot** through woodland of alder and willow to its highest point (2120m) on a spur of the Combeynot massif.

Here the interpretive trail ends and the path turns south to pursue an extraordinary route across the precipitous mountainside. Shortly, a chain bolted to the rocks provides a measure of security past a long drop on the right; there's another, but less vertiginous narrow section within the next kilometre. The path then descends steadily to the valley of the infant **Romanche River**. Continue past signs to Villar d'Arène and Col d'Arsine to the *Refuge de l'Alpe de Villar d'Arène* (☎ 04 92 24 53 18), almost two hours from Col du Lautaret. It's open from spring until mid-September and serves meals of hefty proportions: salads (18FF to 34FF), omelettes (24FF to 41FF), the *plat du jour* (daily special; 39FF) and a variety of drinks (although a beer must be accompanied by at least a sandwich). A night in this spacious, clean *refuge* run by Club Alpin Français (CAF) costs 80FF; breakfast is 32FF. At the time of research there was a fascinating display in the foyer about the history of climbing in the area.

SOUTHERN ALPS

SOUTHERN ALPS

To continue to La Grave, go back to the signposted junction indicating the direction to Villar d'Arène, but descend steeply northwards beside the cascades of the Romanche River and down to an informal car park. From there, follow a path to the right (but not the one to a plantation), comfortably down to a minor road on the edge of the village of Le Pied du Col (two hours from the *refuge*). Walk down the road, past *Gîte et Refuge du Pas de l'Ane*, which may be open for drinks and snacks. At the next car park, cross the bridge over the Romanche River and follow the river bank path downstream. After about 2.2km, mainly through larch and mixed deciduous woodland with a short climb en route, you arrive opposite Villar d'Arène. A sign points the way up to La Grave, and soon you come to a fine view over La Grave and the Plateau d'Emparis. Descend steeply to a broad track and follow it down to a road. Turn right to the bridge and one last short climb to the main road in La Grave (two hours from Le Pied du Col).

Lac du Goléon

Duration	6 hours
Distance	15km
Standard	medium
Start/Finish	La Grave
Public Transport	yes

Summary A sustained climb, passing through quiet traditional villages to a spectacularly sited lake, surrounded by precipitous peaks and with an outdoor autograph album 'written' with stones on its shores.

Lac du Goléon sits in a small valley, overlooked by rugged peaks and ridges, high above the northern side of the Romanche Valley; La Meije and its glaciers are constantly in view during this scenic walk. If you have a car, it's possible to drive to an informal parking area at the end of the minor road *(chemin rural)* at Entraigues, thus saving about 8km and 400m climbing, although the road is quite rough from the village of Les Hières.

The amount of ascent (1000m), mostly steep, merits a medium grading; on the day the walk was surveyed, the ages of people met along the way ranged from about six to well over 70.

THE WALK

See the Parc National des Écrins map (p295). Follow the GR54 northwards out of La Grave and immediately turn right to Ventelon, as signposted. The steep narrow path climbs to a road; turn right towards Les Hières. Bypassing Ventelon, the road affords fine views up the Romanche Valley. About 100m past the easternmost access to Ventelon, a sign indicates an alternative route to Les Hières along a grassy track below the road. However, it's not really worth the effort, given an obscure stream crossing and the loss of height relative to the road on to Valfroide. Walk through **Les Hières** (75 minutes from La Grave); at the far end, the road becomes a chemin rural of rough gravel. **Valfroide** is an elongated group of hamlets of traditional timber and stone buildings on either side of the road; just beyond the last building (at Entraigues) the road ends at a car park.

Continue along the vehicle track (signs point to Lac du Goléon) and cross a stony stream; the track becomes a path leading across the broad meadows – ideal marmot territory, as is most of this walk. Cairns and the odd blue waymarker define the line of zigzags for the steepish climb to the southern end of **Lac du Goléon**.

Before or after lunch it's well worth wandering along beside the lake, round the low bluff at its northern end to the wide, flat valley, where many visitors have created an open-air autograph album by inscribing their names on the grassy flat ground with long slivers of (plentifully available) shaly rock. The path continues up the valley to the private Refuge Carraud.

The descent to Entraigues takes about 1½ hours; allow another hour down to La Grave, after a welcome break at the excellent *Les Trois Évêchés (☎ 04 76 79 90 45)*, with a *menu* for 75FF and fondue 65FF. You can also stay the night here (85FF in the *refuge*, 200FF for a double in the hotel).

Parc Naturel Régional du Queyras

Although within this regional park there are more than a dozen summits above 3000m, the landscape is not rugged and inaccessible. In the absence of glaciers and snowfields, there is generous scope for walking, along narrow ridges, through valleys and to numerous lakes and waterfalls. The 60,000-hectare park was reserved in 1977 to support traditional agriculture and crafts while harmoniously developing tourism and winter sports. Depopulation had blighted the Parc Naturel Régional du Queyras – down to fewer than 2000 people in the 1960s from 8000 in the mid-19th century, but up to 2300 in the mid-1990s. Typically, the villages are clusters of traditional timber houses around an old church; Saint-Véran, at 2040m, is within the highest permanently inhabited *commune* (local government area) in Europe. The origin of the unusual name Queyras remains a mystery, although it has been in use since the 13th century.

The park, bounded in the east by the Italian border, is essentially the naturally secluded basin of the Guil River, a tributary of the Durance River to the west. There is only one way in and out year-round – up the Guil Valley from Guillestre. The main waymarked walking routes are the GR58, the Tour du Queyras, and a section of the GR5; these core routes, with several loops or variants, and many other paths, offer weeks rather than days of first-class walking and the weather is ideal – 300 sunny days annually.

The three walks described in this section are based on Saint-Véran and are entirely or largely within the valley of L'Aigue Blanche Torrent, a tributary of the Guil Torrent, the main river in the Parc Naturel Régional du Queyras. It is worth bearing in mind that all three walks reach an altitude above 2700m, so that without a couple of days' acclimatisation, you may notice that your breathing when climbing is just a little more difficult than usual.

NATURAL HISTORY
In the lower reaches of the valleys, up to around 1500m, the Queyras forests consist of beeches and firs in wetter areas, and pines on drier ground. Higher up, in the subalpine zone, arolla pines and larches thrive; the latter (the main forest tree in the Parc Naturel Régional du Queyras) turn a beautiful orange-gold during autumn. Here you'll find the greatest concentration of wild flowers, making a stunning display during June. Of the 2000 species of flowering plants in the park, 40 species are protected, including edelweiss and arnica. Above 2000m, flowers are few and grasses and stunted bushes of juniper predominate.

The mammal you are most likely to see is the marmot, bounding about on stony ground. Chamois are more elusive; although the park's population of this agile, playful animal numbers around 12,000, they're not often seen around Saint-Véran, preferring to keep to the cliffs on the southern side of the valley. There are also a few mouflon, introduced to the Parc Naturel Régional du Queyras from Corsica. Birds are more numerous, including royal and golden eagles, falcons, ptarmigans on the rocky open ground, black capercaillies – an aggressive bird living in the woodlands – and many smaller species, including woodpeckers.

Geologically, the Guil and Aigue Blanche valleys are dominated by schist – a rather friable rock resembling slate – while limestone is the main rock type in the southwestern Queyras (the junction or contact zone of these two rocks is strikingly evident on the Three Cols walk). The rocks around Saint-Véran are rich in minerals – copper has been mined high in the valley in past times (evidence of which you'll find on the Col de Saint-Véran walk).

INFORMATION
The main tourist office for the Parc Naturel Régional du Queyras (☎ 04 92 46 76 18, fax 04 92 46 81 44, ✉ office.promotion .queyras@queyras.com) is in Aiguilles. The office publishes an excellent magazine *Queyras. Terre d'Émotions*, available free to inquirers.

For information specifically about the park, contact La Direction du Parc Naturel Régional du Queyras (☎ 04 92 45 06 23), BP 3, 05600 Guillestre. The area is also discussed on the Web site at www.queyras.com.

Books

Cicerone's *The Tour of the Queyras* by Alan Castle is now out of date but has comprehensive background information. The FFRP Topo-Guide *Tour du Queyras* (No 505) details the GR58 and GR541 and their alternatives. *Queyras – Pays du Viso* published by Didier Richard has descriptions of 144 walks but no maps (you have to buy its 1:50,000 sheet No 10). The IGN guide *Écrins, Queyras* is good for comprehensive background information.

Two books in French are worth recommending: *Balades et Randonnées en Queyras* by Martine Canet & Pierre Putelat is beautifully illustrated; *Balades Faciles en Queyras-Guillestrois* by Yves Fouque describes walks of up to a half-day's duration and is excellent for families with small children.

PLANNING

The following information is relevant to all three walks in this section.

When to Walk

The same considerations apply to all three walks described here. The best times to visit the Parc Naturel Régional du Queyras are either May and June, or September, when the weather should be settled and there'll be plenty of sun but not the oppressive heat of July and August. Some services, notably local buses, are limited from early September. The hunting season (mainly for chamois) starts on 10 September, but this is unlikely to affect walkers; nevertheless, check locally to be sure.

What to Bring

Carry a cup or water bottle with you to collect water from the troughs with clean piped water (noted in the walk descriptions). Although there are streams along the route, this is grazing country and their purity cannot be guaranteed.

Sundials

One of the distinctive traditions of the Queyras, both artistic and practical, is gnomics – the creation of sundials (cadrans solaires). From at least the 18th century, artists, mainly Italian, painted or carved sundials on the walls of houses and other buildings, and decorated them with eye-catching motifs and a proverb, so that no two are alike. Favourite inscriptions, in French or Latin, reflect religious beliefs or concern with the passage of time: *Il est plus tard que vous ne croyez* – It's later than you think, and *Vita fugit* – Life flies past. Only natural dyes were used: yellow ochre, red iron oxide, sienna earth, mixed with melted wax to ward off the ravages of sun, wind and snow. There are more than 400 sundials in the area and they are particularly striking in Saint-Véran, blessed as it is with 300 days of sunshine annually.

Ancient Greek astronomers perfected the calculations necessary for the accurate design of the sundial and the Crusaders brought back from the Middle East the practice of placing the pointer at an angle. The form of cadrans solaires has changed very little since. To read the time accurately, it's necessary to add about 30 minutes in summer or 1½ hours in winter to the time shown by the pointer.

Despite the trend to electronic counting of the passing moment, sundials are now being restored and maintained, preserving traditional skills.

Maps

To cover the walks, you'll need the Didier Richard 1:50,000 *Queyras: Pays du Viso* sheet No 10. Alternatively, the more detailed IGN 1:25,000 *Mont Viso* sheet No 3637OT covers all the walks in this section with the exception of the Three Cols walk (which extends over onto sheet No 3537ET).

NEAREST TOWN
Saint-Véran

The three walks described in this section start at the village of Saint-Véran, in the heart of the park. It's a traditional village arranged linear-fashion along the hillside to take full advantage of exposure to the sun. One of the most distinctive features of the large, rambling stone and timber buildings is the sundials, painted on walls and gable ends (see the boxed text 'Sundials'). Saint-Véran has made few but sufficient concessions to modern tourism, and walkers will find nearly all the basic necessities here for a stay of several days, or for an overnight stop during an extended walk. The various shops and so on are either on the upper or the lower road, the vertical distance between which is at least 30m (a long way at the end of the day!).

The tourist office (☎ 04 92 45 2 21, fax 04 92 45 84 52), near the large church in the centre of the village, is open daily and provides all manner of local information. The daily France Météo weather forecast is posted beside the entrance.

Several shops sell maps but the best place to go is the Presse-Tabac towards the south-eastern end of the village; it also stocks a wide range of local walking, nature and history guidebooks. Opening hours are 8 am to 12.30 pm and 2 to 7 pm Monday to Saturday, with slightly shorter hours on Sunday.

The post office has a bureau de change service; the nearest ATM is at the Maison de l'Artisanat in Ville Vieille, 11km away in the Guil Valley. The nearest petrol station is also in Ville Vieille.

Places to Stay & Eat The nearest *camping area* (☎ 04 92 45 83 37) is at Fontgillarde in the Agnelle Valley, north of Saint-Véran. To reach there, turn off the Saint-Véran road at Molines-en-Queyras towards Col Agnel; Fontgillarde is about 4km along this road.

There are two gîtes d'étape in the village. *Les Gabelous* (☎ 04 92 45 81 39, fax 04 92 45 86 36), in the Pierre Belle area, is towards the south-eastern end of the village. Prices for a bed in one of the small dorms start at 51FF; doubles are available for 80FF per person. A shower will cost you 9FF. The gîte owners also provide a taxi service.

Le Chant de L'Alpe (☎ 04 92 45 85 59) is beside the road leading north-west from the parking area at the lower entrance to the village. A twin room costs 72FF per night,

or a space in the dorm is 68FF; meals are available by prior arrangement and are recommended by French walkers.

Of the few *chambres d'hôtes* (B&B accommodation in a private house), *Mme Jacqueline Turina* (☎/fax 04 92 45 81 77) offers double rooms with private facilities for 200FF per night; a good French breakfast is 30FF per person. Mme Turina is an extremely knowledgeable native of Saint-Véran and can provide advice about many other walks in the Parc Naturel Régional du Queyras.

Eating out in Saint-Véran need not be unduly expensive. Probably the most colourful place for a meal is *La Marmotte*, beside the upper main road. For lunch it offers *menus* for 68FF and 88FF, fondues (80FF to 90FF) and pizzas (40FF to 49FF). Also on the upper road is *La Fougagno* with *menus* for 70FF and 105FF and steaks (60FF to 80FF), which you can enjoy inside or on the terrace. *L'Aigue Blanche* (☎ 04 92 45 82 61), close to Les Gabelous, offers pizzas *au feu du bois* (wood-fired) for 55FF and *menus* for 85FF and 95FF.

The *alimentation* is open from 9 am to 12.15 pm and 3 to 6 pm Monday to Saturday; it has a small but adequate range, including some pharmacy items and Camping Gaz. There's an excellent *boulangerie* on the lower road, and right down at the entrance to the village is *La Carotto*, which sells local cheeses, meats and wines; it's open daily from 9.30 am to 12.30 pm and 4.30 to 7 pm.

Getting There & Away Saint-Véran isn't the easiest place to get to. The nearest train station is Montdauphin Guillestre on the Gap-Briançon railway line which has good connections from Paris, Grenoble and Marseille. There is also a useful twice-daily bus service run by Société des Cars Alpes Littoral (SCAL; ☎ 04 92 51 06 05) between Briançon and Marseille via Montdauphin.

From Montdauphin train station, Imbert Autocars (☎ 04 92 45 18 11, fax 04 92 45 17 30, ✉ CAR.IMBERT@wanadoo.fr) provides a twice-daily bus service to Saint-Véran in summer; at other times (Monday to Saturday only), the service passes through Ville Vieille (40FF), 11km from

SOUTHERN ALPS

Parc Naturel Régional du Queyras

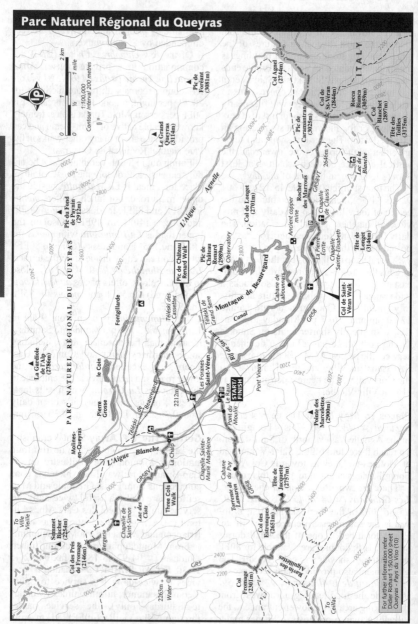

Saint-Véran, from where a taxi can be arranged (☎ 04 92 45 81 39). If all else fails, Waltzer taxis (☎ 04 92 45 00 14) will take you from the Montdauphin station to Saint-Véran for 300FF.

By road, turn off the N91 at Montdauphin, pass the large town of Guillestre and continue along the incredible road winding up the extremely narrow Guil Valley to Ville Vieille, and on to Saint-Véran.

Col de Saint-Véran

Duration	5½ hours
Distance	20.5km
Standard	medium
Start/Finish	Saint-Véran
Public Transport	summer only

Summary A not-too-steep and highly scenic climb to a col on the Italian border, with spectacular views of majestic Monte Viso. Climb to a nearby summit (just above 3000m) for an even grander mountain panorama.

Although these days the border between France and Italy has little political significance, it does offer a distinctive objective for a day walk. The border east of Saint-Véran often also divides good weather in France from low cloud in Italy (or vice versa). From the village, two cols on the border are easily accessible; of these, Col de Saint-Véran (2844m) is slightly easier to reach than Col Blanchet (2897m), and is the highlight of the walk described here.

The walk starts in Saint-Véran and includes 800m of vertical ascent. For a less strenuous outing, if you have a car you could drive up the gravel road to an informal parking area just below Chapelle de Clausis, thus saving 300m ascent, 2½ hours and 10km of walking. However, during the very busy months of July and August the road is closed to vehicles and a daily *navette* (shuttle bus) service is provided, from 6.30 am to 6 pm (with a lunch break from noon to 2 pm). Pic de Caramantran (3021m), 700m north of the col, is well worth the extra distance and 180m climb; allow about 45 minutes return.

There is a water trough with piped deliciously cold, fresh water at the start of the path from the chapel road, so it isn't really necessary to carry water, just a cup or bottle to collect it.

Marmots are plentiful and you can count on seeing some almost anywhere between the road and the col.

Since it was published, the track junctions between Rocher des Marrous and Col de Saint-Véran have been altered: there is now a crossroads near point 2646, rather than two separate junctions (at 2646 and a point 250m to the east).

HISTORY

The copper mine above the upper reaches of the Aigue Blanche Valley had its origin in Neolithic times, but was most actively worked more recently. Some copper was extracted for a time during the later 19th century; the mine was reopened in 1901, mainly to provide local employment. However, it closed once and for all in 1961, as the remote location made extraction too expensive for worthwhile operation. An interesting (and free) display in the village describes the mine's history in detail.

Pilgrimages have been made from Saint-Véran to Chapelle de Clausis and the oratories en route every year since 1846 on 16 July and 8 September.

THE WALK

See the Parc Naturel Régional du Queyras map (p302).

Walk through Saint-Véran south-eastwards to a signposted junction at the crossing of the Rif de Sainte-Luce and descend to the right, following the GR58 red-and-white waymarkers. This vehicle track leads down to Pont Vieux (1km). Cross the bridge and follow the track as it climbs steadily upstream. Nearly an hour's walking brings you to Clot du Faure (not shown on either of the recommended maps) and another 20 minutes to La Pierre Ecrite, directly below the remains of an **old copper mine**. The track narrows and soon climbs steeply to the road, below **Chapelle de Clausis** (1½ hours from Saint-Véran).

To continue, cross the road and follow the path signposted to various cols and the GR58. It climbs steadily across the meadows to a junction, from where the route eastward to the objective, Col de Saint-Véran, is identified with yellow waymarkers. The narrow path leads steadily upwards, creating the feeling of venturing ever farther into a huge amphitheatre, ringed with peaks and bluffs. The next junction is a straightforward crossroads – continue straight on up to the **col** (an hour from the road).

For **Pic de Caramantran** and even better views of the long ridges of rugged peaks, and especially of the soaring cliffs and glaciers of Monte Viso (in Italy) to the east, the best route is closest to the eastern rim. Some large cairns and a fairly well-defined path show the way to the top.

The return to Saint-Véran is straightforward – simply retrace your steps. There is much to be said, however, for going back down the road, avoiding the climb from Pont Vieux and for better views of the valley and peaks beyond. Allow 2¼ to 2½ hours from the col right back to the village.

Three Cols

Duration	8 hours
Distance	19.2km
Standard	hard
Start/Finish	Saint-Véran
Public Transport	summer only

Summary A truly magnificent circuit of the cliff-lined ridge west of Saint-Véran via three cols, mainly along narrow paths, with continuous panoramic views of towering peaks, jagged ridges and deep valleys.

This is a fairly challenging but extremely rewarding walk – a tour at various levels around the high cliff-encrusted ridge immediately west and south-west of Saint-Véran.

The three cols, Col des Estronques, Col Fromage and Col des Prés du Fromage, are quite different in character and mark distinct stages of the walk: the climb from Saint-Véran, the traverse of the precipitous western flanks of the ridge, and the start of the

descent back towards Saint-Véran. You're on good but often narrow paths nearly all the way. Between Col des Estronques and Col Fromage the mountainside drops very steeply to your left, so a head for heights is an advantage. The route is adequately waymarked as part of the GR58 from Saint-Véran to beyond Col des Estronques, and from Col Fromage north for a few kilometres as a sliver of the great GR5. Elsewhere you follow yellow signs and waymarkers.

The detail of the route between Pont du Moulin (below Le Raux) and the bridge over Torrente de Lamaron has changed slightly since the IGN 3637OT map was published (nor does Didier Richard's 1:50,000 map show the route precisely); however this isn't crucial as the route is clearly waymarked.

The amount of ascent (1220m) and the grading may look alarming but this is partly because of the final climb of about 250m from La Chalp to Saint-Véran, 3km up the valley. In summer, you could avoid this sting in the tail by catching the evening bus up to Saint-Véran. The first part of the walk, up to Col des Estronques and back to Saint-Véran, would make a worthwhile easy-medium day walk, especially if you added the ascent of Tête de Jacquette (2757m), the summit immediately south-east of the col. This involves another 110m of ascent for which you should allow about 30 minutes. The panoramic view includes Monte Viso to the east, the village of Ceillac far below to the west, and the massive Aiguille de Chambeyron, complete with a small glacier, to the south.

THE WALK

See the Parc Naturel Régional du Queyras map (p302).

Walk down to the large car park at the entrance to Saint-Véran, past the Hôtel de Beauregard to a sharp bend where there is a large decorated timber cross. Bear left down a path to the hamlet of **Le Raux**, turn right along a road for about 100m to a lane on the left and continue down to cross **Pont du Moulin** over L'Aigue Blanche. There is an informal car park here. Walk up the forest road, signposted among other things for the GR58, for no more than 200m and continue along a waymarked path to the right. This soon joins a track on the right for a short distance, then the route turns right across the meadow to the footbridge over Torrente de Lamaron. The path now starts the serious business of climbing, mainly by describing series of zigzags up the steep side of the narrowing valley.

With the Cabane du Puy in sight, cross the stream (an hour from Pont du Moulin) and continue up through larch woodland, then over a small bluff to a meadow which affords a fine view of Saint-Véran. Another 30 minutes uphill brings you to the narrow **Col des Estronques**. From here you can nip up to Tête de Jacquette and back for even better views.

Descend from the col towards Ceillac but leave the well-used path after about 15 minutes for a lesser one signposted to 'Col Fromage'. It makes a spectacular traverse of the steep mountainside, crossing a couple of scree slopes in the process. Near the Ravine de Rasis there's an abrupt change from the shale you've been walking across to less friable and more colourful limestone. Nearly an hour from the col you come to **Col Fromage** – a pleasant place for lunch. Continue towards Col des Prés de Fromage, and 300m farther on follow the GR5 (not the GR58) through pine woodland, which gradually gives way to more open meadows extending right up to the scree fringing the steep cliffs above.

There's a **wooden trough** with piped fresh water beside the path, south of the point 2263 on the 1:50,000 map, just before the path descends steeply and makes a wide bend to the right. It loses height across meadows and through larch woodland to a stream. Cross this watercourse (nearly an hour from Col Fromage) and continue north along the vehicle track. After a few minutes, where it starts to fall away, turn off along a signposted path on the right to Col des Prés de Fromage. Although meandering cattle have played havoc with the path in places, the surrounding open larch woodland is delightful. About 200m north-east of a bergerie you reach the grassy open spaces of **Col des Prés de Fromage** (25 minutes from the stream crossing). If time is on your side, the

signposted walk to **Sommet Bucher** (2254m) is worth the effort for fine views along the Guil Valley.

To continue, head south-eastwards on a faint track, past a yellow-topped stake and over a low spur to a sign pointing to Chapelle de Saint-Simon. The track is clear from here to the small **chapel**, standing peacefully in a clearing. Every year on 6 August a procession leaves from Molines-en-Queyras to the chapel. A signpost to 'La Chalp de Saint-Véran' and yellow waymarkers point the way forwards, slightly uphill, still in larch woodland. Soon you emerge into open meadows, sloping steeply from the base of the cliffs. Aim for a prominent boulder between the depression (marked on the recommended IGN 1:25,000 map) and tiny **Lac des Clots**. Descend to a vehicle track on the edge of the forest and on downwards through the trees to the next meadow. The final descent starts in earnest from here via a winding path to the bridge over L'Aigue Blanche at the hamlet of **La Chalp**.

For the return to Saint-Véran, the following route takes the inevitable climb more gently than the alternative upstream to Pont du Moulin and then up through Le Raux. At La Chalp cross the road by the church and

A Mountain Observatory

Sitting close to the summit of Pic de Château Renard, housed in a small neat domed building, is the highest telescope in France, maintaining watch over some of the clearest skies in Europe.

A 3.6m telescope was installed here in 1974 by the Observatoire de Paris-Meudon and it operated year-round as a solar observatory until 1982. Eight years later, thanks to the enthusiasm of dedicated astronomers and a group known as Astroqueyras, the observatory was reopened with a *télescope actuel*.

It is now run by Astroqueyras for the Paris-Meudon and Haute-Provence observatories. Staff conduct guided tours daily from June to September. Contact Astroqueyras (☎ 01 45 41 71 41), 4 allée des Hortensias, 75014 Paris, for more information.

SOUTHERN ALPS

go straight ahead, then bend left (north) up a track to an isolated cabin. Turn right (south-east) here along a vehicle track and follow it gradually up through meadows for about 200m to meet a path; here, turn right. A steady climb brings you to a road (30 minutes from La Chalp) and an oratory (tiny chapel). From here, it's only another 15 minutes to Saint-Véran.

Pic de Château Renard

Duration	6½ hours
Distance	18km
Standard	medium-hard
Start/Finish	Saint-Véran
Public Transport	summer only

Summary An exhilarating, extremely scenic circuit above Saint-Véran, including the summit of formidable Pic de Château Renard and an observatory, returning along an old irrigation canal path through marmot territory.

This circuit walk, on Montagne de Beauregard, climbing steeply to the north-east above Saint-Véran, is much less formidable than it looks. About half the climb makes use of well-graded ski tow maintenance tracks; the descent and return to Saint-Véran follow the winding road serving an observatory (see the boxed text 'A Mountain Observatory') and a one-time irrigation canal. In between (along the ridge) there isn't a continuous path, nor is there any waymarking. The final climb to the top of Pic de Château Renard from near the observatory is straightforwards, although impossible from anywhere else, and very well worth the minor detour.

The medium grading is easily earned by the amount of climbing (980m vertical); the fairly easy descent just saves the walk from being a hard one.

A shorter version of this walk would involve walking up the Chapelle de Clausis and observatory roads, either going right up to the Pic or detouring to Col de Longet (2701m), about 500m east of the observatory road (the turn-off is clear on the ground but not signposted), and returning via the canal path.

THE WALK

See the Parc Naturel Régional du Queyras map (p302).

Set out up the lane from the fountain beside the road at Les Foranes (and near the craft shop L'Atelier), climbing steeply beyond the houses, with crosses on either hand, to join a track leading left up to the tiny **Chapelle Sainte-Marie Madeleine**. Go directly uphill from there and at a track junction (at point 2212 on the map) continue northwards. On a clear day you can see some of the glaciers in the Parc National des Écrins to the west.

Climb to the top of the more southerly of the Beauregard *téléskis* (ski lifts) and on up to the grassed track leading north under the longer téléski. About an hour from the track junction, you reach the top end of the téléski. Negotiate the rocky knoll above, then head for the prominent cairn on the ridge, from where a series of sheep paths generally follow the highest ground along the intricate succession of rocky knolls, steadily rising towards the vertical cliffs below. Pass above the next téléski (des Cassettes) and keep to the ridge crest as far as the base of a precipitous shaly peak, then descend slightly to the track leading to the top of the **Téléski Grand Serre** (about two hours from the top Beauregard téléski).

Then, it's not too difficult to make your way across the lower reaches of the scree slopes and rocky ground beneath **Pic de Château Renard**, to grass and the observatory road. Walk up the road to the **observatory**, a smallish white dome; the path to the summit continues northwards, close to the cliff edge and up to the small crest for a superb 360° panorama.

Walk down the road, skilfully engineered to avoid steep gradients, almost to the small timber building that is **Cabane de Labounnais** (about 1¼ hours from the top). The formation of the old **canal** leading west and north-west from here round the mountainside is clearly identifiable. It provides a very pleasant final stage of the walk, with fine views of the valley. Not far beyond a short, steep drop on the path, turn off along a broad track which then descends steeply towards the village via the *Hotel du Château Renard*

(1¼ hours from the cabane). En route to the hotel's bar, Australian walkers may recognise framed photos of scenes from south-west Tasmania; while the Australian co-owner is proud to serve Australian wines, Foster's is not on tap.

Parc National du Mercantour

Protecting the heart of the Maritime Alps, the park's central zone of 68,500 hectares contains many spectacularly rugged peaks, deep sinuous gorges, alpine meadows, lakes, dense forests, a rich array of flora and fauna and an extraordinary assemblage of Bronze Age rock engravings. The long narrow park, created in 1979, extends for 80km south-east from the town of Barcelonette to the road across Col du Tende into Italy, and its northern limits partly share the Italian border. The centre has no permanent settlements; the periphery of 136,500 hectares, home to about 18,000 people, embraces the middle reaches of several valleys: the Verdon, Ubaye, Var, Tinée, Vésubie and Roya. Here you will find almost unspoiled Provençal villages, dominated by churches and often built on elevated sites. The traditional practice of taking large flocks of sheep up to alpine pastures from the lowlands is still carried out on a much smaller scale – the area has long suffered from depopulation.

The glacially sculpted granite peaks, separated by sharply angled ridges, may not be high by alpine standards (only four over 3000m, topped by Cime du Gélas; 3143m), but they lack nothing in scenic splendour.

The park is well served by waymarked routes: the GR5 threads through its north-western half then turns south to head for Nice, and the GR52 (and its variants) more or less continue eastward then south and out of the park to the Mediterranean coast near Menton (see Other Walks at the end of this chapter). There are many other routes,

Parcs Sans Frontières

In practical recognition of the fact that wildlife does not respect national frontiers – artificial lines drawn on maps – the Parc National du Mercantour and Italy's Parco Naturale delle Alpi Marittime joined forces in 1987 to cooperate in their natural and cultural conservation work. Building on success, the link was formalised in 1998 when a threefold charter was signed to improve their understanding and preservation of the area's heritage and to bring people together. The ultimate aim is to create a single large European park under European law.

Back in 1993 the parks' efforts had been rewarded with the Council of Europe's coveted Diplôme Européen, given to internationally important reserves for their nature conservation achievements (see also the National Parks & Reserves section in the Facts about France chapter). The Diplôme was renewed in 1998, testimony to the parks' successes in getting the forestry and pastoral sectors more involved and in preparing management plans.

Among the most notable successes have been the reintroduction of species long absent from the Alpes Maritime. The handsome ibex was virtually hunted to extinction in Italy in the 19th century, and fared little better in France. Between 1987 and 1995, 68 ibex from elsewhere in France and from Italy were helicoptered to several sites in the park and set free. Breeding has been successful and numbers are steadily increasing. A small number are wearing Argos tags which emit a specific signal every other day; this is picked up by a satellite, enabling park staff to check the animals' movements. A small number of bearded vultures were also brought in during the late 1990s, but several years are needed for the birds to settle down and begin breeding.

For walkers, the French-Italian guide, *Montagnes Sans Frontières du Col de Larche à La Mediterranée*, includes four 1:50,000 maps. A great deal of background information sets the scene for descriptions of a variety of walks, the routes of which ignore the dotted France-Italy border line on maps.

waymarked and not, some making use of traditional paths; this section focuses on a sample of these – three varied day walks from a base high in the Vésubie Valley.

NATURAL HISTORY

More than 2000 species of flowering plants, including 200 which are rare and 40 endemic, are found in the park; the orchid population is particularly numerous – 64 of France's 150 species. Forests of holm oak, groves of olives and fields of fragrant lavender clothe the lower southernmost slopes. They give way to firs and abundant larch, juniper, alpenrose and bilberry. Brilliant displays of wild flowers adorn the grassy alpine meadows in spring and early summer, vivid blue spring gentians being among the first to appear, followed by other species of gentian, primroses, lilies and later, various colourful thistles, including the unusual, ground-hugging carline thistle, with a white disc of thin bracts (similar to leaves) surrounding a dark centre.

The lammergeiers, or bearded vultures, have been reintroduced to the park, and royal eagles are also present. In the pine woods, the chewed remains of pine cones on the ground betray the presence of the crossbill, which feeds on the seeds; the male is bright red and usually easier to spot than the green-brown female.

The ibex population, another reintroduction, now numbers more than 400 (see the boxed text 'Parcs sans Frontières'). The wolf returned to the area in the early 1990s after an absence of 50 years, but by the end of the decade its presence and protected status had aroused the anger of mountain farmers who claimed that wolves had slaughtered thousands of sheep. Mouflon were brought in by hunters before the park was established. You should also see plenty of chamois and marmots, and perhaps red squirrels, roe deer and hares; cicadas in the forests and grass snakes near lakes are reminders of the Mediterranean character of part of the park.

PLANNING

The following planning information is relevant to all three walks in this section.

When to Walk

From late June to early July the wild flowers are most prolific and the higher ground should be snow-free. Afternoon showers and thunderstorms are common during July and August; during September and early October, the weather is likely to be more settled.

What to Bring

You may want to carry walking poles (and/or an ice axe early in the season). On two of the walks, Col de Cerise and Mercantour Lakes, you should carry drinking water as the streams are polluted with grazing livestock.

Maps & Books

Didier Richard's 1:50,000 *Mercantour: Massif and Parc National* sheet No 9 covers the eastern part of the park and the walks described in this section, but the IGN 1:25,000 *Vallée de la Vésubie* sheet No 3741OT provides much more detail. The latter is dotted with numbers in small yellow circles, representing the location of an extensive system of numbered signposts along walking paths, set up by the Conseil Général des Alpes-Maritimes. These signs are referred to in the walks described here.

The Didier Richard guide, *Alpes de Sud: Mercantour-Merveilles*, lacks maps, whereas its *50 Sommets sans Corde dans le Mercantour et le Haut-Verdon* by Jean-Louis Daumas has planimetric maps. The FFRP's Topo-Guide *Tinée-Vésubie: Vallée des Merveilles, Parc National du Mercantour* (No 507) covers the GR5 and GR52 through the park and down to the Mediterranean coast, including the area covered here.

It's rare to find a free and useful walking guide, but they do exist. Ask at the tourist office for a copy of *Rando Haut Pays*, published by the Conseil Général des Alpes-Maritimes, which contains exhaustively detailed and beautifully illustrated descriptions of more than 50 walks in the area.

Regulations

Please make sure you're aware of the strict national park regulations which apply to all the areas covered by the walks described here. They're set out in the boxed text 'National Park Regulations' in the Facts for the Walker chapter.

NEAREST TOWN
Saint-Martin Vésubie

The small, old town of Saint-Martin Vésubie, clinging to steep slopes above the Vésubie River, is just within the periphery of the national park, and has all the services you'll need before venturing farther afield. The walks described in detail are based at the peaceful hamlet of Le Boréon, about 8km farther up the valley, where there are just two hotels, a restaurant, a gîte d'étape and a public telephone.

The helpful tourist office (☎/fax 04 93 03 21 28), place Félix Faure, in the centre of Saint-Martin, is open most days throughout the year. Maps, guides and local information are available and the daily France Météo forecast is prominently displayed.

The maison du parc (☎ 04 93 03 23 15), 8 rue Kellermann Sérurier, is open from 9 am to 12.30 pm and 2 to 6.30 pm Saturday to Wednesday from early May to the end of September. You can pick up free leaflets or buy specialised nature and walking guides (in French) for the park (generally 55FF to 65FF). There's also a permanent exhibition about the contentious introduction of the wolf to the park.

The local office of the Association des Guides, Accompagnateurs et Amis des Alpes Meridionales (☎ 04 93 03 26 60), in rue Cagnoli, runs guided walks in the nearby mountains for beginners and experienced walkers alike. The local branch of the outdoor gear chain Technicien du Sport (☎ 04 93 03 26 60) is also in rue Cagnoli; it stocks Epigas, clothing and equipment, and is open daily. A shop called Oceanic, near the prominent town hall, sells Camping Gaz and an incredible array of useful items, including lithium batteries. In rue Cagnoli, Aux Milles Articles is open from 8.30 am to 12.30 pm and 4 to 7.30 pm Tuesday to Saturday, plus Sunday afternoon; it has the widest range of maps and guides in the town. The post office provides a currency exchange service.

The local mountain rescue contact is ☎ 04 97 22 22 22.

Places to Stay & Eat *Le Touron Camping and Gîte d'Étape* (☎ 04 93 03 21 32), in route de Nice, is 1.8km south of Saint-Martin by the main road, where prominent signs indicate its location. It's open all year (by arrangement for the gîte); the nightly tariff for the gîte, which has a kitchen, is 66FF; you'll pay 50FF for a tent and two people in the spacious camping area.

Most convenient for the walks is *Gîte Le Boréon* (☎ 04 93 03 27 27) in Le Boréon, which has single and double rooms and small dorms. You could pay 95FF for B&B, but for 190FF per night you will also have a superb, five-course evening meal. The owners are very helpful and knowledgeable. Rooms at the two hotels in Le Boréon are in the 250FF-plus range, as are most of those in Saint-Martin; the tourist office can provide a detailed accommodation list.

In Saint-Martin, among several reasonably priced possibilities for a meal is *Chez Michele (60 rue Cagnoli)*; it seems positively subterranean from the street but has a quiet, covered terrace which overlooks the Vésubie Valley. It's open from 6 pm daily; the extensive menu includes pizzas (40FF to 48FF) and steaks (55FF to 90FF).

For self-caterers, there's a *Petit Casino* in ave Kellermann Sérurier (close to the maison du parc) which sells Camping Gaz, a *Proxi* supermarket near the bus station, and several *boulangeries* and other *shops* selling local produce.

Getting There & Away By public transport, you need to reach Nice, which is well served by trains from Marseille and Paris' Gare de Lyon, and destinations outside France. Transports Alpes-Maritimes (TRAM; ☎ 04 93 03 20 23, ☎ 04 93 89 47 14) runs a bus service from Nice to Saint-Martin daily during summer (Monday to Saturday only from early September to late June). During summer the service goes on up to Le Boréon on Thursday and Saturday (53FF one way). The bus leaves stand No 7 at Nice's bus station, 5 blvd Jean Jaurès, about 1km south of the train station. This must be one of the most spectacular bus rides in France; after it leaves the broad Var Valley it enters the seemingly impenetrable gorge of the Vésubie River, round blind corners and through curving tunnels. The bus stops at Nice airport, so air travel from most European cities is a possibility. If you're stuck in Saint-Martin without transport, Taxi Teobaldi (☎ 04 93 03 33 92) will take you up to Le Boréon for 95FF.

By road Saint-Martin is 64km from Nice via the N202 towards Digne, then the D2265 up the Vésubie Valley.

Col de Cerise

Duration	5½ hours
Distance	10km
Standard	medium
Start/Finish	Le Boréon
Nearest Town	Saint-Martin Vésubie
Public Transport	summer only

Summary A varied day through pine woodland and a dramatic rocky valley (home to many chamois) up to a col on the Italian border; an optional side trip visits a beautiful alpine tarn.

This day walk is a fine introduction to the Parc National du Mercantour, starting with a steep climb up Vallon du Cavalet, through mixed pine forest with colourful clumps of alpenrose, to a rocky, scree-encrusted valley framed by towering cliffs.

From the narrow Col de Cerise (2543m) on the Italian border, you look across some of the high, rugged peaks of the neighbouring Parco Naturale delle Alpi Marittime in Italy. On the way you pass tiny Lac de Cerise; the much larger Lac du Mercantour, filling a small valley above Vallon du Cavalet, is only 30 minutes, 150m ascent and 1km extra, and well worth the modest effort.

The climb (1000m in total) is pretty steep and unrelenting, with some respite only beside Lac de Cerise. The path is easy to follow and there are intermittent cairns along the way. On the IGN 1:25,000 map, the position of signpost No 376 is incorrect; it's now at the junction of the path to the col and the lesser route north-east to Lac du Mercantour.

Chamois live in this valley, and when the walk was surveyed, a group of eight grazed unconcernedly near Lac de Cerise.

THE WALK

See the Parc National du Mercantour map. From just above Gîte Le Boréon, follow the GR52 up to signpost No 371 and turn left. The long climb is mostly well graded through larch and Scots pine, interspersed with grassy glades and signs of former settlement – ruinous small buildings and stone-walled enclosures. After about an hour, the path crosses a stream and another half-hour takes you up to the edge of the trees.

The path surmounts a scree slope then crosses a grassed, rocky spur with tiny **Lac de Cerise** below. The climbing resumes in earnest up the mountainside, to the right of some more scree. About 30 minutes after leaving the woodland, you come to signpost No 376, at the base of a large granite bluff; on top of this rock the substantial remains of a WWII lookout post gaze over the valley. From here the cairned route crosses to the western side of the now narrow valley and zigzags up the steep slope, past some rusted barbed wire entanglements, to **Col de Cerise** (30 minutes from No 376), where Italian *parco naturale* signs rather than French *parc national* signs tell you where you are (also instructing you to keep out of the derelict barracks building nearby). The peaks in Italy are quite awesome in their density and sheer massiveness, reaching well above 3500m.

Return to signpost No 376 and follow the clear path from there up a steep spur to the edge of peaceful **Lac du Mercantour** (25 minutes), impressively overlooked by Cime du Mercantour (2772m).

The return trip takes about two hours.

Lac de Trécolpas

Duration	6 hours
Distance	13km
Standard	medium
Start/Finish	Le Boréon
Nearest Town	Saint-Martin Vésubie
Public Transport	summer only

Summary Through pine woodlands to awesome rocky valleys and a tranquil lake, overlooked by towering crags; call at an isolated *refuge* for lunch, which you may share with the chamois.

The GR52 in its entirety is a very demand-ing route, as this small sample, climbing 800m, reveals. From Gîte Le Boréon a well-defined path leads through pine woodlands up Vallée du Boréon. A detour from the route takes in the small, bright yellow Refuge de la Cougourde; the highlight of the walk is beautiful, peaceful Lac de Trécolpas. From the lake you can contemplate the incredibly steep climb the GR route then follows up to the extremely narrow Pas des Ladres, 300m above the lake.

Although the walk up the northern side of the Vallée du Boréon is very pleasant, it can be left for another day if you have a car. In this case, drive east along the minor road from Le Boréon to the car park at Vacherie du Boréon and follow the track from there to join the route on the northern side of the river. Even with this variation, a medium grading is warranted by the amount of climbing and the occasional roughness of the path. The GR52 part of the walk is adequately, although not generously, waymarked with the standard red and white stripes; the loop via the *refuge* fol-lows a well-used path, identified by cairns. Numbered yellow signposts at path junctions indicate the times to various destinations.

THE WALK

See the Parc National du Mercantour map. Join the GR52 just above Gîte Le Boréon and follow it steeply up, passing between two chalets in spacious grounds, to a junc-tion and signpost No 371; here, turn right. The path continues to climb steeply in pine woodland. There are two bridged stream crossings and another short climb; it then settles down to traverse the exceedingly steep, timbered slope of the northern side of the Vallée du Boréon on a good grade, for 1km or more. A gentle descent takes you to a junction near Vacherie du Boréon, an hour from the start.

About 500m farther on, the path turns north-eastwards. As the forest opens out, so

SOUTHERN ALPS

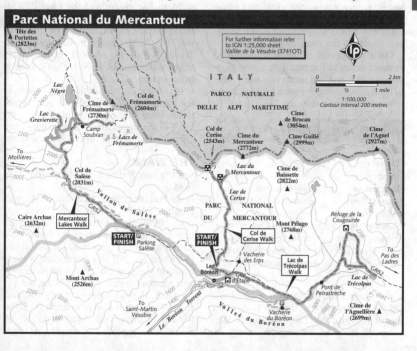

do superb vistas of the cascades on the tumbling Boréon Torrent. The valley widens around the meadows of Peïrastrèche, with major tributaries joining the Boréon from narrow valleys to the north-west and south-east. At signpost No 425 (1¾ hours from Vacherie du Boréon), leave the GR52 and continue north, climbing, but not too steeply, up to the **Refuge de la Cougourde** (☎ 04 93 62 59 99), owned by the CAF. Open from mid-June to the end of September, it serves drinks, sandwiches, soup and fruit tart during the day. The overnight fee is 80FF; evening meals cost 88FF and breakfast 32FF. While you're having lunch on the small terrace, you may be lucky enough to see a local chamois grazing nearby.

Continue along the narrow rocky path on the precipitous eastern side of the valley for about 1km to a track junction where you rejoin the GR52 (30 minutes from the *refuge*). From here it's a fairly short climb to **Lac de Trécolpas** – definitely a place to linger, contemplating the cliffs and peaks and enjoying the tranquillity. There's a causeway to the small island in the south-east corner of the lake.

Once you decide to leave, it's about 35 minutes down to the path junction at signpost No 425, and just under two hours back to Le Boréon along the same route that you followed earlier in the day.

Mercantour Lakes

Duration	6 hours
Distance	20km
Standard	medium
Start/Finish	Salèse car park
Nearest Town	Saint-Martin Vésubie
Public Transport	no

Summary A varied tour to three very different groups of lakes in contrasting settings, following well-defined paths and tracks; the walk described can be adapted to individual abilities.

If the weather is doubtful or if you're looking for a change from climbing to a col (or even a summit), then Parc National du Mercantour's lakes are the answer – many are easily accessible by good paths and are extremely scenic as well. The three featured here are excellent examples; they lie north-west of Le Boréon, between the Italian border and a minor road through Vallon de Salèse linking Le Boréon and the hamlet of Mollières, all overlooked by rugged peaks and rock-plastered ridges. The three together provide for a medium day's walk, or just one or two for an easy outing. In a wooded setting, Lac Gravierette is perhaps the most attractive of the three (it's also the lowest), the Lacs de Frémamorte are colourful and secretive, while Lac Nègre is the wildest and rockiest of the three.

The minor road up the Salèse Valley is closed at the national park boundary and is not serviced by public transport. If you decide to walk from Le Boréon (4km), you can follow the waymarked route of the GR52, partly along the road.

From the parking area, you follow the GR52 to Col de Salèse, from where the paths to Lac Nègre and the Lacs de Frémamorte are signposted and variously waymarked. Lac Gravierette is unidentified, so you'll definitely need a map to find it. Tracks are shown on both recommended maps, although the IGN 1:25,000 map is better option.

If you feel an irresistible urge to climb to the border, a well-defined path leads up to Col de Frémamorte (2604m) overlooking the lakes of the same name – about 200m extra climbing and an hour for the return walk.

THE WALK

See the Parc National du Mercantour map (p311).

From Parking Salèse, it's an hour's steepish climb on the well-used, stony tracks and paths, through pine woodland, to the road near the wide **Col de Salèse**. At signpost No 436, continue along the road for a short distance and turn off at a bend along a stony track (at signpost No 269). It soon narrows and becomes a path which climbs, steeply in places, through pleasant pine woodland, to the junction at Camp Soubran (signpost No 270, nearly an hour from Col de Salèse). From here, an old, well-made and quite stony track leads north up to **Lac Négre**; allow 35 to 40 minutes for the return walk.

Back at Camp Soubran, follow the very well-built path which winds eastwards up through the rocky landscape to a prominent knoll, topped by the remains of a stone chimney, a good vantage point for views of the turquoise **Lacs de Frémamorte** below (nearly an hour from Camp Soubran). Return again to the Camp Soubran junction and walk along the Lac Négre path for no more than 30m, then go left (west) downhill on a stony track. It traverses the flank of a lightly timbered spur, then turns north-west to cross the spur and pass a small, nameless lake, which may be dry at the end of summer. At a track junction here, the track, now grassed, continues generally northwards and gains a little height through scattered larches to reach **Lac Gravierette**. Unless the water level is high (possibly so in spring), it's easy to walk right round the lake, wandering between the low rock and grass-covered hillocks.

Follow the track back to the minor junction near the nameless lake and continue down, generally south and south-eastwards, to meet the track you followed up much earlier in the day, at signpost No 269 (30 minutes from the lake). From here, little more than an hour's walking takes you back to Col de Salèse and down to the parking area.

Other Walks

PARC NATUREL RÉGIONAL DU VERCORS
Cirque d'Archiane

This is an awesome, deep, cliff-bound valley on the rugged southern edge of the Vercors plateau and one of the outstanding features of the regional park. The web of signposted and largely waymarked paths on the Haut Plateau and beyond offers a choice of routes to explore the cirque. One of these, recommended by fellow walkers, is a two- or three-day medium walk, starting and finishing in Chichilianne (the base for the walks described earlier). From the village, climb to the plateau via the Pas de l'Essaure, continue north-west to Refuge de Chamailloux (above Pas de l'Aiguille) then south-west to join the GR91 at Les Quatre Chemins. Follow the waymarked route south, along a ridge

immediately west of the cirque and down to the small town of Châtillon-en-Diois.

Next day, follow the route of the Balcon du Glandasse (see the 1:25,000 map) east and north into the cirque and to the hamlet of Archiane. You can stay here and just soak up the local comforts and the spectacle of the cirque. Alternatively, continue on the route of the GR93 up through the cliffs of the cirque via a long narrow breach in the otherwise almost unbroken ramparts. Return to Chichilianne via either Pas de l'Aiguille (see the Rochers du Parquet walk) or Pas de l'Essaure.

There are gîtes d'étape in Châtillon – try *Le Suel* (☎ 04 75 21 13 49) and *Archiane* (☎ 04 75 21 11 02). For more information, contact the tourist office in Châtillon (postcode 26410; ☎ 04 75 21 10 07).

The map for the walk is the IGN 1:25,000 *Glandasse* sheet No 3237OT; the FFRP Topo-Guide (see Maps & Books in the introduction to this section) would also be useful.

La Grande Traversée du Vercors

All or part of this two-day walk, partly across the central section of the plateau and the nature reserve, offers an introduction to a different, more wooded and pastoral aspect of the Vercors. The route starts at the small town of Corrençon-en-Vercors and follows the GR91 south to Refuge de Pré Peyret. Here it turns west and finishes at Col du Rousset, somewhat unhelpfully a long way from main roads or public transport. However, from the *refuge* it's possible to head off in the opposite direction and then to descend from the plateau via either Pas de l'Aiguille or Pas de l'Essaure to Chichilianne. The overnight stop is at the small *refuge La Jasse du Play*; there isn't a *gardien* (caretaker) in residence, so you'll need to carry your own food. Alternatively, carry a tent in case the *refuge* is full, which is highly likely during July and August.

Corrençon is at the end of a VFD bus service from Grenoble; Chichilianne is 5km west of Clelles on the Grenoble-Gap railway line (see Getting There & Away for Grenoble earlier in this chapter). Contact the Association de Développement Touristique du Vercors (☎ 04 76 95 15 99), 38250 Villard de Lans, for more information about the Traversée du Vercors.

You'll need IGN 1:25,000 sheets *Villard-de-Lans* and *Glandasse*, Nos 3236OT and 3237OT respectively.

PARC NATIONAL DES ÉCRINS
Tour de l'Oisans

This is a challenging, highly scenic and varied circuit of the central zone of the national park, starting and finishing at the town of Bourg d'Oisans in the Romanche Valley, at the north-western corner of the park. The distance is around 200km but the amount of up and down is significant – more than 6000m. From near Bourg d'Oisans (717m), the route stays above 1000m almost all the way, crossing eight passes above 2300m en route. Allow from 11 to 14 days.

The route is that of the GR54, described in the FFRP Topo-Guide *Tour de l'Oisans* (No 508). The relevant maps are the Didier Richard 1:50,000 *Écrins Haut-Dauphiné* sheet No 6, or six IGN 1:25,000 sheets, Nos 3335ET, 3435ET, 3336ET, 3436ET, 3437ET and 3437OT. Accommodation is in *refuges* or gîtes d'étape. For more information, contact the Parc National des Écrins (☎ 04 92 40 20 10, fax 04 92 52 38 34), Domaine de Charance, 05004 Gap.

Access to Bourg d'Oisans is by VFD bus from Grenoble (☎ 04 76 47 77 77); points served by this bus include Vallouise from L'Argentière-la-Bessée (contact the tourist office in Briançon for timetable information on ☎ 04 92 21 08 50), and Le Desert (Valjouffrey) and Venosc (Vénéon) from Grenoble.

Vallée du Vénéon

The village of La Bérarde in this valley, on the western side of the Parc National des Écrins, lies in the shadow of its highest summit, Barre des Écrins. It's an excellent base for several day walks in the middle and upper reaches of the valley, and to *refuges* in the area, some at the edges of glaciers. La Bérarde is hallowed in local mountaineering history as the base for several first ascents in the 19th century, and these days is the starting point for some of the major climbs.

The valley is served by a VFD bus from Grenoble; the narrow D530 road leads to La Bérarde from Bourg d'Oisans in the Romanche Valley. For information about accommodation, contact the Parc National des Écrins (☎ 04 92 40 20 10, fax 04 92 52 38 34) or the tourist office in Saint-Christophe-en-Oisans (☎ 04 76 80 50 01).

For maps, either the Didier Richard 1:50,000 *Écrins Haut-Dauphiné* sheet No 6 or the IGN 1:25,000 sheets, Nos 3436ET and 3336ET, are relevant. *Walking the Alpine Parks of France & Northwest Italy* by Marcia R Lieberman has descriptions of walks in the valley.

PARC NATUREL RÉGIONAL DU QUEYRAS
Tour du Queyras

The Tour du Queyras is a circuit through the northern and central sections of the park, following the GR58 waymarked route. With its

four variants or loops (GR58A to GR58D), two of which cross the border into Italy, and a section of the mighty trans-Alps GR5, you can undertake a comprehensive exploration of the park's valleys, passes, high meadows and several of the villages. It isn't necessary to complete the full circuit, taking eight or nine days, since the loops create at least six shorter circuits of one to four days' duration from such bases as Aiguilles, Abriès and Ceillac. Accommodation is in gîtes and *refuges*; camping is also possible at established sites or in the wild.

For maps you'll need either the Didier Richard 1:50,000 *Queyras: Pays du Viso* sheet No 10 or the IGN 1:25,000 sheets, Nos 3637OT, 3637ET and 3536OT. The FFRP Topo-Guide *Tour du Queyras* is indispensable. For more information contact the tourist office in Aiguilles (see Information in the introduction to the Parc Naturel Régional du Queyras). For details of access, see Getting There & Away for Saint-Véran under the Parc Naturel Régional du Queyras; in addition, for the bus to Ceillac contact Autocars Favier (☎ 04 92 45 07 71).

PARC NATIONAL DU MERCANTOUR
Vacherie des Erps

Dotted about the lower reaches of some Mercantour valleys are *vacheries* (literally, 'cowsheds'), where cows were, and often still are, herded for milking.

Vacherie des Erps, about 1km horizontally and 350m vertically north-east of Le Boréon, makes a pleasant objective for an easy short walk. It could fill up to 2½ hours in an afternoon. The paths are clearly defined and signposting is adequate. From just above Gîte le Boréon follow the GR52 generally east to signpost No 379 and continue up to the vacherie through lightly timbered meadows and broad open areas. For the return go on westwards to signpost No 373 and back down to Le Boréon. The IGN 1:25,000 map is the one to consult.

Vallée des Merveilles

Near the eastern edge of the park, the valley and the nearby Cirque de Fontanalbe constitute a unique, internationally important site where, about 3500 years ago, early Bronze Age people created around 30,000 rock engravings, the biggest such open-air collection in Europe. After years of desecration, access to the most vulnerable part of the valley is now very strictly regulated. You can explore part of the area independently on official paths with interpretive signs; visits to the central protected area are only permitted with approved guides, or on one of the guided walks run from the nearby Refuge des Merveilles. It is forbidden by law to tread on or to touch the engravings; the penalty for so doing is a hefty fine – or imprisonment. For more information contact the Bureau des Guides du Val des Merveilles (☎ 04 93 04 77 73), 18 rue de France, in Tende; or the Bureau des Guides (☎ 04 93 03 26 60), rue Cagnoli, in Saint-Martin-Vésubie. Expect to pay at least 1000FF per person for the trip.

Access to the area is from Saint-Dalmas de Tende, on the N204 from Ventimiglia in Italy, and on the SNCF Nice-Turin railway line. From the limit of vehicle access at Lac des Mesches, 10km from Saint-Dalmas de Tende, it is about 8km on foot to *Refuge des Merveilles* (☎ *04 93 04 64 64*); the valley and the protected site is within an hour's walk from there. The *refuge* is open from mid-June to the end of September and half board is around 160FF.

The valley is covered by the Didier Richard 1:50,000 *Mercantour: Massif and Parc National* sheet No 9 and the IGN 1:25,000 sheet No 3841OT, and features in FFRP Topo-Guide *Tinée-Vésubie: Vallée des Merveilles* (No 507). The valley is traversed by the GR52 linking Saint-Dalmas Valdeblore, Le Bore and Menton on the Mediterranean coast. For more information, contact La Direction du Parc National du Mercantour (☎ 04 93 16 78 88, fax 04 93 88 79 05), PO 1316, 06006 Nice.

Before heading out to the valley, make sure you visit the Musée des Merveilles (☎ 04 93 04 32 50, fax 04 93 04 32 53), ave du 16 Septembre 1947, in Tende. It's open from 10.30 am to 6.30 pm daily except Tuesday from May to mid-October; during the rest of the year the hours are 10.30 am to 5 pm on the same days. As well as comprehensive displays about the valley, the books on sale include a fascinating account of the life and work of Clarence Bicknell, the first person to systematically record and interpret the engravings in the valley: *L'Échelle du Paradis – Clarence Bicknell et La Vallée des Merveilles* by Christopher Chippendale.

Traversing the Park

It's possible to walk right through the park by linking several of the FFRP's waymarked routes. The first stage is along the GR5 (en route to Nice) from Larche to Saint-Dalmas Valdeblore (seven or eight days). The next stage follows the GR52 from Saint-Dalmas to Sospel, another five days, including Vallée des Merveilles. Lastly, another two days will take you through to Menton on the Mediterranean coast. Alternatively, the GR56 from Sisteron (in the Durance Valley, south of Gap) meets the GR5 near Saint-Dalmas-le-Selvage, south of Larche (10 days).

These extremely scenic routes over high passes, along valleys through mountainous and often remote country, require a considerable degree of commitment as public transport connections are few. Sisteron is on the Briançon to Marseille railway line; Larche can be reached by bus from Gap station; Sospel is on the Nice to Turin railway line; and Saint-Dalmas Valdeblore is linked to Nice by bus. Accommodation is in gîtes and *refuges*, or camping where park regulations permit. The relevant FFRP Topo-Guides are *Grand Traversée des Alpes* (No 531) and *Tiné-Vésubie* (No 507). For maps the Didier Richard 1:50,000 *Alpes du sud* and *Mercantour: Massif and Parc National* sheets, Nos 1 and 9 respectively, will suffice, or several IGN 1:25,000 sheets.

For accommodation lists and a helpful *Guide Practique* for the Sisteron-Larche area, contact the Comité Départemental du Tourisme, Maison des Alpes de Haute-Provence (☎ 04 92 31 57 29, @ CDTL04@wanadoo.fr), 19 rue du Docteur Honnorat, 04005 Digne-les-Bains. For information on other areas crossed by the traverse, the Saint-Martin Vésubie maison du parc (listed under Nearest Towns in the Parc National du Mercantour section), and La Direction du Parc National du Mercantour in Nice (see La Vallée des Merveilles earlier in this section) are both useful. Sections of the GR5 are also covered in the Jura & Massif des Vosges and Northern Alps chapters of this book.

Northern Alps

NORTHERN ALPS

Boasting the highest and most spectacular mountains in Western Europe, the Northern Alps are one of the classic walking areas in France, if not the world. Several thousand kilometres of well-maintained and well-signposted paths give access to virtually every valley, meadow and glacier in the region. Most walkers will find something here to suit their level of fitness, whether it's enjoying low-level valley trails with views of the high mountains through the trees, or strenuous outings above the tree line. In the Chamonix Valley, *téléfériques* (cable cars or funiculars) can be used to access high-altitude trails with minimal effort.

This chapter is divided into two areas. In the northern half of the region (Haute-Savoie) the Chamonix Valley gives a wide range of convenient one-day walks dominated by impressive views of the Mont Blanc massif (for the Tour du Mont Blanc, see Other Walks at the end of this chapter). To the south, in the *département* (department) of Savoie, is Parc National de la Vanoise where the multiday Tour of the Vanoise Glaciers affords good mountain scenery and excellent opportunities for enjoying abundant alpine flora and fauna in less developed surroundings. Public transport is excellent in these areas and a liberal scattering of *refuges* (refuges or mountain huts) means that most overnight trips can be made with little more than a day-pack.

CLIMATE

The mountains of the Northern Alps have a huge influence on the climate of the area. In some instances they can enjoy better weather than the rest of France with the Pre-Alps often taking the sting out of the Atlantic weather systems that bring rain to the rest of the country. However, in the strong summer sun, with all the evaporation from snowmelt coupled with localised winds and updraughts created by the deep valleys, summer weather can often be markedly poor. It is not uncommon during summer to experience a fine morning followed by

GARETH McCORMACK

Walkers on the Grand Balcon Sud, with Grand Jorasse and Mer de Glace behind

- Stepping out onto the ice of the Glacier des Bossons on the Montagne de la Côte walk

- Looking out across the Mer de Glace from Signal Forbes on the Chamonix Aiguilles walk

- Views of Mont Blanc from the Grand Balcon Sud and profuse wild flowers near Vallorcine

- Watching a herd of ibex moving beneath glaciers in Parc National de la Vanoise

heavy rain and electrical storms in the afternoon, while just 100km away on the plains west of Grenoble, the skies will be clear and the weather fine. At an even more localised level, a bad storm can generate over the Mont Blanc massif while the sun may still be shining in the Chamonix Valley.

Northern Alps – Maps	
1 Grand Balcon Sud & Lac Blanc	p322
2 Chamonix Aiguilles	p326
3 Montagne de la Côte	p329
4 Vallorcine & Alpages de Loriaz	p332
5 Desert de Platé	p334
6 Tour of the Vanoise Glaciers	p338

Lake Geneva

N1

Évian-les-Bains

Yvoire

Thonon-les-Bains

Mijoux
Lajoux
Gex
Lélex

N5

Abondance

Ferney Voltaire

HAUTE-SAVOIE

Châtel

GENEVA

Annemasse

Les Gets
Morzine
Avoriaz

A40

Martigny

SWITZERLAND

To
Lyon

N201

Cluses

N205

Col des
Montets

Vallorcine

N508

Sallanches

Le Grand
Bornand

Chamonix

Argentière

Annecy

La Clusaz

Saint-Gervais

Mt Dolent
(3820m)

Lac
d'Annecy

Megève

GR5

TMB

A41

Duingt

Mont Blanc
Tunnel

Le Semnoz

N212

Mont Blanc
(4807m)

Courmayeur

SAVOY

To
Aosta

Aix-les-Bains

Le Châtelard

Albertville

Parc Régional du
Massif des Bauges

Col du Petit
Saint-Bernard

Bourg
Saint-Maurice

Seez

ITALY

Chambéry

Tarentaise
Valley

N90

Les
Arcs

GR5

Parc Régional
de Chartreuse

Moûtiers

La Plagne

Tignes

Val d'Isère

ISÈRE

Brides-les-Bains

DAUPHINE

SAVOIE

D915

N6

Courchevel

PARC NATIONAL
DE LA VANOISE

Col de
l'Iseran

Pralognan-la-Vanoise

Bonneval-sur-Arc

Les
Menuires

GR5

Bessans

Val
Thorens

Lanslebourg

Maurienne

La Dent
Parrachée
(3639m)

Col du
Mont Cénis

Isère River

Valley

A L P S

To
Grenoble

0   10   20 km
0   5   10 miles

1:970,000

Modane

To
Briançon

To
Turin

Susa

The walking season in the Northern Alps is all too brief. Typically, people begin to venture onto the trails in early June when the spring thaw is over, avalanche risk has fallen and there is not too much snow on the trails. On many popular routes where the trail is above 2000m, deep banks of snow will persist in localised pockets throughout July and into August (see the Warning). Early October sees the walking season drawing to an end, with snow falling and accumulating below 2000m.

Summer daytime temperatures in the valleys commonly reach 25°C and sometimes go as high as 30°C. At 2000m, summer daytime temperatures will rarely be more than 20°C (although the strong sun will make it feel hotter) with the temperature routinely falling close to freezing at night. June and July are commonly unsettled months. Typically you might experience two days of fine weather followed by three or four days of cloudy weather with evening storms. Moving into August the weather often settles down and September, although cooler, can give long spells of fine weather.

INFORMATION
Maps

The IGN produces two overview maps of the area covered by this chapter. Sheet No 112 of the 1:250,000 series *Savoie/Dauphiné* gives a good overview of the French Alps, while sheet No 53 of the excellent 1:100,000 series *Grenoble/Mont Blanc* is a great reference for trip planning.

For maps covering individual walks, see Planning in the introduction to each walk.

Books

A good overview book is *Walking the French Alps: GR5* by Martin Collins. For details of more specific books see the Planning sections for individual walks.

Information Sources

Agence Touristique Départmentale Haute-Savoie Mont Blanc (☎ 04 50 51 32 31, @ tourisme@cdt-hautesavoie.fr, www.haute savoie-tourism.com), BP 348-74012, Annecy Cedex, provides general tourist information

---

WARNING

Trails at elevations in excess of 2000m can be covered by banks of snow persisting well into the summer. Typical problems with snow banks will be navigation when the trail becomes covered with snow and the cloud is down. In such situations, unless there are cairns in place, staying on course may be tricky. If the snow is icy (first thing in the morning) and/or the slope is steep then a slip may be disastrous. If you expect to encounter icy snow an ice axe would be appropriate and perhaps also crampons if it is early in the season and snow has not had steps kicked into it. On most trails, however, the passing of feet rapidly cuts a trail into the snow and summer daytime temperatures quickly make the snow soft. Following exceptional winters where snowfall has been very high, sections of trail above 2300m may even be difficult throughout July.

---

on the Haute-Savoie. The Agence Touristique Départmentale de la Savoie (☎ 04 79 85 12 45, @ documentaion@cdt.savoie.fr), 24 blvd de la Colonne, 73000 Chambéry, provides similar information for the Savoie. Its Web site is at www.savoie-tourisme.com.

For general information on Parc National de la Vanoise, contact La Direction du Parc National de la Vanoise (☎ 04 79 62 30 54, fax 04 79 96 37 18), 135 rue du Docteur Julliand, BP 705, F 73007, Chambéry Cedex. It's also worth exploring the excellent Web site at www.vanoise.com.

Chamonix Valley

Bounded to the south by the glaciers and soaring rock spires of the Mont Blanc massif, and to the north by the Aiguilles Rouges with their (sometimes) mountain-reflecting lakes, the Chamonix Valley is one of the most popular walking destinations in Europe. More than 300km of trails provide opportunities for walks of all difficulties. Several téléfériques further enhance the potential for walkers of modest fitness, allowing access to high-level trails without the effort of ascent and descent. The mountains are very developed in comparison to Parc National de la Vanoise to the south, and walkers seeking a greater sense of wilderness may prefer to walk there.

The extremely rugged Aiguilles Rouges provide some of the classic walking in the valley and some of the best views of the Mont Blanc range. The Grand Balcon Sud is a two-day trip offering continuous and excellent views, while the one-day trip to Lac Blanc is equally spectacular but a little more strenuous. On the other side of the valley, the Grand Balcon Nord and the walk on Montagne de la Côte bring the walker as high into the mountains as they can go without becoming mountaineers. A little farther from the really popular trails, the walks in Vallorcine and to the Desert de Platé retain the excellent mountain views and boast an abundance of wild flowers.

GATEWAY
Chamonix

Chamonix must be the biggest summer destination for visitors to the Alps. As well as general tourists who come to look at the mountains and take a ride on the highest téléférique in Europe (the Aiguille du Midi; 3842m), the town is also packed by walkers and mountaineers from Europe and beyond. It's hard to escape the sense of purpose in the town as every second person you pass sports a walking pole, or a pack laden with ropes and ice tools. Naturally the town has plenty of accommodation and a concentration of restaurants and cafes in the centre. Note that even the camping grounds may be full in the peak season between mid-July and mid-August. With this in mind, and the convenience of public transport in the valley, it may be easier to seek accommodation in smaller towns such as Argentière (see Nearest Town in the Grand Balcon Sud walk).

Information Chamonix's efficient and helpful tourist office (☎ 04 50 53 00 24, fax 04 50 53 58 90, ☻ info@chamonix.com), 85 place du Triangle de l'Amitié, can provide listings and advice on accommodation, public transport, local events, walking routes, *refuges* and

the téléférique. For more informed advice about trail conditions on the route you intend to take, go to the nearby Maison de la Montagne, 190 place de l'Église, where on the 2nd floor you'll find the Office de Haute-Montagne (☎ 04 50 53 22 08). You'll find a notice board in the entrance with a long-term weather forecast in English.

Chamonix has its own weather centre providing local forecasts for walkers and climbers. For a forecast, call ☎ 06 36 68 02 74 or see the bulletin posted three times daily on a notice board at 134 ave de Courmayeur. Chamonix has around 10 outdoor gear shops. You'll find three Internet terminals at Café Santa Fe, on rue du Docteur Paccard.

Places to Stay & Eat Open from mid-June to mid-October, *Camping Les Molliasses* (☎ 04 50 53 41 06) is across the main road from the Aiguille du Midi téléférique station. It has excellent shade and its own shop and restaurant. However, it is short on toilet facilities at peak times. The charge per person is 26FF with a supplement of 18FF for each tent. Baggage storage is 20FF a night. Other camping grounds close to Chamonix include *L'Île des Barrats* (☎ 04 50 53 51 44) and *Camping Les Arolles* (☎ 04 50 53 10 42).

The *auberge de jeunesse* (☎ 04 50 53 14 52, ☻ chamonix@wanadoo.fr) is 2km south of the centre on the bus route to Les Houches. There is no kitchen, and dorm beds are 70FF a night (closed from October to mid-December). *Gîte La Montagne* (☎ 04 50 53 11 60) has a kitchen and dorm beds for 65FF, breakfasts for 28FF and is only closed from mid-November to mid-December. For other *gîtes d'étape* (hostel-style walkers' accommodation), see Argentière in the Grand Balcon Sud walk later in this chapter. Chamonix has a good selection of hotels.

Le Bumbelbee Bistrot, in the cobbled walkway of rue des Moulins, is an attractive little place with vegetarian dishes and international cuisine. All dishes are a la carte. The bar has Cafferys & Murphys stout for those Irish beer lovers. *Brasserie L'M* (☎ 04 50 53 00 11) is a stylish restaurant at the north end of rue du Docteur Paccard. It does a good range of crepes and has a large a la carte selection. *Menus* (fixed-price meals of two or more courses) start from 100FF. Nearby, **La Taverne de Chamouny** serves food until 1 am. Crepes, pizzas, fondues and plenty of fish are available, with *menus* for 65FF to 99FF. *Café Santa Fe* (☎ 04 50 53 99 14) is a popular hang-out with young, trendy types. It does good Tex Mex and large burgers. *Menus* are 65FF to 80FF. Finally, *Pizza Hop* (☎ 04 50 53 14 86), on ave du Courmayeur, does excellent pizzas for 40FF to 50FF.

Getting There & Away Chamonix has excellent rail and bus connections to its closest international (Geneva, Lyon-Satolas, Turin) and regional (Grenoble) airports. The Chamonix train station (☎ 04 50 53 00 44) is at the end of ave Michael Croz, five minutes' walk from the centre. The narrow-gauge track which serves the valley connects to the main railway network at Saint-Gervais-les-Bains, from where there are connections to all major destinations, including Geneva airport, and also to Moûtiers (129FF) for Parc National de la Vanoise. The line runs north as far as Martigny in Switzerland.

SAT Autocar has several buses each day via different routes to Annecy (95FF). There is also one bus each day to Grenoble (157FF) and two each day to Geneva airport (188FF). The SAT Autocar (☎ 04 50 53 01 15) office is inside the train station building; buses depart from outside the train station.

A SATOBUS (☎ 04 72 35 94 96) service runs twice on weekdays and three times a day on weekends to Lyon-Satolas airport (3¼ hours, 340FF). There is also a twice-daily service into Italy: to Courmayeur (53FF) and Turin (three hours, 138FF). Chamonix Bus (☎ 04 50 53 05 55) runs local services in the valley, which are much cheaper than using the train.

PLANNING
The following planning information is relevant to all the walks described in the Chamonix Valley.

When to Walk
The valley attracts tremendous numbers of walkers during the summer season and you

---

Téléfériques & Télésièges

On long, steep descents you sometimes wonder what's going to be left of your knee joints for later life. If you already have bad knees or simply don't relish 1000m of continuous downhill, then the *téléfériques* (cable cars or funiculars) and *télésièges* (chairlifts) of the Chamonix Valley will probably seem like a godsend. Of all the walks described in the Chamonix Valley section of this chapter only one, Vallorcine & Alpages de Loriaz, is not served by some form of mechanised lift. They are a boon also for the lazy walker who wants the views without the sweat, and on walks like Chamonix Aiguilles you can skip the climb and descent and simply stroll along the balcon path 1000m above the valley floor without too much thought of the difficulty.

I have to confess that I didn't bother too much about the téléfériques to begin with. Indeed I was, and to a certain extent still am, a little bothered by the intrusion (both visually and mentally) they represent, into what I normally like to see as a wild environment. But they are a necessary part of the infrastructure of the ski and tourist industries in the Alps. The access they provide to the mountains attracts people who would normally regard the high mountains as the reserve of the very fit. There is definitely something to be said for the feeling of whooshing silently and effortlessly over the heads of walkers on the trail below, especially when they started out an hour ahead and still won't get there before you.

Gareth McCormack

---

can expect to encounter literally hundreds of people on the trails. July and August are the busiest months; June is quieter, but late-lying snow and poor weather may make walking difficult. September is also quieter and often sees more settled weather than the other summer months. Walks in the evening can be much less busy, plus you can be up high to watch the evening light on the peaks. You should, however, be prepared to descend in the dark.

Alpine orchid.

Alpine harebell.

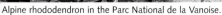

Alpine rhododendron in the Parc National de la Vanoise.

Lac Blanc, Chamonix Valley.

Grand Jorasse (4208m), Chamonix Valley.

GARETH McCORMACK

The high, alpine areas of the Parc National de la Vanoise are breathtakingly beautiful.

GARETH McCORMACK

Stopping for a break at a mountain refuge in the Chamonix Valley.

GARETH McCORMACK

Climbing the Mont Blanc trail.

NEIL WILSON

The soaring pinnacles of the Aiguilles de Chamonix, from the Grand Balcon Nord in Chamonix Valley.

What to Bring

Although all of the Chamonix Valley walks are on paths, many of the paths higher up can be rough and boulder-strewn. Walking boots with ankle support are recommended, preferably light canvas-style boots. Warm clothes and protective gear (even gloves) should be carried on higher walks, and walking poles give good support when crossing snow banks. Early in the season you might consider carrying an ice axe for the walk to Lac Blanc.

Most of the walks cross streams formed from snowmelt, which means there are opportunities to refill water bottles along the way. Most walkers seem to drink the water without purification (including the author). Two exceptions are the Vallorcine and Desert de Platé walks, for which you should carry plenty of water from the start.

Maps & Books

IGN 1:25,000 *Massif du Mont Blanc* sheet No 3630T covers the following walks: Vallorcine & Alpages de Loriaz, Grand Balcon Nord and Lac Blanc. You'll need this sheet and IGN's 1:25,000 *Samöens Haut-Giffre* sheet No 3530ET for the Grand Balcon Sud. Montagne de la Côte is covered by IGN 1:25,000 *St-Gervais* sheet No 3531ET. The *Samoëns Haute-Giffre* map covers the Desert de Platé walk. Didier Richard 1:50,000 *Pays du Mont Blanc* sheet No 8 covers all of the above, although the map detail is very cluttered and can be difficult to read.

Chamonix Mont Blanc – A Walking Guide by Martin Collins gives in-depth coverage of the popular and less popular walks in the valley. *Mont Blanc Trails* by René Bozon is also a detailed guide compiled from local knowledge and is widely available in Chamonix in both French and English editions.

Permits & Regulations

Wild camping is forbidden in the Chamonix Valley, although discreet camping is permitted between 7 pm and 7 am. In practice this means you can camp overnight, but you can't leave your tent up during the day. Although many people appear to flout this rule without any trouble, you do run the risk of having your tent confiscated. See the boxed text 'National Park Regulations' in the Facts for the Walker chapter for other park rules.

In the Réserve Naturelle des Aiguilles Rouges, wild camping and picnicking are forbidden, in order to protect the delicate alpine habitat.

Grand Balcon Sud

Duration	2 days
Distance	20km
Standard	easy-medium
Start	Col des Montets
Finish	Chamonix
Nearest Town	Argentière
Public Transport	yes

Summary A classic *balcon* trail, contouring above a valley floor, with impressive views of Mont Blanc. A steep initial climb leads to easy walking at a high level. The final viewpoint of Le Brévent is followed by a long descent.

Giving spectacular views of the Mont Blanc massif from a relatively easy balcon path, the Grand Balcon Sud is a classic walk and is understandably popular. The Tour du Mont Blanc long-distance walk is routed along it (see Other Walks at the end of this chapter) so you'll be following the red-and-white waymarkers of that walk. It is possible to cover the route in a single day if you can handle 10 or 11 hours of walking, or if you finish the walk at Le Brévent and descend to Chamonix on the Téléférique du Brévent. A two-day traverse will suit most walkers and the easy days give time to include side trips to Lac Blanc (see the Lac Blanc walk description later in this chapter), Lacs Noir and Lac Cornu, and to create your own traverse of the Aiguilles Rouges.

HISTORY

The Grand Balcon Sud was one of the first significant walking paths to be built in the Chamonix Valley, constructed in 1924 by Charles Vallot and originally running between the Col des Montets and Planpraz. It now extends to Le Brévent and down into Les Houches, just south of Chamonix.

NORTHERN ALPS

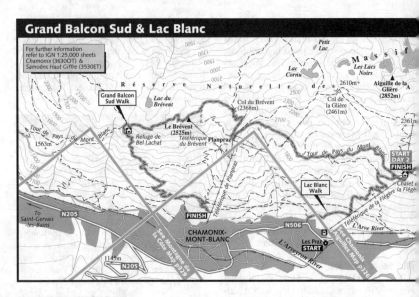

NATURAL HISTORY

The walk passes through the Réserve Naturelle des Aiguilles Rouges. This 3278-hectare reserve was created in 1974 and takes in a large swathe of the northern Aiguilles Rouges. There is a visitor centre (☎ 04 50 54 02 24) at the Col des Montets that is open from June to September from 9.30 am to 12.30 pm and 1.30 to 7 pm (to 6.30 pm in June and September). There is a 2km nature trail beginning from the centre, on which interesting alpine plants are identified. On the walk proper, the diversity of plants and flowers on the climb onto the balcon path is particularly impressive.

NEAREST TOWN
Argentière

For walkers and climbers the small town of Argentière is a popular alternative to Chamonix as a base for activities. There is a good range of accommodation and services, and the public transport connections are excellent. There is a tourist office (☎ 04 50 54 02 33) and several outdoor gear shops.

Places to Stay & Eat The two-star *Glacier d'Argentière* (☎ 04 50 54 17 36) is 200m off the N506, 10 minutes' walk south of the town. It is open from mid-June until the end of September. It is popular with climbers although the pitches are rather sloping and there is no shade. *Le Belvédère* (☎ 04 50 54 02 59) is a friendly and comfortable *gîte d'étape* just downhill from the centre of town. Dorm beds are 60FF and private doubles from 194FF. *Les Randonneurs* (☎ 04 50 54 02 80) is five minutes' walk downhill from the centre of town and caters, as the name suggests, for walkers; the owner takes guided walks every week. Doubles cost from 195FF.

There are several restaurants in town. Worth mentioning is *Le Dahu* (☎ 04 50 54 01 55), which serves local specialities. The *sandwich bar* in the shopping mall south of the town centre serves cheap, filling sandwiches from 20FF.

Getting There & Away Chamonix Bus (☎ 04 50 53 05 55) runs services from Chamonix (20 minutes) to Argentière and beyond to Le Tour and the Col des Montets. Buses run from 7 am until 7.35 pm. There is a train station served by the narrow-gauge line which runs the length of the Chamonix

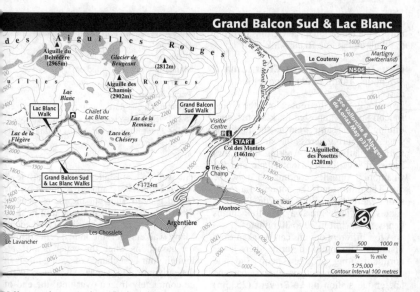

Grand Balcon Sud & Lac Blanc

Valley and across into Switzerland. Call ☎ 08 36 35 35 35 for information.

GETTING TO/FROM THE WALK
To the Start
Take the bus (☎ 04 50 53 05 55) to the Col des Montets (the start of the walk). If you have a car there is plenty of parking at the col. The first bus leaves Chamonix at 8.30 am, arriving in Argentière at 8.50 am. Thereafter there are buses to Col des Montets every two hours. A more frequent bus service runs to Montroc (as does the train), from where you can pick up a path running through Tré-le-Champ and along the road to the Col des Montets (20 minutes).

From the Finish
The walk finishes in Chamonix. For details of transport out of Chamonix, see the Gateway section earlier in this chapter.

THE WALK
Day 1: Col des Montets to La Flégère
4–5 hours, 7km, 690m ascent
Take the path immediately behind the visitor centre and begin to climb onto the open

lower slopes of the Aiguilles Rouges. Turn right at a junction and climb steeply as the trail begins to make switchbacks through rock outcrops and escarpments. The slopes, in the main free of pine trees, are rich in wild flowers (rosebay willowherb grows in large swathes lower down). After two hours the climb eases and the trail stops making switchbacks, flattening out onto the **balcon**. Keep an eye out in this area for ibex.

Easy walking on the balcon follows, rising and descending gently among lichen-covered boulders and rhododendron, while across the Chamonix Valley the whole Mont Blanc massif (in good weather) is laid out in full splendour. After almost 2km on the balcon, a junction is reached. A path to the right is signposted for Lac Blanc, and a short distance farther on, a path to the left descends to Argentière. The Balcon Sud is signposted straight ahead for La Flégère (2km, 45 minutes).

A short descent is made and then the generally flat walking which characterises the balcon routes resumes, to reach the téléférique station and ***Chalet de la Flégère*** (☎ 04 50 53 06 13). This *refuge* is open from 12 June to the end of September. Dorm beds

NORTHERN ALPS

are 70FF and evening meals 80FF. For details of the téléférique, see Getting To/From the Walk in the Lac Blanc walk.

Day 2: La Flégère to Chamonix

6–7 hours, 14km, 650m ascent, 1500m descent

From La Flégère the route along the Grand Balcon Sud is signposted for Planpraz, continuing in the same vein as the previous stage, contouring across the slopes and affording relatively easy walking. The views across the valley to Mont Blanc and the Chamonix Aiguilles continue to draw the eye. The trail rounds the bottom of a rocky spur where the Téléférique de Planpraz comes into view, 1km away. The trail climbs gently to reach it in 20 to 30 minutes.

A few different options can be taken from Planpraz. The routing described here is the normal routing of the Balcon Sud and climbs to the summit restaurants, bar and téléférique station on **Le Brévent** (2525m) via the **Col du Brévent** (2368m). Alternatively, many people climb direct to Le Brévent on a far from aesthetic 4WD track, climbing through a wide gully to reach the summit. Easiest of all is to take the téléférique (☎ 04 50 53 13 18) to the summit and continue on foot from there (a one-way ticket is 47FF). Finally you could continue at the same height on the routing of the Tour de Pays du Mont Blanc for another kilometre before descending to Chamonix from Plan Latchet.

The route to the Col du Brévent is signposted from Planpraz and climbs north steadily before making a few steep switchbacks to reach the col in 30 to 45 minutes. A signpost and snow banks mark the top. The route to Le Brévent climbs a little farther onto a rocky ridge before dropping behind it and across a basin of boulders and shattered rock slabs. The trail then climbs round a rocky shoulder (handrails in places) to meet the 4WD track coming up direct from Planpraz. The summit is 10 minutes' steady climb farther up from this junction. Views from Le Brévent are understandably excellent, taking in the Mont Blanc massif and the limestone cliffs and plateau of the Desert du Plâté.

Lac Blanc

Duration	6 hours
Distance	12km
Standard	medium
Start/Finish	Les Praz
Public Transport	yes

Summary A beautiful visit to a high alpine lake. In still weather the lake gives a classic reflection of the Mont Blanc massif. Views on the ascent are excellent.

The walk to Lac Blanc offers similar views of the Mont Blanc massif to those on the Grand Balcon Sud, but the main focus of the trip is the beautiful alpine tarn held by the rock walls of the Aiguille du Belvédère. Many walkers seek the famed reflection of the mountains when the water is still, although your best chance of seeing this is in the early morning. The lake will most likely be completely frozen over until the end of June. By August, most (but not all) of the lake will be free of ice and snow.

The walk described here ascends on the path and descends on the Téléférique de la Flégère (see Getting To/From the Walk later in this section). Many people however use the téléférique for both ascent and descent, leaving a relatively easy day to get to Lac Blanc and back (grade: easy-medium). But the ascent through pleasant pine forest is worthwhile and provides a much greater sense of achievement when you finally arrive at the lake.

NEAREST TOWN
Les Praz

The village of Les Praz is 40 minutes' walk north of Chamonix. There is an outdoor gear shop in the main street if you need to pick up last-minute supplies.

Places to Stay & Eat

Camping Mer de Glace (☎ 04 50 53 08 63) has excellent facilities and although a bit more expensive than the Chamonix sites, small tents can sometimes be pitched without a site charge, reducing the price and making it excellent value.

Auberge Gîte La Bagna (☎ 04 50 53 62 90) has dorm beds for 70FF and doubles for 200FF. Other than this and the camping ground, accommodation is basically limited to a couple of hotels and it may be easier to stay in Chamonix (see Gateway earlier in this chapter).

La Cabane (☎ 04 50 53 23 27) is a very attractive chalet-style restaurant which includes an outside terrace with good views of Mont Blanc. The *food store* is in the main street.

Getting There & Away

Chamonix Bus (☎ 04 50 53 05 55) runs services to and from Chamonix with a service at least every hour. There is a bus stop in the main street. The train station (☎ 08 36 35 35 35) is at the east end of the village, on the Chamonix Valley railway line.

THE WALK

Go to the west end of Les Praz village and cross the L'Arve River. Look out for a signpost on the right for La Flégère and Lac Blanc. Continue to follow these signs as you pass through several junctions. Sometimes the walking is on the flat, contouring in a north-easterly direction, and sometimes you'll be climbing steeply on switchbacks. The top of the Téléférique de la Flégère is just above the tree line at 1877m and about two hours' walk from Les Praz. Beside it is *Chalet de la Flégère* (see the Grand Balcon Sud walk description for details).

Turn right onto the Grand Balcon Sud, pass under a *télésiège* (chairlift) and then turn left onto a path signposted for Lac Blanc. Climb on switchbacks alongside another télésiège before passing underneath it and climbing more gently to Lac de la Flégère. Passing the lake, a large cairn is reached marking the boundary of the Réserve Naturelle des Aiguilles Rouges, and shortly after this the trail begins to climb steeply. From here a one-hour climb will bring you to **Lac Blanc**. Before mid-July you may be crossing snow banks near the top.

Chalet du Lac Blanc (☎ 04 50 53 49 14) is set above the eastern shore of the lake, recently rebuilt after an avalanche partially destroyed it. Half board is 270FF and

reservations are recommended. The lake itself is actually two lakes, and many people miss this point entirely. Beside the *refuge* is a small lake about 30m across in which you can (sometimes!) see the famed reflection of the Mont Blanc range. It is fed by a small stream which, if followed, leads to a much larger lake above and behind the first, but not visible from the *refuge*.

From Lac Blanc take the path heading east towards the Lacs des Chéserys. The path descends at first over rocky ground with splashes of paint showing the way. It then descends farther on switchbacks to the shores of a westerly outlier of the lakes. From here descend along a ridge from where, if you want to see the other lakes, you'll need to detour off-trail to the left. In another five minutes you reach a junction with the Grand Balcon Sud. Turn right onto it and follow it for 45 minutes, contouring fairly easily to arrive back at La Flégère.

The last descent to Les Praz on the Téléférique de la Flégère (☎ 04 50 53 18 58) is at 5 pm (5.30 pm from mid-July until mid-August) and travel one way is 44FF.

Chamonix Aiguilles

Duration	6–7 hours
Distance	13km
Standard	medium-hard
Start/Finish	Chamonix
Public Transport	yes

Summary A challenging walk on good trails with superb mountain scenery, including a classic view of the Mer de Glace. The walk can be made easier by using a téléférique and/or a mountain railway.

The Chamonix Aiguilles (Needles) form what is probably the most celebrated mountain ridge in Europe. Stretching north-east from Mont Blanc, the 4km ridge is broken and serrated into tremendous pinnacles and spires along its entire length. The Grand Balcon Nord, like its sibling the Grand Balcon Sud, contours across the mountain at a height just above the tree line and just below the level where you need to be a climber to go much farther. It is in essence a great path on which to get really close to the high, alpine environment, and with a superlative lookout across the Mer de Glace glacier, it will appeal to those who appreciate the architecture of these mountains.

The walk described here begins and finishes in Chamonix, going as far north on the Grand Balcon Nord as Montenvers. The difficulty of the walk can be greatly reduced by using the Aiguille du Midi téléférique and the Montenvers tourist train respectively. Doing so would reduce the grade to that of an easy-medium walk. Otherwise

you'll be ascending 1330m and descending the same, which makes for a very solid and rewarding day's walk.

GETTING TO/FROM THE WALK
To the Start
The walk begins in Chamonix (see Getting There & Away for Chamonix earlier in the chapter). You do have the option of using the Téléférique de l'Aiguille du Midi (☎ 04 50 53 30 80) to reach the Grand Balcon Nord, thus avoiding a long climb. A one-way ticket to Plan de l'Aiguille (from where you can access the Grand Balcon Nord) is

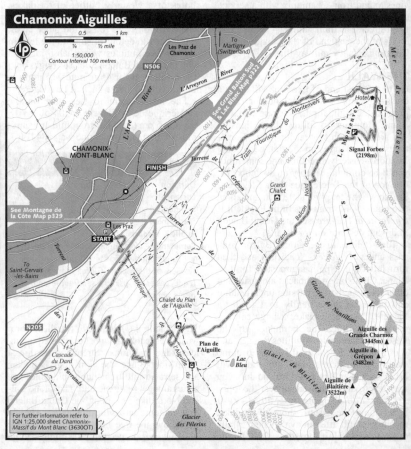

Living Glaciers

The Mer de Glace (on the Chamonix Aiguilles walk) and Glacier des Bossons (on the Montagne de la Côte walk) are two spectacular examples of very different types of mountain glacier.

The Mer de Glace is a classic example of a valley glacier, a slow-moving tongue of ice descending to low elevations from a meeting place of several smaller glaciers. It is probably the best-known glacier in Europe, and at 14km long it is the second longest in the Alps. It is 1800m across at its widest point, and as much as 400m deep. The movement of the ice varies from year to year, but recent movement has been at 45m a year at the edges and up to 90m a year in the middle. Although it is crevassed in places, the moderate gradient of the valley floor means that the Mer de Glace is not as heavily crevassed as some other glaciers. It often serves therefore as a route of ascent and descent for mountaineers on the Grande Jorasses.

By contrast, the Glacier des Bossons is almost entirely an icefall, extremely steep and heavily crevassed, with gradients of 45° in many places. It is in fact the largest icefall in Europe, driven downwards by the weight of snow accumulating in the extensive névés on Mont Blanc. Huge seracs collapse continuously under the pressures of a fast descent: the glacier currently moves at some 250 to 300m a year.

A branch of the Glacier des Bossons, the Glacier du Taconnaz, is typical of a hanging glacier, with its terminal face resting on very steep ground. Violent avalanches from these glaciers are not uncommon, with large sections of serac breaking away and thundering into the valley. You'll see many hanging glaciers on the Tour of the Vanoise Glaciers, described later in this chapter. Below is an explanation of some glacier terminology. For a description of landform features left behind by melted glaciers, see the boxed text 'Signs of a Glacial Past' in the Facts for the Walker chapter.

ablation zone – where the annual rate of melt exceeds snowfall
accumulation zone – where the annual snowfall exceeds the rate of snowmelt
bergschrund – crevasse at the head of a glacier
blue ice – ice compacted and metamorphosed into an airtight mass
crevasse – deep crack or fissure in the ice
firn line – the line between the accumulation and ablation zones
ice fall –the frozen equivalent to a waterfall as the glacier descends over steep ground
lateral moraine – mounds of debris deposited along the flanks of a glacier
névé – masses of porous ice not yet transformed into blue (glacier) ice; also called firn
serac – pinnacle of ice among crevasses on a glacier
sinkhole – depression in the glacial surface where a stream disappears underground
terminal moraine – mound of debris at the end of a glacier

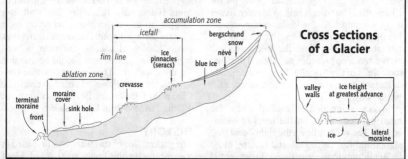

Cross Sections of a Glacier

65FF. Cable cars leave at frequent intervals beginning at 7 am (6 am July and August).

From the Finish

The walk finishes in Chamonix. You have the option of using the Montenvers train (☎ 04 53 50 12 54) to return to Chamonix from the far end of the walk. The last train descends at 6 pm and costs 56FF one way.

THE WALK

A trail enters the forest from the far right-hand corner of a car park opposite and across the road from the Aiguille du Midi téléférique station. There is a signpost for Plan de l'Aiguille. As the trail climbs immediately into the forest, switchbacks lead steadily upwards. Within the first 30 minutes there are two trail junctions. Keep to the right and keep climbing on a long straight section of path, which becomes less shady as you reach the southern flanks of the ridge and the junction with a trail coming up from Cascade du Dard. You now have good views across the Glacier des Bossons and Montagne de la Côte.

The trail now climbs for a long time, back and forth on long switchbacks. The slopes are very open and there is a good deal of new growth after avalanche damage. Pass some large granite boulders and make a traverse back to the left before climbing on tight switchbacks out of the tree line and up to *Chalet du Plan de l'Aiguille* (☎ *06 85 17 31 25*), a small, homely *refuge* 2½ hours from the start.

Follow signposts behind the *refuge* for Montenvers, ignoring a trail dropping off for Chamonix. The balcon path to Montenvers is a joy, winding across wild slopes strewn with jumbles of granite boulders. Here and there a few stunted pines flout the tree line. Just above, moraine precedes glacier and the high rock walls of the Aiguille. There are a couple of streams from snowmelt where you can fill water bottles.

In 2km a junction is reached where the main path continues on the level to Montenvers. The walk follows the right-hand trail signposted for 'La Signal' and leading in 20 to 30 minutes to the superlative viewpoint at **Signal Forbes** (2198m). The view of the Mer

de Glace is probably the classic view in the Chamonix Valley. Keep a look out for chamois on the rocky shoulder above. Descend steeply and quickly (20 minutes) to Montenvers and the *hotel* (☎ *04 50 53 12 54)*, where there is a path and téléférique giving access to the edge of the glacier.

From Montenvers the trail descends steadily through pine forest back to Chamonix, roughly along the same course followed by the railway (1½ hours). Just before halfway on the descent from Montenvers is a small *cabin* selling cold drinks.

Montagne de la Côte

Duration	6 hours
Distance	8km
Standard	medium-hard
Start	Chalet du Glacier des Bossons
Finish	Les Bossons
Public Transport	yes

Summary A tremendous walk with magnificent views of the Glacier des Bossons and the upper reaches of Mont Blanc. The route was originally used by Balmat and Paccard on the first ascent of Mont Blanc.

This walk is similar to the Chamonix Aiguilles in that it brings the walker to the boundary between the worlds of the walker and the mountaineer. At La Jonction (The Junction), the high point of the walk, you can step onto the glacial ice and look out across an ocean of ice and seracs to the summit of Mont Blanc, only 4km away. The walk is a straight up and down route, returning by a slightly different path. Although it involves some 1200m of ascent, the path is well benched and graded and should be suitable for most walkers. The walk is described assuming that the télésiège is used to reach the Chalet du Glacier des Bossons, cutting out 400m of ascent from Les Bossons.

HISTORY

The general line of this walk was first used to gain access to the lower sections of Mont Blanc during early attempts to climb it. On 7

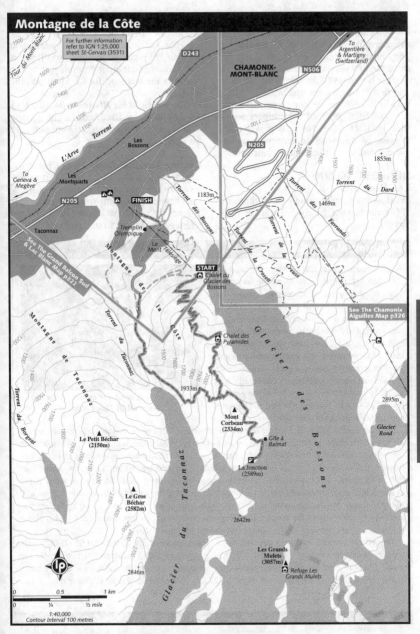

Montagne de la Côte

For further information refer to IGN 1:25,000 sheet St-Gervais (3531)

Tour du Mont Blanc

D243

CHAMONIX-MONT-BLANC

N506

To Argentière & Martigny (Switzerland)

L'Arve

Torrent

Les Bossons

N205

1853m

Torrent du Dard

To Geneva & Megève

Les Montquarts

1183m

N205

Torrent des Bossons

1469m

Torrent des Favrands

Taconnaz

FINISH

Tremplin Olympique

Torrent de la Creuse

Le Mont Téléskège

Montagne

START

Chalet du Glacier des Bossons

Torrent de la Croeti

See The Grand Balcon Sud & Lac Blanc Map p322

de

See The Chamonix Aiguilles Map p326

la

Côte

Chalet des Pyramides

Glacier

2895m

Torrent du Taconnaz

Montagne de Taconnaz

1933m

des

Mont Corbeau (2334m)

Glacier Rond

Torrent du Borgeat

Le Petit Béchar (2150m)

Gîte à Balmat

Bossons

La Jonction (2589m)

Le Gros Béchar (2582m)

Glacier

2642m

du

Taconnaz

Les Grands Mulets (3057m)

Refuge Les Grands Mulets

2846m

0   0.5   1 km

¼   ½ mile

1:40,000
Contour Interval 100 metres

NORTHERN ALPS

August 1786, Jacques Balmat and Dr Michel Paccard climbed Montagne de la Côte as far as the area now known as the Gîte à Balmat. They bivouacked here and the next day became the first people to summit Mont Blanc (see the boxed text 'Climbing Mont Blanc'). The first female ascent was made by Marie Paradis in 1808, on the same route. This trail has now been superseded by others accessible by téléférique. Interesting Web sites relevant to this walk include www.mont-blanc.to and www.glacier-montblanc.com.

NEAREST TOWN
Les Bossons

Les Bossons is really a southern continuation of Chamonix itself, barely five minutes away by bus.

Places to Stay & Eat The shady camping ground, *Les Deux Glaciers* (☎ *04 50 53 15 84*), has flat pitches for 26FF per person with an 18FF charge per tent. You'll see it and two other camping grounds just before reaching the bus stop for Le Mont and the télésiège.

Glacier du Mont Blanc (☎ *04 50 53 35 84, 224 route des Tissières)* is a gîte d'étape also close to the télésiège. Dorm beds are 80/110FF.

Getting There & Away From Chamonix, Chamonix Bus (☎ 04 50 53 05 55) runs services to Les Bossons approximately every hour beginning at 7 am. You may want to get a ticket for Le Mont, where you'll find the *télésiège* and places to stay and eat.

Climbing Mont Blanc

When Jacques Balmat and Dr Michel Paccard became the first people to stand on the summit of Mont Blanc they would never have foreseen the modern summer scene of maybe 100 people or more summiting on a fine day. But Mont Blanc is not a technically demanding mountain if climbed by the popular Gôuter route, and is within the reach of fit walkers with a good head for heights who are prepared to hire a guide. Walkers with some mountaineering experience could easily go it alone, as long as they are heedful of the weather conditions – the route is very exposed and becomes extremely dangerous in poor weather.

Capturing a spectacular sunrise from the summit of Mont Blanc

My own ascent followed a period of poor weather and there were maybe 200 climbers setting off from the Refuge de l'Aiguille du Gôuter at 2 am in a surreal procession of headtorches snaking up the mountain. By sunrise, strong winds had turned many people back as we reached Les Bosses ridge, a knife-edge of snow not far from the summit. The wind was lashing us with a painful spin drift of ice chunks and the altitude was beginning to tell – walking seemed to involve a few paces at a time with rests in between, all the while intently studying the gaiters of the climber in front and trying to ignore the tremendous drops on either side. We summited at 7 am, dazed by the altitude and thinking more about the descent than the view. What took five hours to ascend took an hour to descend, seeing us back at the Gôuter Hut in time for breakfast!

The world-famous Compagnie des Guides de Chamonix Mont Blanc (☎ 04 50 53 00 88) guide the mountain every summer. The cost is 3600FF per person with a maximum of two people per guide. Check its Web site at www.cieguides-chamonix.com. You can find out more about the route at the Office de Haute-Montagne (☎ 04 50 53 22 08), 190 place de l'Église, in Chamonix.

Gareth McCormack

GETTING TO/FROM THE WALK

Télésiège du Glacier du Mont Blanc takes you to the beginning of the walk at the Chalet du Glacier des Bossons. The cost is 30/50FF one way/return, and it starts running at 8.30 am with the last return at 7 pm.

If you want to walk from Le Mont (climbing 400m to the chalet), simply follow the trails crisscrossing the ski slopes to the left of the télésiège. The télésiège is beside the Le Mont bus stop in the south end of Les Bossons.

THE WALK

From the **Chalet du Glacier des Bossons** (☎ 04 50 53 03 89), which serves meals and drinks, there is already a good view of the Bossons icefall and especially the huge, clean and deeply crevassed terminal face. Forty-five minutes on, forested switchbacks lead to **Chalet des Pyramides**. From this small, basic *refuge* there is a view across the middle of the icefall, and a trail leads down from the *refuge* to the edge of the ice. At this point the glacier still seems well below the path, and the views disappear again as the trail climbs steeply above the *refuge*, crossing onto the western slopes of Montagne de la Côte to gain views of the Glacier du Taconnaz. Thirty minutes from the *refuge* there is a junction. To the right (west) a path descends down to the terminal face of the Taconnaz glacier (the return route).

For the moment, keep climbing east from this junction on steep switchbacks, which bring you to a notch in the ridge. Passing through this, an impressive view of the séracs of the upper Bossons icefall appear. The trail contours for a short distance beneath the steep flanks of a ridge and then begins to climb again where the ridge gives way to a clean sweep of rocky ground. The climb from here to La Jonction is rough but generally straightforward, although there are two or three rocky steps where you'll need to use your hands. Yellow splashes of paint mark the line of least resistance.

In 30 minutes from the beginning of this final climb you reach a group of house-sized granite boulders, the historic bivouac site known as the **Gîte à Balmat** (see

History at the beginning of this walk section). **La Jonction** is only five minutes' climb beyond, where the rock of Montagne de la Côte is subsumed by the sweep of ice coming down from Mont Blanc.

Return along the same trail to the junction with the path descending to the Taconnaz glacier. The path to the glacier is rough and awkward in a couple of places, although most walkers will have no trouble. It gives excellent views of the terminal face of Taconnaz. Once past the terminal face, the path descends along a grassy moraine ridge. Note the avalanche deflectors far below – this whole valley sees large and violent avalanches in the spring. The path descends farther and then traverses through pine forest to meet the 4WD track leading from Le Mont to the Chalet du Glacier des Bossons. The top of the télésiège is uphill 500m away. Descend on foot by following the 4WD track downhill to the ski jump and then following tracks down to the finish.

Vallorcine & Alpages de Loriaz

Duration	5 hours
Distance	11km
Standard	medium
Start/Finish	Vallorcine
Public Transport	yes

Summary A very pleasant outing to an alpine meadow profuse with wild flowers. Views of the Mont Blanc massif are excellent. A chance to step across the border into Switzerland.

This walk through lovely alpine meadows is a great way to escape the crowds of the more popular walks in the Chamonix Valley. Just across the Col des Montets, you'll be able to step across the border into Switzerland at the northern limits of the walk. There are good possibilities here for strenuous side trips, and fitter walkers will find an exploration of the great mountain scenery around Lac du Vieux Émosson (via the Col de la Terasse) very rewarding. This variation would merit a grading of hard for a one-day trip. The walk described here starts and finishes at Vallorcine train station.

NATURAL HISTORY

This is an excellent walk for those who appreciate wild flowers. On the ascent to Refuge de Loriaz, the sides of the path are thick with different species, most of them common, but you'll probably find some rarer species in the profusion. Among the more common species are harebell, goat's-beard, vipers bugloss, early purple orchid and pyramidal orchid. Lower down are large swathes of rosebay willowherb.

NEAREST TOWN
Vallorcine

Vallorcine is on the N506 between Chamonix and Switzerland, and the name of this small village is generally used as an umbrella name for the many small hamlets spread throughout the valley both north and south of Vallorcine itself. There is a small tourist office (☎ 04 50 54 60 71) in the car park of the train station.

Places to Stay & Eat Complete with its own restaurant, *Camping des Montets* (☎ 04 50 54 60 45) is about 15 to 20 minutes' walk

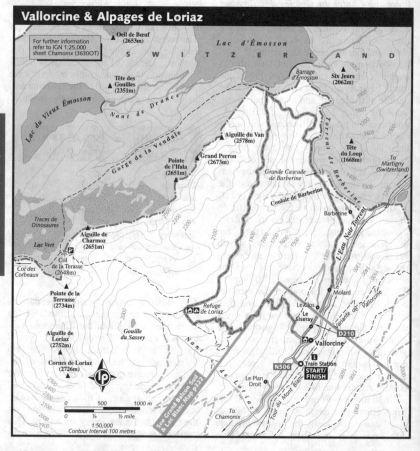

Vallorcine & Alpages de Loriaz

south of Vallorcine train station. The local gîte d'étape, **Chalet-Gîte Mermoud** (☎ 04 50 54 60 03), is on the N506 where the walk leaves the road, and is open all year.

L'Arrêt Bougnête is beside the train station and serves crepes and a small bistro menu. **La Ferme des 3 Ours** (☎ 04 50 54 63 06) serves farm-style dishes and is in Le Plan Droit, 10 minutes' walk south of Vallorcine.

The single **shop** sells bread, fruit and vegetables.

Getting There & Away Trains run between Chamonix and Vallorcine train station (☎ 04 50 54 60 28) throughout the day at almost hourly intervals. The trip takes about 30 minutes and a return ticket costs 44FF.

THE WALK

From the train station and tourist office turn right onto the N506 and walk along it past a shop. After 100m turn left at signposts for Le Siseray and Le Clos. In another 50m you'll see a sign for Refuge de Loriaz (1½ hours) nailed to the side of a small building. Follow this to the left and then another two signs for 'Loriaz' leading you through tidy chalets and, it would seem, someone's front garden before climbing out of Vallorcine on a grassy path lined with rosebay willow-herb. Keep left at two junctions and climb steadily through pockets of pine. In clearings the path is lined with an abundance of flora and associated insect life.

The path climbs more steeply through thicker pine cover before breaking out onto the **Alpages de Loriaz** ablaze with flowers, under wide-ranging views of Mont Blanc. **Refuge de Loriaz** (☎ 04 50 54 06 45) is only another 10 to 15 minutes' climb from here, where you'll find a small restaurant and dorm beds for 62FF.

From here the balcon path is signposted to Lac d'Émosson and it gains another 60m in altitude over the next 2km to reach a shoulder where Lac d'Émosson and its dam come into view. The path descending to the lakeshore is rough. At the lakeshore there is a junction with the Tour du Ruan (a four-day walk, half in France and half in Switzerland). The mountain backdrop to the

glacial green waters of the Émosson reservoir is impressive, and at this point you are also right on the border with Switzerland.

Follow the sign for Vallorcine (1½ hours) and descend a steep and arduous track for 40 minutes, passing through new growth of birch and ash where avalanches have felled significant stands. Follow more signs for Vallorcine as the trail gradually flattens out, crossing a couple of old rock avalanches. In another kilometre you reach a sealed road at Le Molard, only 500m from Vallorcine.

Desert de Platé

Duration	6 hours
Distance	13km
Standard	medium
Start/Finish	Praz Coutant
Nearest Town	Plateau d'Assy
Public Transport	yes

Summary A steep and exciting climb to a high plateau of limestone pavement and wild flowers. This is followed by a circuit across a rocky ridge and a descent by the route of ascent.

The limestone plateau of the Desert de Platé is a wonderful contrast to the granite and glacier of the Mont Blanc massif. Although views on the ascent to the plateau are dominated by the latter, the ambience of the walk is well removed from the other walks described in this chapter. Those interested in rock formations will find the limestone pavement features fascinating (see Natural History following), while there is also plenty of botanical interest.

The ascent of 850m to the plateau is steep and unrelenting. Close to the top the path crosses a slightly exposed section to gain access to the plateau, which from below appears to be barred by huge cliffs. For some, reaching Refuge de Platé will be enough, but others will want to climb a little farther to the Col du Colonney and return via a circuit across the Tête des Lindars.

NATURAL HISTORY

The limestone of the plateau is a good example of limestone pavement. Here, the covering soil of the plateau has eroded away to expose the limestone to the weathering effect of water, to which it is particularly susceptible. Weathering works upon the lines of weakness in the limestone beds, widening and deepening cracks and joints to create deep fissures known as grikes. The slabs of beautiful white limestone in between are called clints. The overall pattern of clints and grikes is known as limestone pavement. The rich, calcareous soils, which accumulate in the sheltered grikes, support an abundance of wild flowers including the tall, late-blooming yellow gentian.

NEAREST TOWN
Plateau d'Assy

This is a quiet and neat village with plenty of facilities. The tourist office (☎ 04 50 58 80 52), in the main street, has plenty of information on shorter walks in the area.

Places to Stay & Eat At the end of the D43 in Plaine Joux, *Aire Naturelle de Camping de Plaine Joux* (☎ 04 50 78 00 03) is open from June to September. From here walkers can follow the route of the Tours de Pays du Mont Blanc west for 45 minutes to reach the path ascending to the Desert de Platé.

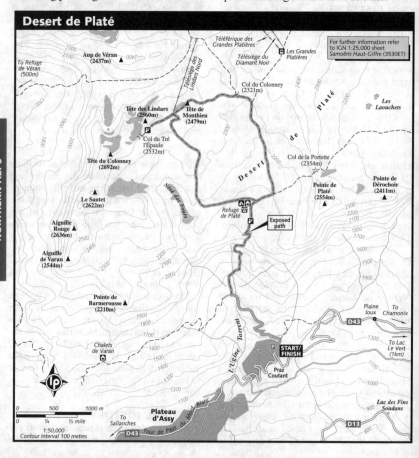

In Plateau d'Assy, *Les Gentianes (☎ 04 50 58 83 91, 740 rue des Granges)* is a pleasant gîte d'étape with good views. A dorm bed with breakfast is 110FF. *Les Charmettes (☎ 04 50 93 84 12, 291 route du Dr Davy)* has double rooms for 100FF.

Both of the gîtes have restaurants. In addition, *La Ferme D'Assy (☎ 04 50 93 82 22)* does pizzas and take-away food. Near the tourist office is a *supermarket*.

Getting There & Away To reach Plateau d'Assy take an SAT bus (☎ 04 50 53 01 15) from Sallanches, on the main train line between Chamonix and Annecy. The first bus is at 8.25 am with departures approximately every two hours after that. The return fare is approximately 80FF.

GETTING TO/FROM THE WALK

The bus that serves Plateau d'Assy continues to the start and finish of the walk at Praz Coutant a few kilometres farther up the road (see Getting There & Away above). If you are driving, simply follow the D43 east from Plateau d'Assy for 3km to a very sharp right-hand hairpin bend, with a parking area on the right and a wooden cross on the left. The walk starts and finishes here.

THE WALK

Just across the road from the layby and to the right of the large cross is a lane with a signpost for Refuge de Platé. Walk up this for 100m, turn left at a small memorial and follow a path, which runs along the top of an avalanche deflector. The path leads onto a 4WD track, which climbs steadily through a mixed forest of pine and beech. After 30 minutes the trees thin out and a path climbs off to the right with another signpost for the *refuge*. At this point you can see the extent and scale of the cliff line apparently barring an ascent onto the upper plateau.

The path climbs steeply and without much respite up scrubby slopes, twice crossing a dry river bed as numerous switchbacks attempt to make the gradient more amenable. Once at the foot of the first cliff the path traverses west beneath it and then climbs round some outcrops and up a ramp

of easier ground above. The path continues across steep slopes of scree, still quite well benched, and then climbs directly underneath an oppressive, dripping rock wall before traversing back to the west. Just ahead is an airy 5m section of metal walkway spanning a gap where the trail has fallen away. The walkway has a good handrail and is quite straightforward. Just beyond it the trail climbs gently onto grassy slopes. In another couple of minutes the first limestone pavement appears and then the **Desert de Platé** itself comes into view, with slabs and outcrops of eroded and fissured limestone stretching off in all directions. The numbers and variety of wild flowers and insects to be found in the fissures confirm that this plateau is anything but a desert.

Refuge de Platé (☎ 04 50 93 11 07) at 2032m is only five minutes away in a small hollow backed by low cliffs. Run by the Club Alpin Français (CAF), it is open from 19 June until the end of September. Beyond the hut the ground rises steadily towards **Col du Colonney** (2321m). A path leads east for a few hundred metres and then swings to the north into a small valley. After 1km the path climbs diagonally across steeper slopes and then swings round to the west above some outcrops to reach the col. From here a signposted path climbs gently west towards the Tête des Lindars (2560m). In 30 minutes, after covering some rocky ground, the trail reaches the top of the Télésiège des Lindars Nord (2484m) and another 20 minutes will see you at the **Tête des Lindars**; from here there are fine views across the Desert de Platé. Return to the top of the télésiège and turn right, descending to the south onto a broad shoulder. From the shoulder the path leads across limestone pavement, turning east to reach the *refuge*. Return by the route of ascent.

Parc National de la Vanoise

Created in 1963, the Parc National de la Vanoise was the first national park to be set up in France. Its fully protected central zone covers almost 530 sq km of 3000m-high peaks, attendant glaciers and high alpine meadows. Alpine flora and fauna are to be found in abundance, especially the ibex (see the boxed text 'The Ibex'), which has been reintroduced to the park.

For the walker this means a markedly different experience from that in the Chamonix Valley, where the development of ski pistes and téléfériques has detracted from the inherent wildness of the alpine environment. With lower mountains (the highest summit in the park, La Grand Casse, is only 3855m) than the Chamonix Valley, the park attracts fewer walkers and you can expect the trails to be slightly quieter than some of the Chamonix trails. However, this is all relative and it will still seem busy to walkers who are used to more remote areas. In 1996 an average of around 7000 walkers used the principal trails of the Tour of the Vanoise Glaciers compared with around 10,000 for the world-famous Tour du Mont Blanc. Regardless of this, the views throughout are generally excellent and the trails are well benched and signposted.

The Tour of the Vanoise Glaciers is the only walk described in detail here. However, there is a great deal more to be done both in terms of one-day and multiday walks. See Other Walks at the end of this chapter for more information.

NATURAL HISTORY

Protected somewhat by the Pre-Alps and Belledonne range from Atlantic rains, the Vanoise massif enjoys a relatively dry and sunny climate. In summer, however, it is subject to the microclimates of high mountain areas, with the high mountains often developing their own bad weather (see Climate at the beginning of this chapter).

More than 1000 species of plant can be found above the 1500m contour, comprising mainly alpine species but also oriental, southern and arctic species. Nationally protected species to be found in the park include Alpine columbine, bicoloured sedge, cortusa, dwarf scorpion-grass, Alpine eryngo and the only French colonies of linnaea.

The fauna of the park is perhaps even more spectacular, with 1200 ibex and 4700 chamois roaming the central area. Rodents such as marmot, mountain hare and snow vole are preyed upon by fox. Other carnivorous mammals include badgers, pine martens, beech martens and stoats. With an eye to the sky you might be lucky enough to spot one of the 16 pairs of golden eagles resident in the park. Other notable bird species include black grouse, ptarmigans, rock partridges, eagle owls, Tengalm's owls and black woodpeckers. Look out too for bearded vultures, or lammergeiers, recently reintroduced into the Haute-Savoie/Mont Blanc region and now spreading south into the Vanoise.

Tour of the Vanoise Glaciers

Duration	5 days
Distance	59km
Standard	medium-hard
Start/Finish	Pralognan-la-Vanoise
Public Transport	yes

Summary A memorable circuit in a national park created to protect the ibex. It has all the flavour of alpine walking: good mountain scenery, abundant wildlife and several tough climbs.

This five-day walk makes a varied and beautiful circuit of an extensive mountain massif with dome-like summits reaching heights of 3500m. The extensive glaciers are an almost daily view and some of the *refuges*, such as Refuge de la Vallette and Refuge de la Col de la Vanoise, are set in spectacular alpine surroundings. Coupled with an almost guaranteed sight of ibex at some point, this walk is a classic alpine outing.

Some walkers complete the walk in four days, but five is a much better schedule, and almost mandatory if you are carrying camping gear. Even six would not seem unduly leisurely given the abundant opportunities to watch wildlife, appreciate the wild flowers and take in the views. There are *refuges* sited at the end of each day, although in July and August you would do well to book a bed in advance. All of the

The Ibex

In five weeks walking in the Northern Alps my most impressive experience was that of following a herd of male ibex *(Capra ibex)*, known in France as the *bouquetin*. We were on the Tour of the Vanoise Glaciers not far from the foot of the Glacier du Dôme de Chasseforêt. In the high alpine setting, among rock slabs and alpine herbs, with a backdrop of snow and ice, these powerful animals with their huge, distinctive curved horns seemed like true lords of their world. As we followed them, they regarded us with a casual indifference, moving together over banks of snow, and pausing where they found patches of greenery.

It is hard to believe that these animals were extinct in France by 1800. From the 16th century they were a prime game animal and supposed medicinal properties in their flesh and horns only exacerbated the hunting pressure on them. The situation of decline was the same throughout the Alps. Just 40 or 50km away from the Vanoise, across the border in Italy, a small population of around 100 ibex held on in the fastness of the Gran Paradiso and this herd was to become the nucleus of reintroduction programs throughout the Alps. The 1963 creation of Parc National de la Vanoise was primarily to provide a protected environment for the new herds of French ibex. From the 50 individuals originally placed in the park, there are now some 1200, representing 50% of the French and 5% of the European populations. The park has also benefited the chamois, with which female ibex are often confused; the chamois have increased from 500 animals in 1963 to about 4300 in 1986.

The ancient domestic ancestry of the ibex has left them with a residual tameness not shared by the chamois, and this lack of fear still brings them into confrontation with mountain villagers. In winter, ibex will often come into villages looking for food and may occasionally mate with goats. For the purposes of watching ibex, it is best to stay downhill of them; doing so, it is sometimes possible to get within 5m.

My second-best ibex experience was watching a pair of ibex calves standing on the top of a small cliff, separated from the rest of the herd (a mixture of females and young) by a group of trekkers. Unsure of themselves for a few moments, instinct kicked in and they launched themselves down the cliff face in what seemed like a controlled fall. They landed upright and in a full run, already true masters of the mountain environment.

Gareth McCormack

refuges can provide breakfasts and evening meals, and all have kitchens for those who wish to self-cater. National park *refuges* charge 70FF per night for a dorm bed, while the CAF huts charge 78FF. Both charge half-rate for camping. Water is never in too short supply, but in the limestone areas between Refuge du Fond d'Aussois and Refuge de l'Arpont it can be a long way between streams, so you should try to carry a litre with you.

NATURAL HISTORY

The Glaciers de la Vanoise descend from a broad mountain backbone ranging between 3000 and 3500m. The extensive high ground has allowed deep and substantial névé (masses of porous ice not yet frozen into glacier ice) to form, pushing down tongues of ice across the steeper ground below and resulting in some beautifully hanging glaciers. See the boxed text 'Living Glaciers' earlier in this chapter.

You'll be unlucky if you don't see ibex on the circuit and you'll find it impossible not to see marmot scampering away across the grass and rocks, especially at the Col de la Vanoise where feeding has left them virtually tame. The best place to see ibex is probably on the day between Refuge de l'Arpont and the Col de la Vanoise. See Natural History earlier in this section for details of other flora and fauna in Parc National de la Vanoise.

Tour of the Vanoise Glaciers

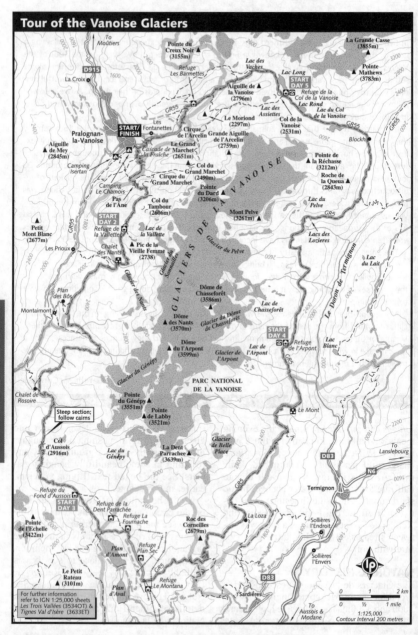

To Moûtiers

La Grande Casse (3855m)

Pointe du Creux Noir (3155m)

Lac des Vaches

Pointe Mathews (3783m)

D915

Refuge Les Barmettes

Lac Long

START DAY 5

Refuge de la Col de la Vanoise

La Croix

Aiguille de la Vanoise (2796m)

Lac Rond

Lac du Col de la Vanoise

Les Fontanettes

Le Moriond (2297m)

Lac des Assiettes

Col de la Vanoise (2531m)

GR55

Blockh

START/ FINISH

Cirque de l'Arcelin

Grande Aiguille de l'Arcelin (2759m)

Pralognan-la-Vanoise

Le Grand Marchet (2651m)

Pointe de la Réchasse (3212m)

Aiguille de Mey (2845m)

Cascade de la Fraîche

Col du Grand Marchet (2490m)

Roche de la Queua (2843m)

Camping Isertan

Cirque du Grand Marchet

Pointe du Dard (3206m)

Mont Pelve (3261m)

Lac du Pelve

Camping Le Chamois

Col du Tambour (2606m)

Pas de l'Âne

GR5

Petit Mont Blanc (2677m)

START DAY 2

Refuge de la Vallette

Lac de la Vallette

Les Prioux

Chalet des Nants

Pic de la Vieille Femme (2738m)

Glacier du Pelve

GLACIERS DE LA VANOISE

Lacs des Lozières

Lac du Lait

Glacier des Sommeilles

Plan des Bôs

Montaimont

Glacier des Nants

Dôme de Chasseforêt (3586m)

Lac de Chasseforêt

Le Doron de Termignon

Dôme des Nants (3570m)

Glacier du Dôme de Chasseforêt

Dôme du l'Arpont (3599m)

Glacier de l'Arpont

START DAY 4

Refuge de l'Arpont

Lac Blanc

Glacier du Génépy

PARC NATIONAL DE LA VANOISE

Lac de l'Arpont

Chalet de Rosoire

Pointe du Génépy (3551m)

Pointe de Labby (3521m)

Le Mont

Steep section; follow cairns

Col d'Aussois (2916m)

Lac du Génépy

La Dent Parrachee (3639m)

Glacier de Belle Place

To Lanslebourg

D83

N6

Refuge du Fond d'Aussois

START DAY 3

Refuge de la Dent Parrachée

Termignon

Pointe de l'Echelle (3422m)

Refuge La Fournache

Roc des Corneilles (2679m)

La Loza

Solliéres l'Endroit

Le Petit Rateau (3101m)

Plan d'Amont

Refuge Plan Sec

Solliéres l'Envers

For further information refer to IGN 1:25,000 sheets Les Trois Vallées (3534OT) & Tignes Val d'Isère (3633ET)

GR5

Refuge Le Montana

Plan d'Aval

Sardières

To Aussois & Modane

D83

0   1   2 km

0   ½   1 mile

1:125,000 Contour Interval 200 metres

NORTHERN ALPS

PLANNING
When to Walk
July and August are the busiest months for visiting the park. June is quieter but the walking may be made difficult by late-lying snow and poor weather (see the warning at the start of this chapter about difficulties with snow). September is also quieter and generally sees more settled weather than the other summer months.

What to Bring
Although all of the walks within Parc National de la Vanoise are on paths, many of the paths higher up can be rough and boulder-strewn. Walking boots with ankle support are recommended, preferably light canvas-style boots. Warm clothes and protective gear (even gloves) should be carried, and walking poles give good support when crossing snow banks. Early in the season you might consider carrying an ice axe for the crossing of the Col d'Aussois on the Tour of the Vanoise Glaciers. As regards water filters and water purification, most walkers seem to drink the water without treatment. Generally the streams crossed are fast-flowing and come from melting snow banks, so have little opportunity to become contaminated.

Maps & Books
The IGN 1:25,000 *Les Trois Vallées* sheet No 3534OT covers the western half of the park and a large part of the Vanoise Glaciers. IGN's 1:25,000 *Tignes Val d'Isère* sheet No 3633ET covers the eastern half to the edge of the Gran Paradiso national park (across the border in Italy). You will need both of these maps when walking the Tour of the Vanoise Glaciers.

The Agence Touristique Départementale de la Savoie (see Information Sources at the beginning of this chapter) produces a useful booklet, *115 Itinéraires Remarquables*, describing a variety of walks in Parc National de la Vanoise and in the Savoie region as a whole. Even better though is *Tour of the Vanoise* by Kev Reynolds, which gives a day-by-day account of the entire 10- to 12-day circuit of the park.

Permits & Regulations
No permits are required to walk in the park, although you will be subject to the usual restrictions governing protected areas (see the boxed text 'National Park Regulations' in the Facts for the Walker chapter). In addition, wild camping is prohibited (discreet camping is permitted between 7 pm and 7 am), outside most of the main *refuges*.

NEAREST TOWN
Pralognan-la-Vanoise
The beautiful and peaceful mountain town of Pralognan-la-Vanoise is an excellent base for walking in the park. This small town is at the head of the steep-sided Pralognan Valley, and arrival to it along the D915 gives a feeling of remoteness and of penetrating into the heart of the mountains. The setting of the town is spectacular: the 1000m rock faces of Le Petit Marchet and Aiguilles de l'Arcelin tower above the town, leading the eye round to the north-west where serrated peaks and hanging glaciers peer over the grass-topped dome of Le Moriond.

Despite its relative remoteness, the town has all the facilities you'll need. There are several outdoor gear shops in the main street, and you'll also find a medical centre. The tourist office (☎ 04 79 08 79 08, fax 04 79 08 76 74, ✉ info@pralognan.com) is in the main street and also serves as the national park office (☎ 04 79 08 71 49). Together they can provide all the information you'll need on the park, including details of *refuges*, general information (some in English) and copies of the free park magazine, *L'Estive*. There are also displays on the history and natural history of the park.

The park wardens organise regular half-day and full-day walks during the summer months. You'll need to reserve in advance with the park office. For other guided walks, contact the Bureau des Guides et Accompagnateurs (☎ 04 79 08 71 21), just opposite the tourist office.

Places to Stay & Eat *Camping le Chamois* (☎ 04 79 08 71 54), on the east side of town, has good facilities and helpful owners: 20FF per person with a charge of 5FF for a tent. Bag storage is free. Just beside Camping Le Chamois is the three-star *Camping Isertan* (☎ 04 79 08 75 24), charging 30FF per person with an additional charge for a tent. Neither camping ground has particularly good shade, unless you're lucky enough to grab the one or two choice spots. However, they are perfectly situated for walks leaving Pralognan-la-Vanoise.

Hotel Gîte – le Petit Mont Blanc (☎ 04 79 08 72 73) is an attractive gîte just round the corner and on the left at the top of the main street. Dorm beds and doubles are 90/200FF.

Peruse the many *menus* in the main street for whatever suits your taste. Good restaurants include *Hôtel La Vanoise* (☎ 04 79 08 70 34) and *Le Chardon Bleu* (☎ 04 79 08 73 07), both in the main street. Elsewhere, you'll also find two *supermarkets*, a good *boulangerie* (bakery), and a host of other restaurants and cafes.

Getting There & Away Transavoie (☎ 04 79 24 21 58) runs a daily bus service between the town of Moûtiers (where there are connections to the main SNCF railway network and even Eurostar) and Pralognan-la-Vanoise. The one-hour bus ride costs 47FF one way, with three services daily (five on Saturday).

THE WALK
Day 1: Pralognan-la-Vanoise to Refuge de la Vallette
5 hours, 1200m ascent

There are two options for beginning the long, steep ascent to Refuge de la Vallette. The more direct route is signposted from the forest edge at the eastern end of Camping Isertan. The option described here is slightly less direct but is the more interesting, taking in a thundering waterfall. From the eastern end of Camping le Chamois follow signposts for the waterfall and the sentier Nanette. The gradient is immediately steep, setting the tone for the rest of the day's walking. Switchbacks lead up through pine forest, passing a couple of junctions where you should follow signs for the sentier Nanette. In a few places the route crosses wooden gangways built into rock faces. There are fastened chains to lend security here. After one hour, pine gives way to birch and, shortly after, you reach a viewpoint at the edge of a ravine. On the far wall of the ravine are a number of powerful **cascades**, one of which pours out of a cave in the cliff face.

The route now climbs above the tree line and then flattens out as it contours beneath rock faces. A brief descent brings you to a junction where you turn left following the sign for Refuge de la Vallette. This path is called Pas de l'Âne (Donkey Steps). Climb steeply through a rocky gully on a rough staircase and at the top look carefully for a couple of cairns, which lead onto a more defined path. Climb steeply on switchbacks for another 30 minutes to reach a junction amid a boulder field. From here you can make out the path climbing up to the **Col du Tambour**, 20 minutes away. There may be patches of snow to cross before the top. From the col, the immediate view of rock spires is backed by the snow peaks of Le Grand Bec and Le Grand Casse. To the north-west several impressive waterfalls can be seen on the rock walls around the Cirque du Grand Marchet. To the south across patches of snow you can see the *refuge* just 1km away. Descend a little and then climb above Lac de la Vallette to reach the *refuge*.

Refuge de la Vallette (☎ 04 79 22 96 38) is surrounded by wonderful alpine scenery. There is plenty of scope for exploration if you have the energy. A path to the south-west leads onto Pic de la Vieille Femme (2738m), a rocky peak with expansive views (one hour return from the *refuge*).

Day 2: Refuge de la Vallette to Refuge du Fond d'Aussois
8–9 hours, 1200m ascent, 1200m descent

From Refuge de la Vallette the trail drops steeply in switchbacks to the Chalet des Nants, a ruined herding shelter. Follow the signpost for the Col d'Aussois and ford several streams before curving round a spur onto a lovely balcon trail right on the boundary of the park. In one hour you reach a small stone shelter above Montaimont. The recommended IGN 1:25,000 map shows a significant detour down towards Plan des Bôs and back up to reach this point. In reality there is a trail all the way along the park boundary.

Now turn left and climb into the **Cirque du Giverny**, at first along a ridge and then contouring steep slopes crossing the beautiful Rau des Traves. At a bridge across a powerful torrent coming down from the Glacier du Génépy, the valley opens out. On the right a few hundred metres ahead is a ridge of moraine. The trail switchbacks up this and then loops back to the west. For the next 30 minutes the trail rises and falls around the 2400m contour and then descends steeply to reach two trail junctions just above the Chalet de Rosoire. This is the beginning of the climb to the Col d'Aussois. Keep left at the junctions – one signpost indicates the top of the col to be 2½ hours. Most walkers will need at least two hours for the steep and unrelenting ascent.

After a large switchback the trail crosses the thundering Ruisseau de Rosoire on a plank bridge and then steepens as it climbs through rocky outcrops. You stand a good chance of seeing chamois and ibex in this area. The trail is well defined and cairns are there to help out; however, some 200m below the col the gradient becomes very steep on loose scree. There are also large snow banks, gullies and rock outcrops. In mist it is very easy to miss the path. Tend left as the path makes a large sweep up to the Col. If you miss this, which is easy to do in the mist, you'll be taking the line of least resistance almost directly south to the col. Keep an eye out for faint trails and one or two small cairns. The ground is steep and loose and some care is needed. Just below the col you rejoin the main path coming in from the left.

The **Col d'Aussois** (2916m) is marked by a small wooden signpost. Follow good cairns to within sight of a wooden cross, which marks the beginning of the descent, which is steep but easy to follow. Cairns lead east and then south between rock slabs and across large patches of snow descending into a large and impressive glacial bowl. The lovely *Refuge du Fond d'Aussois* (☎ 04 79 20 39 83), open from mid-June to

mid-September, is hidden below rocky outcrops where the valley widens and begins to flatten out.

Day 3: Refuge du Fond d'Aussois to Refuge de l'Arpont
7 hours, 18km

The trail leaves the *refuge* across a flat, grassy valley floor. After 1km it reaches a ruin where there are good views down across the Plan d'Amont. The trail for Refuge de l'Arpont breaks off to the left here and climbs through boulders and stunted pines. It then drops to join a 4WD track, which is followed to ski lifts. Follow the signs for Refuge de l'Arpont, contouring steep slopes for 2km on a good path.

The route re-enters the park at a series of limestone escarpments and the trail switchbacks through these and continues to climb for 1km to reach a flat and grassy balcon path leading across to La Loza. Just round a ridge, the nature of the route begins to change, becoming more rugged in character. Shattered cliffs and pinnacles throw down sheets of scree across the path. Early in the season there will be a large snow bank to cross. The trail rounds another ridge and then descends steeply crossing a stream, then climbing round another ridge before dropping down again to Le Mont.

Refuge de l'Arpont (☎ 04 79 20 51 51), open from mid-June to mid-September, is now only 2km away and the final climb to it begins just past the ruins at Le Mont. The final section is in scrub but opens out onto slopes cut through by several glacier-fed torrents. The glaciers are visible not far above.

Day 4: Refuge de l'Arpont to Refuge de la Col de la Vanoise
5–6 hours, 12km

A beautiful day's walking with probably the best mountain scenery on the walk. There is also a very good chance of seeing ibex up close. The trail climbs immediately from Refuge de l'Arpont, crossing very steep and broken slopes and gaining almost 300m in 1.5km. It then flattens out and turns a broad spur to enter a vast **cirque** of moraine, streams and lakes, which the route crosses for the next 3km. The views (given good weather) of the Dôme de Chasseforêt (3586m) and Mont Pelve (3261m) are superb. North of the moraine the trail passes three beautiful lakes among meadows and boulder fields. This is a popular lunch stop.

The route climbs slightly above the lakes and rounds a broad spur to leave the views of Dôme de Chasseforêt behind and descends to a trail junction (three hours). Walkers heading for the eastern half of the park would turn right here. The trail for the Col de la Vanoise stays at the 2300m level heading north across steep scree slopes and then climbs over a boulder field to reach another trail junction overlooking the Vallon de la Leisse. There are good views here of the ridge between La Grande Casse (3855m) and La Grande Motte (3605m). The trail to the Col de la Vanoise climbs to the left past two block shelters and enters the valley of the Ruisseau de la Vanoise.

Three lakes are passed on the gradual 2km ascent to the col and *refuge* with buttresses, scree slopes and glaciers on either side. *Refuge de la Col de la Vanoise* (☎ 04 79 08 25 23) is a large *refuge*. Camping is not permitted and the refuge charges a 30FF surcharge for gas.

Day 5: Refuge de la Col de la Vanoise to Pralognan-la-Vanoise
3 hours, 1400m descent

A long but beautiful descent. Walk west on a path across deep snow banks at the base of Aiguille de la Vanoise and then descend steeply towards the **Lac des Vaches**. The lake at most times will be shallow enough to enable use of the stepping stones across the middle. Late in the season the lake may have dried up altogether. Descend again from the lake with a wild vista of La Grande Casse opening up behind.

Cross a vigorous stream and descend steeply to **Refuge Les Barmettes**. Just after the *refuge* take a left turn signposted for the Cirque de l'Arcelin and descend on this small path into pine forest. In 30 minutes you reach a 4WD track coming up from the hamlet of Les Fontanettes. Above and to your left is the Cirque de l'Arcelin with its glacially carved rock walls and impressive cascade. Descend on the 4WD track, keeping on the left of the Torrent de la Glière, through pine forest to Camping Le Chamois via a good view of the Cascade de la Fraîche.

Other Walks

CHAMONIX VALLEY
Tour du Mont Blanc
The Tour du Mont Blanc (or TMB as it is often called) must be one of the most well known and popular walks in France. If this chapter had room, a full description of this excellent long-distance walk would certainly be included. It will take most walkers eight to 10 days to cover the 160km loop around the Mont Blanc massif, and although the route is generally regarded as being a French walk it has a significantly European feel, with about half of the walking in either Italy or Switzerland.

It is also fairly challenging (medium-hard grade) with a good deal of height gain and loss (six major passes); those who plan to camp will find it particularly demanding. However, the TMB is well provided for by *refuges* at strategic points, so if you can afford to eat and sleep in them you really don't have to carry that much weight. Its popularity does have the drawback of making it a major destination for organised walking holidays and French walkers alike. Every year as many as 10,000 people walk the TMB, so expect *refuges* to be busy (it's wise to book ahead). If you'd prefer a quieter long-distance walk you could try the Tour of the Vanoise Glaciers (see the walk description earlier in this chapter).

As you might expect, the route is very well marked: junctions are well signposted, and trails are marked with distinctive splashes of red and white paint. There are variations to the classic routing, normally marked on maps as TMB Vte (quick TMB). These routings are shorter but generally more difficult. Don't, however, confuse the TMB with the Tour de Pays du Mont Blanc (TPMB), with which it shares routings close to Chamonix and Contamines. The TPMB circuit lies farther west of the Mont Blanc massif.

A good point to begin the TMB is from Les Houches, 15 minutes by bus south of Chamonix. From Les Houches the trail climbs to the Col de Voza (1653m) before descending through alpine pastures, pine forest and alpine hamlets to Les Contamines Montjoie (six hours). From here the route climbs to the head of the Contamines Valley and makes the long crossing of the Col du

Bonhomme (2599m) to reach the settlement and *refuge* at Les Chapieux (six hours). Turning north-east the route climbs the huge valley headed by the Aiguille des Glaciers and, at the end of it, passes Refuge des Mottets and makes a steep ascent of the Col de la Seigne (2516m), crossing into Italy at the top. The trail descends more gradually down the Vallon de la Lée Blanche and then climbs onto a balcon trail above Val Veni where there are tremendous views of the Brevna glacier and the immense rock faces on the south face of Mont Blanc. This balcon trail then descends into Purtud (seven to eight hours).

Still in Italy the TMB passes through Courmayeur and then climbs onto the Mont de la Saxe, a broad ridge with stunning views across to the Grandes Jorasses. After crossing the tops of the Tête Bernarda (2534m) and Tête de la Tronche (2584m), it drops to the Col Sapin and then climbs the Pas Entre Deux Sauts to a pass at 2524m, before descending to La Vachey (five hours). From La Vachey, a flat valley section leads to a steep ascent of the Col Ferret (2537m) and the crossing into Switzerland. A descent into Ferret follows (six hours).

From Ferret a long stretch of lower-level valley walking allows some respite before the trail climbs round the shoulder of the Chaux de Bovine, descends into the valley of the Glacier du Trient, and then climbs to the Col de Balme (2191m) with a return into French territory (two days from Ferret). Looking down the Chamonix Valley from the *refuge* on the Col de Balme you are now on the home stretch. After a descent into Montroc the trail climbs steeply onto the Grand Balcon Sud (see the Grand Balcon Sud walk description earlier in this chapter) and leads south to Les Houches (two days) on a classic balcon path giving excellent views of Mont Blanc.

The Tour du Mont Blanc has several books devoted entirely to it. The illustrated hardback *Tour du Mont Blanc* by Pierre Millon is an excellent armchair read. *TMB* by the Fédération Française de la Randonnée Pédestre (FFRP) gives good, clear map extracts along with the route description (available in French and English), while the route is also covered in *Tour of Mont Blanc* by Andrew Harper. The Didier Richard 1:50,000 *Pays du Mont Blanc* sheet No 8 is probably the most useful map, even though it is somewhat cluttered and the TMB drops off the map for a short distance in Switzerland. Alternatively, you could rely on the map extracts in the FFRP guide.

GR5

Although it actually begins in the Netherlands most people get interested in the GR5 when it

reaches the Alps. From Lake Geneva it climbs into the forests and pastures in the Pre-Alps around Morzine, descends into valleys and then climbs into the Aiguilles Rouges and across into the Chamonix Valley. Passing Mont Blanc to the west it climbs into high country surrounding the Aiguille du Grand Fond, and drops down into Bourg Saint-Maurice. Then, climbing back into the mountains, it enters Parc National de la Vanoise, running south of the Glaciers de la Vanoise and into Modane. The distance from Lake Geneva to Modane is approximately 250km. It is well marked and maintained throughout and is well served by *refuges* and gîtes d'étape. See Other Walks in the Southern Alps chapter for details of the GR5 south of Modane.

There is plenty of literature available on the GR5. *Walking the GR5: Lake Geneva to Mont Blanc* has map extracts and descriptions of not only the GR5 in the Northern Alps, but also the TMB and Tour of the Vanoise. It is published by Robertson McCarta as an English translation of the FFRP guide. There is also *Walking the French Alps: GR5* by Martin Collins.

PARC NATIONAL DE LA VANOISE
Tour of the Vanoise

Taking 10 to 12 days and covering around 160km, the Tour of the Vanoise makes an almost figure-eight shape round and through the entire Parc National de la Vanoise. Utilising large sections of the GR5 and the GR55, it has a wide range of alpine scenery. The western loop, which takes in a good deal of the Tour of the Vanoise Glaciers, is the more rugged and challenging, and is also representative of the best mountain scenery. The slightly longer eastern loop is somewhat more pastoral and follows the Maurienne Valley before turning north through Bonneval and Val d'Isère, completing the loop by descending the impressive Vallon de la Leisse. As usual, the route is well serviced by *refuges*.

For maps and books, see Planning in the introduction to the Parc National de la Vanoise section earlier in this chapter.

Cirque de l'Arcelin

This short day walk starts and finishes in Pralognan-la-Vanoise (see Nearest Town in the Tour of the Vanoise Glaciers walk earlier in this chapter) and features some beautiful waterfalls and impressive views of the mountain scenery around Pralognan. From the town it climbs through forest to the junction of the Torrent du Dard and the Nant de la Crépéna. After views of waterfalls the trail climbs round the back of Le

Moriond (2297m) and then joins the GR55 descending from the Col de la Vanoise. This trail is followed back to Pralognan. The walk takes around four hours. Use the IGN 1:25,000 *Les Trois Vallées-Modane* sheet No 3534OT.

Col de la Vanoise

This is an incredibly popular outing with almost 40,000 people climbing to the Col de la Vanoise (2531m) via this route every summer. The route, which starts and finishes in Pralognan-la-Vanoise (see details for this town earlier in this chapter) is essentially a reversal of Day 5 of the Tour of the Vanoise Glaciers (see the walk description). The climb of more than 1000m gives little respite. Many walkers will overnight in Refuge de la Col de la Vanoise before descending either on the path of ascent, or alternatively via the Lac des Assiettes. Expect a day trip up and down to take eight hours. Use IGN 1:25,000 *Les Trois Vallées-Modane* sheet No 3534OT.

Cirque du Grand Marchet

A challenging and dramatic one-day walk crossing the Col du Grand Marchet (2490m). The route, which starts and finishes in Pralognan-la-Vanoise, follows the same route as Day 1 of the Tour of the Vanoise Glaciers (see the walk description earlier in the chapter), until a trail junction just above the Pas de l'Âne. A left turn is made here leading across rugged ground into the Cirque du Grand Marchet where numerous waterfalls cascade down the rock walls from the glaciers above. A steep climb leads to the top of Col du Grand Marchet and a very steep and difficult descent is made into the Cirque du Dard. From here the route passes through a narrow gap between soaring rock walls and descends into the Cirque de l'Arcelin across what appears from Pralognan to be improbable walking ground. The descent down into Pralognan is straightforward from here. Expect this (grade: hard) walk to take six to seven hours. Use IGN 1:25,000 *Les Trois Vallées-Modane* sheet No 3534OT.

Jura

Much of the Jura, its economy once heavily dependent upon cattle rearing and logging, now relies equally heavily upon tourism for its wealth. Many quite small villages have a tourist office or a *point d'information*, an information service operating from the town hall or post office. There's often also a notice board outlining winter cross-country ski trails. Paths around villages are spattered with paint to indicate summer-season walking and mountain bike routes.

Unlike more popular walking areas such as the Alps, Pyrenees and Provence, visitors remain predominantly French and this medium-mountain region of dense forest and grassy crests remains relatively undiscovered by walkers from other nations.

Damp-loving trees such as ash, willow, poplar and alder flourish in the valley bottoms. On the lower slopes beech and spruce fight for light and territory, together with hazel and boxwood. Where it's higher and drier – for which read 'less damp'! – there are copses and woods of Scots pine plus, growing in isolation, juniper and service tree.

Be warned when planning a foray into the Jura that this region is particularly deficient in public transport. Services are often primarily for transporting children to school and can be nonexistent during vacation time. Fortunately, most major villages have a taxi service, often run on a part-time basis and on demand.

Bear in mind when navigating that what may appear as a clearing or pasture on reference maps, even those recently printed, may have been reclaimed by forest. Conversely, logging may have created open spaces which don't yet feature on the map.

CLIMATE

Summer – from June to September – is mild with temperatures rarely exceeding 25°C. Winters can be severe with snow falling lower and lingering longer than in many places of similar height and latitude. Expect snow on the tops from mid-November

until early April. Rain, while rarely long-lasting in summer, can fall in any season. Jura storms can be as unannounced and as violent as anything the Alps or Pyrenees can throw at you. If the weather forecast even hints at rain, pack a waterproof.

INFORMATION
Maps

The IGN 1:250,000 *Bourgogne Franche Comté* sheet No 109 and Michelin's 1:200,000 sheet of the same name are both reliable general maps of the region.

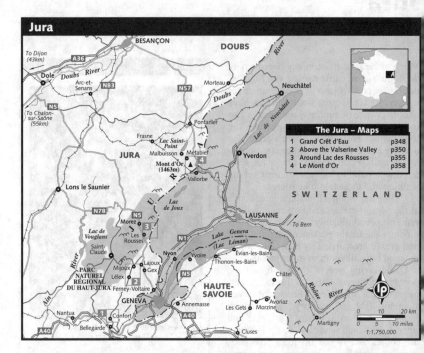

The best overall walking map of the region is the IGN 1:50,000 *Parc Naturel Régional du Haut-Jura* sheet No 3615, on which the Lac des Rousses and Valserine walks feature. These walks and also the Grand Crêt d'Eau fall within Didier Richard's 1:50,000 *Jura Sud*, which covers a much more extensive area.

For maps covering individual walks, see Planning in the introduction to each walk.

Books

Michelin produces a guidebook in English, *Burgundy Jura*, which, while not pitched at walkers, is impressive in its background information and level of detail.

In French, the Fédération Française de la Randonnée Pédestre (FFRP) Topo-Guides *Hauts Plateaux du Jura* (No 001), *Tours dans le Haut Jura* (No 063) and *Lacs et Plateaux du Jura* (No 511) offer a wide selection of possible walks, ranging from half-dayers to treks of a week and more.

Parc Naturel du Haut-Jura (32FF), produced by the park's administration and available in French, English and German, is a good introduction to the park and its features.

Grand Crêt d'Eau

Duration	5–5½ hours
Distance	18.5km
Standard	easy
Start/Finish	Confort
Nearest Town	Bellegarde
Public Transport	no

Summary A 1000m ascent from Confort to Grand Crêt d'Eau via Menthières, doubling back through forest and pasture below its eastern escarpment, with an easy return to Confort down the outbound route.

It's a hard climb from Confort to Menthières but the effort is more than rewarded by glorious crest-walking from Crêt des

In Farmhouse Kitchens

Jura farmhouses are renowned for their flavoursome sausages and hams, smoked over pine woodchips in custom-built chimneys (known as *tuyés*). The famous Morteau pork sausage is cooked in a stew of vegetables, smoked meats and white Jura wine. The large round wheels of hard Comté cheese (over half a metre wide) are another celebrated Jura speciality. Originally made as a way of storing milk over the harsh winters, their quality is now jealously protected. Other well-known cheese varieties include Bleu de Gex, Morbier and Emmental Grand Cru.

Frasses to Crêt de la Goutte, followed by level strolling through alpine pasture and forest. Only the impedimenta of winter ski installations mar the views.

PLANNING

Walking is normally possible from the second half of May until mid-November. At other times the prints on the trails are only of snowshoes and skis.

Maps

The body of the walk is on IGN 1:25,000 *Bellegarde-sur-Valserine* sheet No 3330OT with a northern tongue extending onto *Crêt de la Neige* sheet No 3328OT. The local *Les Chemins de Randonnée du Jura Gessien* is a useful supplement but inadequate alone for navigation. For details of maps at 1:50,000 refer to the Maps section under Information earlier in this chapter.

NEAREST TOWN
Bellegarde

Bellegarde has little going for it except its excellent rail connections. The tourist office (☎ 04 50 48 48 68, **@** otbelleg@cc-pays-de-gex.fr) is on place Victor Bérard.

Places to Stay & Eat If you can't get up the valley before nightfall, pitch your tent at *Camping Le Crêt d'Eau* (☎ 04 50 56 60

81). Beside the stadium and 2km north of the train station, it charges 28FF for a tent and 21FF per person. *Hôtel-Gril Adria (7 ave de Lattre de Tassigny)* has doubles for 165FF, triples for 205FF and does a *menu* (fixed-price meal of two or more courses) for 75FF.

Chez Mireille (☎ *04 50 48 04 75, 78 rue de la République)* does a daily special for around 60FF. Nearby at No 49, *Le Manhattan* (☎ *04 50 48 35 55)* has *menus* (fixed-price meals of two or more courses) from 75FF.

Getting There & Away Paris is three hours away by TGV *(train à grande vitesse).* There's a frequent train service to Geneva (17FF) and over 10 trains a day to/from Lyon (101FF).

GETTING TO/FROM THE WALK

A taxi between the Bellegarde train station rank (☎ 04 50 48 13 20) and Confort or Menthières costs 55/130FF respectively. You might also consider hiring a car from Hertz (☎ 04 50 56 05 32), at 21 ave de la Gare, near the station.

THE WALK

If you have wheels and fancy a shorter walk, drive to Menthières and omit the tranche to/from Confort. This shortened walk still leaves you with an invigorating stretch of about three hours.

The Outside Safe

Until recently, many outlying farms in the Jura would have a *grenier fort*, a small, secure wooden building constructed upwind from the main dwelling. This simple windowless rectangular structure was an insurance against the risk of fire and, to a lesser extent, theft. Here, the family would keep all that was valuable to them – money, deeds of property, Sunday-best clothes and agricultural tools. Under it was a vaulted cellar for storing vegetables and – most important of all – seeds and grain for the following spring.

JURA

Otherwise, leave Confort by the old route to Menthières. Its stony track is a more direct and decidedly more pleasant alternative to the modern winding road. After a steep rise through woodland up the western flank of Combe du Velu and an equally breath-snatching climb up the grassy ridge of Crête de Charmy, the trail levels out to continue through upland pasture to Menthières (1066m). It's a place of little charm, dead as the grave outside the ski season or its brief summer flowering, during July and August, when you may be lucky enough to find one of its several bars and cafes open.

Head south along a sealed road and turn left immediately after a car park at a sign, 'Crêt de la Goutte'. Follow the ski slope beside a chair lift and turn right at a second sign for Crêt de la Goutte. The path now ascends to La Charnaz (1250m), a forest clearing.

Take a steep bend to the left, leaving the main track as it continues straight ahead, then 50m later tack equally steeply right beside an old wooden sign, its writing long since effaced.

As you emerge into open meadow with the lone building of Chalet de Varambon

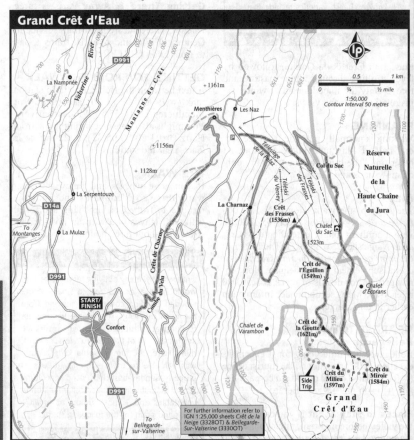

Grand Crêt d'Eau

well to the south, cross a fence, aiming for a lone signpost.

Here on the high pasture, trails are vague and often more travelled by cattle or occasionally chamois than by humans. But the vistas are broad and it's easy just to take a visual bearing and stride out for the next landmark.

At the signpost, turn left (north) following a sometimes indistinct footpath towards Crêt des Frasses. Avoid climbing too high too early. Instead, keep beneath and just east of a low escarpment. Aim for the top of a ski lift before climbing the final few metres to **Crêt des Frasses** (1536m), topped by a large cross, with the first of the day's splendid panoramas.

To the south-east is the rounded hump of a nameless hill (1523m), your next landmark, and beyond the equally bald Crêt de l'Éguillon (Aiguillon; 1549m). Looming behind both is Crêt de la Goutte, its western slopes cloaked in pine.

Drop to the top of the drag lift and aim south-east for that anonymous hilltop. There's little evidence of a path. If you're unsure, simply follow the barbed wire fence which threads along the ridge.

From Crêt de l'Éguillon, drop southwards to a small col. Ascending, keep left (east) of a pronounced rocky spur and cross under a cattle fence to pick up sparse redand-yellow waymarkers which lead you to the summit of **Crêt de la Goutte** (1621m). From it you can distinguish the rounded peak of Crêt de Chalam to the north-west and the more spiky Colomby de Gex along the ridge to the north. To the south is the Grand Colombier and the Rhône Valley, while on a clear day Mont Blanc shimmers white behind Geneva.

From the crest, pick your way south-eastwards down a short ridge to meet the Balcon du Léman GR trail beside a small pond. Turn left to follow its red and white bars. Whenever the track divides, take the left-hand option in order to avoid drifting too far east towards the ruined Chalet d'Écorans.

At *Chalet du Sac* (1381m), an unstaffed *refuge* (refuge or mountain hut) at the head of a wide bowl, don't be tempted along the

distinct path which leads down the valley. Instead, go due north from the rear of the chalet to pick up the wide, still discernible but scarcely used track which once used to serve it.

After around 15 minutes of walking through deep forest, fork left at a sign for Menthières as the Balcon du Léman trail turns right. Ignore a prominent right turn for La Poutouille. Shortly after, the track hairpins back on itself to descend to the Col du Sac. Double back again to leave the 4WD track and head gently downhill over grass. At the base of a drag lift, the wide slope of a ski run opens before you. Follow this down to Menthières, from where you take the morning's route back down the valley to Confort.

A Couple More Crêts
20 minutes, 1.75km

If you fancy bagging a couple more peaks, make the easy extension southwards from Crêt de la Goutte to take in Crêt du Milieu (1597m) and Crêt du Miroir (1584m). Rejoin the route by picking up the signed Balcon du Léman trail as you descend from the latter.

Above the Valserine Valley

Duration	2 days
Distance	37.5km
Standard	medium
Start/Finish	Lajoux
Nearest Towns	Les Rousses, Saint-Claude and Bellegarde
Public Transport	very limited

Summary A rectangle around the Valserine Valley. Predominantly forest on Day 1. From Col de Crozet, above Lélex, magnificent ridge-walking to Montrond. Back down to valley level and a final haul up to Lajoux.

This is a walk of opposites, following the western and eastern flanks of the Valserine Valley. The forest trails of Day 1 are succeeded by breathtaking vistas from the long spine running parallel to Lake Geneva (Lac Léman). At each end of the slim rectangle are a couple of more gentle interludes as the trail cuts across the tranquil Valserine Valley.

JURA

Above the Valserine Valley

To Les Rousses

D436

Septmoncel

sur l'Étain

To Saint-Claude

START/FINISH

Lajoux

La Trace

Trecombe

Mijoux

N5

D936

Col de la Faucille
(1340m)

To Gex

GR9B

D991

PARC NATUREL

RÉGIONAL DU

HAUT - JURA

D292

Petit Montrond
(1534m)

Le Crozat

Montrond
(1596m)

Creux de l'Envers

Mont Chanais

Chalet de la
Chenaillette

GR9

Colomby de Gex
(1688m)
(1627m)

(1680m)

GR9B

Sept-Fontaines

Echenevex

START
DAY 2

Lélex

GR9

Naz-dessous

Les Trois
Cheminées

Le Truchet

Refuge
du Ratou

Col de
Crozet

D984c

Refuge
de la Loge

(1429m)

Montoisey
(1669m)

Crozet

Avouzon

Chevry

Grand Crêt
(1702m)

Villeneuve

Prégnin

Crêt de la Neige
(1717m)

D991

Les Molles

Les Morènes

Sergy

0   1   2 km

0   ½   1 mile

1:100,000
Contour Interval 100 metres

For further information refer to
IGN 1:50,000 sheet *Parc Naturel
Régional du Haut-Jura*

JURA

PLANNING

See Planning in the Grand Crêt d'Eau walk earlier in this chapter for information on the best times to walk.

Wear boots with a deep tread as the forest trails on Day 1 can become very squelchy after rain.

Maps

The IGN 1:25,000 sheet Crêt de la Neige No 3328OT covers 90% of the route, the remainder featuring on No 3327OT. For details of the 1:50,000 maps needed, see the Maps section under Information in the introduction to this chapter. The local map *Les Chemins de Randonnée du Jura Gessien* (28FF) is a useful supplement but has no contours and is inadequate on its own for navigation.

NEAREST TOWNS

Both Bellegarde and Les Rousses are nearby accommodation options. For information on Bellegarde, see Nearest Town in the Grand Crêt d'Eau walk. For information on Les Rousses, see Nearest Town in the Around Lac des Rousses walk later in this chapter.

Lajoux

If you find yourself waiting for a transport connection in Lajoux, there are several accommodation options. ***Chalet Le Triolet*** *(☎ 03 84 41 23 00)* has dorm beds for 67FF (82FF in a room). At the friendly ***Gîte d'Étape La Trace*** *(☎ 03 84 41 27 27)*, with hostel-style walkers' accommodation, it's also 67FF for a bed. Rooms at ***Hôtel Restaurant La Haute Montagne*** start at 183FF and the *menus* at 74FF.

Getting There & Away Public transport provision is lamentable. For Lajoux, take the train from either Dole or Mouchard to Saint-Claude, the station beyond Morez. Both Dole and Mouchard are on the TGV line to Paris.

From Saint-Claude, Jura Bus (☎ 03 84 24 33 07) runs to Lajoux (50 minutes) and on to Mijoux (one hour), leaving at 12.40 pm on Wednesday, 7.30 am and 12.10 pm on Saturday and 5.15 pm on both days. The most convenient return bus calls by Lajoux at 6.25 pm on Wednesday and 7.15 pm on Saturday.

Another possibility is to take a bus from Bellegarde to Lélex and reverse the order of the walking days. During school holidays, a bus (daily except Sunday) leaves Bellegarde at 11 am, and at 5.55 pm on Thursday and Saturday. The return bus leaves Lélex at 6.55 am on weekdays and between 9 and 10 am on Saturday.

Day 1: Lajoux to Lélex

4¼–4¾ hours, 18.5km

Leave Lajoux by the D292, 100m east of the combined post office and tourist office (☎ 03 84 41 24 10). Take a cart track on the near side of Gîte d'Étape La Trace and head south-east across open meadow.

About 30 minutes out, ignore the seductive, descending footpath straight ahead. Instead, stay on the same wide track as it joins the GR9B, passes under an electricity pylon and heads south-west to plunge into the forest.

Just over the hour mark, a large **grassy glade** speckled with wild narcissuses makes a pleasant rest stop. At the end of a second, smaller meadow are the foundations and little more of a couple of stone houses. Beside them, implausibly, are the equally dilapidated, overgrown remains of an old Panhard, a classic 1950s saloon car.

Take particular care a couple of minutes later when the GR makes a very easily overlooked left turn. Towards the end of an even smaller clearing, the only indication is a faded orange chevron on a small rock beside the track which points towards a gap in the conifers. Trust it and, 50m along, the narrow but distinct footpath where you again pick up the GR flashes.

Yet another open patch offers the first clear views over to Colomby de Gex and the bare crests of the valley's eastern flank, to be savoured on Day 2.

In spring and early summer, each clearing is bright with wild flowers: yellow primroses, buttercups, gentians and trolles, and whole colonies of narcissuses.

In many such meadows, the remains of an old stone building are a reminder that the days of pasturage on these slopes are not so distant. Only a little over half a century ago,

JURA

grass grew in profusion and the slopes were as free of trees as those on the opposite, eastern flank. But once cattle were no longer grazed, the forest rapidly reasserted itself on the more sheltered western face.

Notice too the old, crumbling boundary walls, built perpendicular to the valley. Unlike many areas in the Jura where the forest is literally communal (belonging to the *commune* – the basic unit of local government in France), the wooded slopes of the Valserine are divided into private holdings. Cutting property lines across the valley meant that each landowner had a share of the river and a right to its fishing, a slice of fertile river bank, a tranche of forest for firewood and building materials, and upland pasture for summer grazing.

Where the path meets a wide dirt logging road at a hairpin bend, take the right-hand prong. Turn left at a sign 'Les Trois Cheminées' 200m later to cross a grassy knoll and head away south-west up a cart track. Turn left (south) at a junction with a deeply rutted logging track. No more than 100m later, just after a footpath signed 'Sept-Fontaines' heads away east, bear left along a scarcely perceivable track and go left at the intersection with another rutted logging trail.

A little over 30 minutes later, turn left at a wooden sign to begin the long descent

Small-Time Smugglers

Until the 1950s the Valserine Valley, its north-south axis parallel to and west of the Franco-Swiss frontier, was a recognised customs-free zone. In the days before winter skiers and summer walkers brought greater wealth, local farmers and woodcutters would supplement the meagre income the land afforded by a little small-time smuggling. Walking minor trails through dense woodland, they bore goods into France from Switzerland, where the duty levied was low or negligible. Their packs were stashed with items such as tobacco, playing cards, matches, chocolate, sugar, coffee and watches, all of which could command a higher price in France.

towards Lélex. From here on, there's little possibility of going astray as every junction, major or minor, tempting or unremarkable, has its wooden signpost. As you lose elevation, ash, maple and hazel trees, abundant on lower more protected slopes, begin to assert themselves among the beech and spruce.

At the brow of a short, sharp rise 30 minutes later, make the briefest of diversions to the viewpoint of **Le Truchet** (1188m) with its plunging views of the Valserine and Lélex, dominated by the chain of bald crests to the east.

The route turns sharp left (east) to continue descending along a well-banked path. Just before another abrupt left turn for Lélex, a circular cistern is another reminder that the days of cattle grazing in what is now thick wood are not all that distant.

Five minutes later, turn left (north-east) at a wide stony track and left again after about 20 minutes onto a bitumen road to cross the Valserine River and reach **Lélex**.

A bed at Mme Vacher's *gîte d'étape* (☎ 04 50 20 90 98) is a bargain 42FF. *Hôtel Le Mont Jura* (☎ 04 50 20 90 53, fax 04 50 20 95 20) has rooms for between 210FF and 270FF, while those at *Pension La Pomme de Pin* (☎ 04 50 20 90 32) cost from 210FF to 250FF. The tourist office (☎ 04 50 20 91 43), which can give further accommodation suggestions, is at the base of the *téléférique* (cable car or funicular).

A further 45 minutes' uphill walking or a téléférique ride brings you to *Refuge du Ratou* and beyond it, *Refuge de la Loge*. For details see the Day 2 walk description.

Day 2: Lélex to Lajoux
5–5¾ hours, 19km

In July and August, if you want to omit the first strenuous hour, the téléférique (30FF single, 40FF return; last ascent at 5.30 pm) can whisk you from Lélex (900m) to 1450m, just below the Col de Crozet.

From the tourist office in Lélex, walk north up the D991 for 400m. Just beyond a souvenir shop, go right up a narrow lane, past La Cordonnière, a private house, and onto a stony track. Just before the farm of Les Cornes, follow a sign for Crêt de la

Shop sign, Riquewihr, Alsace.

The makings of a good harvest.

Building facade, Riquewihr.

Quaint houses with window boxes are common in Alsace.

Storks nesting in Zellenberg.

The view from near Col de la Schluct, Alsace, on the Grand Crêt d'Eau walk.

RICHARD NEBESKY

A peaceful place to rest, Les Rousses, Jura.

INGRID RODDIS

Walking near Métabief, Jura.

INGRID RODDIS

A traditional grenier fort (external safe) near Les Rousses, Jura.

RICHARD NEBESKY

A church in every village – Les Rousses, Jura.

Neige and head initially north-east into the forest up a steep grassy path.

After more than 30 minutes of unremittingly uphill climbing, the route, brightly blazed in red and yellow, emerges from the trees and turns right at a T-junction to pass under the cables of the téléférique, where it picks up the GR9. Just beyond the *Refuge du Ratou*, which is more often closed than open, the route to Crêt de la Neige continues straight ahead. Leave it to keep following the wide dirt track around to the left (north-east), staying with it as it wriggles under the téléférique cables and back again. (The GR9 describes a sizable dogleg to the east to pass by *Refuge de la Loge* (☎ *04 50 20 90 46*), where a bunk costs between 34FF and 47FF.)

About 1¼ hours from Lélex, you reach the top of the téléférique and, at times when the lift's functioning, the welcome *Bar-Restaurant La Catheline*, which serves draught Murphy's Irish stout.

At the Col de Crozet, just to the north of the northernmost ski lift, the route enters the Réserve Naturelle de la Haute Chaîne du Jura, a nature reserve of 10,780 hectares, where walkers are asked to stick to designated trails.

The rich upland pasture, dimpled, rolling and treeless, is a delight after so much forest. As you progress, each gap in the skyline to the east gives glimpses of Lake Geneva (Lac Léman), the long lateral gash of Geneva airport, the city beyond and the high Alps on the far side of the lake.

The footpath is faint in places and GR stripes are few. About 30 minutes beyond the col, aim for a notch in the hillside ahead to the north-east. Once around the rim of a small coomb (deep hollow), there's an abrupt but brief ascent to the rounded summit of an unnamed hill.

From this peak, follow a crumbling limestone wall which drops without a kink to the intervening saddle (1627m) and up to **Colomby de Gex** (1688m), topped by a rusting metal pylon commemorating some long-forgotten congress. The wraparound view is breathtaking: to the east Geneva and its fountain; just below, the town of Gex with Ségny to its south; Nyon beside the lake; and Ivoire over the water. Looking northwards, the telecommunications tower at the peak of Petit Montrond tests the air like a giant thermometer, while the bulbous dome on the summit of La Dôle awaits some celestial golfer.

Far to the south is Crêt de la Neige, undistinguished in appearance yet the highest point in the massif, while to its southwest rises the pointed peak of Crêt de Chalam. You don't have to take all this in at once; from here until Montrond, the path follows the cliff's edge, from which the vistas are consistently magnificent.

The small cave near Chalet de la Chenaillette was once used as an ice house and, in summer, storage for fresh milk and cheeses.

Just beyond the first of two anonymous hills, recognisable by its cairn and trig point, the route leaves the nature reserve. Some 10 minutes later, it passes over the second and continues to **Montrond** (1596m). From here, you can see Lajoux to the north-west, sitting in a broad swathe of pasture surrounded by forest.

Descend north-westwards to pass by Le Crozat (don't be misled by the series of wooden pegs, painted green and leading too far to the north). Pick up the stony track leading north-east from this active *farm*, where you can buy fresh butter and cheese.

After passing under high-tension wires and the cables of a drag lift, turn left onto a forest track signed 'Col de la Faucille'. Five minutes later go straight over a sealed road and, on meeting it for a second time, turn right along it.

Just before the shops of the small ski station of Col de la Faucille, turn left down a wide stony track beside giant letters painted on a wall, 'Mijoux Village par la Piste Verte'.

After about 25 minutes of easy descent, go right and down a narrow footpath, cutting off a significant bend in the track, rejoining it a few minutes later. Turn right and, a couple of minutes later, left to pass through **Mijoux** along the rather grandly named rue Royale.

Mijoux has several *bars* and *cafes* where you can refresh yourself before the final ascent to Lajoux. Cross the Valserine River, take a small lane beside the church and turn

JURA

left at a T-junction just beyond. Should you be tempted to postpone the last leg to Lajoux until the next day, *Gîte d'Étape La Michaille* (☎ *04 50 41 32 45)*, where a bunk costs 65FF, lies temptingly alongside the route.

Beside the gîte, take the footpath which ascends steadily westwards below a meadow then into deep woodland.

Ten to 15 minutes later, take care not to miss what looks suspiciously like a vandalised signpost. Nothing more than an ankle-height grey cylinder indicates a junction where you turn sharp right (north-east) up a minor trail (both branches, confusingly, bear GR stripes). Where this meets the D436 coming up from Mijoux, follow the road for 100m then veer left onto a track, which recrosses the highway a couple of minutes later just to the east of a telecommunications tower.

Pass by the farm of Trecombe and head along a level track to reach Lajoux some 15 minutes later.

Around Lac des Rousses

Duration	6½–7½ hours
Distance	26.75km
Standard	medium-hard
Start/Finish	Les Rousses
Public Transport	no

Summary A steepish wooded ascent through the Forêt du Risoux. Level striding before a descent to Bois d'Amont. Up the Orbe Valley's eastern flank to Mont Sâla. Down through forest and pasture back to Les Rousses.

It's a potpourri of a day: a slice of the GR5, a longish stretch of the Tour de Haute Bienne trail and a PR incorporating a sliver of Switzerland. We grade it medium-hard primarily because of its length. If you have a vehicle and prefer a less demanding walk, the return leg from Bois d'Amont to Les Rousses makes an attractive half-dayer.

PLANNING

See Planning in the Grand Crêt d'Eau walk earlier in this chapter for information on the best times to walk.

Since the second half of the route dips into Switzerland, pack your passport or ID although the probability of anyone asking to see it is minimal.

Maps & Books

The IGN 1:25,000 *Morez Les Rousses* sheet No 3327ET covers both the French and Swiss elements of this walk. For details of maps at 1:50,000, see Maps under Information in the introduction to this chapter.

The locally produced *À la Découverte du Haut Jura* is a well-produced modular pack of walks between two and four hours long. You can buy single walk sheets or the whole pack of 21 walks.

NEAREST TOWN
Les Rousses

On the north-eastern edge of the Parc Naturel Régional du Haut-Jura, Les Rousses is a popular base for winter sports, walking, mountain biking, and sailing on the nearby lake. The friendly tourist office (☎ 03 84 60 02 55, ☎ 03 84 60 52 03) is on rue Pasteur.

Places to Stay & Eat The nearest camping ground is *Camping Danico* (☎/*fax 03 84 60 78 74)* at Les Jacobeys, 5km to the south. The *auberge de jeunesse* (youth hostel; ☎ *03 84 60 02 80, fax 03 84 60 09 67)*, 3km from Les Rousses at Bief de la Chaille, also has limited camping space. In town, *Hôtel des Rousses* (☎ *03 84 60 00 02, fax 03 84 60 05 89)* has doubles for between 175FF and 230FF.

L'Isatis (☎ *03 84 60 50 26, place de l'Église)* is both pizzeria and restaurant. For more exciting fare, the small *Restaurant de la Fromagerie* (☎ *03 84 60 09 20, 137 rue Pasteur)*, just beside the cheese factory, does a range of salads and cheese-based dishes.

Getting There & Away The nearest public transport link is Morez, 10km away. Three trains daily link Morez with the TGV to/from Paris at either Dole or Mouchard train stations. From Mouchard, there are five daily connections to Lyon.

Alternatively, there's an hourly train from La Cure, 3km from Les Rousses, to

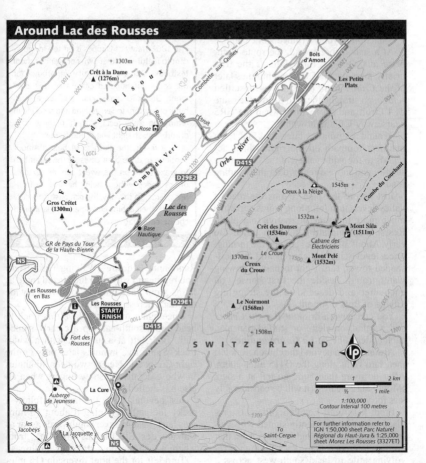

Around Lac des Rousses

Nyon in Switzerland, from where there are frequent trains to Geneva (connecting with the TGV to Paris) and Geneva airport.

Between Morez and Les Rousses, the only option is a taxi (90FF). Phone Les Rousses (☎ 03 84 60 02 53). Morez Automobiles (☎ 03 84 33 71 71), on rue de la République in Morez, rents cars.

THE WALK

From the tourist office, walk north along rue Pasteur, turn right onto rue de Noirmont then left after 10 minutes onto Montée du Rochat. Beside a school, pick up the red-

and-yellow waymarkers of the GRP Tour de la Haute-Bienne and take a muddy track to the right (north-east) towards Lac des Rousses. Turn right to follow a sealed road (D29E2) to the Base Nautique, a grand name for a few pedal craft and a windsurf board or two. Here, take a footpath which heads north-east, away from the road and into the Forêt du Risoux.

Once the winding trail gains height and again turns north-east, it's pleasant, easy walking. About 45 minutes from the lakeside, cross the Combe du Vert, a lateral valley once used for pasture but now being reclaimed by scrub. Soon after, turn left at a T-junction beyond a ruined stone cabin.

At a sealed forest road, the route Combette aux Quilles, turn right as the trail briefly joins the GR5. Fifteen minutes later at the *Chalet Rose* (1235m), an unstaffed *refuge*, go straight ahead to follow the route de l'Étroit and stay with it when the GR5 bears away left and downhill.

Around 15 minutes later, look out for a manifest footpath on the right which descends to the wide valley of the Orbe more steeply and more directly than the winding road.

Just before the path rejoins the road at valley level, turn left along a grassy path, a much more pleasant alternative to asphalt. Resist the temptation to drop down too early. About 30 minutes beyond the turning, once level with the church and its bell-shaped tower, turn right to pass a flowing water trough beside the first house you encounter and descend to the straggling village of **Bois d'Amont**.

You can have a drink at *Bar du Centre* and a salad, omelette or stuffed pancake, each under 40FF, at *La Gourmandine*.

Around 100m beyond the church, fork left then turn right along the D415 after 300m. After no more than 50m, go left at a sign, 'Mont Sâla 2 heures' (it will be considerably less for you).

From here until Les Petits Plats, the revised route, intermittently signed with yellow stripes and diamonds, differs from that on any reference map. Pass through a revolving stile to head south-west across a meadow and into forest. After about 20 minutes, make a significant short cut by leaving the signed route where it turns east beside a wooden bench. Instead, continue straight ahead (south) along a path signed Mont Salat (sic).

About 30 minutes beyond Bois d'Amont, the path emerges at **Les Petits Plats**, a magnificent swathe of pasture dotted with cowherds' summer cabins, most now shuttered and uninhabited.

As you exit from the wood and – as the occasional frontier post tells you – enter Switzerland, look for a sign, 'Chemin de

Treaty of Dappes

The 1862 Treaty of Dappes is far too insignificant to feature in either Swiss or French school textbooks. But it has particular importance for the couple of hundred citizens of Bois d'Amont. Under its terms, France ceded a small hunk of territory to Switzerland and received in return the small rectangle which these days disturbs the straight line of the frontier.

As a result, the farmers of Bois d'Amont continue to drive their cows up the mountain to graze them on the sweet summer grasses of Les Loges without being hassled by frontier guards. To this day, the rich pasture is dotted with their cabins and a pair of abandoned cheese cooperatives.

Randonnée Pédestre' (Walking Trail). Here you rejoin and stay with the blazed route as far as Mont Sâla, initially following a wide dirt track across the meadow.

Once again in forest, leave this track to head south-south-east up a clearly signed path. Bear left at a junction with a wider track. Some five minutes later pass on the right Creux à la Neige, two deep sinkholes in whose depths the snow lingers when all else has melted.

Just beyond, leave the track to follow a rocky footpath, rejoining it about 10 minutes later, heading ever southwards as far as Cabane des Électriciens (1474m), from where a lush meadow stretches north-east.

Turn left for the brief diversion (15 minutes return) to **Mont Sâla** (1511m) which, with extensive views of Lake Geneva and the Alps beyond, makes an inspiring rest stop.

Back at Cabane des Électriciens, take an unsigned track heading south-west. After 150m, fork right onto an indistinct grassy track. Barely 50m later, pass through a gap in the trees to take a stony track westwards through jumbled karstic limestone.

The trail, again grassy, veers south and crosses a barbed wire fence. Just beyond a small pond, continue south-west along a well-defined track. Turn right at a T-junction to reach the tin-roofed chalet of Le Croue.

Now for the only tricky navigation of the day: descend towards a circular sheepfold on the western side of the meadow below the chalet. In a dip, turn right (west) through a gap in the trees. Once over a small rise, cross a high stile to join a path which curls round the northern flank of the spectacular cirque of **Creux du Croue**.

Where two stone walls meet at the coomb's north-west corner, join a major track which zigzags down through forest to the Orbe Valley. Turn left at a T-junction beside a chalet and small water cistern. With Les Rousses again in sight beyond the lake, recross the frontier, its only indication a Swiss customs sign and border stone No 213A, ankle height and choked by grass and wild flowers.

Turn left at a junction and after 20 minutes go briefly left on the D415 then right onto a minor road. Five minutes later, fork right onto a broad path which leads across a golf course and back to Les Rousses.

Le Mont d'Or

Duration	4½–5 hours
Distance	16.5km
Standard	easy-medium
Start/Finish	Métabief
Public Transport	yes

Summary A gradual descent, mainly through woodland, to Les Tavins. Six hundred metres of ascent to enjoy splendid ridge-walking to beyond Le Mont d'Or.

Preceded by a brief step into Switzerland, the long ridge walk at the heart of this route is among the finest in the Jura. The walk can be shortened by roughly 2km if you catch a téléférique down to Métabief from the summit of Le Monrond.

PLANNING

See Planning in the Grand Crêt d'Eau walk earlier in this chapter for information on the best times to walk.

Since the walk very briefly dips into Switzerland, bring your passport or ID although you're unlikely to need it.

Maps

The IGN 1:25,000 *Mouthe Métabief* sheet No 3426OT covers the whole route.

A local pamphlet in French, *Guide de Randonnées Pédestres au Départ de Métabief Mont d'Or* (10FF) gives enough ideas for a fulfilling week and more of walking based around this small but dynamic resort.

NEAREST TOWN
Métabief

Métabief is a small but dynamic resort which attracts winter skiers and walkers during the summer. It regularly hosts the French mountain bike championships. Métabief's tourist office is open only in winter. Les Hôpitaux Neufs tourist office (☎ 03 81 49 13 81, ✉ ot@Métabief-mont dor.com), 2km from the bottom of the Métabief chair lift, functions all year.

Places to Stay & Eat *Camping Le Miroir* (☎ *03 81 49 10 64*) is at Les Hôpitaux Neufs. *Hôtel Restaurant Les Géraniums* (☎ *03 81 49 12 77*) has rooms for between 155FF and 220FF. At *Hôtel L'Étoile des Neiges* (☎ *03 81 49 26 91*) doubles cost from 235FF to 255FF. Both are on rue du Village. There are several cafes and restaurants, many of which are closed outside July, August and the ski season.

Getting There & Away SNCF buses run twice daily (three times on Sunday – or four on Sunday during July and August) between Frasne (25km north-west) and Vallorbe (9km east in Switzerland), passing through Métabief. Frasne's services interconnect with TGV trains to/from Paris. For a taxi, ring Taxis du Mont d'Or (☎ 03 81 49 16 03).

THE WALK
4½–5 hours, 16.5km

This local classic is blazed in blue and yellow as far as the summit of Le Mont d'Or, where the red and white stripes of the GR5 take over.

From the bottom of the ski slopes, take a small road, closed to traffic, which heads south-east from the base of the largest chair lift.

JURA

Le Mont d'Or

For further information refer to IGN 1:25,000 sheet *Mouthe Métabief* (3426OT)

Saint-Antoine

D45

D9

River

Le Miror

Métabief

Les Hôpitaux Neufs

N57

Jougne

Bief

Crêt de la Chapelle

START/ FINISH

Gais Loisirs

Longevilles Hautes

1090m +

Mont Ramey (1087m)

1094m +

Télésiège du Morond

D450

Refuge du Petit Morond

GR5

Chalet du Cernois

Alternative Route

Viaubillon Rau

Le Moulin

Jougeena Rau

Télésiège du Troupezy

Le Morond (1419m)

Refuge du Gros Morond

Les Maillots

La Ferrière

Le Troupezy

Téléskis de Super Longevilles

Télésiège du Chamois

Les Tavins

Les Echampés

1299m +

GR5

Le Mont d'Or (1461m)

Au Chalet du Pisteur

Télésiège des Roches

Refuge de Piquemiette

1463m

To Ballaigues

SWITZERLAND

Les Jurats

Orbe River

Pralioux Dessus

Vallorbe

0   0.5   1 km

0   ¼   ½ mile

1:50,000
Contour Interval 50 metres

After about 20 minutes, having passed a flowing water trough, bear left onto a dirt track and descend to the Chalet du Cernois (1160m). From it, head downhill and eastwards over a short pathless stretch to join a cart track and turn right at a road. After 100m this curls to the south side of a tight, steep valley and becomes track, boggy in places after rain. Turn left at a T-junction then right to rejoin and cross the Vaubillon.

Follow the stream as it drops to the hamlet of Les Tavins (880m), reached after about an hour of walking. Turn right to ascend rue de la Piquemiette to the base of a couple of chair lifts and the bar-restaurant *Au Chalet du Pisteur*, open from the second half of May to the end of September. As you gain height, there are increasingly impressive views to the west of the sheer limestone cliffs beneath Le Mont d'Or. A raindrop falling to their east makes its way to the Mediterranean via the rivers Doubs, Saône and Rhône. Had it fallen to the west, it would have joined the North Sea via the Rhine.

Continue along the same route, now a dirt track, to pass the unstaffed *Refuge de Piquemiette* (1058m) – no charge. About 15 minutes later, go straight ahead (south) onto a footpath where the track describes a tight bend to the right.

Five minutes later, a crumbling stone wall and frontier marker bearing the fleur-de-lys of France and the coat of arms of the Swiss canton of Vaud are the only indication that you've reached an international border.

Cross a meadow, aiming for a metal post in the middle, then a ruined cabin. Climb a wooden stile and descend a lane southwards along the fringe of the forest.

Turn westwards to ascend a steep, well-banked track with fine views of Dent de Vaulion and the Alps rising beyond the southern shore of Lake Geneva. The trail emerges into the broad pasturage of Pralioux Dessus (1314m). From the chalet at its heart, head north-east up a shallow gully along a scarcely discernible path.

A staffed *refuge* (1377m) of the Club Alpin Suisse, where you can stay overnight, serves drinks and snacks. The path behind it heads north-west to border stone No 69 and a swing stile which leads you back into France.

Once you reach the crest, the views are spectacular all the way to Le Mont d'Or and beyond. To the east, Lac de Neuchâtel disappears behind the flanks of an intervening mountain. South-west glints Lac de Joux, with Lac de Saint-Point to the north-west, while the chain of Jura crests tails away north-eastwards.

The summit of **Le Mont d'Or** (1461m) usually swarms with motorists who have made the short stroll up from the nearby car park. Follow them downhill to a junction where the GR5 comes in from the west.

About 15 minutes from the summit, the path leaves the cliff top (the gravel path which stays with it is principally for mountain bikers) to keep heading northwards. Just off the route to the west is *Refuge du Gros Morond (reservations ☎ 03 81 46 59 56)*.

At the summit of **Le Morond** (1419m) there's a small *buvette* (refreshment room), open from mid-June to the end of August. If you want to call it a day, you can, in season, take the chair lift (22FF; daily during July and August, and on weekends during May, June and September) down to Métabief.

To continue, leave by the service road and follow the flashes of the GR5 down the valley as far as the water trough you passed at the outset of the walk. From here, turn left to repeat your first steps. Alternatively, at the second bend from the summit, head straight down the hill keeping a giant aerial to your left and passing by the winter-only

Finding North

When walking through a Jura village, you can often dispense with a compass for orientation. The north facade of many of the older houses – the side which bears the force of the dominant winter winds and lashing rain – is faced with hundreds of *tavaillons*, small protective shingles, usually in wood, sometimes in beaten tin. These days, they're rarely maintained or repaired so many look as though they're moulting or peeling away.

Refuge du Petit Morond. This way, you descend more directly and considerably more steeply to Métabief beside mountain bikers hurtling down their own special trail, which is used annually for the French mountain bike championships.

Other Walks

Ascent of le Suchet

This is a 20km circular walk from Jougne, near Métabief, taking in the summit of Le Suchet (1588m). It's possible to stay overnight at

Refuge de la Queue on the outward leg and continue next morning. There are great views from the summit of the Swiss plain, the town and lake of Yverdon and the Alps.

Grande Traversée du Jura

The winter cross-country ski classic, this is also a popular mountain bike and walking trail once the snows melt. Few are the walkers who accomplish all 370km from Montbéliard in the *département* (department) of Doubs, passing through Métabief and Les Rousses reaching Hauteville-Lampnes, way west of Geneva, but thousands attempt a tranche or two each year.

Alsace & Massif des Vosges

Alsace is at once France, Germany and neither. For centuries it has been fought over and divided up by its powerful neighbours to the east and west. Long sections of the Crête des Vosges walk, for example, follow what was the Franco-Prussian frontier from 1871 until 1918, and it's common to stumble across remains of trenches and fortifications from both world wars.

Nowadays, the mountains are at peace and the only conflict is of nature's making. Forest, primarily of beech, oak and spruce, the original cladding of the whole massif, is fighting to reclaim upland pasture, cleared centuries ago for summer grazing but now too often abandoned.

Villages are trim and tidy with half-timbered houses and window boxes brimming with geraniums and petunias. The food is distinctive and served in huge portions, and the rich, fruity wines are a revelation.

CLIMATE

As befitting this region of great contrasts, the temperatures in Alsace can vary greatly. Summer temperatures are usually in the upper 20s, while winters are cold enough to keep snow on the ground for weeks on end. Snow can linger on higher ground until early July. Temperature inversions sometimes drown the valleys in a sea of cloud, while the bluish peaks of the mountains are bathed in bright sunlight.

INFORMATION

With so much trans-frontier contact and so many locals comfortable with *alsacien* (Alsatian; the traditional Germanic language of Alsace), you'll find a knowledge of German almost as useful as French.

Maps

For a regional overview, choose either IGN's 1:250,000 *Lorraine, Alsace & Sarre* or Michelin's 1:200,000 *Vosges & Alsace* No 87. For maps covering individual walks, see Planning in the introduction to each walk.

HIGHLIGHTS

INGRID RODDIS

Walking alongside extensive vineyards near Riquewihr

- Just about any point you choose on the Crête des Vosges

- Tucking into a steaming plate of *choucroute Alsacienne*, the local sauerkraut

- Up high, the first glimpse of the Rhine Valley and Germany's Black Forest beyond

- The geometrical bars and stripes of vineyards, seen from the village of Zellenberg

Books

The excellent *Guide des Fermes-Auberges* (45FF) gives a comprehensive list of farms in the Hautes-Vosges which provide accommodation and/or meals. Its pictograms mean you don't have to be proficient in French to extract the essential information.

The Colmar tourist office sells a useful booklet, *Proposals of Walking Tours in the Region of Colmar* (10FF), which gives ideas for day hikes.

Place Names

Many topographical features have names in both Alsatian and French. Often the two are so similar that there's little cause for confusion. But sometimes they invite a little lateral thinking (eg, the spring on Day 1 of the Crête des Vosges walk that is known as both Fontaine des Mulhousiens and Milhuser Brennala).

Information Sources

The villages along the route des Vins d'Alsace all have tourist offices, often located inside the town hall. These offices can provide information on wine tastings, accommodation and restaurants in the region.

The special mountain rescue number in Alsace is ☎ 03 89 77 14 22.

GATEWAY
Colmar

The capital of the Haut-Rhin, Colmar is a maze of cobbled lanes and restored buildings from the late Middle Ages and Renaissance. The town comes to life during 10 days in the first half of August, when Alsatian vintners display their wines at the annual Foire Régional des Vins d'Alsace (Regional Wine Fair of Alsace).

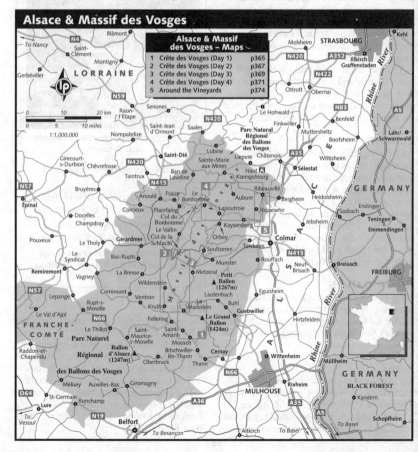

Alsace & Massif des Vosges

Alsace & Massif des Vosges – Maps
1 Crête des Vosges (Day 1) p365
2 Crête des Vosges (Day 2) p367
3 Crête des Vosges (Day 3) p369
4 Crête des Vosges (Day 4) p371
5 Around the Vineyards p374

The tourist office (☎ 03 89 20 68 92, fax 03 89 41 34 13) is at 4 rue des Unterlinden beside the Unterlinden/Point Central bus hub.

Places to Stay & Eat For *Camping de l'Ill* (☎ 03 89 41 15 94), take bus No 1 from the train station or Unterlinden/Point Central bus hub and get off at Plage de l'Ill. Fees are 19FF for a tent and 17FF per person.

The friendly *Maison des Jeunes et de la Culture* (☎ 03 89 41 26 87), also called the Centre International de Séjour, charges 46FF for a bed. It's at 17 rue Camille Schlumberger, just south of the train station.

Hôtel La Chaumière (☎ 03 89 41 08 99, 74 ave de la République), also near the train station, has rooms from 150FF to 180FF (220FF to 240FF with bathroom).

For good Alsatian cuisine, visit *Le Petit Bouchon* (☎ 03 89 23 45 57, 11 rue d'Alspach), which has a local *menu* (fixed-price meal of two or more courses) for 89FF.

Getting There & Away There are around 20 trains a day to and from both Strasbourg (58FF) and Mulhouse (42FF). For Paris' Gare de l'Est (239FF), change in Strasbourg. The

Colmar train station is in place de la Gare, roughly 1km south-west of the town centre.

Colmar's bus terminal for out-of-town services is immediately south of the train station. There are eight buses a day to the trans-border town of Freiburg in Germany.

For a taxi, call Radio Taxis (☎ 03 89 80 71 71). The cheapest option for car hire is Grand Garage Jean Jaurès (☎ 03 89 41 30 26, fax 03 89 41 77 29), 80 ave de la République. Alternatively, try Europcar (☎ 03 89 24 11 80).

Crête des Vosges

Duration	4 days
Distance	84km
Standard	medium
Start	Saint-Amarin
Finish	Riquewihr
Public Transport	yes

Summary A steep ascent from La Thur Valley to Le Grand Ballon, following the ridge through woods and high pasture with descents to Col de la Schlucht and Col du Calvaire, before dropping to Riquewihr.

The walk mostly follows the GR5 as it winds across the rounded summits of the Ballons des Vosges. It's medium mountain-walking, rarely taxing, with fabulous views of the gentler green slopes to the west and, to the east, the wide Rhine Valley and the Black Forest (Schwarzwald), over the frontier in Germany.

The open grasslands above the tree line are known locally as *hautes chaumes*, where for centuries farmers brought their cows to graze the high pasture in summer. These days, however, fewer and fewer make the journey so the grass isn't cropped, allowing shrubs and stunted trees to encroach and reclaim their territory. The hilltops now risk reverting to their natural condition – dense, scarcely penetrable woodland – with the loss of all those sweeping vistas that are the prime joy of this stirring walk.

From the plains up to 700m, vineyards and oak wood predominate. Forest of conifer and beech occupies the middle belt, above which is a narrow subalpine stripe of beech and isolated maple and rowan. Above

How the GR Lost Its Bar

On the occasion of the Club Vosgien's 25th anniversary, its general assembly voted to create and sign a long-distance trail along the entire length of the Vosges Mountains from north to south.

So what's so special? France has over 40,000km of GR trails. What makes that general assembly – the 25th, remember – different is that it was held in 1897.

Volunteers planned, cleared and signed the route with red rectangles exactly 50 years before the name *grande randonnée* was coined in 1947, and almost a century before it became the fashion to plaster red and white bars all over Europe.

That's why the blazes of the pioneer Vosges sector of the GR5 are the only ones throughout France to be red, and only red.

1200m are the upland meadows, scattered with shrubs and stunted trees.

The lakes that you look down on are no more 'natural' than the hautes chaumes. Most were created at the end of the 19th century when streams were dammed to provide back-up power for small-scale textile mills.

For a shorter walk, you could join the trail at Col d'Hahnenbrunnen (early on Day 2) along a waymarked path from Kruth in the Thur Valley (2½ to 2¾ hours, 8km). Kruth is the final stop on the railway line from Colmar that passes through Saint-Amarin.

HISTORY
Thousands of millennia ago, the Massif des Vosges and the Black Forest were part of the same massif. Then, in the same violent movement of the earth's crust which created the Alps and the Jura, the central part collapsed and created the wide Rhine Valley.

The granite massif stretches north-south for about 100km. To the east, the steep Alsatian side with its scree and glacial cirques dominates the vineyards of the Rhine plain. The western slopes of Lorraine and Franche-Comté descend more gently and are more densely populated.

The Parc Naturel Régional des Ballons des Vosges, established in 1989, covers 3000 sq km. It embraces 203 *communes* (the basic unit of local government in France), 250,000 inhabitants and parts of three regions – Alsace, Lorraine and Franche-Comté.

PLANNING
When to Walk
Normally it's possible to walk the crests from mid-May to mid-November. Summer is a delight, with temperatures rarely becoming uncomfortably hot.

What to Bring
If you plan to self-cater, you'll need to pack food for three days as there are no shops between Saint-Amarin and Le Bonhomme.

Maps & Books
Club Vosgien's 1:50,000 *Colmar, Munster, Hohneck, Gerardmer & Les Ballons des Vosges* sheet No 6/8, based upon IGN data,

is superior to the IGN's own 1:100,000 *Parc Naturel des Ballons des Vosges* sheet No 83019 as it includes more walking routes and information. Reliable and covering the whole route, its only disadvantage is that, being so vast, it handles like a spinnaker sail in a high wind.

The Fédération Française de la Randonnée Pédestre (FFRP) Topo-Guide *Crête des Vosges* (No 502) covers the GR5 and GR53 routes from Alsace's northern extremity to south of Belfort. Maybe just worthwhile for its maps at 1:50,000 if you're planning to walk more of the GR route than the Crête des Vosges, it's a thin volume where the text is largely superfluous.

If you plan to spend time in La Thur Valley, pick up the loose-leaf *Promenades et Randonnées Autour de la Vallée de la Haute-Thur* from the local tourist office which describes in detail 39 walks in the valley and is worth the 30FF for its maps alone.

NEAREST TOWNS
Saint-Amarin
With one of the few remaining textile mills in the region, Saint-Amarin – a town which relies increasingly on tourism – makes a good base for exploring the Thur Valley. The tourist office (☎ 03 89 82 13 90, **ℯ** o.t.sant .amarin@wanadoo) is at 81 rue Charles de Gaulle. Both the tourist office and the stationer's at 61 rue Charles de Gaulle carry a small stock of maps and guidebooks.

Places to Stay & Eat The nearest camping ground is *La Mine d'Argent (☎ 03 89 82 30 66)* in Moosch, one train stop south-east of Saint-Amarin (along the N66), which charges 14FF for a tent and 14FF per person.

Rooms at *Hôtel Le Cheval Blanc (☎ 03 89 82 64 80)* in Saint-Amarin cost from 160FF to 210FF.

For pizza and pasta, try *Diligence Pizz' (☎ 03 89 82 79 47, 84 rue Charles de Gaulle)*. *Le Relais de la Vallée (☎ 03 89 82 72 27)*, on the same street opposite the town hall, has *menus* from 70FF.

Getting There & Away Eight Chopin buses (☎ 03 89 42 17 04) link Mulhouse and

Saint-Amarin on weekdays (five on Saturday). The last leaves Mulhouse train station, south of the city centre in ave du Général Leclerc, at 7.05 pm (3.20 pm on Saturday).

There are 10 weekday trains to/from Mulhouse and three on Saturday. The last leaves Mulhouse train station at 7.35 pm (12.16 pm on Saturday).

Riquewihr

The small walled town of Riquewihr, all timbered buildings and bright with window boxes of geraniums, is like a transplant from a Germanic fairy story. It fairly seethes with tourists during the high season. The friendly tourist office (☎ 03 89 49 08 40, fax 03 89 49 08 49) is at the junction of rue du Général de Gaulle (the main street) and rue de la Première Armée.

Places to Stay & Eat The busy *Camping Intercommunal* (☎ 03 89 47 90 08), a 15-minute walk east of Riquewihr, costs 26FF for a tent and 23FF per person.

There's no shortage of places to stay and eat in this tourist-oriented town, where every second house seems to offer B&B, some requiring a minimum stay of two

Crête des Vosges (Day 1)

nights. Ask at the tourist office for a copy of its *Liste des Chambres d'Hôte*. The cheapest hotel is *Au Dolder* (☎ *03 89 47 92 18, fax 03 89 49 04 58)*, on the main street where doubles cost from 250FF to 330FF.

For something snacky, try *Le Bistrot*, also on the main street, which does pizzas and *tarte flambée*, a tasty local version of the ubiquitous pizza, for between 40FF and 52FF. Nearby, in the gorgeous cobbled courtyard of *L'Écurie*, *menus* (fixed-price meals of two or more courses) cost 100FF, 120FF and 135FF.

Getting There & Away Five or six Autocar Pauli buses (☎ 03 89 78 11 78) run between Riquewihr and Colmar, daily except Sunday. The last buses leave Colmar train station at 6.10 pm and Riquewihr at 5.15 pm.

THE WALK
Day 1: Saint-Amarin to Le Markstein

4½–5 hours, 18km

It's work all morning, play all afternoon: a steep, unrelieved and not very varied ascent to the peak of Le Grand Ballon then, once back at Col du Haag, easy striding with great views and little change in elevation all the way to Le Markstein.

From rue Charles de Gaulle in Saint-Amarin (406m), go north up rue Georges Clemenceau. Walk round the south side of the church and head south-east up Kattenbach, a steep lane. Cross over a wider lane and turn left to take a steep track into a wood. After only 20m be careful not to miss a narrow footpath taking off to the right and signed 'Grand Ballon par Col du Haag'. Turn left (north) at a T-junction onto a wide grassy forest track, leaving it after five minutes to fork right onto a footpath. Cross over a wide gravel track and continue heading north-north-west.

Fontaine des Mulhousiens, or Milhuser Brennala, is a spring just below the track, overlooked by a small, rather tacky shrine and spray of plastic flowers, both nailed to a tree. The flowing water, by contrast, is delightfully cool and natural.

Fifteen minutes beyond the spring, leave the houses of Hoehe (763m) on your right, cross a sealed road and take the middle tine of a three-pronged fork. At a junction marked by a picnic bench cross over a forest track. Go left where the footpath meets a stony track, then right (south-east) at a four-way junction 75m later. Just after the track begins to descend, fork left onto a narrow footpath which continues to rise gently as Le Grand Ballon, topped by what

The Ferme-Auberge

There are over 70 *fermes-auberges* (farm-inns) in the Vosges. Farms which are usually still worked, they offer meals and often accommodation too.

Known locally as *marcairies*, they were for centuries the summer home and workplace for *marcaires* (derived from the Alsatian *malker*, (literally 'the one who milks'), or cowherds. You could tell when a marcaire was in residence by the flag flying from a tall flagpole.

Walking in the Vosges is a long-established tradition, and it was back in the 19th century that the fermes-auberges first began opening their doors to hikers. Nowadays, some are accessible by car but travellers on foot are still the main clientele.

The degree of comfort can vary from simple bunks to double rooms with more mod cons than a walker needs. Some allow you to camp for a modest fee or for free if you take dinner with them. Most, especially in the high season, expect you to take half board, which normally costs between 190FF and 230FF.

Regulars salivate at the thought of the *repas marcaire* (80FF to 95FF) which in some fermes-auberges may be the only dish on offer. Expect to receive in gargantuan portions: a sizable hunk of pie, smoked pork and *roigabrabeldi* (sliced potato with onions, slow-cooked in butter), a slab of Munster cheese and a local dessert.

For an excellent directory of fermes-auberges in the Hautes-Vosges, see Books in the introduction to this chapter.

looks like a giant golf ball, looms solid against the sky.

Turn left onto a track which intersects with the GR5 as it comes in from the west only a few metres later. Go straight at a sealed road to reach, after a couple of minutes, *Ferme-Auberge du Haag* (closed Monday) which does snacks and meals and has a couple of dormitories.

From the farm and Col du Haag (1280m), strike south-east along a clearly defined path which goes beside a brimming trough of cool water as it climbs towards the peak. A couple of minutes before the orientation table which marks the summit, it passes the Monument des Diables Bleus, erected in memory of the 'Blue Devils', a crack WWI Alpine regiment from Savoy which fought and suffered massive losses in these same hills.

Le Grand Ballon (1424m) is both the highest and farthest east of the peaks along the crest of the Vosges. From its summit you get the finest views (although the competition's tough) of the Rhine Valley and the hills of the Black Forest beyond the river in Germany.

At the summit, reached after 2¼ to 2½ hours of walking, that strange giant golf ball humming in the high winds which regularly sweep the peak is revealed as an aircraft tracking station. If you look backwards as you descend its flight of steps, it resembles some displaced Inca temple.

Turn left to follow the sign 'Circuit Versant Ouest' and drop to *Chalet Hôtel du Grand Ballon*, which does a three-course 50FF *menu marcheur* (walkers' menu) and also welcomes picnickers, provided that you buy a drink. The optimistically named *Restaurant Bar La Vue des Alpes*, newer and catering primarily to the motorised trade, also does lunches and snacks.

Walk beside the former then follow a footpath running parallel to the sealed road. This is the first of several encounters with the **Route des Crêtes**, originally a military road constructed by the French to supply and control the ridge.

Back at Col du Haag, don't take the old GR trail over the crest of Le Storkenkopf, whose owner does his best to deny access. Instead, go along the left side of Ferme-

Auberge du Haag and take a footpath heading westwards, up into the woods. This makes a shorter if steeper alternative to the more frequented amended GR5 route.

Once over the crest, pass through a revolving stile and descend to join the route des Crêtes where the GR5, coming in from the left, crosses it. Join the GR route to head north-west. From here to Le Markstein, navigation is simplicity itself, aided by the twin clues of the GR's red-and-white waymarkers and the winding course of the route des Crêtes, never long out of sight. There are continuously fine views to the west –

Crête des Vosges (Day 2)

less so to the eastern Alsatian side, as much of the route runs just below the crest.

Outside the ski season, **Le Markstein** (1240m) is a mournful dump whose accommodation options aren't great. But anyone who makes it up here hasn't come primarily for the creature comforts.

At *Hôtel Restaurant Wolf* (☎ *03 89 82 64 36, fax 03 89 38 72 06)*, a rambling old place where the staff could do with a crash course in how to deal with customers, a double is 175FF with washbasin, 255FF with shower and 315FF with bathroom. Its restaurant offers *menus* for between 75FF and 130FF.

One of 20 bunks at *Maison d'Accueil* (☎ *03 89 82 74 98)*, which doubles up as the *syndicat d'initiative* (tourist office), costs 51FF. It's more welcoming than the down-at-heel exterior would suggest. The small bar does snacks and breakfast and can supply meals, if warned in advance. Despite the decidedly limited charms of these two places, it's advisable to reserve on summer weekends and in July and August.

Two kilometres beyond the ski station, *Ferme-Auberge du Steinlebach* (☎ *03 89 82 61 87)* does half board for 210FF.

Day 2: Le Markstein to Les Trois Fours

4¼-4¾ hours, 19km

Follow the GR route as it curves westwards around a small hill (1268m) with a summer sledging run. Cross the route des Crêtes and continue along the clearly defined path (a short detour north-east from the junction brings you to *Ferme-Auberge du Steinlebach*).

A small stone monument just to the left of the route commemorates the spot where in 1940 a company of beleaguered French soldiers burnt their regimental flag rather than surrender it to the German invaders. Here too you see the first of many slit trenches from both WWI and WWII. Nowadays they're banked by bilberries and are being colonised by shrubs and small trees. Violence is difficult to imagine amid such splendid views – back to Le Grand Ballon and eastwards to the wide plain of the Rhine Valley with the dark stain of the Black Forest beyond.

The Killing Fields

From Day 2 onwards, there are constant reminders of man's inhumanity to man. You're walking a small part of the vast WWI and WWII killing fields near the Franco-German border. The slaughter in WWI was infinitely the greater as hilltop after hilltop, vantage point after vantage point, was fought over, lost and regained only to be recaptured. In WWII by contrast, the German forces ripped through Belgium and rolled southwards to attack from the rear the French Maginot Line, running the length of Alsace and believed to be impregnable.

Over half a century since the last shot was fired, nature is stealthily effacing the evidence of trenches, bunkers and gun emplacements.

From Le Rainkopf onwards, you pass the boundary stones which demarcated the frontier from 1871, when Alsace was occupied by Germany, to the treaty of Versailles in 1919. With 'F' for France chiselled on one side and with an often defaced 'D' for Deutschland on the other, these days they mark the boundary between the French *départements* (departments) of Haut-Rhin on the eastern side and Vosges on the west, and between the regions of Alsace and Lorraine.

Recross the route des Crêtes just before the Col de Breitfirst (1280m). As you emerge from the welcome shade of a copse of stunted beech trees, you can see the village of Kruth in the Thur Valley to the west, its lake hidden by the long spine of Le Griebkopf.

At the **Col d'Hahnenbrunnen** (1186m), where the trail briefly follows the sealed road, there's a *refuge* (refuge or mountain hut) whose picnic tables, perched over the upper reaches of the wooded Mittlach Valley, make a great rest stop. From here you can clearly see Le Hohneck, recognisable by the inverted 'V' of the hotel-restaurant that crowns its summit.

Leave the road after 200m to take a wide track beneath beech and a sprinkling of plane trees as you advance in parallel with the clear traces of slit trenches. A small cairn at ankle level marks the highest point of Le Schweisel (1271m).

From the Col du Herrenberg (1186m), the GR5 descends the village of Mittlach with an altitude loss of over 650m. Our route by contrast sticks to the tops, continuing resolutely northwards. Pass a small Club Vosgien unstaffed *refuge* – essentially a hut with a fireplace and space to stretch a sleeping bag.

Along a clear, unambiguous trail, tick off the summits: Batteriekopf (1311m) from where, looking back south-west, Lac de Kruth-Wildenstein is now visible and, 10 minutes later, Rothenbachkopf (1316m) with a stone cairn. Just below the peak is a small wooden cross in memory of two young Germans who, one night in December 1965, perished in a blizzard.

Having dropped to an unnamed col (1205m), instead of the waymarked trail choose the minor right-hand footpath which hugs the lip of the Mittlach Valley, thus retaining the magnificent plunging vista as long as possible. This curves west for the final 200m to the summit of Le Rainkopf (1305m) and the first of the one-time frontier markers (see the boxed text 'The Killing Fields').

Just beyond Collet du Rainkopf (1200m) is the Club Vosgien's staffed **Chalet Refuge du Rainkopf** with a trough and flowing water. It doesn't do meals or drinks but, 150m away, **Ferme-Auberge Firstmiss** (also called Ferschmuss) provides both – but not accommodation. Perfect symbiosis!

At a four-way junction, go left then right (north-east) after 50m to stay in woodland. A left turn would take you to **Ferme-Auberge Breitzhousen** (☎ *03 29 63 22 92, fax 03 29 63 03 21)*, visible below with the inky Lac de la Lande beyond it, once the trail leaves the wood.

Beside the flat, sandy track bordered by meadows of wild flowers, there are a couple of strange phenomena. Groups of giant granite boulders, for all the world like tumbled megaliths, are in fact the work of farmers long ago who, without mechanical assistance, cleared the land for cultivation. The line of large ugly orange lollipops marching parallel to the ridge are designed to guide travellers in winter when snow conceals other landmarks. All the same, they're an ugly stain on the summer landscape and could surely be either removed until snow returns or replaced by something more aesthetic.

At Collet du Hohneck (1280m), also called Col du Wormspel, take a gravel path. The summit of Le Hohneck is topped by an orientation table and *Hôtel Restaurant du Sommet du Hohneck* (☎ 03 29 63 11 47). The bar-restaurant, although often crowded with motorists, makes a welcome rest stop. Open until 7 pm, it serves snacks plus lunch

Crête des Vosges (Day 3)

menus at 50FF, 80FF and 95FF, or you can eat your own picnic inside provided that you buy a drink. In July and August, it also functions as a hotel, where doubles start at 270FF.

Having rejoined the GR5, head initially north-west from the summit – still following those old frontier stones – to drop to Col de Falimont (1239m) where the trail veers north-east around the rim of the steep valley that drops to the east.

At a sign reading 'Champ des Trois Fours', turn right onto a sealed lane. Where the GR5 forks left onto a dirt track after 100m, continue straight as far as the three houses – a farm which makes Munster cheese, a *refuge* and a *ferme-auberge* (see the boxed text 'The Ferme-Auberge') – which constitute Les Trois Fours.

Since Les Trois Fours falls within a nature conservation area, not even bivouac camping is possible. However, there's a choice of accommodation. Half board at *Ferme-Auberge des Trois Fours* (☎ 03 89 77 31 14) costs 195FF, while dinner alone is 84FF. More auberge than ferme, it has a bar and vast dining room that can accommodate 80 (it's closed Monday). Just beyond is the friendly, spick and span *refuge* (☎/fax 03 89 77 32 59) of the Club Alpin Français (CAF). Here, a bunk costs 64FF, dinner is 60FF, or you can use the cooking facilities – including a microwave – for 10FF per person. If you prefer to stay in a hotel, push on for a further half-hour to Col de la Schlucht.

Day 3: Les Trois Fours to Le Bonhomme

5–5½ hours, 20.5km
Return to the point where you left the GR5 and turn right onto a dirt track which drops down through beechwood to **Col de la Schlucht** (1130m).

At the pass, rooms at *Hôtel du Chalet* (☎ 03 89 77 04 06) cost from 160FF to 215FF, while those at *Hôtel Le Tetras* (☎ 03 29 63 11 37) range from 130FF to 250FF.

Turn right on the D417 and take a path to the left just beyond Hôtel Le Tetras. It's 10 minutes of steep, bouldery ascent until a four-way junction, where the GR531 heads off to the right towards Munster.

Pass Rocher du Haut Fourneau (1288m), also called Le Wurzelstein, and on occasion Le Wourzelstein, which is a rocky outcrop popular with climbers. Just beyond a low log bridge over a marsh, the trail enters the Réserve Naturelle de Tanet-Gazon du Faing. Just before a brief scramble over boulders to the marginally higher point of Le Tanet (1292m), reached after about an hour of walking, note the rusting iron and concrete of a wartime pillbox lookout post on the right.

After fleetingly converging with the route des Crêtes, the trail re-enters forest. Emerge to ascend gradually and scarcely noticeably, now on grass, now on dry peat that's bouncy underfoot and jet black.

Once beyond Ringbuhl (1302m), pause at an orientation table planted at the heart of the **Gazon du Faing**, a flat upland grassy plateau. It's a popular spot with motorists who make the short stroll up from Auberge du Faing and its adjacent car park, a 10-minute detour westwards.

There are splendid views looking west of the valley to the east and back towards Le Hohneck, with Le Grand Ballon, topped by what now appears as a tiny pimple, still visible on the south-eastern horizon. Changing focus, note nearer at hand the superior quality of the grass on the chaumes to the right where they're still regularly cropped by cows, and where trees are sparse and bilberry has still to gain a foothold.

Taubenklangfelsen (1299m) lowers over Lac des Truites, all but dried up, with **Ferme-Auberge Lac du Forlet** at its western end, both of them too far below to be tempting. From this granite outcrop, bear briefly east to Soultzeren Eck (1302m) then turn northwards again, staying with the GR route as the trail to Lac Noir goes straight ahead.

From here it's yet more level striding, straight as an arrow for 2.5km, between forest on the right and marsh and open pasture to the left. Where the path re-enters woodland, it's worth making the briefest of detours east to look down over Lac Blanc (White Lake – in fact a mournful grey), glittering at the base of its glacial cirque. Descending through spruce wood, notice how the trees are taller and more mature than their more exposed and stunted cousins on the upland plateau.

Just before a road and large holiday home, turn left for **Col du Calvaire** (1144m). Ignore the GR5 flashes and instead trust a signpost and take a wide level 4WD track, signed 'Cimetière Duchesne'. This passes beside Source Rosalie, an icy cold spring beside the farm of Les Immerlins. Don't worry about the *chemin forestier privé* (private forest track) signs on this and the next day's route; these are for motorists, not walkers.

At a four-way junction fork left and uphill to reach, a couple of minutes later, the sobering **Cimetière Duchesne**, a French WWI military cemetery, its simple stone crosses now dwarfed by tall conifers.

Picking up the GR5 again, continue north-east up a track, originally paved with blocks of granite, now much eroded, to ease the provisioning of the military post on top of Tête des Faux.

About 10 minutes later, you have a choice: to turn left and take the alternative GR532, shortening the day's walk by 2km and avoiding some stiff altitude gain, or to continue to the peak, scene of a fierce battle in December 1914. Continuing, pass a monument to a group of officers of the Chasseurs Alpins (see the boxed text 'The Killing Fields' earlier in this chapter). At the summit of **Tête des Faux** (1208m), a simple white cross seems to grow from the debris of the fortification which once dominated the hilltop and the orientation table appears incongruous amid so much destruction.

Descending north-eastwards, note the rusting coils of barbed wire, slit trenches, craters and bunkers on both sides of the track. Perhaps pause at a second orientation table which looks east over the Rhine and the frontier to the hills of the Black Forest, and hope that in today's and tomorrow's Europe, such carnage may never happen again.

At a T-junction, turn left onto a track to reach Rocher du Corbeau, a megahunk of granite. At a bend two minutes later, take a steep footpath to the left (north-east). Pass a huge concrete cavern, once a store at the top of a *téléférique* (cable car or funicular) constructed by the Germans to transport supplies. From here, the descent through mixed beech and conifer is easy and pleasant after the sombre debris of the mountain's upper reaches.

The path meets a wide 4WD track beside the pool of **Étang du Devin** (926m), which is reverting to bog as grasses and sedges inexorably occupy the site. Here, an old bunker excavated into the hillside offers spartan shelter. Turn left for the superior comfort of *Hôtel Résidences Étang du Devin*, a little over five minutes away, just beyond a former German military cemetery. A dormitory bed costs 55FF (75FF in a room) and the owners allow camping.

Continue along the firm, graded track that becomes sealed lane. Some 50m before the first houses of **Le Bonhomme**, turn right down an easily missed footpath to reach the valley and its main street.

In Le Bonhomme, *Hôtel Restaurant La Tête des Faux* (☎ 03 89 47 51 11) has doubles for between 180FF and 260FF (half board from 180FF to 250FF). *Restaurant Au Chasseur* (☎/fax 03 89 47 51 02) does a *menu* for 65FF. It has a few doubles (130FF) and triples (140FF) and does half board for 180FF. A pizza at *Bar/Pizzeria Le*

Schlitte (closed Wednesday) costs from 30FF to 45FF.

There are five STAHV buses a day to/from Colmar (not Sunday), the first leaving at 8.15 am and the last at 6.08 pm.

Day 4: Le Bonhomme to Riquewihr
5¾–6½ hours, 26.5km

From the church in Le Bonhomme (690m), head north along route des Bagenelles (D48). Fork right after five minutes onto a lane, which soon narrows to overgrown footpath.

Continue straight where this path merges with a wide cart track and cross the D48 a couple of times. (Here, as so often in France's hills and mountains, the walkers' way follows a long-established track while the modern road has to wind and snake to gain the same height).

At a T-junction, turn left along a dirt track which descends towards Les Bagenelles. Just before the farm, the trail describes a 'Z' (not as on the Club Vosgien reference map) to reach Col des Bagenelles (903m) after about 45 minutes' walking. From the pass there's a magnificent view northwards of the valley of La Lièpvrette and the succeeding

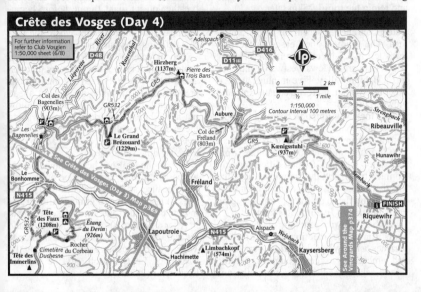

ripples of hills beyond. A Club Vosgien *chalet* offers snacks, drinks and accommodation in high summer and, year-round, a tap and flowing trough.

Take chemin du Haycot, a wide dirt track, then fork left after a little under 10 minutes to stay in woodland. About 30 minutes beyond the col, cross a major track and take a narrow footpath signed 'Ski Club'. Pass a chalet (not open to casual overnighters) belonging to the eponymous club and, five minutes or so later, emerge into a vast forest clearing (1075m) where tracks scatter in all directions.

Just off the clearing and off-route is the stone-carved crest of an infantry battalion from Bonn, another relic of WWI. A little beyond is *Le Haycot (☎ 03 88 73 12 79 for reservations)*, where a bunk costs 43FF. It's worth dropping by for a drink or a snack while savouring the magnificent view of the gentle wooded slopes of the Rauenthal Valley to the north.

From the clearing, it's a brief but steep climb to the summit of **Le Grand Brézouard** (1229m), the last peak of any consequence on the walk. If you prefer to bypass it, simply take the alternative GR532 eastwards and rejoin the trail 1.25km later.

To reach the peak, the main route makes a steep, unrelieved ascent for 10 to 15 minutes. The gradient then eases as the trail turns left at a T-junction to reach a rickety bench with great views westwards and back to La Behine Valley. Five minutes and another bench later, there are equally splendid views to the east.

At a four-way junction beside a trashed, abandoned chalet, continue straight (north-east) then turn left at a T-junction. Ignore all side turnings until, about 20 minutes from the chalet, the route (which differs slightly from the tracing on the recommended Club Vosgien reference map) turns left and uphill, leaving the main track. Turn left again at a similar fork five minutes later.

At the five-way junction of Pierre des Trois Bans, the meeting point of three parishes, a trim wayside *chalet* offers shade and emergency accommodation. Of the three tracks signed 'Aubure', take the one heading south towards Col de Fréland. It's the least travelled route and, once you're beyond the dead zone of factory forestry, the most scenic.

About 15 minutes beyond the chalet, turn left at an intersection to enjoy easy, agreeable walking along a wide forest track. About 25 to 30 minutes later, turn left onto a sealed road then, just after an ugly stone *belvédère* (viewpoint), left again at Col de Fréland (803m) to descend to **Aubure**.

Turn right down chemin du Combattant and follow it as far as the post office. Here the route veers south-west and back on itself then turns sharp left beside the last house in the village. At a junction 20 minutes later, stay with the main track ignoring the sign 'Kœnigsstuhl Variante', then fork right after 150m onto a pleasant footpath bordered by ferns. A further 20 minutes brings you to a jumble of giant granite boulders from where there are the first fine views of wooded hills rolling to the southern horizon, the broad plain to the east and the town of Colmar where hill and plain meet to the south-east.

At Kœnigsstuhl (937m), which literally means 'the seat of the king', you can take a breather on its giant throne before beginning the descent. About 10 minutes from the peak, continue straight where the narrow path merges with a broad logging track.

Say farewell to the GR5 as it veers left beside a small cross. At a four-way junction 100m later, where three of the four options are signed 'Riquewihr', go straight ahead (south-east) then right after 150m to follow red-and-white waymarkers all the way to the end of the walk. Ten minutes from the cross, turn right and go over a track to continue heading south-west.

Unless the trail has been groomed since we passed, this section may be quite difficult because of thick undergrowth. But it doesn't last; around 10 minutes after crossing the track, the route meets a sealed road.

After a further 10 minutes, fork left onto the wide, bramble-free chemin de la Grande Valle, which descends gently, following the stream of Le Sembach, all the way to Riquewihr (283m).

Around the Vineyards

Duration	3½–4 hours
Distance	14km
Standard	easy
Start/Finish	Riquewihr
Public Transport	yes

Summary A circular route taking in six of Alsace's premier wine-growing villages and a memorial to a major WWII battle. Despite little change in elevation, there are fine views of the surrounding plain and Vosges Mountains.

Alsace has as many as 19 wine trails. We've selected the longest and best, not so much from a wine lover's perspective but because it offers good walking – and good tasting into the bargain. The route, indicated by signposts and red circles, passes through six villages: Riquewihr, Hunawihr, Zellenberg, Beblenheim, Mittelwihr and Bennwihr, and links some of Alsace's finest vineyards producing seven varieties of *grand cru* wines (see the boxed text 'Grand Cru Wines of Alsace').

Gentle and with no dramatic changes in elevation, the walk allows plenty of time for exploring the villages and sampling a fine wine or two. Bear in mind that we only take into account actual walking time – the walk could easily and pleasurably fill a whole day. In July and August there's a daily short guided walk organised by each of the six *communes* on a rotating basis. Starting at 5 pm and lasting a couple of hours, they finish with a visit to a *cave* (wine cellar) and tastings. The schedule is displayed around the *communes*, and the Riquewihr tourist office has a leaflet.

When we walked this route, it was generally adequately signed, except around Bennwihr where, the tourist office assured us, new waymarkers were imminent.

PLANNING
When to Walk
The walk is rewarding at any time. Although vines are bare in winter and until the spring growth begins at the end of April, views remain constantly splendid. The optimum time is late September and October when the grape harvest is under way. The precise starting date is determined each year by La Comité Interprofessionelle des Vins d'Alsace, the guild of wine producers, but the harvest always embraces the first two weeks of October.

What to Bring
If you're planning a little *dégustation* (tasting), pack an extra water bottle. There's very little shade en route and alcohol dehydrates the system.

Maps
Pick up *Le Sentier Viticole des Grands Crus*, a detailed plan of the route, from the tourist office in Riquewihr. A free booklet of the same name in French describes the various vineyards en route and their wines.

NEAREST TOWN
For information on Riquewihr, see Nearest Towns in the Crête des Vosges walk.

Grand Cru Wines of Alsace

It was the Romans who first introduced the vine to Alsace, nowadays root and branch (together with tourism) of the regional economy. Among the most prized of all the region's fruity white wines are those known as *grand cru* (literally 'great growth'). The title isn't bestowed casually. The area planted is strictly defined and slopes must face somewhere in an arc between east and south-west.

Their tall, slim bottles must indicate the year of the vintage, the variety (only four – Gewurztraminer, Riesling, Tokay Pinot Gris and Muscat d'Alsace – are permitted) and the vineyard where the grapes were grown. The sentier des Grands Crus takes you through seven such areas.

To average walkers and topers like ourselves they all look the same on the vine. But crack open a bottle back at base camp and you'll understand why a grand cru is indeed grand.

ALSACE & MASSIF DES VOSGES

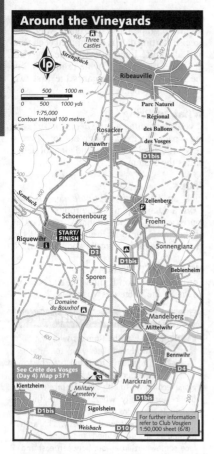

Around the Vineyards

Three Castles

Strengbach

Ribeauville

0   500   1000 m
0   500   1000 yds
1:75,000
Contour Interval 100 metres

Parc Naturel
Régional
des Ballons
des Vosges

Rosacker

Hunawihr

D1bis

Sembach

Zellenberg

Schoenenbourg

Froehn

START/
FINISH

Riquewihr

D3

D1bis

Sonnenglanz

Beblenheim

Sporen

Domaine
du Bouxhof

Mandelberg

Mittelwihr

Bennwihr

D4

See Crête des Vosges
(Day 4) Map p371

Kientzheim

Marckrain

Military
Cemetery

D1bis

Sigolsheim

D1bis

Weisbach   D10

For further information
refer to Club Vosgien
1:50,000 sheet (6/8)

THE WALK

3½–4 hours, 14km

Leave Riquewihr's tourist office, having collected a map, and turn left (south) along rue de la Première Armée. Bear left along rue de Mittelwihr to pick up the first of the route's red dots.

Once out of town, turn right onto a sandy path to pass through the first of the day's vineyards. At a tall wooden tripod indicating the boundary between two *communes*, turn right to pass in front of the imposing Domaine du Bouxhof villa.

Where the sealed road ends just over the brow of a hill, turn left onto a dirt track to diverge very slightly from the signed trail, aiming for a tall flagpole. This marks the **military cemetery** and memorial to troops of the Première Armée (First French Army) who fought the bitter battle of Colmar in temperatures of -20°C in early 1945. Note that half of those who fell were Muslim troops from France's colonies. Just beyond is a monument erected in 1995 by veterans of the First French army to their American colleagues in arms.

Back on the path, turn left (north) after 50m to rejoin the signed route beside a descriptive panel and turn right. After going left at a marker post, look out for an unsigned turning to the right where a footpath passes through a tunnel of trees. Make your way down to Bennwihr. If in doubt, aim for the twin fermentation tanks of Best Heim winery.

Follow the trail through the twin villages of Bennwihr and Mittelwihr. Communities going back to Roman times, both were comprehensively destroyed in 1944, then rebuilt in the traditional style.

Cross the main road and take the lane which ascends to the left of Hôtel Le Mandelberg. The trail, clearly signed from here onwards, then drops through vines to Beblenheim.

Beyond the hamlet, a grassy track leads towards **Zellenberg**, conspicuous on top of its escarpment. Climb a flight of steps to a shaded square (notice the storks' nest on top of the church). Take a short, oval-shaped detour (10 minutes; factored into the walk time) around its lanes and beside the remnants of its chateau, razed in 1791, just after the revolution. There are great views in all directions, particularly towards Riquewihr and the wooded hills behind. There's also a welcome *fontaine* (fountain or spring) at the head of rue du Schlossberg.

Once over the busy D1 (bis), pass beside yet another winery, signed 'Paul Fuchs' (Lucky Paul). Nearing Hunawihr, you can clearly see the chateau of Le Haut Kœnigsbourg on the northern horizon and the trio of castles above Ribeauvillé to the north-west.

The old wash house in **Hunawihr** has a welcome shaded canopy and fine fountain whose water, alas, is not potable. A short detour from Grande Rue up rue de la Fontaine leads to its 15th-century fortified church, now used for worship by both Catholics and Protestants.

Beyond the village, the track enters the first and last woodland of the day. At a four-way junction about 20 minutes from Hunawihr, turn left, then left again after 200m to pass through vines of the Schoenenbourg grand cru and descend to Riquewihr.

Other Walks

GAZON DU FAING

If you want to explore Réserve Naturelle de Tanet-Gazon du Faing (Day 3 of the Crête des Vosges walk) and the biological richness of the high pastures, a five-hour circuit from Auberge du Gazon du Faing takes you to the Belmont-Rocher observatory and back via Lac des Truites and Lac Vert.

Language

While the French rightly or wrongly have a reputation for assuming that all human beings should speak French – until WWI it was the international language of culture and diplomacy – you'll find that any attempt to communicate in French will be much appreciated. Probably your best bet is to always approach people politely in French, even if the only sentence you know is *Pardon, madame/monsieur/mademoiselle, parlez-vous anglais?* (Excuse me, madam/sir/miss, do you speak English?).

An important distinction is made in French between *tu* and *vous*, which both mean 'you'. *Tu* is only used when addressing people you know well, children or animals. When addressing an adult who is not a personal friend, *vous* should be used unless the person invites you to use *tu*. In general, younger people insist less on this distinction, and they may use *tu* from the beginning of an acquaintance. In this guide the polite form is used in most cases; where both forms are given they are noted by the abbreviations 'pol' and 'inf' respectively.

All nouns in French are either masculine or feminine and adjectives reflect the gender of the noun they modify. The feminine form of many nouns and adjectives is indicated by a silent *e* added to the masculine form, as in *étudiant/étudiante*, the masculine and feminine for 'student'. In the following phrases we have indicated both masculine and feminine forms where necessary (separated by a slash, with the masculine form first). The gender of a noun is often indicated by a preceding article: 'the/a/some', *le/un/du* (m), *la/une/de la* (f); or a possessive adjective, my/your/his/her', *mon/ton/son* (m), *ma/ta/sa* (f). With French, unlike English, the possessive adjective agrees in number and gender with the thing possessed, eg, *sa mère* (his/her mother).

For a more comprehensive guide to the French language, get hold of Lonely Planet's *French phrasebook*. It has sections on grammar and pronunciation, and contains all the words and phrases you'll need to cover most of the situations you find yourself in while travelling.

Pronunciation

Most letters in French are pronounced more or less the same as their English equivalents. A few which may cause confusion are:

j	as the 's' in 'leisure', eg, *jour* (day)
c	before **e** and **i**, as the 's' in 'sit'; before **a**, **o** and **u**, as English 'k'. When underscored with a 'cedilla' (ç) it's always pronounced as the 's' in 'sit'.

French has a number of sounds that are difficult for Anglophones to produce. These include:

- The distinction between the 'u' sound (as in *tu*) and 'oo' sound (as in *tout*). For both sounds, the lips are rounded and projected forward, but for the 'u' the tongue is towards the front of the mouth, its tip against the lower front teeth, whereas for the 'oo' the tongue is towards the back of the mouth, its tip behind the gums of the lower front teeth.

- The nasal vowels. With nasal vowels the breath escapes partly through the nose and partly through the mouth. There are no nasal vowels in English; in French there are three, as in *bon vin blanc*, (good white wine). These sounds occur where a syllable ends in a single **n** or **m**; the **n** or **m** is silent but indicates the nasalisation of the preceding vowel.

- The **r**. The standard **r** of Parisian French is produced by moving the bulk of the tongue backwards to constrict the air flow in the pharynx while the tip of the tongue rests behind the lower front teeth. It's similar to the noise made by some people before spitting, but with much less friction.

Greetings & Civilities

Good morning.	*Bonjour.* (pol)
Hello.	*Salut.* (inf)
Good evening.	*Bonsoir.*
Good night.	*Bonne nuit.*
Goodbye.	*Au revoir.* (pol)
	À bientôt/
	À plus tard. (inf)
Please.	*S'il vous plaît.*
Thank you.	*Merci.*
You're welcome.	*Je vous en prie.*
Excuse me.	*Excusez-moi.*
Sorry/Forgive me.	*Pardon.*
Yes.	*Oui.*
No.	*Non.*
Maybe.	*Peut-être.*

Small Talk

How are you?	*Comment allez-vous?* (pol)
	Comment vas-tu/
	Comment ça va? (inf)
Fine, thanks.	*Bien, merci.*
I'm tired	*Je suis fatigué/e.* (m/f)
And you?	*Et vous?*
What's your name?	*Comment vous appelez-vous?* (pol)
	Tu t'appelles comment? (inf)
My name is ...	*Je m'appelle ...*
I'm pleased to meet you.	*Enchanté* (m)/ *Enchantée.* (f)
How old are you?	*Quel âge avez-vous?*
I'm ... years old.	*J'ai ... ans.*
Do you like ...?	*Aimez-vous ...?*
Where are you from?	*De quel pays êtes-vous?*
I'm from ...	*Je viens de ...*

Language Difficulties

I understand.	*Je comprends.*
I don't understand.	*Je ne comprends pas.*
Do you speak English?	*Parlez-vous anglais?*
Could you please write it down?	*Est-ce que vous pouvez l'écrire?*

Getting Around

I want to go to ...	*Je voudrais aller à ...*
I'd like to book a seat to ...	*Je voudrais réserver une place pour ...*

Signs

Entrée	**Entrance**
Sortie	**Exit**
Complet	**No Vacancies**
Renseignements	**Information**
Ouvert/Fermé	**Open/Closed**
Interdit	**Prohibited**
(Commissariat de) Police	**Police Station**
Chambres Libres	**Rooms Available**
Toilettes, WC	**Toilets**
Hommes	**Men**
Femmes	**Women**

What time does the ... leave/arrive?	*À quelle heure part/arrive ...?*
aeroplane	*l'avion*
bus (city)	*l'autobus*
bus (intercity)	*l'autocar*
ferry	*le ferry(-boat)*
train	*le train*

Where is (the) ...?	*Où est ...?*
bus station	*la gare routière*
bus stop	*l'arrêt d'autobus*
metro station	*la station de métro*
train station	*la gare*
ticket office	*le guichet*

I'd like a ... ticket.	*Je voudrais un billet ...*
one-way	*aller-simple*
return	*aller-retour*
1st class	*première classe*
2nd class	*deuxième classe*

Do I need to ...?	*Est-ce que je dois ...?*
change trains	*changer de train*
change platform	*changer de quai*

Can you take me to ...?	*Est-ce que vous pouvez me conduire à ...?*
How long does the trip take?	*Combien de temps dure le trajet?*
Please let me know when we get to ...	*Voulez-vous me dire quand nous arrivons à ...*
I'd like to get off at ...	*Je veux descendre à ...*

left-luggage office	*consigne manuelle*
left-luggage locker	*consigne automatique*

platform	*quai*
timetable	*horaire*

I'd like to hire ...	*Je voudrais louer ...*
a car	*une voiture*
a bicycle	*un vélo*

Around Town

I'm looking for ...	*Je cherche ...*
a bank/exchange office	*une banque/un bureau de change*
the city centre	*le centre-ville*
the ... embassy	*l'ambassade de ...*
the hospital	*l'hôpital*
my hotel	*mon hôtel*
the market	*le marché*
the police	*la police*
the post office	*le bureau de poste/ la poste*
a public phone	*une cabine téléphonique*
a public toilet	*les toilettes*
the tourist office	*le syndicat d'initiative/l'office de tourisme*

Where is (the) ...?	*Où est ...?*
bridge	*le pont*
castle/mansion	*le château*
cathedral	*la cathédrale*
church	*l'église*
(main) square	*la place (centrale)*
old city (town)	*la vieille ville*
quay/bank	*le quai/la rive*
ruins	*les ruines*
tower	*la tour*

What time does it open/close?	*Quelle est l'heure d'ouverture/ de fermeture?*
I'd like to make a telephone call.	*Je voudrais téléphoner.*

I'd like to change ...	*Je voudrais changer ...*
some money	*de l'argent*
travellers cheques	*chèques de voyage*

Shopping

bookshop	*la librairie*
chemist/pharmacy	*la pharmacie*
laundry/launderette	*la laverie*
newsagency	*l'agence de presse*
outdoor equipment shop	*un magasin de sports et loisirs*
stationers	*la papeterie*
supermarket	*le supermarché*

How much is it?	*C'est combien?*
It's too expensive for me.	*C'est trop cher pour moi.*
I'm just looking.	*Je ne fais que regarder.*
It's too big/small.	*C'est trop grand/petit.*
more/less	*plus/moins*
cheap	*bon marché*
cheaper	*moins cher*

Accommodation

Where is ...	*Ou est-ce qu'il y a ...*
I'm looking for ...	*Je cherche ...*
a B&B	*une chambre d'hôte*
a campground	*un camping*
a gite (walker's hostel)	*une gîte d'étape*
a hotel	*un hôtel*
a tent pitch/space	*un emplacement*
the youth hostel	*l'auberge de jeunesse*

Where can I find a cheap hotel?	*Où est-ce que je peux trouver un hôtel bon marché?*
What's the address?	*Quelle est l'adresse?*
Could you write it down, please?	*Est-ce que vous pourriez l'écrire, s'il vous plaît?*
Do you have any rooms available?	*Est-ce que vous avez des chambres libres?*

I'd like to book ...	*Je voudrais réserver ...*
a bed	*un lit*
a single room	*une chambre pour une personne*
a double room	*une chambre double*
a room with a shower and toilet	*une chambre avec douche et WC*

I'd like to stay in a dormitory.	*Je voudrais coucher dans un dortoir.*

LANGUAGE

How much is it ...?	Quel est le prix ...?
per night	par nuit
per person	par personne

Is breakfast included?	Est-ce que le petit déjeuner est compris?
May I see the room?	Est-ce que je peux voir la chambre?
Where is the toilet?	Où sont les toilettes?

Where is ...?	Où est ...?
the bathroom	la salle de bains
the shower	la douche

I'm going to stay ...	Je resterai ...
one night	une nuit
three nights	trois nuits
one day	un jour
a week	une semaine

Health

I'm sick.	Je suis malade.
I need a doctor.	Il me faut un médecin.
Where is the hospital?	Où est l'hôpital?
I have diarrhoea.	J'ai la diarrhée.
I'm pregnant.	Je suis enceinte.
It hurts here.	J'ai une douleur ici.
I have a sprain.	Je me suis fait une entorse.

I'm ...	Je suis ...
diabetic	diabétique
epileptic	épileptique
asthmatic	asthmatique
anaemic	anémique

I'm allergic ...	Je suis allergique ...
to antibiotics	aux antibiotiques
to penicillin	à la pénicilline
to bees	aux abeilles

antiseptic	antiseptique
aspirin	aspirine
blister	ampoule
condoms	préservatifs
medicine	médicament
insect repellant	produit/répulsif anti-moustiques
nausea	nausée
sunblock cream	écran (solaire) total
tampons	tampons hygiéniques

Emergencies

Help!	Au secours!
Call a doctor!	Appelez un médecin!
Call the police!	Appelez la police!
Careful!	Attention!
I've been raped.	On m'a violée.
I'm lost.	Je me suis égaré/égarée. (m/f)
Leave me alone!	Fichez-moi la paix!

Time & Dates

What time is it?	Quelle heure est-il?
It's 10 am.	Il est dix heures.
It's 10 pm.	Il est vingt-deux heures.
It's five past six.	Il est six heures cinq.
It's five to six.	Il est six heures moins cinq.
When?	Quand?
today	aujourd'hui
tonight	ce soir
tomorrow	demain
day after tomorrow	après-demain
yesterday	hier
all day	toute la journée
in the morning	du matin
in the afternoon	de l'après-midi
in the evening	du soir
public holiday	jour férié (m)

Monday	lundi
Tuesday	mardi
Wednesday	mercredi
Thursday	jeudi
Friday	vendredi
Saturday	samedi
Sunday	dimanche

January	janvier
February	février
March	mars
April	avril
May	mai
June	juin
July	juillet
August	août
September	septembre
October	octobre
November	novembre
December	décembre

Numbers

1	*un*
2	*deux*
3	*trois*
4	*quatre*
5	*cinq*
6	*six*
7	*sept*
8	*huit*
9	*neuf*
10	*dix*
11	*onze*
12	*douze*
13	*treize*
14	*quatorze*
15	*quinze*
16	*seize*
17	*dix-sept*
20	*vingt*
21	*vingt et un*
22	*vingt-deux*
30	*trente*
40	*quarante*
50	*cinquante*
60	*soixante*
70	*soixante-dix*
80	*quatre-vingts*
90	*quatre-vingt-dix*
100	*cent*
1000	*mille*
2000	*deux mille*

one million	*un million*
quarter	*quart* (m)
half	*demi/e*
dozen	*douzaine* (f)

FOOD

breakfast	*le petit déjeuner*
lunch	*le déjeuner*
dinner	*le dîner*
I'm a vegetarian.	*Je suis végétarien/ végétarienne.* (m/f)
I don't eat meat.	*Je ne mange pas de viande.*
I'd like the set menu.	*Je prends le menu (à. prix fixe).*
menu (free choice)	*carte* (f)
service charge included	*service compris*

bottle	*bouteille* (f)
cup	*tasse* (f)
fork	*fourchette* (f)
glass	*verre* (m)
knife	*couteau* (m)
plate	*assiette* (f)
spoon	*cuillière* (f)
teaspoon	*petitie cuillière* (f)

bread	*pain* (m)
butter	*beurre* (m)
cheese	*fromage*
chips (french fries)	*frites* (f/pl)
eggs	*oeufs* (m)
jam	*confiture* (f)
oil	*huile* (f)
(thin) pancake	*crêpe* (f)
pasta	*pâtes* (f/pl)
pepper	*poivre* (m)
rice	*riz* (m)
salt	*sel* (m)
snack	*casse-croûte* (m)
sugar	*sucre* (m)

water	*eau* (m)
mineral water	*eau minérale* (m)
orange juice	*jus d'orange* (m)
milk	*lait* (m)
coffee	*café* (m)
decaffeinated	*décaféiné*
coffee with milk	*café au lait* (m)
black coffee	*petit noir* (m)
tea	*thé* (m)
herbal tea	*tisane* (f)
hot chocolate	*chocolat chaud* (m)

baker	*boulangerie* (f)
butcher	*boucherie* (f)
cheese shop	*fromagerie* (f)
delicatessen	*charcuterie* (f)
grocery store	*épicerie* (f)/ *alimentation* (f)
market	*marché* (m)
supermarket	*supermarché* (m)

a carton of ...	*une barquette ...*
a portion of ...	*une part de ...*
a slice of ...	*une tranche de ...*
a small piece of ...	*un morceau de ...*

Menus & Markets

Fruit & Nuts

abricot	apricot
ananas	pineapple
cassis	blackcurrant
cerises	cherries
fraises	strawberries
framboises	raspberries
pamplemousse	grapefruit
pêche	peach
pomme	apple
prune/mirabelle	plum
raisins	grapes
amandes	almonds
cacahuètes	peanuts
châtaignes/marrons	chestnuts
noisettes	hazelnuts
noix	walnuts

Meat & Poultry

agneau	lamb
boeuf	beef
canard	duck
dinde/dindon	turkey
foie	liver
jambon	ham
lapin	rabbit
lard	bacon
poulet	chicken
veau	veal
viande	meat
volaille	poultry

Vegetables

ail	garlic
asperges	asparagus
betterave	beetroot
céleri	celery
champignons	mushrooms
chou	cabbage
chou-fleur	cauliflower
concombre	cucumber
haricots verts	french/string beans
laitue	lettuce
légumes	vegetables
maïs	corn
oignon	onion
petits pois	peas
pomme de terre	potato

Fish & Seafood

coquilles Saint-Jacques	scallops
crevettes roses	prawns
écrevisses	crayfish
fruits de mer	seafood
huîtres	oysters
moules	mussels
poisson	fish
thon	tuna
truite	trout

WALKING

Preparations

Where can I/we buy food?	*Où est-ce qu'on peut acheter de la nourriture?*
We'll return in one week.	*Nous serons de retour dans une semaine.*
Can I leave some things here for a while?	*Puis-je laisser des affaires ici pendant quelques temps?*
Can you repair this for me?	*Pourriez-vous me le/la réparer?*

Clothing & Equipment

backpack	*sac à dos* (m)
battery	*pile* (f)
(walking) boots	*chassures (de montagne)* (f)
camera	*appareil photo* (m)
camp stove	*réchaud* (m)
cooking fuel (gas)	*cartouche de gaz* (f)/ *camping gaz* (m)
cooking pot	*marmite* (f)/ *casserole* (f)
compass	*boussole* (f)
film	*film* (m)/*pellicule* (f)
fleece jacket	*veste polaire* (f)
gloves	*gants* (m)
map	*carte* (f)
matches	*alumettes* (f)
pocket knife	*canif* (m)
rainjacket	*cape de pluie* (f)
sleeping bag	*sac de couchage/ duvet* (m)
sleeping mat	*tapis de sol* (m)
socks	*chausettes* (f)
sunglasses	*lunettes de soleil* (f)/ *solaires* (f)
tent	*tente* (f)

toilet paper	*papier hygiénique* (m)	flat	*plat*
torch/flashlight	*lampe de poche* (f)	steep	*raide*
walking pole	*bâton* (m)	high	*haut*
warm hat/beanie	*bonnet* (m)	low	*bas*
water bottle	*gourde* (f)	near	*proche/voisin*
		far	*éloigné/loin*

Directions

		beside	*à côté de*
How many kilometres/ hours are we from ...?	*Nous sommes à combien de kilomètres/d'heures de ...*	between	*entre*
		level with	*au niveau de*
		opposite	*en face de*
Does this path go to ...?	*Est-ce que ce chemin/ sentier mène à ...?*	north	*nord*
		south	*sud*
		east	*est*
Is there a short cut?	*Est-ce qu'il y a un raccourci?*	west	*ouest*

Weather

What's the forecast?	*Quel est le météo/le prevision de temps?*
Tomorrow it will be ...	*Demain il fera ...*

Can you show me on the map?	*Pouvez-vous me le montrer sur la carte?*	good weather	*beau temps*
		bad weather	*mauvais temps*
What is this place called?	*Comment s'appele ce lieu?*	clear/fine	*beau*
		cloudy	*nuageux/couvert*
Where have you come from?	*D'où arrivez-vous?*	cold	*froid/frais*
		hot	*chaud*
We're walking from ... to ...	*Nous allons de ... à ...*	sunny	*du soleil, ensoleillé*
		overcast	*couvert*
How long did it take you?	*Ça vous a pris combien de temps?*	flood	*inondation* (f)
		fog	*brouillard* (m)/ *brume* (f)
Is there much snow on the pass?	*Le col est-il fortement enneigé?*	ice (icy)	*glâce* (f) *(glâcial)*
		lightning	*éclairs* (m)/*foudre* (f)
Can the river be crossed?	*Est-il possible de franchir la rivière?*	mist	*brume* (f)
		rain (it's raining)	*pluie* (f) *(il pleut)*
Go straight ahead.	*Conduisez tout droit.*	snow (it's snowing)	*neige* (f) *(il neige)*
Turn left.	*Tournez à gauche.*	storm, gale	*tempête*
Turn right.	*Tournez à droit.*	thunderstorm	*orage* (f)
Take the first left.	*Emprûntez la première à gauche.*	wind (it's windy)	*vent* (m) *(il y a du vent)*
		high tide	*haute marée* (f)
one-way	*aller-descente/ascente*	low tide	*basse marée* (f)
round trip	*aller-retour*		
turn off	*bifurcation* (m)		

Features

ahead	*devant*	bend (road, track)	*lacet/virage* (m)
behind	*derrière*	bridge	*pont* (m)
above	*au-dessus*	cairn	*cairn* (f)
below	*au-dessous*	canal lock	*écluse* (f)
before	*avant*	dam	*barrage* (f)
after	*après*	farm	*ferme* (f)
beginning	*le début*		
end	*la fin*		
downstream	*en aval*		
upstream	*en amont de*		

fence	*barrière* (f)
footbridge	*passerelle* (f)
ford	*gué* (m)
forest	*forêt/bois* (m)
highway	*route* (f)
house/	*maison* (f)/
building	*bâtiment* (m)
hut/chalet	*refuge* (m)
jetty/pier	*embarcadère* (m)
lighthouse	*phare* (m)
lookout	*belvédère* (f)
loop	*boucle* (f)
marsh	*marais* (m)
path	*sentier* (m)
quarry	*carrière* (f)
road	*chemin* (m)/*rue/voie* (f)
signpost	*poteau indicateur* (m)
spring	*fontaine* (f)
town	*ville* (f)
tree	*arbre* (m)
village	*village/hameau* (m)
way marker	*balisage/balise* (f)

Landforms

avalanche	*avalanche* (f)
bay/cove	*anse/baie/golfe* (f)
beach	*plage* (f)
bog/swamp	*marais* (m)
cape/	*cap* (m)/
headland	*promontoire* (m)
cave	*caverne/grotte* (f)
chasm	*gouffre* (m)
cliff	*falaise* (f)
coast	*côte* (f)/*littoral* (m)
crag	*rocher* (m)
crater	*cratère* (m)
estuary	*estuaire* (m)
glacier	*glacier* (m)

gorge	*gorge* (f)
hill	*colline* (f)
island	*île* (m)
lake	*lac* (m)
landslide	*éboulement* (m)
moor	*lande* (f)
moraine	*moraine* (f)
mountain	*mont/pic* (m)/
	montagne/tête (f)
mud	*boue* (f)
pass	*col* (m)
peninsula	*presqu'île* (m)
plain	*plaine* (f)/*plan* (m)
plateau	*plateau* (m)
pond, pool	*étaing* (m)
rapid	*rapide* (f)
ridge	*arête/crête* (f)
river	*fleuve* (m)/*rivière* (f)
riverbank	*rive* (f)
rock	*roche* (f)
rock slab	*dalle* (f)
rubble	*rocaille* (f)
sand	*sable* (m)
scoria	*scorie* (f)
scree	*éboulis* (m)
slope	*pente* (f)/*vente* (m)
snowfield	*champ de neige* (m)/
	névé (m)
spur	*épaulement* (m)
strait	*rade* (f)
stream	*courant/ruisseau* (m)
stream junction	*confluent* (m)
summit	*cime* (f)/*sommet* (m)
valley	*val* (m)/*vallée/combe/*
	cuvette (f)
volcano	*volcan* (m)
waterfall	*cascade/chute d'eau* (f)

Glossary

Unless otherwise indicated, glossary terms are in French *(français)*. The (m) indicates masculine gender and (f) feminine gender. Other languages are listed in brackets; English is abbreviated to 'Eng'. Words which appear in italics within definitions have their own entries.

abbaye (f) – abbey

aber (m) – estuary

abri (m) – shelter; a rudimentary building in the mountains for emergency use

aiguille (f) – needle; also sharp rocky peak

aire naturelle (f) – informal camping area with facilities

alimentation (f) – grocery store

allée (f) – lane or path

alsacien (m) – Alsatian language; also a native of Alsace

anse (f) – handle; also natural harbour or cove

AOC – appellation d'origine contrôlée; label of origin, certifying that a wine comes from a designated place and meets certain standards

aqueduc (m) – aqueduct

arête (f) – narrow ridge separating two glacial valleys

arribet/arriou (m) – small stream in the Pyrenees

artigue – a pasture clearing in the Pyrenees

ATM – (Eng) automatic teller machine; cash point

auberge (f) – inn or hotel

auberge de jeunesse (f) – youth hostel

baie (f) – bay

balcon (m) – mountain path contouring above a valley floor, normally above the tree line

balise (f) – waymarker

barrage (m) – dam

bastide (f) – walled town in south-western France

belvédère (m) – lookout or viewpoint

bergerie (f) – shepherd's hut

bivouac (m) – site for spending the night in the open without a tent; also temporary encampment without facilities

bocca – mountain pass in Corsica

bois (m) – wood

borie – small stone building; also farmhouse in southern France

boulangerie (f) – bakery

brasserie (f) – bar or pub; also brewery

breton (m) – Breton language; a native of Brittany

butte – (Eng) isolated, steep-sided, flat-topped hill

buvette (f) – refreshment kiosk serving drinks and snacks

CAF – Club Alpin Français; French Alpine Club

cairn – (Eng) pile of stones, often used to mark a path and/or path junction

camping (m) – organised camping ground with facilities, often including restaurant, shop and swimming pool

calanque (f) – rocky inlet

camping municipal (m) – municipal camping ground

cap (m) – cape or headland; also summit in the Pyrenees

carrefour (m) – crossroads

carte (f) – menu from which a choice of dishes can be made; also map

cascade (f) – waterfall

causse (m) – limestone plateau with low, dense vegetation in south-western France

cave (m) – wine or cheese cellar

CDT – Comité Départemental du Tourisme; tourism committee of a *département*

chambre d'hôte (f) – B&B accommodation in a private house

charcuterie (f) – delicatessen; also cooked pork meats

chemin (m) – path

chemin forestier (m) – forest track

chemin de halage (m) – towpath beside a canal

cime (f) – mountain summit or peak

cirque (m) – head of a glacial valley, usually with an extensive rock wall

cistern – (Eng) underground water reservoir

clôt – deep pool; also head of a valley in the Pyrenees

col (m) – pass; lowest point of a ridge connecting two peaks

combe (f) – *coomb*

coomb – (Eng) shallow valley or deep hollow

commune (f) – the basic unit of local government in France

contour interval – (Eng) vertical distance between contour lines on topographical maps

corniche – (Eng) coastal or cliff road

corrie – (Eng) *cirque*

côte (f) – coast

cour (f) – courtyard or square

courbe de niveau (f) – *contour interval*

crête (f) – narrow rocky ridge

CRS – Compagnie Républicaine de la Securité; organisation involved in mountain rescue

dégustation (f) – tasting

demi-pension (f) – half board B&B with either lunch or dinner

département (m) – department; also one of 96 administrative units of France

dolmen – (Eng) prehistoric burial tomb

eau potable (f) – drinking water

éboulis (m) – scree; mass of fallen rocks

église (f) – church

emplacement (m) – tent site

épaulement (m) – retaining wall; also escarpment

épicerie (f) – *alimentation*

étang (m) – pond or lake

falaise (f) – cliff

ferme auberge (f) – family-run inn attached to a farm or chateau

FFRP – Fédération Française de la Randonnée Pédestre; French Walking Federation

fontaine (f) – fountain or spring

forêt (f) – forest

formule (f) – similar to a menu but with a choice of any two or three courses

fromagerie (f) – cheese-maker

garrigue (f) – cover of aromatic plants

gare (f) – train station

gave (m) – mountain stream in the Pyrenees

gîte d'étape (f) – hostel-style walkers' accommodation

goat – (Breton) forest

GR – *grande randonnée*, a trademark of the *FFRP*

grande randonnée (f) – long-distance, waymarked walking route

grotte (f) – cave

hôtel de ville (m) – city or town hall

hourquette – steep pass in the Pyrenees

IGN – Institut Géographique National; national mapping authority

île (f) – island

itinéraire (m) – route followed by a path, not necessarily waymarked

jeton (m) – token

levée (f) – levee or dyke

mairie (f) – town hall; also town council

maison (f) – office or house

maison du littoral (f) – coastal information centre

maison du parc (f) – information centre in a national park or regional nature park

maquis (m) – scrubland vegitation, composed primarily of broad-leaved evergreen shrubs or small trees

marché (m) – market

mas (m) – farmhouse or small hamlet in southern France

ménez – (Breton) mountain or hill

menu (m) – fixed-price meal of two or more courses

mistral (m) – persistent north wind in southern France

moulin à vent (m) – windmill

névé – (Eng) masses of porous ice not yet frozen into glacial ice

office du tourisme (m) – tourist information office

ONF – Office National des Forêts; National Office for Forests

oratoire (m) – tiny chapel, often found beside paths or tracks

parc national (m) – national park
parc naturel régional (m) – regional nature park
pension complète (f) – full board B&B with lunch and dinner
petit lac (m) – tarn or small mountain lake
petite randonnée (f) – short-distance, waymarked route
PGHM – Peloton de Gendarmerie de Haute Montagne; branch of police force responsible for mountain rescue
phare (m) – lighthouse
pic (m) – mountain peak
pla – area of flat ground in the Pyrenees; also spelt plan
place (f) – square; also place
plage (f) – beach
plat du jour (m) – daily special
pont (m) – bridge
pouy – hill or rise in the Pyrenees; also spelt pouey
pozzi – pits
pozzines (f) – interlinked waterholes
PR – *petite randonnée*, a trademark of the *FFRP*
presqu'île (f) – peninsula
puits (m) – well
puy – plug or cone of an extinct volcano

rade (f) – natural harbour
randonnée (f) – walk; also walking
randonneur (m/f) – walker
ravin (m) – ravine or gully
ravine (f) – small ravine or gully
refuge (m) – refuge or mountain hut providing accommodation and usually meals
réserve naturelle (f) – nature reserve
rond-point (m) – roundabout
rue (f) – street
ruelle (f) – alley or lane
ruisseau (m) – stream

SAMU – Service d'Aide Médicale d'Urgence; Emergency Medical Aid Service
scoria – (Eng) volcanic rock material
sentier (m) – *chemin*
sentier côtier (m) – coastal path
sentier littoral (m) – *sentier côtier*
sentier des douaniers (m) – customs officers' path
serrat/serre – long crest or ridge in the Pyrenees
site naturel classé (m) – classified natural site
SNCF – Société Naionale des Chemins de Fer; state-owned railway company
supermarché (m) – supermarket
syndicat d'initiative (m) – small tourist information office, often seasonal

tabac (m) – tobacco; also tobacconist selling newspapers, phonecards and possibly bus tickets
téléférique (m) – cable car or funicular
télésiège (m) – chairlift
téléski (m) – ski lift or tow
tête (f) – head; also mountain peak
TGV (m) – train à grande vitesse; high-speed train
trez – (Breton) beach or strand
tree line – (Eng) altitude above which trees can no longer survive
true left/right bank – (Eng) side of the riverbank as you look downstream
TVA – taxe sur la valeur ajouté; *VAT*

vallée (m) – valley
vallon (m) – small valley
VAT – value-added tax

zone périphérique (f) – periphery zone; the protected, inhabited zone surrounding the core area of a national park

LONELY PLANET

Guides by Region

Lonely Planet is known worldwide for publishing practical, reliable and no-nonsense travel information in our guides and on our web site. The Lonely Planet list covers just about every accessible part of the world. Currently there are fifteen series: travel guides, Shoestrings, Condensed, Phrasebooks, Read This First, Healthy Travel, Walking guides, Cycling guides, Pisces Diving & Snorkeling guides, City Maps, Travel Atlases, Out to Eat, World Food, Journeys travel literature and Pictorials.

AFRICA Africa on a shoestring • Africa – the South • Arabic (Egyptian) phrasebook • Arabic (Moroccan) phrasebook • Cairo • Cape Town • Cape Town city map • Central Africa • East Africa • Egypt • Egypt travel atlas • Ethiopian (Amharic) phrasebook • The Gambia & Senegal • Healthy Travel Africa • Kenya • Kenya travel atlas • Malawi, Mozambique & Zambia • Morocco • North Africa • Read This First Africa • South Africa, Lesotho & Swaziland • South Africa, Lesotho & Swaziland travel atlas • Swahili phrasebook • Tanzania, Zanzibar & Pemba • Trekking in East Africa • Tunisia • West Africa • Zimbabwe, Botswana & Namibia • Zimbabwe, Botswana & Nambia Travel Atlas • World Food Morocco
Travel Literature: The Rainbird: A Central African Journey • Songs to an African Sunset: A Zimbabwean Story • Mali Blues: Traveling to an African Beat

AUSTRALIA & THE PACIFIC Auckland • Australia • Australian phrasebook • Bushwalking in Australia • Bushwalking in Papua New Guinea • Fiji • Fijian phrasebook • Healthy Travel Australia, NZ and the Pacific • Islands of Australia's Great Barrier Reef • Melbourne • Melbourne city map • Micronesia • New Caledonia • New South Wales & the ACT • New Zealand • Northern Territory • Outback Australia • Out To Eat – Melbourne • Out to Eat – Sydney • Papua New Guinea • Pidgin phrasebook • Queensland • Rarotonga & the Cook Islands • Samoa • Solomon Islands • South Australia • South Pacific • South Pacific Languages phrasebook • Sydney • Sydney city map • Sydney Condensed • Tahiti & French Polynesia • Tasmania • Tonga • Tramping in New Zealand • Vanuatu • Victoria • Western Australia
Travel Literature: Islands in the Clouds • Kiwi Tracks: A New Zealand Journey • Sean & David's Long Drive

CENTRAL AMERICA & THE CARIBBEAN Bahamas, Turks & Caicos • Bermuda • Central America on a shoestring • Costa Rica • Cuba • Dominican Republic & Haiti • Eastern Caribbean • Guatemala, Belize & Yucatán: La Ruta Maya • Jamaica • Mexico • Mexico City • Panama • Puerto Rico • Read This First Central & South America • World Food Mexico
Travel Literature: Green Dreams: Travels in Central America

EUROPE Amsterdam • Amsterdam city map • Andalucía • Austria • Baltic States phrasebook • Barcelona • Berlin • Berlin city map • Britain • British phrasebook • Brussels, Bruges & Antwerp • Budapest city map • Canary Islands • Central Europe • Central Europe phrasebook • Corfu & Ionians • Corsica • Crete • Crete Condensed • Croatia • Cyprus • Czech & Slovak Republics • Denmark • Dublin • Eastern Europe • Eastern Europe phrasebook • Edinburgh • Estonia, Latvia & Lithuania • Europe on a shoestring • Finland • Florence • France • French phrasebook • Germany • German phrasebook • Greece • Greek Islands • Greek phrasebook • Hungary • Iceland, Greenland & the Faroe Islands • Ireland • Italian phrasebook • Italy • Krakow • Lisbon • The Loire • London • London city map • London Condensed • Mediterranean Europe • Mediterranean Europe phrasebook • Munich • Norway • Paris • Paris city map • Paris Condensed • Poland • Portugal • Portugese phrasebook • Portugal travel atlas • Prague • Prague city map • Provence & the Côte d'Azur • Read This First Europe • Romania & Moldova • Rome • Russia, Ukraine & Belarus • Russian phrasebook • Scandinavian & Baltic Europe • Scandinavian Europe phrasebook • Scotland • Slovenia • Spain • Spanish phrasebook • St Petersburg • Sweden • Switzerland • Trekking in Spain • Tuscany • Ukrainian phrasebook • Venice • Vienna • Walking in Britain • Walking in Ireland • Walking in Italy • Walking in Spain • Walking in Switzerland • Western Europe • Western Europe phrasebook • World Food Ireland • World Food Italy • World Food Spain
Travel Literature: The Olive Grove: Travels in Greece

INDIAN SUBCONTINENT Bangladesh • Bengali phrasebook • Bhutan • Delhi • Goa • Hindi & Urdu phrasebook • India • India & Bangladesh travel atlas • Indian Himalaya • Karakoram Highway • Kerala • Mumbai (Bombay) • Nepal • Nepali phrasebook • Pakistan • Rajasthan • Read This First: Asia & India • South India • Sri Lanka • Sri Lanka phrasebook • Trekking in the Indian Himalaya • Trekking in the Karakoram & Hindukush • Trekking in the Nepal Himalaya
Travel Literature: In Rajasthan • Shopping for Buddhas • The Age Of Kali

LONELY PLANET

Mail Order

Lonely Planet products are distributed worldwide. They are also available by mail order from Lonely Planet, so if you have difficulty finding a title please write to us. North and South American residents should write to 150 Linden St, Oakland CA 94607, USA; European and African residents should write to 10a Spring Place, London, NW5 3BH; and residents of other countries to PO Box 617, Hawthorn, Victoria 3122, Australia.

ISLANDS OF THE INDIAN OCEAN Madagascar & Comoros • Maldives • Mauritius, Réunion & Seychelles

MIDDLE EAST & CENTRAL ASIA Bahrain, Kuwait & Qatar • Central Asia • Central Asia phrasebook • Dubai • Hebrew phrasebook • Iran • Israel & the Palestinian Territories • Israel & the Palestinian Territories travel atlas • Istanbul • Istanbul City Map • Istanbul to Cairo on a shoestring • Jerusalem • Jerusalem City Map • Jordan • Jordan, Syria & Lebanon travel atlas • Lebanon • Middle East • Oman & the United Arab Emirates • Syria • Turkey • Turkey travel atlas • Turkish phrasebook • World Food Turkey • Yemen
Travel Literature: The Gates of Damascus • Kingdom of the Film Stars: Journey into Jordan • Black on Black: Iran Revisited

NORTH AMERICA Alaska • Backpacking in Alaska • Baja California • California & Nevada • California Condensed • Canada • Chicago • Chicago city map • Deep South • Florida • Hawaii • Honolulu • Las Vegas • Los Angeles • Miami • New England • New Orleans • New York City • New York city map • New York Condensed • New York, New Jersey & Pennsylvania • Oahu • Pacific Northwest USA • Puerto Rico • Rocky Mountain • San Francisco • San Francisco city map • Seattle • Southwest USA • Texas • USA • USA phrasebook • Vancouver • Washington, DC & the Capital Region • Washington DC city map
Travel Literature: Drive Thru America

NORTH-EAST ASIA Beijing • Cantonese phrasebook • China • Hong Kong • Hong Kong city map • Hong Kong, Macau & Guangzhou • Japan • Japanese phrasebook • Japanese audio pack • Korea • Korean phrasebook • Kyoto • Mandarin phrasebook • Mongolia • Mongolian phrasebook • North-East Asia on a shoestring • Seoul • South-West China • Taiwan • Tibet • Tibetan phrasebook • Tokyo
Travel Literature: Lost Japan • In Xanadu

SOUTH AMERICA Argentina, Uruguay & Paraguay • Bolivia • Brazil • Brazilian phrasebook • Buenos Aires • Chile & Easter Island • Chile & Easter Island travel atlas • Colombia • Ecuador & the Galapagos Islands • Healthy Travel Central & South America • Latin American Spanish phrasebook • Peru • Quechua phrasebook • Rio de Janeiro • Rio de Janeiro city map • South America on a shoestring • Trekking in the Patagonian Andes • Venezuela
Travel Literature: Full Circle: A South American Journey

SOUTH-EAST ASIA Bali & Lombok • Bangkok • Bangkok city map • Burmese phrasebook • Cambodia • Hanoi • Healthy Travel Asia & India • Hill Tribes phrasebook • Ho Chi Minh City • Indonesia • Indonesia's Eastern Islands • Indonesian phrasebook • Indonesian audio pack • Jakarta • Java • Laos • Lao phrasebook • Laos travel atlas • Malay phrasebook • Malaysia, Singapore & Brunei • Myanmar (Burma) • Philippines • Pilipino (Tagalog) phrasebook • Read This First Asia & India • Singapore • South-East Asia on a shoestring • South-East Asia phrasebook • Thailand • Thailand's Islands & Beaches • Thailand travel atlas • Thai phrasebook • Thai audio pack • Vietnam • Vietnamese phrasebook • Vietnam travel atlas • World Food Thailand • World Food Vietnam

---

ALSO AVAILABLE: Antarctica • The Arctic • Brief Encounters: Stories of Love, Sex & Travel • Chasing Rickshaws • Lonely Planet Unpacked • Not the Only Planet: Travel Stories from Science Fiction • Sacred India • Travel with Children • Traveller's Tales

LONELY PLANET

You already know that Lonely Planet produces more than this one guidebook, but you might not be aware of the other products we have on this region. Here is a selection of titles which you may want to check out as well:

France
US$24.95 • UK£14.99 • 180FF

The Loire
US$17.99 • UK£11.99 • 140FF

Paris
US$14.95 • UK£8.99 • 110FF

South-West France
US$16.95 • UK£11.99 • 130FF

Paris condensed
US$9.95 • UK£5.99 • 59FF

Walking in Italy
US$17.95 • UK£11.99 • 140FF

Walking in Spain
US$17.95 • UK£11.99 • 140FF

Walking in Switzerland
US$14.95 • UK£8.99 • 115FF

Western Europe phrasebook
US$6.95 • UK£4.99 • 50FF

Paris city map
US$5.95 • UK£3.99 • 39FF

Read this First Europe
US$14.99 • UK£8.99 • 99FF

Western Europe
US$25.95 • UK£15.99 • 140FF

French phrasebook
US$5.95 • UK£3.99 • 40FF

Corsica
US$15.95 • UK£9.99 • 120FF

World Food France
US$12.99 • UK£7.99 • 99FF

Index

Text

Bold indicates maps.

Boxed Text

Map Legend

BOUNDARIES

━━━━━	International
─ ─ ─	Regional
─ ─ ─	Disputed

HYDROGRAPHY

	Coastline
	River, Creek
	Lake
	Intermittent Lake
	Salt Lake
	Canal
⊙ ⟫	Spring, Rapids
╫	Waterfalls
⊾ ⊾ ⊾ ⊾	Swamp

ROUTES & TRANSPORT

	Freeway
	Highway
	Major Road
	Minor Road
═ ═ ═ ═	Unsealed Highway
═ ═ ═ ═	Unsealed Major Road
─ ─ ─ ─	Unsealed Minor Road
─ ─ ─ ─	Track
	Lane
⇒ = = = :	Tunnel
──●──	Train Route & Station
⊢┼┼┼┼┼┤	Cable Car or Chairlift
A10	Route Number
	Described Walk
━ ━ ━ ━	Alternative Route
●●●●●●●	Side Trip
─ ─ ─ ─	Walking Track
─ ─ ─ ─	Ferry Route

AREA FEATURES

	Beach/Reef
	Forest
	Glacier
	Park (Regional Maps)
	Park (Walk Maps)
	Urban Area

MAP SYMBOLS

✪ **CAPITAL**	National Capital	✈	Airport	℗ Parking
◉ **CAPITAL**	Regional Capital	⚲	Beach	)(Pass
● **CITY**	City	🚏	Bus Stop	☻ Picnic Area
● Town	Town	⌂	Cave	✚ Police Station
● Village	Village	➕ ✝	Church	✉ Post Office
⌂	Camping Area	⌒	Cliff or Escarpment	⊞ Shopping Centre
⌂	Hut/Refuge	500	Contour	⚡ Ski Area
⊡	Lookout	⊢	Gate	+200 m Spot Height
▼	Place to Eat	⊕	Hospital	☎ Telephone
⬤	Place to Stay	🛉	Lighthouse	⊙ Toilet
●	Point of Interest	Ⓜ	Metro Station	ℹ Tourist Information
⬣	Shelter	⚑	Monument	⊖ Transport
🛉	Trailhead	▲	Mountain or Hill	△ Trigonometric Point
		🏛	Museum	🖾 Zoo

Note: not all symbols displayed above appear in this book

LONELY PLANET OFFICES

Australia
PO Box 617, Hawthorn, Victoria 3122
☎ 03 9819 1877 fax 03 9819 6459
@ talk2us@lonelyplanet.com.au

USA
150 Linden St, Oakland, CA 94607
☎ 510 893 8555 or ☎ 800 275 8555 (toll free)
fax 510 893 8572
@ info@lonelyplanet.com

UK
10a Spring Place, London NW5 3BH
☎ 020 7428 4800 fax 020 7428 4828
@ go@lonelyplanet.co.uk

France
1 rue du Dahomey, 75011 Paris
☎ 01 55 25 33 00 fax 01 55 25 33 01
@ bip@lonelyplanet.fr
🖥 www.lonelyplanet.fr

World Wide Web: 🖥 www.lonelyplanet.com or AOL keyword: lp
Lonely Planet Images: @ lpi@lonelyplanet.com.au